W9-AZI-279

PASSION
AND
POLITICS

SANDRA MACKEY

PASSION AND POLITICS

THE TURBULENT WORLD OF THE ARABS

A DUTTON BOOK

DUTTON
Published by the Penguin Group
Penguin Books USA Inc., 375 Hudson Street,
New York, New York 10014, U.S.A.
Penguin Books Ltd, 27 Wrights Lane,
London W8 5TZ, England
Penguin Books Australia Ltd, Ringwood,
Victoria, Australia
Penguin Books Canada Ltd, 10 Alcorn Avenue,
Toronto, Ontario, Canada M4V 3B2
Penguin Books (N.Z.) Ltd, 182–190 Wairau Road,
Auckland 10, New Zealand

Penguin Books Ltd, Registered Offices:
Harmondsworth, Middlesex, England

First published by Dutton, an imprint of New American Library,
a division of Penguin Books USA Inc.
Distributed in Canada by McClelland & Stewart Inc.

First Printing, November, 1992
10 9 8 7 6 5 4 3 2 1

 REGISTERED TRADEMARK—MARCA REGISTRADA

LIBRARY OF CONGRESS CATALOGING-IN-PUBLICATION DATA:
Mackey, Sandra, 1937–
    Passion and politics : the turbulent world of the Arabs / Sandra Mackey.
       p.   cm.
    ISBN 0-525-93499-5
    1. Arab countries—Politics and government—1945–   I. Title.
DS63.1.M24   1992
320.917′4927—dc20   92-52879
                                                                           CIP

Printed in the United States of America
Set in New Baskerville
Designed by Leonard Telesca

In memory of my father
Velt Sherman

For how many arbitrary unities have collapsed,
even before they had seen the dawn of life?
—King Abdullah of Jordan

CONTENTS

LIST OF MAPS

ACKNOWLEDGMENTS

No writer works in isolation. And no writer can accurately list all of those who in some way contributed to a project. An inclusive thank-you goes to all those people in the United States, Europe, and the Arab world who helped me make contact with those I needed to see and to others who added their special part to the huge mosaic that became this book.

I owe a debt of gratitude to Dr. Donald Reid of Georgia State University, who read the manuscript and offered so many valuable challenges and insights, and to W. Scott Harrop of the University of Virginia, who was such a valuable sounding board. I, however, bear total responsibility for the final product.

I also want to thank my diligent and tireless research assistant Kevin Fain, whom I have forgiven for deserting me for the University of Chicago Law School. Much gratitude goes to Bob and Hedy Lodwick, who so often opened their home in Geneva to me as I trudged between the United States and the Middle East; to Bettye Sue Wright for her help on so many points, great and small; to John and Ione Lee for the use of their mountain house; to Cheryll Tobin for handling so many telephone calls for me; to Brenda Kilgore for her help in making my always complicated travel arrangements; and to Issac Bryant, who kept my house running all those hectic months.

My loving appreciation goes to my husband, Dan, who is not only a first-rate editor but an interested and caring participant in the arduous process of book writing. A special thanks to my editor, Kevin Mulroy, and Helen Rees, who is not only my agent but such a special friend.

Finally I have to thank the Arabs themselves for their fascinating, fatiguing, and often frustrating world.

AUTHOR'S NOTE

When one is writing about as vast a subject as the Arab world in a single volume, one must explain the scope and focus of the book. The Arab world can be defined in different ways. In its broadest sense, it reaches from Iraq on the Persian Gulf to Morocco on the Atlantic and splits between the *maghrib*, the Arab west, and the *mashriq*, the Arab east. The *mashriq*, composed of Egypt, Lebanon, Jordan, Syria, Iraq, Saudi Arabia, Yemen, Oman, the United Arab Emirates, Qatar, Bahrain, and Kuwait, constitutes the core of the Arab world culturally and politically. Within the *mashriq*, the major power points are Egypt, Syria, Saudi Arabia, Iraq, and geographically important but politically weak Jordan. Both at the edge and in the center of the region is a nation but not a state—the Palestinians. It is the *mashriq* with which this book deals.

The focus is on the fundamental conflicts in the region that pit the Arabs' historical and cultural sense of unity against their parochial and national interests. Out of this clash between oneness and separateness comes the unique world of the Arabs.

Having stated what the book is about, I must also state what it is not about. This is not another examination of the Arab-Israeli dispute. Rather it is an exploration of the Arabs' relationship with each other and their relationship with the West. Yet it is impossible to write about the Arab world without also touching heavily on the issue of Israel, since Israel plays such an integral part in the dynamics of Arab politics. No attempt has been made to argue the Israeli points of the Arab-Israeli dispute. That is another subject. Rather, Israel is portrayed from the Arab perspective in order to explain how the Jewish state contributes to hostilities between Arab and Arab and between the Arabs and the West, particularly the United States. Nor does the concluding chapter intend to examine the full relationship between the United States and Israel; it merely demonstrates that by ignoring Arab problems and Arab concerns, American foreign policy in the Middle East has failed to serve the interests of the United States.

A note about language. The transliteration of Arabic to English is problematic at best. There is no standard system recognized for either academic or general audiences. Since no method of transliteration is without critics, I have chosen to use the simplified forms of Arabic words, names, and locations commonly used by newspapers in the United States. The diacritical marks, glottal stops, consonant sounds unique to Arabic, and marks for long vowels have been omitted. (However, transliterations in quotations from other writers have not been changed.) Perhaps no other example of the imprecise nature of Arabic-English transliteration is more graphic than the spelling of the name of the Prophet Muhammed. Although newspapers generally continue to use the form Mohammed, an evolution is under way to adopt either Muhammed or Muhammad to correspond to the already widely practiced style of spelling Muslim with a *u*. Again, these are choices of style, not dictates of either Arabic or English.

One further word. Because of the heavy hand of internal security organizations in several countries explored in this book, the names of people I interviewed who are neither historical nor public personages have been changed for their protection.

The story about al-Mamun and Aristotle in Chapter 3 is from *Islam and the Arab World: Faith, People, Culture*, edited by Bernard Lewis (New York: Alfred A. Knopf, 1976).

INTRODUCTION:
WORLD OF
THE EAST,
WORLD OF
THE WEST

THE SIXTEENTH-CENTURY STONE battlements of Muscat stared out over the pale blue waters of the Gulf of Oman—the link between the Persian Gulf and the Arabian Sea. As I strolled in their shadows, I felt with quickening senses the vast separation in distance and culture between this place and my world of the West.

Below me the gentle sands fanning out from the foot of the bare, stark hills played host to the life of the eastern side of the Arab world. Four- and five-man crews of fishermen, hiking their white *disdashas* above their knotty knees, heaved ashore the ageless high-backed wooden boats that fish these waters. Behind them, their barefoot sons of ten and twelve race toward the water to empty nets filled with sardines and to cart ashore one or two sleek, heavy king mackerels. And their wives, waddling palettes of color carrying plastic buckets, follow to scoop up each family's share of the catch.

All that is exotic and foreign moved around me as I aimlessly walked. I approached a wrinkled and leathery woman with heavy brass and coral rings in her nose squatting by a washtub filled with chipped ice. As I passed she reached in her hennaed hand, pulled out a dirty can of fruit juice, and thrust it forward, crying, "*Asir,*

asir"—juice. Before I could respond, a slightly built man with a full beard and a magnificent silver dagger at his waist barreled toward me with a woven carpet balanced on his turbaned head. The crenellated roofs and carved wooden window screens, the sweet and pungent aroma from dozens of tubs of spices mixing with the penetrating smoke of braziers, and the scent of heavy perfume trailing behind the colors and costumes of half a dozen tribes placed me unmistakably in the realm of the Arabs. As the haunting wail of the muezzin's call sounded from half a dozen mosques, I looked out over the dhows and the little reed-hull *badans* to the Gulf and on to the far horizon. There an enormous mass slowly and ponderously began to encroach on my line of vision. At last, out of the low-hanging mist created by rapidly evaporating water, a mammoth oil tanker presented its whole bulk. Seemingly suspended between sea and sky, it erased all illusions of separation between the Arab world and the West.

With the collapse of the Soviet empire in the late 1980s and early 1990s, the Middle East, dominated by a series of nation-states collectively known as the Arab world, took its place at the top of the United States' security agenda. The reasons exceed oil. The Arab world is 90 million people in an ever more interrelated world. It is the bridge of land connecting Europe, Asia, and Africa. It is warehouse to arsenals of weapons that in less than half a century have gone from rifles to tanks to missiles to nuclear weapons. Over the same period, events in the region, like jagged pieces of glass in a kaleidoscope, have tumbled, paused and reordered, tumbled, paused and reordered, in dizzying sequence. Red, green, blue, and yellow translating into passions, interests, ambitions, and fear build ever larger designs. And with increasing rapidity and menace, they reach out to pull the United States with its own, often disruptive, interests into their tangled, multifaceted patterns.

The forces driving these events layer one upon the other. They are cultural. They are religious. They are historical. They are economic. They are neatly reasoned and they are wildly irrational. Thus perceptions and realities fall one over the other forging ever stronger the inescapable link between the Arabs and the West.

In 1991, the United States fought a war in the Persian Gulf. In 1991, it also brokered a peace conference between the Arab states and Israel. In pressing a reluctant Israel, which for more than forty years had claimed a special, almost sacred relationship to the United

States, the conference spoke as never before to the realities of American interests in the Arab world. Yet in the wake of war and attempted peace, the world of the Arabs floats through American perceptions like an amorphous mass. It defies the architects of foreign policy and escapes Congress after Congress, whose constituents demand a world divided between simply defined white hats and black hats. But time and circumstances no longer allow a nescient public and a complacent government to escape the apparently chaotic world of the Arabs.

Once the Arab world hovered only as a vague image at the farthest periphery of American thought. In the mid-nineteenth century, God-fearing Christians clutching their well-worn Bibles sat in hard, straight-backed pews to hear the story of young David confronting the hulking Goliath. But beyond the Biblical "Promised Land," the Arab east was nothing but endless sand seemingly as far away from the shores of the United States as the moon. Universally Arabs, if they ever arose in the conscious mind, loomed as uncivilized "Mohammedans," robed and turbaned fanatics who lived in tents and survived on the caravan trade. It was this basic attitude that led Americans to concur with the judgment of the British scholar Sir William Muir that "the sword of Muhammad, and the Kor'an are the most stubborn enemies of Civilisation, Liberty, and the Truth which the world has yet known."*

Yet in the mid-nineteenth century, a few widely scattered Christian groups with budding global interests began to dispatch missionaries into the Arab world charging them with revitalizing the gospel in Christian churches tracing their histories back to the first century.† Failing to recognize that the energies of the Christians of the Muslim Middle East went into survival, the Rev. Justin Perkins in 1842 goaded the eastern Christian churches to "send forth faithful missionaries of the cross, in such numbers and with such holy zeal, as shall bear the tidings of salvation to every corner of benighted Asia."‡

---

* Albert Hourani, *Europe and the Middle East* (Berkeley: University of California Press, 1980), p. 34.
† The American Board of Commissioners for Foreign Missions sent its first missionaries, Pliny Fisk and Levi Parsons, to the Middle East in 1819. Both had died in the field by 1825.
‡ R. Park Johnson, *Middle East Pilgrimage* (New York: Friendship Press, 1958), p. 92.

Despite the cultural myopia of the Rev. Mr. Perkins, there were some among the mission contingent who understood and savored the Arab world in which they lived. In 1866 the mild-mannered Presbyterian missionary Daniel Bliss argued before the American Board of Commissioners for Foreign Missions that America's duty to the Arabs was education. Accepting the argument, the board voted funds to construct a college on a deserted stretch of sand dunes that served as Beirut's garbage dump. Through what would become the American University of Beirut, the United States first entered the realm of the Arabs.

Before the closing decades of the nineteenth century, small contingents of tourists followed the missionaries into the Arab world. Americans enriched by the proceeds of the Second Industrial Revolution began to creep out of the cocoon of North America to join their wealthy European cousins in the Grand Tour. Sailing east out of Marseilles on luxurious cruise ships, first-class passengers danced their way across the Mediterranean. Disembarking at Haifa or Jaffa, they followed the path of the Crusaders to historic Jerusalem, trudged the Via Dolorosa, and squinted into the gloom of the Church of the Holy Sepulcher. Then they moved on to Cairo, where in broad-brimmed sun hats they clung to the humps of ugly, plodding camels winding around the great Pyramid of Cheops and down to the Sphinx. And they shopped the bustling souks piled high with golden brassware, boxes inlaid with mother-of-pearl, and fat leather ottomans that they would lug home to New York and Boston, Chicago and San Francisco to attest to their immersion into the Arab world. It was an age of innocence in which American naiveté about the Arab east mattered little.

But as the twentieth century proceeded, the relationship between the world of the Arabs and the world of the West shifted like tectonic plates. New ships of war sliding out of the docks of Glasgow, Devonport, and Bremen ate oil rather than coal. And horseless carriages propelled by gasoline revolutionized transportation. Before the Great War began in 1914, all suspected that oil, that most precious commodity of the twentieth century, lay under the sands and marshes surrounding the Persian Gulf. Oil now joined the geography—the imperative of protecting the Suez Canal, the route to India, and securing the strategic bridge between Europe and Asia—to lure the West to the Arab east.*

Europe responded more than the United States. Within the bounty bequeathed to them by their geography, Americans possessed their own oil. During the 1920s, the lands of the Osage and Cherokee felt the bite of drills wielded by Oklahoma wildcatters. And in Texas the towns of Lubbock, Midland, and Odessa boomed in a topography and climate much like those of the deserts of the Middle East. Even when the second great war came, U.S. priorities in the Arab east limited themselves almost exclusively to supply lines for the enemies of Hitler and Mussolini. Yet war and time had once more altered the affairs of nations. World War II marked the last point at which Americans could remain oblivious to the Arab world.

Harry Truman inherited from Franklin Delano Roosevelt a nation that had had thrust upon it global responsibilities and an aggressive adversary armed with ideology as well as guns. Having taken possession of eastern Europe, the Soviet Union pressed against Iran, Turkey, and Greece. Each sat on a perimeter of the Middle East. And beyond each lay the invasion routes followed west for centuries by invaders from the east. And at the end sat the Suez Canal. Britain and France, the lingering colonial powers of the region, were so enfeebled by World War II that they were incapable of providing the countervailing force to Soviet expansionism. Only the United States could block the breach.

Military responsibilities fed economic interests. Americans, the isolationists of the 1920s, now tasted the elixir of foreign profit. The Middle East's 32 billion barrels of proven petroleum reserves beckoned a nation embarking on the greatest economic expansion of modern times. By luck and the foresight of a few swashbuckling oil pioneers, U.S. petroleum companies held the concessions on Saudi Arabia's petroleum.† Discovered in 1938, it remained untapped through World War II. But as soon as the guns ceased and the sea lanes opened, geologists, engineers, and drillers landed on the sandy dunes of Dhahran to open the richest oil field in the world. By

---

* Iran was producing oil by 1914. Concessions in Iraq were granted in 1912 but the German, Dutch, and British consortium became paralyzed by the politics of World War I, delaying major production until 1927. It was the 1930s before oil was discovered in Saudi Arabia.

† U.S. oil companies also had a piece of the action in Iraq.

October 1945, the Arabian-American Oil Company (Aramco) had spread northward and westward implanting ice cream machines, jukeboxes, and crews of drillers at Ras Tanura and Abqaiq. The prewar pioneering period of exploration gave way to full production, mighty growth, and great profits.

At the same time, American bankers, salesmen, and entrepreneurs moved into beautiful, brash Beirut and from there fanned out into markets never before plowed by Americans. By 1948, American interests crept like vines through that part of the globe called Arab.

The affairs of men never begin at a precise time and place isolated from all that went before. But if a time and place must be chosen to signal the United States' political entanglement in the Middle East, it is 1948 in Palestine.

If Oman is the eastern end of the Arab world, pre-1948 Palestine lay near its western perimeter. As part of the Levant that bordered the Mediterranean, it formed the buffer between the West and the Arab hinterland.* Harboring Christians, Jews, and Muslims, Palestine was nonetheless distinctly Arab. But Arab Palestine vanished in 1948 when Jewish Israel claimed its land.

Tel Aviv, a Jewish town in an Arab environment before 1948, is today a heavy concentration of buildings and highways that stretch for miles along the Mediterranean, a celebration of the creation and survival of the state of Israel. All that is left of the perished Palestine in this part of Israel is Jaffa, just south of Tel Aviv's beaches. The flat docks reaching like long fingers into the Mediterranean across which the trade of Palestine flowed are still there. So are the limestone buildings rising like stair steps from the sea to the bluff above where families lived and merchants plied their trade. Both are quiet now—preserved as a museum by the government of Israel.

The breeze always blows cool across the top of Jaffa. There is no better place to buy an ice cream, find a bench, and enjoy the long sweep of ocean running north to Tel Aviv. At the point between what was and what is, the last forty-plus years in the Middle East come back.

In 1948, the victorious Allied powers from World War II played midwife at the birth of Israel. For the West, its symbolism was pro-

* The Levant is the eastern end of the Mediterranean that encompasses Lebanon, Israel, and the coastal areas of Syria.

found. The starving, tortured remnants of European Jewry released from Hitler's concentration camps proved the justice of six long, bloody years of wrenching warfare. And if the defeat of Nazism proved the worth of Western values growing out of the Judeo-Christian tradition, then the emaciated, lame, and destitute who went to Palestine to join the Zionist drive for a Jewish national homeland must attest to the vigor of those values. The descendants of Americans who sat in their pews hearing the story of how the boy David felled the giant Goliath bought into the Zionist dream.

Jews out of the diaspora, armed with Western money and diplomatic support, set out to rebuild the kingdom of David. And as in Biblical times, this modern day tribe of Jews would have to defeat the tribe already there—the Arab Palestinians. In a reversal of the exile at the hands of the Romans, it was the Jews who stayed in Palestine while others exited under a force stronger than themselves. As a result, the central conflict of the Middle East was born. If ordinary Americans did not understand the ramifications, neither did their government. The United States, directly and indirectly, playing patron or policeman, acting from national interests and raw emotion, drew the state of Israel to itself.

In 1955, Arab humiliation at the loss of Palestine found its voice in Egypt's Gamal Abdul Nasser. From Cairo to Baghdad, Nasser's passionate rhetoric against the West pulled the masses of the Arab world to the man and his message of Arab pride and Arab power. On July 26, 1956, the thirty-eight-year-old army colonel turned president shouted to 100,000 people jammed into Alexandria's Liberation Square, "The Suez Canal belongs to us!" Tanker mileage from the rich Persian Gulf oil fields to New York threatened to increase 3,500 miles. Oil stocks in London nose-dived $168 million. And shares in the Suez Canal Company plummeted, forcing the French franc into another postwar relapse. The West took its first hit from the Arabs.

Britain and France joined by Israel struck back. British bombers and French warships pounded the Canal Zone, crippling the port city of Ismailia while Israeli tanks raced across the Sinai gobbling up Egyptian territory mile after mile. And then Dwight Eisenhower said no. Nasser lost the battle of 1956 but he won the war.

Across the Arab world, pictures of the handsome, smiling Nasser papered public buildings and dark hovels and his voice poured from the airwaves into cheap radios. He dined with Nikita Khrushchev in the secrecy of the Kremlin. And he talked nonalignment with Yugoslavia's Tito and India's Nehru. With $200 million worth of weapons delivered by the Soviets, he grew larger than life. The Arab world had become part of the cold war, a vital piece in the strategic maneuvers of the superpowers. In July 1958, Nasser's emboldened followers were among those who murdered Iraq's King Faisal, the symbolic anchor of the West's defensive alliance against Soviet incursion into the oil-rich Middle East. The next day, American Marines in full battle gear stormed across the soft, wide beaches of Beirut. For the first time but not the last, United States military power injected itself into the puzzling, far-off world of the Arabs.

In 1967, Israel stilled Nasser's power to incite millions against the "imperialist West." In six days the Arab world was reordered politically and geographically. Nasser, the Arab messiah, stood naked. The West Bank of the Jordan River, the narrow strip of territory along the Mediterranean known as Gaza, the Golan Heights overlooking the rich valleys of the Galilee, and eternal Jerusalem passed into the eager hands of the Israelis. These lost territories became the new focus of Arab unity and propelled a new symbol of Arab resolve—the Palestinian commando. It would be in the person of the commando that Arab grievances would thrust themselves on a complacent world.

Beginning in 1968, middle-class Americans traveling on cheap package tours to the "Holy Land," American businessmen plying their Middle East markets, and ordinary U.S. citizens going nowhere beyond Europe became caught up in the storm of Arab politics. Angry men carrying automatic weapons and hand grenades attacked the airport in gentle Zurich. Other angry men boarded TWA and Pan Am to engrave the fear of "hijacking" into the mind of every passenger, every airline, and every airport.

Terrorism was death, but it was also theater. In September 1970, three hijacked airliners carrying the national flags of the United States, Switzerland, and Britain brooded on a crude desert airstrip in Jordan. While the $28 million worth of aircraft sat in hundred-degree heat, the lives of 439 passengers served as the currency of negotiation for those empowered by terror. Masked men commanding no force beyond hand weapons and nerve had rendered kings and presidents helpless and laid low conventional military might. It was only the beginning of the United States' awakening to the limits of its power in the Arab world.

As guerrillas continued to hit far-flung targets deemed enemy territory, it seemed no place was any longer safe from the Middle East's quarrels. And then on September 5, 1972, terrorism hit the twentieth Olympiad in Munich. Just before dawn, masked men entered the athletes' village and quickly forced their way into an apartment housing the Israeli Olympic team. Television cameras already in place to beam the victories of the world's greatest athletes trained instead on a hooded figure on a balcony challenging the existing order in the Middle East. The world of the Arabs, once so far away, injected itself directly into the living rooms of average Americans.

The next year, the world of the Arabs would invade American pocketbooks and alter forever the relationship between the West and the Arab east. On October 20, 1973, Arab oil producers embargoed shipments of oil, the most crucial commodity in the Western economic system, to those countries supporting Israel. In the United States, panicked car owners lined up to buy gasoline refined from petroleum that jumped from $3.01 a barrel on October 15 to $11.65 a barrel on Christmas Eve. While the oil sheikhs filled their coffers, the United States experienced soaring inflation, strangled business, and mounting unemployment. Americans now knew in real terms what they had known in intellectual terms for the last decade and a half—the economic health of the West lay at the mercy of Arab oil suppliers. No longer could the fields of Texas, Oklahoma, Louisiana, and California feed the United States' voracious appetite for petroleum. The United States along with the rest of the industrialized world was dependent on the resources of the Persian Gulf. As a result, the United States could allow no force to interrupt Western access to Arab oil.

In 1979, the threat to oil supplies came from raging Islam. On February 1, a fragile, bearded man enveloped in black crept down the steps of an Air France 747 parked on the tarmac of Tehran airport. The Ayatollah Ruhollah Khomeini had returned to Iran to complete the Islamic revolution. Nine months later, a ragtag lot of four hundred Iranian students marched through the streets of Tehran chanting, "Death to America." Reaching the American embassy, the hated "nest of vipers," they bridged the gates to lay claim to fifty-two hostages. For the next 412 days, the United States itself became hostage to passions it did not understand. Militant Islam, coming out of Persian Iran, spread to the Arab side of the Persian Gulf, threatening to separate the West from its lifeblood. But it was in Lebanon that crusading Islam slammed against the United States.

Little Lebanon, the Switzerland of the East, always symbolized what the West wished the Arab world to be. But since 1975, Lebanon had delineated all of America's negative attitudes toward the Arab world—tribal, irrational, chaotic, brutal. By 1982, the endemic conflicts with each other had been exacerbated by Palestinians, Syria, Israel, and the Islamic Republic of Iran. It was this Lebanon, a Lebanon wracked by communalism, rivalry, and hatred, to which the United States military returned almost a quarter century after America's first military incursion into the Middle East. But this time U.S. Marines would not casually patrol beaches strewn with bikini-clad swimmers or stroll the shops on Beirut's Hamra Street. They would hole up in bunkers guarding against an enemy they did not understand. And on October 23, 1983, they would be struck down by a shadowy force calling itself the Islamic Jihad.

At 6:20 A.M. on that Sunday morning a big yellow Mercedes truck turned into Beirut airport's Aviation Safety Building, housing the American contingent of the Multinational Force summoned to Lebanon to try to restore order. As the truck reached the guard at the gate, the driver flashed a smile and hit the accelerator. Moments later the "Beirut Hilton" collapsed, destroyed by two thousand pounds of explosives. Across the United States, Americans grimly watched 241 young Marines in the prime of life dug from the ruins. And again few knew why.

They understood even less why Terry Anderson, Benjamin Weir, Jeremy Levin, Thomas Sutherland, and Father Lawrence Jenco—journalists, educators, and clergymen—disappeared off the streets of Lebanon to become hostages to amorphous organizations claiming a grim assortment of political agendas. Or why the battered corpse of a Navy diver named Robert Dean Stethem was kicked out of the rear door of the hijacked TWA flight 847 sitting on the runway of Beirut airport.

Yet even before hostages, individual and collective, became the coin of conflict in Lebanon, the United States had already surrendered to forces it could not control. On February 26, 1984, seven Marines with their battle gear strapped to their backs waded through the gentle surf of Green Beach and onto a landing craft silhouetted against the ravaged city scape of Beirut. From the pack of the last man, a three-foot rod extended upward. On it hung a small American flag. The United States was leaving Lebanon and the Arab world behind. But it would be back.

A little over three years later, the frigate USS *Stark* moved through the night patrolling the Persian Gulf's shipping lanes, which were imperiled by the Iraq-Iran war. At 10:08 P.M. two Exocet missiles from an Iraqi Mirage ripped through its thin steel hull midway between the deck and the waterline. Another thirty-seven flag-draped coffins bearing Americans came home from the Middle East. Ronald Reagan and more than a thousand mourners gathered in a sweltering helicopter hangar in May Port, Florida, to say goodbye. A grieving president recounted the sorrow of an Iowa couple who lost all five of their sons in World War II—"In some ways, it was easier to bear then because it was easier to understand why we were there, why we were fighting."* The next time Americans died in the Middle East they knew why they were fighting.

In the dark hours just before the dawn of August 2, 1990, hundreds of Iraqi tanks, trucks, and armored personnel carriers rammed across the sand and scrub border of Kuwait. Before they reached Dasman Palace, Emir Jaber al-Ahmed al-Sabah and his family jumped into a fleet of cars and sped toward Saudi Arabia. Block by block the invading Iraqi forces took the palace, the airport, and the cash-rich central bank. Within twelve hours, Kuwait was Saddam Hussein's. To the south lay Saudi Arabia's rich oil fields, contributing 17 percent of the industrialized world's oil supplies.

It was the crisis American policymakers had dreaded since the early 1970s, and they were ready. Six days after Iraq invaded Kuwait, American troops and treasure began to pour into the most desolate reaches of the Arab world.

In the summer of 1978, I stood alone just above a broad dip in the terrain outlining the dry riverbed of Wadi al-Batin in northern Saudi Arabia. Around me, the desert stretched out in every direction—empty, featureless, void of color. And above me the vast arch of perfect blue sky spanning the horizon dwarfed the earth that it crowned. It all spoke of another planet afloat in the endless universe. Other than the lone black donkey that stood suspended on the horizon, there was nothing—nothing but heat and silence.

In the late summer of 1990, that silence disappeared. This same desert crawled with growling half-tracks and honking jeeps. Tents and artillery emplacements fanned out across the flat landscape, conquering its emptiness. And that hollow yet exquisite sense of

---

* *Time*, June 1, 1987.

loneliness was gone, replaced by the gnawing sense of anxiety that comes with the threat of war. In January 1991, war came. Spectacular military victory gave way to an imperfect peace. The following October the United States succeeded in convening a tumultuous peace conference in which Arabs faced Israelis on one level and faced each other on another level. Americans found themselves confronting head-on the world of the Arabs—a world they had never understood.

Over the last four decades, the United States has been called to the Middle East to protect the Zionist dream; roused to stop the perceived march of communism into the heart of Islam and the Soviet Union into the Middle East's oil fields; lured into Lebanon in the naive belief that order could be imposed on a tribal war; coaxed to keep the oil flowing out of the Persian Gulf; and finally called to intervene against ambition and naked aggression. The Arab world once was so far away from everyday American life that it existed only in old stereopticon photos and the articles of travel writers plying obscure backroads that had no relevance to real life. But the Arab world is no longer some indistinct place somewhere east of Europe. It is here. It is now. And it is difficult.

The Arabs are tortuously trapped between their deep sense of unity as a people and their constant conflicts over competing parochial and national interests. The result is seeming chaos in which the Arabs constantly unite and divide, unite and divide.

The Arabs' unity is found in part in the long history of their region that can be felt from the Nile to the Persian Gulf. In Egypt's poverty-ridden villages, blindfolded oxen trudge around and around drawing to the surface the water that sustains fields cultivated since the time of the pharaohs. And women, as they always have, sit outside their small square houses pounding dough into flat loaves while their children run barefoot along the dusty lanes. But the sense of continuity comes most forcefully when the prayer call goes out from the flat roof of a mud brick mosque just as it has every day for over a thousand years.

People, plants, animals, ways of life—everything in the world of the Arabs has about it the feeling of long, uninterrupted time. Even the land on which the Arabs live refuses to give much that is new. The coastal plains, river valleys, and oases produce in their season. But most of the dry, rock-hard land simply marks time— year to year, generation to generation, century to century. Nor do the skyscrapers that the Kuwaitis built in the heyday of the 1970s oil boom erase the aura of tradition that arises when a single-sail dhow is spotted rocking in the Persian Gulf's shallow waters.

Time, religion, and tradition give the Arab world its great emotional unity. It is a unity that binds all those who identify themselves as Arabs into one powerful, mystical whole. In this sense, the Arab world is one, a mighty nation aligned against all who would seek to humble it.

Yet this same world resonates with its own discord. While so much that is the Arab world is locked in time and tradition, the rest is ensnared in rivalry and conflict.

Arab society is tribal. It is anchored in vast and not so vast extended families that trace their exact and inclusive histories back over centuries. I have listened to an illiterate Bedouin in a tent on the desert recite his lineage generation after generation, and I have heard a Palestinian in a refugee camp place his family exactly in the hierarchy of pre-1948 Palestine. But family is more than genealogy. It is life itself. For it is from the family that an Arab draws his identity and his security.

Families coalescing in villages and neighborhoods become clans; clans coagulate into regions or religious sects or sometimes pseudopolitical parties or military organizations which drive the political process. Arabs are not citizens of a nation-state. They are members of self-contained groups who compete peacefully or militarily to mold the nation to their particular will. This is how society functions, for family and tribe are part of the ancient fabric of the Arab world. But the nation-state is an alien in Arab culture, a Western idea imposed on the Arab world in the twentieth century by the forces of Europe. The Arabs came to nationhood late, and they came with their tribalism intact. And it is as tribes that they largely manage their countries.

Arab states often survive because strongmen hold them together by force of arms and will. These authority figures in pushing their own interests or the interests of their group or their nation as defined by themselves compete politically, militarily, economically, and psychologically. Thus Egypt's Gamal Abdul Nasser battled with charisma. Jordan's King Hussein duels with cunning and brains. The House of Saud stands behind the bulwark of religion. Syria's Hafiz Assad connives. And Saddam Hussein unleashes brute force. But all ultimately face the painful process of building states that can function in the late twentieth century. It follows, therefore, that as respective states develop their own specific identities, their rivalries over national interests intensify.

Yet no Arab leader or Arab state is willing to surrender "Arabism"—a phenomenon that only Arabs truly understand. The emotional commitment to unity works itself into every dispute and every crisis in the Arab world. The Arab states, at odds over competing interests and quarreling with one another over their own vision of events, are nonetheless irresistibly drawn together in the search for an "Arab solution." This coming together is a ritual in which nations and leaders seek once again to reaffirm their identity as Arabs but fail to admit their differences as nations. Thus the Arabs are united by the senses, not the limbs. They are essentially linked by a huge invisible nervous system that lives outside a skeleton. When pressure is applied at one point, reaction can occur at some wholly different place.

The Arabs move rapidly back and forth between the realm of brotherhood and the recesses of betrayal, between unity and conflict. The forces of unity, so strong, and the reasons of disunity, so powerful, constantly war with each other. It is this juxtaposing of conflict and unity that fuels the turmoil of the Arab world. And it is in the understanding of both the mythology of unity and the reality of conflict that the United States and the West can learn to live with the Arabs.

Any conference of Arab states fires the mechanism that seeks unity in discord. In early 1979, I watched as an inter-Arab conference convened at the new King Faisal Conference Center in Riyadh, Saudi Arabia. Sleek black Mercedes-Benzes responding to the direction of a bevy of security officers frantically blowing whistles and waving their arms turned off King Saud Street and inched toward the door of the gold-toned geodesic dome that is the meeting hall. As each car stopped below the canopy extending out from the glass-and-chrome front, ushers in brilliant white dresslike *thobes* jerked open car doors, releasing the representatives of the Arab world. They came in the name of revolutionary leaders and hereditary rulers, presidents and the chairman of the Palestine Liberation Organization. They wore business suits, military uniforms, and flowing robes. They came from countries possessing ancient cultures and countries boasting new wealth. They were part of regimes that nudged democratic philosophy and regimes that survived only by crushing opposition beneath steel heels.

In the grand conference center dominated by a massive crystal chandelier, they sat around a circular table that nodded to the equal status of all from proud, impoverished Egypt to rich, revolutionary Iraq. They were rivals. They were enemies. They held competing interests and harbored corroding grudges. But they were there together because they were Arabs. In this place at this time, as in all places at all times, the Arab mystique superseded all else—economics, politics, and logic. The reason lay in the very origins of the people called Arab.

PART I

THE
MYTHOLOGY
OF
UNITY

CHAPTER 1

THE NOBLE BEDOUIN

IN HIGH SUMMER ON THE ARABIAN peninsula, the broiling afternoon sun pounds the desert's rock-strewn floor with a force that defies man to challenge its brutal dominance. And man surrenders. Through the barren, ragged hills, the dry wadis, and the rolling oceans of sand, a breathless quiet reigns during the heat of the day. Nothing stirs—not human, not beast, not breeze. In this stillness, all patiently wait for release from the sun's fury. At last late afternoon comes, when shadows lengthen and temperatures soften. And then comes twilight, bringing its own magic to the desert. Broken strings of stately camels move as silhouettes past towering escarpments painted in rich pinks and purples by the sunset, and the first brilliant stars appear in a cloudless sky untouched by the pollution of man. On the desert at dusk, centuries compress, bringing into union past and present.

The fiery furnace of the Arabian peninsula produced the original Arabs. At the dawn of history, the Arabian peninsula was a vast junction where migrating people coming out of Africa and other pockets of human development mingled and merged into a people known as Semites. By the advent of the Neolithic Age, waves of these Semites had moved north and west out of the barren peninsula. And by 3000 B.C., some had settled in the flat, fertile lands between the Tigris and Euphrates rivers, where they pressed the history of Mesopotamia into tablets of clay. Others found their way to the Nile. Drawing from the river's fertile gifts, they merged into the great Egyptian civilization of the pharaohs.* In later waves, the Semitic Assyrians, Canaanites, Phoenicians, Nabataeans, Amorites, and Hebrews made their way out of Arabia into the Levant. But others stayed behind on the wide peninsula between the Red Sea and the Persian Gulf. As early as 854 B.C., Assyrian records identified them as "Arabs."

United in language, they divided into two groups claiming a different ancestor. The Qahtan, short with round heads, lived as a settled population in the rain-fed uplands in what is now northwest Yemen. The Adnan, angular with elongated skulls, inhabited the great northern reaches of the peninsula. It was the Arabs of the north who sat on the crossroads of the frankincense and spice trade between Yemen and the Mediterranean. From the first century B.C. to the sixth century A.D., they held this pivotal position, exercising their influence from the cities of Mecca and Medina. But it was the Bedouin, the nomads of the desert, who infused Arab society with its values.

What is today described as Arab culture did not develop until after the Islamic conquests of the seventh century A.D. It grew out of a mix of different ethnic groups, languages, and traditions that were encompassed in the Islamic empire. And it was a product of the cities, not the desert.† But who and what Arabs are today began with the Bedouin of the Arabian peninsula.

Long after other Semitic groups moved northward, the Bedouin of Arabia remained the most unsoiled repository of the values that the ancient Semites carried with them into the valleys of the Euphrates, the Nile, and the Jordan. Transported north again by the armies of Islam, Bedouin ways were diluted by and integrated into civilizations far more sophisticated than their own. But over time, the Bedouin, uncorrupted and untamed by civilization, became

---

* Ancient Egyptian showed some kinship with Semitic languages. There was also some Semitic influx into ancient Egypt but the exact relationship between the Egyptians and the Semites remains unclear.
† See Chapter 2.

a bloodbank of new vitality for the jaded urban society beyond Arabia. Today Arabs both disdain the Bedouin and, at the same time, harbor a romantic love for the nomadic life and the simplicity, dignity, and virtue of the desert. As a consequence, the Bedouin exists beyond the bounds of reality to become the legendary knight of Arab culture.

Century after century, the Bedouin roamed free across central and northern Arabia. From the time they domesticated the camel in the eleventh or twelfth century B.C., the Bedouin used the desert as an impenetrable fortress behind which they guarded their unique way of life. Living on the livestock they herded from one oasis to another, providing their own protection, disappearing at will into the endless sand, the Bedouin lived free of all authority.

Convinced of their own superiority, the Bedouin held themselves contemptuously above the farmers of the oases and the merchants of the towns. For they held sway in the desert with a nobility that few could explain but all perceived. As late as the 1940s, the British explorer Wilfred Thesiger, who had crisscrossed the Arabian peninsula for five years with no companions other than the Bedouin, testified that among no other people did he feel the same sense of personal inferiority. "All they possessed were their camels and saddlery, their rifles and daggers, some waterskins and cooking pots and bowls, and the very clothes they wore. . . . [Yet] they met every challenge, every hardship, with the proud boast: 'We are Bedu.' "*

Bedouin pride rose out of an incredible ability to survive. Gaining their only shelter in long, open-front tents woven from the wiry black hair of their goats, they sucked like parasites on the sour milk of their animals and on dates from the palms of the widely scattered oases. They covered their bodies with a simple long shirt, or *thobe*, that dropped from their thin shoulders to just above the ankle and draped their heads against the sun and wind with the square *gutra* held in place by a looped cord that doubled as a camel tether. On their calloused feet, they wore crude sandals cut from the dried skins of their stock. Hewn out of sand and dust and rock, the Bedouin claimed neither cities nor pharaohs, only an endurance to survive in the environment nature had bequeathed them. Some have never surrendered to the dictates of government.

---

* Wilfred Thesiger, *The Life of My Choice* (New York: W. W. Norton, 1987), p. 398.

Saudi Arabia once resonated to the migrations of the Bedouin. But today less than 5 percent of the population still clings to a migrating life-style. Defying a government that holds out seductive incentives to settle, they continue to live in solitary camps that are fortresses without walls, defended by an arsenal of antiquated and modern rifles. Only the rare outsider is ever invited in.

It was a sparkling clear winter day. A group of us from the King Faisal Specialist Hospital in Riyadh, where my husband was a physician, were camping on the desert. We always stayed clear of the Bedouin camps, and the Bedouin always stayed contemptuously clear of us. But on this day, a battered white Datsun pickup chasing a stray camel skidded to a stop. The driver had recognized among us the surgeon who had recently operated on him. To our total astonishment, we were all invited to his camp just over the hill. I threw a long skirt over my jeans and hopped into our Nissan Patrol as my husband swung in behind the pickup.

In the middle of this great empty desert, a long, low, black goat-hair tent floated between the gray of the sand and the blue of the sky. From its open front, children poured out, excitedly waving at the approaching vehicles. Inside a dozen or so men put down the narghile, the old hubbly-bubbly, got up from woven mats strewn with foam-rubber bolsters, and moved out to greet us. Finally the women, swathed in black, their faces hidden by veils that left only their kohl-rimmed eyes exposed, tentatively emerged. The patriarch waved them forward to escort me and the other women into the female quarters of the long tent.

A Bedouin camp in the last decade of the twentieth century juxtaposes the past and the present and overlays both against the Bedouin's timeless sense of themselves. Colorful Bedouin weavings, wooden bowls, and pounded copper pots no longer compose the whole of the Bedouin's belongings. Foam-rubber sleeping mats purchased in a Riyadh souk lay in the far corner. Imported aluminum trunks held the group's possessions. And battered enamel utensils made in Taiwan served the tea. The children who clustered around my feet wore knits from Hong Kong, while their mothers hid multi-hued polyester from China under their black *abbayas*, or cloaks. Sitting not on old, worn tribal rugs but on woven plastic mats imported from Yemen, we watched the men, wearing Western-style shoes and knock-off Rolex watches, pull a roasted lamb from an oven created from an oil drum. Yet in spite of the eclectic origins of their possessions, the Bedouin proved they had not lost touch with their past.

As day faded into evening and the chill of a desert night set in, the three-foot-high collection of gnarled sticks that had sat in the center of the camp through the day suddenly burst into flame. In its light and warmth, the feeling of isolation of this single camp on an empty plateau in the center of the Arabian peninsula dissipated. The women still stayed apart, relegated by their culture to the role of spectator. But the men, filled by roasted lamb, rice sprinkled with pine nuts, flat Arabic bread, and endless cups of tea consumed through the long afternoon, gathered to dance. They locked arms and began a slow rhythmic pattern around the fire, voicing the monotones of the songs that had rolled over this barren landscape for centuries. They became one with their past. The cities from which they had escaped, the television sets projecting cartoons and images of Mecca, the shopping centers and huge, glittering airports, the new government bureaucrats who planned their integration into Saudi society, faded away as the Bedouin celebrated their heritage. At that moment, a sense of eternity hung over that camp. The pride of the Bedouin—his innate sense of independence, his confidence in his ability to endure physical hardship, his commitment to family, his faith in himself—was still there.

Bedouin culture has implanted in the Arab society that arcs from the Persian Gulf to the Mediterranean powerful forces of both division and unity. Arab society is at all times both fractured and whole as the energies that divide it play against the energies that join it. Societal schisms that torment all contemporary Arab states vary in specifics and degrees and are often complicated by forces beyond Arab society itself. Nonetheless they follow the general patterns found in the Bedouin's deep commitment to family and tribe, the dictate of vengeance, and the concept of honor. At the same time, these societies claim a solidarity that is rooted in the language of the Bedouin and the religion birthed on the Arabian peninsula.

The desert was capable of supporting nothing more than a subsistence economy. In its most rudimentary form, government, even on the level of the small city-state, required nonagricultural administrators, soldiers, and craftsmen, who demanded to be fed. But the desert did not yield surplus food. As a result, no governments capable of either binding the Bedouin together or acting as arbitrators in the fierce competition for scarce, life-giving water and pasture developed. Life on the desert was only possible if individuals and groups joined in tight, cohesive units bound by ties of blood.

It was this overwhelming need for security that led the Bedouin over the centuries to build their society around patrilineal families locked in steadfast fidelity and sacred obligation to one another. Exact and inclusive, bloodlines united all who traced their descent from a common male ancestor. Thus in the open desert, the family, like a fort, gathered its members within walls built on consanguineous solidarity. Together, father and son, brother and brother, cousin and cousin, wandered in search of pasture, camped together, practiced ingroup marriage, and perpetuated the sacrosanct bonds of kinship. Within the group, cohesion was maintained by instilling into each member, as the supreme and unquestioned value of life, a commitment to group integrity and the assumption of mutual responsibility. In small social units in which every person knew every other person, in which all were related by blood, or at least by a fiction of common descent, the imperative of family took hold. Pressures to conform, to uphold the collective good, and to live by the unwritten but universally recognized moral code of the group bound every member. The message was so effective because the reality was so stark—without the support and protection of the kin group, the individual would be lost.

The price the individual had to pay for this protection was strict conformity to the family's values and code of behavior. A Bedouin internalized these to the extent that he ceased to identify himself emotionally as an individual. Rather his wishes reflected the wishes of his father; his interests matched those of the group; and he, like it, distrusted and disliked people outside his own kinship group.

Little in this set of attitudes has changed either on the Arabian peninsula or in the rest of the Arab world. "The family is the alpha and omega of the whole system; the primary group and structural model for any possible grouping, it is the indissoluble atom of society which assigns and assures to each of its members his place, his function, his very reason for existence and, to a certain degree, his existence itself."*

To understand the Arab world is to come to terms with family.

---

* Pierre Bourdieu, quoted in David Pryce-Jones, *The Closed Circle: An Interpretation of the Arabs* (New York: Harper Perennial, 1991), p. 27.

While I was living in Saudi Arabia in the late 1970s and early 1980s, I was invited to dinner at the home of a sheikh. The car he sent to bring me to the Sulaminiyah section of Riyadh bumped over streets torn up by sewer installations, drove around rubble from construction piled high in the road, and finally turned at what proved to be a final corner. Expecting a house, I saw instead a miniature village. At the center, a large villa sat like a giant centerpiece. Fanning out behind it were four identical but smaller houses that fronted on a central swimming pool in the middle of a large garden. In a mammoth sitting room in the main house, scattered with heavy leather sofas on soft blue and beige Persian carpets, I met my host and his four sons. Each of the sons was in his late twenties or early thirties, married with his own children, and occupied one of the houses enclosed within the family compound. All over Saudi Arabia, similar family compounds exist, striking reproductions of the desert camp.

The compound concept is somewhat special to wealthy Saudi Arabia, but throughout the Arab world large extended families link in mutual loyalty and obligation. Weddings and births, illness and death bring the family together. In between, family members visit back and forth, engage in business or occupations together, transfer money from the best off to the worst off, connect into political configurations, and pair their children in the time-honored practice of arranged marriages that perpetuate the family's size and strength.

In pre-Islamic Arabia, families bought additional protection by joining clans that grafted onto tribes formed through links of common blood.* Although important in expanding the pool of marriage partners, the ultimate function of the tribe was the same as that of the family—to supply the crucial protection that members needed. Survival, in its most literal sense, depended on the tribe, because beyond it there was no political structure or policing power capable of enforcing order. In the desert, each man and his kin group stood against the rest of the world.

Since every facet of life on the desert revolved around the protection of family and tribe, the Bedouin developed interlocking social controls that made life on the desert possible. They began with vengeance and ended with hospitality.

Every group on the desert was hunter and prey at the same

* An entire tribe, even if numbering thousands, considered itself the offspring of one single mythical ancestor.

time. There was only so much vegetation, so much water, so much livestock. Tribes claimed grazing lands and wells that they had to defend with their lives, because they were, in fact, life itself. And their camels, sheep, and goats were fair game for the hit-and-run raids of rival tribes buying their own security against starvation.

The only way to survive "was by letting others know that if they violated you in any way, you would make them pay and pay dearly. . . . You had to make sure that if someone violated you in any way—even the smallest way—you would . . . punish them in a manner that signaled to all other families, clans, or tribes around that this is what happens if anyone tampers with me. . . . 'I am my own defense and I am good.' "*

Any group's security depended on numbers. This is precisely why the birth of a son so delighted a Bedouin family while the birth of a daughter meant just another mouth to feed until she married to produce sons for her husband's family. It is also why marriage between cousins was so desirable, for their offspring stayed within the kinship group. With numbers so crucial, the loss of even one person weakened the whole. Consequently, death at the hands of a rival tribe impacted on every kin of the dead man. Only by killing a member of the offending group could numbers be evened out and the weakness redressed. Thus the vengeful cry "blood demands blood" called every male member of the victims' kin group, the *khamsa*, to wreak revenge. From year to year and generation to generation, the demand for vengeance passed. Time meant nothing, as demonstrated by the sheikh who bragged to another that he had achieved revenge for a minor slight suffered by his tribe forty years earlier. Instead of congratulations, he got reproof: "You acted hastily."

Vengeance has its psychological as well as its practical side, for it is on one level an expression of honor. Honor is the driving force of the Arab psyche. It is a demanding master that stalks its vassal with a broadsword called shame. Honor, if it can be adequately defined in Western terms, is self-respect that comes not so much from the behavior of the individual but from the approval that he draws from his peers. The desire for respect is a basic human emotion that infects all cultures. The difference between many societies

---

* Thomas L. Friedman, *From Beirut to Jerusalem* (New York: Farrar, Straus & Giroux, 1989), p. 88.

and Arab society is the degree to which that need of approval is felt and the lengths to which it is pursued. In Arab culture, self-respect which is manifested in personal honor bestows worth on life. Shame, on the other hand, is like living death. Intolerable to the sufferer, it demands that any loss of honor be avenged. Thus in Arab culture, pride constantly plays against defensiveness, creating within Arabs and among Arabs a level of ongoing tension.

In ancient Arabia, the concept of honor imposed some order between competing tribes. If storming into a rival camp had simply been a matter of robbery, the weaker tribes, deprived of their animals by stronger ones, would have soon disappeared. But raiding carried with it a system of rules and the sanction of honor. Raids took place only between tribes, or sections of tribes, which were each other's equals, or near-equals, in both status and strength. With the Bedouin code of honor, a tribe considered noble within the hierarchy of the desert would never raid a tribe ranked far below it in status, nor would a large tribe attack a notably smaller tribe. To do so would have been so shameful that the noble tribe would have chosen to starve. The Bedouin meant what he said in his proverb "It is better to die with honor than to live in humiliation."

In contemporary terms, Bedouin do not smuggle across Jordan's long, open borders for the simple and at the same time complex reason that the chance of being caught poses an intolerable threat to personal honor. According to a Captain Zani who gave up the desert for employment in the border patrol, "There is great fear of being stopped and put in prison. We are very proud and cannot tolerate humiliation, and prison would be the ultimate humiliation."*

All different kinds of honor from bravery in battle to generosity extended to guests to the sexual chastity of his sisters and daughters interlocked to surround the Bedouin ego like a coat of armor. The smallest chink in that armor threatened to unhinge it, leaving the individual exposed to the greatest of all threats—shame. The values of tribal society demanded in the strongest terms that individual shame be avoided. If it occurred, then it must be hidden; if it was exposed, then it must be avenged. In the end and at any cost honor had to be restored.

---

* *New York Times*, December 13, 1990.

If honor was individual, it was also collective. The dishonor of any single member of the family imposed disgrace on the whole. For the Bedouin saw life as a caravan designed to carry the family over the dunes of the desert's combative society. As long as all members of the family obeyed the rules of conduct, the tightly knit caravan enabled them to survive. However, if one member allowed his camel to stray, the caravan would dissolve, leaving the family adrift in the open desert. It was therefore up to the adult males of the family to see that no member committed any act that would spell disaster for all. Defense of collective honor lay only on males. A woman could most readily imperil family honor through sexual misconduct, but it fell to the men to restore that honor even if it meant killing the offending female.

The restoration of honor in Arab society is not necessarily bloody or ugly. It can amount to nothing more than the reordering of a disrupted hierarchy in an office. Or it can mean a game of meaningless titles bestowed by a political entity, a practice not unknown in the West. It can also carry the appearance of sport. I was once in a small village built of yellow-veined stone that clung to a steep slope in the rugged and stark mountains of north-central Yemen. Across the valley, an almost identical village held to its own steep incline. As I climbed up narrow twisting steps that connected one house to another, three of the village men acting as self-appointed guides motioned me forward through a swarm of children, shouting "*Yellah, yellah!*—This way!"

Reaching the summit, I saw that the top of the mountain had been leveled enough to create an open area maybe forty by a hundred yards. Commanding its center were two aging cannons left over from Egypt's adventures in Yemen during the early 1960s. I sensed they were there as something more than pieces in an open-air museum. This led me to ask if there were difficulties with the opposite village. All around me heads, young and old, nodded an emphatic yes. The eldest of the men spoke. "There is always trouble with this village. They graze their sheep on this side of the valley, and the merchants are dishonest in trade." At that point, I asked what turned out to be the wrong question: "Do you ever fire the guns?" The spokesman of the group with a quick swoop of his arm motioned one of the boys toward a square stone hut just behind us. The child, maybe ten years old, ran and within seconds came staggering back carrying a heavy, corroded artillery shell. The elder then motioned two of his companions forward. One took the shell while the other slid open the breech. The shell went in. The gun roared, sending its missile hurling toward an open spot just below the offending village. My host, exposing his qat-stained teeth in a wide smile, turned to me and said, "Oh, yes, we sometimes fight. We must preserve the honor of our village."

The contest for honor takes place on every level of life in Arab society—who succeeds in avoiding dirtying his hands with manual labor, who yields in traffic, who secures the favor from a government official. All establish status from which vaunted self-esteem is delivered.

Honor builds from the individual to the nation to interstate relations and back down again in a constant battle of one Arab to get the better of another. This contest for honor fractures nations and divides countries. The tribes in southern Iraq feel superior to the market people, government employees exert their self-assigned status over the very people they are supposed to serve, and one dispossessed Palestinian holds his lineage above another dispossessed Palestinian. When Anwar Sadat criticized his predecessor, Gamal Abdul Nasser, the thrust was honor, not policy. "Members of the Committee [for the Liquidation of Feudalism] played havoc with life in Egypt everywhere, their gravest and most heinous crime being the shattering of human pride—which our people could never accept. The Egyptian people may endure poverty, deprivation, even starvation, but they can never accept hurt to their pride."* Nasser himself in an extreme exercise to protect the honor of Egypt kept from his ally King Hussein for thirty-six hours the truth that Israel in the opening hours of the 1967 War had wiped out his air force. Within what the Arabs claim as the Arab nation, Lebanese insist they are superior to Palestinians; Palestinians claim their superiority to Syrians; Syrians exhibit arrogance toward Saudis; while Egyptians question if they are even Arab because they consider themselves so superior to everyone else.

Even the Arabs' famous hospitality is an exercise in honor. The host in lavishing elaborate attention on his guest establishes himself as the master of the situation. While honor accrues to the guest, it accrues even more to the host. The exact origins of the Bedouin's

---

* Anwar el-Sadat, *In Search of Identity: An Autobiography* (New York: Harper & Row, 1978), p. 165.

famed practice of hospitality are lost, but its development was probably a response to dire need. In the wasteland of the desert, a man pursuing a straying camel could easily become separated from the protective circle of his kin and tribe. If the desert itself did not kill him, the first group he stumbled across probably would. Under the tribes' commonly accepted rules of hospitality, a wanderer coming upon a camp entered as an honored guest. The rule applied to everyone, including the son of a hated enemy or the target of bitter revenge. But mere protection was not enough. Generosity in food was also demanded. Poverty, even at its meanest, did not excuse a man from fulfilling the sublime duty of hospitality—to shelter and feed a guest for three days.

The ritual of hospitality fed into the strength of the group, because generous behavior secured for the giver a potential client and political ally in tribal disputes. Like other Bedouin values, it ultimately served the one great goal of Bedouin life—the invigoration of the group. Although the imperative of self-protection has passed, hospitality remains one of the dominant features of Arab culture. Just before ground troops attacked Iraqi lines in the 1991 Persian Gulf War, Saudi military officials refused to allow American intelligence analysts to interrogate hundreds of captured Iraqi prisoners because they were Saudi "guests."

Vengeance—a deterrent to indiscriminate slaughter—and hospitality—the guarantee of safety to someone separated from his group—were joined by the third restraint on the constant conflict of the desert: mediation.

In disputes and blood feuds, both sides would call in a mediator, someone who carried prestige and wielded influence. His job was to take both groups into his tent to strike a mutually acceptable accord or to arrange a truce that would last until broken by one side or the other. The function of the mediator was to allow the fighting sides to separate without incurring the shame that came from an exhibition of weakness or admission of defeat. By the same token, the failure of a settlement dishonored neither, only provided a new opportunity for mediation.

Mediation still stands as a time-honored tradition among Arabs. In crisis after crisis, Arab diplomats shuttle between capitals or presidents, and military rulers and kings meet at the summit to negotiate an "Arab solution" to disputes rocking the Arab political realm. Often they succeed in patching together some type of consensus, which lasts a few weeks, a few months, or even a few years. When that collapses, the mechanisms go into effect once again. Even when the quarreling parties fail to agree on any point in their dispute, the door always remains open for yet another try. Arabs, in search of a highly prized but elusive unity, always seek consensus. In its absence, they meet and meet and meet and issue one statement after another praising in the most eloquent Arabic the successful pursuit, although not the completion, of a united Arab position. If necessary, issues of discord are simply avoided in order to achieve some degree of unity. At the end of March 1991, shortly after Saddam Hussein had been forced by a coalition containing most of the other Arab states to withdraw from Kuwait, the Arab League meeting in Cairo agreed in advance to drop all reference to the Gulf War in the interest of Arab unity.

Family and tribe, retribution and vengeance take their toll on the nation-states of the Arab world. Nationalism, whether seen as good or bad, simply does not exist in the sense that an individual feels a strong primary loyalty to his country. Nor do political organizations which exercise real political power cross family or tribal lines to embrace broad political philosophy or the common interest. The Arabic word for the emotion that binds together the clan is, in fact, the same as the word for nationalism, *qawmiyah*. The great weakness of Arab states generally is that they are still deeply fragmented into families, clans, and tribes that protect their interests, both great and petty, as if their very survival depended on it. Just as in the harsh environment of Bedouin life, the family is security, the external world is strife. His tribe, whether it be a tribe based on kinship, religious confession, or region, writes his political agenda. Consequently, politics in the Arab world is too often competition between families and tribes for dominance in a contest in which higher goals are often lost.

Yet while the Arabs constantly war against the forces that so profoundly divide them, they hold high above the battle the great emotional symbols of their unity—first language and then religion. Both have their roots in the Bedouin past.

The Bedouin call themselves the "sons of Arabic," the most celebrated employers of language in the Arab world. Early in history, exceptional beings who possessed the ability to arrange words in such a way that the act of communication rose to an art inexplicably appeared in Bedouin culture. The *shair*, the illiterate Bedouin poet, gathered words like precious gems and strung them together in verses of incredible beauty. Others endowed with prodigious memories stored thousands of these poems in their minds. Around the sparse fires of the camps, they recited line after line to enraptured audiences. Still others exhibited the uncanny ability to engage in long debates entirely in verse. Over time, illiterate camel breeders, living in scattered tribes, lacking the most elementary political and economic structures, developed a language of incredibly rich texture and expression.

Every year Saudi Arabia holds a poetry contest in honor of former King Faisal. Tough, desert-hardened men in snowy white *thobes* and traditional red-and-white-check *gutras* stand before television cameras. In their rhythmic recitations, often delivered with their eyes closed, they transport themselves and their audience to an artistic level unmatched by anything else in Arab culture. In four years in Saudi Arabia, I never missed a poetry contest, even though my Arabic was no match for the nuances and subtleties that hid in the play of words. For me, simply listening to the rich sounds, one following on another, was enough.

The poet acted as the tongue and sword of his tribe. Every tribe had its poets, whose unwritten words flew across the desert faster than an arrow. For the *hija*, an insulting poem, was as much a weapon in the tribe's arsenal of weapons as the bow. It attested to the Bedouin's faith in the power of the word, the unshakable belief that an insult that found its mark caused great damage. It therefore followed that the more violent the insult, the more effective the result in striking the enemy low. Insults did not have to contain a grain of truth, only to be clad in the poetic form. Thus insults directed against an individual drummed out accusations that cut to the very quick of Bedouin disrespect—cowardice, timidity, avarice, and being of mixed blood. Against the group, the poet hurled charges of its weakness, deprecated the sexual conduct of its women, and the mediocrity of its poets and orators, and accused it of detestable habits such as eating the flesh of a dog. The grosser the insult, the more effective the *hija*.

Although tamed, the *hija* still exists. During the late 1970s, a spat between two of Saudi Arabia's military commanders ended when one contender struck down the other with a humiliating insult to the quality of his poetry. Ghazi A. Algosaibi, the former health minister and Saudi Arabia's most noted contemporary poet, subtly bragged in one of his poems, "May God protect me from the evil of my enemies, who suffer because of your gifts to me and who cause me to suffer with them."*

For all Arabs, Arabic—reaching its perfection in the Koran—represents the ideal of higher self. At their best, Arab writers and political orators make full use of all the vast linguistic resources of the Arabic language including emphasis, exaggeration, and elaborate metaphor. The result is that a column in a daily newspaper or remarks given at the inauguration of a village water pump can intoxicate its audience. Just as Westerners can be enraptured by Italian opera without knowing a word of Italian, Arab audiences can be moved more by how something is said than what is said. The two-hour-long songs of the famous Egyptian singer Umm Khalthum were more exercises in language than music. And the long speeches of Arab politicians aspire to beautiful, powerful language, not necessarily reasoned, rational arguments. A Lebanese once said about a famous Arab politician, "Yesterday I heard him speak for two hours without pausing or looking at any notes. He was magnificent." As to what he said: "Oh, I don't remember."†

The poetry of the Bedouin breathed with bravery and celebrated the glories of raids run against rival groups to steal the herds and the water that sustained life on the desert.

Whoever is in terror of the ways Death may come, Death shall yet slay him, though he aspire to mount to heaven on the rungs of a ladder.
Whoever suffers people always to be riding upon him, and never spares himself humiliation, shall come to rue it.
Whoever defends not his water-tank with his goodly weapons will see it broken; whoever assaults not others is himself assaulted.‡

Language—emotional, powerful, and artistic—provided the Bedouin a sense of identity and a degree of unity that was missing elsewhere in an environment in which the only imperative was sur-

---

* Ghazi A. Algosaibi, *Arabian Essays* (London: Kegan Paul International, 1982).
† Peter Mansfield, *The Arabs* (Middlesex, England: Pelican, 1985), p. 493.
‡ The poet Zuhayr ibn Abi Sulma, quoted in Bernard Lewis, ed., *Islam and the Arab World: Faith, People, Culture* (New York: Alfred A. Knopf, 1976), p. 202.

vival. Religion added protection from evil spirits and conservation of his values.

By the beginning of the Christian era and probably long before, the Bedouin were a minority on the Arabian peninsula. The majority of the population farmed the oases, tilled the rain-fed slopes of southwestern mountains, or plied the trades in widely scattered towns or in the peninsula's major trading center—Mecca. A scant fifty miles inland from the Red Sea, Mecca sat at a crossroads of the trade routes that brought the spices and frankincense from Yemen north to the seaports on the Mediterranean. Lying on the margins of the civilized world dominated by the Byzantine and Persian empires, Mecca was the subject of neither. But because of the wealth of these empires, Mecca experienced an economic boom as more and more caravans shifted goods from the south to the north. Taking advantage of their position at a major crossroads, Meccan merchants organized trade fairs, added more caravans, and scurried to capitalize on the spinoffs from increased commerce. The results were social as well as economic. Radical change moved Mecca from a partly Bedouin society into an urban society. In the process, traditional loyalties eroded and old values declined. Tribal culture—the most basic element to survival on the desert—gave way to a society that glorified individual initiative and wealth.

Removed from the new influences engulfing Mecca and other settled areas experiencing the same changes, the Bedouin still clung to the revered values of desert life—honor, bravery, hospitality, and the sacredness of family and tribe. Pagans, they worshiped various gods dwelling in rocks and other elements of nature and lived in terror of a swarm of spirits, or *jinn*, that lurked everywhere, ready to attack the hapless desert dweller. With no priesthood or other trappings of an organized religion, the Bedouin's only ritual was to come to Mecca from time to time to fulfill an ill-defined pilgrimage at a square, windowless building known as the Kaaba. The Kaaba was under the guardianship of Mecca's ruling tribe—the Quraysh.

The Quraysh, an extensive tribe linking a covey of mercantile families, personified the gulf between the ethical system of the Bedouin and the new materialism that gripped the ruling class. Around it a volcano of clan infighting spewed which threatened to unravel the old tribal system that had knit the competitive and fractious society into some kind of order. As clan undercut clan, life became a cycle of attack and vengeance.

The city and the desert confronted each other in a way that has never been resolved. About 1950, King Abdullah of Jordan spoke to the same issues that had divided seventh-century society on the Arabian peninsula. "The town dwellers represent a group of those who have spoken Arabic since the rise of the Arabs in the distant past. They, however, have lost the true Arab feeling and have become confused and insensible, striving like the others for self-gain and self-aggrandizement."*

It was into this social disruption that Abu al-Qasim Muhammed ibn Abdullah ibn Abd al-Muttalib ibn Hashim was born in A.D. 570 or 571. His father died on a caravan journey before Muhammed was born. His mother died six years later, leaving Muhammed an orphan. After two years with his grandfather, he passed to the care of an uncle, Abu Talib, who claimed like Muhammed and his father before him membership in the Bani Hashem, a poor powerless clan within the Quraysh. As a young adult, Muhammed's destiny as the progeny of respectable bloodlines with little money or power was fulfilled when he became a driver of caravan camels. But Muhammed, whether by luck or divine intervention, married the widow who owned the camels.

Relieved of the need of daily toil, inspired by the teachings of Judaism and the ministry of Jesus, Muhammed began to retreat into the desert for long periods to meditate on the sins of Meccan society. In 610, when he was approaching his fortieth year, a troubled and distracted Muhammed heard a call in the solitude of the desert. According to the classic biographies of the Prophet, the Angel Gabriel came to Muhammed on a night in the month of Ramadan while he slept alone on Mount Hira. The messenger said one word: "Recite!" Muhammed hesitated. And three times the angel commanded, "Recite!" The shaken Muhammed asked, "What shall I recite?" And the angel said, "Recite in the name of the Lord who created all things, who created man from the clots of blood." Muhammed came down off the mountain carrying with him this first revelation. With it and the others that followed, he admonished the people of Mecca to abandon their idolatrous practices and accept the one, universal God—Allah, the all-powerful, the creator of the universe, the everlasting.

---

* King Abdullah of Jordan, *My Memoirs Completed: "al Takmilah"* (London: Longman, 1978), p. 3.

Muhammed, a product of the city, preached to the city. But his message spoke of the simplicity of Bedouin life. There is paradise and there is hell. Splendid rewards come to those who obey Allah's commands. Terrible vengeance awaits those who disregard them. He won some converts, for like every successful preacher Muhammed gave voice and form to the restiveness of his time. He denounced the quest for wealth, attracting the poor. He gathered in the young who were shut out of the councils of power. He rid the Bedouin of the dreaded *jinn*. And he restored the ethics of the tribe. "Look to those moral practices you had in the *jahiliyya** and apply them in Islam: give security to your guest, be generous toward the orphan and treat the stranger who is under your protection with kindliness" (Sura 4:36). But in attracting the lowest classes—the "meanest of society"—Muhammed threatened the aristocracy. The tribes, too, divided—those whose members were part of the establishment remained pagan while many of those outside the power structure became Muslims. The Quraysh was no exception. The Quraysh establishment, controllers of the caravan trade and masters of the city, possessed special reasons for detesting Muhammed's message. The once-poor orphan not only jeopardized the pagan pilgrimages to the Kaaba, the Quraysh's main source of income next to trade, but threatened the entire economic system by preaching dangerous doctrines such as the rightful claim of the destitute to a share in the wealth of the rich. Finally, in substituting faith for blood as the bond of society, Muhammed tore at the structure of clan and tribe on which Quraysh prestige and wealth rested. The Quraysh saw the writing on the wall. If the revolutionary doctrines of Islam triumphed, the Prophet would catapult into the seat of power in Mecca.

The pagan Qurayshis declared war on Muhammed and his small community of faithful. Poets in their employ hurled their verbal assaults at the Muslims. Their hirelings dumped garbage on doorsteps of the Prophet's followers and beat them in the streets. When all failed, the Quraysh establishment tightened the economic screws. In 622, Muhammed with his community left Mecca for Medina.† Known as the *hijra*, or flight, the move to Medina transformed

---

* *Jahiliyya* translates as the pre-Islamic period, the "time of ignorance."
† In the tradition of mediation followed on the Arabian peninsula, Muhammed was invited to Medina as an arbiter between quarreling tribes.

Muhammed from a private person preaching a new faith to a ruler wielding political and military authority.

Without a source of income, the Prophet ordered his community to take up the desert's most time-honored profession—raids on caravans. In late 623, Muhammed, leading a band of 305 men, seventy camels, and two horses, waylaid a caravan belonging to Mecca's powerful Umayyad family, part of the Quraysh. With eight hundred armed men, the Meccans counterattacked. The outnumbered Muslims, shouting "God is Great," beat back the assault, capturing 115 camels and the Quraysh's highly prized coats of mail. The clash, celebrated in Islamic legend as the Battle of Badr, instilled in the Muslims the belief that God led the victory. Over the next four years, Muhammed through alliances with the Bedouin tribes around Medina and repeated successes in repelling attacks from the Meccans strengthened his community in Medina.

But in 627, the Muslims of Medina once more faced the power of the pagan Meccans. Muhammed in preparation for the attack ordered a wide ditch dug around the city's least defensible side. For two weeks, the Meccans laid siege to the city. They then withdrew, claiming the ditch a tactic to which no honorable Arab would resort. But the pagan Qurayshis could not dishonor Muhammed and his new faith.

In January 630, Muhammed, backed by a thousand followers, made his triumphal entry into the city of his birth. Realizing the futility of any further opposition, the Quraysh yielded. The once humble camel driver entered the Kaaba, believed by Muslims to have been built by Abraham. With his spear, he touched its 360 idols one by one, causing each to fall to the ground. He ordered the pictures of the false prophets painted on the walls washed away with water from the Zamzam well, the well that saved Hagar and Ismail from death. In purging the Kaaba of idolatry, Muhammed also cleansed Mecca. In his defeat of the Quraysh, Muhammed restored many of the values of the desert and delivered to future generations who would embrace Islam much that is essentially Arab.

Muhammed raised the Kaaba to the central point of Islam.* But he retained Medina as his political capital. After fourteen cen-

---

* By keeping the Kaaba as a place of pilgrimage, Muhammed protected the material interests of those dependent on its income and therefore assured their political loyalty, primarily the Quraysh.

turies, Medina still seems an unlikely spot from which to build a mighty empire. Even with the multilane superhighways that run toward it across the flat, open plain and the always busy pilgrim traffic that plies through it, Medina, a town of 412,000, is isolated and somewhat alone. Sitting among a cluster of mud-and-stucco villages named Qaba, Arwah, Abyar Ali, and Bir Tujah, 100 miles from the shore of the Red Sea, 250 miles from the historic seaport of Jeddah, 500 miles from Jerusalem, and 600 miles from Damascus, Medina is in the middle of nowhere. But Medina, possessing the second holy site of Islam, ranks in status above any of the Arab world's leading cities. The huge Prophet's mosque sits at the end of a wide boulevard extending off Abizar Street northeast of the city's center. Early in this century, the mosque, marked by four minarets of different styles and heights, recalled in some ways the Medina of Muhammed. The rectangular courtyard in which two domed buildings stood was surrounded by a series of linked structures that recreated the walled enclosure so typical of the Arabian peninsula's traditional mud-walled towns. When Saudi Arabia's House of Saud took possession of Medina in the early 1920s, it became one of the marks of the monarchy's legitimacy. By the 1950s, escalating petroleum sales provided revenues to continue earlier renovations and expansions of the mosque. In 1982, when he became king of Saudi Arabia, Fahd commissioned construction of a massive expansion of the Prophet's mosque. Now huge courtyards define the new boundaries of the Holy Harem and elaborate designs in marble cover fine arabesque arches. It is an imposing statement of the triumph of Islam.

In the beginning of his ministry, the Prophet harbored no ambition to found either a new religion or a government. He saw himself as nothing more than an ordinary man chosen by God to convey to the people of Mecca the truths that would save them from divine wrath on the Day of Judgment. But by the time the Prophet died on June 8, 632, near the age of sixty, he had gone beyond delivering Allah's message to the people of Mecca. Presenting himself as the culmination of the Old Testament prophets and the New Testament prophet Jesus, Muhammed had brought a monotheistic religion with precise ethical doctrines to most of western Arabia. He had given believers a book of revelations that would over the centuries provide the guide to thought, faith, and conduct for countless millions. And he had established in Medina a new community, in essence an organized and armed state. The Bedouin remained un-tamed, but for the first time in history a force beyond the family exerted influence in their lives.

The victory of Islam was religious and it was social. Muhammed had not only defined God for human beings but redefined relations between one human being and another. While Islam incorporated some of the basic values of Bedouin life, it rejected the Bedouin's fierce tribalism. Replacing fragmentation with the unity of religious belief, Muhammed instilled the idea of the *ummah*, the nation of believers. Thus "Islam was not merely a matter of each individual's obeying God; it was a compact in which all Muslims were bound to each other as well."* The Koran spoke to religious kinship as the Arab poet spoke of his tribe. "Hearken, O ye men, unto my words and take ye them to heart. Know ye that every Muslim is a brother unto every other Muslim, and that ye are one brotherhood" (Sura 49:10). It is this injunction and this theology that place polished business shoes side by side with battered sandals at the door of the mosque. In lining up one next to the other to face Mecca together in prayer, Arab Muslims close the chasms between family and family, city and country, ignorance and education to become one with their God.

Religiously Islam was a completion. In the Koran, Muhammed had delivered the complete word of Allah. There would be no more prophets and no more revelations. But Islam was also a new beginning—the foundation of a new empire and a new civilization. At Muhammed's death, the Arabs—the townsmen, the farmers, and the Bedouin—poised to take their religion and their culture out of the Arabian peninsula into the world. Their isolation had ended.

---

* Marshall G. S. Hodgson, *The Venture of Islam: Conscience and History in a World Civilization*, Vol. 1 (Chicago: University of Chicago Press, 1974), p. 197.

CHAPTER 2

THE SONS
OF ISMAIL

THE LITTLE DATSUN PICKUP BACKED into a wide, sloping trench dug into the sand of the camel market in Riyadh. Out of an adjacent wooden-railed pen, a bawling chocolate-brown camel responded to its lead rope. When it reached the pit, a clump of men in soiled *thobes* and limp, worn *gutras* began yelling, gesturing, and shoving as they tried to force the eight-foot-tall dromedary into the six-by-five-foot truck bed. Finally, they succeeded in collapsing the leggy beast for transport to the desert pasture of men still called Bedouin.

From outside its boundaries, the Arab world is perceived as a monochrome. All Arabs are perceived in Western stereotypes as Bedouin following their herds through the waste of the desert or devout Muslims kneeling in prayer or swarming mobs of humanity shouting their anger at some unseen object. Yet from inside their world, the Arabs fracture into a multicolored prism. People and place and history all combine to make a variegated collage that lays out its contrasts for all to see.

Nine hundred miles west of Riyadh's camel market I watched an Egyptian archaeologist in a gray-blue polyester safari suit lead a group of uniformed schoolchildren through the dimly lit exhibits of the Cairo museum. Case by case, he explained Egypt's pharaonic past that reached its glory two thousand years before Muhammed. In Baghdad, I saw a style-conscious young woman wearing a knee-length skirt and spiked heels lead another group of children through their history, the history of Mesopotamia. At the door of a Greek Orthodox church outside Damascus, I stepped aside for a priest in gold-embroidered vestments hurrying to begin services for a Christian community that traces its existence to the time of Christ. And in Beirut, I followed a bearded militiaman of the Shiite Hizbollah as he picked his way through the rubble of a fifteen-year-long civil war fought to confirm Lebanon's Arab identity. In each of these places, with all of these people, one communality held them together—the sense of being Arab.

The Arab world stratifies ethnically, historically, and religiously. It segregates by family and tribe. And it divides by nation. Yet the Arab world is one, joined by the sense of what it means to be Arab. And being Arab means in part drawing identity from an age when the Islamic empire defined high culture for the world.

Stretching from Asia to Europe, the Islamic empire was won by the Arabs of the Arabian peninsula and welded together by their language and religion. Yet as the armies of Islam spread east and west in wars of conquest, the simple values and traditions of the Bedouin merged with the civilizations of Byzantium and Persia. And out of the amalgamation of Bedouin, Semite, Greek, and Persian, a synthesized culture speaking Arabic as the mother tongue, adhering almost exclusively to the precepts of Islam, and expressing in its society many of the basic values of the Arabian peninsula emerged. Although the Islamic empire at its zenith encompassed Indians, Persians, Chinese, Mongols, Turks, Berbers, Slavs, and Moors, the Arabs see the Islamic empire as their golden age. Ignoring both the reality of the empire as a celebration of many ethnic groups cross-pollinating each other and the political turmoil that bedeviled it, those who now call themselves Arab have for almost a thousand years pointed to the Islamic empire of the eighth and ninth centuries as a touchstone of their unity.

Arab culture cannot be separated from Islamic culture. Arabic, the language of Islam, binds emotionally, if not theologically, all Arabs. And the history they shared from the seventh to the twentieth century is largely the history of Islam. Islam, which began as a religion in the Arabian peninsula, became a state governing an empire and finally a culture that now defines the Arab world.

When Muhammed died, he bequeathed to his followers the

mission of defending the faith and delivering its message to the rest of mankind. Rallying to the Koranic injunction "Fight those who believe not in God and the Last Day," a man named Khalid ibn al-Walid took to the field at the head of a ragtag Muslim army drawn from the deserts and towns of the Hijaz, the western coastal plain of what is now Saudi Arabia. Having accepted Islam near the end of Muhammed's life, Khalid charged across the peninsula with the zeal of a new convert. In a lightning campaign consuming a few months, the "sword of Islam" brought the tribes of southern, central, and eastern Arabia to Islam. For the first time in its history, the peninsula knew a kind of unity.

With Arabia subdued and its inhabitants put off limits to attack by fellow believers, Muslim energies strained for an outlet. The grinding hunger that always gripped overpopulated Arabia and the sheer love of spoils fueled the call to conquest. For the Muslim warriors the quest for booty posed no contradiction to Islam. From the day he descended from Mount Hira, Muhammed's divine revelations contained within them the secular currents of economics and politics. The supernatural ideas of paradise and hell preached by religion also concerned land and hunger.

A year after the Prophet's death, two columns of Islam's soldiers raced north. One drove east toward Iraq and the empire of the Persians, the other west toward Syria and the empire of Byzantium. Understanding little about the tactics of war except the siege, the Muslims surrounded Damascus. Six months later, Christian Byzantium's "pearl of the East" surrendered. The terms of the treaty signed by Khalid ibn al-Walid became the model for most treaties between the Muslims and their new subjects: "In the name of Allah, the merciful, the compassionate. This is what Khalid ibn al-Walid would grant the people of Damascus if he enters it: He shall give them security for their lives, property, and churches. This city['s] walls shall not be demolished and no Moslems shall be quartered in their dwellings. Thereunto we give them the pact of Allah together with the protection of His Prophet . . . and of all believers. So long as they pay poll tax, nothing but good shall befall them."*

The fall of Damascus was the prelude to the decisive encounter between Islam and the Christian empire. On a broiling hot August day in 636 the army of Allah and the army of Byzantium stood face

* Quoted in Philip K. Hitti, *Capital Cities of Arab Islam* (Minneapolis: University of Minnesota Press, 1973), pp. 46–47.

to face on the banks of the Yarmuk, the eastern tributary of the Jordan River. Fifty thousand Christians commanding the technology of war stood ready to do battle with a Muslim army half its size, armed with bows and curved-blade axes. But the victory was Allah's. The way was opened for the Muslim conquest of all of Syria.

The first Muslim armies were nothing more than tight masses of tribesmen operating without discipline or organization. Lightly armed, highly mobile atop swift camels or horses bred for endurance and speed, they dashed across the desert. Moving with ease in vast expanses of territory, the Muslims lived frugally off the plunder from the countryside and operated like self-sufficient bands of raiders. Their speed and mobility made a mockery of conventional armies weighed down with heavily mailed cavalrymen and an infantry encumbered by massive baggage trains. But as they gained experience on the Syrian and Iraqi frontiers, the Muslims learned to hurl missiles from mangonels and ballistas, to batter down walls with rams, and to scramble over walls from scaling towers. Still, the Arabs' major weapon remained the great, open expanses of desert.

The Muslims were so successful because they rode into a vacuum. Centuries of internecine wars between Byzantium and Persia had enfeebled both. Thus once mighty armies faded before the Arab invaders emboldened by the promise of paradise for those who died on the "path of Allah."

From Syria, the Muslims wheeled toward the Byzantine province of Egypt. In 640, four thousand rugged, battle-hardened Bedouin soldiers crossed the Syrian-Egyptian border and laid siege to the border fortress near what is now Cairo. Surrounded by a double wall and wide moat, defended by a fifty-thousand-man garrison, and backed up by a fleet of ships, the fortress seemed impregnable. But like Damascus it fell to the desert invaders.

The Muslims rode on toward the Nile Valley, Alexandria, and on across Africa. With each new victory and each new tactic of warfare they learned, the armies of Islam moved faster and faster. They reached Spain in 710 and within eight years occupied most of the Iberian peninsula. As the Muslim army crossed the Pyrenees into France, it seemed nothing could stop them. But in 732, the centennial year of Muhammed's death, "the Hammer," Charles Martel, checked a border raid by Muslims at the French town of Tours which the Europeans came to regard as the historic point at which the Muslim advance into Europe was stopped.

In 651, the Sassanid empire, an empire that was the latest

incarnation of the thousand-year-old Persian imperial tradition, and one that only a few years before had stood against the best that Byzantium could throw against it, crumbled before the Arabs. Booty that came out of the exalted cities of Persia poured on the Arabs unimagined riches. Fabulous objects such as a life-size silver camel and a golden horse with emerald teeth and a garland of rubies draped around its neck passed from the cultured Sassanids into the rough and calloused hands of the Arab warriors and on to Mecca. From the palace of Ctesiphon, the army sent a royal banquet carpet measuring 105 by 90 feet woven with gold and silver threads and sprinkled with diamonds, rubies, and cascades of pearls.* With each mile they advanced, the Arabs saw and seized treasures they never imagined existed. Before the eastward advance of Islamic influence ended, it had crossed the threshold of China.

By the eighth century, the great wave of Arabic expansion had reached its uttermost limits. The wars of conquest in both the east and the west subsided as the Muslim armies accepted coexistence with the non-Muslim states beyond them and settled down within more or less permanent frontiers. *Jihad*—the perpetual and obligatory holy war conducted by the Muslim state—would remain enshrined in Muslim mythology, but as time wore on its imperative became defensive, not offensive.

Islam had made heroes out of weaklings. Despite their inferiority in numbers and weaponry, the backward sons of the Arabian peninsula had defeated two powerful empires and incorporated their territories into the *ummah*.

The old mud palace of Abdul Aziz in Riyadh is a good place to consider just how remarkable the Islamic conquests actually were. Except for the old, single-shot Turkish rifles, Abdul Aziz unified Saudi Arabia in the early part of the twentieth century with equipment very much like that of the first Islamic armies. The Bedouin king's camel saddle lies astride a tall sawhorse inside a dusty glass case. It is a simple open wooden frame that encloses the hump of the animal. The rest is nothing more than animal-hair weavings folded and laid on top to provide some cushion. Weapons line the wall—short-handled battleaxes, daggers, and spiked iron balls on a chain attached to a wooden handle. Except for a wicked-looking

---

* Since earthly goods were considered passing things by the religious leaders of Islam, the carpet was cut into pieces.

sword with a sharp central point and a curved double-edged blade that not only stabbed but gutted an opponent and the bow and arrow, this was the arsenal of the first Arab armies that rode north out of the peninsula.

I browsed the exhibit with a young veiled woman and her brother, students respectively at the female and male branches of Riyadh University. She and I talked of the weapons and the marvels of the early Islamic conquests. Suddenly the brother stopped fingering his prayer beads and snapped at us, "It was not amazing at all. They carried the sword of Allah." Western historians can point to Arab mobility and a vacuum of power north of the Arabian peninsula as causes of the rapid expansion of Islam. But for many Arab Muslims the force engendered by faith in Allah is the only explanation necessary for one of the most extraordinary events in the history of mankind.

As remarkable as the speed and order of the conquests were, the ease with which the conquered people underwent Arabization is even more astounding. The religious wars of the seventh to ninth centuries created the mold from which the Arabs as they are now known were cast. When the conquering tribes swept out of Arabia, they encountered a patchwork of languages, religions, and ethnic identifications. The Fertile Crescent—the expanse of geography from the Nile to the Tigris, from the southern Taurus mountains of Asia Minor to the northern deserts of the Arabian peninsula— lay on the historical invasion routes between Europe, Africa, and Asia. For almost three thousand years—from the days of the pharaohs to the arrival of the Muslim armies—the Fertile Crescent had been subjected to one invasion after another. Armies moved from the west and then they moved from the east, conquering, occupying, and finally withdrawing in response to a greater force. They all came—the Egyptians, Hyksos, and Hittites; the Macedonians and the Persians; the Romans and the Assyrians; the Byzantines and once more the Persians. And when each of them retreated, they left a little of themselves behind.

Across what is now the core of the Arab world, pockets of language and ethnicity left by the invaders separated village from village. One religion and then another reflected the ideas of the many who had passed through as soldiers, philosophers, or missionaries. But no one faith encompassed the whole. In fact, the seventh century A.D. represented a particular time of doubt and a period of searching. Faith in the gods of the Greeks and Romans had died. Magic and astrology encased in cults of mystery flared and then faded. In the second century A.D., Christianity based on love and the promise of immortality began to take hold. But by the fifth century, it was captive of a political empire. The Byzantine state had wed the spiritual and secular and set above it an autocracy composed of ethnic Greeks. For the masses in the eastern reaches of Byzantium's empire, religion delivered by the Greek language and justifying Greek political institutions engendered little commitment.

Despite the bombardment of different empires with all their accompanying languages and philosophies, the people of the Fertile Crescent did possess a certain fragile cultural unity. Semitic tribes had been some of its earliest immigrants. By the first millennium B.C., each had added something—writing, metallurgical skills, political organization, societal mores—to the region's common pool of knowledge and way of life. The Fertile Crescent remained basically Semitic in culture until the Indo-Europeans came from the east out of Persia and from the west out of Greece, Rome, and Byzantium to subdue it. When the Arabs entered Syria in the first wave of the Islamic conquests, Semitic culture was freed again. These first conquests were so swiftly successful, in part, because the Semitic people of Syria and western Iraq identified more with their Semitic cousins from Arabia than with either the Greeks of Byzantium or the Sassanids of Persia. Non-Semites saw the Arab armies not so much as conquerors as emancipators from the tyranny. As a result, groups, cities, and regions more often than not surrendered to the armies of Islam.

Muslim warriors seldom converted by the sword. With most of the region's older religions discredited, mass conversions to Islam took place on the battlefield.* Carrying the banner of the Prophet, the Muslim armies thundered toward a town. Halting at the perimeter, the commander ordered the horns to sound the summons to Islam. And then they waited. In the stillness, doors flew open and new converts flocked out to surrender to Allah. Jews and Christians—as monotheists protected by Koranic injunction—kept their religion and paid tribute. All others were subject to enslavement or

---

* Christianity still commanded a number of followers. The major Christian groups were Greek Orthodox following their own eastern rites, the Copts of Egypt, the Jacobites, and Nestorians.

ransom. With no ideology or political authority for which they were willing to die, the people of Alexandria, Damascus, Baghdad, and thousands of towns and villages in between simply accepted the invaders and hoped they would fare well under the new regime. Yet it would take two centuries for Islam to establish itself firmly in the Fertile Crescent. Arabization of the Islamic empire came through language, not religion.

The language of the unlettered, poetry-loving Arabs imposed itself on the most sophisticated cultures of the ancient world with a speed and ease that has yet to be adequately explained. There were contributing factors. Arab soldiers married non-Arab women and produced offspring who spoke the Arabic of their fathers. Conquered people gained access to power by learning Arabic in order to attach themselves as clients to the people who now controlled the territory in which they lived. Clientage in turn promoted an adherence to Islam, which demanded a knowledge of Arabic. Ignoring the old, exact genealogical standards of the Arabian peninsula, anyone in the new empire who spoke Arabic considered himself an Arab. Conversion to Islam itself implied for many the status of Arab. In 750, a non-Arab laid claim to Arabism for the conquered people. "If Arab means a language, we came to speak it; if it means a religion, we have embraced it."* By the eleventh century, less than four hundred years after the first Islamic conquests, Arabic as a cultural vehicle had completely supplanted such old and distinguished languages as Coptic, Aramaic, Greek, and Latin. Through language, people out of different regions, different histories, and different ethnic roots became Arabs. And it is as Arabs that they have remained.† And it was Arabic, both in linguistic and cultural terms, that drew the geographical boundaries of what is now the Arab world. Arabic was such a powerful unifying force that from the beginning of the Islamic conquests it constituted the essence of the Arab ethos.

The Anglican Cathedral of St. George just outside the walls of

---

* A. A. Duri, *The Historical Formation of the Arab Nation: A Study in Identity and Consciousness* (London: Croom Helm, 1987), p. 46.
† There are a number of groups living within the Arab world, such as Armenians and Kurds, who are not Arabs either linguistically or culturally. The Maronite Christians of Lebanon are culturally Arabs, but they prefer to speak French rather than Arabic and identify themselves more with the West than the Arab east. Defying history, anthropology, and logic, many claim they are non-Arab descendants of the Phoenicians.

Jerusalem's Old City is a mirror of an English rural church. The dining hall of its hostel drips its Gothic gloom over crucifixes and long plank tables that belong more to Oxford than Jerusalem. The bishop wears a purple rabat and clerical collar and presides over a staff trained in the theology of the Church of England. But St. George's is unmistakably an Arab church conducting services in the Arabic language. If I had any doubt it was dispelled in the cramped, crowded study of one of the senior priests. He pointedly reminded me that Christianity in the Middle East preceded Christianity in Europe and that the Christians in adopting the language of Arabic added their part to the development of Arab culture. At the end of the discourse, the priest got up from his desk and stood in front of the window that framed the cathedral's famous bell tower. Fixing me in his piercing gaze, he said, "A man is no less an Arab because he is a Christian."

It is this merging of religion and ethnicity under the language of Arabic that creates so much of the confusion over who the Arabs were originally and who they are now. The best explanation of who is an Arab I ever heard came from the son of the last Ottoman governor of Palestine. Although his pale skin and gray eyes place him in the fairer strains of the Turks and despite the fact that he grew up speaking Turkish, he is an Arab. Delighting in the contradictions, he unleashed a sly grin. "I choose to speak Arabic, therefore, I am an Arab."

The unity that the nascent Islamic empire achieved through language played against political and theological dissension within Islam itself. The first crisis in Islam came with the death of the Prophet. Although making no claim to immortality, Muhammed left his followers without instruction as to who was to succeed him as the leader of the Islamic community. All his disciples had to guide them was the raw political structure of pre-Islamic Arabia—the tribe. Traditionally tribes selected their leaders from among themselves, choosing the man who commanded the most respect. For respect evoked the loyalty and confirmed the authority necessary to hold the allegiance of the tribe. Drawing on custom, the Prophet's closest companions selected as caliph, the commander of the faithful, the ablest among them. The choice fell to Abu Bakr, a cloth merchant who was among Muhammed's first converts and by common consent the most respected man in the Muslim community of Medina. Gathering around, those who chose clasped the hand of the chosen in the time-honored ceremony of *bayah*, or oath of loyalty.* In one act, the men of Medina confirmed their leader and made of the caliph an institution of Islam.

Between 632 and 661, the sole function of the caliph was to carry out God's will. The only model known by those attempting to do that was the Prophet's government, a one-man affair unencumbered by specialized bureaus, officials, or other trappings of administration. In Abu Bakr's two-year reign, government remained tribal and patriarchal. It was with the second caliph, Umar (634–644), that Muhammed's successors began to face the problems of administering a far-flung empire comprising a plethora of languages, religions, and people. Umar, scarcely more experienced in governing than Abu Bakr, nonetheless began to elaborate some of the governing institutions of the emerging empire. While administering Medina and other cities of the Arabian peninsula under the precepts laid down by Muhammed, he left virtually intact whatever governmental framework his generals found in the territories they conquered.

By the third caliph, Uthman (644–656), Islam's theology could no longer contain the new strains of conflict created by empire or the old pre-Islamic fractionalism of the Arabian peninsula. Unlike Muhammed, who considered bread a rare treat and most often made a meal of dates or milk but never enjoyed the luxury of both at the same time, Islam's leadership in Mecca and Medina had begun to live like an idle aristocracy on the booty of war. In the territories, a second generation of Bedouin warriors was coming to full manhood. Still inspired by the message of the Prophet, they had nonetheless strayed from the simple life exemplified by the Prophet. Subjected to the temptations of Alexandria and Damascus or the raucous life of the new camp cities, they tasted wine, women, and gambling. But sumptuous living was only the symptom of the underlying forces. The drive for personal power, prestige, and position had begun to eat at the vitals of Muslim society. Questions of how to govern an empire, what its mission should be, and how its leadership would be chosen opened the old tribal divisions that predated Islam and drew in new groups and new conflicts competing against each other

---

* The king of Saudi Arabia is still chosen by the "tribe" composed of the royal family, selected notables, and religious leaders and participates in the ceremony of *bayah* with his subjects. See Chapter 8.

in the far-flung empire. They all came together in a devastating series of civil wars that ended the egalitarian principles established by Muhammed's immediate successors and split Islam itself.

Uthman, noted for his mild manner and piety, was a member of the powerful Umayyad family, part of the Quraysh tribe of Mecca. Although seventy years old when he became caliph, Uthman administered the empire with vigor. He installed energetic governors and generals in the provinces with instructions to push forward Islam's frontiers and secure its unquestioned power. But Uthman could not free himself from the bonds of kinship. High office and the spoils of war went disproportionately to Umayyads, opening Uthman up to charges that the caliph was reverting to the old order of Arab society in which blood ties ruled. A dozen years after Muhammed last preached the social, economic, and political equality of all believers, the Arab predilection for the family reasserted itself.

As a result of the controversy surrounding Uthman, three political groups formed within the still-young Islamic state. The first considered itself the party of Muhammed. Led by members of the less important families of Mecca, it incorporated those who had originally gathered around the Prophet. The first two caliphs, Abu Bakr and Umar, had both been members of the first Muslim community, and now Ali, the cousin of the Prophet and the husband of his only child, Fatima, claimed its leadership.

The second group was composed of members of the Umayyad family and their allies among the Quraysh who came to Islam late. Politically, they held the most powerful administrative posts in the empire. Philosophically, they still regarded the Quraysh as an aristocracy.

Bedouin soldiers who had surrendered to Islam just before or after Muhammed's death composed the third group. Outnumbering the other two parties, they commanded neither their organization nor their prestige. However, it was their swords that had created Islam's empire. As such they bitterly resented the inferior position forced on them by both the Prophet's inner circle and the Umayyad caliph.

Malcontents far and wide across the new empire fed on the stories and rumors about Uthman's sale of positions and the growing power and wealth of his favorites. In 656, the supporters of Ali lifted the banner of revolt by laying siege to Uthman's residence in Medina. At the end of several months, they stormed the palace and took the caliph. With Abu Bakr's son raising the first dagger, the insurgents hacked the caliph to death. Islam was once more without a leader. Out of the anarchy that resulted, Ali emerged as caliph.

Distinguished in the early conquests and esteemed as the son-in-law of the Prophet, Ali was generally recognized everywhere as caliph. The exceptions were Syria, where a Umayyad still held on as governor, and within the house of the Prophet. Aishah, Muhammed's favorite wife, hated Ali.* Accusing him of cowardice in refusing to punish those who had killed Uthman, she rallied to rebellion the Bedouin troops encamped near Basra at the head of the Persian Gulf. Ali headed toward Kufah, a rival Bedouin garrison town two hundred miles northwest of Basra. In between, the two Muslim forces met. The battle swirled around a camel from which Aishah, in a litter, commanded her forces. Against all of Muhammed's precepts of the brotherhood of believers, the Battle of the Camel threw Muslim against Muslim.

Ali won. But he never went back to Medina, and he never really established himself at the head of the Islamic state. The governor of Syria and his Umayyad relatives claimed the caliphate. Having lost most of his supporters in the Battle of the Camel, Ali was forced to depend on the army in place at Kufah to defend him against the Umayyad usurpers. But elements within it disliked Ali as much as the Umayyads. Known as the Kharijites, the Seceders, they were largely Bedouin who, feeling shut out of the new empire, sought their own power. Calling forth their poets to weave together vindictive words, the Kharijites hurled the same charges at Ali as they had at Uthman—nepotism. In 661, Ali left his house to go to the mosque for prayers. On the way, he fell to a Kharijite assassin.† His son Hassan, surrendering all claim to the title of caliph, retired to the pleasures of his palace in Medina. The era of the "Rightly Guided Caliphs," the companions of the Prophet, came to an end. The short republican tradition of the Islamic state established at Muhammed's death ceased as the Umayyads, the aristocrats of Mecca, established

---

* The reason may have been an incident years before when she dropped behind the Prophet's entourage to look for a lost necklace. When she arrived late in Medina in the company of a young Bedouin, Ali openly suspected her of infidelity.
† Shiite tradition holds that as Ali lay dying from his stab wounds he whispered that he was to be placed on a camel and laid to rest wherever it knelt. Najaf, now in Iraq, became his burial place.

themselves in power. In an important sense, Islam's age of innocence also ended. The capital of Islam moved to Damascus in the newly conquered province of Syria, one deeply marked by the often devious political and administrative traditions of the ancient Middle East.

Damascus was separated from Mecca by more than miles. Mecca was of the desert and of tradition. Damascus was of the Fertile Crescent, a city that knew that it connected west to the Mediterranean and east to the Euphrates. It was a city that had understood and lived other ways long before there was Islam. In 680, the way of the tribe and the way of the city would face each other for final control of the caliphate.

The success of the Umayyads in wooing Ali's son into retirement failed to settle the issue of how the caliph was chosen. Defending tribal tradition, opponents of the Umayyads held that any believer, of whatever origin, was worthy of the office of caliph if the believers chose him. Rejecting the Umayyad caliph Muawiyah as having no authority because he was not a direct descendant of the Prophet and had not been chosen by the community of the faithful, Ali's followers and the Kharijites made alliance against the Umayyads. They brought with them subject peoples who had embraced Islam but remained relegated to a social class lower than that of the Arabs descended from the tribes of the Arabian peninsula and lower still than that of the aristocratic Umayyads. If the assassination of the caliph Uthman was Islam's first civil war, the rebellion against the Umayyads was its second.

Hussein, second son of Ali, grandson of the Prophet, placed himself at the head of an insurrection against Umayyad power. The Umayyads responded, isolating Hussein's forces at Karbala on the open plain south of what is now Baghdad. The army of the Umayyads, by now a professional force fully employing the tactics of both the Byzantines and the Sassanids, butchered Hussein and most of his forces. Waves of anguish and anger flowed with the blood of the Prophet's scion, splitting Islam into its two great branches—the orthodox Sunnis, who accepted the Umayyad caliphate, and the breakaway Shiites, the followers of Ali and Hussein. Karbala transformed what had been a protest movement within Islam into a sect inspired by the potent themes of sacrifice, guilt, and death.

Every year on the tenth day of the Islamic month of Muharram, the anniversary of Hussein's death, Shiites observe the ceremony of Ashura. Shortly after first light, men crowd around the hardware stalls in the souks to buy wooden handles from which hang links of chain with barbed ends. Women, dressed in black appropriate to mourning, lay out prayer rugs, woven mats, and blankets along the street to wait for the coming procession.

In midafternoon, at the hour Hussein was beheaded, the hypnotic rhythms of religious songs commemorating the bloodshed at Karbala rise out of the assembled crowd. As the singing builds in intensity, bodies visibly tremble with emotion in anticipation of the coming procession. Finally it comes. Men wrapped in white to symbolize their readiness to die hit themselves time after time on top of their shaven heads with the flat sides of swords. The point of impact swells as blood pools under the skin. Then in one dramatic moment, the marchers turn their swords to the sharp edge and strike their crowns once more, sending blood cascading down their faces. As the smell of blood mixes with the scent of rose water sprinkled from the crowd, they continue to beat on the wound with the palm of their hands and to hit themselves with the barbed flails purchased in the souk. In Ashura, the macabre, the bizarre, and the beautiful blend in the consummate celebration of Shiism's central theme—martyrdom.*

The Shiites' position as a despised minority within Islam helps perpetuate this theme of martyrdom. Shiism stayed east in Iran and southern Iraq, in clusters around the Persian Gulf, in Syria, northern Yemen, and the Maghrib, and later in southern Lebanon. Comprising only 10 percent of Islam, the Shiites in the Arab world live as second-class citizens within societies and political systems that make little attempt to incorporate them into the whole.†

The midsize Shiite town of Qatif hugs the north side of a finger of bay that juts in from Saudi Arabia's Persian Gulf coast. Until the political upheavals sparked by the 1979 Iranian Revolution forced in more government money, Qatif lived like a stepchild in a house of plenty. The stores and office buildings that led down the main

---

* Government regulation and changing custom have made the shedding of blood in Ashura observance a symbolic rather than actual act in most places west of Iran.
† The Shiites form the majority in both Iraq and Bahrain but they do not control the political system.

street toward the souks were shabby, the schools few, the new street-lights and sewer projects that were going into other towns late in coming.

To the north, the Qatifs of Iraq are poverty-ridden villages scattered over the treeless wastes of the south. Bypassed by whatever government happens to be in power, the people eke out a living from the salty soil or survive on a low level of trade. Not even the presence of Iraq's oil-exporting facilities does much to close the economic gap between the Shiites and the politically dominant Sunnis. Denied the material rewards of life, the Shiites gain spiritual sustenance from pilgrimages to their holy places of Najaf and Karbala.

Other Qatifs dot the south of Lebanon. Before the Lebanese civil war, peasants worked the fields for absentee landowners and did without schools and clinics. While the wealthy bought Italian leather handbags and designer clothes in the boutiques in Beirut, the women of the south drew a few coins out of plastic purses to buy what essentials they could off half-bare shelves in village shops. After fifteen years of war in which the Shiites fought for their fair share of Lebanon's economy and political system, they have yet to establish themselves as equals.

For thirteen hundred years, the Shiites have floated in the ocean of orthodox Islam represented by the Sunnis. A distrusted minority accused of heretical practices by mainstream Islam, they are the religious descendants of the Caliph Ali.

In spite of ruthlessly putting down the Shiite revolt, the Umayyad caliph Muawiyah (661–680) was a man of vision and tolerance.* His philosophy of rule was summed up in his own words: "I apply not my lash where my tongue suffices, nor my sword where my whip is enough. And if there be one hair binding me to my fellow men I let it not break. If they pull I loosen, and if they loosen I pull."†

Beginning in 685, the Umayyads presided over the rapid Arabization of the subject people. But in 715 after the death of the talented al-Walid, the Umayyad caliphate began to totter. His successors proved inept at best, dissolute at worst. Gathering into their

---

* Muawiyah translates as "howling bitch," a name his parents gave him to keep away the evil eye.
† Quoted in Hitti, *Capital Cities of Arab Islam*, p. 68.

bathhouses and pleasure palaces, they made a mockery of the example the Prophet set by mending his own clothes in the courtyard of his simple mud house. But more than a religious issue, court life was the catalyst of rage over political and social grievances most held against the Umayyads.

Across the empire, the white banner of the Umayyads turned in retreat before the black banner of the Abbasids, yet another branch of the Prophet's family. In January 750, the forces of the Abbasids utterly destroyed twelve thousand troops of the Umayyads on a tributary of the Tigris. The fourteenth Umayyad caliph, Marwan, fled to Egypt. Caught hiding in a church, he was decapitated, and his head was sent back to the Abbasids' temporary headquarters in Kufah. Meanwhile in Damascus, the gates swung open to the forces of the new caliph while mobs frenzied with hatred scattered the bones from Umayyad tombs.

The shift from the Umayyad to an Abbasid regime represented more than a dynastic change. The caliphate and the empire altered geographically and politically. The capital moved once more, from Damascus to Baghdad. The distance between Mecca and Islam's capital lengthened again not only in miles but culturally as the new regime oriented itself more to Persia than to Arabia. The Arab aristocracy of Medina and Mecca that had exercised control over the empire since its first days gradually diminished. Pensions paid to Arab warriors descended from those who had come out of the peninsula in the early conquests gradually ceased. And Arabs as a separate, identifiable group faded into the geography of the Islamic empire. There would no longer be any distinction drawn between the Muslims of the Arabian peninsula and the Muslims of the rest of the empire. People whose heritage lay in Mesopotamia and Egypt, who were Muslim and Christian, all came together under the mother tongue of Arabic. They would forever more be known as Arabs.

The Baghdad caliphate saw the full flowering of the Islamic culture to which Arabs attach so much of their identity. Unlike ancient Damascus, Baghdad was a new city created by the Abbasid caliph al-Mansur (754–775). ". . . he came to the area of the bridge and crossed to the present site of Qasr al-Salam. . . . He spent the night there, and awoke the next morning having passed the sweetest and gentlest night on earth. He stayed, and everything he saw pleased him. Then he said, 'This is the site on which I shall build.' . . . So he laid it out and . . . laid the first brick with his own hand saying, 'In the name of God, and praise to Him. The earth is God's; He causes to inherit of it whom He wills among his servants, and the result thereof is to them that fear Him.' "*

Construction of Baghdad employed 100,000 laborers, craftsmen, and architects for four years. Circular in shape, it lay behind a moat and double brick walls rising to a height of ninety feet. Four gates opened on four highways that radiated like spokes of a wheel to the corners of the empire. At the center of all stood the imperial palace.

In 917, an emissary from Greece described the court of the Caliph al-Muqtadir. The palace was composed of halls, courtyards, and parks where elephants paraded in caparisons of peacock silk brocade. In one room, a tree stood "in the midst of a great circular tank filled with clear water. The tree has eighteen branches, every branch having numerous twigs, on which sit all sorts of gold and silver birds, both large and small. Most of the branches of this tree are of silver, but some are of gold, and they spread into the air carrying leaves of different colours. The leaves of the tree move as the wind blows, while the birds pipe and sing." The caliph "was arrayed in clothes . . . embroidered in gold being seated on an ebony throne. . . . To the right of the throne hung nine collars of gems . . . and to the left were the like, all of famous jewels."† In less than three hundred years, the model of the caliphate had passed from an Arabian sheikh to a dynastic ruler to a Persian despot.

But the Islamic empire's enduring strength was in its culture, not its political institutions. Baghdad, its splendor fed by the prosperity of the empire, was a city without peer. The court of the Caliph Harun al-Rashid (786–809) was the court of *A Thousand and One Nights*. And like the tales that came from it, it sparkled with intellectual vigor and extraordinary art. The learning of Persia combined with the learning of Greece and Rome. Together they erased the rough edges of primitive Arabia to create the Islamic culture that all Arabs now claim and celebrate.

In 1983, I attended the opening of an exhibit of objects from the golden age of Islam at a gallery in Jeddah, Saudi Arabia. An

* Muhammed ibn Jarir al-Tabari, quoted in Albert Hourani, *A History of the Arab Peoples* (Cambridge: Belknap Press of Harvard University Press, 1991), p. 33.
† Ibid., p. 34.

army of Pakistani waiters circulated among the guests carrying tea, coffee, fruit juice, honey-filled pastries stacked on large trays, and big silver bowls of expensive chocolates. The room was crowded with minor members of the royal family, Saudi entrepreneurs, and high-ranking government officials as well as an array of prosperous Lebanese, Egyptians, Palestinians, and Syrians working and doing business in Saudi Arabia. At the time, the Arabs, especially the Saudis, were just short of obsessed with pushing high Islamic culture as certification that the Arabs possessed something more than oil money. Jeddah's mayor, Muhammed Saeed Farsi, sounded the theme in his words of welcome. Sweeping the room with an outstretched arm, he said with a satisfaction that hovered at the edge of arrogance, "The collection proves how much Islamic art and science were developed when the kings and emperors in Europe were wasting time in small wars and had not learned from the Roman Empire."

The Islamic empire began as a society of believers. Islam constituted its unifying theme and its raison d'être. As long as the Islamic community existed only within isolated and insular Arabia, its members contented themselves with functional and unspeculative piety. But once that community burst out of the peninsula and swelled through its early conquests, the face of Islam changed. In Syria, the Bedouin mind collided with Greek philosophy and Christian theology. It met the Gnostic doctrines in Iraq and dualism in Persia. These Muslims fresh from Arabia could have chosen to wipe out the last vestiges of "pagan" culture.* But somehow these sons of the desert realized that beyond Islam and Arabic, with its emerging literary florescence, they had little to teach and much to learn. Neither rejecting nor merely tolerating the learning of others, they embraced the intellectual traditions they found and nurtured their seeds. The result was that while Europe sank into the Dark Ages, the Islamic empire preserved the legacy of the Greeks and funneled into it the knowledge of India and Persia. For three hundred years, from the seventh to the eleventh centuries, the Islamic empire tended the lamp of learning for the West.

The Muslims' quest for learning from non-Muslim sources be-

---

* The legend of the burning of the library of Alexandria by Arab invaders, which was invented by a zealous Christian at the time of the Crusades, has gained in plausibility largely because of the expectedness of the alleged event.

gan in earnest with the Caliph al-Mamun (813–833). According to tradition, al-Mamun had a dream in which he sat on a couch by a bald man with a fair complexion, pink cheeks, wide forehead, joined eyebrows, and light-blue eyes. "Who are you?" al-Mamun asked. "Aristotle," the man replied. If legend is to be believed, the commander of the faithful on waking summoned the books of the ancient philosophers. Beginning with the works of Aristotle and Plato, translators soon rendered almost the whole of Hellenistic philosophy into Arabic.* From al-Mamun's "House of Wisdom," groups of translators and copyists moved on to Euclid and Ptolemy and writings in Persian and Hindi. For the first time in history, scholars transmitted the results of the intellectual inquiries coming out of different regions and cultural traditions in one language—Arabic. But it was not all imitation. Muslim intellectuals spewed out theology and jurisprudence, philology and linguistics, mathematics, medicine, and natural science. During the ninth and tenth centuries when their creativity crested, they had no peers in either Europe or Asia.

The mathematician-astronomer Muhammed ibn Musa, al-Khwarizmi, explored Greek but especially Hindi mathematics. Out of the Hindi sources, he devised the system of calculating by means of nine figures, adding what was probably his own invention, the zero. He incorporated it all in a book roughly titled "the book on addition and subtraction Hindi-style." By the time the system made its way to Europe, Hindi numerals had become "Arabic numerals."

With al-Khwarizmi's astronomical tables, Muslim astronomers went into the Syrian desert to measure the terrestrial degree. Based on the assumption that the earth is round, their measurement missed the modern measurement of the length of a degree (about sixty-nine miles) by a mere 2,877 feet. Other Islamic astronomers delved into spherical trigonometry, rectified the calculations of the orbit of

---

* Al-Mamun's insistence on a primary role for reason in Islam did not win without a struggle. "Foreign science," which included not only mathematics, astronomy, and medicine but also magic, alchemy, and astrology, was generally felt by many Islamic scholars to constitute a serious threat to religious beliefs and the values of religious life. Ibn Taymiyya, a leading Islamic jurist of the thirteenth century, considered the whole system of Aristotelian logic to be based on a metaphysical doctrine that threatened the Islamic worldview. Yet others ardently within the folds of tradition believed and repeatedly declared that the study of religious jurisprudence must be preceded by a sufficient grounding in Greek logic.

the moon, determined with greater accuracy the obliquity of the ecliptic, proved the possibility of annual eclipses of the sun, and produced non-Ptolemaic models for the planets that were comparable to those of Copernicus.*

While the astronomers explored the heavens, other Arabic scholars explored the human body. Ibn Sina, known as Avicenna in the West, developed a veritable medical encyclopedia entitled *The Canon* that summed up what the Arabs knew of Greek, Syriac, Persian, and Hindi medicine and enriched it with their own experiments. The physician al-Razi, for one, hung shreds of meat all over Baghdad to test the degree of putrefaction before choosing a new hospital site. Primitive though it was, the method gives clues to Muslim thinking of the time. Centuries before the germ theory of disease, the *Canon* speculated on the contagious nature of tuberculosis and the spread of disease through water. It covered general medicine, pathology, and pharmacology; gave instructions on how to treat diseases affecting all parts of the body; provided the first clinical account of smallpox, distinguishing it from measles; put forth original work in optics and ophthalmology; recognized the importance of diet and climate on general health; and speculated on the close relationship between emotional and physiological conditions. Until the mid-seventeenth century, the *Canon* defined medicine for most of the world.

But it is architecture that remains the most eloquent monument to Islam's golden age. As befit an empire held together by religion, architecture reached its height in the great mosques. The mosque builders arrived on the heels of Islam's conquering armies. In 691, they changed Jerusalem's landscape with the great and ponderous Dome of the Rock. Located on the traditional site of Muhammed's ascension into heaven, the Dome of the Rock stands sentry over the Haram al-Sharif, the third holy site of Islam. The arched roof, constructed of wood and covered with a glass mosaic laid over a glittering gold background, dominates all around it. It looms above the Jews' Wailing Wall; it overpowers in scale and grandeur the Church of the Holy Sepulcher. It is visible from Mount Scopus and the Mount of Olives. Perhaps nowhere is its power as art and religion more striking than from the rooftops of the Muslim quarter of the Old

---

* Unlike Copernicus, Muslim astronomers made no attempt to abandon the Ptolemaic geocentric system of the world.

City. Late one summer afternoon, I climbed onto the vaulted roof of a fifteenth-century house to watch the sun set. The gold-and-blue mosaics of the dome captured and then intensified the fading light before throwing it back toward the sky. Its effect was what its architects intended—the connecting point between earth and heaven.

Islamic culture celebrated in art and learning the unity that the empire, except for limited periods of time, never achieved politically. Inquiry, scholarship, and language created the illusion of oneness. Distance, intrafamily strife, dynastic rivalries, and regional secessions engendered the reality of disjunction. In 788, an independent ruler backed by his own professional army took Morocco away from the caliph. North Africa and Egypt followed in the tenth century. By the end of that century, northern Persia and northern India no longer answered to the caliph in Baghdad. In time, the caliph himself ceased to be the master. Having built slave armies to protect themselves from their own subjects, the caliphs fell under the control of their military commanders. At the beginning of the eleventh century, the Islamic empire was no longer an empire but a patchwork of semi-independent provinces, each ruled by its own sultan. Yet the theoretical unity of Islam remained in the symbolism of the caliph. In 1258 that too was challenged.

Mongol hordes coming out of the steppes of Asia overran Baghdad's defenses. Flashing swords, they slaughtered 800,000 people. Among them was al-Mustasim, the thirty-seventh and last Abbasid caliph. For the first time in the history of Islam, the caliph's name would not be intoned at the Friday prayers.

The Mongols retreated. Islam's cultural traditions lived on to the west in Granada until 1492, when the Catholic monarchs Ferdinand and Isabella drove the seven-hundred-year-old Moor presence out of Spain. In 1502, the Safavids created a new Persian empire with Shiism as the state religion. In 1520, Suleiman the Magnificent began his reign at the head of the Ottoman Empire of the Turks. The Islamic empire built first around the Umayyads and then the Abbasids fragmented, leaving the Arabs at the mercy of others.

There are those who argue that the Islamic empire was never an empire at all, only an emotional attachment to the ideal of Islamic unity. The Arabs who now cherish the memory of Islam's glory never celebrated the empire in the fabled poetry of the Bedouin. In fact, during the golden age of Arabic literature, not one epic poem emerged. The reason is perhaps that the necessary background of a national life richly embroidered in heroic deeds was never there. For the Arabs' heroic period came in the early conquests with the Arab armies. In the Islamic period, the Arabs drew their sense of identity more from the empire's religious overtones than from feelings of nationalism coming out of a shared cultural history. Still, the ideal of the Islamic empire as a celebration of Arab language and culture is there, and it is powerful. "The Mongol invasion threw concepts of consciousness into confusion and limited prospects for their reinvigoration. Nonetheless, the essential elements that had formed this consciousness persisted in the cultural heritage, to reappear in the movement of national awakening in modern times. The Arabic language remained the foundation of Arabism; and the cultural heritage, embracing the idea of the Arab nation in a cultural sense linking Arabism with Islam, remained a fundamental common ground. From these roots, and in the compass of internal challenges and foreign ideas, the modern Arab consciousness emerged to proceed from Arabism in a socio-cultural sense to Arabism in a nationalist political sense."*

The Islamic empire of the eighth and ninth centuries—religiously and culturally—stands in the Arab mind as an Arab achievement. Regardless of the input of so many other cultures and traditions, it was in Arab eyes the people of the Arabian peninsula and the Fertile Crescent who originally created the empire and gave it its intellectual drive. And it is because of the Arabs that the Alhambra in the fourteenth century, seven hundred years and three thousand miles from Muhammed and Mecca, spoke of Arabia.

The Alhambra, poised on the hill of La Sabica between the bare, brown Sierra Arana and crowded, vibrant Granada, is meant for twilight. Its arching porticoes and intricately carved stone walls, its quiet reflecting pools and gentle fountains release their magic in the serenity of evening. For it was in the evening that the thousand and one tales of the *Arabian Nights* were retold and the nightingales sang. It was in the evening when those most learned in science, architecture, philosophy, and literature met to ponder the questions of the universe. And it was in the evening that the Muslim rulers ensconced within the Alhambra's walls retold the breathtaking history of the Islamic empire.

---

* Duri, *Historical Formation of the Arab Nation*, p. 125.

Arabs, like all people, choose to remember their history at its moments of glory. The Islamic empire was a time of glory. But by the eleventh century, the empire in the east had died, taking from the Arabs their sense of preeminence. If the Alhambra is the symbol of Arab glory, the university in Zabid is the symbol of Arab decline.

The university is a white stucco building with a squat, square tower that hides within lush blue-green foliage in the town of Zabid on the flat coastal plain of southwestern Yemen. In the ninth century, it boasted a reputation as a center of education. Students flowed in and out, bringing with them their intellectual curiosity and leaving with the gifts of learning. It was in this university among the trees that a man named Ahmed Abu Musa, al-Jaladi, devised a mathematical system called *al-jabr* which some claim was the precursor of modern algebra. Now the excitement of discovery is gone, and the university sits quietly reflecting the poverty of the town around it. Zabid lives hand to mouth from farming and an erratic handicraft trade. Except for the two-lane asphalt highway that runs from Taiz to Hodieda, the streets are nothing more than wide swatches of thick red dust stirred only occasionally by a passing car. On this day, all that is in sight are four adolescent boys wrapped in checkered Yemeni sarongs, who hang on a donkey-drawn flatbed wagon mounted on four old automobile tires. Zabid has been bypassed by time; just as time bypassed the golden age of the Arabs.

If in the Arab mind the Alhambra lives as a credit to Arab brilliance, then Zabid is the representation of Arab woes. When the Abbasid dynasty fell, the Arabs lost the ability to govern their own destiny. Control of Arab land and Arab people passed to others, notably the Ottoman Turks. And it is the Ottomans that most modern Arabs blame for what they see as their cultural decline in the sixteenth, seventeenth, and eighteenth centuries. In the nineteenth century, it was the West that the Arabs began to blame for their stagnation. Ever since the West has served as the flaming symbol of all that is wrong in the Arab world. Thus as the Islamic empire united the Arabs culturally, hostility toward the West unites them psychologically.

CHAPTER 3

INVASION OF
THE INFIDEL

THE CAFÉ MODCA SITS ON A PROMINENT corner of Hamra Street, not far from the oceanfront in Beirut. Before the civil war, it enjoyed a clandestine reputation gained from pumping coffee and pastries into the zealous Arab nationalists who congregated there. The Deuxième Bureau, Lebanon's combined FBI and CIA, knew all about the Modca. But for those who frequented it, the risk of arousing the suspicions of a less than efficient security service increased the café's appeal.

When I was last at the Modca, Lebanon had suffered so much from communal violence that the days before 1975 when people crept out of the alley to see who was about before entering seemed like an age of innocence. There was no longer that atmosphere of intrigue. Political debate had been carried out with guns for so long that the Modca had become just another café trying to survive in war-weary Beirut. As I approached, the busboy lethargically swept debris from in front of the door, pushing it around the corner toward a tall mound of jagged pieces of glass blown into the alley by bombs and artillery during the years of the Lebanese civil war. Entering the door, I noticed that all the pockmarks of those years had yet to be removed and the chairs showed the battering the long war had inflicted on Beirut. But in the grimness, political passions still burned. I made my way to a back table where Hassan, Hamid, Faisal, and Kamal sat sipping coal-black coffee and smoking one cigarette after another. Two Sunni Lebanese, a Syrian, and a Palestinian, they shared the despair of the Arab condition and laid its fault at the feet of the West.

Hassan punched his cigarette into the air as he unrolled a litany of charges that although differing in their examples were identical in tenor to others I had heard so often before. "There is this conspiracy in the West to make the Arabs weak. That's the purpose of the CIA. I know and you know that everything that happens in the Middle East is caused by Washington's CIA."

Faisal impatiently interrupted, "The CIA destroyed Nasser. It pays people to hijack airplanes and then blames it on Arabs. Look at Lebanon. The CIA started plotting against us in 1958." Four heads nodded in agreement.

Hassan retook the conversation. "It's not just the United States."

Before he could go further, Hamid jumped in. "Europeans plot against us. They want Arab oil but they don't want Arabs to share their technology. Why?" He shrugged, a look of disdain crossing his face. "To keep us weak and poor, of course."

Kamal, a listener rather than a talker, leaned back in his chair to pronounce the final word on Western iniquities: "Ever since the Crusades, the West has tried to destroy the Arabs."

The Arabs live in the distressing shadow of the West. They see Western power and Western ways always lurking on the horizon ready to enslave them economically and destroy them culturally. However exaggerated and irrational these perceptions may appear to the Westerner, they go to the very core of the Arab psyche.

In one sense, the Arabs' pervading suspicions of the West are defensive, an acceptable explanation of all that has gone wrong since the Arabs' golden age. They are applied like a salve to Arab honor, which the Arabs believe grievously suffers when Arab nations are swayed by Western standards such as GNP and the ability to successfully manage government and business according to twentieth-century modes. They excuse societies unable to break the burden of traditionalism or to overcome the Arabs' myriad forms of tribalism. The West thus becomes the scapegoat on which the intolerable weight of collective Arab shame can be unloaded.

But in another sense, Arab hostility to the West carries within it the seeds of rationality. Arab experience with the West is composed of a chain of encounters in which the Arabs, in some way, always lost. In perceptions and realities that span almost ten centuries, the Arabs see themselves as having been subjected to a series of invasions in which they, superior in culture and morality, have suffered at the hands of the West's aggressive nature and technological know-how. From the Crusades of medieval Europe to European economic intrusion in the nineteenth century, from the period of European colonialism in the early to middle twentieth century to the United States' determined support of the state of Israel, the Arabs see themselves as having been murdered, raped, pillaged, and humiliated by a West intent on subjugating the Arabs culturally, politically, and economically. Rational or irrational, distrust, hostility, and even hatred of the West constitute a major element in Arab unity. One of the great icons of that unity is the medieval Crusades.

As the eleventh century dawned, Western Europe and the Arab world had hardly met. While Islam had flowered, Christian Europe had slumbered in the darkness of ignorance. But the height of the great Islamic empire passed, and the map drawn by Islamic warriors and intellectuals lay broken. The region of Palestine was under the sway of the Fatimids, a dynasty coming out of the Ismaili sect of Shiism that ruled Egypt. Christians within its borders enjoyed a level of security, freedom of worship, and a measure of respect from the Muslim majority. When al-Hakim, the mad caliph of Cairo, all but destroyed the Church of the Holy Sepulcher in 1010, Muslim money helped in the restoration of the church's gold-threaded Byzantine brocades and the portrait of Jesus riding into Jerusalem. "Palmers," Europeans seeking penitence in the pilgrimage to Jerusalem, came in peace. But in the midpoint of the eleventh century the tranquillity ended. The Seljuq Turks, a nomadic tribe from the steppes of Asia, thundered into the Arab world. In 1070, they stormed Jerusalem and expelled the Fatimids. Christian pilgrims now returning to Europe with their palm leaves also brought with them frightful tales of oppression and desecration of Christian holy sites. Thus a worried Christendom watched and waited as the wild men of the steppes wheeled their ponies northward toward Constantinople.

For seven centuries, the Byzantine Empire, through its days of glory and its years of decline, functioned as Christianity's bastion against invaders from the east. By the eleventh century the Byzantines, bled by their internal conflicts, were no longer strong enough to stem the tide. In 1085 when the Seljuq Turks stood on the Bosporus looking across at Constantinople and beyond it toward all of eastern Europe, the Byzantines knew they were helpless to stop them. Pushing aside a half millennium of struggle between Constantinople and Rome for dominance over Christianity, the Byzantine pope, Alexius, sent out a call for help to the Latin pope, Urban II. Envisioning the reunification of Christendom under the rule of Rome, Urban answered.

In the cold November of 1095, thousands of people from across Europe congregated for the great Council of Clermont. The mighty, housed in tents flying the colorful flags of the nobility, and the masses, huddled in the open, spread out like an ocean across the broad fields. From a raised platform at the center of the congregation, the voice of Urban II rang out. "O race of Franks! race beloved and chosen by God! . . . From the confines of Jerusalem and from Constantinople a grievous report has gone forth that an accursed race, wholly alienated from God, has violently invaded the lands of the Christians, and has depopulated them by pillage and fire. Jerusalem is a land fruitful above all other, a paradise of delights. That royal city, situated at the center of the earth, implores you to come to her aid. Undertake this journey eagerly for the remission of your sins, and be assured of the reward of imperishable glory in the Kingdom of Heaven."* Knights fell to their knees to receive the cross and pledge themselves and their property to the great mission to which their pope called them.† Blacksmiths and cobblers, bakers and merchants joined the knights in putting on the cross. Serfs and vassals, released from the obligations of feudalism, prepared to leave for the Holy Land. Monks emerged from their monasteries and hermits from their caves to join the army of Christ. Even the gates of the prisons opened to provide more soldiers for Christianity. In one burning idea, the needs and desires of the ambitious Urban II and a restless Europe met. Jerusalem would be wrested from the hands of the heathen "Muhammedans."

Thousands strong, the Crusaders marched from France to Constantinople, where they descended like locusts on the treasure of churches, palaces, and shops. Shocked, the Byzantines realized

---

* Will Durant, *The Age of Faith* (New York: Simon & Schuster, 1950), p. 587.
† The word "crusade" came from the Spanish word *cruzada*, meaning marked with a cross.

that the western Europeans they had summoned to defend them were odorous barbarians centuries removed from the intellectual and cultural standards of the East. And once called, it was they who took charge of Christendom's campaign against the Seljuq Turks.

From Constantinople, the Crusaders marched five hundred miles toward "Jerusalem the Golden," raping and pillaging on the way. On June 7, 1099, the twelve thousand survivors of heat, exposure, and battle finally reached the outer walls of Jerusalem. For three years, they had marched and fought toward their goal. Now they paused before storming the City of God, unaware that the Muslim population of Jerusalem suffered under the Seljuq Turks no less than the Christians. The Crusaders slaughtered those they judged wicked. Babies, snatched from their dying mothers' breasts, were flung against the stone of walls and streets. Mounds of mutilated bodies were put to the torch. The soldiers of Christ killed seventy thousand Muslims before they flocked to the Church of the Holy Sepulcher to weep with joy and thank the God of Mercy for their victory. A thousand years of Arab anger against the West had begun.

Jerusalem, including most of Palestine and Syria, became a sovereign state of European Christendom.* Divided into four feudal principalities—Jerusalem, Antioch, Eddessa, and Tripoli—Christian territory was parceled into fiefs which would breed the same ambitions and greed as their models in Europe. Jealous lords collected taxes, coined money, and made war on each other. Assuming all ownership of land, they reduced the former owners—Christians as well as Muslims—to the condition of serfs, imposing on them feudal obligations. All Arabs regardless of religion fell under the harsh edicts of the Europeans. Thus the Crusades, more than pitting Christian against Muslim, stood European against Arab in a war of cultures. In Arab perceptions, the West is still attacking.

In the contemporary Arab world, religion often provides the code words for what the Arabs believe is Western determination to destroy a whole way of life. In flashes of rhetoric, the terms "Muslim" and "Arab" are emotionally interchangeable. In 1980, Sheikh Muhammed Ali al-Harakan, the secretary-general of the Muslim World League, spoke the feelings of all Arabs in the words and imagery

---

* The Knights Templar used the Haram al-Sharif as their capital.

of Islam. "Muslims [are] besieged by enemies and unbelievers who wish to put out the Light of God with a puff of mouth. But the Light of God cannot be put out even though unbelievers detest it."* In more blunt terms a headline in Saudi Arabia's daily *Arab News* in November 1983 screamed, "West's scorn of Mideast people assuming race prejudice forms."

After a few decades in the balmy climate and easy ways of the Levant, the Crusader state softened and tamed. It survived because of the schisms dividing the Muslims around it. But in the twelfth century, the Arabs found a leader capable of solidifying sufficient territory and men to challenge the Franks.†

Salah-al-Din Yusuf ibn Ayyub was born in Tikrit in what is now Iraq, the same area that claims the twentieth century's Saddam Hussein. Ironically, Salah-al-Din, the man to whom every Arab pays homage, was a Kurd, an ethnic group with fierce loyalty to its own identity that has for centuries resisted Arabization. Salah-al-Din grew up in the cities of Baalbek and Damascus, both part of a demi-empire ruled by the Kurd Nur-ur-din. On Nur-ur-din's death, Salah-al-Din, as the empire's most successful general, became its head. Consolidating the territories he inherited, Salah-al-Din moved into northern Iraq. Eventually, he was accepted as the sultan of the Hijaz, Nubia, and Egypt. Mighty in war, Salah-al-Din lived a personal life of ascetic simplicity. His clothes were made of coarse woven cloth, and he drank nothing but water. Shunning the booty of war, he ruled his conquered territories with integrity. In possession of the qualities embodied in the ideal of the caliph, Salah-al-Din went to war against the European Christians.

If Salah-al-Din symbolized the best of the Muslims, Reginald of Chatillon exemplified the worst of the Crusaders. From his castle of Karak, fifteen miles northeast of the Dead Sea, Reginald repeatedly violated the truce in place between the Christians and Salah-al-Din. In 1183, he announced his intention to invade Arabia to destroy the tomb of the "accursed camel driver" and smash into fragments Mecca's Kaaba. An infuriated Salah-al-Din sounded the

---

* *Saudi Gazette*, March 13, 1980.
† Symbolic of the war of misunderstanding that divided Christian and Muslim, the Arabs referred to the Europeans as "Franks" and the Europeans referred to the Arabs as "Saracens," a name that was originally applied to a tribe on the Arabian peninsula.

call for holy war. On July 4, 1187, in the crucial engagement of the two-hundred-year contest between Islam and Christianity, Salah-al-Din wiped out the cream of the knights' armies at Hittin, near Tiberias in Palestine. The defeated Reginald was captured. Hauled before Salah-al-Din, he was given the choice of acknowledging Muhammed as a prophet of God or death. Reginald, true to his own character, chose death.

The castle of Reginald of Chatillon at Karak is still there. It sits high on a soft hill south and a bit west of Amman. The great, heavy outer door is gone, but the main portal still reaches high, as if expecting Reginald mounted on a white horse to charge through. The long, narrow slits in the stone of the turrets that accommodated the long bow and the small stone perches from which the pigeons flew forth with their messages have survived the ravages of time. It is as if a medieval castle had been picked up out of France or Germany or Britain and transplanted here in the Levant. Like Reginald himself, it somehow does not fit its surroundings. Perhaps it is the brown terrain or olive trees in the orchard across the asphalt road. Maybe it is the people along that road wearing headcloths and dresses embroidered in the designs unique to the Levant. Although the castle has been there for a thousand years, it is of another place, another way of life that came to the world of the Arabs but could not stay.

Salah-al-Din left the battlefield of Hittin and charged on toward Jerusalem. After a siege of only twelve days, the city's Christian defenders surrendered to the Muslim commander. In reclaiming Islam's holy site, Salah-al-Din reverently entered the Dome of the Rock. Slowly he walked around its octagonal walls sprinkling rose water to purge the Christian taint. Then he watched as the golden cross atop the cupola came down. Salah-al-Din had driven out the pigs and crosses and vile odors of the Europeans. Jerusalem once more belonged to Islam. Except for a brief period in the thirteenth century, it would stay in Muslim hands until 1917 when Britain captured it during World War I.

The fall of Jerusalem brought the most famous of all the Crusades—the Third (1189–1192). Setting Salah-al-Din against Richard the Lionhearted, it was perhaps the last heroic contest between the Muslim East and the Christian West. In the character and motivation of these two men, the Arabs see the great cultural confrontation between themselves and the West.

Richard I became king of England at the age of thirty-one. The son of Henry II and Eleanor of Aquitaine, he incorporated the impulsive, irrepressible personality of his mother. Wildly indulgent, he sucked taxes from his subjects to squander on drunken banquets and showy splendor. Possessing a boisterous sense of adventure, he sold an acknowledgment of Scotland's independence to finance his own crusade to recapture Jerusalem from Salah-al-Din.

Actions and recriminations of Richard and Salah-al-Din, one against the other, were brutal. Richard slew 2,500 Muslims at the outer walls of Acre. Salah-al-Din countered by ordering all English prisoners taken in battle put to death. Richard imposed a two-year siege on Acre, and Salah-al-Din sustained the besieged. Salah-al-Din burned with the fire of belief, Richard with the sheer love of battle. Yet between these two a degree of respect existed which demanded that when Richard lost his horse in battle Salah-al-Din sent him a charger so that so gallant a warrior would not be shamed by fighting on foot. Respect existed because they fought as equals, a situation the Arabs feel they have not experienced with the West since.

In the end, Richard was forced to turn home, leaving Salah-al-Din and the cause of Islam victorious. In 1193, Salah-al-Din died at the age of fifty-five, leaving an empire that stretched from Egypt through most of Palestine across Syria, ending on the plain between the Tigris and Euphrates.

For the Arabs, the legendary Salah-al-Din never really died. He remains the reigning symbol of Arab power against the West, the noble emblem of Arab history in the centuries after the decline of the Islamic empire. The search for the new Salah-al-Din, the hero who can defeat the West, constitutes the great ongoing quest of Arab politics. The Arabs saw Salah-al-Din in Nasser during the 1950s and 1960s. After his death, the quixotic Muammar Qaddafi unsuccessfully tried to pick up the mantle of the Arabs' long-dead hero. For a time in the 1980s, many Arabs allowed Iran's Ayatollah Khomeini, a non-Arab, to serve as their symbol of defiance against the West. In the first year of the 1990s, Saddam Hussein grabbed for Salah-al-Din's legacy.

For a hundred years after Salah-al-Din defeated Richard the Lionhearted, Christendom's shrinking territory in the Levant survived, drawing to it one crusade after another. The Fourth Crusade, the "Children's Crusade," killed or dispersed fifty thousand of Europe's children. The Fifth, the last real crusade, accomplished nothing for the Europeans. The Seventh and Eighth Crusades of Louis IX of France were nothing but anemic efforts of a saintly man. Finally they ended. In 1291, Acre, the strongest Christian outpost in Palestine, fell. The Mediterranean ports of Tyre, Sidon, Haifa, and Beirut followed. Eventually the Europeans either went home or did what invaders have always done in the Fertile Crescent—they merged with the people they had come to conquer. Traces of what the Arabs claim are their descendants are still there.

I found one in the Palestinian refugee camp of Kalandia on the Israeli-occupied West Bank. Picking my way through the narrow paths of the crowded camp toward the school, I saw ten or twelve lively adolescent boys waving their arms and shouting, "Me, me, you take picture of me." Dark-haired, dark-eyed, slightly built, all were physical stereotypes of "Arabs," except one. He was a little taller than the others, a little more angular in his build. But what made him stand out from the rest was his ash-blond hair and blue-gray eyes. He was what is known in the Arab world as a "Crusader child," an actual or fictionalized descendant of the Franks who entered, plundered, and permanently scarred the world of the Arabs.

The Crusades imposed a profound change in Muslim society. Before the arrival of the crude, uneducated Europeans, Muslim governments and Muslim populations had been reasonably tolerant of the Christians and Jews living among them. But after two centuries of ruthless Christian occupation, little charity toward Christians remained. The Jews, viewed as part of the fabric of the Levant and not directly connected by religion to the European interloper, fared somewhat better than the Christians. Rulers, drawing from the hostility of their own people, adopted harsh attitudes toward anyone suspected by reason of faith of collaborating with the infidels. Discounting the fact that most identified more with their Arab neighbors than the invading Europeans, all Christians became suspect. The heavy hand of government fell on churches and schools and reached into the pocketbooks of those professing to be Christians. It was all part of the pattern in which the Arabs became increasingly insular and xenophobic.

After the Crusades, the Arabs retreated into an isolation that would characterize their whole future and explain some of the Arabs' collective condition today. Although this isolation was, in large part, imposed by Turkish occupation in the fifteenth century, the Arabs had already deliberately separated themselves from the West. While

Europe took home from the Crusades what it had learned from the Arabs and fed it into the Renaissance, the Enlightenment, and finally the Industrial Revolution, the Arabs retreated further into the legalisms of Islam and the security of their own way of life. In many ways, they have never recovered.

Isolation was fed by a belief eating into the Arabs' collective consciousness that it was the armies of Christian Europe that ended the golden age of their intellectual and cultural life. This is the stuff of popular myth. When the Crusaders arrived, the Fertile Crescent was in political shreds. An array of groups energized by the scent of decline had already assaulted what had been the Islamic empire from the east, north, and south. It was still in fragments when they departed. Salah-al-Din had united the Muslims in the interim. But when he died, his empire was dismembered by his own family. One son held Damascus, another Cairo, another Aleppo. A brother ruled Transjordan and competed with his nephews for Egypt and Syria. Yet the belief that it was the Europeans who doomed the Arabs to a position of humiliating impotence is so powerful and so persuasive that it still grips the Arab psyche. The image of the Crusader as an ignorant, ruthless semibarbarian is still so strong that the threat to summon "Richard the Lionhearted" provides Syrian mothers a potent weapon to frighten their children into behaving. The Crusades, a faded episode in the history of the West, lives in the mind of the Arabs. Its power and immediacy are something no Westerner ever fully comprehends, only experiences.

I once sat in a small room in the Tunisian seaside town of Sidi Abu Said with Yasser Arafat. Opposite his desk, a giant-screen television sitting on top of a high, heavy metal stand projected a 1950s grade B Hollywood movie. Medieval knights, lining a long plank table, tore meat with their teeth and tossed the bones to large, shaggy dogs waiting at their feet. It was the perfect backdrop for Arafat's conversation. With lightning speed, he verbally leaped between the sins of the West against the Palestinians and the sins visited on the Arabs by the European Crusaders. In his fervor, it was as if he were speaking of simultaneous events. Far from being unique, Arafat mirrors the Arab attitude that the Crusades created the model for all relations between the West and the Arab world from early-eighteenth-century European colonialism to the state of Israel to the Gulf War.

During the early days of the 1990 Persian Gulf crisis, when

American troops were pouring into Saudi Arabia, Jordan's minister of religious affairs, an unmistakable product of Arab culture, proclaimed, "We cannot retaliate against the United States itself because vast oceans separate us. But we now have the opportunity to retaliate against the American troops and other crusaders who are a stone's throw from us. I assure you that we will take them captive and shackle them with chains as Muslims did with the Crusaders."* And so the Arab mind moves back and forth across the centuries drawing up its own images of Christendom's invasion of Islam.

Absent from the myth is the reality that the long-term threat to the great Islamic civilization came from tribes of Asia's northern steppes. They came first as slaves caught or purchased beyond the Central Asian frontiers of the Islamic empire. Imported at an early age, these young boys were trained, educated, converted to Islam, and eventually enrolled in the armies of the empire. During the Abbasid dynasty of Baghdad, it was the Mamluks, the Asian slaves, who dominated the military. But they were only the prelude to the Turkish tribes who would come under their own leaders.

Nomadic Turks brought to Islam by tenth-century missionaries and led by the descendants of a chieftain named Seljuq drove into the Islamic heartland in 1040. Tough, uncultured, infused with energy and zeal, the Seljuq Turks rolled over the broken and deteriorating Islamic empire in their path. By 1042, they were masters of the Iranian plateau. In 1055, they took Baghdad, the religious and administrative capital of the Islamic world. Although they propped up the caliphate, the Seljuq Turks gave themselves the title of sultan, under which they exercised power and authority in their own interest. But like those who had come before them, they succumbed to the powerful influence of high Islamic culture.

For more than a century and a third (1055–1194), the Seljuq Turks held together the realm of Islam from central Asia to the eastern border of Egypt. It was they who stood at the threshold of Constantinople triggering the Crusades.

In the thirteenth century, at the time the Europeans were launching the Fifth Crusade, a new threat to Islam arose in the east. The legendary Genghis Khan had forged the nomadic tribes of Mongolia together and stood poised to sweep west. Between 1219

---

* *New York Times*, December 16, 1991.

and 1221, he drove through Turkestan into Iran and Afghanistan and on into the Caucasus and southern Russia. The great Genghis died in 1227 and the Mongol advance paused. Twenty-nine years later, Prince Hulagu, the mighty Genghis's grandson, pushed the Mongol hordes on west. "Like a cyclone, the warriors swept from their habitat through the steppes of Asia into the world of Islam, leaving a crimson stream bordered with heaps of ruin in their trail."* Practically overnight the Seljuqs became vassals of the Mongols.

In 1258, the Mongols took Baghdad, looting and plundering the public buildings that so exemplified the intellectual vigor of the Islamic empire. In 1259, Hulagu's armies rode into Syria, took Damascus and Aleppo, and went on to the Mediterranean. More barbaric than the Christians ever were, the Mongols stanched Islam's period of glory in the cradle of its birth.†

Gradually the Mongols, like others who invaded the vast region between Asia and Europe, melted into the whole. They converted to Islam. And with the Arabs, they merged into a new empire that would rule the Arab world until the end of World War I—the empire of the Ottomans.

The Turks, an amalgam of the Seljuqs and other Turkish-speaking tribes, brought a new vigor into Islam. Laying claim to the caliphate, the Turks once more pushed Islam's borders, this time into the Balkans and to the door of Europe. On May 29, 1453, the Ottomans captured Constantinople, ending at last the debilitated Byzantium. For Europe, the fall of Constantinople marked the end of the Middle Ages. For Islam, it inaugurated a new imperial age.

The Ottoman Empire enjoyed its own golden age in the sixteenth century under the forty-six-year-long reign of Suleiman the Magnificent. Suleiman's empire sprawled from the River Dniester through the Balkans, across Anatolia into the Fertile Crescent, down the coasts of the Arabian peninsula and across North Africa to Al-

---

* Philip K. Hitti, *Islam: A Way of Life* (Minneapolis: University of Minnesota Press, 1970), p. 101.
† The Mongol advance westward into Egypt and North Africa was stopped by the Mamluks. Turkish slaves who guarded the sultan, they killed their master in 1250 and took over. They would rule Egypt for three centuries. It was the Mamluks who drove the last of the Crusaders out of the Levant. And it was the Mamluk sultanate in Egypt that remained the stronghold of Arab culture. Egypt became a kind of Arab Byzantium—a bastion of the older culture holding out against the new wave represented by the Turks, Mongols, and their successors in the north who by the beginning of the sixteenth century incorporated Egypt into the Ottoman Empire.

geria. Within its borders resided a population of twenty to thirty million, a staggering array of languages, and the adherents of three of the world's major religions.

Yet with all the glories it delivered to the Turks, the reign of Suleiman failed to reverse the downward drift of Arab culture. The Ottoman Empire was the revival of the Islamic state, not Arab culture. The Turks formed a military/political caste that ruled over a miscellany of subject peoples, of whom the Arabs were only one. Turkish, while joining Arabic and Persian as a language of Islam, ranked as the sole language of the state. And the caliph, now revived in Constantinople, was no longer a descendant of either the Prophet or those tracing their origins to Mecca. He was not even an Arab. Yet as the Arabs mourned the passing of the caliphate from Arab hands, they accepted the Ottoman Empire, which breathed new life into the ideal of the Islamic state. It was in this state that the Arabs found unity between themselves and the Turks. For four hundred years, the Arab identity linked to the Ottoman Empire. But the union of Arab and Turk was rooted in neither politics nor culture. Only Islam and the recognition of the caliph as the religious heir of the Prophet Muhammed held the Arabs within the folds of the Ottoman Empire.

Torn by the centuries-long progression of alien invasions, suspended between the West and Constantinople, the Arabs slumbered under the Ottomans. Intellectual curiosity, the passion for knowledge, and the joy of discovery that had characterized the Arabs during Islam's golden age slowly evaporated. And then it was gone, snuffed out under a heavy blanket of dogma and traditionalism. Having lost touch with its creativity and liberalism, a whole culture retreated into the security of its religious past.

The Arabs kept alive the image of their past greatness through roving poets who migrated from village to village retelling stories of the glorious past. Fact represented a seed that when fertilized by longing and embellished by imagination produced the Arabs' heroic myth. "The model was a simple popular image that embodied all the traits that the Arab—the imagined one, this is—had lost along the way. As a result, history intermingled with myth and produced a primitive, simple ideology removed from the necessities of the modern age."*

---

* Fouad Ajami, *The Arab Predicament: Arab Political Thought and Practice Since 1967* (Cambridge, England: Cambridge University Press, 1981), p. 47.

If Islam at its best had raised Arab society to a new height of human progress, at its worst it reached a low point of stagnation. The Arabs replaced the concept of progress with a self-complacency which was rendered more perilous by their own exaggerated feeling of superiority that came out of the Bedouin ethos and the confidence of faith. As a result, achievement and self-satisfaction existed in reverse order. Rather than pursuing the future, the Arabs stayed in the past cultivating their cherished pride in Islam, the source of their greatness and glory. While Europe moved into the Industrial Revolution, the Arabs drifted on the periphery of one of the defining events of history, living in the twilight of what was rather than participating in what was to be.

But no matter how much they may have wished it, the Arabs could not live forever in isolation from the West. Just over five hundred years after the Crusaders withdrew from the Levant, the West again descended upon the Arab world as a conqueror. And once more the cultures of East and West would clash on the soil of the Arabs. This time the West would win.

On the eve of 1798, Napoleon Bonaparte threatened Europe in the name of the French Republic. Driven by an unquenchable need to expand, striving to gain the upper hand in the imperialist contest with Britain, Napoleon turned his ambitions toward the eastern edge of the Mediterranean—to Egypt. With Napoleon aboard the first ship, the French fleet sailed out of Marseilles toward Malta and then south and east in the direction of Alexandria. En route, the seasick Bonaparte studied the Koran and indulged his fantasies. "I saw myself founding a religion, marching into Asia riding an elephant, a turban on my head and in my hand the new Koran that I would have composed to suit my needs."*

With the fleet anchored in the warm waters offshore, Napoleon and a party of five thousand stepped onto an unprotected beach near Alexandria. Bonaparte, swelled by the success of his mission, announced his intention to deliver the philosophy of the French Revolution to the Egyptians. "Henceforth, with God's help, no Egyptian shall be excluded from high office. Those who are the most intelligent, educated, and virtuous shall govern, and thus the people

---

* Quoted in Mansfield, *Arabs*, p. 104.

shall be happy."* He then marched to Cairo to wrest Egypt from its Mamluk rulers.

Napoleon knew as little about the Arab world as most Europeans. For a time, he outwardly addressed the culture by praising al-Azhar, the great depository of Islamic law and tradition, and daily conversed with the learned sheikhs. But he was a man who believed in the power of technology over the assurance of tradition. When Napoleon tried to impress his occupied people by launching a gas-filled balloon, the glitz of French technological achievement, the Egyptians saw it with Arab eyes and Arab attitudes. A sheikh pronounced the collective judgment: "The French fabricated a monster which rose up into the sky with the intention of reaching and insulting God. But it rose only to a feeble height, then fell back, ridiculously impotent."†

While Napoleon played with Islamic symbols and Western technology, the people filled with anger. Underground, secret documents passed from mosque to mosque charging that Napoleon's respect for Islam was a lie. "The French, . . . may the Almighty in his wisdom destroy their accursed country, are obstinate infidels, denying the existence of a supreme being, mocking at all religions and creeds. . . . Let the servants of Islam unite and march to battle."‡

Egyptian hostility to Napoleon had less to do with military power and materialism than with the whole interpretation of knowledge and the very essence of existence. The confrontation between Napoleon and the Egyptians "was one between Europe, which believed in the power of man's will to change the present and determine his future, and Islam, which conceded all knowledge as given and the process of learning as accumulation of the known rather than a process of discovery."§

It was not long before Cairo, in defense of Arab culture, revolted. Mobs screaming Allah's vengeance on the infidel severed the heads from resplendently uniformed officers and bore them through

---

* Marshall B. Davidson, ed., *The Age of Napoleon* (New York: American Heritage, 1963), p. 56.
† Raphael Patai, *The Arab Mind*, Rev. ed. (New York: Charles Scribner's Sons, 1983), p. 270.
‡ Lt. Col. P. G. Elgood, *Bonaparte's Adventure in Egypt* (London: Humphrey Milford, 1931), p. 155.
§ Michael Youssef, quoted in Thomas W. Lippman, *Egypt After Nasser: Sadat, Peace and the Mirage of Prosperity* (New York: Paragon House, 1989), p. 242.

the streets in triumph. Napoleon, stunned by the uprising, ordered his troops into the streets to shoot on sight Egyptians carrying arms. Matching Arab terror with French terror, Napoleon's soldiers threw decapitated Egyptian bodies into the Nile.

Napoleon restored order in Cairo, but he never controlled Egypt. Attempts to expand the French presence into Syria failed. And then he retreated back toward France, forced out by Britain's control of the seas and the challenge of the anti-French alliance to Napoleon's empire in Europe.* The whole episode lasted a little over three years. Its aftermath has consumed generations.

Nowhere else in history did an invasion of so little military consequence have such profound and durable psychological results. Napoleon invaded Egypt with more than an army. Possessing an arsenal produced by an industrializing economy, he accentuated the gap between the West and the Arabs. The teams of scientists, agricultural experts, and administrators he brought from France injected the accumulated ideas of the Renaissance and the Enlightenment into the tightly closed, moribund world of the Arabs. The French occupation, in essence, laid before the Arabs their own backwardness. Memories of the glorious centuries of the early Islamic empire were anemic challenges to Western superiority in organization, economics, and technology. While the prolonged medieval struggle between Western Christendom and the world of Islam was a conflict between the learned Muslims and the semibarbaric Europeans, the new Western invasion brought Europeans who far surpassed the Arabs in accumulated knowledge. With that knowledge they judged the world of the Arabs a failure. The resulting shock brought into question all the assumptions concerning morality and religion on which the Arabs had built their inner feelings of power and their outward assurance of superiority. The painful transformation of Muslim society from one in which eternal truths alone proved its validity to one which could compete with the West under standards imposed by the West forms the dominant themes of Arab history in the nineteenth and twentieth centuries. From the moment Napoleon set foot in the Arab east to the present, the Arabs have

---

* The most solid accomplishment of the French adventure resides in the British Museum. The Rosetta Stone, stumbled across by one of Napoleon's soldiers thirty miles from Alexandria, unlocked Egyptian hieroglyphics, revealing for civilization the complex and highly developed culture of ancient Egypt.

wrenchingly searched for an Arab response to the challenges of the West. They have yet to find the path to their own modernity. And in this feeling of impotence, the Arabs find an element of their unity.

Possessing his own measure of arrogance and blindness, a Westerner in the Arab world is swept up in the tension the Arabs suffer in their relationship with the West. It assumes many guises, inflicting itself in different forms. There is the defensiveness of the Saudis that comes across as insufferable arrogance. There is the anger of the Palestinians that carries with it the unmistakable hint of haughtiness. There are the Muslim Lebanese who revel in arguing their view of history. And there is the Egyptians' assurance that the Arab commitment to family and religion is the only valid measure of society. Yet no nationality corners one particular attitude. All ebb and flow from one group to the other and have in common a proud defensiveness. I see it most intimately among middle- and upper-class educated women.

Arab women, like Arab men, divide the world into the material and the spiritual. The products of the West fall into the category of excellent. At social functions, possessions are discussed in terms of points of origin. A blouse was purchased in New York, a wristwatch in Geneva, shoes in a shop that sells only Italian imports. From each woman comes the declaration "I only buy Western-made goods, of course. Their quality is so much superior to anything else." But when the conversation turns to values and the worth of society, any question of Western superiority evaporates. Contrasts and comparisons between Western and Arab culture never touch individual rights or the rule of law. Instead, Western society is seen as lacking any real values, tolerant of attitudes that degrade the family and relegate religion to the trash heap of a godless culture. It is in the arena of morality and values that the Arabs feel their societal strength in comparison to the West. As I left an afternoon tea party, one of my acquaintances told me with assurance but no venom, "You do not seem like most Westerners, who think they have everything but really have nothing." She spoke not only for herself but for a whole culture.

Under Ottoman rule, Arab society functioned as it had for centuries. The peasants worked their fields with hand-held plows and moved their produce by donkey. Artisans created traditional crafts with the same techniques as their fathers, grandfathers, and great-grandfathers. In the nineteenth century, both were hit by the winds of European economic interests that blew through the door opened by Napoleon. The industrial output of Birmingham and Lille pushed aside the Damascene brocades and copperware of the Mediterranean coast. European bankers took charge of governing authorities unwilling or unable to resist their lines of credit. This intrusion of the West not only damaged the Arabs economically, it gravely violated the Arab psyche, values, religion, and sense of historical and cultural integrity. In the Arab mind, the modernization being forced by the West translated into an assault on religious and cultural Islam.

In response, the Arabs first invented and then accepted as the explanation for their arrested development the argument that the Muslims had for a long time distorted their own values. Tapping into the ideas of earlier revisionists, nineteenth-century Islamic reformers contended that the prevailing values within the Arab world were different from what Islam had taught centuries before. For them, Arab salvation lay in the rediscovery and purification of Muhammed's original teachings. It was through Islam that the Arabs would transform the humiliating backwardness of their own society and create a new, progressive culture capable of confronting the West. Reaching into the past, they brought forth the heroic myth that would energize Arab society. But the ideas of seventh-century Arabia could not stop the Western avalanche. Yet the Islamic revivalists in failing to find an answer for Western dominance in science and industry raised the whole question of the relationship between Islam and the modern world. What generally emerged from their philosophical explorations was an affirmation of the exalted status of Islam in the moral realm and an appeal to Arabs to find in Islam a way to incorporate those things of the West deemed beneficial to Arab society.

In the second half of the nineteenth century, relentless Western economic penetration continued to imperil Arab culture and Arab existence. Western trade and capital subjugated states with more efficiency than armies. The Ottoman Empire itself declared bankruptcy in 1875; Egypt in 1876; Tunisia in 1881. Britain imposed its protectorate on Egypt in 1882, the year after France seized control of Tunisia.

A new wave of Islamic reformers sent out the call for a national awakening of the Arabs and for an Arab caliphate that could confront the Western invasion and turn back its disintegrating effects on Islamic society. Rather than using Islam as the rationale for withdrawing into the past, they pushed open the door on Islamic legal reasoning, expanding its scope and reinterpreting certain Islamic concepts that would enable Islam to meet the modern world. By emphasizing the Arabic language and the Arabs' living heritage, these nascent Arab nationalists clothed traditional concepts with modern meaning.

This was the right wing of emerging Arab nationalism.* Its left wing was composed of the educated elite who would in the next century stand at the front of an Arab nationalist movement.† For them, Arab success in modernization demanded the separation of religion from political life. In the last two decades before World War I, their nationalism argued that through language and culture Arabs of different regions and faiths should be bound together for the benefit of all.

All nationalists need a myth and an ideal. For the Arabs, it was the unification of all Arabic-speaking peoples into a single nation that would create a common ground between families, tribes, regions, and religions. In the unification and glorification of a mythical Arab nation, the Arab intelligentsia began to search for a system that would break the shackles of tradition and drive out the poison and power of the West. From their efforts, a general consensus developed among educated Arabs that the peoples of Arabia, Iraq, Syria, Egypt, and North Africa composed a nation held together by the concepts and realities of descent, homeland, and religion, but above all by language. Lacking a precise definition, Arab nationalism promised power where there was weakness, mission where there was alienation.

As the twentieth century opened, Arab nationalism that began as a response to the West moved on to question the position of the Arabs within the Ottoman Empire. A verse of the tenth-century poet al-Mutanabbi illuminated the call for a specific Arab identity outside Islam. "Like subjects, like King, the sages maintain. Can Arabs then thrive o'er whom non-Arabs reign?"‡

---

* Not all Islamic reformers were nationalists. Many attacked the idea of nationalism as a kind of secular heresy that divided the universal Muslim community. This same opinion is often expressed in the Islamic political movements currently found in the Arab world.
† See Chapter 4.
‡ Duri, *Historical Formation of the Arab Nation,* p. 191.

The Arabs could sing a litany to the abuse under the Otto-mans—poor administration, a deplorable lack of education, repressive despotism under local governors. Out of the maltreatment, a vague sense of Arab patriotism hovered around the image of *watan*, or homeland. The words of the writer al-Kawakibi cried out to the native speakers of Arabic: "You there! Leave us to manage our own affairs, to communicate among ourselves in eloquent Arabic and to show respect and understanding for each other as brothers. . . . Leave us to lead our own earthly lives and to make religion the arbiter in the hereafter only. Leave us to rally around the same message. Long live the nation! Long live the homeland!"* Yet after enumerating the instances of Turkish mistreatment and celebrating the image of an Arab nation, most Arabs still felt compelled to stay within the empire of the Ottomans, within the house of Islam. For the overriding reality was that the Islamic bond between the Arabs and the Ottomans represented the Arabs' only viable defense against the Western menace.

From the beginning of the Arab awakening in the early nineteenth century, the Ottomans had kept their distance from the Arabs' soul-searching. But ultimately the form Arab nationalism assumed resulted more from the actions of Istanbul than from tactics of the Arabs themselves. During the last decade of the nineteenth century, the Young Turks, an underground group of reformers, demanded that the whole Ottoman system be liberalized.† By 1907, they had become the driving force for change within the decaying Ottoman system. Many Arab nationalists looked on the agenda of the Young Turks as their own, interpreting it as a movement to decentralize the empire and to place the Arabs, with a population of 10.5 million, on an equal footing with the 7.5 million Turks. But in 1908, a pure Turkish nationalism exploded at the heart of the Ottoman Empire. The Young Turks, now in power, abruptly shifted the Ottoman Empire from an empire united under Islam to an empire promoting Turkish interests and culture. Long-standing tolerance for local customs and traditions became buried under edicts from Constantinople. In the face of Turkish nationalism, Ottomanism faded for the Arab intellectual elite. Yet for most Arabs—peasants, merchants, and intellectuals—fragile Arab nationalism could not replace the Ottoman Empire, still considered the Arabs' bulwark

---

* Ibid., p. 193.
† Also known as the Committee of Union and Progress.

against Western encroachment. The irony was that during World War I the Arabs would revolt against Ottoman rule, led by the caretaker of Mecca in alliance with the West.

In 1914 as the war clouds gathered in Europe and the Ottoman Empire gasped its last breaths, Hussein, the sharif of Mecca, began to think in terms of an independent Arab state.* The imperious sharif emitted the aura of authority. His distinguished white beard and white-banded turban served as staging for piercing black eyes that paralyzed those who came within his gaze. Although born in Mecca, Hussein had been raised in Constantinople as an urbane and cultivated descendant of the Prophet. For fifteen years, he lived as a well-kept hostage of the caliph Abdul Hamid, who rightly distrusted Hussein as a devious schemer. Finally, the schemer succeeded. On November 1, 1908, Hussein at the age of fifty-five became the sharif of Mecca, its religious custodian. By consolidating his position with the tribes of the Hijaz, Hussein built political power that soon exceeded that of the Turkish governor, who was forced to humble himself in public by kissing the hem of the sharif's robe.

In early 1914, Hussein dispatched his second son, Abdullah, to Cairo to hint vaguely to Lord Kitchener, the British resident, that the sharif, with British support, might mount a rebellion against the Turks. Although discreet in nature, the message indicated that Hussein wanted the same deal the British maintained with the Arab sheikhs strung along the western coast of the Persian Gulf. In each of these petty states, a British resident minister doled out gold sovereigns or Maria Theresa silver dollars and stood ready to summon the British fleet on the horizon at the first sign of encroachment by a hostile power.

When World War I broke out, Kitchener, recalling his 1914 conversation with the Emir Abdullah, sent a messenger into the Hijaz to make contact with Hussein on the question of a British-Arab alliance against the Turks. Messenger "X" left Suez on October 5 and reached Jeddah three days later. On arrival in Mecca astride a donkey he found that "every man he met, even if he possessed an insufficiency of clothes, was armed to the teeth and bristling with weapons."† Anxious to disrupt the Ottoman Empire's front on the

---

* A sharif is a descendant of the Prophet. In the Ottoman system, a sharif could be appointed to a specific function as the caliph's standard-bearer.
† Randall Baker, *King Husain and the Kingdom of Hejaz* (New York: Oleander Press, 1979), p. 51.

Red Sea, Britain decided to commit to some form of Arab independence as long as the Arabs, under Sharif Hussein, effectively helped the British war effort. So began the celebrated correspondence between Sir Henry McMahon, British high commissioner for Egypt and Sudan, and Hussein, Keeper of the Holy Places, Prince of Mecca. McMahon began: "To the excellent and well-born Sayid, the descendant of the Sharifs, the Crown of the Proud, Scion of Mohammed's Tree and Branch of the Quraishite trunk, him of the Exalted Presence and of the Lofty Rank . . . the lodestar of the Faithful and cynosure of all devout Believers . . . may his Blessing descend upon the people in their multitudes."* To Hussein and those who supported his cause, this exchange of letters meant a British promise of an Arab state when the Ottoman Empire was defeated.† The letters also were taken to mean that Britain solemnly promised to refrain from signing any peace treaty that did not specifically include an Arab state. Hussein, in the correspondence, categorically stated that under no circumstances would he consent to any part of Arabia becoming the possession of any power.

While McMahon and Hussein exchanged their letters, Britain and its wartime allies negotiated the secret agreements that would divide the territories of the Ottoman Empire among themselves. In February 1916, the infamous Sykes-Picot Agreement apportioned the lands the Arabs thought were theirs among the Europeans. But it would not be until after the Bolsheviks released the documents that the Arabs knew the full extent of British perfidy.‡

Believing he had the promise of an Arab state, Hussein himself lowered a rifle on the Turkish barracks at Mecca and fired the first shot in the Arab Revolt against Turkish rule. The secularism and zealous nationalism of the Young Turks, combined with the seduction of Britain and France and the spirit of Arab nationalism, broke the Arabs' emotional ties with universal Islam, enabling them to rebel against the Ottoman Empire in support of a Western alliance.

---

* Mansfield, *Arabs*, p. 165.
† The state Hussein envisioned and believed the British had promised extended from Alexandretta eastward to the Iranian frontier and south to the Persian Gulf. It was to include the entire Arabian peninsula. Excepted from this Arab state were the British port at Aden and the districts of Syria west of Damascus, Homs, Hama, and Aleppo.
‡ The Hussein-McMahon correspondence and the Sykes-Picot Agreement also contained stipulations regarding Palestine. See Chapter 4.

But the Arabs would soon learn that they were not a part of the Allied war effort but one of its targets. Deceived, the Arabs were sold like slaves.

What the Arab Revolt was or was not was largely in the eye of the beholder. Jordan's King Hussein, great-grandson of the sharif, says, "The whole Arab revolt was for the defense of Arab identity —to secure Arab freedom and Arab unity."* The king speaks with hindsight and a tailoring of history. What the sharif wanted was an independent Arab nation ruled by himself and his sons. He had never been an Arab nationalist, only an ambitious man with religious credentials. In attempting to define Arab nationalism and draw Arabs outside his own political alliances to the cause, he argued, "We are Arabs before being Muslim, and Muhammed is an Arab before being a prophet. There is neither minority nor majority among us, nothing to divide us. We are one body, we were Arabs even before the time of Moses, Muhammed, Jesus, and Abraham."†

But the Arab Revolt and the Sharif Hussein never meant very much to anyone other than the sharif's own followers. The better measure of Arab sentiment was the 1915 Damascus Protocol, which defined the conditions under which Arab leaders were prepared to support the Arab Revolt. The protocol, which came out of a broad conclave of Arab leaders, called for complete Arab independence from any foreign power. It drew the boundaries of an Arab state to encompass the Arabian peninsula, Palestine, and what is now Syria, Lebanon, and Iraq. This Arab state would commit to a defensive alliance with Britain and would grant the British Empire economic preference within its borders. Rather than total independence, the Arabs were seeking a kind of commonwealth arrangement with another imperial power, which addressed the reality that the Arabs were still unsure of what Arab nationalism actually meant. Arabic, in fact, did not even provide a word meaning nationalism. In many ways, what those at Damascus were engaged in was an ideological search for something to replace "Ottomanism." So long accustomed to membership in the universal Islamic state, the Arabs were incapable of developing a sense of national identity overnight. Nor were they willing to accept the Sharif Hussein as the Arab caliph.

---

* Quoted in Milton Viorst, "The House of Hashem," *The New Yorker*, January 7, 1991, p. 46.
† Mansfield, *Arabs*, p. 223.

The Arab Revolt was in essence a British-Hashemite adventure. The British financed it and the Hashemites led it. On November 2, 1916, the Sharif Hussein declared himself King of the Arab Lands at a ceremony in the Great Mosque at Mecca. As he spoke, the Turks were threatening to march to Mecca to hang the "old gray devil." Possessing only light arms, Hussein's largely Bedouin army, numbering somewhere between ten thousand and forty thousand men depending on the day and place of battle, were no match for Turkish artillery. Engaging in battle with the wisdom of the Bedouin, Hussein's forces chose to fight only when victory was certain, withdrawing to make coffee when it was not. Desperate to bring some order and direction to the Arab war effort, the British command in Cairo sent in several British officers, including the legendary T. E. Lawrence—Lawrence of Arabia.

The story of Lawrence is the story of the complex relationship between an English misfit and a scion of Islam's most distinguished family. In important ways, it is a romantic adventure that exemplifies the exaggerated expectations, the crosscurrents of interests, and the bitter disappointments that keep the Arabs united against the West.

In the autumn of 1916, T. E. Lawrence, a young British eccentric, educated at Oxford, experienced in the ways of the Arab world, met Faisal, the third son of the Sharif Hussein, educated in the ways of the desert, ignorant of the ways of the West. When Lawrence arrived at Arab headquarters in Hama in Syria, the dashing, white-robed Faisal stood in the garden, framed between the uprights of a black doorway. According to Lawrence, "I felt at first glance that this was the man I had come to Arabia to seek—the leader who would bring the Arab Revolt to full glory."[*] Faisal—tall, dark, Arab—and Lawrence—small, blond, English—hit Turkish rail lines and garrisons in lightning raids that would forever celebrate the guerrilla fighter. Elated with the results, the British still regarded the Arab effort as little more than a contributory element in bringing about the defeat of Germany's ailing ally, the Ottoman Empire. But if the British commander Allenby thought of Faisal's army only as his own right flank, Faisal and Hussein saw themselves as the central force in the movement to liberate the Arabs.

None of the targets the Arab forces hit was strategic until

---

[*] T. E. Lawrence, *Seven Pillars of Wisdom* (Garden City, N.Y.: Doubleday & Company, 1966), p. 64.

Aqaba. On June 19, 1917, Lawrence and forty men of the sharif's forces left from the Arabian coastal town of Wejh and turned into the desert. Men and camels became one under the pounding heat of the summer sun. Over eight hundred miles they rode, spreading the promise of victory and glitter of British gold among the Bedouin tribes. Finally, with more than a thousand men, Lawrence and the Arabs from the landward side attacked Aqaba, the Turkish port at the head of the Red Sea. It was a major victory for the Allies on the front with Ottoman Turkey.

The Arab Revolt had immobilized thirty thousand Turkish troops along the railway from Amman to Medina and prevented Turkish forces in Syria from linking up with the Turkish garrison in Yemen. The Allies benefited further by keeping the Turks in Arabia from linking up with the Germans in East Africa to shut off the Red Sea to Allied shipping. The Arabs had earned their place in the peace settlement. The Emir Faisal and perhaps the sharif himself believed Lawrence and the British would deliver them independence. If the Arabs believed that this was the reordering of the world of the Arabs and the world of the West, they were wrong. The fate of the Arab states decided in the Sykes-Picot Agreement would be sealed in the smoke-filled rooms of Paris.

When the Paris Peace Conference convened on January 18, 1919, Faisal, accompanied by Lawrence, joined the politicians and diplomats, bankers and oilmen, bondholders and missionaries gathered to push their respective interests in the peace accord. The American president, Woodrow Wilson, was perhaps the only honest broker present. While the other victors schemed for territory, Wilson argued for peace based on his Fourteen Points, which the Allies had embraced in the heat of war. But with peace, Lloyd George, the British prime minister, abandoned the Fourteen Points to aggressively pursue the interests, power, and possessions of the British Empire. George considered Egypt, Mesopotamia, Arabia, Palestine, Iran, Cyprus, and the Caucasus legitimate British prizes. In essence, the entire Middle East, with the exception of Syria and the Christian areas north of Beirut, was regarded as a necessary economic adjunct of the British Empire. The balance to the ravenous hunger of the British was the equally hungry Georges Clemenceau, the French premier. He insisted that France hold Syria and southern Anatolia and envisioned placing a French adviser at the elbow of the sultan of shrunken Turkey. Amid receptions, gay dinner dances, and week-ends at rented châteaux within easy motoring distance of Paris the future of the Middle East was decided.

Although the conference opened in mid-January, it was not until March 6 that Faisal was reluctantly allowed to speak—for twenty minutes. Younger and less experienced than his brother Abdullah, Faisal was the sharif's representative only because of his close relationship with Lawrence, in whom the sharif had such faith. Dressed in his exotic robes of Arabia, Faisal was on his first visit to Europe. His experience in political maneuvering was confined to his own region. Therefore he depended on Lawrence, who sat at his elbow garbed as an Arab. Lawrence, the comic actor, the oddball of the Middle Eastern theater, commanded meager respect within the British delegation. His presence meant little as Faisal explained to the Western-dominated conference that his father was asking for the right of self-determination for the Arabs and recognition of an Arab state as an independent geographical entity.

While the conference listened to petitions from those who populated the lands of the former Ottoman Empire, British and French mapmakers were behind closed doors drawing the boundaries of what would become the Arab states of Lebanon, Syria, Transjordan, and Iraq. They tinkered with other boundaries here and there— Egypt, Palestine, Kuwait, and the other sheikhdoms of the Persian Gulf. Only the near-empty center of the Arabian peninsula escaped European cartography. In every instance, boundaries met the needs of European colonialism. And it was in pursuit of Western interests that ethnic groups, tribes, and religions were thrown together in political entities often void of logic. Except for Palestine and minor adjustments here and there, none of these boundaries has ever changed.* The Arab states created by the will and whims of others are still paying the price.

Britain and France, restrained somewhat by international support for Woodrow Wilson's declaration against colonialism, connived to create a system of mandates under the League of Nations by which they could secure their coveted Middle East territories. Reflecting a measure of guilt, Britain recognized Hussein as king of the Hijaz and would eventually place two of his sons on the thrones of the British protectorates of Iraq and Transjordan. Hussein,

---

* The 1991 Gulf War was prompted by Saddam Hussein's attempt to annex Kuwait to Iraq.

refusing to concede to reality, still believed himself king of the Arabs—a king with no territory beyond the Hijaz.

All that is left of the Arab Revolt lies in the desert north of Mecca. The blackened remains of three passenger coaches protrude at angles out of drifts of red-orange sand. From time to time, a violent windstorm brings to the surface a segment of track of the old Hijaz railroad that once ran from Damascus to Mecca. In pursuit of their own vision of the Arab nation, Hussein's Arabs led by the dashing Lawrence rode across the drifting sands to strike the Turkish presence from the world of the Arabs. The debris they left behind is both the monument to their success against the Turks and a stone on the grave of Arab expectations. To touch the hot metal is to touch history and the failed Arab Revolt. At midafternoon when the heat sends waves over the landscape, I could almost hear the cry of the rebels as they swept down out of the dunes—"Death has become sweet, oh Arabs."

The Arabs came out of World War I not as an autonomous entity in the Ottoman Empire nor in possession of an Arab nation extending from Egypt to Persia and from Alexandretta to Aden. Instead the Arabs were divided into small territories that were in reality colonies under British and French lordship. In the collapse of the Ottoman Empire, the Arabs changed masters from Muslim Turks to European Christians.

CHAPTER 4

NATION AND COLONY

THE TWENTIETH CENTURY WAS breaking over ancient Palestine. From the west and from the east, roads of dirt and rock climbed up toward eternal Jerusalem. Depending on who gazed upon its thick stone ramparts, the sacred city stood on the hill of God, of Yahweh, of Allah.

The city's gray outer walls, laid in the sixteenth century by the Ottoman Suleiman the Magnificent, defined Jerusalem territorially and Palestine epochally. For four hundred years, time in Palestine had been measured by little more than the slow, twisted growth of the olive trees. Seasons turned into years and then generations as the enduring peasants, wrapped in Biblical-vintage robes, patiently harvested their wheat and herded their sheep. But as the twentieth century began, the rhythm of life altered perceptibly. Knots of aliens, Jews primarily from eastern Europe, settled in increasing numbers on Palestine's coastal plain. Their presence caused disquiet but no exaggerated alarm among their Arab neighbors. What transformed Palestine toward the end of the second decade of the twentieth century was the arrival of the British.

On December 11, 1917, khaki-clad British soldiers escorting Field Marshal Edmund Allenby covered the last mile before Jerusalem. As they approached, the city's population, shrunken to half its size by hunger, exile, and deportation inflicted by the desperate Ottoman governor Izzet Bey, opened the long-closed Jaffa Gate to the liberator. For the first time since the brief restoration of Crusader rule in the early thirteenth century, Western boots marched across the ancient cobblestone streets of what the Muslims call al-Quds. Allenby, intelligent, sensitive to the ways of the Arabs, perhaps grasped the moment. He came on foot, his head bared. Standing at the citadel below the Tower of David, he uttered the prophetic words "Lest any of you be afraid." But for the Arabs, there was much to fear.

As British military forces moved through Palestine at the end of World War I, they were greeted as liberators by a people tyrannized by Ottoman rule. Around them hovered the vague promises of Arab independence that had fueled the Arab Revolt. And in them the Arabs for a moment saw their deliverance. But British imperial interests joined by those of France destroyed this promise, not just in Palestine but across the Fertile Crescent.

At the end of World War I, the Arabs moved from the control of one empire, that of the Ottomans, to the empires of the West. But the change involved more than switching colonial masters. The Ottoman Empire, no matter how flawed, carried with it the aura of Islam on which Arab culture rested. The Arabs' new colonial masters bore with them the abhorrent label of the West. Like new Napoleons, they arrived as occupiers to fuel again the Arabs' sense of technological inferiority and to prick anew their defensive pride. The West's rank as master energized the Arabs' ongoing search for a definition of nationalism that could move the Arab nation from the philosophical to the functional plane. But before the Arabs answered the question of how to find and express their nationalism, they would achieve their unity in anger. In Palestine, Arab nationalism faced both British imperialism and Zionism. In the years before World War II, it was this competition between the nationalism of the Arabs and the nationalism of the Jews that began to stitch the great offending banner around which all Arabs circle—Israel. To comprehend the emotion and the rage of Arab unity is to understand from the Arab perspective what happened in Palestine between 1920 and 1948. For it was events in Palestine and the imagery of Western power and Arab impotence that they projected that have fed the passion of Arab unity ever since.

When the Ottoman Empire surrendered in 1918, three forces

controlled the Fertile Crescent. The guerrilla army of the Sharif Hussein commanded by his son Faisal held sway from the Hijaz to Damascus. France through influence extending back to the mid-nineteenth century controlled Beirut and the Christian area to the north known as the Mountain. With an army stretched from Mosul, in what is now northern Iraq, to the Persian Gulf, Britain was master of Mesopotamia. Allenby's military forces to the West held Egypt, what is now southern Lebanon, and Palestine.

Each army represented a political interest. For the Sharif Hussein, it was an independent Arab state ruled by his own Hashemite family. For France, it was the pursuit of Middle East territory that rose as much from French chauvinism as French economic interests. For Britain, it was empire. Mesopotamia promised oil to fuel the British fleet and a transportation and communications link to India. Egypt formed the right flank of the Suez Canal, Palestine the left flank.

In April 1920, the San Remo Conference ratified the secret territorial bargains struck during World War I in the Sykes-Picot Agreement. Under the guise of mandates from the League of Nations, Britain took charge of the new entity of Iraq and Palestine, including what is now Jordan.* With Egypt under British domination as a result of the debt crisis of 1882 and the sheikhdoms along the western side of the Persian Gulf locked in alliances dating back to the nineteenth century, Britain controlled both ends of the Arab world.

At San Remo, France got Syria. On July 14, 1920, General Gouraud, backed by French regulars and Senegalese reinforcements, gave the Emir Faisal four days to vacate Damascus. Deprived of British support, he had no choice but to surrender. French machine guns, tanks, and airplanes rolled over an unorganized Arab resistance to occupy all of Syria and to claim France's prize from World War I. Intent on strengthening its Christian allies on the Mediterranean, France sliced off western Syria from Tripoli south to the border of Palestine, and attached it to the Mountain to create

---

* The mandate system of the League of Nations placed former colonies of the Ottoman Empire and Germany under the supervision of a politically developed country. That country was to prepare the mandated territory politically and economically for independence. Because of the deathblow dealt to the League by the United States' refusal to join, the mandate system became what Britain and France always envisioned it to be—a screen for traditional colonialism.

Lebanon. The new map of the Fertile Crescent was now complete. The possessive hand of the West held the Arab world from the Nile to the Euphrates.

As British and French administrations snapped into place in the mandated territories and renewed themselves in the West's existing territories, the Arabs took stock of just what the nascent Arab nationalism that struggled toward life in the nineteenth century actually meant. Discontented with centuries of stagnation, humiliated at being forced to adopt the ways of their conquerors, frustrated by their inability to direct their own affairs, the Arabs reacted with a combination of wounded pride and self-condemnation. At first, the Arabs resisted and then most grudgingly submitted to imperial domination, transferring to their new Western masters the habit of acquiescence and obedience nurtured by centuries of Ottoman rule. At the same time, imprecise and ill-defined Arab nationalism labored to birth some viable framework in which the cultural and ethnic unity of the Arabs could find a political focus. Flailed both by the Arabs' own traditionalism and the West's model of modernization, Arabs faced their own confusion. As a result, Arab nationalism swung between the simple—a total rejection of the West—and the complex—a well-devised philosophy in which the Arabs could embrace aspects of the West without debasing themselves either personally or culturally. Through the 1920s, 1930s, and 1940s, the debate raged as the Arabs tried to release themselves from Western colonialism. And it followed them into independence. The Arabs have yet to find either the philosophy or the formula to answer the emotional demands of Arabism.

Ironically, the Arabs, who have yet to develop strong political institutions, breathe politics. In the days before the American University of Beirut was forced to exist on a battlefield, political groups ranging from Islamic fundamentalists to Marxists chased their political destinies across the tree-shaded campus and into the coffee shops that populated the streets on its landward perimeters. There was no better way to spend an evening than to sit and listen as the political rhetoric flowed. Fact, perception, and fantasy swirled through rooms choked with cigarette smoke exhaled by the products of a culture that celebrates verbal prowess. The Islamic fundamentalists stayed hidden in tightly controlled cells, but everyone else competed for an audience. Over my time in the Arab world, I have heard Maronite Christians carefully explain how they belong with the West, how they came out of the mountains to meet the first Crusaders and led them to Jerusalem, and how their nationalism can only be expressed in terms of separation from the Arabs. I have listened as Nasserites search for a philosophy that can take the place of the dead Nasser's personal charisma. I have followed discussions of Arab socialism and the Arab version of Marxism. And over and over, I have watched as the emotional appeal of Arab nationalism grips men and women trying to find Arabism's response to the West.

The period between World War I and World War II called for an Arab awakening and provided a fertile proving ground for the ideas of Arab nationalism. It was Arab writers and thinkers rather than statesmen who developed these theories of Arab nationalism. They came from different perspectives and took different paths of thought, yet all propagated a vision of an Arab renaissance. Out of this river of Arab thought, several main currents formed. Two still play a role in Arab political thought.

Between the two great world wars, the Islamic fundamentalists continued to hold that the Arabs' salvation lay in Islam. In 1928, a charismatic Egyptian schoolteacher named Hasan al-Banna founded the Ikhwan al-Muslimin, or Muslim Brotherhood. Burning with the fire of a reformer, al-Banna challenged his followers to reject the secularism of Islamic society and return to the original teachings of Islam. Al-Banna moved beyond rhetoric to build a militant, highly organized movement dedicated to sweeping away secular government and Western influence. Initiation into the Brotherhood was a solemn ritual in which the neophyte was taken into a darkened room to confront the Koran and a revolver. Plugged into networks of cells, new members were indoctrinated about the degeneration of Arab society and turned into cadres of idealists girded to do battle with corruption and oppression. Exactly what that new order was in social, economic, and political terms remained vague. When Hasan al-Banna was asked about the Muslim Brotherhood's explicit policies, he would reply with such statements as "Our program is the Koran" or "Our program is Islamic government. When the secular government is overthrown we will consider what to do in the light of existing circumstances. Until then, we are not going to be pinned down by details."

In the 1940s, the Brotherhood turned its paramilitary units to terrorism against Egyptian government officials and foreigners. In the period of its greatest power, membership reached half a million activists with unknown numbers of members and sympathizers in other Arab countries. Most were unskilled and semiskilled workers or the poorer class of students, those most exploited by Egypt's *haute bourgeoisie* and their European allies.

The Brotherhood planted cells everywhere—factories, schools, and trade unions. It owned business enterprises, including textile and insurance companies. It ran a publishing house that papered the country with tracts and pamphlets. It operated paramilitary camps and provided a wide array of social services. It was therefore a significant threat to the government of King Farouk. At 9:00 P.M. on February 12, 1949, Hasan al-Banna was killed on Queen Nazli Street by two policemen in civilian clothes. The leader was dead but the movement went on.

In the name of Islam, the Muslim Brotherhood tried to assassinate Gamal Abdul Nasser in 1954 and a radical offshoot succeeded in killing Anwar Sadat in 1981. In 1982, Muslim Brothers in Syria came close to overthrowing Hafiz Assad. In 1990, they won a sizable block of seats in Jordan's parliamentary elections. The strong currents of fundamentalism that run through the Arab world in the 1990s continue to be agitated by the ideas of Hasan al-Banna. Whether the Brotherhood exists as a single organization operating in different countries or whether groups outside Egypt seeking to replace secular government with the rule of Islam simply adopt the Ikhwan's name is unclear. Yet whether connected organizationally, all Muslim Brothers are linked ideologically. Austere, puritanical, xenophobic, the Muslim Brothers envision the Islamic *ummah* encompassing all believers. Only in a nation transcending politics can Muslims build the community decreed by Muhammed and escape the satanic tools with which they perceive the West manipulates the Islamic world.

If the Islamic fundamentalists were on one end of the religious spectrum, the Arab Christians were at the other. Arab Christians have always felt awash in the sea of Islam. For this reason, much of the intellectual vigor of Arab nationalism in the 1920s and 1930s came from Christians, primarily the Greek Orthodox.* They, after all, held a vested interest in turning Arab nationalism away from

---

* The Maronites of Lebanon and to a lesser extent the Catholic Melkites rejected Arab nationalism, finding their protection from the overwhelming numbers of Muslims in their strong ties to France.

Islam in the direction of the Arabs' common language and culture. Therefore Christian intellectuals often argued that the Arabs, made up of Babylonians, Assyrians, Phoenicians, and other Semitic races, were united more by a common history, language, and culture than by religion. And it was these commonalities that muted the distinction between Christian and Muslim, between Druze, Sunni, and Shiite. In 1938, the Lebanese writer Amin al-Rihani summed up this Christian viewpoint: "The Arabs existed before Islam and before Christianity. Let the Christians realize this, and let the Muslims realize it. Arabism before and above everything."*

Christian intellectuals spawned the two dominant ideologies in Arab nationalism to emerge before the end of World War II. The first, the Parti Populaire Syrien (PPS), or Syrian National Party, was founded in the 1930s by Antoun Saadeh, a thirty-year-old Greek Orthodox teacher from Syria. A secularist who demanded the separation of church and state, Saadeh's political theory revolved around the concept of a Syrian national identity that encompassed the original inhabitants of present-day Syria, Lebanon, Jordan, Israel/Palestine, Iraq, part of Turkey, and the island of Cyprus, the "star within the Crescent." To escape the threat of Islam's numbers, PPS's Greek Orthodox ideologues postulated that the people living in this geographical area of "Syria" constituted a unique ethnic unity. Saadeh reasoned that the Syrians were not Arabs but an ethnic fusion of the Canaanites, Akkadians, Chaldeans, Assyrians, Aramaeans, Hittites, and Mitannis that was well formed by the time the Arabs arrived in the seventh century A.D. It was in this context that PPS ideology called for a single Syrian state rather than a state embracing all Arab people as the Arab nationalists envisioned.

The PPS commanded more notoriety than its numbers warranted. And by the end of World War II, its ritualistic greeting "Long Live Syria" had waned. In 1949, Antoun Saadeh was executed for masterminding an attempted coup against the Lebanese government. The PPS survived his death and attempted another coup in 1961 before fading into political insignificance. In 1982, the PPS claimed another moment when it was implicated in the assassination of Lebanon's newly elected president, Bashir Gemayel. Today it is little more than one of the minor players in the political chaos in Lebanon.

---

* Mansfield, *Arabs*, p. 225.

The second ideology to come out of attempts of Arab nationalists to move away from Islam was more potent and enduring. The ideology of the Baath, or Renaissance Party, has rumbled through Arab politics for five decades. Its originators, Salah Bitar, a Sunni Muslim from Damascus, and Michel Aflaq, a Syrian Christian, studied together at the Sorbonne in Paris between 1928 and 1932. Returning to Damascus, they prowled the city in crumpled clothes, torn collars, and dirty fezzes. Unmarried, sometimes unemployed, forced to live on a pittance, they planned the Arab renaissance. By 1940, a year after World War II began in Europe, Aflaq and Bitar had gathered around them a cadre of intellectuals who met on Fridays, the Muslim day of rest. From the beginning of their political odyssey, Bitar played accompaniment for Aflaq.

Withdrawn and eccentric, Aflaq is often called the Gandhi of Arab nationalism. Taking something from Marxism and something from nineteenth-century romantic German nationalism, and superimposing on them an Arab character, Aflaq poured out reams of nationalist rhetoric. Through his writings, he described the Arab nation as stretching back into the mists of time. Within its boundaries, he included both the *mashriq* and the *maghrib* as well as Celicia and Alexandretta in Turkey and Khuzistan, bridging northern Iraq and northwestern Iran. For Aflaq's Arab nation to achieve deliverance from backwardness and foreign control, the Arabs had to break the shackles of religion, traditionalism, tribalism, and sectarianism. To Aflaq, the Baath Party he created was less a political organization than "an artistic creation that took the place of a novel or a poem . . . and he loved it as an artist would love his own creation."*

Aflaq's ideology stressed nationalism, unity, secularism, and a vague theory of socialism, but most of all he talked of the Arab renaissance. "In the conditions of the Arab nation today we need a party and a movement that represents in the first place the element of spirit. . . . The true party, the living party, the one that can perform its message for the Arab nation today, is the party that makes its goal the birth of a nation, or its renaissance. . . ."† In pursuit of this renaissance, Aflaq coined slogans that ranged from

---

* Ajami, *Arab Predicament*, p. 44.
† Samir al-Khalil, *Republic of Fear: The Inside Story of Saddam's Iraq* (New York: Pantheon, 1989), p. 220.

the visionary—"One Arab nation with an eternal mission"—to the banal—"Arabism is love."

Aflaq's call for an Arab revival came up against the classical problem of how to reconcile the transformation of Arab society with the orthodox values of Islam. Aflaq approached the dilemma by asserting that Islam was the most sublime expression of Arabism. One grew out of the other. Islam originated as an Arab religion, spoke through the Koran in the language of Arabic, embodied ancient Arab values, and launched the Arabs on the establishment of empire. Islam thus advanced beyond religion to become a culture that unfolded in the flowering of Arab genius.*

Aflaq's rhetoric and writings stayed largely encased in the educated class, where his vision of a single, independent Arab nation capable of transforming the Arab intellect and soul, its politics and society, found a following. For those drawn to the Baath, the slogan "Unity, Freedom, and Socialism" pulled the Arabs above their own unresolved conflicts and lifted from the collective psyche the burden of inferiority imposed by contact with the West. Finding in Aflaq's often quixotic writings the answer to the impotence of the Arab world, they made of themselves the vanguard of a new age, rebels against all the old values. As such, they vowed to banish tribalism and other outmoded characteristics of Arab society to make way for the future Arab state. Yet they remained a small elite. It was not until April 4, 1947, that the First Baath Congress convened in Damascus, drawing 250 people. Baathism found prominence in the 1950s and finally came to power in Syria and Iraq in the 1960s. For those left from its beginning years, none believed that the romanticism and idealism of the Baath Party would end up in the hands of repressive regimes presided over by Hafiz Assad and Saddam Hussein.

One constant ran through the whole panoply of nationalist ideologies—the vague and amorphous feeling that the Arabs constitute one people destined to form one great nation. But simplicity often defies truth. While Europe consumed centuries cultivating a sense of allegiance to a nation-state, the process in the Middle East

---

* Aflaq's arguments offended both Muslims and Christians. The Muslims found unacceptable Aflaq's contention that Islam was anything other than the revelation of God. And Christians, bristling that his ideology sold out to Islam, dubbed him "Muhammed Aflaq."

telescoped into two short decades. Between 1900 and 1920, Arab intellectuals vainly attempted to shift deep-rooted allegiances to family, village, and religion to the virgin concept of a nation stretching from the Nile to the Euphrates. But the drive to develop Arab nationalism faltered, unable to mount the existing realities. Arab nationalists were either unable or unwilling to seriously attack the cultural obstacles standing in the way of unity. The passion aroused by nationalist rhetoric was never able to surmount the group mentality that chains Arab society and drives its politics. As a consequence, Arabs throughout the Middle East floated between the mystique of the "Arab nation" and the security of parochialism within each of the Arab territories. In the end, the overwhelming strength of local priorities won out. Nationalism on any level other than the emotional ceased to be the glorification of the Arab nation and instead linked itself to a specific piece of land and a specific group of people. Although they nursed a desire to revive the wholeness they had possessed under Ottoman rule, the Arabs' unity lived most in their hostility to the West. And it was strategies to break the Western hold on Arab land that fed the search for Arab destiny between the two world wars. Instead of operating in tandem, a near impossibility under the heel of colonial administrations, each territory on the new map of the Middle East trod its own path. Elements in Syria and Lebanon rebelled against French rule in 1925. Iraq won a form of independence from Britain in 1932, and Egypt in 1936 slipped some of its bonds of colonialism. In Palestine, the Arab population pulled against both the heavy load of British colonialism and the deadly threat of Zionism. It was this death struggle that kept before all Arabs the cause of pan-Arabism.

Palestinians dwell in the past, in the time before Western imperialism, Jewish nationalism, and their own mistakes combined to take their land. As if talking might somehow assuage their wounds, Palestinians pour out their personal and collective story to those who will listen. Over the years, I have covered Palestinian issues from the Persian Gulf to Beirut to the Israeli-occupied territories to Tunis. I have talked to Palestinians from every walk of life from refugees to Western-educated businessmen to the founding members of Yasser Arafat's Fatah faction of the PLO. It is an exercise that is both fascinating and repetitious. Whether he or she is old enough to remember or not, each Palestinian has a personal or family story to tell about life in Palestine before the invasion of

Zionism and the West. In the decades of exile and occupation, Palestine has assumed historic proportions for those who claim its soil. Over and over, those who retell the stories report that the fields produced the most golden of grain, the orchards the sweetest oranges, the groves the fattest olives. In Palestine, the sky is bluer, the ocean greener than anywhere in the world. These are images of people longing to return to the land of their ancestors or to break the shackles of alien rule. In their minds, desire and repetition combine to transform what was into a beauty beyond what the reality ever was. Usually the retelling of Palestine's legend consumes significant amounts of time. But once I asked the well-dressed, middle-aged wife of a successful banker in Jordan to describe her vision of life in Palestine. She thought for a moment and then answered in one phrase. "We lived in paradise."

Historic Palestine was a fragment of jagged geography lying east and west between the gentle shores of the eastern Mediterranean and the Jordan River, the dramatic dividing line between the verdant coastal plain and the bare, crusty hinterland. From north to south it extended from the soft pine-covered hills of the Galilee southward to the Dead Sea and on into the harsh dun of the Negev desert. Its precise boundaries were undefined in political terms because Palestine, by the measure of the modern nation-state system, never existed.*

Hugging the Mediterranean coast and reaping the benefit of the rains carried in on the winds of the sea, Palestine shone like a jewel to the disparate tribes that moved out of the Arabian peninsula thousands of years ago. It was during the twentieth century B.C. that the Canaanites, a collection of tribes sharing a common language who are part of the mixed heritage of the present-day Palestinians, exercised dominion over Palestine. Then the Hebrews, led by the bearded, magnetic Moses, wandered out of the bleached hills of the eastern wilderness to assert a God-given right to the land of "milk and honey." For generations, Canaanite defied Hebrew and Hebrew challenged Canaanite for ascendancy. Eventually, the Hebrews emerged dominant.

A thousand years before the Christian era began, David, the Hebrew king, proclaimed from his capital in Jerusalem the kingdom

---

* Palestine is a name derived from the Philistines of the Bible.

that still marks the high point of Hebrew history. Yet it would not last. Wracked by internal dissension and assaulted by outside powers, David's kingdom eventually fell.

Lying at the Levantine crossroads of empires, Palestine for centuries served as a battleground for competing powers. By 63 B.C., the Romans possessed Palestine. And for several decades, it enjoyed a stability unknown during many of its years of independent existence. But on the death of Herod in A.D. 4, Palestine once again plunged into disorder. With the challenge to Roman rule coming from the Jews, Rome moved against them with vengeance. In A.D. 70, the Roman rulers demolished the Second Temple, leaving only its western wall. By A.D. 135, following a second revolt under Bar Kochba, the Jews had scattered into their diaspora, leaving behind only a remnant. That remnant took up life side by side with the rest of Palestine's indigenous population, creating another of those heterogeneous societies by which the Levant is defined.

Little changed in this relationship with the arrival of Islam. Most in Palestine were Christian when the Muslim armies arrived. In the centuries that followed, 10 percent of the population remained Christian. All in Palestine, Muslim, Christian, and Jew claimed a common ancestor—Abraham. Called Ibrahim by the Muslims, Abraham sired Ismail through Hagar and Isaac through Sarah. Each went on to found a nation, Muslim or Jewish. Yet both sprang from the same source, a fact central to the theology of Islam. An inscription that once hung over Jerusalem's Jaffa Gate perhaps best described general Arab attitudes toward Jews in the years before the twentieth century: "There is no God but Allah and Abraham is his friend."

The Ottoman Turks never colonized Palestine in the sense of planting large numbers of their own people within its borders. Nor did they even rule Palestine as a unit. The two northern districts were attached to the province of Beirut; areas across the Jordan River formed part of administrative Syria; while Jerusalem, a religious symbol central to the legitimacy of the Ottoman sultan, was governed directly from Constantinople. The Jews, secure in their identity as a distinct and unique people, regarded the Ottomans as nothing more or less than another colonial master, as did the Christian Arabs, 7.5 percent of the population. But the Muslim Arabs of Palestine, like other Arabs, found symmetry with an empire centered in Islam and balanced against the West. They did not even claim a name for themselves beyond "Arab." Yet they recognized themselves as an amalgam of the indigenous people of their ancient land—Canaanite and Philistine and Ammorite, and some would claim even Hebrew.* In the waning years of the Ottoman Empire, they were Arabs sharing Palestine with a small Jewish population. Three decades before the twentieth century reached midpoint, they would be Palestinians locked in a desperate fight for survival against a new group of Jews—the Zionists.

The watershed year in Palestine was 1877, the year before Jews out of the diaspora established the colony of Petah Tikva. The population of Palestine at the time stood at 600,000—roughly 515,000 Arab Muslims, 60,000 Arab Christians, and 25,000 Jews. The Jewish population, almost exclusively Orthodox, were the descendants of that remnant left behind in the great Jewish migration of A.D. 73. Clustered within close-knit communities in and around Jerusalem, they adhered to a traditional way of life. They posed no threat to Palestine's Arab majority nor its Arab character, for culturally they also formed part of the collage that was the Levant.

In 1881, other Jews from outside began to arrive on Palestine's shores. The first wave came out of Orthodox communities in eastern Europe. Like the Jews already living in Palestine, most were pious and apolitical, seeking only to live in the land of Abraham. But in 1882, Jews aflame with the Zionist ideology of Jewish nationalism and the vision of establishing a Jewish homeland on the ancient stones of Palestine began to arrive. Coming principally out of Poland and Russia, they followed the example set by Petah Tikva, the original Zionist colony, established near what is now Tel Aviv. Establishing small agricultural communities, the new influx of Jews scattered over the coastal plain, into the hills of Galilee, and over the western approaches to Jerusalem. Ignoring both the existing Jewish communities and the region's dominant Arab population, they remained separate. For these new immigrants were not in Palestine to assimilate but to reclaim Eretz Israel.† The whole pattern of invasion and assimilation that had marked the long history of the Levant changed, and with it the Levant itself.

---

* Although the distinct term "Palestinian" did not come into common usage until after 1948, it will be used throughout this chapter and the remaining chapters of this book to distinguish the Arabs of Palestine from the Arabs of the rest of the Arab world.
† Hebrew for "land of Israel."

Zionism was born of the pogroms of eastern Europe. The earliest Zionists who stepped ashore in Palestine with a few pitiful possessions carried in cloth sacks or battered bags possessed neither money nor political influence. As Russians and Poles, they were outside the parameters of power exercised by western Europe in the age of imperialism. Thus for the Palestinians, the early Zionists stood apart from the grasping power of the industrialized West.

But in 1894, Zionism came to life in western Europe. France's insidious anti-Semitism, laid bare in the scandalous Dreyfus Affair, led a young Jewish reporter named Theodor Herzl to articulate in *Der Judenstaat* the passionate vision of a Jewish state. In 1897, Herzl convened the First Zionist Congress in Basel, Switzerland, which drew up the new Zionist agenda—the colonization of Palestine by Jews for the purpose of creating a Jewish homeland. In 1903, the first contingent of Western Zionists landed in Palestine carrying their political agenda.

At first, Palestinian antagonisms toward the Zionists revolved around economics. For the merchants, the Zionists, commanding some skills in the economic practices of industrialized Europe, struck at an indigenous economy already wrecked by the cheaper products of Europe's industrial revolution. For the *fallahin*, the peasants, the threat was greater. The Zionist demand for land threatened to separate families from fields they had cultivated for centuries. With many already living as tenant farmers of Arab moneylenders, the *fallahin* watched as the new Zionist colonies gobbled up property from these same moneylenders at prices the Palestinians could never pay.

But the brewing contest between Zionist and Palestinian involved, at its most basic level, a conflict of cultures. Coming from Europe, Zionism constituted another invasion of the Arab world by the West. Ignorant of Arab ways and insensitive to the local customs of Palestine, too many of the European Jewish newcomers enraged those they lived among. Although outsiders, the Zionists attempted to impose Western customs on an ancient and traditional society. Fencing off Zionist colonies, they blocked the customary pasture rights of the adjacent villages. And if Arab farmers defied the ban, the settlers often rounded up trespassing flocks and exacted fines from the peasants who owned them. Conflict over grazing rights appeared inconsequential to the Zionists, yet for the Palestinians the issue represented a form of foreign domination. Unlike the Jews who had always lived in Palestine or even the earlier Zionist immigrants, the Jews who were attached to political Zionism loomed as proponents of a culture and ideology that menaced Palestine's Arab character. In 1914, the nonpolitical Zionists of Ahad Haam criticized the political Zionists for waxing "angry towards those who remind them that there is still another people in Eretz Israel that has been living there and does not intend at all to leave."* But within the Zionist movement, the political Zionists, those seeking a Jewish homeland in Palestine, buried those Zionists who had come to Palestine for purely religious reasons.

Strengthened by their organizations in western Europe, the Zionists used the war years of 1914 to 1917 to put in place the essential building blocks for the Jewish homeland in Palestine. From the bloody stalemate on the Western Front that drained away Britain's youth and its resources, the Zionists drew the British government toward a public commitment to a Jewish homeland in Palestine. Within the offices and country homes of Britain's political elite, Zionists such as the imposing Lionel Walter Rothschild, scion of the British banking family, and the captivating Chaim Weizmann, leader of Europe's Zionists, transmitted promises of international Jewish support for the British war effort in return for some commitment to a Jewish homeland in Palestine. The wartime pressures of money, the alluring prospect of creating a fifth-column movement of Germany's Jews, and the tantalizing possibility of a Western-oriented Zionist state strategically placed near the all-important Suez Canal seduced Britain into issuing the now-famous Balfour Declaration, another watershed in the history of Palestine.

In a letter to Lord Rothschild dated November 2, 1917, Lord Balfour, the British foreign secretary, issued the notorious words that would torment Palestine for the next three decades. "His Majesty's government views with favor the establishment in Palestine of a national home for the Jewish people and will use their best endeavors to facilitate the achievement of this object." The great caveat followed: ". . . it being clearly understood that nothing shall be done which may prejudice the civil and religious rights of existing non-Jewish communities in Palestine. . . ." With the flourish of a pen, Palestine became a thrice-promised land. Britain had already pledged Arab independence in the Hussein-McMahon documents.

---

* William B. Quandt, Fuad Jabber, and Ann Mosely Lesch, *The Politics of Palestinian Nationalism* (Berkeley: University of California Press, 1973), p. 12.

It then determined Palestine's future as a British colony in the Sykes-Picot Agreement. Now, in a statement with the profile of Janus, the British embraced the Zionist agenda. Even the British themselves were puzzled. At the time, Prime Minister Herbert Asquith observed, "Curiously enough the only other partisan of this proposal is Lloyd George, who, I need not say, does not care a damn for the Jews or their past or their future, but thinks it will be an outrage to let the Holy Places pass into the possession of . . . 'agnostic, aesthetic France.' "*

The die was cast. However subtly it might be stated, the British government had anointed the concept of a Jewish homeland in Palestine. Recognizing the import, the Zionists seized the Balfour Declaration as holy writ.

In 1919, the year of the Paris Peace Conference, Palestine's population numbered 620,000—550,000 Muslims, 70,000 Arab Christians, and 50,000 Jews, many of whom looked on political Zionism as a blasphemous assault on prophecy. At most, the Zionists constituted 5 percent of the population. Yet in the summer of 1919, Lord Balfour announced that Britain, Palestine's new overlord, was committed to Zionism. Furthermore, nothing bound His Majesty's Government to consult the wishes of the Arab inhabitants of Palestine on this issue. Somehow the ugly fact that the ratio of Palestinians to Jews ordained that the realization of the Zionist agenda would entail bloodshed and military repression never intruded into the realm of British policymaking.

As the decade of the 1920s opened, Arab Palestine resided in a thousand villages and a score of towns built of hard, buff-colored stone pulled out of the rockbound hills. Its society was agrarian, rigidly structured on a squat pyramid built on the mass of *fallahin*, layered with thin strata of workers, merchants, and professionals and capped with a cluster of landowning families.

The *fallahin* tilled the red-brown fields that checkered the fertile valleys and tended scattered flocks of fat, shaggy sheep on the steep hillocks. Generation after generation, the same families worked the same land, drawing out of its rocky soil and coastal plain plump red tomatoes, fat black green cucumbers; melons, grapes, and dates; tart

---

* Ibrahim Abu-Lughod, ed., *The Transformation of Palestine: Essays on the Origin and Development of the Arab-Israeli Conflict* (Evanston, Ill.: Northwestern University Press, 1987), p. 46.

lemons; and sweet Jaffa oranges harvested from orchards with histories as long as the families who tended them.

In towns like Jaffa, Nablus, and Hebron, craftsmen and artisans huddled within the narrow, arched stone passageways turning out the same products as their ancestors—rugs, intricate hand-painted pottery, fragrant soaps, and finely worked jewelry. Others plied the trades created by modernization—electrician, plumber, mechanic. In offices beyond the souks, the tiny middle class engaged in overseas trade or practiced the professions. In Jerusalem, the seat of most of Palestine's major families, the great landowners lived on the incomes from their properties.

On rare occasions, glimpses can be caught of pre-1948 Palestine. Each in its own way paints a picture of traditional Palestinian society. In the early 1980s, I was driving at random along an asphalt road beyond East Jerusalem. Without warning I came upon a crude stone house tucked into a crevice of a hill. I stopped the car and got out for no purpose except simply to look into the past. The house faced out on a plot of golden grain. A few olive trees wound down toward the valley. Below them, a man in a *khaffiyeh* and baggy trousers, his hand wrapped around an old, worn staff, watched a half-dozen goats pull at the weeds that bordered his tiny field. He is probably gone now, consumed by Israeli expansion into the occupied territories. But for that moment, he stubbornly held to the life of Palestine's *fallahin*.

The residue from the other end of traditional Palestinian society is more enduring, enshrined inside the walls of Jerusalem's Old City. One evening just a few summers ago I was invited to dinner in a house once owned by one of the great landowning families of Palestine. I walked into the Old City through St. Stephen's Gate, turned left, and carefully made my way down a narrow cobblestone street. Under an arch connecting one multistoried house to the one across the street, I found a narrow door. I sounded the heavy knocker and waited for my host and hostess to usher me in. We climbed up through what had once been the eighth-century level of the old house and continued up through the tenth and twelfth until we reached the sixteenth-century rooms at the top. The sitting room was thirty by thirty, its ceiling reaching up twenty feet or more toward the point of an onion-shaped dome. Beyond it was another huge domed room that had once served as a reception chamber where tenants and clients of the man who once lived here came to pay their rents or collect their patronage. When I returned to the sitting room from the roof garden, I saw a short, fat woman primly sitting on a straight-backed sofa, her ankles crossed over each other and her wrists meeting across a large plastic pocketbook resting against her expansive bosom. Her adolescent daughters, copious amounts of organza enveloping their stout frames, surrounded her. Their mother had once lived here as a young child. Too young to remember much, she told me the stories that had come down to her from her family. They were one of those who had sat at the top of the Palestinian social pyramid. Richer in status than money, they guarded the old order.

At the time of the mandate, as it had for centuries before, Palestinian society organized itself into family and place. A vast chasm separated the rural *fallahin* from the workers, merchants, and landowners of the towns and cities. Rural and urban, they lived separate lives, touching only as tenants and landowners, producers and consumers. Within this broad rural/urban split burrowed the most basic source of being in the Arab world—the family. A Palestinian's identity began with his extended family, or *hamuleh*, reached to his village, and finally to his region. The little political organization that existed followed vertical lines of family, locality, and sometimes faith. The horizontal lines of class functioned only as a by-product of the vertical forces.

Loyalty and allegiance fixed to personalities—the head of the family, the elder of the village. These local leaders in turn welded themselves and their followers to a more influential leader to form a clan. There were Muslim clans, Christian clans, and religiously mixed clans which in turn swore fealty to one of Palestine's dozen or so major landowning families. And it was out of these landowning families, several steps removed from the peasant masses, that all Palestine's political leadership emerged.

Palestinian society dwelled in its long traditions. While the Zionist immigrants purposefully left their established social structure and traditional culture behind to turn themselves into "new men" dedicated to the building of the Zionist state, the Palestinians carried with them into the mandate their "web of belonging"—the social and cultural characteristics that resided in Palestine. And while Zionist settler society assumed a relatively flat form, indigenous Palestinian society remained wedged in its pyramid. And this is how the Palestinians met the combined forces of the British and the Zionists.

From the moment they grasped the reality that independence

would not come to the Arabs, the Palestinians locked British colonialism and Zionism together. Protest against one was protest against the other, for Britain held in its hands the future of Zionism in Palestine. Before Sir Herbert Samuel, the first British high commissioner, stepped onto the worn limestone of Jaffa's old quay, Palestinians had already massed in the port's narrow streets to protest the first official public reading in Palestine of the hated Balfour Declaration. On the July day of 1922 when the League of Nations officially bestowed the mandate of Palestine on Britain, the Palestinians went on strike. In 1925, angry, hostile Arabs boycotted Lord Balfour's visit to Jerusalem to dedicate the Hebrew university. And every year on the anniversary of the detested Balfour Declaration, iron doors on Palestinian shops slammed shut, black flags of mourning hung from Palestinian owned buildings, and broad, sober black bands bordered the front pages of the Arabic-language newspapers. All were symbols of the Palestinians' furious sense of being victimized by the West. On one level, the implacable foe of the Palestinians' nationalist aspirations was Britain, the imperial power. On another level, it was Zionism, the colonizing force.

The challenge the Palestinians faced at the end of World War I was how a small, traditionally organized, and impoverished people could gain independence against the combined weight of the British Empire and the determined Zionist movement. Many saw their only salvation in Arab unity. Consequently, desperate calls went forth to Syria, to Egypt, to Iraq, and to any other Arab area willing to listen. All came back with expressions of sympathy or suggestions that the Palestinians convene a conference of Arab nationalists or the Islamic *ummah*. But little else followed. Held captive to Western colonialism, the "Arab nation" in which the Palestinians sought their salvation was not there. Palestinians still remember with a combination of bitterness and regret.

The National Palace Hotel wraps around a corner not far from the Damascus Gate. A wide veranda opening onto the activity of the street makes it one of the best places in East Jerusalem to sit. I had been at the hotel for maybe a week, occupying one of the comfortable molded white plastic chairs almost every afternoon. The grayed and stooped manager of a small nearby shop that sold olive-wood crucifixes and nativity scenes to tourists was a regular on the veranda. He was a quiet man who politely nodded but seldom spoke. This day he decided to talk. "I was just a small boy in 1923. I didn't understand what was happening, who these Zionists were, but I knew my parents were worried. In the evening when the work was done, men from the neighborhood would come here to sit under the trees that grew on this property." Pointing left to a stand of pines down the street, he said, "They would sit under trees like those and talk a lot and smoke many cigarettes. Over and over, they would say, 'All Arabs are brothers. Our struggle is their struggle. They will come from Damascus and Aleppo and maybe even Alexandria and they will help us.' Then someone would puff up and say, 'The British and the Zionists will not be able to defy the whole Arab nation.' But of course, they never came."

For the first five years of the mandate, four separate but parallel governmental entities governed Palestine. The first, the British colonial administration, ruled over all as the bureaucracy administering the civil affairs of Palestine. The Jewish community inaugurated the second. The Vaad Leumi, a Jewish national council indirectly elected by the Jews living in Palestine, presided over the secular as well as the religious affairs of the Jewish community. Exempted were the Jews from Palestine's indigenous Orthodox Jewish communities, who chose to remain outside the new Zionist institutions. The third was the most unique and most destructive to Arab claims in Palestine. Thirty organizations representing worldwide Zionism and headquartered in London constituted part of the mandatory government of Palestine. Between 1920 and 1929, a cadre of its officials operated in Palestine directing the spectrum of Zionist policy from immigration to industry. Although the governmental structure of the mandate designated the Vaad Leumi as the representative of the Zionists in Palestine, Zionism's real power rested in London with the international Zionist organizations. Any British colonial official attempting to interfere with Zionist policy in Palestine came face to face with the well-financed, well-connected Zionists in London, who aggressively and effectively challenged within the halls of Westminster or inside 10 Downing Street any decision infringing on Zionist activity in Palestine.

Against this combined power of British imperialism, Palestine's Zionist settlers, and world Jewry, the Palestinians could mobilize the Arab Executive, the fourth and weakest of Palestine's governmental entities. Although it attempted to duplicate the Vaad Leumi, the Arab Executive never approached in staff or resources its Jewish counterpart.

The British inflicted political impotency on the Palestinians because they could. While the Zionists wielded power through world Zionism, the Palestinians had only themselves. But as important, the Palestinians crippled themselves with their own internal divisions. Competitors for generations, the two most prestigious families in Palestine, the Husseinis and the Nashashibis, locked horns over leadership of the Palestinians' nationalist movement. Throwing aside the logic of unity, the two families reached into region, village, and family in the contest for patronage, prestige, and that oldest of Arab imperatives—honor. Out of this contest of loyalty and will, Haj Amin al-Husseini emerged to lead the Palestinian cause.

Haj Amin was an aristocrat. He was born into Jerusalem's Husseini family, more prestigious but less wealthy than the Nashashibis. Educated in Jerusalem and Constantinople, he moved to the hallowed al-Azhar University in Cairo for his advanced religious training. On the eve of World War I, he made the pilgrimage to Mecca, thus winning the coveted title Haj. As a person, Haj Amin could be charming, affable, almost hypnotic or crafty, treacherous, unscrupulous, and cruel. As a result, his followers adored him and his enemies loathed him. Demonstrating his love of intrigue, he began World War I as a Turkish artillery officer and finished as part of the Arab Revolt. By the time the revolt ended, Haj Amin had focused on the single purpose of his life—to secure Palestine for the Palestinians. In the failed process he would prove to be both a patriot and a scoundrel.

In 1921, Sir Herbert Samuel, the British high commissioner who was himself a Jew, had appointed Haj Amin al-Husseini to the post of grand mufti of Jerusalem and president of the newly created Supreme Muslim Council, a body structured by the mandatory government to oversee Muslim religious affairs. In bestowing on him the most prestigious religious title of Palestine, Samuel gave Haj Amin the indispensable commodity necessary to claim political leadership of the main body of Palestinians—religious authority. Haj Amin mustered his religious title, his control over *waqf* funds, or religious endowments, his status as a scion of the largest landowners in Palestine, and his own personal magnetism, ability, and talent for intrigue to become the embodiment of Palestinian nationalism.

During the 1920s, the field of battle for Palestine was London, in the arena of British policymaking. Haj Amin, distinguished by his trim, faultless beard, black patent-leather shoes, and impeccable white spats, led delegations of Palestinians and dignitaries from surrounding Arab territories to London in the losing fight to change Britain's pro-Zionist policies in Palestine. For weeks at a time, the Arabs meekly knocked on government doors or glumly sat in cheap hotels waiting for permission to make a perfunctory visit to a lower-level official in the colonial office. At the same time, the Zionists floated through the drawing rooms of Britain's political elite. The contrast starkly reflected imperial Britain's own entrenched prejudices. To the British, the Palestinians sprang from an alien race that somehow failed to measure up to the West's perceptions of the worth of non-Western societies. When the Palestinians came to London, it was as suppliants carrying the odious labels "Arab," "Eastern," and "Muslim." For the Zionists, it was far different. Although the eastern European Jews who lived in Palestine also came to London, it was the upper-class western European Jews practiced in the etiquette of the aristocracy who conducted Zionist diplomacy. They were, after all, of the same culture and the same class as those they petitioned. With their Western mores and European manners, they sold Zionism to those who controlled Palestine.

In the unequal contest, the Palestinians and the Zionists pulled at British colonial policy over the most vital element in the survival of Arab Palestine—Jewish immigration. Population and land formed the core of Zionist strategy in Palestine. In the Zionists' carefully devised game plan, mass migration acted as the vehicle to create a Jewish majority in Palestine in as short a time as possible. When that majority was realized, Britain would be pressed to relinquish its mandate and Palestine would emerge as the Jewish homeland. Its simplicity of concept reduced to a mathematical formula —immigration equaled numbers of Jews in Palestine and Jews in Palestine equaled a Jewish homeland. So from 1920 until the state of Israel came into being in 1948, political peace in Palestine between Arabs and Jews fluctuated with the rate of Jewish immigration. And it was the rate of immigration, controlled by Britain, which most bared the fallacies of the mandatory power's "even-handed" policy in Palestine and turned Zionism, from an Arab perspective, into a Western plot against the Arab nation.

Jewish immigration with its demand for land taxed Palestine's lean capacity for absorption. Small, bound by the sea, hemmed in by more powerful neighbors, and weighted by a high birthrate, Palestine in the 1920s already approached the population limits of an agrarian economy. Without even basic public education in the village to prepare peasants for nonagricultural jobs and no industrial base in capital-starved Palestine to create new jobs, the peasants struggled to survive on dwindling plots of land. For the *fallahin*, immigration of Jews equaled displacement of Arabs.

Throughout the 1920s, the British Colonial Office insisted that it tied the level of Jewish immigration to the absorptive capacity of Palestine. But the criteria chosen to determine the economic impact of an immigrant meant almost nothing. Any Jew possessing a skill or $2,500 in cash secured the needed permit to enter Palestine. With Zionist organizations in the West recruiting skilled workers or providing the prescribed funds, the rate of immigration marched on. In 1925, 35,000 Jews arrived as legal immigrants. Yet the number of illegal immigrants, those who came to Palestine in response to Zionism's appeal for the "ingathering" of Jews out of the diaspora, far exceeded those entering legally. With the principle of the "ingathering" turned with consummate skill into a moral issue by the Zionist organizations in London, those who came to Palestine under its auspices essentially enjoyed immunity from deportation.

The land issue, like the second horse of a team, harnessed itself to the issue of immigration. The very core of the Zionist ideal was the establishment of an agrarian society in Palestine. Impassioned Zionist writers and speakers wove the dream of a Jewish state, drawn out of the ground of Palestine by Jewish labor. But the moshavahs (the colonies) and the kibbutzes (the collectives) needed to fulfill the dream required large amounts of expensive land. Land lying fallow often demanded irrigation. Fields on the coastal plain required draining or flushing to counter salinity, while those in the hills needed to be cleared of the rock that lined them like furrows. Even without these costs, agricultural land in an area of relatively dense population cost four times what it cost in the United States. Basic economics dealt the *fallahin* and most other Palestinians out of the game.

Ownership gave way to an even more basic issue—tenancy. For decades, many of the *fallahin* had worked as tenant farmers on land owned by families living in Beirut, Cairo, and Damascus. In this classic example of peasant and absentee owner, land changed hands from time to time. But what happened now was an exchange of owners, not tenants. Poor crops and the incessant demands of the tax collector dominated *fallahin* fears, not eviction. Even in some of the early Zionist land purchases, Arab peasant families stayed rooted in place, hired as laborers by the new Jewish owners. But when the Jewish National Fund began to purchase large tracts of land from absentee landowners, that land became the exclusive property of the Jewish community, its cultivation restricted to Jewish hands. Arab tenant farmers whose families had tilled the same fields for generations, whose fragile security clung to its furrows, suddenly found themselves evicted. Uprooted from ancestral homes, pushed onto marginal land unable to support an already meager standard of living, denied employment on Jewish land, the *fallahin* fell victim to Zionism. Jewish land purchases came to hang like the sword of Damocles over every peasant. In the length and breadth of Palestine, the *fallahin* exchanged their frightened whispers—"Who will be next?"

In 1929, the Palestinian masses exploded in a sudden, raging expression of pent-up frustrations against the British mandate— against its pro-Zionist policies, against the Palestinians' own worsening economic plight, and against the ever growing anxiety that Zionism stood poised to become the overlord of Palestine's Arabs. A dozen incidents could have ignited the violence, but as it happened the cause was no less than the long-festering difficulties over the Wailing Wall, the remaining wall of the Second Temple, a boundary of the Muslims' Haram al-Sharif.

Of all the ironies in the Arab-Israeli dispute, none is greater than that of the proximity of the Wailing Wall and the Dome of the Rock. To come at sunset and stand above the plaza fronting the ancient wall of the Jews is to visualize the entangled destinies of Jews and Arabs. The Dome of the Rock, radiating the setting sun, is like a jewel. Its shadow juts out to the right, falling on part of the worn, ancient stones that Jews vowed for almost two thousand years in exile to reclaim. The monument to high Islamic culture and the remains of high Jewish culture sit one on top of the other.

Although the Wailing Wall in 1929 nestled against the Haram al-Sharif, Jews had prayed there for centuries, their customary rights barring only the full accouterments for a religious service. But with swelling Zionist nationalism during the 1920s, the issue of the wall and the Jews' unrestricted access to it ceased to be a religious question and instead coalesced into a symbol of Zionist power in Palestine. On a hot Saturday in August 1929, zealous Zionists from Tel Aviv marched chanting and singing through the narrow, twisted streets of old Jerusalem toward the sacred wall. Leaving the main contingent to sing the "Hatikvah," the Zionist anthem, the core scaled the rough, ancient stones and unfurled the Zionist flag. To the Palestinians, political Zionism had claimed al-Quds.

The next day, Haj Amin ordered his followers into the streets. Marching on the Wailing Wall, they jerked out prayer-petitions wedged into the crevices and flung them to the ground. It was as if by destroying bits of paper, the Palestinians could destroy Zionism. Arab anger raced through Jerusalem's Jewish section and on to Hebron, Safad, and other towns, where Arab mobs vented their fury against Jewish communities. Before it ended, 133 Jews were dead. But so were 116 Palestinians, most slain at the hands of the British troops called in to restore order. In the shorthand that records the struggle for Palestine, 1929 came to mean the time that Arab peasant and worker, the primary victims of Britain's pro-Zionist policies, drew blood.

Although emotionally satisfying to Palestinian passions, the revolt of 1929 only crippled the Palestinians' cause in the eyes of their British overlords. Ignoring the fundamental economic grievances of the peasantry and failing to question the whole premise of a Jewish homeland in Palestine, the British government eagerly cited the violence as clear evidence of the Arabs' "backwardness," their unfitness for independence. Only within verbiage buried in official papers did the British government conclude that opposition to Jewish immigration prompted the riots and acknowledge that the Palestinians saw in that immigration a menace to their livelihood but even more threatening a possible overlord of the future. Despite ten years of communal unrest and two government reports calling into question Britain's blessing for Zionist immigration and land acquisition, British policy in Palestine stood. With the Palestinians unable to end British countenance of Zionism, the best they could hope for was to freeze Zionist gains. The triangular contest between the Palestinians, the Zionists, and the British that would span the 1930s centered on the status quo—the Palestinians determined to defend and preserve it, the Zionists to subvert and revolutionize it.

But the momentum was with the Zionists. Utilizing secret negotiations to attain their ends, the Zionists in the winter of 1930–31 reaped a harvest of concessions from Britain—permission to build a hydroelectric power complex on the Jordan and Awja rivers to serve as the basis for the industrial development of Palestine's

Jewish community; to extract mineral salts from the Dead Sea; to drain and settle the Hulah marshes; and to reclaim the sand dunes along the Mediterranean coast below Haifa. Having granted the Zionists the right to build an exclusive Jewish economic infrastructure, the British colonial office conferred on Jewish institutions the right to hire only Jews. It also sanctioned the Haganah, an autonomous Jewish military force, to protect Jewish colonies and urban quarters. And finally, British colonial policy allowed the Jewish Agency to mobilize its funds from abroad to build schools, hospitals, and a whole network of social services for the exclusive use of Jews. Left outside, the Palestinian population was forced to scrape by with nothing beyond the meager resources that the British government channeled into the mandate.

As the 1930s unfolded, Jewish immigrants increasingly lived entirely within a Jewish community, dependent in no respect on the Arab majority of Palestine and coming into contact with Arabs only by chance. Tel Aviv, a dingy town of two thousand people in 1918, had by 1935 blossomed into an industrial city touted as the "only purely Jewish city in the world." The Zionists lived within a society that stressed the Jews' absolute right to possess Palestine as their own, buffered from the uncomfortable issue of whether the Arabs might have comparable or prior rights.

It was this exclusiveness of Jewish society fed by Zionism's foreign network that stoked Palestinian rage against the West. To the Palestinians, Jewish Palestine existed in essence as a project conceived in the West, nurtured and sustained by Western money. Between 1919 and 1936, Zionist Palestine gathered in $400 million from foreign sources. Because of this money, Jews within Zionism's fold enjoyed a standard of living far in excess of the mandate's resources. In 1935, Jews claimed an annual per capita income equivalent to £34 in British currency. For Arabs, it was £7. Rather than benefiting from any trickle-down phenomenon from the Jewish economy, the Palestinian faced a steeply escalating cost of living brought about by the infusion of foreign money to which he had no access.

There is a small house on an obscure road between Nazareth and Haifa in Israel. The little walled-in garden overflows with flowers and the sweet aroma of orange blossoms. When I arrived I ducked under a grape arbor that shaded an old weather-stained cane chair supporting a man in his late seventies. Slow to rise, stooped by his advanced years, he radiated a sure dignity as he came to greet me. Over the inevitable cups of strong black coffee, Rashid Khalil told me about a youth spent in Haifa.

"Before I was born, my father and my grandfather lived beside the Palestinian Jews. We worked together. And because everyone was poor, I could say we suffered together. We were not against them and they were not against us." He stopped, convulsed by a racking cough. When it subsided, he went on, "That was before the Zionists came. It was the Zionists who chose to live apart." His shaking hand reached into his pocket to extract a worn handkerchief. Wiping tears from his eyes and spittle from his mouth, he again took up the conversation. "By the time I was a young man, the Zionists had built their own schools and hospitals. They owned big farms, or at least big for Palestine. And they ran factories like we had never seen before." Again he paused, this time in thought. I waited. Finally he turned his head away from me as if he were ashamed. "What do you think it felt like for a Palestinian to pass new apartments built for Jews and to see nice playgrounds where only their children could play?" Turning back toward me he said, "I cannot tell you what it was like to see a new Jewish hospital and to know that if someone in my family was sick the only place for them was a little clinic with nothing but a few bottles of pills. Or to see Jewish children sitting inside their nice schools while my children tried to learn in one crowded room with an untrained teacher." The coughing returned. Still gasping, he said in a tone that combined anger and pathos, "The Zionists had so much and they gave the Palestinians nothing, not even a job."

But life in Palestine, even for the Jews, was difficult. The great worldwide depression that began in that fateful year of 1929 hit the economy hard, stemming the flow of immigrants and draining the colonies. Then in 1933 the tide turned as Adolf Hitler consolidated his new order in Germany. Propelled by a gripping fear of what the future held, Jewish immigration to Palestine reached new levels— 30,327 in 1933, 42,359 in 1934, 61,854 in 1935. Britain's anemic efforts to restrict the flow of Jews into Palestine disintegrated in the face of Hitler's evil stratagem against Germany's Jews. As a result, the Jewish population of Palestine, which was 11 percent in 1922 and 16 percent in 1931, jumped to 28 percent in 1935. Suddenly the Palestinians found themselves ensnared in a world they had not made and did not understand. They asked for independence and got the British mandate. They asked for the protection of their land from an alien people and got instead the products of an order created by a madman. Yet in 1935, it was still unclear just how much the events that would determine the future of Palestine were moving beyond the sphere of Britain. Britain still stood sentry at the gates of Palestine. Only Britain held in its hands the ability to stay the Zionist assault on Palestine. And so it was against the British that the Palestinians struck.

Since 1929, Haj Amin's fiery rhetoric had accomplished nothing in the struggle for an Arab Palestine. Although Palestinian nationalism ruled the mufti's life, deep flaws marred his leadership and corrupted his ability to unite the Palestinians against the British. The ancestors of Haj Amin, like the ancestors of most of Palestine's leading families, reached Palestine in the wake of the Arab conquest. They possessed no military tradition, so they never exercised military power within the Ottoman system. Instead they filled the role of bureaucrat, religious figure, judge, or scholar. Their status emanated from land, lineage, and the symbolic functions of guarding holy places. Thus their political style was that of intermediary between their clients and those who held power.

Faced with the threat of Zionism, Haj Amin acted within the parameters of his experience. With the exception of the 1929 riots, he persisted in the only strategy he was capable of—persuasion. Through argument, warnings, and reluctant hints of eventual violence, he steadfastly insisted that he could persuade Britain to abandon its commitment to Zionism. The problem was that in spite of his reputation as a fierce, anti-British demagogue, the mufti essentially balanced his fiery nationalist stance against his own acceptability to the mandate government as an instrument the British could use to diffuse popular discontent. In the final analysis, Haj Amin was a nationalist unwilling to jeopardize his access to government, the rock on which his status depended. Others, not so timid, moved into the breach to challenge Britain's pro-Zionist policies.

Palestine, at least on the emotional level, ranked as an Arab cause. Haj Amin's delegations to London in the 1920s included a range of dignitaries from other Arab territories. And the rising Arab nationalists intoned Palestine as a graphic example of Western designs against the Arabs. In December 1931, a congress of delegates from twenty-two Muslim countries convened in Jerusalem to warn against the dangers of Zionism. Two years later, Arabs, in retaliation against the guardian of the Zionist evil, called for a boycott of British goods. The Palestinian issue began to serve as a medium culturing Arab nationalism. But beyond emotional support the Palestinians were left to carry their own fight against the twin threats of colonialism and Zionism.

Even before the 1929 riots exploded, Sheikh Izz al-Din al-Qassam, a bearded, turbaned Muslim religious teacher and reformer from Haifa, had organized a covey of secret revolutionary cells. Under the name Holy Martyrs, al-Qassam and his cadres swooped down on isolated British troops and installations to hammer out Palestinian anger. On a dark night in early November 1935, a British bullet killed the sheikh. Overnight, Izz al-Din rose to the revered status of martyr, and others took up his cause.

On April 15, 1936, a knot of al-Qassam's disciples crouched in the dark along the Tulkarm road waiting as three Jews walked toward their ambush. When they came in sight, the Palestinians rose as one and fired their guns. Following a funeral in Tel Aviv charged with Zionist rhetoric, Jews went in search of revenge. They found it in a hut near the original Zionist colony of Petah Tikva where two Palestinians were working. In this one incident, Palestinian anger and frustration over British rule and Zionist encroachment erupted. Haj Amin, scrambling to preserve his leadership, called a general strike that would stretch into a three-year-long armed resistance to British rule. In towns across Palestine, shop owners slammed shut their doors and workers walked off their jobs. In the countryside, men of whole villages threw down their rakes to take the oath of allegiance to the only government they could claim—the British-sanctioned Arab Higher Committee. Crying "no taxation without representation," the Palestinians demanded the suspension of Jewish immigration, prohibition of land sales to Jews, and organization of a national government responsible to all the people. Even at this late stage in their nationalist struggle, the Arabs' aim was not to drive the Jewish community out of Palestine, only to force the British to acknowledge that the Zionists constituted a minority in a predominantly Arab area. To stay, they had to agree to submit to majority rule—Arab rule.

The general strike united Palestine's fractured society across lines of family, class, region, and religion. Shouting "Down with Balfour, down with Balfour," protesters virtually shut down commercial activity and transportation in the Palestinian sector of the economy. In Jaffa, Palestinian protesters and British riot police clashed in hand-to-hand combat, splashing Britain's troubled mandate across the front pages of every newspaper in London.

If Haj Amin was the face of the rebellion, the *fallahin* were its backbone. And if Haj Amin was its spiritual leader, Abd al-Qadir al-Husseini was its hero.

The son of the former mayor of Jerusalem, the man who would become the celebrated al-Qadir gathered a guerrilla army to fight the British as the Arabs had fought the Turks in 1918. But where British money and arms underwrote the Arab Revolt, the rebellion of 1936 had to depend on its own resources and a few men and arms smuggled in from the surrounding Arab territories.

In village after village, men unearthed antiquated weapons and rushed to join a patched-together army brandishing the red, green, white, and black flag of independent Palestine. Galloping on horseback or trudging on foot, the guerrilla army, composed of hundreds of *fallahin* following a handful of military regulars from an assortment of Arab states, derailed trains, sabotaged the crucial oil pipeline running across Palestine from Iraq to the port of Haifa, and torched Barclays Bank, the very symbol of imperial England. No longer totally impotent, the Palestinians wielded their newfound power.

The strike lasted six months. Not defeated, the Palestinians succumbed to the entreaties from neighboring Arab leaders to accept British promises to redress Palestinian grievances. But in July 1937, the uprising breathed new life when His Majesty's Government published the Peel Commission's report on the unrest. While mimicking other such reports in assigning the disturbances to the Palestinians' desire for national independence and their anxiety about the establishment of a Jewish national home, the commission recommended the partition of Palestine between the Arabs and Jews. According to the provisions of the Peel Commission report, the Zionists, with only 28 percent of the population, acquired 33 percent of the total area of Palestine, including the fertile regions of Galilee and the coastal plain from the Lebanese border south to Jaffa. In hundreds of Arab villages falling within the Jewish state, thousands of Palestinians would either be reduced to a subject minority or forcibly transferred out of the Jewish state. Finally, the proposed area designated for the Palestinians faced incorporation into Transjordan, to be ruled by the pro-British King Abdullah. The Peel

Commission confirmed the Palestinians' worst fears. Once again they rose as one against the British.

From the summer to the early fall of 1938, the whole Palestinian countryside from Lake Huleh in the far north to Beersheba at the edge of the Negev rumbled with rebellion. Government offices, banks, postal service, and police stations in such central towns as Ramallah, Bethlehem, and Nablus closed down, forcing the British military to report reluctantly to London that civil administration of Palestine was, to all practical purposes, nonexistent. It was a frank admission that Britain no longer controlled the mandate.

Fighting to recover, the British government threw tanks, air power, and heavy artillery against untrained and poorly armed guerrilla bands. Dispatching an additional twenty thousand of their own troops to crush the rebellion, the British enlisted the Zionists' now matured paramilitary organizations to join the war against the Palestinians.

Still failing to quell the rebellion, Britain clamped on the "emergency regulations." The governor dissolved the Arab Higher Committee and stripped Haj Amin of his offices, forcing him to flee to Lebanon. Military tribunals exiled the rest of the Palestinians' political leadership, passed summary sentences, including death by hanging, on Palestinians arrested for the possession of arms, and flung thousands into special detention camps. Spanning the spectrum of society, the detainees—professionals, civil servants, clergymen, students, and peasants—defied their jailers from behind the barbed wire. Intellectual and peasant, the high and low of the social order, donned the same traditional Palestinian dress. And Christian priest and Muslim religious leader sat shoulder to shoulder as a symbol of Palestinian solidarity.

Moved to Draconian measures by the continued resistance, Britain imposed harsh collective punishment on towns and villages. The army systematically blew up houses in entire sections of rebellious towns, closed schools, levied fines on whole communities, and billeted troops at the expense of the residents. No place was spared the heavy hand of imperial Britain, not even the Old City of Jerusalem. The citadel of Christian, Jewish, and Muslim holy sites shuddered under five days of siege aimed at rooting out rebels holed up in its narrow streets and alleyways.

At last, the deportations, arrests, fines, economic disruption, deaths, and executions broke the Arab community politically, economically, and psychologically. In 1939, with Abd al-Qadir and the mufti both in exile, the rebellion ended. Defeat had descended on the Palestinians because of Britain's superior power and their own failed leadership.

In the revolt, the people drove their leaders. None of the rebellion's military commanders came out of the ruling class. For in Palestine's traditional society, the ruling class shrank from the masses, shrank in horror at the prospect of violence from below, violence that might conflict with the interests of those on top. Steeped in the traditions of notable and peasant, those of the upper class recoiled from any obligation to the lower class, even in the cause of Palestinian nationalism. They could relate to the lower classes only in terms that fell short of conflict with their own vital interests. In 1939, Haj Amin reigned as the prototype of the upper-class Arab pretending to lead a political revolution without dirtying his hands in mobilizing the bulk of his people. At the end of the revolt, he along with the Arab Higher Committee threw away all the practical wisdom that they might have learned from the rebellion—unity, organization, and the potent political potential of popular uprising. Yet the Palestinians still won a victory of sorts. For three years, they had forced Britain to confront a painful, costly insurrection that challenged British policy in Palestine and British interests across the Arab world. At its end, the British offered Haj Amin one more opportunity to prove himself a visionary.

Consumed by the need to restore stability to the Middle East in order to concentrate its energies on Nazi Germany's creeping shadow, Britain retreated from the three main points of the Peel Commission report—partition, an independent Jewish state, and Transjordanian rule of the Arab part of Palestine. After three long years of civil war, Britain now offered the Palestinians a single state of Palestine, Arab and Jewish; independence after ten years; the prohibition of land sales to Jews in large areas of Palestine; and a drastic cutback in Jewish immigration for five years, after which the Palestinians would retain exclusive control over immigration policy. Most important, the 1939 White Paper implied retreat from the Balfour Declaration and an acceptance of the Palestinians' right to self-government. Unless the angry and aroused Zionists in London could torpedo the plan, the Palestinians had won. Yet with Arab leverage at its peak, Haj Amin, speaking from exile, rejected the plan by insisting on independence in five years rather than ten.

Lacking the qualities of an astute politician and dominated by the stubborn maximalism of his political outlook, Amin squandered the Palestinians' best chance for a state. The Arab Higher Committee followed the mufti's lead, a move tragically consistent with the pattern of senseless rejectionism for which it was notorious. As if by fiat, the sacrifices of the rebellion were lost.

Haj Amin is seldom mentioned by the Palestinians. But the memory of Abd al-Qadir still lives. His son, Faisal al-Husseini, came to prominence as a Palestinian leader at the time of the 1987 Palestinian uprising and accompanied the Palestinian delegation to the 1991 Middle East peace conference. Faisal al-Husseini's house sits on the edge of a shallow valley at the bottom of the Mount of Olives in East Jerusalem. Its furnishings are simple, the walls almost unadorned. Between two doorframes in a parlor flooded with sunlight, a carved olive-wood plaque hangs from the white plaster wall. Two crossed swords provide a cradle for the head of a man. The strong profile and the draped *khaffiyeh* identify it as Abd al-Qadir. As he led the Arab armed resistance to British colonial policy that so favored the Zionists, so Abd al-Qadir would lead the Arabs' last stand against the Zionists in the 1948 war for Palestine.

CHAPTER 5

THE WAR FOR PALESTINE

THE ROAD RUNNING NORTH OUT OF Ramallah on the Israeli-occupied West Bank breaks away from the congested town and curves into rugged hills and deep-red-brown fields dotted with olive trees. It was the third year of another Palestinian uprising, the Intifadah. Gray-green trucks of the Israeli army and battered pickups carrying Palestinian produce toward Jerusalem jockeyed for position on the narrow straightaways. The taxi in which I rode followed in dogged pursuit. Just past a newly graded helicopter landing pad, the driver slowed and then turned left at a three-sided wooden lookout post dug into a hill. Inside, a half-dozen Israeli soldiers manned enormous night-piercing binoculars mounted on tripods and a bank of communications equipment linked to the nearest military encampment. Below in the valley was Jalazone, a jumble of cement and concrete block containing the human remnants of the 1948 war for Palestine.

The taxi bumped over the rutted road, slowed for a thin girl balancing an aluminum tray stacked with bread on her head, and stopped at the small store that marked the entrance to the refugee camp. I got out and started down the hill. At the bottom of the steep dirt path that constituted the camp's main street, a squat man with balding head and a neatly trimmed mustache waited. His name was simply Khalil, and he was a teacher of English. He had been ten years old in 1948.

"My family lived in a village between Tulkarm and the sea. There were six of us—my mother and father, three sisters, and me. I was the oldest. We heard the Zionists coming and we were very afraid. My father told us, 'Hurry, run toward the hill behind the village.' My sisters and I started toward the door but my mother would not come. She sat on a chair in the middle of our small front room and said she was going to stay. She thought, I don't know why, that she could protect her home. We cried and begged her to come but she just sat there. My father told her we were only going for a little while. That was when she reached down and picked up my youngest sister. Tears were coming from her eyes when she said she would come with us."

Khalil stopped, reached over to the low table in front of him, pulled a cigarette from a crumpled pack, lit it, and drew deeply. "We lived under the trees on the hill for four months. When the cold weather was coming, we found a small house to rent. Then our money ran out and we came here. We thought that was temporary too." He shrugged his shoulders. "But you see I am still here. And every day that I am here I remind the Arabs about what the Zionists did to the Palestinians—not just the Palestinians but all Arabs."

For Arabs, the 1948 war for Palestine confirms as nothing else the Arab sense of betrayal at the hands of the West. While the West sees the birth of Israel as the culmination of the Jews' heroic effort to overcome oppression and extermination and to return to the land of their forefathers, the Arabs see it as the most odious act of imperialism the West ever inflicted on the Arab nation. 1948 represents in the Arab mind another of those unequal contests in which Western money and technical skills, this time in the hands of Western-financed Zionists, brought the Arabs to their knees. There is a strong basis of truth in Arab perceptions. The Zionists could never have won or survived without Western support. But they also might not have won if the Arabs had achieved the unity that their mythology celebrates. The power that the issue of Palestine exercised over Arab nationalism competed with the power exerted by the interests of individual Arab states. Thus the war for Palestine was both an Arab war against the Zionists and an Arab war against other Arabs. The

Palestinians became victims of Arab ambition as well as Zionist expulsion. Yet in the loss of Palestine, the Arabs found in the state of Israel the most visceral symbol of their unity.

On the eve of World War II, Palestine, exhausted by three years of turmoil, paused between its past and its future. The past was the Palestinians' shackled effort to preserve Palestine and its Arab character. The future was the Zionists' zealous determination to possess Palestine, to create within it the Jewish homeland.

Like some prophetic omen, World War II erupted the same year the Arabs' revolt against British rule in Palestine collapsed. With the Levant marginal to the conflict in Europe, the Palestinians, but even more the Jews, recognized that the war years would serve as a time to prepare for the coming showdown over the future of Palestine. Each community knew that once peace returned to Europe, the Palestine problem would demand a solution. And each knew that only one side could win. But what neither side fully perceived was that the outcome of the contest for Palestine would ultimately have more to do with the war in Europe than with events in the Levant. In his perversion, Adolf Hitler sealed the fate not only of Germany's Jews but of Palestine's Arabs. For it was the worldwide revulsion at the Nazi death camps that secured wholesale Western political support for Palestine as a homeland for the Jews and, in the process, turned the Palestinians into a nation of refugees and the Arabs into a people united in anger against Zionism.

As Europe reverberated with the sounds of war, Palestine slumbered in the sun of the Levant. Jewish immigration had diminished, a macabre result of the Jews' plight in Europe. But the relative peace was also a reflection of what had happened to the Palestinians. The collapse of the 1936–39 revolt against British rule had marked the end of the Palestinians' ability to affect the course of their own history. Exhausted, denied the right to organize politically, deprived of their exiled leadership, and shut out of the international political arena, the Palestinians were politically paralyzed. The best they could do was play weak defense against the Zionists' strong offense.

While the Palestinians languished, the Zionists feverishly prepared for the coming collision over Palestine. Yet one inescapable fact loomed over all Zionist plans—the reality of their numbers. The Jewish population of Palestine in 1939 was 445,000, a bare 30 percent of the population. If Zionism was to triumph, the war years had to be used to multiply the size of the Yishuv, the Jewish community in Palestine. Only immigration, massive immigration, could produce the numbers necessary to win the Jewish homeland. But Britain still guarded the portals of Palestine. Anxious about the buffeting that British interests in the Arab world were taking over the issue of Jewish immigration, London no longer played the pliant partner of Zionism. Therefore, what Zionism demanded was a Western sponsor that was even stronger than the faltering British Empire.

As if the power configuration of the West had already begun to shift from imperiled Britain to mighty America, American Zionists meeting at the Biltmore Hotel in New York in May 1942 unveiled Zionism's new agenda. Dropping the term "Jewish homeland," the so-called Biltmore Program declared Zionism would settle for nothing less than the establishment of a Jewish "commonwealth" in Palestine, in other words a Jewish state. All that was left to decide was the timetable. David Ben-Gurion, speaking with the force of a prophet, pronounced the end of World War II as the signal for the Zionists to begin their final push for Palestine.

As the war in Europe wound toward its close, Western backing for a Jewish state grew to proportions even the most ardent of the early Zionists could never have predicted. Allied armies driving toward Berlin verified for all the unspeakable torments the Nazi regime had visited on Jews and others considered unfit for the Third Reich. Day after day the front pages of the West's newspapers were blanketed with pictures showing hollow eyes staring blankly at liberating armies, emaciated hands meekly reaching through barbed wire to take a chocolate bar, withered legs the size of reeds sticking out of dirty striped prison uniforms. But nothing spoke more forcibly of the horrors of Hitler's "final solution" than Auschwitz's abandoned ovens and its mass graves. Western society so long deaf to the rumors of genocide was outraged.

The Allies moved inmates out of Hitler's concentration camps into new camps designated for "displaced persons." Soon hundreds of thousands of the survivors idled in olive-green tent cities and converted army camps waiting for settlement. While those victorious against Hitler's evil anguished over the dispossessed, organized Jewry in the West movingly evoked the memory of the Jews massacred by the Nazis and claimed a "divine impatience" over the West's procrastination in finding a haven for those who had escaped.

But finding a home, any home, for the displaced was not necessarily the objective. To those building the Zionist state, the only point at which the progeny of the Holocaust should gather was Palestine. Europe's refugees formed the wellspring of the population the Zionists needed to create the critical mass necessary to claim their state. It was with this goal that American Zionists lobbied the U.S. Congress to hold strongly to the already existing quotas on immigration of Jews to the United States. Thus with the golden doors to postwar America largely closed, the refugees descended on Palestine.

There they collided with the immigration quotas the British had erected to keep the peace. Refusing to abide by British restrictions, the Zionists assailed the embargo by filtering thousands of Jews out of the refugee camps and through the sievelike lines manned by the Jewish brigade in Italy. They sent others to Palestine on rusting, belching hulls claiming to be ships. Britain, finally trapped in its long-conflicting policy of attempting to affirm Palestine for the Zionists while reserving it for the Palestinians, tried vainly to stem the tide. As the decaying ships approached the shores of Palestine, British patrols turned them back. It was a tactic awaiting execution by some ill-starred incident. When that incident came, it was as a pair. Refused permission to land, the SS *Patria*, with its load of woeful refugees, sank off Haifa and the SS *Struma*, overloaded with its cargo of displaced, went down in the Black Sea. Both sides of the Atlantic raged with indignation. And the pressure to open the gates of Palestine to the homeless of World War II relentlessly increased. From Jerusalem, David Ben-Gurion thundered that if the British government returned to the provisions of the 1939 White Paper restricting Jewish immigration and land acquisition it would suffer "bloody terror" and "constant and brutal force" in Palestine.

Ben-Gurion could afford to challenge Britain in Palestine because the configuration of allies and adversaries had radically altered. Through the twenty-five-year history of the mandate, power relationships in Palestine were triangular—the British, the Zionists, and the Palestinians. But in reality, power between 1920 and 1940 was bipolar—the British/Zionist axis and the Palestinians. By 1944, two things had happened to modify these power relationships. Britain, husbanding its own interests in the Middle East, came to acknowledge that there existed an Arab as well as a Jewish question in Palestine. And secondly, the United States emerged from World War II as the Zionists' new champion.

Under intense congressional pressure, the spent and ailing Franklin Roosevelt, returning from the Yalta Conference, lobbied Arab leaders to drop their opposition to Jewish immigration. Cautious himself about the issue of Palestine, Roosevelt nonetheless met with Abdul Aziz ibn Saud, the legendary king of Saudi Arabia, aboard a U.S. cruiser anchored in the Suez Canal's Great Bitter Lake in February 1945. It was a meeting of opposites. Roosevelt—Western, patrician, surrounded by the might of the American military —sat for the official portrait with Abdul Aziz—Arab, Bedouin, accompanied by seven-foot-tall Nubian slaves armed with swords. Exuding his famous charm, Roosevelt went to work. In his deep resonant voice, he enumerated for Saudi Arabia's king and the guardian of Mecca all of the horrors Hitler had inflicted on the Jews, ending with an emotional plea to allow a Jewish homeland in Palestine. Abdul Aziz looked directly at Roosevelt with his one good eye and replied that the Arabs had never injured the European Jews. It was the Germans who had taken their homes and lives, and it was the Germans who should pay. "Give them and their descendants the choiciest lands and homes of the German who had oppressed them."* Roosevelt pressed on in his attempt to win the king's help in meeting Zionism's dream. And Abdul Aziz held firm. "Make the enemy and the oppressor pay; that is how we Arabs wage war. . . . What injury have Arabs done to the Jews of Europe? It is the 'Christian' Germans who stole their homes and lives. Let the Germans pay."†

Franklin Delano Roosevelt died two months after this stalemated meeting with Abdul Aziz. In April 1945, Harry Truman assumed the American presidency, and with him came an emotional commitment to the ideals of Zionism. With the diplomatic front covered and thousands of immigrants waiting to come to Palestine to bolster the Jewish population, the Zionists broke their corroded link with battle-worn Britain. Britain, still holding Palestine as a mandate from the defunct League of Nations, ceased to be an ally of Zionism and instead became its adversary. To deliver Palestine

---

* Colonel William A. Eddy, *FDR Meets Ibn Saud* (New York: American Friends of the Middle East, 1954), p. 34.
† Ibid.

as a Jewish state in the shortest time possible, the Zionists would force Britain to relinquish its claim.

In the fall of 1945, the three Zionist armed forces in Palestine—the Haganah, the Irgun Zvai Leumi, and the Stern Gang—began their separate operations against British installations and personnel. The Haganah, with a membership of about sixty thousand, had been organized in the 1920s as an underground army to defend isolated Jewish settlements from Arab attacks. During the 1930s, as the British winked, the Haganah spread into every Jewish community in Palestine. By the mid-1940s, it operated a sophisticated arms network that purchased from abroad and smuggled into Palestine everything from small sidearms to mortars to equipment for manufacturing ammunition. While the Haganah approached the status of the army of the Jewish Agency, the Irgun and the Stern Gang were more in the mode of guerrilla organizations. Both were factions of the Revisionist camp of Zionism.

Led by Vladimir Jabotinsky, the Revisionists were a right-wing chauvinistic movement emulating the European fascist movements of the 1920s and 1930s. They attracted followers with their military uniforms, martial ceremonies, and emotion-charged rallies that promised to deliver through force of arms greater Palestine, spanning the Levant from the Mediterranean to the eastern border of Transjordan. Brandishing an escutcheon bearing a rifle thrust aloft by a clenched fist ringed by the motto "Only Thus," the Irgun and its offshoot, the Stern Gang, became the terrorist wing of the Zionist movement.

With Menachem Begin as the strategist of the Irgun and Yitzhak Shamir as a leader of the Stern Gang, they at first targeted British policemen. Then in the summer of 1944, the Stern Gang upped the price Britain would pay to stay in Palestine by dealing in political assassination. On August 8, the group failed in its attempt to assassinate the British high commissioner, Sir Harold Mac-Michael. But in November, it succeeded in killing Lord Walter Moyne, British resident minister of state in Cairo and friend of Winston Churchill.

Working as separate parts of a general strategy in October 1945, the Haganah's Palmah commandos, the Irgun, and the Stern Gang made war on the British. Under the assault, Britain vacillated, caught between the Arabs' demand that Jewish immigration to Palestine be halted and the United States' insistence that 100,000 Jewish immigrants be immediately admitted. And while His Majesty's Government wavered, the violence spread. Munitions thefts, bombings, sabotage, bank robberies, destruction of bridges, and more deaths of English soldiers served as confirmation of Zionism's assault on Britain. Finally, the British retaliated. The army arrested leaders of the Jewish Agency, rounded up members of the Palmah, and seized caches of arms, including one hidden in the Great Synagogue of Tel Aviv. In all, 2,675 Jews landed behind bars. From the court docks, they shouted defiantly, "In blood and fire Judah fell; in blood and fire it will rise again."*

In August, the Zionists sent Britain another message on immigration. Jerusalem awoke to find one wing of the stately King David Hotel, the home of the British military command, reduced to dust by Irgun bombs planted in the basement. Ninety-one more people had joined the growing list of victims of the struggle for Palestine.

Palestine had become an intolerable burden for Britain. Just the cost of keeping a minimum of 100,000 men in the mandate to enforce any kind of order constituted an enormous burden for a country drained by a global war and verging on bankruptcy. Ensnared in its own economic problems, pressed by the persistent demands of Western opinion to drop the barriers on immigration, and powerless to stop the escalating violence between Zionist and Palestinian, enfeebled Britain searched for a way out.

In January 1947, Ernest Bevin, the British foreign minister, summoned the leadership of both the Arab and Jewish communities to London to discuss the partition of Palestine into two states—one Arab, one Jewish. Facing each other across a heavy oak table, both sides refused partition. Bevin thanked each delegation for coming and bid them goodbye. His Majesty's Government had made its last try. In February 1947, Britain passed the tangle of Palestine over to the fledgling United Nations.

Events in Palestine, driven by the Nazi affront to the West's moral code and the interests of more than a few of its political leaders, were nonetheless taking place within the environs of the Arab world. The shocks of World War II lifted colonial rule from

* *Time*, July 8, 1946.

the last two Arab territories of the *mashriq*—Syria and Lebanon.*
Independence had finally come to the Arabs, not as one nation but
as separate states. United by common language and culture, they
straddled strategic communications and transportation routes, possessed great potential wealth, and claimed a large combined population. But they were politically and militarily weak.

In the autumn of 1944, conversations began on a strategy by
which the Arab states could face the great powers. On March 22,
1945, Egypt, Iraq, Syria, Lebanon, Transjordan (Jordan), Saudi Arabia, and Yemen formed the Arab League. The League, like Arab
unity, was heavy on symbolism and light on substance. It essentially
affirmed cooperation in communications and in economic, cultural,
social, and health affairs. Embodying a guarantee of the sovereignty
of each member, it stopped short of committing members to collective security or mutual defense. The League's most definitive
commitment was cooperation against the partition of Palestine. Abdul Rahman Azzam Pasha, the League's first secretary-general,
threw the Arabs' contempt at Zionism. "Our brother has gone to
Europe and to the West and come back something else. He has come
back a Russified Jew, a Polish Jew, a German Jew, an English Jew.
He has come back with a totally different conception of things, Western not Eastern. . . . our old cousin [is] coming back with imperialistic
ideas, with materialistic ideas, with reactionary or revolutionary ideas
and trying to implement them first by British pressure and then by
American pressure, and then by terrorism on his own part—he is
not the old cousin, and we do not extend to him a very good welcome.
The Zionist, the new Jew, wants to dominate, and he pretends that
he has got a particular civilizing mission with which he returns to a
backward degenerate race in order to put the elements of progress
into an area which has to progress. Well, that has been the pretension
of every power that wanted to colonize and aimed at domination.
The excuse has always been that the people are backward and that
he has got a human mission to put them forward. . . . the Arabs
simply stand and say 'No.' We are not reactionary and we are not
backward. Even if we are ignorant, the difference between ignorance
and knowledge is ten years in school. We are a living, vitally strong

---

* France tried to retain its rights after the war, but British, American, and Arab
opposition forced the French government to grant both countries independence
in 1946.

nation, we are in our renaissance. . . . We have a heritage of civilization and of spiritual life. We are not going to allow ourselves to be controlled either by great nations or small nations or dispersed nations."* Thus Abdul Rahman Azzam Pasha articulated the Arabs' passion concerning Palestine. When the United Nations was called on to decide the future of Palestine, it was also deciding in emotional terms the future of the Arabs.

From its squat, flat-roofed temporary quarters in Flushing Meadow, New York, the General Assembly of the United Nations sent its eleven-nation Special Committee on Palestine (UNSCOP) into the field to explore ways of resolving the decades-old contest for Palestine. Linking Palestine to the problem of Jewish refugees, UNSCOP toured the refugee camps in Europe before going on to Palestine. During June and July 1947, while UNSCOP conducted its hearings in Palestine, the Zionists paraded their power. In reprisal for British execution of three Jews, the Irgun, as the avenging hand of Zionism, kidnapped and hanged two British sergeants, leaving their booby-trapped bodies dangling from olive trees for all to see. Yet the major act staged for the benefit of the UN visitors was the arrival in the waters off Palestine of another rusted, leaking ship— the *Exodus*. Packed with 4,554 Jews garnered from the displaced persons camps, it floated off Palestine as the perfect symbol of the synonymous issues of refugees and immigration. Although the British authorities seized the ship at Haifa and turned it back to Marseilles, the Zionists won their point.

UNSCOP returned to the United Nations recommending the partition of Palestine. Like a modern-day Solomon, the committee divided Britain's former mandate into three sections for Jews and three for Arabs, with Jerusalem and Bethlehem, important as religious sites to three religions, "internationalized." As proposed, 45 to 50 percent of the population in the Jewish state would be Arab and 1 percent of the Arab state Jewish. To the Arabs, this partition plan was worse than the one proposed by the Peel Commission in 1937. The Jews made up only 35 percent of the population. They owned only 7 percent of the land. Yet they were to inherit an area of Palestine that was a thousand square miles bigger than what the United Nations was willing to leave with the Arabs. Even worse from the Arab perspective, nearly all the citrus land, 80 percent of the

---

* Quoted in Mansfield, *Arabs*, p. 474.

cereal land, and 40 percent of the few industries belonging to Arabs were in the Jewish state. And Jaffa, the major port, was cut off from the rest of the Arab territory. The Palestinians rejected the plan and the Arab states supported them.

According to Arab attitudes shaped by a history of occupation and deception, no international body or other foreign power had the right to deliver Arab land to an alien people. But beyond that, the Arabs raged at the very idea of partition, which had been tailored by the Western powers to meet the needs and demands of the Zionists of Palestine, 80 to 90 percent of whom were Europeans. The old imagery of the Crusades rose up to haunt a people long suspicious of Western intentions in the Levant. A Jewish state in Palestine went beyond the division of Palestine to raise once more the specter of Western colonialism. In doing so, it touched the very core of the Arab psyche.

Arabs still see the partition of Palestine in terms of Western manipulation of the Arab world. On November 29, 1947, when the United Nations voted to divide Palestine between Arabs and Jews, countries claiming a Western culture (including the Soviet Union and Latin America) held thirty-six seats in the General Assembly, the Arabs six. Although not all the "Western" countries were rich and industrialized and not all that were economically developed voted for partition, the image has stood over the years. In Arab mythology, the decision to grant the Zionists part of Palestine was another attempt of the West to inflict on the Arabs "death by a thousand cuts."

Mansour is a roly-poly man who runs a little restaurant at the foot of a hill in Amman. He seems always to be wrapped in his own good humor, throwing off quips faster than he can quarter the tomatoes that decorate his platters of tabouli. Mansour's forte is politics. Because past and present are always so closely intertwined in the Arab mind, discussion of today's events is a discussion of the last ten centuries. I have no recollection of the particular subject, but Mansour held up a big butcher knife: "Do you see this?" I said, "Yes." He pointed to a strip of meat laid out on a heavy wooden chopping block and asked, "Do you see this?" Again I answered, "Yes." In lightning strokes the knife severed the meat—chop, chop, chop vertically, chop, chop, chop horizontally. Within seconds it was a pile of cubes. Mansour roared with laughter. "That's what the West does to the Arabs."

With partition decided, Britain was to be freed of the mandate on May 15, 1948. In the months between November 1947 and May 1948, the years of coalescing fury in Palestine solidified into outright war. Violence marked every day, like the rising and setting of the sun. On the part of the Zionists, the malignity was organized. On the part of the Palestinians, it was random. Palestinian bands struck at Zionists without plan, only with purpose. They lacked strategy or direction in part because they had no leader.

Carrying the Palestinian banner into British-imposed exile in 1937, Haj Amin had used his refuge in Beirut and then Iraq to build anti-British sentiment. Forced out of Baghdad by British pressure, he fled to Iran and finally to Rome. Seeing World War II only in terms of the old Arab adage that the "enemy of my enemy is my friend," he joined the propaganda machine of the Axis powers. Thwarting attempts to bring him to trial at Nuremberg on the unconfirmed charge that he authored the Nazi's plan to exterminate the Jews, he escaped in disguise to Egypt to the protection of King Farouk. Discredited by his wartime activities, the mufti was rejected first by Britain and then by the United Nations as a spokesman for the Palestinians, denying them their flawed but logical leader.

The question of who would lead their cause in Palestine hobbled the already enfeebled Palestinians. The Muslim Brotherhood, at the peak of its influence in Egypt, constituted the most visible force in the Arabs' fight against Zionism in 1947.* But when the United Nations voted partition, a joint Arab effort established itself in Damascus. Fawzi Bey Kawukji, a Lebanese with experience in the Turkish army, was sent to Palestine to command the ten thousand volunteers of the Arab Liberation Army. In March 1948, Kawukji, a fleece-lined cape draped from his shoulders, stepped out of a black sedan in Jerusalem. A Syrian observing the arrival exclaimed, "Arab history is repeating itself. In the Crusades, Saladin had to free Jerusalem from the infidels. Today Fawzi Bey is our Saladin."†

Pulled from the slums of Baghdad, Damascus, and Beirut, filtering into Palestine in fits and starts, the ragtag force that was the Arab Liberation Army never put more than five thousand men in

---

* The Brotherhood was in Palestine under the auspices of the Egyptian government. Sending the Brotherhood to Palestine to fight against Zionism was an attempt by the government to control the Brotherhood's increasingly violent behavior in Egypt.
† *Time*, March 15, 1948.

the field at one time. Uneducated, untrained, and meagerly armed, it was more of a statement of the Arab rejection of Zionism than a fighting force.

Haj Amin resisted the Arab League's decision to recruit volunteers. Always protective of his own power, the mufti wanted to retain control over the funds and training of those who fought in Palestine. Unable to exercise that total control, Haj Amin saw the volunteers under Kawukji as a dangerous rival to his own volunteer force, the Jaish al-Jihad al-Muqaddas ("Forces of Struggle"), led by Abd al-Qadir al-Husseini.

In January 1948, al-Qadir, the celebrated hero of the 1936–39 rebellion, had returned from exile. Immediately he began to organize the Arab resistance to the partition of Palestine. It had been ten years since the dashing, bandoliered al-Qadir led the Palestinians. But they remembered. Out of the villages men once more came carrying their banned rifles and their sparse stores of ammunition. With no uniform other than their *khaffiyehs* draped about their heads, the *fallahin* again followed al-Qadir into battle against the Zionists.

Yet as the war for Palestine would prove, the Palestinians were prepared neither militarily nor politically to confront the highly financed, organized, and motivated Yishuv. Although Palestinian bomb squads executed some damaging blows against the Zionists, the war from the beginning proved an uneven contest.* Burdened by the legacy of the mandate's misrule and crippled by the fissures in its own society, the Palestinians furiously drove into war lacking any clear vision other than an impassioned desire to drive out the Zionists before they seized the land of Palestine. But it was not enough to thwart the Yishuv, united around a sacred call to statehood embroidered on the backdrop of the Holocaust. While the Palestinians threw themselves into hit-and-run guerrilla raids, sporadic firefights, and random attacks, the Zionists extracted their weapons stores from underground hiding places and unrolled their carefully conceived strategic plans. Before the war for Palestine ended, the "transfer question," which had intrigued the Yishuv for two decades, would be answered.

In December 1947, the Haganah launched Plan Gimmel, de-

---

* The most infamous of Palestinian bombs blew up on Jerusalem's crowded Ben Yehuda Street, killing eighty-nine people, almost all Jews.

signed to occupy strategic positions on Palestine's coastal plain. In Jaffa, Haifa, and even Jerusalem, the fear that had gripped the Palestinians since the partition vote turned into frenzy. The rich drew down their bank accounts, locked their imposing homes, and loaded into ships and automobiles for Beirut, Cairo, or Damascus to wait out the war. The middle class, carrying suitcases and children, strung eastward to join relatives in towns a safe distance from concentrated Jewish settlement. With the greater and lesser notables went the *fallahin*'s only political identification, their allegiance to the personages of the clan. Almost overnight, the struts had been pulled out of Palestinian society, leaving behind a tottering shell.

In February 1948, the Haganah in the first planned, organized expulsion of Arabs emptied the ancient town of Caesarea of its Palestinian citizens. The choice of a town that provided vegetables to the Haifa market and that was recognized for its efforts to avoid the conflict was enough to send other villages isolated from Arab centers of population into panicked flight. Yet it was not the Haganah that infused the Palestinians with overpowering fear. It was the ignoble Irgun.

Nadia al-Hatar is a strikingly good-looking educator in her late forties who lives in East Jerusalem. I never go to Israel without having at least one cup of tea with her. Over the years, I have found her to be a person steeped in the Palestinian experience but free of the hyperemotional language that pours out of so many Palestinians. On one particular day, we drove north and west out of Jerusalem. Pulling to a stop in front of an old square stone house, we got out and walked across the road, where heavy trucks loaded with cement groaned up a steep incline. Neither of us said anything; we just looked down on the site where the most famous village of the 1948 war for Palestine once stood. After a few moments, Nadia turned to me and said, "You know, the Jews have this saying that unless you are a Jew you cannot begin to comprehend the Nazi Holocaust. I'm sure that must be true. But we Palestinians also have a saying. Unless you are a Palestinian, you cannot completely grasp the meaning of the massacre at Deir Yassin. It was nothing more and nothing less than an eviction notice served on a whole people."

On April 9, 1948, the Irgun, along with operatives from the Stern Gang, crept in on Deir Yassin, an unremarkable Arab village hugging a rocky promontory west of Jerusalem. At dawn, the commandos quietly eliminated the village's guard and invaded its stone-

and-cactus perimeter. Families pulled from their beds stood dazed as fifteen houses within the village core collapsed, reduced to rubble by the Irgun's dynamite. The pale stone walls of the remaining houses became backboards for Jewish bullets systematically riddling Palestinian bodies. In an orgy of destruction and death, Irgun and Stern Gang operatives slashed open villagers with the cold steel of their knives, spilling blood and entrails across the dusty ground. Women running with wild-eyed fear fell to the ground and were raped by the attackers. By noon, the operation had ended and Deir Yassin belonged to the Zionists. Its cost—254 Palestinians, most of whom were women and children.

As the sun set that evening on what was left of the grieving village, the heavy question hung—why Deir Yassin? It was nothing but a small community with no particular strategic value that had labored to avoid the conflict raging around it. Ironically, this was the reason Deir Yassin suffered its tragic fate. Deir Yassin was the Irgun's bloody message to the Arabs to get out of Palestine.

Although the Palestinians wreaked their revenge three days later by killing seventy-seven doctors, nurses, university teachers, and students bound for the Hebrew University and the beleaguered Hadassah Hospital on Mount Scopus, Deir Yassin, a typical Arab village, proved to be the single most devastating psychological blow to the Palestinians of the entire struggle for Palestine. Although the mainstream Zionist leadership publicly denounced the massacre, when Zionist forces moved on Tiberias and Haifa, Haganah jeeps equipped with loudspeakers preceded them to broadcast prerecorded shrieks, wails, and anguished moans of Arab women. Over the wail of sirens and the clang of fire-alarm bells, a sepulchral voice called out in Arabic, "Save your souls, all ye faithful! Flee for your lives! The Jews are using poison gas and atomic weapons. Run for your lives in the name of Allah!" And the Palestinians fled.

Abandoned by its traditional leadership, terrified by rumors of Jewish atrocities, threatened by Haganah artillery, the Palestinians surged out of Palestine's coastal cities and villages.* In the pandemonium, Britain's illusions of an orderly transfer of the mandate lay shattered. British troops, unable to inject themselves effectively

---

* A small percentage of Palestinians fled at the urging of their leadership seeking to create chaos in Palestine's Jewish dominated economy. The actual number of Palestinians fleeing for this reason is disputed.

into the chaos, huddled in their barracks while the villages of the eastern Galilee tumbled like dominos. And there was no one else to stem the tide. Three months earlier, the same day the Irgun massacred the residents of Deir Yassin, the legendary Abd al-Qadir, the symbol of Palestinian resistance, died in the battle for the Tel Aviv–Jerusalem road.

The sun was about to set on the British mandate of Palestine. On May 14, 1948, four Scottish bagpipes on top of the Hill of Evil Council outside Jerusalem wailed their lament for Britain's years in Palestine. On the coast where they had turned back so many shiploads of Jewish immigrants, British soldiers protected by the steel of their tanks rolled through the rubble-strewn streets of Jaffa making their final patrols. In Haifa, eager British soldiers abandoned their wooden barracks overlooking the harbor and packed aboard barges headed for ships waiting to take them home to England. Although the mandate still had eight hours to run, General Sir Alan Cunningham, the last British high commissioner, had already retired to the cruiser *Euryalus*. There he sat waiting for the night to creep across the eastern Mediterranean. In 1917, Allenby had taken the British triumphantly into Jerusalem. Now they were departing, unhonored and unsung, leaving Jerusalem under the flag of the International Red Cross and Palestine to a new war.

In Jewish Tel Aviv, crowds in the streets chanted the ancient "Hatikvah"—"We have not forgotten, nor shall we forget, our solemn promise." Inside, in the main gallery of the modern two-story Tel Aviv Museum of Art on Rothschild Boulevard, David Ben-Gurion, flanked by his twelve fellow ministers of the national council, stood beneath a portrait of Theodor Herzl. At precisely 4:00 P.M., he struck a blow on the long speakers' table before him. "We proclaim the establishment of the Jewish state in Palestine, to be called Israel." Within sixteen minutes of Ben-Gurion's announcement, U.S. President Harry Truman, against the advice of his State Department and to the total surprise of the United Nations General Assembly, debating at the moment the question of Palestine, announced the United States' de facto recognition of the state of Israel.

The following day, May 15, the war for Palestine became an Arab war. The Egyptians moved out of the Sinai and along the coast toward Tel Aviv and through the Negev to Beersheba. An Iraqi force crossed the Jordan River and advanced toward the Mediterranean. A few thousand Syrians came down through Galilee, perceptibly reducing the fear spreading through the Arab villages. Even Lebanon sent a small force to join in the Arab cause, a profound symbol for a ruling elite that held as a sacred trust the determination to stay out of Arab politics. All the while, the Arab Legion of Transjordan held the center of the line. The only effective fighting force on the Arab side, it occupied areas east of the Jordan River and held Arab Jerusalem. Control of the Arab side of the war had passed from the Palestinians to the Arab states. And each of these states possessed its own jealous interests in Palestine, but none more than Transjordan, ruled by King Abdullah.

Abdullah in secret meetings with Israel's Golda Meir had already agreed that in case of war between the Zionists and the Arab states, Abdullah's army would stay out of that part of Palestine assigned to the Jews by the United Nations partition plan in return for Zionist agreement to Abdullah's seizure of the Arab part. The Zionists in effect granted Transjordanian sovereignty over the West Bank of the Jordan River north of Nablus and south of Hebron, including the Old City of Jerusalem. When Transjordan appeared to be joining the Arab states in the invasion of Palestine, a worried Golda Meir sent a message to Abdullah asking if he intended to abide by his word. Abdullah responded with indignation, reminding her of three things—he was a Bedouin, a man of honor; he was a king doubly endowed with honor; and he was a man who would never break a promise made to a woman. Thus while the Palestinians and the Arab armies fought against the Zionists, Abdullah fought for himself.

Although the Arab radio and press claimed victory after victory, the Arab armies were losing. Lacking equipment, leadership, and zeal, the Arab League's main failure evolved from the absence of a commonly agreed on objective. Arab rulers had decided on an invasion of Palestine as much to thwart any attempt by Abdullah to use victory there to establish his own hegemony over Syria and the Levant as to save Palestine for the Palestinians. And Abdullah knew it. As the Arab forces met the Israelis, Abdullah kept his own well-equipped and well-trained Arab Legion on a tight rein, waiting for the war to end so he could claim his prize. Thus with Abdullah's Arab Legion effectively neutralized, Israeli forces by October had driven the Egyptians from most of their positions in the Negev, cleared northern Palestine, and forced the Arab Liberation Army into Lebanon and Syria. In December, Israeli mechanized forces pushed the Egyptians into a narrow corridor at Gaza and crossed into the Sinai Peninsula. The Egyptian government sued for peace.

In February 1949 a UN-negotiated truce between Israel and the Arabs took hold. Israel held in its hands all the land allocated to the Jewish state by the United Nations partition plan plus half the territory originally assigned to the Palestinians. Gaza, a narrow strip of territory fronting the Mediterranean, passed to Egypt. King Abdullah of Transjordan took what was left of Arab Palestine. Coiled barbed wire stretched the length of Princess Mary Avenue, dividing the city of Jerusalem between Arabs and Jews. With the truce in place, all that was left for Israel to do was clear out the last of the Palestinians deemed dangerous to the state of Israel and seal the borders.

Through the painful summer of 1948 and on into the desolate fall, the human debris of the war for Palestine had trekked across the ancient rock-strewn hills en route to some unknown destiny. They moved as families, even as villages, toward Transjordan, toward the strip of land along the Mediterranean known as Gaza, across the heights of Golan into Syria, and over the open border into Lebanon. Within these moving herds of people, a few rusting cars burdened with tightly rolled mattresses, sacks of flour, and the sick wheezed along the rough roads. But mostly those fleeing Palestine walked. The fit and the halt, the young and the old marched at a pace set by the most vulnerable among them. They stopped only for a racking birth or an exhausted death. And then they walked on. When the exodus finally ended, 700,000 Palestinians were homeless; 60 percent of the people of an entire society were refugees.

Today on a hilltop in the Galilee just west of Nazareth, the wind moves like a ghost through a stand of broad pine trees. Although traffic speeds by on the nearby road to Haifa and children laugh as they play on a colorful playground in the Jewish town below, here there is a peculiar quiet. The lonely wind sweeps the low boughs of the trees across deserted ground and bends the weeds atop rectangular mounds that were once houses. Even the spring that flowed below an outcropping of rock is quelled and dry. All that still stands in what was once a Palestinian Christian village is a deserted church. Vines tangle across its thick stone walls, entwine the bare rafters that once supported the roof, and choke the nave.

Israel claimed this land not only by military force but by expunging from the landscape with dynamite and bulldozers every evidence that these hills were once alive with Palestinians. Only a church remains as a haunting reminder of Palestine before 1948.

The refugees might have starved that first winter if the Quakers and a few other benevolent organizations had not intervened. Claiming tents out of the surplus of World War II, the relief organizations threw together the camps that would shelter the refugees until Israel and the Arab states struck the permanent peace that would return them home. In the meantime, they waited in vast cities of olive-green canvas that sprang up along the borders of Israel. Refugee tents flowed over the sandy plain of Gaza, trapping their residents between the border of Israel and the Mediterranean. On the West Bank of the Jordan River, just as the road from Jerusalem to Jericho drops off the steep escarpment onto the flat floor of the Dead Sea valley, acres of canvas and shoddy burlap blanketed the bleached landscape. On this one site were 25,000 people; another 8,000 crowded into 500 circular tents over the hill; another 5,000 to the north; and 13,500 more billeted within the teeming streets of Jericho itself. The 170,000 refugees in Lebanon took shelter in what they could afford. The rich leased apartments in Beirut. Those with less rented small houses, and sometimes only huts, in the villages of southern Lebanon. One hundred and fifty people squatted in caves in the hills. The rest went to the camps.

The refugees hung suspended between the land to which they could not return and the lands in which they could never belong. Egypt, strapped by overpopulation and an arrested economy, segregated its share of refugees in the Suez Canal Zone and the Gaza Strip, separated from Egypt's own population centers by the Sinai desert. Syria, with ample room but no resources, held Palestine's dispossessed near the Golan Heights as if dangling a piteous bargaining tool before the eyes of Israel. Lebanon's political establishment, fretting that the presence of the predominantly Muslim Palestinians would upset the delicate balance between Christians and Muslims on which the country's political existence rested, denied the refugees all services of government, including education and health care. Only Jordan incorporated the Palestinians. For Abdullah, the refugees represented a valuable demographic commodity. They doubled Jordan's minuscule population, and as citizens they legitimated Abdullah's claim to the West Bank. Yet what Abdullah could deliver politically he could not deliver economically. Although a portion of the refugees escaped into the Jordanian economy, the rest stayed imprisoned in the camps.*

Regardless of its location, every camp presented the same deadening sameness. The tents leaked. The cold of winter seeped through blankets that were too thin. The rains of spring washed the waste of thousands of people from inadequate latrines into canals that served as the source of water for drinking, bathing, and washing. The threat of dysentery, malaria, typhoid, and dengue lurked. Yet it was the absence of kerosene that created the most poignant symbol of refugee life. Every day as the sun set, the camps sank into darkness.

It all took its toll. Children ran through the camps like wild yearlings, because there were no schools. Women turned into scavengers, searching every day for the few sticks of wood that would turn scanty doles of flour into bread to feed their families. Still with their families for which to make some kind of home, women experienced purpose in their desperate lives. The men, without work, without the dignity that came with providing for their families, sat in the tattered tents whiling away the time. With the fear that propelled their flight gone, a debilitating listlessness consumed them. Stripped of their dignity, they sat emotionally naked.

Most of the refugee population were *fallahin* who knew little but how to bring forth crops out of the soil of Palestine. Their land was their universe, their identity. When it was lost, everything was lost, even the ability to create some order out of the chaos. Sadly there was none among the peasants able to take charge. The *muktars*, the village elders, suffered the same numbness as those they led. The old Arab adage "One day older, one day more experience" held no relevance in a society torn asunder.

The impassioned utterance "next year in Jerusalem" would sustain the Palestinians in their diaspora as it had the Jews through their diaspora. Wherever Palestinians settled, they wailed the lament for their lost land and wrote the poems of the Palestinian tragedy.

---

* Some Palestinians refused to leave the camps when opportunities presented themselves. Of these, most insisted on staying on the borders of Israel in preparation for "the return." Others regarded the camps as a statement of the injustice visited on the Palestinians.

Evil was made more evil by a nation
That ruled us by oppression and deceit.
Created out of Zionist fancies a home
Which grew to monstrous size:
Let the homeland of the natives be usurped,
Let the Arabs be herded out.*

1950 was a time when everyone except perhaps the Israelis still believed that some of the Palestinians would go home as soon as Israel and the Arab states signed a treaty of peace. But the formal peace that held the Palestinians' only hope of return never came. The Lausanne Protocol of May 12, 1949, in which both sides agreed to accept the partition boundaries of 1947 and Israel agreed to the return of 100,000 refugees, was rejected by both sides. It was rejected because peace presented risks for both Israel and the Arab states. For Israel, any peace treaty meant compromise on the refugee issue, and such compromise not only brought Palestinians back into the Jewish state but opened up the question of Zionist territorial claims. In 1949, Yigael Yadin, the Israeli Defense Forces chief of staff, joined together the issue of the refugees and Israel's final borders: "My opinion is that we must say with all cruelty: The refugee problem is no concern of the Land of Israel."†

Peace with Israel presented the Arab countries with their own series of sobering handicaps. Lebanon, the least hostile to Israel politically, would economically be forced to share Beirut's lucrative transit trade between the Levant and the West with Israel's port of Haifa. Furthermore, a portion of the income both Lebanon and Syria derived from the pipelines and refineries they provided for the burgeoning petroleum industry in the Persian Gulf might divert southward to Israel. Israel as an accepted nation in the region would likely prove a strong competitor for Middle East markets that countries like Egypt, awakening to industrialization, eyed for itself. Beyond economics, a gnawing fear existed that Israel was bent on expanding its borders beyond its 1948 boundaries. Formal peace

---

* Mahmed al-Hut, quoted in A. L. Tibawi, "Visions of the Return: The Palestinian Arab Refugees in Arabic Poetry and Art," *Middle East Journal* 17 (Late Autumn 1963): pp. 507–26.
† Quoted in Benny Morris, *The Birth of the Palestine Refugee Problem 1947–1949* (Cambridge, England: Cambridge University Press, 1987), p. 261.

would only usher Israel into the Middle East political arena, freeing it to maneuver among rival Arab states and with outside powers, especially the West, to fulfill its suspected expansionist ambitions. Yet the overpowering obstacle to peace from the Arab perspective remained psychological. Azzam Pasha, again speaking for the Arab League, said it best: "We have a secret weapon which we can use better than guns and machine guns, and this is time. As long as we do not make peace with the Zionists, the war is not over; and as long as the war is not over there is neither victor nor vanquished. As soon as we recognize the existence of the state of Israel, we admit by this act that we are vanquished."* More than four decades after the 1948 war for Palestine, peasant women in southern Iraq still lament, "Elizabeth, great queen Elizabeth, why did you desert us in Palestine?"† And a king of Saudi Arabia declares, "Palestine is a firebrand burning in our hearts—its occupation is like a deep bleeding wound."‡

The loss of Palestine translated into an intolerable loss to the honor of the Arab nation. Carrying the distinction of being recovered from the Crusaders, Palestine crystallized into a tormenting symbol of the Arabs' final humiliation at the hands of the arrogant West. The birth of Israel for the Arabs was nothing less than a Western-sanctioned crime against the Arab nation that has been neither forgotten nor forgiven. Suckled on Western diplomatic and economic support, Israel loomed as the new citadel of the West, and the Palestinian refugee as the emblem of Arab outrage at forces Arabs could neither overcome nor vie with successfully. Thus Israel became the new Crusader state, the insidious surrogate of Western imperialism. And in Israel, nine centuries of invasion, war, economic servitude, colonialism, and cultural conflict between the Arabs and the West came together, fusing all of their emotional and psychological power. The Zionist conquest of Palestine awoke as nothing before the passions of the Arab world. Ignoring the levels of Arab complicity in the loss of Palestine and the refusal of most Arab states to accept the Palestinian refugees, the Arabs felt belittled, humili-

---

* Quoted in Nadav Safran, *From War to War: The Arab-Israeli Confrontation 1948–67* (New York: Pegasus, 1969), p. 39.
† Elizabeth Warnock Fernea, *Guests of the Sheik: An Ethnography of an Iraqi Village* (Garden City, N.Y.: Anchor Books, 1969), p. 121.
‡ *Arab News*, February 12, 1980.

ated. They grieved that they once again had failed to stand against the onslaught of aliens. It is in this vein that Arab hatred of Israel began. And with the actions and attitudes Israel would later employ against its Arab neighbors, the Jewish state became the flaming crucible of Arab unity.

INTERLUDE:
UNITY AND
DIVISION

TWO CONSTANTS ARE ALWAYS AT work in the Arab world—unity and division. The components of the Arabs' near mystical sense of oneness constituted the preceding section of this book, the elements of their disjunction comprise the next. In religion, culture, history, and language, the Arabs find the powerful forces of their unity. In Islam and Arabic that unity is fed. In the distrust and bitterness of the Arabs' relationship with the West, it is reinforced. In the failure to challenge successfully the Israeli claim to land the Arabs regard as Arab, it is sustained. Dwelling deep within the Arab psyche is the concept of the Arab nation which promises to affirm the honor, power, and influence of the Arab people. This vision takes form in Arab nationalism which is neither a political party nor a political movement but the ideal that the Arabs are one. Yet the Arabs are inescapably divided into nation-states which are tormented by profound problems, some of the Arabs' own making, some the making of others.

The Arab nation-states reflect basic differences in temperament, character, and behavior and variations in climate, topography, history, and economics. They express the ancient enmities that existed between the Nile and the Euphrates, between the Ummayads and the Abbasids. And they testify to the reality that, with rare exception, they are not natural political entities.

The Arab states are largely the creation of the West that the Arabs so resent. Their borders, mapped out to meet the needs of the European imperialist powers of the nineteenth and early twentieth centuries, encompass groups possessing few of the commonalties demanded of nationhood. Complicating their futures, these artificial entities came late into the world of independent states. It was the mid-twentieth century before all of the Arabs of the *mashriq* broke the chains of colonialism. While the nations of Europe went through centuries of political experimentation and maturation before entering the twentieth century, most Arab states leapt within fifty years from being neglected provinces in the decaying Ottoman Empire to being colonies of Britain and France to becoming independent. While these fragile states were trying to take root, they were surrounded by debilitating regional instability that came out of the colonization of Arab land by an alien people and the rivalries of the superpowers.

In this environment created by outsiders, societies steeped in tradition and inexperienced in twentieth-century Western-style political systems faced the challenge of rapid modernization. Before that challenge, the Arabs themselves see the failure of their recent history. Within each of the states of the Arab world, neither the modernists nor the traditionalists have yet to resolve the question of the relationship between God and state in the twentieth century. Nor have they yet developed a form of nationalism that adequately defines the nation-state for the vast majority of people who still largely find their identity in family, clan, sect, and ethnicity. Government is still more of men than of institutions. As a result, strong men hold fragile nations together and drive them to satisfy their particular vision. It is for this reason that the following section of this book explores each of the current Arab states as well as the stateless Palestinians through a particular leader. Each of these men has operated or continues to operate in a region where ideology, systems of government, uneven distribution of resources, conflicting national interests, personal animosities between powerful leaders, and even the self-generated assurance of superiority of one nationality over another tear at Arab unity. In those rivalries, Arabism, rather than speaking to the wholeness of the Arab world, becomes a weapon that one state or leader wields against another.

Arab unity is real and it is myth. The Arabs are one in their deeply felt brotherhood, but at the same time, they live in societies and states that are in continual conflict. It is in this milieu that the proverb "My brother and I against my cousin, my cousin and I against the stranger" speaks of the myth of Arab unity rather than the reality.

PART II

THE REALITY
OF DIVISION

CHAPTER 6

NASSER: THE ARAB MESSIAH

IT WAS EARLY SEPTEMBER 1962, AND Cairo was flaunting its seductive powers. From a balcony on the fifth floor of the Nile Hilton, I looked out across the legendary river toward the great pyramid of Cheops and the lesser pyramids of Chephren and Mykerinos, rising like distant hills out of the surrounding desert. The Nile Hilton, a unique combination of classical Egyptian decor and American plumbing, reigned as the queen of Cairo's hotels. With its clean, modern lines and multistories of glass overlooking the Nile, it claimed status that Cairo's graceful old hotels could no longer match. But even more, the Nile Hilton reflected Egypt itself in the seventh decade of the twentieth century. The archways and fountain-cooled courtyards of the elegant old Mena House were places for sitting, for drinking in thousands of years of Egypt's history. In contrast, the balconies that hung from the Nile Hilton were for looking, for experiencing Egypt's present.

At just after four o'clock, an hour after Cairo awoke from its afternoon slumber, I began to hear from the street a chorus of voices rising and falling in measured cadence. Gradually the noise moved closer, and then it was upon me—"Nas-ser, Nas-ser, Nas-ser." From the hotel balcony, I watched hundreds of university students, mid-level civil servants, some shopkeepers, and a miscellany of unemployed march beneath me waving red, black, and green placards carrying the picture of a smiling Gamal Abdul Nasser. And then they were gone. It amounted to nothing more than another popular demonstration in support of Nasser. Yet it said everything about Egypt in the years when Nasser was just past the peak of his power. In 1962, the splendid, magnetic Nasser was Egypt, and with Nasser most Egyptians believed they had shed their past, found their present, and paraded toward their future.

However, in the years 1955 to 1967, Gamal Abdul Nasser was more than Egypt. For the masses of the Arab world, he was the embodiment of Arab nationalism, the pied piper of the Arab renaissance. He was the descendant of Khalid ibn al-Walid, "the sword of Islam," and of Salah-al-Din. Calling the Arabs once more to greatness, he rallied the masses against Western power injected into the Arab world by Napoleon and sustained by the hated Zionist usurper. In the magnetism of his rhetoric and his persona, Nasser promised to deliver the unity Arab history and culture seemed to demand. These were the years in which much of the Arab world believed Nasser would transform the mythology of Arab unity into political reality.

But Nasser was an Egyptian before he was an Arab. That which was specifically Egyptian had molded his political philosophy. It was conditions created by Egypt's long history of foreign occupation and repression that brought him to political power. And it was Egypt's interests, combined with his own lust for power, that turned Gamal Abdul Nasser into the Arab messiah. In the ruins of the Six-Day War in 1967, the Arab world discovered what many Arabs already knew—Nasser was less an Arab nationalist than a promoter of Egypt's particular interests. In the aftermath of that war, Nasser came full cycle. He dropped the banner of Arab nationalism to more firmly grasp the flag of Egypt.

Egypt is the Nile. In the thousands of years before the Aswan Dam harnessed its waters, the river set the rhythm of life. In June, it began to rise; by September it overflowed, inundating the surrounding fields; in mid-October it receded back within its banks; by late April it reached its lowest mark; and in June it began the cycle again. Rising in Wadi Halfa in the south, the river's gray-brown waters flow north for over a thousand miles, divide at the delta above

Cairo, and empty into the Mediterranean. Without a single tributary on its route across Egypt, the Nile creates a narrow fertile strip of habitation squeezed between two vast deserts. To speak of Egypt is to speak of fifteen thousand square miles, 5 percent of its land area, on which 98 percent of Egyptians are born, work, procreate, and die.

The river and its valley geographically and psychologically divide Egypt from the other Arab states. Unlike the Arabs, who until the mid-twentieth century lived in undefined or shifting administrative areas controlled by succeeding empires, Egyptians possessed a distinct national identity that reached back to 3000 B.C. In the earliest eras of man's recorded history, the people of the Nile produced a culture of astounding richness and variety. Under a succession of pharaohs, they built the pyramids, majestic temples, and imposing tombs that stretched for miles along the edge of the western desert. They sent seagoing ships into the Mediterranean, gave architecture the column and the colonnade, and impressed on religious thought the idea of judgment in the afterlife. That magnificent past can easily become lost in the grime, congestion, and decay of contemporary Egypt. Too often it is reduced to gaudy figures painted on shredding papyrus and cheap stone silhouettes of Queen Nefertiti that are thrust into tourists' faces by dirty, ragged, barefoot boys. These are paltry representations of a civilization that still sets standards for cultural achievement. The glory of ancient Egypt is found away from the crowded tourist sites, on the bank of the Nile opposite the Valley of the Kings. There a sloping bit of ground has escaped the relentless pressures of Egypt's constantly exploding population. And it is from there that it is possible to watch in solitude the feluccas silently pass by. Imposed against the low hills where Egypt's past is buried, the words of the French writer André Malraux come to life: "It was Egypt who invented eternity."

In 525 B.C., the pharaonic period died when Egypt fell to the forces of Persia. With its end, the Egyptians lost control of their political destiny but not their essence as Egyptians. In less than two centuries, Persian rule in Egypt fell to Alexander the Great. On his death, the Macedonian Ptolemy founded the dynasty that ruled to the death of Cleopatra in 30 B.C. During their reign, the Ptolemies adopted more of Egypt than Egypt adopted from Hellenism. And when the Romans came, they changed little beyond imposing another alien ruler class on Egyptian culture. Cultural invasion came more from Christianity than from Rome. And it was Christianity that provided the Egyptians a vehicle through which to express their own national identity within the Roman Empire. Much of the urban opposition to Roman rule came from the Alexandrian church. At the same time, the Christian church in rural areas in the Nile Delta revived Coptic, the last form of ancient Egyptian language. It is largely through the Copts that Christianity in Egypt survives. Today roughly 10 percent of Egypt's population is Coptic. Historically the Copts' influence has exceeded their numbers, giving Egypt a more dualistic society than is found in most other Arab countries. Yet Egypt has managed to escape much of the destructive tribal and sectarian divisions that plague so many other Arab countries. In spite of conflicts and tensions between Muslims and Christians, Egyptians are in essence a distinct and homogeneous population.

In A.D. 641, the Arabs invaded Egypt. Like other peoples touched by the Arab armies, the Egyptians embraced Islam and Arabic culture. Most of the population surrendered Coptic for Arabic, Christianity for the faith of Muhammed. Within a period of five hundred years, Egypt became Arabic in thought, belief, and tradition. By the ninth century, it had become an essentially Arab Muslim society, a center of Islamic-Arab culture. Yet fragments of Egyptian culture remained, ensuring Egypt's special essence.

Concentrated in the Nile Valley, separated from the Arab hinterland by the eastern desert, Egyptians generally see themselves as a part of the Mediterranean as well as the Arab world. As a result, they suffer from a degree of cultural ambivalence. They are Arabs and they are distinctly Egyptians. They are 90 percent Muslim and a fierce 10 percent Christian who see themselves more as Egyptians than Arabs. They are of the Arab world and they are of Egypt. Louis Awad, the cultural critic, once summed up the dilemma between the pull of the Arab world and the Egyptian sense of its own uniqueness: "Are we in Egypt going to be multicultural, to be party of the large body of humanity, or are we going to live in the isolated inferno called the East?"* Others may not say it so forcefully but they convey the same message. One cold winter evening, I sat in a small restaurant on the East Side of Manhattan with Camelia Sadat, Anwar Sadat's daughter by his first marriage. Conversation wandered

---

* Quoted in Lippman, *Egypt After Nasser*, p. 263.

through many subjects and finally touched on what it means to be Arab. Camelia hesitated and then said it was difficult for her as an Egyptian to discuss her feelings as an Arab. "You see, Egyptians are not Arabs at all. We belong to the Mediterranean." Many Egyptians, probably most, would argue with this perception. Yet there has always existed in Egypt a distinct sense of nationalism that sets Egyptians somewhat apart from their Arab identity. Bound to the Arab world by language and culture, Egypt has had a history that has differed markedly from that of the Fertile Crescent. And it is that historical experience which explains the rise of Gamal Abdul Nasser.

From the end of the last dynasty of the long pharaonic period until Nasser reclaimed the Egyptians' birthright, Egypt lived under one form of foreign rule or another.* Between 1250 and 1798, it was the Mamluks, "the possessed." Originally slaves brought from Asia Minor by Salah-al-Din to bolster his army, the Mamluks ended up supplanting his heirs. For five centuries, first as their own masters and then as surrogates for the Ottoman sultan, the Mamluks ruled the Egyptians. Following the French invasion of Egypt in 1798, they fell under the rule of Muhammed Ali.

Muhammed Ali came to Egypt in 1801 as a young Ottoman officer with the Albanian detachment in the Turkish expeditionary force sent against the French. By 1811, he was the outwardly loyal governor of the Ottoman sultan. In the 1830s, he revolted against Ottoman control, establishing a dynasty that would sit on the throne of Egypt until the 1952 revolution that brought Gamal Abdul Nasser to power. While ruling in the name of the Ottoman sultan, Muhammed Ali, competent, shrewd, and progressive, kept Egypt politically, economically, and financially independent. But in 1882, Ismail, grandson of Muhammed Ali, mortgaged Egypt to another suzerain—Britain. Ismail shared the great Muhammed Ali's vision of creating in Egypt the economic and cultural bridge between the Ottoman Empire and Europe. Unfortunately, the economic power bestowed on Europe by the Industrial Revolution made that bridge a one-way route for Europe's economic imperialism. The process was accelerated by Ismail's own economic excesses. When Ismail came to the throne in 1863, Egypt's foreign debt amounted to three million Egyptian pounds. Over the next twelve years, Ismail laid

---

* Politically, Egypt was ruled by others. Religiously, Egyptian Muslims felt part of both the Islamic and Ottoman empires.

railways, dug canals, and reclaimed land. To ensure his virtual independence from Constantinople, he sent millions of dollars' worth of gifts to the Ottoman sultan. Perhaps he could have sustained his expenditures on infrastructure and political autonomy if he had not layered on top his personal extravagances. Ismail swirled through European society in his frequent trips abroad scattering munificent presents, while at home he stocked his palaces with a vast array of treasures, including gold dinnerware encrusted with diamonds. In November 1869, he spent a million pounds on an extravagant spectacle to celebrate the opening of the Suez Canal. Empress Eugénie of France, symbolizing Egypt's tie to Europe, sailed aboard the first in a procession of sixty-eight ships through the canal and sat in Cairo's opulent opera house to hear *Rigoletto*, substituted when Verdi failed to finish the commissioned *Aïda* on time. By 1875, Ismail's drive to modernize and Westernize Egypt had driven his foreign debt to 68 million Egyptian pounds. The rhino whips on the backs of the *fallahin*, the peasants, could bleed no more money from those who had no more to give.

Ismail desperately needed money, and the only thing he had to sell was his 44 percent interest in the Suez Canal Company. It was marketable. Imperialist Britain, seeking to secure its vital line to India, lusted for a greater share in the Suez Canal. The Rothschilds, the great banking family, stepped forward and lent the British government the money to buy Ismail out. In that one financial transaction, Britain jammed its foot in the door of Egypt. By 1879, the rule of Britain had imposed itself on the Turko-Circassian line already on the throne, which in itself was theoretically tied to the Ottoman sultan. Now at least two layers of aliens separated the Egyptians from control of their own country.

Egypt of 1880 was dramatically different from Egypt of 1840. Ismail's love of European ways had imposed a Western aura on Alexandria and Cairo. With thousands of Europeans living in Egypt and the royal sons educated in Europe, Ismail had loved to say that Egypt was part of Europe. But Egypt was of the villages and of Islam and of its own special self.

In a sense, the 1952 revolution that would thrust Gamal Abdul Nasser into the center of Egypt's political life began in May 1882 when an Egyptian army officer named Ahmed Arabi demanded the return of Egypt to the Egyptians. Arabi's nationalist cry struck the deepest chords of Egyptian alienation. Within the cities, the populace flocked to Arabi and the army. On June 11, 1882, riots broke out in Alexandria, and several hundred people, including the British consul, were killed or injured. Using the security of the canal as the excuse to intervene, Britain injected a force of thirty thousand men into Egypt. Sailing up the canal, it engaged the Egyptians in the Battle of Tel al-Kebir. When it was over, ten thousand Egyptians were dead as compared to fifty-seven British. In the uprising, Tewfik, the reigning khedive, chose to stand with the British rather than the Egyptians. As a result, everything snapped into place, allowing Britain to turn Egypt into a colony. But to annex Egypt in the competitive fervor of late-nineteenth-century imperialism meant war with Britain's European rivals. Consequently, Britain ruled Egypt from behind the throne and a screen of Egyptian ministers in a system which even the British imperialists dubbed the "Veiled Protectorate."* British troops needed to ensure the British presence in Egypt would stay seventy-four years, finally withdrawing in 1956 after failing to topple Gamal Abdul Nasser in the Suez War.

Egyptian nationalism festered within the British protectorate. At the end of World War I, the nationalists petitioned Britain for permission to send a delegation to the Paris Peace Conference to present the case for Egyptian independence. Rebuffed by their overlords, they were sent into exile in Malta. Strikes by students and government officials engulfed Cairo and spread into the countryside, where the docile peasant momentarily laid down his hoe and raised his voice in protest. What is known as the 1919 revolution was the product of Egyptian society attempting to resurrect its spirit and civilization. Faced with a popular uprising it was not prepared to meet, Britain granted Egypt a measure of autonomy. In the aftermath, Egyptian nationalism flowered among the elite.

Between 1919 and 1930, a distinctive stream of nationalist thought developed in Egypt. Dividing from pan-Arab thinkers who propagated unity among Arabs across governmental boundaries, the "Pharaonists" postulated a specific Egyptian nationalism. Seeing Egypt as the "gift of the Nile," they argued that nowhere had territory defined a nation more definitively than Egypt. Despite its multiplicity of eras and diversity of regimes, Egyptians were a homogeneous people possessing a collective historical experience

---

* In 1914, when war engulfed Europe, Britain officially declared Egypt a British protectorate.

stretching back fifty centuries. For the Pharaonists, contemporary Egyptians, poor and downtrodden by generations of foreign rule, were nonetheless the direct descendants of the ancient Egyptians. All the characteristics and qualities that made the ancient Egyptians great still lay within their genes. The writer Muhammed Zaki Salieh proclaimed that "the blood of Ramses has not ceased to flow in the veins of Egyptians. These are not the assumptions of fantasies of writers, but scientific truths which many scientists are now accepting."* And Ahmed Hussein, a prominent writer among the Pharaonists, declared that "it is completely absurd to claim that Egypt is Arab, or that Egyptian blood has become Arab; its absurdity is confirmed by science and history. The contemporary Egyptian is Pharaonic by nature—so Pharaonic in his blood that no other blood has been able to overcome or influence this."†

Ideology became art as plays, operettas, and musicals such as *The High Priest of Amun* and the *Glory of Ramses* celebrated pharaonic themes. In 1923, Pharaonism hit its emotional peak when archaeologists uncovered the tomb of Tutankhamen. From beneath the dusty soil of the Valley of the Kings came the gold burial mask of the boy king, the exquisite statue of the goddess Selket, the alabaster urns, and beautifully executed chests. All confirmed once more the extraordinary heights to which ancient Egypt had ascended. For a people already stirred by the rising tide of nationalism, the treasures of Tutankhamen confirmed the greatness Egypt could once more achieve when it was shorn of foreign control.

Gamal Abdul Nasser fell under Pharaonist philosophy through Young Egypt, an organization founded in 1933 by the writer Ahmed Hussein. Although calling up a fanatic nationalism based on Pharaonism to revive Egypt, Hussein at the same time refused to deny Egypt's place in Islam. Influenced by pan-Arab thinking of the time, he put Egypt into the context of the Arab world. "Egypt is at the center of the Eastern world and the leader of Islam. It must be resurrected. . . . The task requires those who are prepared to die, suffer hardship and welcome sacrifice. These qualities cannot be found among the older generation. It is the youth, the new generation, soldiers of Young Egypt, upon whose shoulders falls the

---

* Quoted in Israel Gershoni and James P. Jankowski, *Egypt, Islam and the Arabs: The Search for Egyptian Nationhood, 1900–1930* (New York: Oxford University Press, 1986), p. 155.
† Ibid.

task of resurrecting our old glory."* The young Nasser listened and
prepared to one day lead the new generation to which Young Egypt
called.

Despite the romance of Pharaonism, Egypt in the 1920s and
1930s wallowed in corruption and confusion. Between 1922 and
1936, as Nasser grew up, three major political forces battled for
control of Egypt—the British; the nationalist Wafd Party, a bizarre
coalition of reformers and wealthy landowners who opposed reform;
and the king. The British, distrusting the nationalism of the Wafd,
attempted to bolster the king while the king hated the British almost
as much as the Wafd.

Fuad, the descendant of Muhammed Ali who sat on the throne,
provided no voice for the ills of his own population. Brought up in
Italy, he knew so little about the country he ruled that he never
became fluent in Arabic. When he died in 1936, he left his only son,
Farouk, a handsome, spoiled sixteen-year-old, to defend the throne.
Separated by position and wealth from his poor, populous country,
Farouk knew even less about the real Egypt than his father. Yet
when he ascended the throne he was received with wild enthusiasm
by the Egyptian masses as a new hope for the future. After all, he
at least felt at home in Arabic.

Farouk took up life as king in the same manner he had grown
up—isolated in palaces built by his predecessors. They still stand as
testaments to the dynasty of Muhammed Ali. Two particularly draw
razor-edged distinctions between the ruler and the ruled. Abdin
Palace in Cairo reflects the Western inclinations of the spendthrift
Ismail. Of cream-colored stucco with graceful porticos, its Italian
renaissance splendor sits among gardens dotted with towering
palms. And like Ismail, it is more of the Mediterranean than of
Egypt. Ras al-Tin in Alexandria was begun by the mighty Muhammed Ali in 1834 and served as the official summer residence of
his successors. The six tall granite columns once topped by the royal
crown of Egypt and bearing inscriptions from the Koran mark its
eastern gate. In Farouk's time that gate was always closed to the
ordinary of Egypt's people. In 1952, Farouk spent his last day as
king of Egypt at Ras al-Tin. When it ended, he descended the steps
on the palace's seaward side to leave Egypt forever.

Farouk, already fatally flawed by his own character, came to

---

* Ahmed Hussein, quoted in P. J. Vatikiotis, *Nasser and His Generation* (New
York: St. Martin's Press, 1978), p. 73.

the throne in a maelstrom of raging nationalism and chaotic politics. Alarmed by Mussolini's African ambitions, the British lion, the ultimate villain to the nationalists, reluctantly lay down with the Egyptian nationalists. In 1936, the Anglo-Egyptian Treaty gave Egypt full control of its government and limited the British occupation to ten thousand troops stationed in the Suez Canal Zone.*

A more subtle but as great a change in Egyptian politics came in 1937 when the military academy opened its doors to students from outside the landowning aristocracy. Gamal Abdul Nasser, the eldest son of a postal clerk from Assiut in Upper Egypt, entered with the first class. Unlike their aristocratic predecessors, members of the class of 1937 had tasted street politics and consumed a plateful of nationalist views ranging from the Muslim Brotherhood to European fascism. And all came into the academy nourishing bitter resentment against Egypt's whole decayed and corrupt political system, from the British to the king to the petty bureaucrats surviving on the favors of the privileged.

By 1950, Egypt was ripe for revolution. An immensely rich 2 percent of the population owning 50 percent of the land sat on top of millions of destitute, land-hungry peasants. Unable to survive in the villages, the landless flocked to the cities, where they clawed to survive, one stacked upon the other. While they scratched out an existence, Egyptian politicians representing the existing order squabbled and plotted against one another, leaving the country with no real leadership. At the same time, 200,000 foreigners engaged in business, commerce, and finance reigned as a privileged elite over a cadre of Egyptian entrepreneurs and a multiplying number of university graduates grabbing for a greater slice of a shrinking economic pie. On top of it all sat Farouk—corpulent, corrupt, and decadent—the symbol of everything plaguing Egypt. The country of the Nile awaited a new pharaoh who would purge Egypt of the old order dominated by the foreigners and the privileged elite.

In 1951, a half decade after the countries of the *mashriq* had gained independence, British troops still occupied Egypt. On the fifteenth anniversary of the 1936 Anglo-Egyptian Treaty, Egypt's seventy-four-year-old nationalist prime minister, Mustafa Nahas

---

* Britain reserved the right of reoccupation with unrestricted use of Egyptian ports, airports, and roads in the event of war. This right was exercised in World War II.

Pasha, twisted the imperialist lion's tail by demanding Britain pull its last 35,000 troops out of the Canal Zone and quit Egypt. Seizing Britain as a symbol, Egyptians poured into the streets to vent their raw emotions against colonialism, against economic deprivation, against the still palpable shame of the Arab defeat in 1948. Dependent on the Suez Canal as its lifeline to Middle East oil, Britain ordered its troops to don battle gear and the British fleet to steam full speed ahead from Malta toward Suez. Ismailia, in the heart of the Canal Zone, exploded. In restoring order British soldiers backed by British tanks attacked the headquarters of a lightly armed police unit, killing forty-six Egyptians in the process. Egypt screamed for revenge.

On January 26, 1952, legions of enraged Egyptians joined by a scattering of Arabs living in Egypt took to the streets of Cairo to destroy the symbols of Britain, ranging from the petty to the profound. Every bar that catered to Westerners was wrecked. Three British- and American-owned movie theaters disappeared in flames. Barclays Bank burned. Mobs invaded, vandalized, and finally torched the Turf Club, the playground of the British establishment. But the most symbolic casualty of the rampage was Shepheard's Hotel. The 350-room structure, a curious mixture of Western and Moorish architecture, had stood in the heart of Cairo's European district since 1891. For generations, the notables of the West had stopped there. Lord Kitchener came to Shepheard's after the Battle of Omdurman. Explorer Sir Henry Morton Stanley stayed over after finding Dr. Livingstone. And John Pierpont Morgan ate his last meal in the hotel's stately dining room. To the Egyptians, Shepheard's was the embodiment of British influence in Egypt. Now it was a smoldering, wasted ruin.

"Black Saturday," a day in which sixty-two people died and $300 million in property perished, failed to expel the British from Egypt. Instead it acted as the fiery prelude to the Egyptian army's coup against King Farouk, a revolution that changed the dynamics of the Middle East and delivered to the Arabs a new Salah-al-Din.

For months prior to July 1952, a group of military officers known as the Free Officers spearheaded by Gamal Abdul Nasser laid their plans. Lacking any firm organizational structure, the group had a core of perhaps a dozen, a second tier of fifty or so, and a third level that might have approached two thousand consisting of those who vaguely supported the goal of the Free Officers in overthrowing the government but held no formal membership in the group. Captains, majors, and lieutenant colonels ranging in age from twenty-eight to thirty-five, they claimed no common political ideology beyond raw nationalism. They were half-learned revolutionaries coming out of a confused mixture of religious faith, patriotism, and muddled notions acquired from fascist political pamphlets of the 1930s. But they had generational links. As part of the Egyptian military, they had fought in the Palestine war. And they had all suffered the humiliation of defeat, a defeat they laid at the feet of the politicians in Cairo. In toppling the corrupt government and removing the yoke of Western economic and military power, the Free Officers would liberate Egypt. Only then would thought be given to the strategies necessary to solve Egypt's myriad of other problems.

On the night of July 22, word came to Nasser that Egypt's military elite were meeting at general headquarters to plan their defense against the revolt brewing in their own ranks. Nasser, hurriedly driving his black Austin from unit to unit, alerted the conspiring commanders that this was the night the new generation would take Egypt. With a cadre of only ninety officers, the Free Officers seized general headquarters, military units, government buildings, radio stations, and telephone exchanges. At seven o'clock the next morning, Egypt was informed that the coup was completed. Anwar Sadat, chosen because of the quality of his voice, read the Free Officers statement. "People of Egypt. Egypt has lived through one of the darkest periods of history. The army has been tainted by the agents of dissolution. This was one of the causes of our defeat in Palestine. Led by fools, traitors, and incompetents, the army was incapable of defending Egypt. This is why we have carried out a purge. The army is now in the hands of men in whose ability, integrity, and patriotism you can have complete confidence."* Without knowing anything about the aims or intentions of the new government, Cairo erupted with joy.

The politicians of the old order would be systematically ousted. It began with the king. On the morning of July 26, the military regime delivered an ultimatum to Farouk, demanding his abdication. By six o'clock that evening, Farouk, his queen, his infant son,

---

* Quoted in Hugh McLeave, *The Last Pharaoh: Farouk of Egypt* (New York: McCall, 1969), p. 21.

and two hundred trunks containing the booty and the trivia of his reign boarded the *Mahroussa* at Alexandria. The 150-year-old dynasty founded by the Albanian Muhammed Ali had finally ended.

Egyptians for the first time in nearly 2,500 years ruled the land of the Nile. Through the reigns of ancient Persia, Greece, Rome, and the Byzantine Empire, on to the Arabs, Mamluks, Turks, French, and British, Egypt had been ruled by foreigners. Subjected to so many centuries of someone else's whip, the ordinary Egyptian had come to accept that the perverse hand of fate had relegated him in perpetuity to the status of vassal to whatever foreigner occupied the throne. Now the despised and decadent Farouk was gone, along with the vestiges of the old regime. But as Nasser mused in 1952, "Egypt cannot do without a king for long."* And Nasser intended to become the new king.

From the time the army moved against the government, Gamal Abdul Nasser was the driving force of Egyptian politics. The Free Officers, conspirators under the guiding hand of Nasser, became the Revolutionary Command Council (RCC), an oligarchy dominated by Nasser. Their charge was to chart the revolution—Nasser's revolution. Between 1952 and 1954, Nasser step by step consolidated his power. The army, purged of the old order within forty-eight hours of the revolution, was again purged six months later of those who might question Nasser's direction. In April 1954, General Muhammed Naguib, the respected elder of the Free Officers and the prime minister chosen by the RCC, was placed under house arrest. With Nasser as the new prime minister, political parties were abolished, opposition leaders put in prison, liberal newspapers closed, professional syndicates, trade unions, and student organizations emasculated or suppressed. By June 1956, Nasser held the title of president, the undisputed leader, the caudillo of Egypt.

Gamal Abdul Nasser was born at 18 Anawati Street, Bakos, Alexandria, on January 15, 1918. The death of his mother when Nasser was eight began a troubled childhood in which the young Nasser shunted back and forth between relatives, his father's house, and a series of boarding schools. It was at al-Nahda, a school known as a hotbed of Egyptian nationalism, that the political Nasser first emerged. At al-Nahda, one of his teachers resurrected Muslim he-

---

* Vatikiotis, *Nasser*, p. 124.

roes. Another wove the ideology of Pharaonism with its theme of Egyptian resurrection under an idolized, charismatic leader. By the age of seventeen, Nasser had become obsessed with the idea of the hero in the five-thousand-year history of Egypt. In letters to friends, Nasser poured out his passion. "Egypt . . . is in a state of hopeless despair. Who can remove this feeling? . . . Where is the man to rebuild the country so that the weak and humiliated Egyptian people can rise again and live as free and independent men?"* This vision of Egypt freed from foreign domination propelled Nasser through the military academy, into clandestine politics, and finally into revolution. The image of Egypt—proud, powerful, respected—drove him to leadership of the Arab world.

From the beginning, Nasser promised Egyptians *al-izza wa'l-karama*—dignity and self-respect. And dignity remained the central focus of Nasser's nationalism. In a speech on March 3, 1955, Nasser sounded the theme. "We are a people that never forgets if it has been injured, but the injury to us increases our determination and stubbornness."† In almost every address and interview in his eighteen-year political career, Nasser pounded home to his audiences that dignity required independence and independence required the final and total elimination of all foreign occupation and interference in the affairs of the Arabs. Depending on the year, the major culprit blocking Arab independence could be Britain, the United States, or Israel.

The paradox of Nasser is that until the fall of 1954, he was a shy, interior man who read wooden speeches to restless audiences. Then on October 26, 1954, as he was plodding through an address to an audience of ten thousand workers gathered in the open in Alexandria, a member of the Muslim Brotherhood named Mahmud Abdel Latif raised a gun and fired six shots directly at Nasser. Somehow they all missed. Suddenly Nasser, still standing in place on the podium, transformed into an orator. "O men, let everyone remain in his place. . . . my life is yours, my blood a sacrifice to Egypt. I speak to you with God's help after the mischievous tried to kill me. Gamal Abdul Nasser's life is your property; I have lived for you, and will do so until I die, striving for your sake."‡ The attempted

---

* Quoted in Anthony Nutting, *Nasser* (New York: Dutton, 1972), p. 7.
† Ibid.
‡ Quoted in Vatikiotis, *Nasser*, p. 144.

assassination of Nasser was precipitated by his crackdown on opposition political groups that forced the Muslim Brotherhood underground. This incident provided Nasser with the pretext for crushing the Brotherhood, the only remaining viable threat to Nasser's power. By ordering six Muslim Brothers hanged and several hundred arrested, Nasser effectively quelled the Brotherhood as a political force in Egypt. Gradually Nasser developed into a hypnotic speaker who combined neoclassical Arabic with the language of the man in the street and the peasant in the fields and added to them the chatty confidences of a father speaking to his family. As a result, he became the accomplished master of the spoken word, the most successful Arab communicator of modern time. In a culture in which language is magic, his voice was his power. Resonance, cadence, and image mesmerized people and pulled them to him. But Nasser delivered not only style but also a message.

Nasser was a nationalist in the image of the 1950s, when Nehru, Nkomo, and Sukarno railed against Western imperialism. And it was as an Egyptian nationalist that Nasser went to the conference of nonaligned nations in the sleepy West Java city of Bandung in April 1955. Courted by India's Jawaharlal Nehru and China's Chou En-lai, Nasser commanded center stage. When he spoke, he spoke not only for the Arabs but for the 1.4 billion have-nots of the world. When he said, "There is a striking similarity between the conditions prevailing in our countries; a similarity that operates as a unifying force, we have emerged from a long period of foreign influence, political as well as economic,"* Nasser sounded a clarion call against the West that rang through most Third World countries. In far-off Indonesia, Gamal Abdul Nasser resurrected Egypt to a place of prominence on the world stage and delivered to its people a dignity that they had hungered for for so long. As a result, he returned home a hero to his own people—the new pharaoh.

Nasser was to become the idol, the worshiped of "heaps of humanity without a mind or thought of their own, without an independent voice emanating from their gatherings. They became a collection of waving arms and applauding hands, and cheering mouths. And the Chief in his dominating presence, towering over them from his podium, spoke alone for long hours, interrupted only

* *Vital Speeches*, June 1, 1955, p. 1256.

by the hysterical cries: 'Nasser, Nasser, Nasser.' "* The adulation reached the point that whenever Nasser rode through the streets in his fin-tailed pink Cadillac convertible, near-hysterical men in the loose-fitting *galabia* of the peasant broke through police lines to climb on the car and embrace *al rais* (the boss). Out of the public adulation a cult of personality fed by his own propaganda machine coalesced around Nasser. At its peak, twenty-foot-high plywood cutouts would be lashed to Cairo's light poles showing Nasser—handsome, dashing, waving a hand to his adoring people—with a banner at his waist that read "Allah sent him to help our country."

In his new role, Nasser lusted for arms, arms he needed to replace an obsolete arsenal in order to face the challenge of Israel. Nasser's interest in arms was intensified by events in the Egyptian territory of Gaza, which Israel invaded and occupied in February 1955. Western sources of weapons had closed in 1950 with the Tripartite Agreement between the United States, Britain, and France. Attempting to reduce the threat of war in the Middle East, the three powers limited arms sales to both Israel and the Arab states. But by the mid-1950s the Tripartite Agreement was conveniently serving as the stopper on arms sales to Nasser and what the West regarded as his raging anti-Westernism. Then in October 1955, Nasser rocked the West by announcing that Egypt would buy arms from Czechoslovakia, the major arms manufacturer of the Soviet bloc of eastern Europe. The deal electrified the Arab world. By challenging the whole concept that the Arabs were a subordinate part of the Western system, Nasser launched the second Arab revolt. Yet for most of the Arab world's ruling regimes, Nasser was no more acceptable as a leader than the Sharif Hussein had been in the first revolt. Nasser was a revolutionary, anathema to the monarchies in Jordan, Iraq, and Saudi Arabia. He was anti-Western, upsetting the pro-Western, Christian government of Lebanon. For Syria, Nasser's gathering of power in Cairo meant diminished power for Damascus. But Nasser's appeal to the masses of the Arab world effectively neutralized his opposition at the top. In defying the West, Nasser overnight became the master of the Arab street.

By early 1956, a procession of ships carrying arms from the Soviet Union and the eastern bloc had landed at Alexandria. With

---

* Tawfik al-Hakim, quoted in Vatikiotis, *Nasser*, p. 291.

them came a whole new strategic scenario for the Middle East. In turning to the Soviets for arms, Nasser catapulted the Russians into Egypt and the Middle East into the framework of the cold war.

If Egyptian nationalism had propelled Egypt into the cold war, Nasser, a gifted politician, meant to make the most of it. In the intense gamesmanship of the 1950s cold war, the United States was pouring economic aid into Europe, Asia, and Africa to block the Soviets wherever they moved. Sensing the moment and patterning his moves after India's Nehru and Yugoslavia's Tito, Nasser played the United States against the Soviet Union. Dreaming of electrical power and irrigation from a dam across the Nile at Aswan, Nasser wrung a $70 million grant out of the United States' foreign aid budget. A shrewd negotiator, he cleverly delayed his acceptance and hinted that the Soviets were prepared to offer more. Then in March 1956 he upped the stakes by recognizing Communist China. John Foster Dulles, the American secretary of state, jerked back the aid package, and Nasser retaliated by nationalizing the Suez Canal, one of Europe's lifelines to Middle East oil. In taking the canal, Nasser trumpeted his theme of Egyptian dignity. "At the moment, some of your brethren, the sons of Egypt, are now taking over the Egyptian Suez Canal Company and directing it."*

While Nasser postured and the British and French threatened to rip Nasser's thumb from Europe's windpipe, John Foster Dulles labored to defuse a crisis caused in part by American ambiguity. But in October 1956, the interests of Britain and France in protecting the Suez Canal merged with Israel's interests in laying hold of the Sinai peninsula. The Zionist usurper joined hands with the Western imperialists in a war designed to topple Gamal Abdul Nasser.

On October 29, 1956, Israeli paratroopers rained into the Sinai desert near the Mitla Pass, only thirty miles from the Suez Canal. As they hit the ground, mobile columns of the Israeli army dashed toward southern Sinai and Britain issued its declaration—Britain and France would invade Suez to protect the canal. As the world cried collusion, a grim-faced Anthony Eden denied that the actions of Britain and the actions of Israel amounted to anything more than the pursuit by each of its own narrow interests.

Two days later, British and French jets pounded Egyptian air-

---

* Quoted in Robert Stephens, *Nasser: A Political Biography* (London: Allen Lane/ Penguin, 1971), p. 197.

fields and military concentrations, severing the main rail line from Khartoum to Cairo. Three days further into the crisis, British and French troops stormed ashore at Port Said while the Israelis launched an all-out attack along their entire front in the Sinai.

The air power of Israel and its Western allies rained destruction on Port Said, smashed Egypt's air force on the ground, and chewed up a quarter of Nasser's army. While Egypt headed toward defeat, leaders of most of the Arab states stood by and watched, satisfied that Nasser would be crushed before his broad popularity posed a threat to their own regimes. Only by blowing up his own ships to block the Suez Canal could Nasser retaliate against the onslaught of power far greater than his own.

However, the decisive battle of 1956 was not fought in the Canal Zone but in the United Nations. Dwight Eisenhower, enraged by the actions of the United States' allies, which he saw drawing the Soviet Union into the Middle East, threw American power behind a series of UN resolutions aimed at removing Israel and its Western allies from Egypt. Publicly he castigated Britain and France, and privately he informed Israel that it was alone if it annexed the Sinai. With the Western alliance strained to the breaking point, a gray and exhausted Anthony Eden led his French counterpart in agreeing to an immediate cease-fire on November 5. Israel resisted. On November 6, David Ben-Gurion thundered like a prophet from the floor of the Knesset, "And the words of Isaiah the Prophet were fulfilled. In that day shall the Egyptians be like unto women, and they shall tremble with fear because of the shaking of the hand of the Lord of Hosts which he shaketh over them." Sinai was Israel's. No one would force it to evacuate. Yet two days later, Ben-Gurion took the floor of the Knesset once more to announce the Israeli withdrawal from Sinai as soon as United Nations peacekeeping forces assumed their places.

Britain, France, and Israel had gambled on a quick knockout of Nasser. They failed. In essence, they won the battle of Suez but lost the war to control Nasser's passionate nationalism. American displeasure, the threat of Soviet intervention, and the moral indignation of a majority of the free world forced all three powers to pull back short of their objectives. But their real loss occurred on the psychological plane. Israel's 1956 collusion with Britain and France confirmed the Arabs' steadfast conviction that Israel was, as they had always believed, the handmaiden of imperialism, determined to hold the Arab world hostage to Western interests. The rhetoric of Gamal Abdul Nasser bore the truth. His hammering axiom that the eradication of imperialism demanded the destruction or dismemberment of Israel gained new passion. Rather than toppling Nasser, the three confederates in the Suez War birthed "Nasserism," the blend of Arab nationalism, anti-imperialism, the codewords of socialism, and the cult of personality built around Gamal Abdul Nasser. As foreign forces withdrew from Egypt, Nasser stood before Cairo's al-Azhar mosque to receive the adulation of hundreds of thousands of his frenzied followers. Beyond Cairo and Egypt, Arabs turned their eyes and their hearts to Nasser as the long-awaited leader capable of repelling the West.

In four years, Gamal Abdul Nasser had risen from an obscure lieutenant colonel in the Egyptian army to the undisputed leader of the Arab world. He began his career as an opponent of a weak and dissipated monarchy, emerged as a defender of Egyptian interests, established himself as the leader of the nonaligned movement, and now he was about to embark on a new era in which he would become the adored leader of a pan-Arab movement that reached from northern Africa to the border of Iran. It was an era in which his wishes and his priorities would set the agenda for both his allies and his enemies. For nothing that happened in the Middle East between 1956 and 1967 happened in isolation from Nasser.

Nasser unfurled his pan-Arab agenda at Port Said the day after the final withdrawal of the Anglo-French expeditionary force. His speech, a clever fusion of Islam and Arabism, spoke to a new, wider Arab constituency. Before Nasser, the doctrine of pan-Arabism had been the realm of the intellectuals and the elite. With the Suez victory, Nasser took the theory and emotional appeal of the Arab nation and gave it to the masses. Through his powerful oratory, he translated to the peasant, the laborer, the underemployed of the Arab world the excitement of transformation, the illusion of a better tomorrow. In so doing, he gave pan-Arabism its moment in the sun. In return, the Arabs helped create the Nasser myth.

The irony was that Nasserism came about as an almost accidental by-product of Nasser's success in moves and policies he had undertaken on behalf of Egypt's own particular national interests. Although Arabs from across the Middle East mobilized behind him and he reaped his greatest glory as an Arab leader, Nasser remained an Egyptian who coupled his pursuit of Egypt's national interests with pan-Arab themes. Yet as Nasser climbed to ever higher heights as the charismatic leader of the Arab world, he brought the Egyptians' faith in their special national identity into question. Egypt was the least Arab of the Arab states. In defiance of history and singularity, Nasser was calling on Egyptians to lose themselves in the greater Arab nation, to lay on the altar as a sacrifice to a wider Arab identity Egypt's unique perception of itself. Throwing away a whole school of Egyptian national thought, Nasser proclaimed, "Arabism not Pharaohism is our political ideology."*

In 1958, Nasser charged toward the pinnacle of his power by arousing Arab nationalism as no other leader before or since. He did it by commanding two potent weapons—an elaborate propaganda machine and a terrifying intelligence network. One sought control of the Arab streets, the other of governments or the machinery of state in Arab countries. Across the Middle East, cheap radios delivered into the hands of the masses by the technological revolution carried Nasser's words broadcast over his own radio station. The *Voice of the Arabs* reached from Morocco to Iran, from Cyprus to Portuguese Mozambique. On four wavelengths, it poured out Arab songs reverberating with the passion of the Arab cause and incendiary comment that rolled with the hypnotic insistence of a political muezzin. Words and music wove together to arouse within the Arabs all of their resentments against the old colonial powers. In his defiance or at least in his assertion of some equality with the "Franks," Nasser played to the deepest emotions of the Arab masses. Playing to Arab paranoia, Nasser dredged up the imagery of the Crusades as the beginning of the Arabs' dark ages and portrayed the United States and Israel as the modern successor to the Crusaders. He preached subversion, rebellion, intransigence, and hatred of "imperialists." He promised that Arab honor, honor destroyed by the West and its Israeli stooge, would be restored. Through Arab unity, the Arabs would once again take their exalted place within the world. "Follow me, follow me!" And follow they did. From the coastal villages of Yemen to the camps of the Palestinian refugees to the hallowed halls of the American University of Beirut, the image of the dashing Nasser plastered walls and bobbed among loud street demonstrations.

---

* Quoted in Vatikiotis, *Nasser*, p. 235.

Once Nasser controlled the streets, he moved to control Arab governments. Between 1959 and mid-1961, no Arab state escaped Nasser's attention and/or intervention. His agents plied every capital, and his shadow hung over every regime. Those who refused to embrace Nasser and his agenda lived in terror of revolt bubbling up from the streets. In his speeches, Nasser pumped out his poison against the Hashemite regimes of Iraq and Jordan, the "lackeys of Western imperial designs."* Squads of subversives directed from Cairo fanned out through Lebanon, Libya, Iraq, and Jordan carrying the message of Nasserism. Even the Baath Party, the keeper of the flame of Arab nationalism, embraced Nasser as its champion. Gamal Abdul Nasser became larger than life for both the Arabs and the West.

In early 1955, the United States, alarmed by Nasser's growing influence, had attempted to contain Egypt with the British-sponsored Baghdad Pact, a regional security agreement anchored in the pro-Western Hashemite regime of Iraq. With justification, Nasser screamed imperialism; yet in objecting to a Western alliance with an Arab country, Nasser was also denouncing the West's attempt to create a rival for his leadership of the Arab world. On February 1, 1958, Egypt and the Baathist regime of Syria stunned the West and the tottering anti-Nasser Arab regimes by announcing the union of Egypt and Syria into the United Arab Republic (UAR).† Nasserites from Amman to Aden agitated for their own country's unity with Nasser's Egypt. During May, Lebanon rumbled with strikes and protests against the pro-American policies of the Christian president Camille Chamoun while delegations from Iraq and Jordan joined Lebanese Muslims in trekking back and forth to Cairo for audiences with the revered Nasser. In July, Nasser's vendetta against the pro-Western king of Iraq came to fruition. In the early hours of the 14th, two Iraqi army brigades swept into Baghdad and surrounded the palace. The twenty-three-year-old King Faisal was killed in the act of surrender.‡

It was a moment of high triumph for Nasser. His most for-

---

* The thrones of Iraq and Jordan were still occupied by the descendants of the sharif of Mecca, installed by the British at the end of World War I. Both monarchies looked to the West for support in maintaining their regimes.
† See Chapter 10.
‡ See Chapter 11.

midable Arab rival had been eliminated and Iraq, once the keystone
of Western influence in the Arab world, had joined the neutralist
Arab states. Nasser, speaking in Damascus, declared that "Arab nationalism has at last been unchained. The Arab peoples are confident
of themselves and in their fatherland . . . The banner of freedom
will also fly high over Amman and Beirut."* But the following day,
five thousand American Marines stormed across the beaches of
Beirut. Amid the pleasure boats and the beachfront cafés, the
United States made its statement—Nasser would not topple the pro-
Western government of Lebanon.

In the summer of 1958, Nasser's Egyptian brand of Arab nationalism seemed close to a historic triumph. But then in September
1961, things began to unravel. Syria, unable to countenance Nasser's
obsession with power, seceded from the UAR. The following year,
Nasser put his army and his prestige into a tribal war with ideological
overtones in Yemen. Yemen, sitting on the tip of the Arabian peninsula, was the cellar of the Arab world. Backward, divided between
the southern coastal plain and the northern mountains, its internal
feud between the modernized lowlanders and the outmoded imam-
ate of the highlands meant little outside the politics of Nasserism.
This civil war in far-off Yemen, which Nasser cast as a struggle
between revolutionary Arab nationalism and a reactionary regime
backed by Saudi Arabia, promised to give him the opportunity to
restore the prestige lost with the rupture of the UAR. Instead it
sank him into a quagmire. Attacked by those tired of his meddling
in the affairs of sovereign Arab states and criticized by a new constellation of conservative regimes led by Saudi Arabia, Nasser by
1966 was in decline. In 1967, he fell off the precipice during six
days of war with Israel.

Nasser's attitude toward Israel was always linked primarily to
his pursuit of Egypt's interests. It was in this context that one of his
basic objections to Israel formed. The Jewish state towered as a
geographic barrier between Egypt and the Arab hinterland, denying
Egypt a land link with Syria. Otherwise, until 1954, Israel for Nasser
represented a satellite to the real threat to the Arabs—Western
imperialism. But once Nasser committed himself to an Egyptian-led
pan-Arabism, he was forced to promote the idea of the Arabs' "permanent struggle" against Israel. It was only then that Zionism trans-

---

* Stephens, *Nasser*, p. 290.

formed into the forward outpost of imperialism, the deadly threat to the Arab nation, and the alien intruder to be expunged from the Arab heartland.

Beginning in 1956, Nasser's speeches became consumed by the theme of Western imperialism's complicity with Zionism. Britain armed the Zionists and in so doing handed Palestine over to Zionism. The United States armed and aided Israel, enabling "world Jewry and Zionism to conquer a beloved part in the heart of the Arab fatherland, so as to be the tip of imperialism's bayonet inside the Arab nation, a source of danger and terror."* With the United Nations Emergency Force (UNEF) implanted on the Egypt-Israel border at the end of the Suez War, Nasser was allowed a decade of militancy without the risk of another military clash. But Nasser could not sustain "no war, no peace" forever.

Tangled in a war of wills since the Suez crisis of 1956, Israel and its Arab neighbors inched toward war. In this instance the Arabs were led more by the Baathists than by Egypt. In 1963, Baathism, the pan-Arab ideology propagated by Michel Aflaq, came to power in Syria. By 1966, a zealous and unpredictable regime in Damascus was charging Nasser had gone soft on the issue of Israel. Intent on precipitating war with Israel at any cost, the Syrian government ran or condoned commando raids across its border into the Jewish state. Fearing the price of war, Nasser tried and failed to put the brakes on the reckless men of Damascus. When Israel threatened Syria with retaliation, Nasser found himself forced to come to Syria's aid or watch his declining prestige drain away.

Nasser's enemies, sensing his weakness, jabbed their pins into the thin skin of the mighty man who had so long attacked them. Saudi radio gloated, "Anyone who imagines that Egypt will wage any kind of battle against Israel to defend Syria or anyone else will wait a long time."† And Jordan's King Hussein sniped at Nasser's duplicity in posing as the Arabs' champion while letting Israeli ships pass through Egyptian waters to their own southern port of Elat. Nasser found himself faced with the decision of entering the ring or losing his title. Since his enormous ego denied him the option of retiring, he charged ahead.

By the spring of 1967, Nasser's fiery rhetoric, guerrilla attacks

---

* Vatikiotis, *Nasser*, p. 252.
† Quoted in Patrick Seale, *Asad: The Struggle for the Middle East* (Berkeley: University of California Press, 1988), p. 129.

launched from Syria against settlements in northern Israel, and Israel's tough threats of retaliation propelled Nasser and the Arabs onward through a chain of events that led to war more rapidly than even the Syrians had foreseen. In June, a swaggering Nasser sent more troops into Gaza, trained guns atop the heights of Sham al-Sheikh on the narrow Tiran Strait, and boastfully declared the Gulf of Aqaba closed to ships headed for Israel's port of Elat. Rattling its own sabers, Israel angrily responded that a blockade of the Gulf of Aqaba constituted an act of war.

With the two sides at the brink, United Nations Secretary-General U Thant rushed to Cairo to see Nasser. When he arrived the quiet, bespectacled diplomat found himself running a gauntlet of workers outside Nasser's office chanting, "God is great, long live Nasser, Egypt will win."

The miscalculations had already begun. Nasser, who had repeatedly and publicly warned that the Arabs lacked the strength to challenge Israel, had made the first mistake by signing a mutual defense pact with rival Syria. Intended as a ploy to stop Syrian-sponsored commando attacks on Israel, the pact in essence made Nasser hostage to Syrian misadventures. Levi Eshkol, Israel's prime minister, made the second mistake by threatening war against Syria if those very attacks that so frightened Nasser did not cease. Syria, taking Eshkol at his word, ordered Nasser to honor their mutual defense treaty. Nasser, intent on remaining the Arabs' champion, had no choice but to comply with Syria's demand. But his ace in the hole was the UN peacekeeping force sitting since 1956 on his border with Israel. Nasser, maneuvering to force a crisis in which the United Nations would intervene to force a settlement, ordered the peace-keeping troops out. At this point, U Thant made the final mistake. To everyone's astonishment, the secretary-general, without consulting anyone else, complied. The border between Egypt and Israel was open. Syrian infantry and armor moved onto the Golan Heights. In Cairo, Soviet-built tanks and half-tracks rumbled through the streets en route to the rugged Sinai. Cairo radio trumpeted martial music and called the Arab states to join in the defense of Syria in the "sacred march on Israel" while the call of *jihad* rang out to the faithful from the mosques. Even cautious, Nasser-hating King Faisal of Saudi Arabia proclaimed that "any Arab who falters in this battle is not worthy of the name Arab."* King Hussein of Jordan, fearing

---

* *Time*, June 2, 1967.

revolt among his own population, swallowed his abhorrence of Nasser and entered a military pact with Egypt on June 1, 1967. As tensions built to their climax, Umm Khalthum sang in her smoky contralto,

> We are going back by force of arms.
> We are going back like morning after the dark night.
> Army of Arabism, may God be with you.
> Oh, how great, splendid and brave you are.
> The tragedy of Palestine pushes you toward the borders.
> All are with you in the flaming battle.

At dusk on June 5, 1967, Uzi-toting Israeli foot soldiers followed by half-tracks strung out along both sides of a dusty road leading into Sinai. Bored with routine patrol, they kicked at the dirt with their heavy boots to startle excited flocks of small birds out of the sun-bleached scrub. It was another ordinary day on Israel's borders.

Dawn broke on June 6. Before the blazing orange sun crested the rim of the Moab hills, Israeli fighter planes, one after another, streaked down long ribbons of runway and out over the calm, inky waters of the Mediterranean. One by one, they peeled off to the east and to the west, turned, and screamed back toward land. Dropping low, they unloaded their explosive cargoes on the airfields of Bir Gifgafa, Bir Hasana, Fayid, Ismailia, Helwan, Cairo, and Alexandria, wasting Egypt's Russian-supplied planes; on al-Mafraq and the air base near Amman, destroying the Royal Jordanian Air Force; and on Syria's lone airfield for fighter planes just north of Damascus. When it ended, 350 MiG-16s, Hawks, and a miscellany of other aircraft were splayed across their runways like so many smashed flies. Israel had destroyed the air power of the Arab states before most realized there was a war.

With Israeli fighter planes returning from their first bombing run, armored columns under the blue-and-white Israeli flag plunged south into the sands of the Sinai. The main force pushed toward the Suez Canal, along the same roads the Israelis had taken in 1956. A secondary force curled north to seal off the Gaza Strip. To the northeast, Israeli artillery laid a barrage on Syrian gunners perched on the commanding heights of the Golan above the Huleh Valley. And in the east, tanks rolled across the seventy-five-mile-long border of the West Bank, where they met Hussein's Arab Legion.

With no air cover, Egypt's army dissolved. By the second day of the war, ten thousand Egyptian soldiers lay trapped in a pocket along Gaza's border with the Sinai. All along the road to Suez, Egyptian prisoners by the thousands squatted on their haunches or lay flat on the hot ocher sand under the vengeful eyes of Israeli infantrymen. The rest, deserting their tanks, guns, sometimes even their shoes, fled in panic toward Egypt.

Only Jordan's Arab Legion, defending Jerusalem, stood effectively against the Israeli onslaught. Through the second day of the war, Jordanian artillery laid its shells on Jewish West Jerusalem. With terrifying force, they hit near Premier Eshkol's home, landed in the garden of the King David Hotel, and pierced one of Chagall's stained-glass windows at the Hadassah Medical Center. Yet while the Jordanians punished Jerusalem, Israeli air power pounded the poppy-studded hills of Amman and Israeli ground forces ceaselessly closed their three-pronged pincer around the Old City, house by house, block by block.

At dawn on the war's third day, Israel's final assault on the walled city of Jerusalem began. Busloads of Israeli troops slowly crawled up the piney slopes of Mount Scopus and the Mount of Olives. At the top, they waited while four Israeli jets dropped napalm canisters on Jerusalem's last Jordanian defenders. And then they moved. Approaching the thick stone defenses of the Old City from the east, the Israeli advance stopped at St. Stephen's Gate just long enough for a Patton tank to rumble forward, aim, and fire, reducing the ancient portal to rubble. Eager, shouting soldiers with the Star of David sewn on their khaki shirts poured through. Rabbi Shlomo Goren, chief rabbi of the Israeli army, followed, carrying the Torah. Within minutes, he was standing before the Wailing Wall. "We have taken the city of God. We are entering the Messianic era for the Jewish people."* And then he blew the shofar. The hated Israelis had conquered al-Quds.

On the fourth day of the war, a haggard and hollow-eyed King Hussein sued for peace. The subdued Gamal Abdul Nasser followed. Egypt had lost the Sinai and Gaza, Syria the Golan Heights, and Jordan the West Bank of the Jordan River. With it, Islam had lost Jerusalem. On June 9, the great charismatic figure of pan-Arabism

---

* *Newsweek*, June 19, 1967.

acknowledged a defeat larger in scope, more dramatic in impact than that of 1948.* Not only the achievements of Nasser's reign stood in question but the logic and symbols of an entire era of Arab political thought and practice.

The six days of the 1967 war marked the end of the Egyptian era of Arab politics. Egyptian pride in itself was forced back into balance with its limited material resources. In defeat, the aura of glory gave way to the certainty of poverty. Without Nasser as the Arabs' high priest, Egypt would no longer seem to mold the Arab nation to its will. And Nasser himself would face the reality of his shrunken stage. "Pushed against the wall, devoid of hope and resources, men and societies do not rebel: instead they give up, they surrender, they make compromises. And that is what Nasser had to do. . . . Nasser's game was to become purely defensive: how to deal with his own legacy and previous ambitions; how to shore up the popular will in the face of despair; how to absorb the frustrations and anger of youth; how to tackle the Israeli occupation, inter-Arab matters, and the frustrations of international diplomacy. His revolution, like him, was exhausted and finished."†

A part of Nasser died on June 5, 1967, but the living corpse somehow survived. Although the magic relationship between Nasser and the Arab masses formed during the glorious days of Bandung and Suez faded, he would stay in power as a tragic figure, a symbol of the Arabs' will to resist those they believe are intent on destroying them. In a sense, Nasser survived because he was all the Egyptians had. For eleven years, from 1956 to 1967, he had roused their passions and promised a better future. Thus in defeat, they still looked to him to pick up the pieces, to give meaning to the Arab disaster. Caught between those who wanted him to negotiate with Israel to end the turmoil between Arabism and Zionism and those who screamed for revenge and the recovery of honor, trapped between one superpower always ready to defend his enemy and the other superpower interested only in using him in its own service, Nasser walked a tightrope.

To recover Arab honor, Nasser had to recover Arab land. But he could not move the United States to pressure Israel to give up

---

* Although Nasser resigned on June 9, mass popular demonstrations on June 10 and 11 restored him to power.
† Ajami, *Arab Predicament*, p. 85.

its conquered territory nor withdraw from the Suez Canal without Arab recognition of Israel's existence. This the Arabs refused to do from the depth of their humiliation. Wringing more arms out of the reluctant Soviets, Nasser dug in for a war of attrition against Israeli forces along the Suez Canal. Probing raids against Israeli positions brought heavy retaliation, but they also bought time for Nasser to find some salve for the Arabs' damaged honor. In the bloody exchanges, Egypt suffered more than Israel. But Egyptian firepower inflicted enough casualties to cause the Israelis pain. By the summer of 1970, both sides were ready for compromise under the so-called Rogers Plan of the United States secretary of state. On August 7, 1970, the man who had assumed mythical and heroic proportions by defying the West accepted an American-sponsored cease-fire with Israel. Nasser had come to terms with those he loathed.

Gamal Abdul Nasser was politically debilitated and physically sick. He had suffered from diabetes since 1958. His health had started to deteriorate in the early 1960s, becoming progressively worse each year. The diabetes triggered arteriosclerosis. His upper legs, swollen and extremely painful, plagued him through many of the glory years. In 1965, he suffered a mild heart attack. In the summer of 1968, he spent several weeks in the Soviet Union undergoing hydrotherapy to shrink his swollen legs. In 1969, a more serious heart attack put him in bed for six weeks. All the while, he smoked as many as sixty cigarettes a day.

Nasser died of a sudden, massive heart attack on September 28, 1970, at the age of fifty-two. Ironically, he spent his final hours negotiating a cease-fire in the Jordanian civil war, surrounded by Arab heads of state, proving to his fellow Egyptians that despite the June War Egypt's primacy in Arab councils was still a reality.

On the day Nasser was buried, hundreds of thousands of Egyptians, clinging to the roofs of trains, loaded on ancient trucks, riding donkeys and bicycles, or walking on foot, flocked out of the delta, Aswan, and the upper reaches of the Nile toward Cairo. By the time Nasser's simple wooden coffin draped with the Egyptian flag was placed on a gun carriage, four million people lined the six-mile route from al-Qubbah Palace to the hastily completed tomb. Weeping hysterically, thrusting forth portraits of their dead leader, Egyptians said goodbye to the man who had given them a sense of pride. Somehow they knew that in their lifetimes it would never be recaptured. And so they mourned for Nasser, for Egypt, for themselves. A weeping government official perhaps said it all: "Nasser was everything to Egypt—friend, father, president, king, even our God. And now we are alone."*

If Nasser was a god, he was also a despot. A complex man, excessively secretive and cautious, he had no intimate friends. After his death, Anwar Sadat said of him, "It wasn't easy for Nasser to have anybody for his friend, in the full sense of the term, because of his tendency to be wary, suspicious, extremely bitter, and highly strung."† Throughout his life, Nasser seemed to constantly suffer acute feelings of shame and accept psychological enslavement to a highly exaggerated sense of dignity. Yet he remained in his tastes and living habits very much a simple man of the lower classes. He read no literature, only newspapers. His musical tastes were filled by the mother of Egyptian popular singers, Umm Khalthum, who groaned out the laments of her people. Alien indulgences entered his life only in the forms of tennis, American cigarettes, and the occasional Hollywood movie.

Nasser was not corrupt in the common sense of the term. A faithful husband and devoted father, he lived in a simple house in a Cairo suburb. Like most Egyptians, he ate native white cheese, cucumbers, tomatoes, rice and vegetables. Business ventures and land speculation were left to family and cronies. His one great indulgence was clothes, especially neckties. At least 250 hung in his closet. And like most Arabs who achieve a level of success, Nasser cluttered his bathroom with scores of bottles of colognes and perfumes. Nasser's vices were not material, they were psychological.

Nasser's political life amounted to a ceaseless quest for power. It was a quest in which he shut out personal relationships, crushed his political opposition, quelled potential opponents through a massive security force, and closed the political process to the people. Nasser always had to reign supreme, exalted as the reincarnated pharaoh. "Nasser in Egypt came closest to being a Kingfish. He appeared to the people as the virulent xenophobe, the skilled politician most readily identified with the poor downtrodden rural and urban masses, the rabble-rousing anti-Establishment man, the affable demagogue who welded together a fanatically loyal following

---

* *Newsweek,* October 12, 1970.
† Sadat, *In Search of Identity,* p. 101.

to his own person; the captain who constantly rhetorically inquired of his team if he had kept faith with them and they hypnotically yelled back in unison in the affirmative."*

Despite his revolutionary aura, Nasser's regime did little to change the deference of the lower orders to the upper ones. Nor did he eliminate exploitation. The old ruling class simply gave way to a new class of his sycophants. "Socialism" under Nasser accomplished little beyond destroying the landowning elite, decimating the small commercial bourgeoisie, and firmly establishing an unrivaled—almost militarized—public sector in the state economy. Like an eighteenth-century Mamluk, Nasser built a pyramid of intelligence and security services connected under the feared Mukhabarat. His political prisons—the Citadel, Abu Zaabal, Tura—held those who refused to take part in the acclamation of Nasser. Thus Nasser, in quest of his personal power, failed his own revolution.

That leaves the question of whether or not Nasser ever believed in the doctrine of Arab nationalism. On his own terms, yes. But in the final analysis, Nasser's Arab nationalism was more a tool to promote Egypt's leadership of the Arab world than an ideological commitment to the united Arab nation. Nasser believed that an Arab world free of foreign influence would allow Egypt a leading role in its affairs and destiny. And as leader of Egypt, Gamal Abdul Nasser would himself lead the Arab nation.

The Nasser era was a mixture of Egyptian nationalism and Arabism. They came together in Nasserism, becoming the Arabs' modern-day grand epic.† For many Egyptians, Nasser died a pharaoh, a god-king, the worshiped idol of the nation. But after his distinctive voice was silenced by death, little remained of his ideas, his views, and especially his resentments.

In a country that has produced the greatest monuments in human history, almost nothing can be found of Nasser. The billboards and plywood cutouts that celebrated his reign disappeared within a year of his death. Today only a few in Egypt know or care

---

* Vatikiotis, *Nasser*, p. 349.
† On the death of Nasser, Muammar Qaddafi took up the call of Nasserism. Claiming that Nasser had designated him the trustee—*al-amin*—of Arab nationalism, he was furious when the Arab world went through a period of de-Nasserization following Nasser's death. In 1980, Qaddafi made an offer to pay Egypt $500 million to allow Nasser's remains to be moved to Libya to be entombed in a shrine for the faithful.

where to find his grave. In a country that fused itself to Nasser's person, there is a street here and there that bears his name but little more. It is almost as if Nasser never existed. His memory lives in faded, fly-specked photographs hung on the walls of dilapidated apartments in the working-class sections of the cities and in Lake Nasser, behind the high dam at Aswan built during the years Nasser so effectively defied the West. The old photographs continue to decay and the lake to fill with silt. Someday they too may be gone.

CHAPTER 7

KING HUSSEIN: THE ENDURING MONARCH

THE FIRST TIME I SAW KING HUSSEIN, he sat at the center of a large stage, engulfed in a high-backed chair with his small feet lined up precisely on a low, square stool that put him in contact with the floor. His posture was erect, drawing every millimeter out of his five-foot-three frame. When he spoke, his deep, resonant voice belied the 125 pounds or a little more that produced it. As I sat listening to the very proper editorial "we" of royalty, I could not help speculating that if King Hussein met the devil himself he would undoubtedly extend to him that same exquisite politeness and perfect demeanor that so characterize the public man. Yet behind the studied grace, Hussein reflects in his dark, brooding eyes a deep melancholy born of four tumultuous decades on the throne of Jordan.

On May 2, 1953, Dwight Eisenhower sat in the White House; Winston Churchill presided over 10 Downing Street; Charles de Gaulle brooded in Colombey-les-deux-Églises waiting for the call to lead France; Gamal Abdul Nasser gathered the reins of power in Cairo; and Hussein ibn Talal at the age of seventeen rose from a satin chair to take the oath of allegiance as king of Jordan.

After the simple ceremony, the boy king rode through the

streets of his capital in a blue Lincoln convertible. Wearing a blue uniform with gold epaulets, Hussein followed ranks of Bedouin warriors mounted on white chargers proudly bearing the pennants of the Arab Legion. As the procession passed beneath the triumphal arches of wood and paper that spanned Amman's modest streets, excited, flag-waving Jordanians poured out their affection for the thirty-third-generation descendant of the Prophet Muhammed. It boded well for the waiflike king. But within the diplomatic corps, the survival time of "the plucky little king" was estimated at perhaps a year.

It was not only the king's youth that challenged his survival, it was also the nature of his kingdom. Barely larger than South Carolina, three-quarters desert, denied by providence almost all natural resources, Jordan eked out a living from the phosphate industry and subsidies doled out by the British government. Split into two territories—the East Bank and the West Bank, separated by the shallow Jordan River—its population of two million fractured into thirds. On the East Bank, a people with Bedouin roots saw themselves as the true Jordanians, the loyal subjects of their king. The Palestinians, settled in the towns and villages on the West Bank, looked to Jordan and Hussein as little more than a way station to their undefined future. Across both banks, the refugees of the war for Palestine caged in camps considered Hussein and his kingdom part and parcel of their bitter plight. It was a heavy burden for an adolescent, and it has never gotten better. Hussein has spent almost forty years politically trapped between his own concept of his duty to hold his country and his throne for the Hashemite dynasty and a Palestinian population that has never been reconciled to his rule. Economically, he has struggled with a land without resources and a nation always at the edge of the financial abyss. Diplomatically and militarily, he has battled a host of forces that he can sometimes contain but never neutralize. Following a lonely and difficult path, Hussein has survived by defending the particular interests of his dynasty within the ideological demands of Arab unity. By standing apart when possible and entering the Arab tent when necessary, Hussein has outlasted Eisenhower, Churchill, and de Gaulle, the British colonialists and Gamal Abdul Nasser. But with each passing year, the forces undercutting his kingdom and his throne move farther beyond his control. Becoming less the player and more the victim, he must constantly respond to the policies of others—the

Arab states, Israel, the United States and its Western allies, and finally his own Palestinian population. In the end, neither the man nor his kingdom may survive.

Within its boundaries, Jordan lays out an extraordinary mosaic of the past. Amman, resting in a bowl created by seven surrounding hills, dates back to the Bronze Age. In Biblical times it was Rabbath. But the drama of Jordan's Biblical past plays itself out on Mount Nebo, west and south of Amman. From the summit of a steep hill rising out of barren nothingness, the whole Jordan River Valley presents itself—from the Sea of Galilee in the north to the Dead Sea in the south. Between the two, the Jordan River draws a green belt in the otherwise desolate landscape. It is at this point that Judeo-Christian tradition holds that Moses first saw the "land of milk and honey."

In the time of the Romans, Jordan formed part of the rich granary that sustained the empire. The weathered stones of the six-thousand-seat Roman amphitheater still whisper of the time when Amman, then known as Philadelphia, ranked high among Roman cities. But the queen was Jerash, twenty-three miles north of Amman. To enter Jerash is to enter into the grandeur of ancient Rome. The triumphal arch of Hadrian leads inward to the towering Co-rinthian columns that delineate a circle three hundred feet in diameter at the center of the city. The baths, the markets, but most of all the wide cobblestone streets still bearing the ruts of a thousand chariots wheels raise the ghosts of Roman power at the frontier of its empire.

To the south toward Aqaba, the Nabataeans, who monopolized the rich caravan trade between the Arabian interior and the coast of the Red Sea, established their own grandeur during the third century B.C. in the harsh desert near Petra. Beyond a final bend in the high red sandstone walls of Wadi Musa, through a passage just wide enough to clear a horse and rider, the dry riverbed widens to present its gift of porticos, columns, and cupolas etched in the towering walls. In the twelfth century, the Crusaders came and built their own monument—the castle at Karak. And then the Ottomans came and Jordan sank into oblivion.

By the nineteenth century, Jordan simply existed as a remote, formless corner of the Ottoman Empire. It was an unnamed wilderness where perhaps 350,000 people either worked the land around the northern hilltowns of Irbid, Ajlun, and Salt or roamed

the south as nomadic Bedouin. Steeped in conservatism and traditionalism, farmer and Bedouin idled in their own ignorance, barely
touched by events in the Levant. The First World War and the Arab
Revolt held no relevance for them until these events paralyzed trade
and visited on the landscape hunger and disease. When the British
arrived in 1920, what is now Jordan knew little of being governed.
Untamed, living under the Bedouin mandate of absolute freedom,
the territory newly designated by the British Colonial Office as
Transjordan refused to submit to Britain as it had refused to submit
to the Ottomans. It yielded finally to the Hashemites, first Abdullah
and then Hussein.

In November 1920, Abdullah, the second son of the sharif of
Mecca and the man who argued the Arab cause at Versailles, climbed
aboard the old Turkish rail line at Medina and headed north. When
the little steam-driven train pulled into the station at Maan in southern Transjordan, Abdullah, accompanied by three hundred men
and six machine guns, stepped out on the platform and announced
his intention to conquer Syria in the name of his brother Faisal.*
Without an army, military ingenuity, or any real will to march to
Damascus, Abdullah settled down in Maan to compose delicate Arabic poetry, play chess, and build a political base. In March 1921,
he moved north to Karak, where the British resident, confused about
what to do with a Hashemite prince, greeted him in the name of
the crown. Donning British protocol like a cloak of political recognition, Abdullah descended on Amman, where he summoned the
Bedouin tribal leaders to declare that he intended to become their
new king. For the Bedouin, Abdullah's lineage established his
legitimacy.

Moon-faced with a hint of an epicanthal fold, sporting chin
hair and a turban, Abdullah looked more like a descendant of
Genghis Khan than the Prophet. But as a member of the Bani
Hashem clan of the Quraysh tribe, Abdullah traced direct descent
from the Prophet Muhammed through his daughter, Fatima, her
husband, Ali, and their martyred son, Hussein. And it was the Hash-

---

* Faisal, Abdullah's younger brother, had claimed the throne of Syria and the
British government, embarrassed by its own double dealing in World War I,
recognized his interim government. But at the second round of double-dealing
after the war, France gained suzerainty over Syria and ousted Faisal. See Chapter 10.

emites who had presided over the Hijaz as guardians of Islam's holiest sites since the thirteenth century. Reflecting the region in which his genealogy lay, Abdullah, although a ceaselessly cheerful extrovert, was a staunch traditionalist, deeply imbued with the morals, mores, and values of Bedouin society. Thus charm, heredity, and the time he had spent in Maan combined to give Abdullah the support of the Bedouin tribal sheikhs. Securing the allegiance of a force of eight thousand armed men, he presented Britain the solution to its concerns about governing this wilderness with a minimum of men and money.

Winston Churchill, Britain's new colonial secretary, drew the boundaries of Transjordan and put Abdullah "temporarily" in charge with an annual British subsidy and British advisers. Writing to General Gouraud, the French governor of Lebanon, in March 1921 Churchill explained, "I have made an arrangement with Abdullah of an informal and temporary character whereby he is to use his whole influence to prevent any disturbances in the French zone arising out of Transjordania."* By 1923, the arrangement between Abdullah and his British patron had become permanent.

When Abdullah took charge, the Bedouin were the dominant force in the confusion of Transjordan. And it was in the best Bedouin tradition that Abdullah ruled his kingdom. A son of the Hijaz, a field commander in the Arab Revolt, he understood how Bedouin loyalties worked. The men of the desert demanded accessibility to those who wished to lead them, and they expected generosity in return for their loyalty. Therefore Abdullah spent what money he could scrape together buying the allegiance of the sheikhs. If he could not buy them, he fought them. And when he came to form an army, it was from the Bedouin that he took his recruits. In return, the Bedouin developed a fierce devotion to their king, one of their own stock, a descendant of the Prophet himself. When Hussein became king, the tie between the Bedouin and the Hashemites passed unbroken.

One day in the late 1970s, I was traveling the long ribbon of highway from Amman to Aqaba. Off the road in the distance, I saw a black goat-hair Bedouin tent hugging a low, barren hill. It was an

---

* Quoted in Anne Sinai and Allen Pollack, eds., *The Hashemite Kingdom of Jordan and the West Bank* (New York: American Academic Association for Peace in the Middle East, 1977), p. 328.

increasingly rare sight in an era when economics and government policy were pulling the Bedouin out of the desert and into the towns. I slowed, hesitated, and then stopped the car. Quickly covering my hair with a scarf, I began a careful approach toward the ramparts of the camp. As I got nearer, I saw a wizened old woman wrapped in an *abbaya* sitting on a worn rug shuttling thick skeins of odorous black goat hair through dozens of strands of warp loosely tied to a beam supported by two large rocks. I could hear the men over the next crusty hill rounding up strayed sheep. As I looked around it seemed they had left only one old man, dangling a withered arm, with the women.

No one enters a Bedouin camp without elaborate preparation. I extended a whole string of greetings, commented on the commanding view from the top of the hill, and complimented the family's fine stock of animals. After carefully weighing his decision, the camp's defender called for cushions and tea and motioned me to sit down. The conversation wound around for some time before I could come to the central question—what is life like for you under the Hashemites? He paused, adjusted his position against the foam-rubber bolster he lay against, and then answered, "Bedouin are too proud for the politics of the cities. We ask only to be free, to live in the open. Abdullah understood this. Hussein understands this."

By the early 1930s, Abdullah had put his stamp on Transjordan by building Raghadan Palace on a hill north of Amman and beside it a small house where his grandson Hussein was born in 1935. For a Hashemite, Amman represented a humiliating comedown from the cities of Mecca and Medina. With no status derived from either religion or geography, it was nothing but a small town on the desert focused around the old Roman theater. Perhaps because of the modesty of his capital and his kingdom, Abdullah never learned to love this rocky, desolate land as Hussein loves it. For Abdullah, Transjordan was always a wilderness that provided him the kingdom fate had decreed to him. Proud of his race and descent, Abdullah believed as Hussein believes that the Hashemites are destined to rule. Thus Transjordan represented only the first link in Abdullah's grand plan to resuscitate the Islamic caliphate. Abdullah envisioned gathering Transjordan, Palestine, Syria, and Lebanon under the Hashemite crown. The idea of this "Greater Syria," which Abdullah called "that great half moon which opens on two seas," infuriated the French ensconced in Syria and Lebanon, the Syrian nationalists who held their own vision of Greater Syria, and Haj Amin al-Husseini, the grand mufti of Jerusalem, whose own flaming ambition was to rule Palestine. The opposition did little to dampen Abdullah's determination. So obsessed with his dream of empire and talking of it so much, Abdullah prompted a story to circulate in Amman's souks that claimed that the king's old one-eyed cat Kutna ("Fluff") would yawn and walk out of the room at the mention of the words "Greater Syria."

Abdullah coveted Palestine above all else, and for Palestine he was willing to sacrifice the sacred unity of the Arabs. In the interim between the United Nations vote to partition Palestine and the British withdrawal, Abdullah declared, "I must hold strategic positions in Palestine. These are indispensable to Transjordan, both from military and economic points of view. I cannot give up Mediterranean ports in Palestine. I have rights and claims in Palestine without which Transjordan cannot live."* To win those positions in Palestine and to shut his despised rival Haj Amin out of Palestine's political constellation, Abdullah struck a deal with the Zionists. If war came to Palestine, Abdullah would not lend his Arab Legion to the Arab forces if the Zionists, for their part, would stand aside to allow the Hashemite king to annex the territory assigned to the Arabs by the 1947 United Nations partition plan.

As the war for Palestine built, the thirteen-year-old Hussein watched his grandfather Abdullah dance around the Arabs and court the Zionists. And when war broke out between the new state of Israel and the Arabs, Abdullah annexed the West Bank of the Jordan River, including Hebron, Jericho, Nablus, and East Jerusalem. Shedding the shackles of Arab unity, Abdullah faced the Arab League's threatened expulsion of Jordan for his duplicity. Abdullah essentially had to choose between the lesser of two evils—isolation in the Arab world or the territories he had occupied in Palestine. He chose to preserve his gains in Palestine. Demonstrating little respect and less confidence in the Arab leaders arrayed against him, Abdullah proceeded to cement his relations with Israel and his new Palestinian subjects.

In December 1948, Abdullah convened a body of pliant Palestinians in the Jericho Congress. Endorsing Abdullah's contention

---

* *Time*, February 16, 1948, p. 36.

that Palestine and Jordan shared historical connections, the Palestinian delegates granted Jordan's king full authority to represent them. The congress was rigged. The Palestinians were deeply divided in their attitudes toward Abdullah's role in their political future. But in 1948, many Palestinians were willing to accept Abdullah because they had nowhere else to go. Count Folke Bernadotte, the United Nations mediator for Palestine, had reported in September 1948, "The Palestinian Arabs have at present no will of their own. Neither have they ever developed any specially Palestinian nationalism. The demand for a separate Arab State in Palestine is consequently relatively weak. It would seem as though in existing circumstances most of the Palestinian Arabs would be quite content to be incorporated into Transjordan."*

Thirty years after the Jericho Congress, I stood at the ancient ruins of Jericho and looked across a shallow wadi toward the crumbling mud-walled cubicles that once housed thousands of Palestinian refugees who fell under Abdullah's control. Row after row of huts, divided from their neighbors only by lopsided walls defining a little space, crawled up the bare, treeless hill. In 1948 these empty shells had teemed with angry, confused refugees adrift between the hated Israel and the scorned Abdullah. They were now empty, their inhabitants pulled into the economy of the West Bank or pushed onto the East Bank. Standing on that deserted place, I mentally bridged the years. With the gift of hindsight, this abandoned camp became a graphic statement of the forces that Abdullah through his cunning incorporated into his kingdom.

Almost immediately, Abdullah's subjects divided between Jordanian and Palestinian. And the change in the name of the country, in June 1949, from Transjordan to the Hashemite Kingdom of Jordan, was only a reflection of Abdullah's pride in the expanded size of his country rather than a coming together of the people within those expanded boundaries. By 1950, Abdullah and the Jordanians felt the full impact of 900,000 West Bank Palestinians and almost 500,000 Palestinian refugees. Palestinians granted full citizenship by Abdullah in 1948 now outnumbered Jordanians two to one. Since very few Jordanians lived west of the river, the electric social tensions between the native Jordanians and the incorporated

---

* Quoted in Avi Plascov, *The Palestinian Refugees in Jordan 1948–1957* (London: Frank Cass, 1981), p. 10.

Palestinians concentrated on the East Bank, where Abdullah's original subjects held the population edge. There hostilities festered against the Palestinians, many of whom, as ripened products of the Levant, quickly moved into the professional classes, became merchants, landowners, artisans, and shopkeepers. Plowing a wide economic gap between themselves and the less skilled Jordanians, the Palestinians became unwelcome guests guilty of depriving the Jordanians of their status and rights as masters of their own country. The Palestinians for their part felt little in the way of gratitude or loyalty to Jordan. Those with education and skills established a stake in Abdullah's kingdom. Yet, regarding themselves as infinitely superior to the Jordanians, middle- and upper-class Palestinians, drawing on the Arab imperative of honor, considered it inconceivable that they should be governed by "a Bedouin." The rest of the Palestinians—the unskilled, often illiterate, and always poor segment of the refugees—did not even feel the allegiance to Abdullah born of economic interest. Seen as the handmaiden of Israel, the source of their catastrophe, he was nothing but another foreign ruler.

As for Abdullah, he neither trusted nor particularly respected the Palestinians. Yet at the same time, his political and territorial interests demanded that he build some base among those who, at the least, disdained him. Drawing some support from privileged Palestinians, Abdullah attempted to erase any sense of separate Palestinian identity within his kingdom. Palestinian history and culture as well as the Palestinian flag were banished from the schools and public forums. In defense of his own interests, Abdullah renounced Palestinian separatism as a "blow to the meaning of the sacred unity in the conscience of every Arab."* Yet Haj Amin al-Husseini, seething in exile, would not let Palestinian identity die.

On the hot summer day of July 20, 1951, Abdullah left Amman to go to Jerusalem for Friday prayers. He knew of a plot to kill him. Both the American and British ambassadors had begged him not to go to Jerusalem and especially not to al-Aqsa mosque. But Abdullah knew he could never cement the West Bank to the East Bank by cowering in Amman.

Just before noon, Abdullah, wearing a spotless white *thobe* and

---

* Ibid., p. 29.

beige ankle-length *bisht* (cloak), and fifteen-year-old Hussein, dressed in a military uniform, slipped off their shoes at the door of al-Aqsa as they prepared to join four thousand other Muslims in prayer. They had just crossed the threshold when Mustafa Shukri Asho, a tailor's apprentice who belonged to Haj Amin's "Forthcoming Salvation Army," stepped from behind an iron grille and pumped five bullets from an American-made automatic weapon into Abdullah's face and chest.* Within seconds, panic-stricken worshipers rushed forward, trampling the body of the fallen Abdullah underfoot. Arab Legionnaires, assigned to guard the king, waded into the melee, firing guns and slashing with bayonets. In their frenzy, they killed at least twenty bystanders. At last, Abdullah's pierced and broken body, wrapped in a bloodstained carpet, was carried out of al-Aqsa. Behind it, John Pasha Glubb, the British adviser to the Arab Legion and intimate friend of Abdullah, led the young, shaken Hussein from the scene and back to Amman.

In the aftermath of Abdullah's assassination, the festering resentments between Jordanians and Palestinians broke open. Arab attacked Arab as Palestinians bearing arms in the name of Haj Amin fled into the northern hills and the Arab Legion followed. The adolescent Hussein, wearing the red-and-white-checkered headdress of the Bedouin, toured the East Bank to shore up support. In the custom of the desert, he courteously called on the local sheikhs, dispensing favors among those whose loyalty would be decisive in the future. But it was Talal, Hussein's father and the eldest son of Abdullah, who was king.

Lonely and moody, Talal was a schizophrenic who periodically flew into fits of uncontrolled rage.† In May 1952 at a quiet dinner party in the palace, the king suddenly jumped from his chair, swept the tablecloth along with the dishes and glassware off the table, and turned on his wife, striking her across the face. Bundled off to Paris, the sad Talal sometimes escaped his attendants to wander alone while his frantic family and entourage searched the streets. On August 11, 1952, the parliament, recognizing the seriousness of his condition, deposed him. Abdullah's other son, Naif, who lacked

* The last bullet hit Hussein and ricocheted off a medal pinned to his uniform.
† The night Queen Zein gave birth to a daughter, a screaming Talal rushed into her hospital room. Wielding a knife, he tried to kill his wife and newborn to repent for bringing a child into a disordered world.

statesmanship and drive, and devoted himself to chasing women, was deemed unfit to rule. Thus at the age of sixteen, Hussein ibn Talal became king of the Hashemite Kingdom of Jordan. A brief regency and a stint at Sandhurst got Hussein to the age of seventeen, eighteen as reckoned by the Islamic calendar, when he stood before his subjects to take the oath as king. Thrust into adulthood by fate, he never experienced an adolescence.

Hussein is as melancholy and introverted as Abdullah was cheerful and extroverted. He is haunted by a deep sense of fatalism that comes from knowledge born of eleven documented assassination attempts that his odds of perishing exceed his odds of surviving. Yet he boasts a natural confidence in himself as a king that manifests itself in a powerful sense of honor and discipline.

Aside from his regal demeanor, little that is royal surrounds Hussein. He grew up in a house with little heat and only one bathroom. At the age of ten, he was forced to sell his British-made bicycle because his family needed money. Today what he calls his palace is a modest complex of low-lying buildings held together by a series of unexceptional gardens. The one touch of majesty in Hussein's environment is the ceremonial Circassian guards who patrol the halls in magnificent fur hats, high boots, and black uniforms with silver daggers sheathed at the belt.

As a direct descendant of the Prophet and the great-grandson of the man who ignited the Arab Revolt, Hussein by lineage is among the most Arab of all the current rulers in the Middle East. Yet he is the most Western. His English is impeccable, the result of an education provided by a Christian missionary school in Amman, Victoria College in Alexandria, Eton, and, of course, Sandhurst. Two of his four wives have been Westerners, and all were educated in the West.*

---

* At the age of nineteen, Hussein married his cousin Dina Abdulhemied, whom he divorced eighteen months later. In 1961, he astonished his Arab subjects by marrying Antoinette Gardiner, the daughter of a British army officer serving in Jordan. Known as Princess Muna, she was divorced in 1972. The same year he married Alia, the jet-setting daughter of a notable West Bank Palestinian family named Tuqan. A graduate of New York's Hunter College, she was the first of Hussein's wives to carry the title of queen. In February 1977, she was killed in a helicopter crash. Hussein married Lisa Halaby, an American and a graduate of Princeton, in June 1978. As Queen Noor, she is the most politically active of his wives. Hussein and Noor have four children. He has seven other children from his previous marriages.

Yet Hussein seems to encompass the very soul of Abdullah. Like his grandfather, Hussein believes it is the Hashemites' destiny to rule. In profound ways, belief in the survival of the Hashemite line and the family's divine duty to guide a poor, basically defenseless country through the treacherous shoals of Middle East politics has propelled Hussein through almost forty years of conflict and crisis.

Hussein is a monarch in a region struggling with the pains of modernization. He rules an artificial country in which most of the population considers itself distinctly Palestinian, not Jordanian. He lives wedged between Syria on the north, Saudi Arabia on the south, and Iraq on the east. To the west he faces the most powerful military force in the Middle East—Israel. Although his grandfather's violent death warned him that direct negotiations with Israel without Arab sanction spelled death, Hussein inherited enough of Abdullah's realism to acknowledge that a tacit acceptance of Israel is the only rational policy if Jordan is to survive. But survival also challenges Hussein to endure the blows Arab politics and Arab emotions thrust at him. In pursuit of his own interests, Hussein has more often than not swum against the current of Arab politics. At the same time, he has assiduously protected his Arab credentials in order to remain part of the Arabs' encompassing identity. It has never been easy, nor will it ever be. Over the years, in hundreds of interviews, Hussein has sounded one constant theme: "I am pessimistic."

From the beginning of his reign, Hussein as king of Jordan faced a series of interrelated needs. He had to reconcile the Jordanians and the Palestinians. He had to keep his country economically afloat with the largess of British aid. He had to maintain a Western alliance that would protect his small kingdom from its more powerful Arab neighbors. And he had to play to Arab nationalism while at the same time keeping himself out of its wake. All of these factors collided in the era of Gamal Abdul Nasser.

Hussein was only twenty years old when he confronted the passion of Nasser's Arab nationalism. While Nasser railed against Western imperialism and made his arms deal with the Soviet Union, Hussein remained dependent on British advice and British subsidies to keep his Bedouin army and his kingdom afloat. Labeling Hussein an anachronistic tool of the imperial West, Nasser vowed to drown him in Arab nationalism. Thus when John Foster Dulles lay the Baghdad Pact before him in 1955, Hussein saw it as a natural refuge for a conservative monarch facing an impassioned revolutionary movement. But nothing is ever natural in Jordan. While the East Bank Jordanians supported an alliance between the kingdom and the West, the Palestinians of the West Bank and the refugee camps pulsated to Nasser's rhetoric. In its golden age, Radio Cairo vented its wrath against the Hashemite king, branding Hussein a "whore" and a "prostitute" to the desires of the West. In late 1955, mobs of schoolchildren, incited by their teachers, rampaged through the streets of both the East Bank and West Bank armed with the slogans of Nasser's revolution. Off the streets, their parents plotted the fall of the government. Hussein stood at the brink. Recognizing that he could call on no Arab government for help, he summoned the British. Anthony Eden ordered parachute battalions to Cyprus and dispatched Vampire jets to Amman. On the ground in Jordan, Hussein's Bedouin of the Arab Legion cleared the streets with tear gas and warning shots. But before he became irretrievably entangled with his Western protector, Hussein struck a deal with Nasser that allowed him to get back into the Arab fold. If Nasser stopped his propaganda attacks against Hussein, Jordan would stay out of the Baghdad Pact. Hence Hussein saved himself in the first episode in what would prove to be an ongoing battle between Nasser of Egypt and Hussein of Jordan. From 1955 until both were brought to their knees by the 1967 War, Nasser postured and threatened while Hussein ducked and maneuvered in a contest of interests and wills. At stake for Nasser was his vaunted prestige as leader of the Arab world; for Hussein the stake was the survival of the Hashemite throne.

In 1956, Hussein at the age of twenty-one again became wedged between Arab nationalism and his Western patrons. Although he had refused to join the Suez War, its aftermath forced Hussein to jettison his British benefactor. In shucking Britain, he also shucked a little over half of Jordan's total budget, cash crucial to maintaining the bulwark to the throne—the Arab Legion. Money thus became an obsession for a country chronically dependent on foreign aid. Arab aid was ephemeral—floating before the beleaguered king and then disappearing when he reached out to grasp it. And American aid carried with it the same stench of Western collusion as British aid. To provide a cover under which he could escape the charge of collaboration with the West and still receive American arms and money, Hussein went on the offensive against "Godless communism" as a menacing threat to Islam and Arab culture. With U.S. interests and Jordanian interests on parallel tracks,

American aid and weaponry moved in as the guarantor of the Hashemite regime. By the summer of 1958, the twenty-three-year-old Hussein had committed Jordan to an American alliance and the full force of Gamal Abdul Nasser's fury.

Nasser was riding the crest of his power, molding Arab politics to his needs and desires. Calling Hussein "that idiot dwarf in Amman," Nasser pronounced the political sentence of death on the Hashemites. Going beyond politics, Nasser's followers goaded on those who murdered Hussein's cousin, the king of Iraq. That brought American troops into Beirut to shore up Lebanon's pro-Western government and by implication Hussein in Jordan. With oil shipments from his Arab neighbors suspended under pressure from Nasser, Hussein was under siege. Elite units of the Arab Legion formed a protective ring around the entire city of Amman. At night, companies of Jordanian soldiers armed with clubs, riot shields, and Sten guns bedded down on roofs of public buildings. During the day, they drilled, often to the music of Scottish bagpipers. In an arrangement that was both humiliating and dangerous for Hussein, American oil and British paratroopers came in by air over Israel. In the end, Hussein persevered. By October, the crisis subsided. The British troops went home and oil tankers once more docked at Aqaba. But Nasser's disciples did not forget Hussein's treachery. On November 10, 1958, they reached out from the Syrian sector of the Egyptian-controlled United Arab Republic.

Hussein was flying his Dove aircraft over Syria en route to a European vacation when Damascus ordered him to land. Turning the controls over to his Scottish pilot, Hussein watched the plane dive out of radar sight, skimming the ground at two hundred miles an hour, and racing two Syrian MiG-17s to the border of Jordan. The incident was only the beginning of an insidious campaign by Nasser to rid Jordan of its king.

Between 1958 and 1960, Hussein's life lay in the hands of Arab nationalists wedded to Nasser. Within his palace, Hussein's cook was uncovered as an agent of Nasser's after he killed fifteen palace cats experimenting with various doses of poison. Someone else put acid in the king's nose drops only to be discovered when a housekeeper who was pouring the remains of one bottle into another bottle noticed the sink corrode. Plots were also afloat outside the palace. By stopping to review the site of the new university of Amman, Hussein missed a bomb carried into the prime minister's office, where the king was to meet with the eleven people killed when it exploded. With each incident, Hussein's fury against Nasser increased and his search for protection became more desperate. While carefully playing to the rhetoric of Arab unity, he laid his alliances elsewhere.

By 1960, Hussein was boldly projecting himself as the West's bulwark against the pounding waves of Nasser's militant anti-Westernism and Soviet arms shipments to the Arab world. Playing on fears of communism, which was as dreaded by Muslims as by the West, Hussein put himself at the center of American policy in the Arab world. As a result, a grateful United States injected money on a regular basis into the Jordanian economy. The new source of money and a defensible image as the Arab champion against creeping communism made Hussein's life a little easier.

Hussein had even worked out a palatable response to Arab nationalism. Opposing Arab unity in the sense of one Arab state, Hussein passionately promoted the view that the ideal of Arab unity could best be served by preserving existing Arab frontiers. Picking up a theme similar to that of Egypt's Pharaonists of the 1930s, Hussein eloquently argued that Arab strength lay in diversity, that the mix of monarchies and republics gave strength and vitality to the whole of the great Arab nation.

During the early 1960s, even the internal dynamics of Hussein's kingdom improved. Palestinian refugees were increasingly leaving behind the grim environment of the camps to join the economic mainstream. Although in small numbers relative to their percentage of the population, Palestinians entered the ruling establishment. As prosperous suburbs built with Palestinian money went up around Amman and Jerusalem, it seemed that Hussein, given enough time, might actually be able to turn Palestinians into loyal Jordanians.

But Hussein could only pacify, not escape, his Palestinian population. In 1964, Gamal Abdul Nasser conceived the Palestine Liberation Organization, the structure under which the dispersed Palestinians would gather.* Hussein reluctantly went along on the condition that the PLO not become a rival to Hussein's authority over the Palestinians in Jordan. What he failed to secure was the promise that Jordanian territory would not be used for Palestinian guerrilla raids into Israel.

---

* See Chapter 12.

Commando groups operating from the West Bank pierced the Israeli frontier, inflicted their damage, and withdrew back into Jordan. Fearing reprisals, Hussein put his Bedouin army on the border to intercept guerrillas passing between Jordan and Israel. Hussein's army ultimately killed more Palestinian commandos than the Israelis killed, but that was not enough for an Israeli government intolerant of the limitations under which Hussein ruled. Just as the sun broke on November 13, 1966, an Israeli force of four thousand men and five Patton tanks rumbled toward the West Bank village of Samu. In the name of security against commandos, Uzi-wielding Israeli soldiers herded Samu's frightened citizens into the streets. While they watched, Israeli demolition squads systematically destroyed houses, a clinic, a school, and the village's mosque. Then the Israelis withdrew, leaving behind eighteen dead Palestinian subjects of King Hussein.

The West Bank thundered with denunciations of Hussein for refusing to attack Israel. Egypt and Syria took up the cry. Overnight, the pent-up grievances of the Palestinians against Hussein's regime exploded. His enraged Palestinian subjects took to the streets, tearing the king's photographs from public places and ripping them to shreds as they screamed their recriminations against the Hashemite throne. As demonstrations turned into riots, Egypt, Syria, and the PLO danced around the flames engulfing Hussein. While his Bedouin army stamped out the anarchy, Radio Cairo shrieked "whoremonger" at the embattled king.

The last thing Hussein wanted was war with Israel. Like Abdullah before him, he sought accommodation with the Zionist state. But after Samu that option vanished, at least in the short term. With the full support of the Arab world, Jordan's Palestinians were baying for Israeli blood. Hussein could do nothing beyond distributing yet another load of American weapons to the Arab Legion.

During the 1960s, Hussein painstakingly tended the morale and welfare of his troops. Almost any given week in Amman presented an opportunity to follow the king as he worked his military constituency. It was always an interesting spectacle to observe the bonding between ruler and defenders that was the purpose of these occasions. Donning aviator glasses to protect his eyes from the blazing sun, Hussein would watch the air force streak through the sky in training exercises. Wearing the *gutra* and *igal* of the Arab Legion, he pinned insignias on new graduates from the military academy.

Less frequently, he dropped out of the sky in a helicopter to join night patrols along the frontier. The king lavished time, attention, and money on his military forces because these forces, crowned by the Bedouin of the Arab Legion, were Hussein's only weapon against his host of enemies. But not even the Arab Legion could protect Hussein from events whirling beyond his control.

During the spring of 1967 as Nasser bluffed his way to the brink of war with Israel, Hussein became caught as never before in the snare of Arab unity. Popular will, especially on the West Bank, demanded that Hussein support Nasser's challenge to Israel. Facing his fate, Hussein knew that if Nasser went to war he would have to follow or face a civil war with the Palestinians within his own borders. At the end of May 1967, Hussein surrendered and entered the lion's den with Gamal Abdul Nasser.

In the early morning of May 30, thirty-two-year-old King Hussein of Jordan climbed behind the controls of a Jordanian Airlines Caravelle and took off for Cairo. Two Royal Air Force Hunters escorted him to the border. Then he flew on alone. When he arrived in Cairo, Nasser joked about Hussein's military uniform and revolver strapped at his waist. The grim-faced soldier-king retorted that he had been dressed that way for a week.

Hussein had sustained years of insult over Radio Cairo. Now he faced Nasser directly. What happened next cannot be explained even by Hussein himself. Nasser suggested that a pact be drawn up "between our two countries right here and now." Someone was dispatched "to find the file containing the bilateral defense pact between Egypt and Syria which had bound the two nations together since April. I was so anxious to come to some kind of agreement that I merely skimmed the text and said to Nasser: 'Give me another copy. Put in Jordan instead of Syria and the matter will be settled.' In an atmosphere of growing relaxation and cordiality, Nasser agreed, and a little later, I signed."[*]

With the stroke of a pen, Hussein committed himself to a five-year defense pact that would put an Egyptian general in charge of his precious military forces if war came. Radio Cairo immediately broadcast the news, upgrading Hussein from a "Hashemite harlot" to a hero.

---

[*] Hussein of Jordan, *My War with Israel* (New York: Morrow, 1969), p. 46.

Hussein flew back to Amman the same day. When he emerged from his plane, thousands of demonstrators who had rushed in from every corner of Jordan raced to greet their king. He escaped into his car only to have the mob lift it in triumph. To the man on the street, the king had mounted the obstacles to Arab divisiveness.

In 1967, Jordan only fought a three-day war. By the early afternoon of the first day, Israel had destroyed twenty-one of Hussein's twenty-two Hunter fighters. Israel had not wanted war with Jordan any more than Jordan had wanted war with Israel. Although Premier Eshkol sent a message to Hussein through the United Nations commander in Jerusalem to the effect that Israel would not initiate hostilities against Jordan if Jordan did not attack Israel, the message did not reach Hussein in time. As a result, the first wave of Israeli air attacks left Hussein with only his ground forces.

Four infantry brigades held the West Bank. Two more armored brigades lay back, one at the Damiya Bridge over the Jordan River and the other at Jericho. The rest of the army was on the East Bank. Under the terms of Hussein's agreement with Nasser, all of them were under the command of the Egyptian general Abdel Moneim Riad. On the second day of the war, Riad became pessimistic, urging Hussein to withdraw all his forces to the East Bank and sue for peace. Hussein refused. Riad ordered withdrawal, and Hussein countermanded. Jordanian soldiers, pulled between two commanders, retreated and advanced, sometimes fighting, sometimes surrendering to the confusion. The crucial unit holding Jerusalem's walled Old City evacuated, leaving only a handful of men behind as snipers. On the third day of the war, Hussein lost Jerusalem and all of the West Bank. His need to evince loyalty to the Arab cause had cost him the legacy of Abdullah. Populous Arab towns like Bethlehem, Hebron, Ramallah, and Nablus passed from Jordan to Israel. And Jerusalem, including the sacred Dome of the Rock, slid from the grasp of the Hashemites.

Hussein's sense of shame and despair was terrible to behold. Seldom out of uniform, he constantly traveled his kingdom accompanied by a heavy bodyguard of Bedouin troops. Emotional stress caused him to grind his teeth so badly that by January 1969 he was forced to undergo a jaw operation in London. As Hussein suffered, so did Jordan. Politically, the June War shoved into the kingdom another 255,000 Palestinian refugees, who came toting the baggage of their rage. Socially, Jordan lost the better-educated, more industrious West Bankers, who were the backbone not only of Jordan's civil service but of its intellectual life as well. Economically, 85 percent of the kingdom's agricultural yield and 48 percent of its industrial output vanished with the West Bank.

Jordan's economy was shattered. To save what was left of his kingdom, Hussein had to have new infusions of money. While holding on to his Western aid, he gleaned another roughly $112 million from Libya and the monarchies in the Persian Gulf. And he wooed his educated population toward jobs in the Persian Gulf's oil states in order to generate cash that would flow into Jordan's ailing economy through remittances. Gradually Hussein restored a precarious economic balance. But it was no substitute for his precious West Bank.

Hussein desperately wanted to open negotiations with Israel that might return his territory. Yet he could not openly meet with the Israelis outside of an Arab conference. The publisher of an Amman newspaper explained why: "The minute the king sits down with the Jews, he signs his death warrant. He'd be killed by some Palestinian just as surely as his grandfather was."*

Hussein, imperiled so many years by the radicalism of Nasser, now faced the radicalism of the Palestinians. Discredited by the defeat of 1967, the leadership of the PLO put in place by Nasser gave way to the commando organizations that had been running guerrilla raids into Israel. The *fedayeen*, the "men of sacrifice," became the Arabs' unspent hero, the new icon of Arab unity. With the Fatah organization of Yasser Arafat leading the way, the commandos settled on Hussein's kingdom like a plague of locusts. Erecting new fences of barbed wire and placing *fedayeen* carrying automatic weapons at the entrances, the commando organizations shut Jordanian officialdom out of the Palestinian camps. Step by step, they took full control of these camps, establishing a state within a state in Jordan. Rejecting Hussein's reminders that Jordan had given the displaced Palestinians vastly greater opportunities than they enjoyed in other Arab states, the *fedayeen* mounted a virulent propaganda campaign against Hussein's attempts to subject them to Jordanian rule. By the beginning of 1968, Hussein faced twenty thousand armed commandos and a population that was 50 percent Palestinian.

---

* *Newsweek*, July 24, 1967.

As Hussein struggled to hold his authority, commandos toting their automatic weapons turned up on the streets of Amman and other towns throughout Jordan. Timid at first, by the autumn of 1968 they strutted about jostling Jordanian soldiers and policemen, many of whom had Bedouin roots and abhorred the town-bred *fedayeen*. Hussein reacted to the commandos' audacity by instituting roadblocks and vehicle searches, bringing down on his head *fedayeen* allegations that he intended to stop commando operations against Israel. Undeterred, the king sanctioned press gangs of Jordanian soldiers to pick up Palestinian youths from the streets and dispatch them to remote desert camps to keep them out of the ranks of the guerrillas.

If the *fedayeen* movement had been a unitary bloc, perhaps King Hussein and Yasser Arafat could have struck a compromise. But Arafat and Fatah were only an anemic majority within a movement split between personalities and ideologies. While Arafat was content to coexist with Hussein, the destruction of the Hashemite regime lay at the very core of the leftist ideology of other factions within the commando movement—the Popular Front for the Liberation of Palestine (PFLP) and the Democratic Front for the Liberation of Palestine (DFLP). A confrontation with Hussein, the "reactionary," the "slave to Western imperialism," the "Zionist puppet," was not only desirable but an ideological necessity for those who combined Marxism with the crusade to return to Palestine. With tensions between Hussein and the commandos running high, George Habash of the PFLP sent his supporters into the streets chanting, "The road to Jerusalem goes through Amman."

Hussein and the commandos circled around each other throwing exploratory jabs. In December 1969, commandos stopped the king's wife, Princess Muna, as she was driving through Amman and held her until urgent appeals of the royal guard secured her release. On February 10, 1970, Hussein issued an eleven-point decree banning *fedayeen* weapons in the towns and ordering the commandos to license their vehicles and carry identity cards. It was enough to ignite a four-day riot that left eighty people dead and the guerrillas in control of half of Amman.

In late June 1970, Hussein's army and the *fedayeen* clashed again when a guerrilla shot a Jordanian army officer of the Saiqa regiment, a unit especially faithful to Hussein. The next day the Arab Legion wreaked its revenge against guerrilla encampments, and the commandos fought back. Violence between Hussein's army and the *fedayeen* rolled across the landscape as the fighting spread toward Amman. On July 9, 1970, the king evacuated his summer villa outside Amman and raced toward the capital. Rounding a bend in the road, he drove into an ambush of Palestinian commandos firing a Russian 50mm machine gun into his motorcade of six armored Land Rovers and the king's Mercedes. Thrusting his gun from the window of his car, Hussein fired back. Finally, he escaped by opening his door and rolling toward a ditch along the road. The next day, the army answered the insult against their king by laying barrages of artillery shells on Palestinian camps.

Hussein had lost control of his kingdom. In the escalating violence, the Popular Front for the Liberation of Palestine invaded Amman's imposing Intercontinental Hotel and grabbed sixty-two foreign guests as hostages. The youngest son of Lebanon's former president Camille Chamoun, fourteen Americans, a covey of Europeans, and a smattering of other nationalities huddled in the hotel's basement, where they lived on hamburgers, cold beer, and ice cream until *fedayeen* rockets hit Amman's principal power station. The leftist commandos also took the Philadelphia Hotel with another fifteen hostages before moving on to attack the Amman radio station. Their fury mounting, they stole cars and looted houses. And then they struck at Hussein's patron—the United States. PFLP commandos seized Morris Draper, the first secretary of the United States embassy, on his way to a dinner party and murdered Robert P. Perry, a thirty-four-year-old Arabic-speaking U.S. Army attaché, when he answered the door of his apartment.

Hussein vacillated between two poles—accommodation with the commandos and all-out war. But the decision was not Hussein's alone. His proud Bedouin army, humiliated by badgering inflicted on it by the *fedayeen*, edged toward mutiny. When Hussein inspected an armored unit at Zarka, one of the tanks flew a brassiere from its radio antenna, a scathing statement of an army that thought it was being treated like a woman. Back in his palace, the thirty-four-year-old king endured the cursing and then the pleading of his generals to unleash the army on the *fedayeen*. An obviously depressed Hussein told a dinner party, "I cannot hold my army much longer."*

---

* *Newsweek*, September 18, 1970.

Hussein's decision was forced on September 6, 1970, as TWA's around-the-world flight 741 hummed over West Germany. At the Luxembourg border, commandos jumped from their seats and ordered the pilot to turn toward the Mediterranean. Hours later the Boeing 707 circled in a black night sky over Jordan. Suddenly, flaming oil drums and jeep headlights pointed the way down to the rock hard desert floor. It touched down and bumped to a stop on a deserted World War II airstrip known as Dawson Field. In another forty minutes, the engines of a Swissair DC-8 commandeered west of Paris sounded in the same night sky. Men running with flaming torches again lighted the drums of oil and the headlights switched back on. The plane came down, rolling to a stop a mere fifty yards from the 707. Three days later, a BOAC VC-10 hijacked between Bahrain and London took its place on "Revolution Airstrip."

In the ensuing crisis over the fate of three planes and 439 passengers, it was as if the Jordanian government no longer existed. Even the Red Cross negotiators dealt directly with the commandos, not the government. At a news conference, a PFLP spokesman identified simply as Bassam said, "The government can do nothing to stop us. If they move the army closer to the planes, they will be responsible for the consequences. We are calling the shots in Jordan, not the government."[*] On September 12, the PFLP released all but fifty-six of the hostages. In the final act of the Dawson Field drama, the hijackers blew the three explosive-laden planes into the unclouded sky. The freed passengers went to hotels in Amman, and the remaining hostages disappeared into the Palestinian camps, spending the last nine days of their captivity in the midst of war between Hussein and the Palestinians.

On September 16, 1970, King Hussein went on Amman radio to declare martial law. "It has become our duty to take a series of measures to reestablish law and order to protect the lives, property, and honor of all citizens."[†] "Black September" had begun.

Amman shut down. Shopkeepers rolled heavy shutters down over their shopfronts and hurried home. Buses and taxis parked. Police abandoned their posts. The airport closed. Just before dawn broke on September 17, fifty tanks of Hussein's Arab Legion

[*] Edward R. F. Sheehan, "In the Flaming Streets of Amman," *New York Times Magazine*, September 27, 1970, p. 27.
[†] *Newsweek*, September 28, 1970.

and scores of armored personnel carriers pulled out from the multimillion-dollar sports stadium at the eastern edge of the city and began rolling into the city. Within minutes, the long dusty columns were rumbling into the narrow streets of Jebel Amman and Jebel Wehdeh and spreading out over the seven dun-colored hills of Amman. In a city built of limestone, the mechanized army cleared its path with a blistering hail of artillery shells that smashed into the Palestinians' entrenched positions and leveled entire buildings in order to put a single rooftop sniper position out of commission. The outgunned *fedayeen*, fighting from sandbagged buildings and street barricades, retaliated with hails of machine-gun fire and antitank rockets.

Hussein expected his lightning thrust to produce a victory within hours. The war had to be short, because a long conflict against the current symbol of Arabism threatened to bring united Arab opinion down on Hussein's head. But instead of capitulating, the guerrillas holed up behind thick stone walls of a hundred buildings throughout Amman and other towns. Hour after hour, day after day, the two sides remained locked in battle while Yasser Arafat and King Hussein frantically tried to find a formula that would save them both. But when the king called for a cease-fire, his generals issued a "final ultimatum" to the guerrillas to surrender or be exterminated.

Using its superior firepower, Hussein's Bedouin army slowly blasted its way from house to house in search of Palestinian commandos. Jordanian as well as Palestinian civilians desperate for food and water crouched in basements and inside rooms. Unable to reach them, the Red Crescent, the Arab Red Cross, sent out a message: "Your children are expiring of thirst. We cannot help you except by telling you that you may be able to save their lives by letting them drink their own urine."*

Exhibiting a single-minded determination to wipe out the commandos completely, soldiers of Hussein's elite units revived the old Bedouin custom of breaking the fingers of their prisoners so they would not soon be able to pull a trigger against them. Still the war went on.

The commandos held out by merging with the Palestinian pop-

---

* *Newsweek*, October 5, 1970.

ulation. Thus the camps became prime targets of the Jordanian assault. From the first days of the war, tanks rolled up to refugee camps known to be strongholds of the PFLP and opened fire. Sections of the sprawling Wahdat refugee camp instantly turned into a charnel house. At the al-Husseini camp, where 45,000 Palestinians lived, tin refugee huts melted into twisted masses of scrap. After four straight days under the hail of shells, only 20 percent of the ramshackle housing remained standing. Still the commandos did not break.

To the fatalistic Hussein, the situation looked hopeless. His own driver turned out to be a commando. Another of his cooks tried to poison his food, and when the cook was arrested he was found to be in possession of a hand grenade. Iraq and Syria, in the name of Arab unity, put forces into position to aid the commandos. Preparing himself for the end of his dynasty, Hussein ordered all the women and children of his family to Aqaba.

Over the summer of 1970, as events in Jordan edged toward Black September, President Richard Nixon had mapped the United States response. With the September hijacking of the TWA plane, American contingency plans unfolded. U.S. military forces in the eastern Mediterranean and Europe went to a state of combat readiness. By the time the civil war began, the United States had amassed enough clout in the region to back up Hussein. Israel followed suit by boldly staging elaborate military maneuvers along its border with Jordan. On the Arab front, Iraq vacillated and then decided to hold back its troops stationed in northern Jordan. That left Syria. But when the Syrian tanks crossed the Jordanian border from the north, the United States upped its combat readiness once again as a warning to the Soviets to call off the Syrians. The interests of the USSR and the interests of Hafiz Assad, the Syrian defense minister and an opponent of the PLO leadership, merged. The tanks retreated back north. Finally Nasser, the godfather of Arab nationalism, declared, "I am not prepared to send troops to Jordan."* Broken by the 1967 war, Nasser was willing to do nothing more than play mediator in a war that tore at the very soul of Arab unity.

On September 27, a smiling Nasser stood between Arafat and Hussein in the Hall of the 1001 Nights in Cairo's Hilton Hotel to

---

* Quoted in Vatikiotis, *Nasser*, p. 245.

announce the war between the king and the commandos was over.* On November 7, the last guerrilla handed over his gun to Hussein and reluctantly left the center of Amman. Hussein was now separated from the commandos and much of his Palestinian population "by twenty-five thousand dead and wounded and by a river of blood."† Hussein had won because the almost mystical bonds the Hashemites had built with the Bedouin held and enough Palestinians sided with the king against the PLO to allow Hussein to retain the political balance. Finally, the Arab states had done nothing to help the embattled commandos, the darlings of the Arab masses.

Yet Hussein came out of the war weakened everywhere except with his own Bedouin. The Israelis, those who possessed his territory, held him in contempt for the turmoil in his kingdom. The Syrians and Iraqis, with their revolutionary governments, hated him, coveting sections of his desert for themselves. The Americans, to whom he had steadfastly held for fourteen years, resupplied his weapons losses with largely obsolete equipment. And then there was the Arab nation.

Although the Arab states had watched with a certain satisfaction as Hussein destroyed the out-of-control Palestinian commandos, the demands of Arab unity dictated that once the commando movement was reined in, the one who achieved it be expelled from the Arab fold. Hussein became an Arab pariah. Showing the physical effects of another crisis, Hussein, still only thirty-five, checked into a London hospital with an irregular heartbeat.

In the aftermath of the civil war, the king tended the Palestinians who supported him and locked in under close surveillance those who did not. Simultaneously, he searched for a way to reach some accommodation with Israel that would restore the West Bank. From time to time, the king and Abba Eban, Israel's foreign minister, mysteriously turned up at the same hotel in London. And on at least one occasion, two boats, one Jordanian and one Israeli, coincidentally idled late at night in the waters off Aqaba. In March 1972, Hussein laid out his plan for a "United Arab Kingdom," a federation of the two banks of the Jordan that would allow the Palestinians a

---

* As Nasser was bidding goodbye to the last Arab chiefs of state at the Cairo airport, he experienced sharp chest pains. Rushed home by aides, he died four hours later.
† *Journal of Palestine Studies*, Vol. IV, No. 1.

large measure of autonomy under the Jordanian flag. Hussein was, in essence, reasserting his claim to the West Bank in language that he hoped would appeal to moderate Palestinians. But Israeli rejection killed it before Hussein knew how his former West Bank subjects would react.

While King Hussein pondered the future of his kingdom and waited out his expulsion from the Arab fold, Anwar Sadat plotted the Arabs' 1973 war against Israel. This time Egypt's war would not be Jordan's. Hussein, acutely aware of the disaster of 1967, agreed at the last moment to pose as a third front for Egypt and Syria. Yet he did little but place his army on a state of alert and wait. When the Jordanian army finally committed to the battle, it was to keep Hussein's domestic front quiet, not to carry the banner of Arab unity. Losing only twenty-eight men, eighteen tanks, and nineteen armored vehicles, Hussein came out of the war with martial honor satisfied and his East Bank kingdom intact. But the West Bank remained beyond his reach. If he was to persuade the Israelis to relinquish it, he had first to persuade the Palestinians to allow him to represent them.

Since 1967, Hussein had argued to the Palestinians and to the other Arabs that Jordan provided the only vehicle by which the Palestinians could exercise any type of self-determination. It was a message no Arab wanted to hear. In October 1974, the Arab League gathered in Rabat, Morocco, to determine just who represented the Palestinians. Between 1970 and 1974, Yasser Arafat and the PLO had crawled out of the hole of defeat in Jordan to once more preside over the Palestinian issue, still the crucible of Arab unity. The PLO came to Rabat wearing the mandate of the Palestinians. As Hussein sat helplessly by, the Arab League, speaking as the voice of the Arab nation, declared that the Palestine Liberation Organization was the sole legitimate representative of the Palestinian people. The Arab states, playing to an illusionary unity, had buried Hussein in humiliation. But he, at least in public, accepted the decision. "There is an Arab verse which says . . . Where my tribe goes, I go. . . . As part of the Arab nation, ever seeking its unity, I go with the general consensus—regardless of any previous feelings."*

Hussein's dignified acceptance of the Arab decision began his

---

* *Newsweek*, November 11, 1974.

restoration to Arab politics. The political realists among the Arabs and even a segment of the Palestinians realized that Israel would never negotiate with the PLO. Thus the best chance for West Bank Palestinians to escape Israeli occupation and exercise any political will rested with Hussein. As one refugee from the 1967 War said, "Arafat can cause a lot of trouble for Israel but he can't take us home."* It was a premise the PLO would not accept. From 1974 to 1988, Hussein and the PLO locked in battle over the issue of which represented the Palestinians of the West Bank, who seven years after the 1967 War still lived under Israeli occupation. The contest was crucial for both Hussein and PLO chairman Yasser Arafat. For Hussein, the Palestinians' acknowledgment of his right to negotiate with Israel in their behalf gave him some opportunity to recover the West Bank. For Arafat, an agreement with Hussein meant surrendering the Palestinians' control over their own destiny to the hated perpetrator of the 1970 Palestinian defeat. For the Palestinians of Jordan and the West Bank, Hussein presented some opportunity to break Israel's grasp on Palestinian territory, while Arafat irresistibly held high the elusive promise of a Palestinian state.

Sampling Palestinian opinion in Jordan is always an imprecise and somewhat risky business. The camps by government decree and internal Palestinian control are almost entirely off limits to journalists. And Hussein's security services are effective enough to turn any Palestinian with a stake in Jordan's economy into a warm supporter of the king in the presence of a foreigner. It is only after long-term contacts establish a basis of trust that the depth of the Palestinians' yearning for their own government comes into the open. Once that bridge is crossed, one Palestinian passes you to another.

I was once staying at the Jerusalem Inn Hotel in Amman. Coming in just after dark from a series of appointments, I was startled by a "pssst" from behind one of the lobby's fat pillars. A rather heavyset, prematurely gray man, half hidden between the column and a plant, motioned me over. I acknowledged his inquiry that I was "Sandra." Looking furtively around, he whispered, "Nadia sent me. I wanted to tell you I, as a Palestinian, do not want Hussein to be my king." Before I could utter a word, he turned and fled out a side door.

---

* *Newsweek*, July 22, 1974.

The acceptability of Hussein as a negotiating tool of the Palestinians climbed and plunged according to the fortunes of the PLO and Hussein's ability to keep the door open to Israel without shutting himself off from the Arabs. The first critical test occurred in 1979, when Egypt's Anwar Sadat and Israel's Menachem Begin met U.S. President Jimmy Carter at Camp David. Hussein was not invited to Camp David. And he refused to follow Egypt as the second Arab state to make peace with Israel. The Camp David Accords were unacceptable to Hussein because they failed to address his most vital concerns—the future of the West Bank and Arab Jerusalem. Jimmy Carter, angry, dispatched his national security adviser, Zbigniew Brzezinski, to Amman to threaten Hussein about the future deliveries of American weapons. But Cyrus Vance, Carter's onetime secretary of state, understood. "[Hussein] walks a very difficult line. The pressures he faced at the time of Camp David were such that it isn't surprising that he wouldn't undertake the risks—the economic risks to the country, the physical risks to himself. He depends heavily on subsidies from the Saudis. And it's a tough balancing act with Syria and Iraq, plus the well-known problems with the Palestinians."*

Following the lead of the Arabs' "rejection front," Hussein broke diplomatic relations with Egypt over Anwar Sadat's treachery to the Arab cause.† Yet while he hewed to the line of Arab intransigence, Hussein maneuvered himself toward a pivotal position in which he would become indispensable to a solution of the Palestinian issue for the moderate Arab nations, for the United States, and for the Palestinians themselves.

It all seemed to come together in the summer of 1982 when the Lebanese civil war turned into a war between Israel and the PLO. The PLO lost. The death knell sounded over Yasser Arafat and the PLO at the same time that King Hussein looked more secure in his own kingdom than he had ever been. The economy, for once, was good, the result of $1 billion in remittances that the 350,000 Jordanians employed in the Persian Gulf sent home. A booming real estate market spread palatial homes and spacious apartments, many owned by Palestinians, across the Amman hills. Hussein's confidence was such that when the PLO was expelled from Beirut in

---

* John Newhouse, "Monarch," *The New Yorker*, September 19, 1983, p. 100.
† See Chapter 9.

August 1982, he accepted two thousand of the guerrilla fighters into Jordan.

On September 1, 1982, the United States, looking for a way to stabilize the Middle East after a summer in which Israeli air power had turned Beirut into an inferno, launched the Reagan initiative, which in essence revived Hussein's own 1970 proposal that called for Jordan to take charge of the West Bank and its Palestinians in return for Arab recognition of Israel. Hussein embraced the plan, as he would have embraced any plan that would return the West Bank to Jordanian control. Yet he could not go forward without PLO acquiescence to an agreement that would allow Hussein to lead a joint Jordanian-Palestinian delegation to talks with Israel. Yasser Arafat flew into Amman, where for two days he and Hussein hammered out the details. But Arafat, facing the opposition of Syrian-backed factions in his own organization, could not deliver the PLO. On April 10, 1983, Hussein, his eyes filling with tears, admitted his efforts to persuade the PLO to join him had failed. As a result, "We in Jordan . . . will neither act separately nor in lieu of anybody in the Middle East peace negotiations."*

The following November, the weary king, defeated by a reluctant PLO and militarily threatened by Syria's Hafiz Assad, who for his own ambitions was intent on preventing any Jordanian-Palestinian cooperation, granted an interview to the *Arab Times*. He looked tired, the pain and disappointment written on his face. Hussein laid the blame for his failed talks with the PLO on his Arab brothers. "It is painful to see our disunity which makes us the target for the ambitions of many."†

When illness appeared to have eliminated Syria's Hafiz Assad from the political equation, Hussein again tried to pull the Palestinians into the negotiating process. Throughout 1984, he freed Palestinians from his jails, met openly with Arafat, fostered Jordanian social projects on the West Bank, canvassed support in Washington, restored diplomatic relations with Egypt, and hosted the Seventeenth Palestine National Council in Amman, all in an attempt to persuade the Palestinians to negotiate with Israel under Hussein's auspices.

By the beginning of 1985, Arafat was back in Amman clutching

* Ibid.
† *Arab Times*, November 5, 1983.

an agreement borne of two tumultuous years of infighting in the PLO.* On February 11, the patrician Hussein and the grizzled Arafat signed an agreement stipulating that Jordan and the PLO would jointly pursue a peace initiative based on the concept of trading with Israel peace for land. Out of the disaster of 1967, the isolation of 1970, the rejection of 1974, Hussein was now delivered his best chance to regain the West Bank. The agreement with Arafat gave him credibility in the eyes of the Arab world that would allow him to begin talks with Israel. And the Israeli government under Shimon Peres appeared willing to put these negotiations with Jordan into some kind of international framework to give Hussein another measure of legitimacy to the Arabs. Suddenly Hussein seemed poised to salvage the Hashemite kingdom of Abdullah.

But the pact was doomed from its birth. Its language was so vague it left the Jordanians envisioning a permanent bond between the two banks of the Jordan with Amman exercising control over defense and foreign policy, and the PLO envisioning a "confederation," a voluntary association of equal and independent nations, dissolvable at the whim of either one. Yet for the moment, the parties ignored the basic flaws.

Embracing the vision of Hussein as an acceptable monitor for the Palestinians, Israel allowed the Hashemite king to reassert a measure of authority over the territory he had lost in 1967. With the Peres government seizing the chance to weaken the PLO's grip on the West Bank's inhabitants and Hussein willing to work within the framework of Israel's occupation, Israel and Jordan slipped into harness together. In the grand strategy of the partnership was a Jordanian-sponsored five-year $1.3 billion development plan for the occupied territories. On the operational level was the reopening of the Cairo-Amman Bank in Nablus. In October 1986, painters applied the last coat of paint on a bank that had been closed for nineteen years. When the cleanup began, workers had stepped into a place frozen in time. Dust-laden pictures of babies who were now adults sat on desks next to calendars opened to June 6, 1967. On the wall of the manager's office, a grimy gilt-framed picture of a much younger King Hussein still hung on the wall. Symbolic of the new era, it was taken down, carefully cleaned, and returned to the

* See Chapter 12.

wall, as if the years between had simply collapsed. But too much had changed on the West Bank. The Palestinians, never at ease with the Hashemites, could not be drawn back.

A year after Hussein and Arafat signed their agreement, division within the PLO on just what it meant broke into the open. Without a Palestinian endorsement, Hussein could not go forward. As a result, in February 1986, he broke off all negotiations with the PLO that would have made Jordan the umbrella under which the Palestinians went to an international conference on the future of the occupied territories. This was only the first piece to fall out of Hussein's carefully worked political puzzle. The Israeli government was about to pass to the leadership of the hard-liner Yitzhak Shamir, replacing the Israel dominated by the Labor Party that Hussein knew and understood. And finally, the United States did its part to undercut Hussein. As the PLO bolted in one direction and Israel in another, the U.S. Congress postponed indefinitely a promised arms sale to Hussein until he agreed to negotiate with Israel. Though later waived by presidential order, the restriction left King Hussein shipwrecked.

But it was the Palestinians on the West Bank who would sever the last link between Hussein and the occupied western half of his kingdom. On December 9, 1987, the Intifadah, the Palestinian uprising in the Israeli-occupied territories, began. With stones, ordinary Palestinians profoundly challenged Israeli power both politically and morally in a way the Arab nation had never approached. As rock-throwing teenagers battled Uzi-carrying Israeli soldiers, the Arab world rushed to bestow its blessing. In June 1988, members of the Arab League filed to Algiers, where they once again affirmed the PLO as the sole and legitimate representative of the Palestinian people. Subtly accused of seeking to undermine the influence of the PLO among the Palestinians, Hussein as so many other times in the past found himself at odds with mythical Arab unity.

Hussein faced the grim truth that the uprising in the Israeli-occupied territories was a flaming expression of Palestinian nationalism that was aimed as much against him as against Israel. As such, it threatened to spill over into the Palestinian population of the East Bank. Concern turned to reality in May 1988 when riot police clashed with stone-throwing youths on the East Bank. Although contained, violence continued to boil within Hussein's Palestinian population and sporadically broke to the surface. The moment of truth had arrived. On July 31, 1988, Hussein ibn Talal, king of the Hashemite Kingdom of Jordan, went on television to renounce all claim to the West Bank. "Since there is a general conviction that the struggle to liberate the occupied Palestinian land could be enhanced by dismantling the legal and administrative links between the two banks, we have to fulfill our duty and do what is required of us. These steps were taken only in response to the wish of the Palestinian Liberation Organization, the sole legitimate representative of the Palestinian people, and the prevailing Arab conviction that such measures will contribute to the struggle of the Palestinian people and their glorious uprising."*

The Intifadah had put the final nail in the coffin of the Jordanian solution of the Palestinian issue. Hussein now had to save his East Bank kingdom. This meant cultivating the Palestinians of his kingdom, for the Jordanian population, the mainstay of his power, was shrinking as a percentage of the total. The Jordanian army that was once so fanatically loyal to Hussein was no longer a sure defense of his regime. With urbanization and the need to supplement the ranks with Palestinians, links between king and soldier had gradually weakened. Even the loyalty of the Bedouin themselves seemed to give way in April 1989 when riots protesting declining living standards engulfed Maan, the southern town where Abdullah had first established his presence in Jordan. The disorders prompted the first elections in twenty-two years, which delivered the largest number of seats to the Muslim Brotherhood. Added to all his other problems, Hussein now faced Islamic fundamentalism. Yet a greater problem soon followed. On August 2, 1990, Iraq's Saddam Hussein invaded Kuwait.

While most of the Arab world lined up against aggression of one Arab state against another, King Hussein sided with Saddam Hussein. With the same sense of fatalism he had expressed in 1967 when he followed Nasser down the road to disaster, Hussein now followed Saddam.

Amman's ties with Baghdad first blossomed during the 1980–88 Iraq-Iran War. From the beginning, Hussein saw the Iraqi army as a check on both his longtime nemesis Hafiz Assad and the Ayatollah Khomeini, who in the name of revolutionary Islam had de-

---

* *New York Times*, August 1, 1988.

clared death to all Arab monarchies with Western ties. In Khomeini's revolutionary rhetoric, Hussein as the "shah of Jordan" was near the top of the list. As the war dragged on year after year, Hussein allowed fleets of Jordanian trucks to haul tons of weapons and supplies overland from Aqaba to the war front, allowing Iraq to escape the Iranian blockade of its Persian Gulf port. By the end of the war, wounded but still potentially rich Iraq was pumping into the Jordanian economy the foreign money that is always a basic necessity of life.

But economics played a less important role in Hussein's decision to back Iraq than politics. Judging the invasion of Kuwait the defiant rejection of a privileged, Western-linked regime, the Palestinians seized Saddam Hussein as their latest savior. With the Palestinian population of the East Bank approaching 70 percent, Hussein could risk angering the Arab states better than his own subjects. Two decades after Black September, the PFLP's George Habash and the DFLP's Nayef Hawatmeh made their way down the carpeted aisle of Amman's Royal Cultural Center, packed with hundreds of frenzied Palestinians. It was the first time either had set foot in Jordan since their leftist commandos had tried to overthrow Hussein in 1970. Now they were back with the king's blessing.

Responding to the emotions of his Palestinian population, Hussein reaped the benefits. Demonstrators marching through the streets shouting "We sacrifice our blood for you, Saddam" also hoisted the picture of their king. The fault line between Hussein and his Palestinian subjects appeared, for the moment, to close.

Securing the home front, Hussein frantically scrambled to erect some protection against the wrath of those Arab states who opposed Iraq and to shore up his international standing. He grandly announced that Jordan would observe the United Nations embargo against Iraq, his largest trading partner. It was a decision that would cost Jordan an estimated $280 million a year in exports and another $250 million in transit fees for goods moved from Aqaba to Iraq. Yet this was only one of Jordan's economic problems to spring out of the disorder in the Gulf. Tourism collapsed, creating another $230 million loss. Thousands of refugees requiring food and shelter poured over the border. Saudi Arabia and Kuwait, furious at Hussein's support for Iraq, shut off their economic aid and severed thousands of Jordanians from their well-paid jobs. In all, Jordan's government predicted its losses from the crisis would exceed $2 billion, more than half the GNP. The once solid Jordanian dinar began its precipitous decline.

Hussein, seasoned by crisis, would work his way back into the Middle East's political constellation. Within months of the end of the Gulf War, some Arab oil money began to flow back into Jordan's ravaged economy. And in one of the great ironies of Arab politics, Hussein took the Palestinians into the first rounds of the 1991 Middle East peace conference as part of the joint Palestinian-Jordanian delegation he had tried so hard to structure in the mid-1980s. Hussein weathered the storm of 1991 in part because Jordan's geographic position makes the Hashemite kingdom central to regional politics. Yet perhaps even more, Hussein has been an actor on the Arab scene for so many years that he has earned a measure of respect from those who are his enemies as often as friends. In all probability, Hussein can continue as he has for almost forty years to skillfully juggle his own interests with the demands of Arab unity—if he can hold his country.

In 1982, Ariel Sharon, the town crier of hard-line Likud policy, began his insistent cry: "There is a Palestinian state. It is called Jordan." Hussein answered, "Jordan is the homeland of the Jordanians. Just as there is pride in the Palestinian identity, so too is there pride in the Jordanian identity. Yes, we are brothers, but Jordan will not be a substitute homeland for Palestinians."* But as in so much of his troubled reign, the future of Jordan is hostage to events and conditions Hussein cannot control. In the search for a solution to the Palestinian problem, Hussein's kingdom may ultimately become the Palestinian state. It could happen in two ways. In the highly unlikely event that Israel surrenders the West Bank and it becomes the Palestinian state, Hussein's Palestinian population will attach itself to the new Palestine, pulling Jordan with it. Or more likely, Jordan may be surrendered by the international community to the argument of the current-day Zionists that would give the Palestinians a state and allow Israel to annex the West Bank. A. M. Rosenthal made the often-voiced case for making Jordan into a Palestinian state as well as anyone: "[There is a state], the one that Britain sliced off from the Palestine mandate in 1920 and now goes under the alias of Jordan. As for a Palestinian state, it exists already,

_____

* *Arab Times*, November 5, 1983.

just across the narrow River Jordan, and one day will be known by its real name."*

Hussein is not yet sixty. He looks older. His hair has thinned and his face is lined. Admitting to fatigue and discouragement, he nonetheless carries on in defense of the Hashemite throne. He holds his audiences as he has always done and moves around his deeply troubled kingdom to touch his subjects in the Bedouin way that was handed down to him by Abdullah. To watch Hussein is to watch a figure of tragic proportions whose poor, fragile kingdom never matched the considerable talents of its ruler. Not the least of Hussein's assets is his ability to forgive his enemies. The question is whether Hussein's enemies and the interlopers on his territory will forgive him enough to allow him to win his lifelong battle of political survival.

The road west out of Amman winds down a steep escarpment to the Allenby Bridge over the Jordan River. On a hill on the other side, a concrete-and-steel skeleton that faces Jerusalem broods in the solitude of its abandonment. Begun as a palace from which Hussein could look toward the majestic Dome of the Rock, it was never finished, severed from Jordan by the 1967 War. Hauntingly it speaks of Hussein's past. Perhaps it also speaks of his future.

---

* A. M. Rosenthal, *New York Times*, March 26, 1991, p. A15.

CHAPTER 8

THE HOUSE
OF SAUD:
THE COLLECTIVE
MONARCHY

I T WAS 1984, THE LAST YEAR OF MY
four-year stint in Saudi Arabia. For-
bidden to drive because I am female, I was striding along al-Aasimah
Street on the western edge of the Naziriyah district of Riyadh. I
stopped to watch a Yemeni work crew attach, one by one, the multicolored national flags of at least a dozen different Arab countries
to poles lining the wide driveway of the government's grand conference center. Built in the late 1970s, it is an overwrought testament
to Saudi economic power. The day before it officially opened back
in the '70s, one of the contractors had smuggled me past the loose
Saudi security for a grand tour.

The gold-domed meeting hall is paneled in rich, dark walnut
and graced with a massive crystal chandelier that cost in excess of
$1 million. It connects with a multistory hotel that provides lodging
and hospitality to the Saudis' guests. It is there that salon after salon
spreads out through the first level, overfurnished in the Arabized
version of Louis XIV that the Saudis so love. Behind the salons is
a huge banquet hall where lines of tables, each seating at least fifty
people, groan under the weight of heavy German crystal, Limoges
china, and Christofle flatwear. Upstairs is the *pièce de résistance*—the

grand suite of King Fahd. The ceiling of his audience room sweeps up at least twenty feet, dwarfing an exquisite wood desk inlaid with the crossed swords and palm tree that constitute the emblem of Saudi Arabia. In his private dining room, the walls are covered in deep apricot silk and the table set with gold flatware. Befitting the richest country of the Arab world, the whole complex becomes a stage on which the Saudis reign over their poorer Arab brothers.

My reverie ended as the last flag went up and a string of long black Mercedes limousines swung off the street and through the gates. They carried the delegates of yet another of the obscure inter-Arab conferences that the House of Saud so generously funds and uses to carry out the rituals of Arab unity. But Saudi Arabia's real alliances lie elsewhere. As I turned to continue on down the street, I saw an AWACS, distinguished by the big, flat plate of sensitive radar equipment extending above its fuselage, coming in low to land at the old Riyadh airport. Owned by Saudi Arabia, it carried a largely American crew that fed its data to ground bases discreetly supervised by Americans. Even in 1984, everyone knew that if the kingdom needed to be defended, the House of Saud would call the Americans, not the Arabs.

Saudi Arabia is tormented by the demands of Arab unity. Isolated by its topography from the Fertile Crescent, steeped in Islamic traditions, divided into hostile tribes, the great interior of the Arabian peninsula lived its own life for centuries. Although it was largely unified in the 1920s and took its place among Arab nations in 1932, Saudi Arabia chose not to connect with those beyond its burning, empty deserts. But the discovery of oil and oil's escalating importance to the global economy began to end Saudi Arabia's self-imposed isolation. In the 1950s, Arab nationalist ideology made an implicit claim on Saudi resources while radical politics pounded on the door of the conservative kingdom. In defense of its wealth and way of life, Saudi Arabia circled around the ideal of the Arab nation and searched for security beyond its boundaries. In the process, the House of Saud dexterously balanced three imperatives—to support and defend Arab unity; to escape radical Arab politics that threatened the kingdom's stability and treasure; and, as an underpopulated, resource-rich country, to anchor its defense in the United States. In 1990, when Iraq stood at the kingdom's threshold, Saudi Arabia, forced to choose between the mythology of Arab unity and the reality of the American defense commitment, activated its American alliance, ushering the armed might of the hated West into the Arab world. The House of Saud survived the immediate threat of Saddam Hussein and the wrath of those across the Arab world who cursed it for its collusion with the West. The whole series of events showed that after four decades of great riches, the House of Saud has yet to devise a formula that protects Saudi Arabia from the jealousies, resentments, and threats its wealth breeds within the Arab nation.

The aura of timelessness that envelops much of the Arab world reaches its pinnacle in the deserts of Saudi Arabia. Out of the wide wadis that wander through the baked landscape come the relics of a past that stretches back far beyond the beginning of the age of man. With a basic knowledge of geology, a durable sun hat, and unflagging stamina, that past can be seen and touched and gathered. Fossils of nautilus, scallop, and conch hide within the steep walls of what were once undersea valleys. And prints of ferns, lichens, and moss secreted within the shale of limestone cliffs tell of the time this desert was covered with lush green foliage.

Man came to the Arabian peninsula after the oceans receded. Those who did not migrate northward established themselves in the scattered oases or roamed the desert in search of sparse pasture for their herds of animals. And for thousands of years little happened on the desert that is Saudi Arabia until Muhammed delivered his religion in the seventh century A.D. Yet the great alteration in the tide of history that Islam forced occurred outside the Arabian peninsula. Arabia itself incorporated the faith of Muhammed into its own way of life. The coastal areas on the Persian Gulf and the Red Sea were touched by traders and empire builders. But the Nejd, the great, near-empty heartland of the peninsula, stayed with the tribes. In the Nejd, a camel wandering across empty wastelands remained the symbolic constant.

In the eighteenth century, the Nejd stirred. Muhammed ibn Abdul Wahhab, an Islamic reformer, zealously pulled the Bedouin and the town-dwellers back to Muhammed's original teachings. Before his death in 1787, he won a little-known tribal dynasty in the small oasis town of Diriyah, just north and west of the present city of Riyadh. Joining religion and politics, the Saud family pulled much of the fractured Arabian peninsula together to challenge the Ottoman sultan in the name of Wahhabism. The sultan responded by sending forces to lay siege to Diriyah. Six months later, the Emir

Abdullah surrendered.* Delivering the sultan's anger on the Sauds, Ottoman troops razed Diriyah, felled its life-giving date palms, and shipped Abdullah to Constantinople to be beheaded.

The Sauds, drained by their losses, moved fifteen miles southeast to the oasis of Riyadh. In 1824, they rose again behind the zeal of Wahhabism to challenge their rival family, the Rashids. The desert divided between two contending families until 1865, when Saud turned against Saud. Between 1871 and 1876, leadership of the family changed hands seven times, debilitating Saud power. In 1891, the reigning emir, Abdul-Rahman, lost Riyadh to the rival Rashids. Placing a large woven bag holding his ten-year-old son, Abdul Aziz, across the back of a camel, Abdul-Rahman al-Saud fled to Kuwait.

A ragged piece of limestone with a large elliptical hole near the top called the Camel's Eye stands on the fringe of Riyadh. In the days before the government closed access to its crumbling shale, I sometimes crawled into the open cavity, leaned against its rough side, and looked out toward Riyadh. I was literally sitting in a cradle of history, for it was from the Camel's Eye that Saudi Arabia's nationhood was launched.

In 1901, Abdul Aziz ibn Abdul-Rahman al-Saud at the age of twenty-two left Kuwait intent on retaking Riyadh and returning the Sauds to the Nejd.† Taking forty men with him, he skirted the settled coastal plain before heading across the desert toward Riyadh, the family's former seat of power. Riding under the banner of Wahhabism, he called men to his cause. On the dark night of January 15, 1902, an army of several hundred paused at the Camel's Eye. Accompanied by fifteen handpicked men, Abdul Aziz crept over the mud walls of Riyadh. Before the morning ended, he proclaimed God's will had been done, the Sauds were again the masters of Riyadh. The cornerstone of Saudi Arabia had been laid.

No one took much note. The Nejd lay beyond the interests and the politics of the great powers. The Ottomans claimed both coasts of the peninsula but shared the eastern side with a string of British protectorates. The Nejd belonged to the Bedouin. Hostile to outsiders, intolerant of any ideas beyond Wahhabism, they lived behind

---

* "Emir" translates to "prince." It more accurately refers to a leader chosen by the common consent of the community.
† In the West, Abdul Aziz ibn Abdul-Rahman al-Saud is known as Ibn Saud. In Saudi Arabia, he is called Abdul Aziz, "the servant of God."

the oceans of their desert. Literally untouched by World War I or the Arab Revolt, they never thought in terms of nation or secular politics. The same was not true of Abdul Aziz.

When World War I ended, Abdul Aziz cast his eye toward the territories formerly held by the Ottomans. Lacking resources to support an army, he mobilized Wahhabism. The teachings of the Prophet in their most pristine form became the basic bond between the emir of Riyadh and the men who would help him secure a kingdom. Tribe by tribe and settlement by settlement, Abdul Aziz marched across the peninsula. Anchored in Riyadh, he swung north, south, and then east toward the Gulf. Finally he went west, into the lands of the Hashemites, the guardians of the holy cities of Mecca and Medina. The British, allied with both families, judiciously decided the tide of history was with Abdul Aziz. Deserting the leader of the Arab Revolt, they left the sharif of Mecca to stem the Wahhabi tide alone. He failed. In October 1924, Mecca surrendered to the Wahhabis and guardianship of the holiest site in Islam passed from the Hashemites to the Sauds. Two weeks later, Abdul Aziz, shorn of his *gutra* and wrapped in a seamless white cloth, entered Mecca. His words were those of every pilgrim: "Here am I, O God, at Thy Command."*

Abdul Aziz and his Bedouin warriors rode on. They joined the Hijaz and the mountainous Assir to the eastern coastal plain and the Nejd. In September 1932, the one-eyed, battle-scarred Abdul Aziz proclaimed himself king of Saudi Arabia—Arabia of the Sauds.

Except for the people in the coastal areas, Abdul Aziz's subjects were among the most insular people in the world. Totally bound to family and tribe, suspicious if not frightened of anyone beyond the kinship group, they were tied together by only two concepts—the perception of themselves by blood and language as the true Arabs, and Wahhabism. In their own eyes, genealogies, untainted by the ethnic mix of the Fertile Crescent, confirmed them as the only authentic Arabs. The language of the Bedouin, which is the most closely related to classical Arabic, ordained them as keepers of the

---

* The Sauds and the Hashemites remained rivals. In 1924, Abdul Aziz's warriors invaded the Transjordanian kingdom of the sharif's son Abdullah. They advanced in large numbers in a swirl of dust toward Amman, only to be repelled by two aircraft and four armored cars under the command of a British military adviser. Until the day he died, Abdullah called the House of Saud "the Wahhabite beast."

true tongue. Their Wahhabi sect confirmed them as the most pure among Muslims, the guardians of the orthodox tenets of Muhammed.

Lineage, language, and sect combined to create in the Saudis a withering arrogance. In the early 1970s, great wealth that descended like a gift from paradise served as the Saudis' final confirmation of their superior position among Arabs. While other Arabs possess their particular feelings of preeminence, none can sneer at those they regard as their inferiors with quite the same contempt as the Saudis. Egyptians, Jordanians, Syrians, and the whole range of Arabs can testify to the Saudis' insufferable pride. Although the Saudis may mouth the words of brotherhood, they prefer to travel alone in the world of the Arabs.

The kingdom Abdul Aziz had forged stretched west to east from the Red Sea to the Persian Gulf and north to south from southern Iraq to the mountains of Yemen. Containing untamed tribes and the sacred cities of Islam, it defied government. Facing a population possessing no common loyalties, Abdul Aziz bid for his people's allegiance by making himself the guardian of Islam. Thus Wahhabism became the substitute for nationalism. Under the tutelage of the king, the puritanical tenets of Wahhabism pervaded society's customs and actions, it dominated images and attitudes, it motivated policies, and it embodied the system of values upon which the legitimacy of the House of Saud rested. The *ulema*, the religious elders, joined the king and the tribal chieftains in a triumvirate that would hold this wild land together. As a result, Saudi Arabia became a demi-theocracy in which such questions as whether Islamic law permitted the use of the bicycle within the Wahhabi kingdom became ponderous issues of government.

With the personalized rule of the Prophet at Medina as the only example of government he knew, Abdul Aziz became the patriarch of the community, the father who disciplined and rewarded. He traveled his vast kingdom with the national treasury in a wooden chest swinging from the back of a camel and administered through the *majlis*, the audience of the sheikh. Holding court most often in a tent, the tall, imposing monarch personally dispensed justice and government services to his population while tying the tribes to his person through the marriage bed he shared with more than three hundred wives.

Abdul Aziz always needed money for the simple reason that a

sheikh could hold the loyalty of his people only as long as he could care for them. Every day, people came asking their king for a sack of rice, a cloak, or just a meal. None went away disappointed, even though Abdul Aziz, as the ruler of a country with no known natural resources beyond dates, had little to give.

The Haj, the pilgrimage to Mecca, was Abdul Aziz's molting, half-starved golden goose. Fees pilgrims paid for guides, transportation, food, lodging, and the sheep or goat for the Eid al-Adha, or festival of sacrifice, went into Abdul Aziz's wooden treasury chests. In the 1920s, those fees provided the king with annual revenues of perhaps $725,000. His only other measurable income came from an annual British subsidy of just under $300,000 a year. Abdul Aziz and his state were paupers.

In 1933, providence delivered new revenues when Abdul Aziz eagerly granted a sixty-year oil concession to Standard Oil of California in return for $257,000. The agreement did more than give the king some money—it tied his kingdom to the West more tightly than he understood at the time. Western technology and Western demand for Saudi oil created Saudi wealth, and Saudi wealth created the need for a national defense that the Saudis could not provide for themselves. In the 1950s, rich, Western-connected Saudi Arabia confronted Arab nationalism in the era of Gamal Abdul Nasser.

In 1952, the year Nasser's Free Officers took control of Egypt, Abdul Aziz was past his seventieth year. He often sat on the roof of his new palace in the wheelchair Franklin Roosevelt had given him when they met in the Great Bitter Lake to discuss the future of Palestine. Denied oil revenues by World War II, Abdul Aziz had built a palace that was not much grander than the old mud-walled structure from which he had ruled his poverty-riddled kingdom. Riyadh, which stretched beyond the new palace's scraggly garden, was still little more than a village set within the wide expanse of the Arabian desert. But Abdul Aziz's humble capital belied the accomplishments of its king. In the fifty years of his reign, Abdul Aziz ibn Saud had proved to be the greatest ruler of Arabia since the Prophet himself. He had wooed the villages and towns with his promise of stability. Combining his example of religious purity with paternalistic rule and a strong hand, he had tamed the wild Bedouin. Almost alone, he had built the only nation this part of the Arabian peninsula had ever known. It was a nation whose vast, barren geography, history almost unsoiled by foreign intervention, government wedding secular and religious authority, and people obsessed with a fear of outsiders joined to make it unique among the Arab states. By experience and choice, Saudi Arabia stood apart. For the other Arabs, the kingdom was the outback, a barbarous wilderness beyond their interest or desire where the untamed and unlearned Saudis were at liberty to remain in their self-imposed isolation. When Abdul Aziz died at Taif on November 9, 1953, it fell to his heirs to ensure that his kingdom remained free of the growing turbulence of the Arab world.

No precedent existed for passing the mantle to a new king. Abdul Aziz had been Saudi Arabia's one and only ruler. Therefore the House of Saud turned to the only model it knew—the procedure by which the successor to Muhammed was chosen. The royal family, the tribal leaders, and the *ulema* came together to mold a consensus. Together they chose Saud, the oldest son of the great Abdul Aziz. Unfortunately, the tall, bespectacled Saud was hopelessly unprepared to be king. At a time when Saudi Arabia was taking its first tentative steps out of isolation, Saud knew almost nothing of the outside world. He knew even less about how to manage the affairs of his state, from its finances to its foreign affairs.

Western demand for cheap Saudi oil after World War II had solved the chronic economic problems of the Saud kings. In 1954, ARAMCO, the Arabian-American Oil Company, was generating $234.8 million annually, all of which went into Saud's personal coffers. Shunning the simple life-style of Abdul Aziz, he moved his family into Naziriah, a bright pink mini-city on the edge of Riyadh. There he surrounded himself with a cunning royal court committed to waste, decadence, corruption, and intrigue. To Saud, being king meant little more than drawing the finest females of the kingdom to his marriage bed, holding court, and spending the kingdom's ever-escalating oil revenues.

Saud set the standard for royal excess. When he went abroad, whole department stores opened exclusively for the royal entourage, which bought everything from bath towels to fur coats. The king himself purchased Cadillacs, the premier car of the 1950s, in lots. When he went to Boston in 1962 for cataract surgery, Saud took two floors of the very proper Copley Plaza Hotel. Every day, Boston's Nile Restaurant hauled roast peacock, squab, whole roasted lambs, and quarts of hummus, mashed chick peas, up the king's private elevator, which was carpeted with an Oriental rug. When Saud left, he passed out $11,000 worth of watches as tips. It all seems tame compared to the royal extravagances the world observed during the oil boom of the 1970s. But this was over a decade earlier, a time when Saudi Arabian oil sold at less than $2 a barrel.

Saud strayed further and further into the moral abyss defined by Wahhabi puritanism. In a society bound by stringent codes of conduct, he flaunted a stable of concubines and consumed so much alcohol that an ARAMCO plane routinely flew him from Riyadh to the company's hospital at Dhahran to dry out. Finally corruption, personal and public, brought Saud to the political gallows. Having no precedents to remove him, those who "tie and untie"—the family, the tribal leaders, and the *ulema*—jerryrigged a regency headed by Prince Faisal. After six subsequent years of family infighting, the *ulema* issued a *fatwa*—a religious ruling—that declared Saud unfit to rule. Seven months later, on November 1, 1964, Saud resigned and went into exile.

Faisal, second son of Abdul Aziz, was left to clean up the monarchy and a $2 billion national debt. Thin, hawk-nosed with large, protruding, soulful eyes, Faisal was as personally virtuous as Saud was corrupt. The most famous portrait of Faisal, one that dominates every publication that the Saudi government prints on its former king, shows Faisal dressed completely in white kneeling in prayer, his long fingers rising in supplication to the one god. Setting an example with his own piety, the dour king banned Cadillacs, the most visceral symbol of royal corruption, and shut down the ostentatious living of the royal family. In forcing the constraints on his family, Faisal was looking at both the Wahhabi critics of the House of Saud and the revolutionary, antimonarchial ideology of Nasser.

Nasser's revolution had burst out of the boundaries of Egypt in 1955, three years after the death of Abdul Aziz. Its energy quivered against the ramparts of Saudi Arabia. The high tide of Nasserism forced the House of Saud to walk a dangerous tightrope between fidelity to the wider Arab world and preservation of the kingdom's own interests. "Arab oil for the Arab people" was the stuff of politics of the 1950s and 1960s. It was born of an Arab nation divided between those with pools of petroleum beneath their sands and those without. Thus the have-nots led by Nasser's Egypt trumpeted the message of the Arab nationalists—national boundaries are artificial, meaningless lines imposed by the colonial powers. The Arabs are one people, one nation, one economic unit.

Few Saudis philosophically identified with Arab socialist movements. Saudi Arabia was a country of traditionalism and the orthodoxy of Wahhabism. Most Saudis who possessed enough education to understand or acknowledge Nasser's brand of Arab nationalism rebelled against it as a secular force undercutting the primacy of religion. This was on the philosophical plane. On the economic level, consternation gripped the Saudis when Nasser, whipping his audiences into a fevered pitch, called Saudi oil Arab oil. Together, ruler and subject rejected any political theory that implied that the wealth from the oil-rich Arab states should be distributed among their poorer Arab brothers. The Saudis, in essence, hated pan-Arabism. The harassing idea that Saudi oil revenues should diffuse through the Arab world appalled a people who had endured centuries of abject poverty. Although Nasser and pan-Arabism held a certain appeal among opponents of the House of Saud, that appeal was republican politics, not cooperative economics.

In 1958, the year Saud had nearly bankrupted Saudi Arabia, the mystique of Gamal Abdul Nasser reached its zenith. With Radio Cairo leading the way, revolutionary pan-Arabism shook the sealed gates of the kingdom of the Sauds. The pincers of Arab radicalism pressed in from Cairo, Damascus, and Baghdad. Egypt and Syria were one in the United Arab Republic. Revolution had beheaded the monarchy in Iraq. And the inept King Saud had fallen into a farcical plot to assassinate Nasser. *Einkreisung*, the myth of threatening encirclement, stalked the House of Saud. As radical Arabs built their links to the Soviet Union, the House of Saud bound itself closer to the United States.

By 1962, Prince Faisal was in control of the kingdom's foreign policy. Easing the country out of its isolation, he placed Saudi Arabia squarely against Nasser and the radical Arabs. Using Islam as a rationale and a shield, Faisal drew a line around the small, weak states on Saudi Arabia's eastern and southern borders. He declared this Saudi Arabia's sphere of influence, to be defended against pan-Arabism by diplomacy and money. Thus the stage was set for the showdown between Nasser's radicalism and Faisal's conservatism. It took place on the farthest edge of the Arab world—Yemen.

Yemen, a rugged and beautiful land, curves around the tip of the Arabian peninsula like a sleeping cat. The mountains in the north fall onto a coastal plain that runs into the port of Aden. In the valleys and on the hills, stacked stone houses decorated with heavy, circling cornices that make them look like wedding cakes stand in clusters between patches of deep green qat bushes, which produce the mildly narcotic leaves that are the national obsession. Yemen is tribal. And it is violent. For a whole population, the symbol of manhood is the *jambia*, a menacing curved dagger worn at the waist. For those too poor to buy a knife, an empty wooden scarab serves as a badge declaring a willingness to fight. This is the milieu in which the Yemen war was waged.

In a round of feuding during 1962, the lowlanders of Aden and the surrounding sheikhdom massed behind an army spouting republican and Marxist slogans and challenged the mountain men of the north gathered to defend their imam, Muhammed al-Badr. On September 26, 1962, the army from the south lined up its tanks around the imam's palace in Sanaa, fired, and took off the second story. It amounted to little more than a tribal dispute with ideological overtones in a corner of the Arab world that was so remote that it had never seen a Coca-Cola. But in the highly charged atmosphere of the early 1960s, no dispute involving Arabs stayed isolated. Within days, Nasser committed troops to Yemen in the name of social revolution and Arab nationalism. Faisal countered by shoring up the imam and royalism with petrodollars. For the next five years, Yemen served as the battleground on which Nasser's forces of revolution and Faisal's forces of conservatism confronted each other over the future direction of the Arab world.

Nasser put fifteen thousand men, one-sixth of the Egyptian army, into the steep, jagged mountains of northern Yemen. While tribes fiercely loyal to their imam holed up in caves in familiar terrain to live on Saudi-supplied food and ammunition, convoys of trucks and armored cars carrying Egyptian troops and supplies crawled up the tortuous highway from the Red Sea port of Hodeida to Sanaa. A sweating Egyptian army colonel, yelling instructions to his men, was asked by a reporter what the Egyptian army was doing in Yemen and replied, "We are Arabs and we must help our brothers. That is our duty."*

Unable to dislodge the forces of the imam, Nasser in 1963 ordered Egyptian planes to hit the Saudi Arabian border town of Najran and the coastal plain around Jizan, forcing forty thousand

---

* Quoted in David Holden, "At Cross Purposes in the Sands of Yemen," *Reporter*, February 14, 1963, p. 37.

people into panicked flight. But the strategy failed to shut down Faisal's pipeline to the imam. By 1964, Nasser had forty thousand men in Yemen, draining his reserves of money and material.

A war that neither sponsor could win or withdraw from dragged on, demanding new tactics. Beginning in November 1966, Egypt infiltrated Yemeni agents deep into Saudi Arabia to plant bombs at the Ministry of Defense in Riyadh, two royal palaces, and the vital Tapline that transported Saudi oil to Mediterranean ports. The political damage proved greater than the physical damage. Encouraged by the sabotage, various "liberation movements" declared themselves, and fissures within the House of Saud broke into the open. While Faisal sent one of his republican-leaning brothers into exile, the deposed King Saud tried to reclaim his throne over Radio Cairo. It all ended with Nasser's humiliation in the 1967 War.

Militant pan-Arabism died in 1967. The power and self-confidence of the radical states were shattered by the Six-Day War, allowing a deal to be struck between the dynastic order in the Gulf and the Egyptian state. Although prevented by the requirements of Arab unity to declare so openly, the House of Saud was "on some level relieved that the people who had disrupted stability for so long had paid for their sins, that as a result of the defeat [the Saudis] could now enjoy a period of relative peace."*

But for the Saudis there was also pain associated with the Arabs' 1967 defeat. The Saudis, sharing in the collective honor of the Arabs, shared in the humiliation of the Arab rout. And there was Jerusalem. The third-holiest site of Islam had been lost to the Muslims. For the rest of his life, King Faisal dreamed of once more being able to perform the prayers at al-Aqsa. And it was the issue of Jerusalem rather than the issue of the Palestinians and their lost land that consumed the Saudis after 1967. But the Saudis could not ignore the Palestinians.

In the wake of the Arabs' 1967 disaster, the Palestinian guerrillas stormed out of the refugee camps to declare vengeance on Arab regimes tepid in support of their demands to return to Palestine. The House of Saud cowered before these new messengers of Arabism. Against a political movement fed by commando attacks, the House of Saud had to defend a highly exposed oil delivery

* Ajami, *Arab Predicament*, p. 71.

system, thousands of members of the royal family, and its American alliance. On May 30, 1969, the Popular Front for the Liberation of Palestine demonstrated how vulnerable the kingdom actually was. The Tapline, the pipeline that carried 23 million tons of oil a year to Mediterranean ports, ruptured, blown apart by a terrorist bomb.

Exposed to radical attack because of its American alliance, the House of Saud had to do something in support of the Palestinian cause to protect itself from angry men beyond its borders. For the subjects of the Sauds, once the Palestinian issue moved beyond possession of Jerusalem its emotional appeal ceased. In Saudi perception, the commandos who were so celebrated by the rest of the Arab world were little more than ruffians upsetting the peace and order the Saudis so desperately craved.

In a series of moves intended to give Saudi Arabia cover against Palestinian radicalism and to confirm its Arab credentials, Faisal pressed the Nixon administration on the Arab-Israeli dispute, arguing that it lay at the core of Saudi difficulties in sustaining the American alliance in the Arab political arena. At the same time, he poured money into the coffers of Fatah, the most moderate of the Palestinian commando groups, and ordered the kingdom to aggressively enforce the Arab boycott against Israeli-made goods and Western companies doing business with Israel. It was the Arab boycott that gave the Saudis the safest means to affirm their Arabness. For the richer Saudi Arabia became, the more the boycott spoke of the Saudi commitment to the Arab stance against the Zionist enemy.

Faisal not only wanted peace between the Arabs and Israel to dampen Arab radicalism, he also sought to dilute Soviet influence among the Arab states. Faisal the Muslim and Faisal the conservative monarch wanted the Soviet Union out of the Arab world. When Nasser died, he grabbed the opportunity to steal Egypt away from the Russians.

Together, King Faisal and Anwar Sadat laid plans for an Arab war against Israel. In return for expelling the Russians from Egypt in July 1972, Faisal collected in addition to the Saudis' annual $250 million subsidy to Egypt close to $500 million from the other Gulf monarchies for Egyptian arms purchases and another $400 to $500 million in balance of payments support. In the summer of 1973, Faisal went to Cairo to promise that Saudi Arabia would embargo oil against the supporters of Israel if Egypt attacked Israel in the

232 / PASSION AND POLITICS

territories occupied in the 1967 war.* Saudi Arabia had only play-acted oil embargos before—in the Arab-Israeli wars of 1956 and 1967. First Saud and then Faisal refused to hand the dreaded Nasser the Arabs' ultimate weapon against the West. But Sadat was different. He had neither the ability nor the will to take Nasser's place as the mythical hero of the Arab masses. Leading Egypt away from Nasser's policies, willing to dance to the Saudi tune in return for help for his economically ravaged country, Anwar Sadat posed no threat to the House of Saud. As a result, when Egypt and Syria on October 6, 1973, launched war against Israel, Saudi Arabia was a silent partner in the coalition.

While others fought, King Faisal issued dire warnings to the United States that an oil embargo was imminent if Israel did not withdraw from Arab land conquered in 1967. Ignoring the reality that the United States consumed foreign oil at the rate of one million barrels a day, the Nixon administration decided that mobilizing the comic-strip character Snoopy as the spokesman for a voluntary conservation drive was all the crisis management the United States needed. As far as the American government was concerned, Saudi Arabia's most basic defense and economic interests would never allow the kingdom to confront the United States. And these factors might have restrained the Saudis' hand if the Arab forces on the ground had held their positions and if the United States had held back its resupply of Israeli losses.

Two days after the October War began, Cairo and Riyadh were linked by a direct telephone line. Taking no chances on Nasser's trick of keeping King Hussein in the dark about the military situation in 1967, Saudis with access to Egyptian intelligence were on the ground in Cairo monitoring the war. Into the second week, they reported to Faisal that the Arab armies were losing their early gains. On October 19, Richard Nixon, looking at the war only in terms of the U.S.-Soviet rivalry, asked Congress for $2.2 billion in military assistance to Israel. Suddenly King Faisal confronted the certain danger of Saudi Arabia's becoming isolated in a sea of Arab anger ignited by American support for Israel. The next day he unsheathed the oil weapon, shutting off the 600,000 barrels of oil a day that helped fuel the American economy. Immediately lines of cars like

---

* See Chapter 9.

giant snakes wound around gas pumps. Skyrocketing oil prices drove the economy into peril. And an aroused President Nixon warned a conference of environmentalists that "if one freezes to death, it doesn't make any difference whether the air is clean or dirty."* Under a cartoonist's pen, Saudi Arabia became a hawk-nosed sheikh holding a half-bare American eagle in one hand while he plucked out the rest of its feathers with the other. For the Arabs, Saudi Arabia took its place in the Arab ranks. The conservative, timid Saudis had confronted the United States in the name of the Arab nation.

The embargo went on into the new year. Oil prices climbed from a prewar price of $3.01 a barrel to $11.65 while the Arab oil producers vowed to sustain their boycott until Western support for Israel stopped. Faisal was not so sure. While he fervently believed that the United States must face the fact that the Middle East would never be stable until the Palestinian question was addressed, he was not willing to push the United States to the wall for what he saw as the socialism and radical politics of much of the Arab world. Faisal and his brothers, who made the decisions for the House of Saud, understood that in the last resort they were dependent on American will and muscle to protect themselves from their enemies—domestic and foreign. In March 1974, as Egyptian, Syrian, and Israeli forces disengaged under American diplomatic efforts, Saudi Arabia lifted the embargo against its longtime ally. The following month, a United States Department of Defense team arrived in Riyadh to put together a joint American-Saudi military strategy to ensure the security of the kingdom.

The oil embargo gave new meaning to the term "Arab." The predatory imperialists of the unconquerable West had been brought to their knees. Humbled, they would be made to pay for the psychological, political, and cultural dislocations they had inflicted on the Arab world. Centuries of shame and humiliation dissipated as the mighty of the industrialized world bowed before the Arab oil producers. The embargo had delivered to the Arabs not only the honor they so long had sought but something they had never known before—power. From the Gulf across the Arab heartland and on into the *maghrib*, the Arabs were reborn.

The Arab era, linked inevitably with the name of Nasser, gave

---

* *Newsweek*, October 22, 1973.

way to the Saudi era, when most believed Saudi riches and influence would be put at the service of all Arabs. But Arab wealth and power proved to be only fleeting for those Arabs outside the oil states. The explosion of petroleum prices in 1973–74 in effect opened further the gaping chasm between the Arab world's rich and poor. In 1974, while per capita income in Saudi Arabia was $6,991, it was $428 in Jordan, $340 in Syria, and a bare $240 in Egypt. The Saudis had become a wealthy people in a neighborhood of paupers. The suggestions of the 1960s that Saudi oil was Arab oil now escalated to calls for Saudi Arabia to distribute its wealth to the Arab nation. However, it soon became clear that Saudi Arabia's phenomenal new riches would not be transferred to the Arab nation except in terms of aid to compliant governments and an Arab labor force imported to the kingdom to do the work the Saudis could not or would not do for themselves. Ahmed Shuqairi, the former leader of the Palestine Liberation Organization, summed up the disappointment and enmity: "The Arabs' petroleum triumphed over the Arabs."*

To understand what Saudi wealth did to the psyche of the non-oil Arabs, one only had to spend an afternoon in the lobby of almost any hotel in Beirut. Between 1973 and 1975, Beirut was a paradise of worldly delights where the Saudis came to make their deals and escape the strictures of their own society. A typical newly rich Saudi, his fat stomach straining against his tight white *thobe*, would sit in the corner of the lobby dangling a sandal off one fleshy foot. A son, a cousin or two, and a retainer flanked him, sitting just beyond the space allowed petitioners. Into that space, ubiquitous entrepreneurs clutching contracts would approach in a half-crouched position as if they were ready to fall to their knees on command. Jewelry merchants bearing velvet cases would be fawning over those who could afford their gold necklaces, bracelets, and brooches set with diamond chips. Around it all, waiters shuttling trays of tea, coffee, and bottled water would bow and scrape as they swooped up the large bills contemptuously tossed on the table by the Arab world's new rich. And so it would go through the late afternoon and on into the

* Ajami, *Arab Predicament*, p. 86. The oil boom was not unique to Saudi Arabia. It affected all the sheikhdoms of the Persian Gulf. The same tensions that oil wealth created between the Saudis and the other Arabs also affected relations between the Arabs and the other oil-producing monarchies.

evening. As each suppliant withdrew, he would curse the need to go begging to the Bedouin.

I spent the oil boom in Saudi Arabia. It was a time when the term *nouveau riche* took on new meaning. Bedouin rode their camels into town, dismounted in a corral erected by a car dealership, and drove off in new white pickups. Young men who overnight had leaped from student to entrepreneur prowled the gold souks carrying big brown paper grocery bags filled with riyals. Out of this new and unearned wealth, a new social order developed, encompassing the hundreds of thousands of foreigners working in the kingdom. At the top sat the Saudis, overlords of the whole system. Next came the Westerners. We existed as a privileged class, tolerated because in the late 1970s it was the Westerners who possessed the skills and technology that the Saudis needed to build their new world. Below us was a layer of Arabs, as educated and trained as the Westerners. At the bottom were the unskilled of dozens of nationalities. Ironically, the psychological dynamics were not between the Saudis and the Westerners but between the Saudis and the Arabs. Relegated for centuries to one rung above the Yemenis on the Arab status ladder, the Saudis demanded from their fellow Arabs the honor they had been so long denied. Lebanese, Palestinians, Syrians, and Egyptians, all proud products of ancient cultures, found themselves bowing down to those most still regarded as uncouth inferiors.

One day in a fit of rage, Musa, a good-looking, clean-cut practical nurse from Lebanon who had worked in several hospitals in different parts of the kingdom, said to me, "I will tell you what every Arab will tell you. The Saudis treat us like shit. They don't pay us as much as they do Europeans. That is only one part of it. What makes me really mad is that they won't have anything to do with us. They act like we are not good enough to associate with them. Ask any Arab. He will tell you that Saudis are bad."

The situation within the kingdom between the Saudis and their Arab workers reflected the Arab world as a whole. In the oil boom that made Saudi Arabia vastly wealthy, a few Arabs prospered and the others lost out. And the losers were not convinced that the winners deserved all that they got. The Arabs of the Fertile Crescent, the propagators of the great Islamic civilization, seethed with resentment that the "shoeless goat herders" of the Arabian peninsula should be so rich while they were so poor. Bridling at the perceived parsimony that the governments of oil states exhibited toward other Arab states, they recoiled at the vulgarity individual Saudis displayed when they came to Cairo and Beirut to flaunt their money.

The House of Saud felt the hostility. If 1973 was marked by the Saudis' emergence into the limelight of Arab affairs, the era after 1973 was marked by the Saudis' search for escape from the claims of the Arab nation. Refusing to allow Saudi Arabia's resources to drain into the bottomless pit of Egypt, seeking protection from the Baathist governments of Syria and Iraq, and fearing the anger and vengeance of the stateless Palestinians, the House of Saud looked for an ideal larger than the Arab nation. They found the answer in the 1969 writings of a fundamentalist writer who called for resurrection of the Islamic caliphate under King Faisal. Mustering his position as the revered leader of Islam's religious conservatives, Faisal designed a foreign policy based on Islam. The House of Saud would mobilize its money and its status as the guardian of Mecca and Medina to fill the ideological vacuum left by the demise of pan-Arabism with a policy that can be best described as "petro-Islam." It emerged not as a religious revival so much as the entrenchment of a conservative moral and political ideology backed by oil wealth. Islam became the shield behind which the House of Saud and its kingdom would take shelter from the hostile winds of the Arab world.

King Faisal, the symbol around which petro-Islam was to be built, fell to an assassin's bullet on March 25, 1975.* Once more the undefined and tenuous process of choosing a successor unwound. This time the choice fell to Khalid, the fourth son of Abdul Aziz.

Khalid was king when I arrived in Riyadh in the spring of 1978. And I was there when he died in June 1982. He was an unpretentious man, untainted by the royal family's blatant percentage-taking on government contracts. His palace was simple, a two-story stucco structure on the Diriyah road which always needed a coat of paint. Although he lived in Riyadh, his spiritual home was on the desert

---

* Faisal's assassination came about as a result of a violent demonstration by religious fundamentalists in 1965 over the king's decision to introduce television into the kingdom. In the melee between demonstrators and police, a man was killed. A decade later, that man's brother shot King Faisal as he left the Red Palace in Riyadh following his weekly *majlis*.

with the Bedouin. As in the days of Abdul Aziz, hundreds came to his weekly *majlis*. Greeting him *"ayah Khalid"* (hey, Khalid), his subjects pressed on him soiled bits of paper bearing requests for everything from cash to pay minor debts to a water truck. Khalid lacked the status of Faisal, but his pious demeanor and Saudi Arabia's $37 billion in annual oil revenues made him an effective administrator of petro-Islam.

Since I lived on the grounds of the King Faisal Specialist Hospital and worked in the Ministry of Planning, two stops all visiting dignitaries took on their grand tour of Riyadh, I watched the procession of Islamic political figures dressed in their national costumes troop through the Saudi capital to collect their dues as members of the Islamic community. Week after week, they came from central Africa, Asia Minor, and southern China; from the Philippines, Eritrea, and the southern Soviet Union. Arabs from the *mashriq* came too, not as Arabs laying on the Saudis their fundamental duty to the woes of the Arab world but as members of the Islamic world over which the House of Saud was striving to reign. Yet despite $16 billion distributed in the name of Islam, the House of Saud could not escape the claims of Arab unity or secure its exclusive hold on Islam.

In 1978, Egypt agreed at Camp David to make peace with Israel. The Carter administration expected Saudi Arabia to follow. For weeks, the House of Saud was paralyzed over its decision. Rumors of infighting in the royal family grew exponentially from whispers to a widely accepted story that Crown Prince Fahd had shot Prince Abdullah, the head of the National Guard contingent of the Saudi military. Then Fahd was reported to have flown off to Spain in a rage because the king and much of the royal family refused to join the peace process. It was Saudi politics in the grand tradition of decision-making behind palace walls while those outside fed on rumor. No one, including the doctors for the royal family, ever confirmed a bullet wound in Abdullah, and Fahd went to Spain, at least in part, to undergo a crash diet. Even so, the Camp David Accords, in which the most populous Arab country decided to end its state of war with Israel, struck the House of Saud like a bolt of lightning, confronting it with the perilous decision of whether to address the wishes of the United States or stand with the Arab states massed against Egypt. In the end, King Khalid and the senior princes decided that it was safer for Saudi Arabia to face the displeasure of

238 / PASSION AND POLITICS

the United States than to risk leaving the Arab fold. What Jimmy
Carter's plan for Middle East peace failed to calculate was that Saudi
Arabia stayed just beyond the tumult of the Arab world by never
getting out in front of Arab opinion. The Saudis would follow but
they would never lead.*

Petro-Islam, having failed to protect Saudi Arabia from the
demands of Arab unity, took an even greater hit from the Islamic
revolution in Iran. In January 1979, the exiled Ayatollah Ruhollah
Khomeini crept down the steps of an Air France 747 to take personal
charge of a revolution being fought in the name of Islam. The
Western-tainted Muhammed Reza Shah Pahlavi was gone. On the
horizon stood an Islamic republic dedicated to an Islamic revival.
The words of the ayatollah went forth: "We shall export our revolution to the whole world. Until the cry 'There is no God but God'
resounds over the whole world, there will be struggle."† In Khomeini's messianic vision, Islam's universe would be cleansed of the
"Great Satan," the same Satan that provided Saudi Arabia its security
umbrella—the United States. Suddenly the House of Saud's careful
tending of Mecca, its gifts of mosques and religious grants, its expensive courtship of Islam's leaders paled against the passion of the
ayatollah. One American diplomat described the upstaging the
House of Saud had suffered: "It's like the Russians being outflanked
on the left, or George Wallace, in the old days, being outsegged in
the South."‡ For the House of Saud, militant Islam in terms of
emotion and danger exceeded the threat posed by Arab nationalism
of the 1950s and 1960s.

The House of Saud shuddered when holy Mecca temporarily
fell to religious rebels in November 1979. It quaked as Saudi Arabia's
Shiite population in the eastern province rattled its chains of religious and political oppression. It fretted when bombs laid by clandestine groups following Khomeini's message exploded next door
in Bahrain and Kuwait. The threat to a regime that claimed its
legitimacy through Islam was real and it was serious. If Nasser's

---

* In 1981, Saudi Arabia in a move to repair its American alliance presented
the Fahd Plan at the Arab conference in Fez. Implying recognition of Israel,
it was rejected, only to be adopted in 1982.
† Quoted in Robin Wright, *In the Name of God: The Khomeini Decade* (New York:
Simon & Schuster, 1989), p. 108.
‡ Quoted in Joseph Kraft, "Letter From Saudi Arabia," *The New Yorker*, July 4,
1983, p. 46.

charges that the House of Saud was a lackey of Western imperialism had been unnerving, the accusations hurled by the ayatollah that "these vile and ungodly Saudis are . . . not worthy of being in charge of the haj and Kaaba affairs" were terrifying.* Under the mesmerizing message of the white-bearded Khomeini, the House of Saud became as tainted by its Western connections as the shah. As a result, it scrambled for cover from Khomeini's ideological assault.

Shunning pleas by the United States for military bases from which to organize a defense for the kingdom, the House of Saud moved back toward the Arab tent. When Saddam Hussein launched war against the Islamic Republic of Iran in September 1980, Saudi Arabia found itself uncomfortably stranded between socialist Iraq and theocratic Iran. Ever since Baathism had triumphed in 1968, the Saudis had feared Iraq, the seeming giant on their borders that proselytized Arab nationalism. But when forced to make a choice between Arab Iraq and Persian Iran, the Saudis went with the Arab. Consequently, Saudi money poured into the Iraqi war effort as King Fahd declared that "the Gulf states are Arab states and their interests are the same as other Arabs."†

Yet the House of Saud still looked for an alternative to Arabism. They found an opening through the Gulf Cooperation Council (GCC). Born in May 1981 under the guiding hand of the House of Saud, the GCC brought Saudi Arabia, Kuwait, Bahrain, Oman, Qatar, and the United Arab Emirates into a mutual defense organization. Through it, Saudi Arabia hoped to build a regional security system, free of a dangerous American involvement, that could buffer Iran and to forge an alliance of Arabs in which Saudi Arabia dominated. From its inception, the Saudis made clear that the GCC was not a part of the Arab League, that it was a separate entity outside the traditional bounds of Arab politics.

When Fahd became king in 1982, Saudi Arabia began, inch by inch, to assume a greater role in affairs outside its borders. I reported on Fahd through the first two years of his reign. He is like no other king of the Saud line. Possessing neither the genuine devotion of Faisal nor the integrity of Khalid, his strength is not religion but administration. From the beginning of his reign, he defined himself as Saudi Arabia's first technocrat king and his passion has been

---

* *New York Times*, August 4, 1987.
† *Saudi Gazette*, December 2, 1980.

hardware and diplomacy, not tribal politics. Big like his father, over-
weight, evincing the Saud characteristic of strabismus in his right
eye, Fahd emits great charm in person. As he came and went on
his official duties, he often flashed his engaging smile if you threw
him a wave. Fahd is tainted by corruption and deeply distrusted by
many of his kingdom's fundamentalists, but he understands Saudi
Arabia's problems within its region.

Fahd had recognized in his seven years as crown prince that
Saudi Arabia's enormous petroleum reserves and economic power
dictated a role in regional affairs. From time to time he acted as
mediator in the carnage in Lebanon that began in 1975 and moved
around the periphery of other Arab disputes. It seemed that Saudi
Arabia could successfully play in the Arab arena without being captured by forces larger than itself. And it seemed that the kingdom
could maintain its Arab credentials and its American defense agreement as long as U.S. troops stayed over the horizon and out of sight.
But not everything was manageable.

In June 1984, the Iraq-Iran War had dragged on for forty-five
months. Both Saddam Hussein and the Ayatollah Khomeini were
desperate—one to win, the other to force a cease-fire. The solution
for both lay in cutting off the other's oil shipments to starve the
enemy into submission. As a result, the huge oil tankers moving
black crude through the Persian Gulf became giant targets for Iraqis
firing missiles and Iranians hurling grenades from rubber dinghies.
Shipping much of its own oil from the Gulf port of Ras Tanura,
Saudi Arabia became caught up in a war that seemed to have no
rules. In one week, the Iraqis hit the Saudi tanker *al-Ahood* and
Iranian fighters penetrated Saudi airspace.

When darkness fell on the day a Saudi F-15 shot down an
Iranian F-4, anxiety gripped Saudi Arabia. It was different from the
excited confusion that reigned when Muslim fanatics took over the
mosque at Mecca. And it was different from the deep disquiet that
crept through both Saudis and foreigners when a series of bombs
exploded in next-door Kuwait. This crisis carried with it the threat
of war with powerful, high-tech weapons. From the upstairs balcony
of my house, I looked into a black sky alive with blinking lights from
military planes. They came from the east, landed at the old Riyadh
airport, and took off again, heading back toward the Gulf. Intellectually I had always known Saudi Arabia was essentially defenseless.
Now I felt it.

The United States offered naval and air forces to defend Saudi shipping and territory, but both required ground facilities within the kingdom. The House of Saud refused. To call on the Americans would open the royal family up to attack from both the Islamic militants and the Arab nationalists. Riding the odds, the Saudis kept their U.S.-made F-15s on patrol, hunkered down behind the fragile shield of the GCC, and pumped millions of dollars into Saddam Hussein's war chest. In the summer of 1987 when Kuwait asked the United States to reflag its tankers and escort them through the troubled waters of the Gulf, the Saudis kept their distance, choosing to take their chances rather than risk Arab and Iranian anger by inviting the United States into the Persian Gulf. Finally, after eight years of war had bled both Iraq and Iran nearly to death, the cease-fire came.

In protecting themselves from Iran by holding to the Arab line in support of Iraq, the Saudis helped make a monster of Saddam Hussein. The result was that one Gulf war led to another. In 1990, Saddam Hussein pressed Kuwait on concessions on the Rumaila oil field and relief from its Kuwaiti-held war debt.* While summer wore on, Saddam pushed, Kuwait resisted, and Saudi Arabia mediated. When Iraq invaded Kuwait on August 2, the emir, Sheikh Jaber al-Ahmed al-Sabah, fled to Saudi Arabia as Abdul Rahman had fled to Kuwait in 1891. In the refuge of the al-Sabahs in the mountain resort of Taif, the House of Saud saw sitting before it its own vulnerability. If the vanguard of Iraq's million-man army now in Kuwait crossed the border, the state bequeathed to the House of Saud by Ibn Saud would be up for grabs. Compared to a calamity of this magnitude the political and cultural disorders caused by a foreign military presence on Saudi soil became minor irritants.

On the sixth day of the crisis, U.S. Secretary of Defense Dick Cheney flew into Riyadh armed with maps and reconnaissance data. Cheney, King Fahd, and the senior princes huddled behind closed doors. When they emerged, the king announced that Saudi Arabia was calling in American troops to defend the kingdom. To save itself and Saudi Arabia, the House of Saud had decided to break with the great political and cultural taboo of the Arab world and invite Western troops onto the soil of an Arab state.

---

* See Chapter 11.

Between August and December 1990, an American force of half a million men and women poured into Saudi Arabia and the Persian Gulf. Convoys of tanks, jeeps, and personnel carriers pushed into the northern reaches of Saudi Arabia and fanned out across the desert where a few days before the Bedouin and their flocks had roamed alone. They confirmed that the House of Saud had chosen the reality of American military power over the mystique of Arab unity. And in their presence, the House of Saud declared that although Saudi Arabia was a part of the Islamic world and a member of the Arab nation it was first and foremost a state determined to protect its own interests.

Islamic fundamentalists, seizing the American arrival in Saudi Arabia as an affront to Islam, released their venom against those responsible for calling in a new wave of crusaders. Audiotapes aimed at discrediting the House of Saud, sold clandestinely in the dark corridors of Riyadh's Baatha souk, described in graphic terms how Jewish female soldiers deployed in Saudi Arabia as part of United States military forces deposited "their menstrual rags at the base of the Kaaba."* In Amman, the Jordanian cleric Abu Zant railed from his pulpit, "The battle is not between Iraq and America but between Islam and the Crusaders. . . . The Saudis have lost their credentials as Muslims, by allowing foreign forces to come to our Holy Land. . . . They have brought the Americans, and what the Americans have brought to the Holy Land is VD and AIDS! The Royal Family of Saudi Arabia is a traitor to Islam!"†

The House of Saud gave back as good as it got. On the religious front, Sheik Abdul Aziz ibn Abdullah ibn Baz, the revered head of the *ulema*, issued a *fatwa*, or religious ruling, declaring holy war against Iraq. "The *jihad* that is taking place today against the enemy of God, Saddam, the ruler of Iraq, is a legitimate *jihad* on the part of Moslems and those assisting them."‡ With the stroke of a pen, the Wahhabi hierarchy turned American soldiers into warriors for Islam.

On the economic front, the House of Saud wielded its golden

---

* Saudi orders and American sensitivity kept Americans five hundred miles away from Mecca.
† Quoted in Viorst, "House of Hashem."
‡ *New York Times*, January 1, 1991.

club against Arabs and their states that supported Saddam Hussein. Subsidies and oil shipments to Jordan stopped. The kingdom's borders slammed shut on Jordanian truckers whose livelihood came from transshipping produce across Saudi Arabia to the Arab Emirates along the coast of the Persian Gulf. The large number of Jordanians working in Saudi Arabia found life difficult if not impossible as Saudi security and Saudi vengeance struck against suspected members of its foreign work force.

The PLO, the beneficiary of undisclosed millions of dollars per year, lost its Saudi funds. And Palestinians working in the kingdom lost their jobs or simply decided it was too uncomfortable to stay. Others suffered also, but none more than the Yemenis.

The tiny Yemenis had literally raised the modern infrastructure of Saudi Arabia on their backs. Like beasts of burden, they carried stone and mortar, unloaded ships and trucks, carted air conditioners and refrigerators. As many as two million Yemenis lived in Saudi Arabia until October 1991, when the Saudi government ordered them out. Sparing the small percentage that held citizenship and those with a Saudi sponsor willing to assume responsibility for individuals, the order forced 350,000 Yemenis south across the border in a period of two weeks. When its citizens lost their jobs and businesses, Yemen itself lost an estimated $350 million a month in remittances. It all happened because the government of Yemen sided with Saddam Hussein. At the border, one man in a car packed with his worldly possessions reflected, "Yesterday we were brothers. Today we are enemies."*

The war raced to its conclusion. The House of Saud and its kingdom were saved. But it was not a tidy ending. Although American troops began to pull out within days of the cease-fire, the House of Saud was left to defend itself against the charge that it had hired Western mercenaries to do its dirty work. Ignoring that it was Saddam Hussein who had split the Arab nation, many Arabs attacked Saudi Arabia not as much for what it had done but for what it is.

The Arab world has never recovered from the 1973 economic boom that raised some Arabs to such heights of grandeur and power and demeaned so completely the dignity of others. For those left out, the phenomenal wealth of the Saudis made a mockery of the

---

* *New York Times*, October 21, 1991.

brotherhood of man that Muhammed had practiced at Medina. It diminished Wahhabism's claim on Islam's pristine past. It even left behind the legacy of Abdul Aziz, who had built a nation as the bearer of Islam's original simplicity. By the time the Gulf War began, Saudi Arabia's riches and its collusion with the West had already made it, in Arab eyes, a compromised, corrupt society. The Gulf War simply confirmed the perception in the most graphic terms. With nostalgia more than reality, Arabs beyond Saudi Arabia and the other oil-rich monarchies still cling to a time when all Arabs had less but shared it more equitably. Still it is the well from which the resentments of the have-nots flow. King Hussein of Jordan spoke for the have-nots at the height of the Gulf crisis: "At the grass-roots level, long-submerged feelings of resentment on the part of most Arabs toward the Saudis are now out of the bottle. We resent the fact that they buy everything—technology, protection, ideas, people, respectability. For years, the Arabs have resented America's unlimited support of Israel. Now they are saying that the United States and Saudi Arabia are indistinguishable, and from this they conclude that the Saudis are backing Israel. Have the Saudis no shame? The Saudi monarchy, when this is over, will find it very difficult to shake that association."*

It is still possible to drive an hour beyond any of Saudi Arabia's cities and disappear into the desert. Late at night, after the campfire has died and the stars have appeared, modern Saudi Arabia seems an illusion. No lights or noise break the perfect silence. And in every direction, the empty desert seems to have no end. This is the Saudi Arabia of Abdul Aziz, haunted by hunger but untouched by the problems and demands beyond its borders. That Saudi Arabia is gone, mourned only by the romantics. The gift of oil is washing away poverty and disease, hunger and deprivation, yet its largess has also summoned the outside world. Just beyond the boundaries drawn by Abdul Aziz, coveteous eyes look in. They are Western, they are Asian, and they are Arab. It is the Arabs, holding high the mythology of Arab unity, who believe that they hold first claim on Saudi wealth.

---

* Viorst, "House of Hashem," p. 46.

C H A P T E R   9

ANWAR SADAT:
RETURN OF THE
PHARAOH

IT WAS NOVEMBER 1979, AND EGYPT, at least on the surface, throbbed with promise. The preceding March, President Anwar Sadat had put his signature on a treaty with Israel that ended thirty years of war. With peace, Egypt erupted in a frenzied tourist boom. Flights from London, Paris, Geneva, Frankfurt, and Rome flew into Cairo's international airport fully loaded with Europeans and Americans. The hotels flagrantly overbooked, forcing us veterans of Egypt's ways to discreetly tuck a bit of currency into our passports before we handed them to the registration clerk. I continued to stay at the Nile Hilton, although it was now rather frumpy compared with the Meridien and the Sheraton. From my balcony, I watched herds of tourists wearing sun hats and sensible shoes climb on and off chartered buses in the frantic search for Egypt—the Egypt of the pharaohs and Anwar Sadat. They swarmed through the Khan al-Khalili, Cairo's covered bazaar, toting crudely made camel saddles and narghiles, the legendary "hubbly bubblies." They spread out over the Pyramids and mounted nasty-tempered camels for the obligatory photograph provided as part of economy package tours. Those on superior-class tours floated down the Nile aboard a bargelike boat operated by the Sheraton hotel chain. In the eternal chaos of Egypt, these trips, like the hotels, were so overbooked that tour operators roused their moneyed clients from bed before dawn, drove them through semidarkness, and deposited them as squatters in the boat's lounge to wait to take possession of rooms due to be vacated at noon. Egypt had arrived on the exclusive list of "musts" in the travel business. But few of those who came comprehended the real Egypt— the Egypt of the peasant, the civil servant, and the shopkeeper who floundered between his perception of himself as both an Egyptian and an Arab.

In the nine years since Nasser had died, Anwar Sadat had moved Egypt out of the Arab nation and attached it to the West. Among the tourists in their palatial hotels, the Egyptian president, celebrated from Tel Aviv to Washington as one of history's great statesmen, ranked in status beside the great Ramses II. But Egyptians dwelling in dingy, cramped apartments in Cairo and smoky mud huts along the waters of the Nile were infected by a gnawing sense of alienation. They had seen Egypt pass through the heady heights of the Nasser era and the emotional triumph of the 1973 war against Israel. Now they stood on the outside of the Arab nation, shut out by a separate peace with Israel. Some simply shrugged when asked about the path Egypt had taken. Others verbalized their feelings well. One evening I was visiting with a midlevel army officer and his wife in their modest four-room apartment in one of the sprawling high-rise developments that had been built in the suburbs of Cairo to house the Egyptian military. We talked about Sadat's decision to make peace with Israel. What this veteran of the 1967 and 1973 wars said reflected how many Egyptians felt at the time. "We welcome peace. We sacrificed too much too long for the Arab cause. We all knew for a long time that Egypt was carrying too much of the burden in the Arabs' war with Israel. As a military man and an Egyptian, I say peace is good. Still, I must tell you I wonder if we are paying too much for peace—as we paid too much for war. Egypt is alone. This isn't good. Egypt is Egypt. But Egypt is also an Arab country." He put down his cigarette and put both hands to his chest. "I am an Egyptian but I am also an Arab. This I think Sadat does not understand. He is too much for the West. He doesn't anymore think like an Arab."

In 1979, Egypt was afloat between its two constant geographic and cultural realities—the desert and the Nile. The desert bequeaths the legacy of the Arabs with its deep sense of shared destiny. The Nile defines Egypt, pulls it into itself. The desert shaped Nasser's universe; the Nile molded that of Anwar Sadat.

Until the day Gamal Abdul Nasser died and he ascended to the presidency, few people outside Egypt had ever heard of Anwar Sadat, the obscure vice president of the United Arab Republic. Dwarfed by Nasser, characterized by his obsequiousness, Sadat was the buffoon of Egyptian politics. Few thought he would survive more than a few weeks.

Anwar Sadat was born December 25, 1918, in the Nile Delta village of Mit Abu al-Kom. Despite the image he would later create of being a simple village boy, Sadat was actually brought up in Cairo as one of thirteen children of an educated family. His father, a clerk for the army, was poorer in money than in status. Working his contacts within the military, he secured a place for his son in that first class of nonaristocrats that entered the military academy in 1937, the same class to which Nasser belonged.

When Sadat graduated in 1938, he was already a hotheaded nationalist scheming to drive the British out of Egypt. In 1942, as a young captain, he joined in an absurdly bungled plot to smuggle over to the Germans a former Egyptian general knowledgeable about British war installations. As in some Laurel and Hardy movie, a getaway car broke down, the escape plane crashed on takeoff, and in the finale a belly dancer betrayed Sadat to British intelligence. He along with two Nazi spies went to the Aliens' Jail.

Unchastened, Sadat between 1944 and 1949 spearheaded a group of radical officers within the Egyptian army. Adopting terrorism as an acceptable tactic against the hated Farouk government, he hurled a grenade through the window of Prime Minister Mustafa Nahas's car and stood in attendance at the assassination of Amin Osman, Egypt's finance minister. Sadat went back to jail for thirty-one months as prisoner #2151 in Cairo Central Prison.

Emerging in late 1951, Sadat managed to be reinstated in the army. Almost immediately, he was recruited into Gamal Abdul Nasser's Free Officers movement.* Yet after years of nationalist activity, incarceration, and underground preparation, Anwar Sadat almost missed the Free Officers revolt. Summoned for the long-awaited

---

* In his autobiography, Sadat claims that he, not Nasser, founded the Free Officers and it was only his imprisonment that allowed Nasser to take control.

coup, he arrived in Cairo from his post in Gaza on July 22, 1952. Unable to locate any of the conspirators, he took his wife, Jihan, to one of Cairo's outdoor movie theaters to see a Ronald Reagan film. Returning home at 12:45 A.M. on the 23rd, he found a hastily scrawled message from Nasser asking where he was. Sadat threw on his uniform and rushed into the night. By the time he arrived at general headquarters, it was already in the hands of the Free Officers. All that was left for Colonel of the Signal Corps Anwar Sadat to do in the seminal event of modern Egyptian politics was to read the announcement of the coup on the radio.

After 1952, Sadat more or less disappeared from Nasser's revolution. But after the 1967 disaster, Sadat surfaced again to become Nasser's lapdog. In the trauma of defeat, Nasser apparently found in Sadat a trusted, undemanding friend. Yet while valuing Sadat's loyalty, he was also irritated by his excessive docility. Calling him Bikbashi Sah, "Colonel Yes-Yes," behind his back, Nasser grumbled that he wished Sadat would occasionally vary the way in which he agreed with him. Those around Nasser joked that the rough patch of skin on Sadat's forehead came not from praying but from Nasser so often reaching across the conference table to slap him on the forehead and shout, "You, shut up!"

Sadat's elevation to vice president simply happened. When Nasser went to the Rabat Conference in December 1969, he appointed the eager and seemingly harmless Sadat vice president. According to intimates, Nasser believed that if anything happened to him Sadat could fill the ceremonial role as president while Nasser's Socialist Union Party and the army governed. There the matter rested until September 28, 1970.

Called once more to announce a momentous event in Egyptian history, Anwar Sadat as acting president broke the news of Nasser's death to the nation. He waited three hours, allowing time for a "red alert" for possible Israeli attack to flash through to army units. Then, weeping openly, he went before the television cameras. "The UAR, the Arab nation, and humanity have lost the most precious man, the most courageous and most sincere man."

Anwar Sadat, maliciously disparaged as the "black donkey" because of his dark skin, possessing no discernible ideology and no personal following, now stood at the helm of Egypt. He seemed a jester trying to succeed a king. But it was precisely because Sadat had never staked out an independent position that he had survived

Nasser's pathological suspicion. Anwar Sadat was president of Egypt for one reason—he was Nasser's dutiful vice president who had stood with him through thirty years of conspiracy, revolution, and finally national tragedy. It was only because he was a weak man that Nasser's inner circle reluctantly laid its hands on Anwar Sadat. But there was no enthusiasm. *Al-Ahram*, the mouthpiece of Nasser's political organization, could summon only enough zeal to say Sadat's nomination was "a mature and responsible expression of the exigencies that govern the current complicated situation." Only the strong desire for continuity on the part of Nasser's coterie allowed Sadat to survive a constitutionally decreed plebiscite to become president in his own right. At that point, Anwar Sadat came face to face with Egypt and the legacy of Nasser.

Egypt lives within tight, unyielding ecological boundaries. In 1970, the country was reaching for the limits. When Napoleon arrived in 1798, Egypt had a population of 2.5 million. In 1970, it was 34 million. By 1980, it was estimated that there would be another 50 million Egyptians demanding to be fed, housed, clothed, and employed.

The population increase pressed ceaselessly on Cairo. In 1962, when I first came to Egypt, Cairo was large and it was congested, but it still retained some of that easy atmosphere portrayed by the novelists of the 1930s. In midafternoon, the traffic circle in front of the National Museum could be empty except for a donkey cart and a lone car leisurely passing through. In 1970, the city roared with traffic and throbbed with the pressure of too many people in too small a space.

People flocked to Cairo because there was nothing for them in the villages. The neglect of agriculture during the Nasser years left rural Egyptians no better off than in the days of the corrupt Farouk. In the villages, blindfolded cattle yoked to the forked wooden center post of a primitive water-raising device continued to tread an endless circle while men still toiled in the fields from dawn to sunset. Women, as they had always done, carried water in heavy clay pots from the river to their mud-brick houses, where in stifling heat they baked flat bread in open-fronted ovens that poured gray smoke into the all but windowless cubicles in which they lived out their lives. The only thing that had changed in the Nasser years was the teeming numbers along the riverbank. Unable to absorb any more population, the country pumped its excess numbers into the cities.

But conditions in the cities were little better than those in the rural areas. Misguided economic policy had created an industrial base capable of supporting only half the population. Those that it employed often lived eight to ten in one room in unheated tenements with communal plumbing. The cities had become so crowded that even the mosques overflowed, leaving people to congregate on the sidewalks to pray.

Nasser's ill-considered socialist schemes had channeled the country's resources into industrialization at the expense of agriculture and had left both impoverished. Furthermore, comprehensive nationalization in 1961 had put virtually every commercial and industrial enterprise with fifty or more employees under state control. By the time Sadat became president, the state owned the banks and insurance companies, the oil refineries, the utilities, the railroads, the airline, most maritime transport, the fertilizer industry, all major construction companies, the newspapers, the department stores, and even the film studios. While Nasserism disemboweled the productive sector, it committed itself to ever growing government subsidies to maintain a shaky floor under the poverty-plagued peasants and urban workers and to put the struggling middle class to work in the bureaucracy. Between the 1952 revolution and Nasser's death the number of government employees grew from 250,000 to over a million. In short, Nasser's economic system created all of the disasters of a strict, state-run economy. And Anwar Sadat inherited the mess.

From the day he took office, economic realities shaped Anwar Sadat's agenda. Yet Egypt's despair came as much from its psychological needs as from its physical needs. An economic renaissance depended, in part, on the restoration of Egyptian dignity. For Anwar Sadat to confront Egypt's economic distress he had first to assuage the shame of 1967.

Three years after the Six-Day War, the Arab states and Israel remained stranded between war and peace. Neither side had essentially moved since November 22, 1967, when the Security Council of the United Nations passed Resolution 242, calling on Israel to swap the territorial gains of the June War for recognition by the Arab states of Israeli "sovereignty, territorial integrity, and political independence." But negotiations never began. Egypt, seeking insurance on return of its conquered land, insisted that Israel withdraw before the start of negotiations. And Israel, determined to win recognition of the Jewish state, demanded face-to-face talks with the Arab states before any territory changed hands. Shortly before he died, Nasser accepted a cease-fire under the U.S.-sponsored Rogers Plan. But real peace never came.

Three months after becoming president, Anwar Sadat journeyed to the dusty Nile Delta town of Tanta to address his first mass rally. Before a crowd of twelve thousand people he revived the style of the great Nasser: "There will be no compromise and we will not give up one inch of our land. The battle will extend to our farms, our factories, in the towns, cities and on the streets. Are you really tired of fighting?" The crowd roared back, "We shall fight! We shall fight! O Sadat, lead us to liberation!"* But before Sadat could confront Israel, he had to consolidate his own power base in order to strengthen his tenuous hold on Egypt.

Anwar Sadat, accepted by Nasser's inner circle as the meek, compliant companion who had stood by Nasser like a faithful dog, turned out to have very large teeth. In early 1971, Ali Sabri, a Nasser intimate and the Soviet Union's strongest ally in the Egyptian government, attempted to restrict Sadat's right to rule by presidential decree as Nasser had done. Before he succeeded, a clutch of papers outlining a leftist plot to overthrow Sadat handed the president the excuse he needed to execute the "corrective revolution" of May 1971. Sadat ousted Sabri and threw the rest of Moscow's men in jail. With the hard-line leftists gone, Sadat edged a constellation of Nasserite personalities out of power, including some of his old comrades in conspiracy—the Free Officers. By May 15, 1971, Anwar Sadat, a man formerly thought of as a clown, had destroyed the political apparatus left by Nasser. Then he moved on to the Russians.

During Nasser's last years, Egypt's relationship with the Soviet Union, born in such promise in the mid-1950s, floundered in a sea of disappointments. The alliance had not delivered victory over Israel. And it had clamped the cherished independence Egypt had won in the 1952 revolution into irons forged from Soviet economic and military aid. By the time Nasser died, nearly fifteen thousand Soviet military advisers directed the training of the Egyptian military, Soviet pilots flew Egypt's MiG-21s and manned its air defense system, and Soviet military commanders controlled access to Egypt's

* *Time*, January 18, 1971.

most important military installations. Soviet officers held posts in the intelligence service, the police, and sensitive civilian ministries. In his ability to wield influence over Egyptian decision-making, the Soviet ambassador mirrored the British high commissioner in the days of British colonialism. In the barracks and cafés, Egyptians grumbled that the Russians might prove even harder to get rid of than the British.

No Egyptian's love was lost on the "ugly Russians." In Egyptian eyes, Russian arrogance was exceeded only by Russian stinginess. Vendors fumed as stout Slavic women wearing shoddy garments bought out of the Eastern bloc prowled the vegetable souks squeezing every orange, feeling every tomato, haggling over every piaster. And tour operators, hotels, and shopkeepers groaned that most of their business came from Russian and eastern European tour groups who traveled cheap and bought nothing but a few tacky, low-profit handicrafts. Egyptian judgment of Soviet frugality crystallized in the story of a taxi driver who was ordered to stop at a soft-drink stand where three burly Russian men bought one Pepsi to share among them.

Sadat hated the heavy hand of the Russians. The Soviet leadership consistently lied to him by promising weapons it could not or would not deliver. But above all, the alliance with the Soviet Union pulled Egypt into the poisonous rivalry between the superpowers. The Soviet Union would broach no war in the Middle East that brought it toe to toe with the United States, and the United States would tolerate no war between Egypt and Israel as long as Egypt stayed tied to Moscow. If Anwar Sadat was to avenge the humiliation of 1967, he had to place his actions beyond the consuming interests of the superpowers. On July 18, 1972, five days short of the twentieth anniversary of the 1952 revolution, Anwar Sadat ordered the bulk of Soviet military advisers out of Egypt. Nasser had embraced the Soviets out of frustration with the United States' refusal to supply Egypt with arms. Now Anwar Sadat expelled the Soviet Union in order to neutralize American arms. Events had come full circle.

Before the end of his second year as president, Anwar Sadat had triumphed over his rivals and curbed Soviet influence in Egypt. Only one other thing stood between him and the new order he envisioned for Egypt—the ghost of Gamal Abdul Nasser.

Nasser's spirit haunted Sadat. For Anwar Sadat had never excited a pan-Arab audience. He had never been a hero to the Arab masses from Baghdad to Casablanca. Beyond Egypt's border, Sadat was paralyzed by the Nasser legend. Nasserism itself became a weapon with which Sadat was bludgeoned by his rivals in the Arab system, particularly Muammar Qaddafi. Yet inside Egypt, Sadat could compete with Nasser.

Sadat exhorted Egyptians to debunk the myth, to purge Nasser from their political being. And they responded. Nasser's police state had betrayed much of the 1952 revolution. If the peasants refused to see that, the educated classes did. They packed into theaters in 1971 to see the movie *Karnak*, based on Naguib Mahfouz's novel. Karnak was not the great temple of pharaonic Egypt but a coffee-house frequented by student dissidents of the 1960s. In it, Nasser's secret police operated as sadistic torturers who brutalized innocent people while neglecting Egypt's real interests. Any doubts about the story's message disappeared in a scene in which prison guards standing below a portrait of a smiling Nasser beat a young student to death while Israeli jets bombed a defenseless Egypt during the 1967 war.

Sadat could de-Nasserize Egypt for the deceptively simple reason that Egyptians were tired of camouflaging their poverty and impotence under the banner of pan-Arabism. Sadat pointed the way to a new order by riding at the head of the "Egypt-firsters," those who would minimize the claims of Arabism in favor of Egyptian interests. None of those interests ranked higher than the recovery of the Sinai and accommodation with Israel that would lift from Egypt the economic burden of war.

Anwar Sadat declared 1971 the "year of decision," the year when Egypt would recapture its territory lost in 1967. Denied military supplies by a Soviet leadership smarting from Russia's expulsion from Egypt, Sadat flipped the calendar and 1972 became the "year of the inevitable battle." The calendar was turned again, and 1973 became the "era of total confrontation" with Israel. Actually Sadat, if not his military, had had every intention of breaking out of the stalemate with Israel in 1971. But his fifty fighter-bombers destined to fly a deep-penetration raid into occupied Sinai to capture the world's attention had to be held back when another India-Pakistan crisis seized the stage. In 1972, Sadat ordered a parachute brigade into the Sinai to hold a beachhead for a week to ten days. Sadat envisioned the mission catapulting the United Nations Security Council into session to unlock the diplomatic stalemate in the Middle East, paving the way for Libya to shut off its oil taps, which were dispensing 25 percent of Western Europe's petroleum needs, and forcing the United States to broker an Israeli withdrawal from Arab territories. Sadat's own military squashed that plan. In 1973, Sadat was again beating the war drums, and this time the Soviet Union, perhaps expecting that another humiliating Arab defeat would topple Sadat and bring back a pro-left government, agreed to resume the flow of military hardware and spare parts that had been halted in the USSR's humiliating eviction from Egypt. With a weapons supply secured, Sadat warned, "Everyone has fallen asleep over the Mideast crisis. But they will soon wake up. . . ."*

Between 1970 and 1973, Sadat had put together the alliance of Egypt, Syria, and Saudi Arabia that would fight the 1973 war. Saudi Arabia rather than Syria was Sadat's more important ally. Under Sadat, Egypt's relations with Saudi Arabia's King Faisal improved measurably. Gone were the Soviets, the purveyors of Marxism into the Arab world that King Faisal so feared.† Gone was Nasser's rhetoric that viciously divided the Arab regimes into progressives and reactionaries. To Sadat, it made no difference. "My clear and declared policy was that Egypt could not distinguish one Arab country from another on the basis of so-called progressive and reactionary or republican and monarchial systems. We should be committed to one thing only—our Arab character, pure and simple."‡ Thus the breach between the Arab world's most populous country and its most wealthy closed.

With the House of Saud convinced that Anwar Sadat planned to use a limited war to force an end to the stalemate with Israel, not a lengthy military venture that would plunge the whole region into chaos, the gates to the Saudis' monetary reservoir opened. At the same time, King Faisal used his American alliance to warn Washington that Sadat was not bluffing and that if war came Saudi Arabia would have to join its fellow Arab states in a "gesture of solidarity with Egypt."

In September, Sadat reached out to Syria's president, Hafiz

---

* *Newsweek*, April 9, 1973.
† The Saudis were so happy when Sadat gave the boot to the Soviet Union that they presented him with a $12 million personal plane similar to Air Force One.
‡ Sadat, *In Search of Identity*, p. 239.

Assad, who agreed to join the coalition in an attempt to recover the Golan Heights. Finally, Jordan's King Hussein, the other big loser in 1967, was forgiven his 1970 war against the Palestinians and coaxed into becoming a limited partner.

Still war seemed impossible. In October 1973, Egypt was broke, unable either to service its foreign debts or to buy additional wheat to feed its people. On the battlefield, Israel commanded overwhelming military power. And the United States and the Soviet Union built toward détente, removing a guarantee of Russian help to offset the American commitment to Israel. That Sadat even thought in terms of war confirmed just how desperate he was to find a way out of the self-flagellation and economic urgency engulfing Egypt. For the Egyptians to grasp their future, their self-doubts had to be resolved. A limited war, if successful, promised Egypt a bridge to the future and Anwar Sadat his great act. "I reckoned it would be 1,000 times more honorable for us—40,000 of my sons in the armed forces and myself—to be buried crossing the Canal than to accept such disgrace and humiliation."*

The early days of October idled in normalcy. It was Ramadan, the month of fasting for Muslims. A few soldiers and airmen of the Egyptian military routinely left their units to go to their families for this most holy time of year in Islam. The president's order to send additional food to the troops smacked of a political gesture by a weak government, not a call to arms. It was all a ruse.

At 2:00 P.M. on October 6, 1973, Arab forces threw a two-front assault against Israel. On Yom Kippur, the Day of Atonement, the holiest day of the Jewish year, the Arabs accomplished what Israel had never believed possible—a surprise attack.† Syrian heavy artillery rained shells on Israeli settlements on the Golan Heights while five hundred tanks and two infantry divisions smashed through the 1970 cease-fire lines and on toward the border of Israel. But the real glory for the Arabs awaited in the Sinai, where the Egyptians launched their long-rehearsed crossing of the Suez Canal. Massive dynamite charges laid by Egyptian frogmen the night before tore holes in Israel's sixty-foot-high defensive sand embankment on the east side of the canal. On the Egyptian side, a hundred soldiers of

---

* Ibid., p. 215.
† The 1973 Arab-Israeli war is most often called the October War. It is also known as the Yom Kippur War and the Ramadan War.

the 7th Brigade leaped into waiting boats, sped across the canal under heavy artillery fire, and stormed through a gaping hole in the embankment to plant the Egyptian flag once more on Sinai. Employing high-pressure water pumps especially made in West Germany to widen the opening in Israel's wall of sand, the vanguard of the Egyptian attack forces received three tanks ferried across the canal. Behind them, pontoon bridges from south of Qantara to north of Ismailia spanned the narrow waterway dividing Egyptian from Israeli-occupied territory. As the last links clanked into place, trucks carrying troops, clad in light parkas and hoods to protect against the wind-whipped sand, crested the bank on the west side of the canal and inched their way down and onto a bridge. As they touched the other side, the men who remembered 1967 broke into shouts of "Allahu Akbar." The helmeted, fatigue-clad infantrymen who followed on foot touched the gritty soil of Sinai and raised their automatic rifles to the sky. The canal was crossed, Arab honor restored.

The Arabs, the vanquished, the humiliated, were reborn. Arab pride and the spirit of Arab unity once more infused the Arab world. It did not seem to matter that the odds of ultimate victory remained heavily with Israel. On this day, in the wastelands of the Sinai, Arab honor was vindicated. The editor of one of the myriad of Lebanese newspapers quietly said, "We have won. We have won, even if our cities are turned into ruins in the weeks ahead."*

Twenty-five Israeli fortifications rapidly fell, and then the whole Bar Lev line, Israel's Maginot Line in the Sinai. Mangled and twisted steel girders in scorched bunkers testified to the intensity of the battle on the front line. Farther on, abandoned boots lay on the desert as symbols of a hasty retreat before the relentless, grinding advance of tanks. Long lines of dazed prisoners of war, sitting on their haunches, their hands tied behind their backs, spoke of defeat. But this time the material and human refuse of battle was Israeli, not Arab. This time Israeli radio, not Arab radio, shouted its panic. "We shall turn your days into nights, and show you the stars at high noon. We shall put your faces and noses in the mud. We shall make the enemy leaders pay heavily for this. We shall crush your bones."†

---

* *Newsweek*, October 22, 1973.
† Ibid.

On the second day of the war, the Israeli counteroffensive began. For hours, Israeli and Egyptian tanks wheeled and fired across the Sinai. When it ended, the Egyptians had won, completely destroying the 190th Israeli Armored Brigade. That night its stunned commander and the crews of twenty-five captured tanks were paraded like trophies of war on Cairo television. With collective horror, Israel realized that its crack ground forces and overwhelming superiority in air power that had so decisively won the 1967 war had been reined in by Soviet missiles and the surprising discipline and spirit of the Arab armies. The encompassing confidence of 1967 shattered.

The war went on into its third day. The Golan Heights rumbled as Israeli and Syrian tanks stood barrel to barrel on the barren, bramble-covered plateau, while in the Sinai the Egyptians marched on thirteen miles east of the canal, only nine miles west of the Mitla Pass, the festering symbol of the Arab drubbing in the 1967 war. The words of Nasser's resignation speech after that war came back: "The imperialists believe this was a personal defeat for Nasser. But it was a defeat for the whole Arab people, and the Arab people will not accept that defeat."

But by the third week, the tide turned decisively against the Arabs. At al-Arish, the Sinai town directly behind the front, American transport planes had been disgorging tanks and sophisticated weapons gathered out of the stores of American combat troops to replace Israel's devastating losses and to redress the balance on the battlefield. The Arab oil producers had hit back by embargoing oil to the United States. But shutting down the flow of oil had produced no immediate effects on the ground war. Rearmed, the Israelis threw their own bridges over the canal, quickly putting two hundred tanks and fifteen thousand troops onto its west bank. Fanning out along a fifteen-mile stretch of the waterway, Israeli units wiped out surface-to-air missile batteries, opening a hole in Egyptian air defenses. Almost immediately, the sky over Sinai swirled with dogfights in which Israel's American-supplied jets generally took the Egyptians' MiGs.

On the Syrian front, Israeli forces paused at the village of Saasa, only twenty miles from Damascus. And on the east bank, the Egyptians barely clung to their narrow beachhead in the Sinai. In New York, the United Nations Security Council produced Resolution 338, calling for an immediate cease-fire and negotiations for a peace settlement under "appropriate auspices."* It was the moment Anwar Sadat had been waiting for. Egypt accepted the cease-fire without prior consultation with Syria. With no choice but to follow suit, the Syrians agreed to a cessation of hostilities. The cease-fire went into effect at 7:00 P.M. on October 22 only to break down as Israeli troops raced for Suez City on the west bank to cut off the Egyptian Third Army. On the 23rd, the guns finally fell silent.

The war had lasted eighteen ferocious days—three times longer than the disgrace of 1967. All the participants suffered heavy losses in both men and material. But the Arabs won the psychological war. Regardless of the war's ultimate outcome, the Arabs found their emotional victory in the crossing of the Suez Canal, the grand symbol of the break with the debilitating past. In his poem "The Deliverance," Egyptian writer Yusuf Idris spoke for all Arabs.

With one stroke of a decree the miracle was accomplished:
We were transformed from an honorless existence, an exis-
     tence of beasts and animals, into human beings possessed of
     honor.
With one stroke of a decree our honor returned to us, and
     our humanness came back. . . .
With his [Sadat's] decision not only our army crossed over the
     canal,
But our people crossed over the emptiness and the ignominy,
Crossed over the agonies which man cannot endure. . . .†

Cairo's Panorama continues to celebrate what is now known simply as "the crossing." It is housed in a stately gray-domed building that stands in solitary splendor within a fenced, carefully groomed square set beyond the noise and grime of Cairo. I arrived at the tall black wrought-iron gates about six o'clock one evening in the late fall. After surrendering my admission permit, I stepped through. An atmosphere of reverence I had never experienced in Egypt, even in al-Azhar, enveloped me as I walked past the relics of the 1973

* Resolution 338 essentially reaffirmed Resolution 242, passed after the 1967 war, which called for Israel to exchange territory for peace. These two reso-lutions have formed the basis of the elusive peace that has escaped the Arabs and Israel ever since.
† Yusuf Idris, "The Deliverance," as quoted in Patai, *Arab Mind*, p. 316.

war. The bronze statues of Egypt's heroes of the war flanked a captured Israeli tank that was overshadowed only by a fighter plane of the Egyptian air force mounted on a massive angular base that thrust it toward the sky. Climbing wide stone steps toward a pair of towering copper doors, I entered what is in reality a pink-marble-and-gray-granite temple to the October War. Unlike the rest of Cairo, it was clean, pristine, and quiet. Toward seven o'clock, a group of people dressed in the style of the Persian Gulf surged in, followed by dark-skinned Africans, who were followed by a cluster of Pakistanis. Interspersed among them were well-dressed Arabs from here and there in the Arab world. I was the only Westerner.

Uniformed guards herded us toward a narrow, winding stairway to the auditorium above, where I found a seat between a retired Egyptian army officer and a Jordanian businessman. The lights dimmed. Powerful martial music overlaid with a deep, booming voice blasted forth from dozens of speakers implanted in the circular ceiling. Suddenly brilliant lights flashed on, and there it was—the first section of a 360-degree painting created by a Korean art group that drew on the very worst of Disney. The platform on which the audience sat began to inch around the overdone painting. As we moved, the music and the narrative built toward the climax—the crossing of the canal. Then it ended. The Africans and Asians excitedly chattered as we descended the stairs. But the Arabs remained silent, savoring once more the restoration of Arab pride, the celebration of Arab unity.

The October War rekindled the vision of the most ambitious pan-Arabists, who saw before them a united Arab world overpowering impotence and international neglect. It lasted two years.

The dreams of resurrecting the Arabs' golden age faded as the Saudis, the Kuwaitis, and the sheikhdoms of the United Arab Emirates found more satisfaction in airports, highways, palaces, and consumer spending than in Arab unity. The glorious chapter in Arab history written by the October War that, on the psychological level, belonged to every Arab faded as it became grievously clear that the drastic rise in oil prices and the treasure it generated aggrandized only the fortunate few. The rest stood outside, have-nots burdened by frustration and impotence. No people felt this more than the Egyptians. Those who had shouldered the burden of war would gain no relief from their grinding poverty. Instead, "the rich got richer, whereas those who initially spilled their blood had to turn around and spill their dignity asking for a little of the material wealth that others had acquired because of the sacrifices made by the poor."* The oil boom struck a deep wound in the collective psyche of Egypt. From its pain came a bitter belief that the rich Arabs wanted Egypt "to starve alone, die alone, fight alone and go bankrupt alone."† Egypt and its president had had enough. They wanted out of the Arab quagmire.

Anwar Sadat had never structured the October War as a total Arab endeavor. For him and the Egyptians who understood the war's meaning, the 1973 war marked neither the beginning of a new, sustained struggle with Israel nor another phase of Egypt's submission to inter-Arab politics. The 1973 war might belong to the Arabs psychologically—politically it belonged to Egypt. In a sense it was never a conventional war but a military exercise designed to secure a nonmilitary objective—a settlement of the territorial issues coming out of 1967.

Yet after the 1973 war, Egypt as part of the Arab political constellation faced the same dilemmas it had faced before the canal was crossed. Israel demanded direct negotiations with the Arab states, which amounted to Arab recognition of the Zionist state without guaranteeing a return of territory. The Arab nations insisted on negotiating collectively and pledged to reject any agreement that failed to create a state for the Palestinians. Egypt could not afford to wait for either the Israeli or the Arab position to change. It needed peace immediately. By traumatizing Israel and restoring the shattered pride of the Arabs, Sadat created the authority to leave Nasser's pan-Arab path forever. Rivaling, for the moment, the mighty Nasser, he could ignore the protests of other Arabs and begin to seek peace with Israel. For it was he, not they, who had challenged the enemy, and it was he who was the hero of the war. In the midst of his triumph as an Arab leader, Anwar Sadat began to search for his own peace with Israel. In the final repudiation of Nasserism, he embraced as his partner the United States.

On November 6, 1973, Henry Kissinger, President Richard Nixon's secretary of state, arrived in Cairo. In late October, Egypt and Israel had met in a tent at Kilometer 101 on the road between

---

* Rifaat al-Said, "The Arabs: United by War, Will They Now Be Divided by Peace?" *al Talia* (Cairo), August 1975.
† Ajami, *Arab Predicament*, p. 8.

Cairo and Suez to sign a cease-fire. But their armies stayed entangled along the Suez Canal. By January, Kissinger, shuttling between Tel Aviv and Sadat's retreat at Aswan, had convinced Israel to move back fifteen miles off the west bank of the canal, springing eighteen thousand men of Egypt's strapped Third Army. Egypt's part of the bargain, which was sealed by an agreement known as Sinai I, was to break off from Syria, leaving Hafiz Assad to find his own deal with Israel over the issue of the Golan.

Richard Nixon himself came to Cairo in February. The same crowds that had once hailed Nasser's anti-Westernism now raised their voices in joyful greetings to the American president and the resumption of diplomatic relations between the United States and Egypt. It seemed Anwar Sadat had correctly analyzed the war-weariness that hung around the nation of the Nile.

Nixon left and Kissinger returned. Through the summer, Sadat's friend, "dear Henry," once more shuttled between Middle East capitals. By September, he had negotiated the Sinai II agreement, which returned two thousand square miles of Sinai to Egypt. But in gaining Egypt's territorial goal, Sadat made his break with the Arabs. In a statement with profound implications for collective Arab policy toward Israel, Egypt pledged not to "resort to the use of the threat of force to resolve disputes with Israel." Arab unity, territorial imperatives, and the Palestinian issue faded as Egypt, with its American partner, staked out its own ground. "Throughout the Nasser era it was in Cairo that the banner of Arabism was hoisted and to it that non-Egyptian Arabs turned for material and moral support. Cairo's friends were the believers in Arab unity and solidarity, its enemies the stooges of imperialism, lackeys of the West and secessionists who failed to abide by the imperatives of Arab unity."* But Egypt would no longer sound the rallying cry of Arabism. Instead Anwar Sadat, the hero of 1973, had struck a deal for Egypt in defiance of the collective Arab will. If Sadat's October War marked the zenith of Arab unity, the Sinai Accord of September 1975 signaled the beginning of its disintegration.

Disengagement in the Sinai failed to stop Egypt's slide into the economic cesspool. In spite of the efforts of Henry Kissinger, Egypt was still spending close to $2.2 billion a year on its armed forces.

---

* Fouad Ajami, "Between Cairo and Damascus: The Arab World and the New Stalemate," *Foreign Affairs*, April 1976, pp. 444–45.

And it still needed another $2 billion a year in foreign aid just to stay afloat. Rod al-Farag, not far from downtown Cairo, swarmed with 261,348 residents per square mile—ten times the population density of New York City. Throughout Cairo, housing was so scarce that squatters took over the tombs of the cemetery known as the City of the Dead. The government, regarding the situation as a solution rather than a problem, ran electrical lines to mausoleum-apartments. With too many people and too few jobs, the average urban worker earned 30 BP [$72] a month. Government subsidies on basic commodities helped most people survive, but they sucked the blood out of Egypt's chronically anemic treasury.

In the spring of 1974, Sadat had tried to improve the economy by chiseling a piece out of Nasser's socialism by initiating the *infitah*, the open door to Western investment. The *infitah* gave some energy to Egypt's economy, but it also created a new breed of pashas and fat cats. Collecting commissions and other payments, licit and illicit, from foreign investors, a bourgeoisie arose that became known by the odious designation *"infitah* class." It was a class that derived its livelihood from trade with the West and its identity from its slavish imitation of things Western. Its most visible member was the president, Anwar Sadat. Although producing some trickle-down effect, the *infitah* did almost nothing to alleviate the abject poverty that made government subsidies so critical to so many people.

On January 18, 1977, Egyptians woke up to the piercing news that the government was binding its hemorrhaging budget by reducing the average Egyptian's precious subsidies. Overnight, prices on such basics as flour, rice, soap, and gasoline jumped by as much as 31 percent. By midafternoon, the country reverberated with the worst riots since Black Saturday of 1952. Over the next two days, mobs in every large town burned and looted while crowds chanted their displeasure with Anwar Sadat and his Dunhill pipes, Parisian ties, and London suits. "You live in style and we live seven to a room; you change clothes three times a day and we change once a year." Surviving Nasserites surfaced to shout, "Arise, O hero, we are now ruled by a donkey." While the presidential plane stood by at Abu Suweir airport ready to transport the president and his family to Tehran, Sadat sent the army into the streets. Force, but even more the restoration of the subsidies, brought order. Although Sadat blamed the trouble on communists, the 160 dead testified to the terrible desperation of ordinary Egyptians. Egypt had to find a way out of economic paralysis and military stalemate. But no formula lay on the horizon to coax Egypt, Jordan, Syria, the PLO, and Israel to the bargaining table, much less to a settlement. And Sadat could afford even less than in the past to wait through round after round of rhetoric, posturing, and threats masquerading as diplomacy. For Egypt and its president to survive, he had to break the logjam immediately.

Through confidence or desperation, Sadat believed Egypt could act alone. After all, Egypt was the center of gravity of the Arab world. Regional peace required its participation; war required its leadership. If the Arab states refused to help Egypt extricate itself from the burden of confrontation with Israel, then Sadat would remove Egypt from the military equation, thereby reducing the Arabs to less than a credible force. But he needed a vehicle. It was provided by Walter Cronkite, the American television newsman.

Through the fall of 1977, talk of a summit meeting between Anwar Sadat and Menachem Begin had whiffed through the air. Sadat even announced to his own parliament that he would go to Jerusalem in search of peace if he was invited. But no invitation came. At 9:00 A.M. on Monday, November 14, Cronkite taped an interview with Sadat for the CBS Evening News. When asked if he would be willing to go to Jerusalem in search of peace, Sadat replied, "I'm just waiting for the proper invitation." Cronkite followed up by asking how such an invitation could be transmitted between countries maintaining no diplomatic relations. Sadat hopped on the answer: "Why not through our—our mutual friend, the Americans?"

Over the next six hours, CBS's Tel Aviv bureau filmed a similar interview with Menachem Begin. After some probing, the dour prime minister said he planned to send a letter to Sadat the next day through the U.S. ambassadors in Tel Aviv and Cairo. "Let us sit together . . . and talk peace." That evening, technology paired the interviews, putting Begin and Sadat on a split screen as if they were in simultaneous conversation with Cronkite. The next day Begin's letter arrived in Cairo and the pilgrimage of Anwar Sadat to Jerusalem was on.

Anwar Sadat acted as the instrument, not necessarily the creator of Egyptian history. He seized the moment to go to Jerusalem not because he was a great visionary but because he understood that Egypt's clerks and shopkeepers, its students and obedient peasants were no longer willing to fight and bleed for the Arab nation. But if Sadat understood Egypt's exhaustion, the rest of the Arab world did not. From one Arab capital after another, accusations came forth that Sadat was undercutting the whole Arab system. It was intensified by Sadat's failure to prepare the groundwork with other Arab leaders before making his startling announcement. The Saudis, Egypt's bankers, were particularly incensed at not being consulted. King Khalid, in Mecca for prayers on the eve of Sadat's departure, later revealed, "I have always before gone to the Kaaba to pray for somebody, never to pray against anyone. But on this occasion I found myself saying, 'Oh God, grant that the aeroplane taking Sadat to Jerusalem may crash before it gets there, so that he may not become a scandal for all of us.' I am ashamed that I prayed in the Kaaba against a Moslem."* Jordan's King Hussein simply described the trip as Sadat's "adventure."†

November 19, 1977, was a chilly night faintly lighted by a pale half-moon. Anwar Sadat, dressed in a gray checked suit and a conservative silver tie, climbed aboard a helicopter at his rest house in Ismailia on the Suez Canal to fly to the military airport at Abu Suweir. For security reasons, the hour and place of his departure remained secret. Alighting from the aircraft with a bouncing step, he greeted his cabinet and the few members of parliament in attendance before inspecting an honor guard of lancers. Suddenly he stopped, broke into a broad grin, and roared, "Barbara, so you did come." As he stretched out his hand to greet Barbara Walters of ABC, he shouted, "Walter!" to CBS anchorman Walter Cronkite. For Sadat, those who really mattered were in attendance. Sadat was a master of the media, a phenomenon in Arab culture. Claiming a natural home under the television lights, he had wooed the West and in the process become captive to his own ego. The Arabs could sulk. He had with him those who could convince the United States government and American public opinion that Egypt, like Israel, was a friend deserving of its favors.

The president's plane lifted into the night sky. Less than forty minutes later, at 7:58, the Boeing 707, its red trim glistening under blazing floodlights, rolled to a stop at Tel Aviv's Ben Gurion Airport.

---

* Mohamed Heikel, *Autumn of Fury: The Assassination of Sadat* (New York: Random House, 1983), p. 98.
† Sadat also faced internal opposition. He lost his foreign minister, Ismail Fahmy, over the decision to go to Jerusalem.

Israeli army trumpeters blared out a welcoming fanfare. As thousands of Israelis waved red-white-and-black Egyptian flags, Anwar Sadat, president of Egypt, stepped through the door to begin his "sacred mission."

On the tarmac he stood at attention as a military band played the Egyptian national anthem and the Israeli "Hatikvah," the song that sparked the 1929 riots in Jerusalem. And then he started down the receiving line—former prime ministers Golda Meir and Yitzhak Rabin; Moshe Dayan, foreign minister and Israel's hero of the Six-Day War; and Ariel Sharon, commander of Israel's Sinai forces in the October War. At its head stood Menachem Begin, the old warrior of the 1948 war for Palestine.

Sadat spent the night at the King David Hotel, the hotel Begin's Irgun bombed in 1946. The following day, Eid al-Adha, the Islamic holy day that commemorates the willingness of the patriarch Abraham to sacrifice his son, Sadat prayed at al-Aqsa mosque. As a gesture to Egypt's Coptic Christians, he went to the Church of the Holy Sepulcher and on to Yad Vashem, Israel's memorial to the victims of Hitler's Holocaust. In one of the great ironies of the improbable trip, the president of Egypt laid a wreath at Israel's Unknown Soldier memorial.

At four o'clock in the afternoon, Sadat mounted the rostrum of the Knesset to deliver a fifty-seven-minute speech in Arabic. In the strongest acknowledgment ever made by an Arab leader of Israel's right to exist, Sadat said, ". . . we agree to live with you. Israel has become a *fait accompli* recognized by the whole world." Yet he held the Arab high ground by calling on Israel to return all Arab territory occupied during the Six-Day War—including the Old City of Jerusalem—and to recognize that a Palestinian homeland constituted the core of the problem between Arabs and Jews. Anwar Sadat carefully protected his shrinking place in the Arab constellation, for to negotiate a separate agreement with Israel "would split the Arab world and put Egypt and myself in an impossible position."* The next day he flew home.

Five million Egyptians—stout women who believed their sons would no longer be taken from them; jeans-clad students who saw in the new order the promise of meaningful jobs; tough-skinned

---

* *Time,* December 5, 1977.

farmers in *galabias* ready to grab at anything that might reduce the burdens of their lives—exploded in joy and hope. People of a spent country who had borne the burden of the Arab struggle for thirty years were saying yes to peace. "Welcome Sadat." "Welcome hero of peace." "We are with you, Sadat, hero of war, hero of peace." Those who had cheered Nasser when he reigned as the prophet of pan-Arabism now hailed Sadat and Egyptian self-interest. At the moment, they cared little whether the Syrians or the Saudis approved of what they were doing. The Palestinians, the icon of Arab unity, were all but forgotten. Egyptians were following Anwar Sadat on the path back into "pharaonic nationalism." On this day, the era of the pharaohs had returned.

Anwar Sadat's pilgrimage to Jerusalem challenged as nothing else had challenged the dogma of Arab unity. Although the Arabs desperately wanted to ignore their own fragmentation and to reaffirm the mythology of wholeness, Egypt had thrown up the harsh confirmation of the Arabs' disintegration. "The Arabs wanted to persist in their unionist myths. The intellectuals wanted to engage in the same polemics; the leaders had spoken the languages of Arabism for so long that it was difficult for them to change to a new idiom. Egypt forced on all of them an encounter with their own disparateness. The storm over Sadat's policy was a fight to keep the myth alive."*

Anwar Sadat, presiding over a populous, largely homogeneous society claiming a distinct sense of itself outside the bounds of Arabism, could pursue a path denied others. If he had been less insistent on traveling alone and more sensitive to the problems of King Hussein or Hafiz Assad or even the fragile House of Saud, he might have won a measure of tolerance. But this was not Sadat's style. Once he made his historic gesture, he demanded that others follow Egypt's lead. As a result, Egypt's alienation from the Arab sphere progressed step by step between 1977 and 1979. When Egypt entered into a separate peace with Israel, it became complete.

Saudi Arabia mildly rebuked Sadat's mission to Jerusalem, and Syria vehemently denounced it. Yet no Arab leader wanted to punish Sadat to the point that the Egyptians, rallying around their flag, would throw themselves at Israel. Even the hard-liners—Syria,

---

* Fouad Ajami, "The Struggle for Egypt's Soul," *Foreign Policy*, Summer 1979, p. 28.

Libya, Iraq, Algeria, and South Yemen—meeting in Tripoli in December 1977 would go only so far as freezing diplomatic relations with Egypt and announcing that they would boycott Arab League meetings held in Cairo. Sadat charged like a wounded bull, breaking diplomatic relations and expelling the diplomats of offending governments.

As a result, Sadat's separation from the Arab world increased. When the Arab states gathered at the Baghdad Summit in October 1978, Syria and Saudi Arabia, the hard-liner and soft-liner of Sadat's opposition, offered to buy Egypt out of its budding Israeli-American alliance. Sadat refused. Within Egypt, the population went on the offensive about the agreement with Israel. The Egyptian media accused other Arabs of having allowed Egypt to always fight its wars against Israel. Newspaper cartoons jabbed at Palestinians who carried on their revolutionary struggle from the nightclubs of Beirut. The novelist Naguib Mahfouz and nationalist writer Tawfik Hakim suggested that Egypt had suffered only disaster as a result of its association with the Arab world. But the most scathing attack on the Arabs was the car stickers that popped up in Cairo reading, "Egypt: Like it or leave it."

Beneath the bravado the peace process with Israel was stalled until September 1978, when U.S. President Jimmy Carter captured Menachem Begin and Anwar Sadat in the woods of Maryland.

For thirteen days, the three leaders huddled in the rustic cabins of Camp David, the presidential retreat, while the outside world waited. With Jimmy Carter playing midwife, the eager Sadat and the obstinate Begin chipped away at an agreement. For Egypt, Sadat bargained for the return of Sinai and an end to the costly state of war with Israel. For the Arabs, he argued for Jerusalem, for the halt of Jewish settlements in the Israeli-occupied territories, and for the Palestinians.

The conference swayed back and forth, almost collapsing on Thursday, September 14. On Friday, Sadat told the Americans that it was hopeless and he was leaving. Carter persuaded him to stay. Finally on Sunday, September 17, an ashen-faced, exhausted Carter emerged to announce that agreement had been reached. Egypt and Israel would sign a peace treaty within three months with normalization of relations between the two countries taking place within a year. In return for a treaty of peace, Israel would withdraw from the Sinai within three years. These were the Egyptian issues. Absent were the larger Arab issues—return of the West Bank, Gaza, or the Golan; freezing of Jewish settlements in those territories; some recognition of the PLO; and the status of Jerusalem—al-Quds. All Sadat achieved in these areas was a nebulous agreement in which Israel agreed to hold autonomy talks with the inhabitants of the West Bank and Gaza with the goal of achieving self-government at the end of five years and a freeze on new settlements while negotiations progressed. The Palestinians of the diaspora got nothing. The next day, Menachem Begin reneged on his promise about freezing settlements.* Sadat had jettisoned the great symbol of Arab unity—the Palestinians. For him, the question was not Palestine but Egypt.

In American thinking, the Camp David Accords were to begin the process for a series of peace agreements between Israel and the Arab states. According to the plan, King Hussein would be the next to step forward to make peace with Israel, then the Saudis, and finally the hard-liners led by Syria. The United States well understood that nothing in the accords appealed to any of the Arab states except Egypt. To have any chance of success, Anwar Sadat had to sell peace with Israel to the other Arabs. He had promised Carter he would go to Jordan and Saudi Arabia to explain the agreement. But he never did. Overpowered by his enormous ego and protecting his American-made image as the great peacemaker, Sadat refused to approach those who might become rivals for Washington's affections. As a result, he closed the door on possible allies. King Hussein would later say of Camp David, "Let's be very clear, I was never consulted or invited to take part."†

The Saudis dithered and then rejected the agreement on the basis of the House of Saud's tribal mentality, which held that Arab states should stay within the Arab consensus. And the "Steadfastness and Confrontation Front" composed of Syria, Iraq, Libya, Algeria, South Yemen, and the PLO met at the Sheraton Hotel in Damascus to erect its barricades against Egypt's collusion with Israel.

Nevertheless, on March 26, 1979, a bright yellow-and-orange tent stretching across the south lawn of the White House received

---

* See Chapter 13.
† Sadat had shut Hussein out of Camp David. He felt superior to Hussein and did not want to share his chapter in history. He asked, "Who, after all, is Hussein?"

Anwar Sadat and Menachem Begin. Fifteen hundred invited guests watched as the scion of Zionism and the scion of the pharaohs penned their names to a treaty of peace between Egypt and the state of Israel. Toasts, smiles, and hugs, emblems of rejoicing, illuminated the state dinner that followed. But to the east, the mood in Egypt was subdued. The time when Anwar Sadat could act as a solitary figure, when he represented Egypt's inner feelings, its willingness to set aside the sacred struggle to live beyond its Arab identity, was ebbing. The peace treaty was a personal triumph for Anwar Sadat and Jimmy Carter. For Egypt, it was uncertainty. By taking Egypt into a separate peace with Israel, Sadat completed, literally and metaphorically, Egypt's turn away from the Arab world. In his arrogance, Sadat refused any attempt to repair the damage. Instead he thundered back, "Without Egypt, the Arabs are zero." Those who refused to follow him into his new order were ridiculed as "dwarfs" and "shoeless goat herders," "mice and monkeys." When he scorned the princes of the House of Saud as clowns and impostors who surrendered to pressure to other Arabs, the corporate monarchy remained silent. When he denounced King Hussein as the grandson of King Abdullah, Hussein responded with his usual courteous restraint, "It is a little hard for Sadat to denounce my grandfather for his reported contacts with the Zionists when he himself has signed a separate peace with Israel."* Only Syria's Hafiz Assad, the leader of the rejection front, threw back the rhetoric. But Sadat never let up. Although the Egyptians accepted much of what he said about the other Arabs, Sadat's intemperate language inflicted its wounds on a people suffering a profound sense of alienation.

Sadat's decision to opt out of the Arab arena tore at the Egyptians' sense of self. However imperfectly understood or pursued it might have been, the vision of Gamal Abdul Nasser, which celebrated Egypt as the leader of the Arab world, held its own reality. Although Sadat tried to maintain that image of Egypt even after the Arab League had moved out of Cairo, his people knew he had, in essence, made Egypt the center of nowhere.

Egypt survived economically because of American aid that was part of the Camp David Accords and because the Arab states made a distinction between the Arab people and the Sadat government.

---

* Quoted in Heikel, *Autumn of Fury*, p. 174.

The 800,000 Egyptians working in the Gulf kept their jobs and continued to send their savings home. And in the name of the Egyptian people, the moderate Arab states kept the trade and air links to Egypt open. For regardless of Sadat's policies, to most of the Arab world the Egyptians were still Arabs.

The issue of a separate peace with Israel inevitably became a cultural issue. Shut out of the Arab political sphere, Anwar Sadat slipped into ever greater dependence on his American partner. As the United States fulfilled the role that its own interests and those of Sadat required, the Egyptians' old fears and doubts about the powerful West and its ways revived. Questions about the integrity of their own culture followed. The warning of the leftist Khalid Mohieddin issued at the time Egypt established diplomatic relations with Israel took on new significance: "[We are observing] the loss of the distinct identity of our national culture and consequently of our personality, which rests on the nationalist, ideological, liberationist concepts hostile to foreign colonialism and economic subjugation; [and] the isolation of Egyptian culture from the broad Arab base in which the Egyptian intellectual finds inspiration for his thinking and to which he directs his technical experience and his literary, artistic, and scientific creativity."*

In opting for peace, the Egyptians had not intended to forfeit their cultural and political leadership of the Arab world. Nor did they choose to separate from their Arab consciousness. No matter how much the Egyptians believed in their innate superiority over the Arabs of the desert, they shared with all Arabs what Boutros Boutros-Ghali calls a "common market of the mind." They were part of the cultural web spun by language, religion, and common experience. The knowledge came gradually but forcibly that in leading Egypt away from the Arab world, Anwar Sadat had severed Egypt from its spiritual roots.

By the beginning of 1981, Sadat was an isolated man. Over the span of his political career, he had undergone an immense psychological transformation. The man who complained in the early 1950s that "the West hates the Arabs because they think they are Negroes" had become one of the West's most popular figures, especially in the United States. And the man who had once hated the West now

* Lippman, *Egypt After Nasser*, p. 264.

embraced its emblems of popular culture. He put off state business to go to Ismailia to greet the actress Elizabeth Taylor, the celluloid Cleopatra, when her ship docked in Egypt. He remained silent while the American rock group the Grateful Dead took over the sound-and-light theater at the Pyramids. And he welcomed Frank Sinatra to Cairo to perform in concert at the foot of the Pyramids before four hundred wealthy Western tourists and prominent Egyptians. While Sinatra sang, tattered Egyptians hung on the fence and looked in. The date was September 28, the anniversary of the death of Nasser.

Sadat faced the charge from many of his own people that he had become a Westerner intent on making Egypt part of Europe. It was an overblown accusation. But the reality still existed that in reestablishing Egypt's pharaonic consciousness, its pre-Islamic identity, Sadat miscalculated the extent to which Egyptians, however envious and contemptuous of their Arab brethren, cherish their Arab heritage. Egypt turned out not to have as authentic a national identity as some supposed.

Two years after Sadat signed the peace treaty with Israel, little remained of the euphoria. Grand gestures had failed to prevent either Israel's incorporation of Jerusalem into the Zionist state or its creeping annexation of the occupied territories. As Israeli expansion menacingly ate away at Egypt's geographical link to the Arabs of the east, Egypt lived as a restless and disappointed nation confused about its role in the region and the world. The heralded peace agreement had turned out to be exactly what its critics said it would be—a separate peace between the lonely nation of Egypt and the state of Israel. Nor had the grand alliance Sadat forged with the United States delivered prosperity. For most Egyptians, it had done little beyond clamping on once more the foreign yoke that Nasser had cast aside in 1952 and Anwar Sadat himself had discarded in 1973.

Egypt's grievances against Anwar Sadat came as much from domestic causes as Arab causes. Some involved his wife, Jihan. In a country where there is no equivalent of a first lady, Jihan's rise as a Western media star, her stylish clothes, her public campaigns to change aspects of the traditional position of women, deeply offended conservative Egypt. Others grew out of the president's toleration of corruption that enriched his cronies and sometimes besmirched the honor of the country. In the interest of commerce and commission,

Sadat saw nothing wrong with a deal that would have allowed foreign developers to build what they called a "Palm Springs for the Arabs" at the feet of the Great Pyramids. More important, Sadat shut everyone but his own out of the political and economic system. All pretense of democracy ended in May 1980 when the Law of Shame outlawed the last anemic centers of power independent of the president. Its name, devised by Sadat himself, drew on Egyptian villagers' custom of describing improper behavior as shameful.

On September 3, 1981, Anwar Sadat, the hero of 1973, ordered mass arrests of his political opponents. Inside two days, 1,286 ordinary people followed 250 of Egypt's most prominent political, intellectual, and religious figures into jail. The spectrum of Egyptian political opinion—Nasserites, leftists, rightists, and the Muslim Brotherhood—found itself behind bars.

October 6, 1981, was the eighth anniversary of the 1973 war. Anwar Sadat rose at eight-thirty, early for the increasingly indolent president. He ate a light breakfast and began dressing for the annual military parade in a new field marshal's uniform that had just arrived from London. The bulletproof vest he often wore in public spoiled the uniform's cut, so he put it aside. After he left his residence in Giza, his field marshal's baton, his lucky omen, was found on the table beside the door. Somehow it had been forgotten.

A cheerful Sadat relaxed as his black Cadillac convertible eased through Cairo's streets on the way to Nasser City, an ugly modern suburb. He placed a wreath on the pyramid-shaped Tomb of the Unknown Soldier and crossed the parade ground to take his seat in the reviewing stand. October 6 was Anwar Sadat's favorite day of the year, the day the glory of 1973 was relived. Despite the political turmoil of September, this year was no exception.

The two-hour parade began in a cacophony of noise punctuated by fireworks. Mortars sent mini-parachutes carrying tiny Egyptian flags and portraits of Sadat upward to drift back down into the hands of the delighted crowd. Tanks and artillery rumbled before the president, and sky divers floated in free fall toward the parade ground. It all built toward the finale. French-made Mirage 5-E fighters spewing red, blue, orange, and green smoke swooped low as a Soviet Zil-151 flatbed truck pulled out of line and stopped in front of the reviewing stand. Khalid Ahmed Shawki al-Islambouli, a young lieutenant linked to an offshoot of Egypt's outlawed Muslim Brotherhood, got out and approached Sadat, apparently to pay his respects. Instead he tossed a grenade before leaping over the railing of the grandstand. Anchoring himself before the front row of chairs, he fired bullet after bullet toward the president. At the same time, two accomplices raced to the flanks, firing their own weapons and hurling grenades. In a little over three minutes, six men were dead and twenty-eight wounded. Anwar Sadat, his body covered with blood, lay on the floor clinging to a bare thread of life.

At 1:20 P.M., the mortally wounded president, still wearing his blood-soaked uniform, was wheeled into Maadi Hospital. His unresponsive eyes stared upward. There was no trace of a pulse, no reflexes. At 2:40 P.M., he was pronounced dead. For the first time the people in the long history of Egypt had killed their pharaoh.

Anwar Sadat returned to the parade ground on a caisson drawn by six horses that bore his body to a sarcophagus in the Tomb of the Unknown Soldier. The mourners followed—former U.S. presidents Richard Nixon, Gerald Ford, and Jimmy Carter, French President François Mitterrand, West German Chancellor Helmut Schmidt, Britain's Prince Charles, and Israel's Prime Minister Menachem Begin. Of the Arab states only Sudan, Oman, and Somalia sent representatives. The Egyptian people were not there either, for Egypt did not mourn for Anwar Sadat.

Ten years after a beaming Anwar Sadat sat at a table on the lawn of the White House to sign the Egyptian-Israeli peace treaty, I was once more in Cairo. The central city looked a little shabbier, and the overcrowded buses weighted by passengers hanging out the door still listed to one side. The old Garden District that borders the Nile had deteriorated further. Paint and plaster peeled off the once-elegant apartment buildings, and the gardens from which the area draws its name lay ravaged by urban congestion. The side streets were all but impassable, turned into parking lots by residents and commerce. Even so, Cairo as a whole seemed perhaps a little better than I had found it in 1979. New expressways had alleviated a bit of the massive traffic jams, and attractive shopping areas boasting restaurants and movie theaters dotted the more affluent suburbs. The corniche along the Nile still beckoned strollers to contemplate the majesty of the river. But off the main thoroughfares, desperate poverty and unrestrained population growth strangled the city.

Yet somehow the Egyptians seemed to be more at ease with themselves. Hosni Mubarak had succeeded Anwar Sadat as president. As colorless as his predecessor was colorful, Mubarak set about restoring Egypt to the waiting Arab nation. The Iraq-Iran War had established once more Egypt's importance in the Arab constellation, and improved relations with Saudi Arabia created a sponsor for Egypt's reentry into the Arab fold. In 1984, the door to the Organization of Islamic Conference opened to Egypt. In 1987, the Arab League restored diplomatic relations, once more acknowledging Egypt's centrality in the Arab system. By 1990, when the crisis in the Persian Gulf exploded, Egypt was once again a full partner in Arab affairs. Before that crisis subsided, the Arab League had voted to return its headquarters from Tunis to Cairo, always regarded as the League's natural home.

But Mubarak, like Nasser and Sadat, has protected Egypt's national interests. While culturally returning Egypt to its Arab roots, he has politically and economically retained, if not strengthened, the link to the United States. American aid delivered by the series of peace agreements with Israel keeps Egypt economically dependent on the United States, and when the U.S. military force sent to Saudi Arabia needed an Arab partner, Mubarak was there. The separate peace with Israel, while sometimes strained to the breaking point, still stands. Egypt, although shouldering enormous internal problems that constantly eat at the country's stability, is nonetheless where it is most comfortable—playing its role in the Arab nation yet defining and protecting its own unique interests. Just as the Egyptians of Nasser's era found they could not be pan-Arabists at the expense of Egypt's own interests, they found in Sadat's era they could not be Egyptian nationalists seeking a separate destiny from the Arab world to which they are bound historically and emotionally. In the careful balancing that only the Egyptians truly understand, Egypt has found that it must live with the desert and the Nile.

The last light of day streaked the darkening western sky with deep shades of pink. The Egyptian public's lack of interest in the site created a haunting emptiness. I walked from the reviewing stand where Anwar Sadat held court for the last time toward his tomb. The wide plaza surrounding it was softly lit with amber lights, giving the buff-colored stones a sense of age and continuity with the desert that had just received the sun. I turned toward the tomb itself. There in the glow of a gas flame stood the pyramid holding the remains of Egypt's last pharaoh—Anwar Sadat.

C H A P T E R   10

HAFIZ ASSAD:
THE LION
OF DAMASCUS

S WISSAIR FLIGHT 302 FROM ZURICH
whined to a stop on the tarmac of
Damascus airport. I gathered up my tattered, overloaded flight bag,
inched down the aisle, and stepped off the plane. Briskly walking
through the chilled winter evening, I entered a door marked "Immigration" and handed my passport to a grim-faced official encircled
by sullen, khaki-clad guards cradling automatic weapons. It was
February 1988. Since my last extended trip to Syria, Hafiz Assad
had crushed his internal opposition and established Syria's dominance in Lebanon. The sober reception committee was only the first
indication of what had happened to Syria in the process.

Although it was only eight o'clock on a Tuesday night, the
main terminal in this international airport was almost deserted. In
the eerie quietness, a lone floor sweeper pushed his broom across
the vacant space. Here and there, a few waiting passengers stood
in silent little knots. Except for the passengers off my flight and two
men leaning against a board advertising the Umayyad Hotel, the
terminal was empty. Looking around, I spotted an arrow, wedged
between the frame of a door and an enormous, badly painted portrait of Hafiz Assad, pointing to ground transportation. I went

through, found a Coaster bus, paid the driver, and crawled through the dark to a seat. When the bus was full, we pulled out and headed toward Damascus.

The road from the airport into Damascus was dark, flat, and open, broken only by empty traffic circles weakly illuminated with backlighted boxes on four-foot poles that presented bold line drawings, painted in black on glass, of Hafiz Assad. The only other lights came from the signs of the occasional "Hafiz Assad Elementary School" or "Hafiz Assad Training Facility."

Eventually the bus entered Damascus and pulled into the Sheraton Hotel, where I got out. Under the scrutiny of the desk clerk and another portrait of the exalted Hafiz, I registered. As I walked toward the elevators, a couple of poorly disguised members of one of Assad's several security forces watched me, sizing up my potential threat to the regime. The elevator stopped on four. I got off, turned right, and found room 418. I was putting the key in the lock when I felt someone watching me. I turned and looked down the short hall. There in the conjunction of two passageways stood a man in the proverbial trench coat. He looked me straight in the eye, saying with his piercing gaze, "I am here to keep watch on you." I had arrived in the Syria of Hafiz Assad.

Syria is the realm of one man—Hafiz Assad. For over two decades, Assad, in pursuit of Syrian interests, has been both the ultimate Arab nationalist and the maverick of Arab politics. With his iron will and masterful manipulation of the balance of power, he has bent the Arab order to his specifications and in the process has made Syria the dominant Arab voice in the Levant. Yet the Syria that cannot be long ignored in Arab affairs is itself a fragile, fragmented, and contentious country held together by little except the heavy hand of Hafiz Assad.

Historic Syria arcs the Fertile Crescent from the Taurus Mountains to the Mediterranean coast. Geographically, it stood at the center of the Arab world, forming the east-west bridge between the Mediterranean and the Euphrates and the north-south link between the water-fed hills of the northern Levant and the harsh deserts of the Arabian peninsula. It encompassed what is now Israel, Lebanon, Jordan, part of western Turkey, and Syria. It was through Syria that the trade of the ancient world flowed. Century after century, great caravans of dusty, quarreling camels carried their costly cargoes up the old spice route from Yemen to Damascus and on to Aleppo into

Asia Minor. And square, squat caravanserais offering water and rest to processions of pack animals and their handlers on the east-west routes thread across the desert from Damascus to Palmyra to the central Euphrates.

Syria's trading cities—Damascus, Homs, Hama, Aleppo, Sidon, and Tyre—were rich by the standards of the region. Every man and every animal that passed through their gates contributed to their wealth. Inside their walls, craftsmen and artisans created the products that made them famous—purple dyes, fine damask fabrics, damascene steel for keen-edged fighting weapons, utensils of brass and copper, and intricately inlaid wood.

Lying between the Nile and the Euphrates, Syria commanded power but also invited invasion. Through the centuries, Syria's cities felt the heel of the Egyptians, Hittites, Assyrians, Babylonians, Persians, Macedonians, Romans, and Byzantines. Then the Arabs and Islam came to conquer—this time religiously and linguistically as well as territorially. Damascus rose to glory as Islam's capital under the Umayyads. But when the Islamic empire weakened, Syria was overrun by the Seljuk Turks in the eleventh century, grazed by the Crusaders in the twelfth, raped by the Mongols in the thirteenth, and finally incorporated into the Ottoman Empire in the sixteenth century. Even Ottoman rule was interrupted when Muhammed Ali invaded from Egypt in 1832, occupying Syria until 1840.

Pummeled from the east and west, Syria continues to feel its vulnerability. To the east beyond the cities, the countryside opens up to offer not only its space but its loneliness. Sparsely populated, deprived of natural barriers, the western desert seems to summon intrusion. Even the heavily populated region bisected by the main road running south out of Damascus toward the border of Jordan seems naked. Only when one approaches Damascus through the mountains of Lebanon does Syria unfurl its natural defenses. Through history, Syria's largely flat topography has allowed tribes and nations more powerful than itself to invade and conquer. The experience has left the Syrians hypersensitive to perceived threats to their security. While they share with all Arabs the resentments bred by occupation by powerful nations, the Syrians hold their own special grudges born of dismemberment.

It was the ancient Greeks who first named Syria, that area encompassing what is now Syria, Lebanon, much of Israel, and a slice of Turkey. The concept has survived. To most Syrians, Syria is Bilad al-Sham—the land of Damascus. Within its ill-defined borders, a gifted people gave birth to or nourished three great religions. They cradled philosophies and ideologies that ranged from Aristotle's logic to Arab nationalism. Together they shaped a homogeneous culture girded by extended family networks and enduring economic ties that reached from Damascus, Homs, and Hama to Jerusalem, Haifa, and Jaffa and to Tyre, Sidon, and Beirut. When the British explorer Gertrude Bell wrote in 1908 of her travels from Jerusalem to Damascus to Beirut, she titled the work simply *Syria*. Yet with the fall of the Ottoman Empire in 1919, the territory of Greater Syria began to be picked off piece by piece. Britain took title to the mandate of Palestine, denying what the Syrians regarded as their southern province. France claimed the rest, promptly amputating Syria's western reaches to attach to the Christian enclave north of Beirut and create what is now Lebanon.* At one stroke, Syria lost its gateway to the West, its outlets to the sea, and its claim of independence. In 1921, France presided over the second contraction of Syria—the surrender of Alexandretta-Antioch to Turkey. The Syrians helplessly watched as historic Syria was dismembered by forces they could not control, just as their forefathers had not been able to stop the Egyptians or the Assyrians, the Babylonians or the Romans. Within a period of two years, boundaries drawn through Greater Syria by others traumatically divided families and communities, dislocated economies, destroyed livelihoods, and created an enduring bitterness.

But the reality of Greater Syria defied the myth. Bilad al-Sham never existed politically. And the present country of Syria is a collection of hostile, quarreling communities enclosed within national boundaries whose parochial interests war against their sense of being Syrian. City stands against country, religion divides from religion, ethnic group resents ethnic group, and tribe opposes tribe. Loyalties lie in location, faith, and blood. Consequently, the nation represents only an arena in which group seeks to best group.

Division in the macro sense pits city against countryside. Syria is agricultural. Historically, villages practiced collective farming. But under the Ottomans, the system altered. Taking advantage of the tax system adopted in the seventeenth century, powerful families

---

* Known as the Mountain, the region was populated largely by Maronite Christians and had been tied to France since 1861.

within the cities gathered vast amounts of land into their hands. By 1858, Ottoman land records ceased to compute landholdings in acreage. Instead, the number of villages and peasants in his service stated a man's worth. With their peasants working as sharecroppers, the large property owners, living in pale yellow limestone and black basalt mansions in the towns, siphoned off money from the land. The cities—principally Damascus, Homs, Hama, and Aleppo—became citadels of economic and political power. Overwhelmingly populated by Sunni Muslims, they defined the traditional society in which the "notables" built and maintained a series of alliances with merchants and petty clan chieftains linked to the peasants. Existing as separate, autonomous entities, these cities bred rivalries that matched those of the Italian city-states at the time of the Renaissance. Even today, a Syrian is first of Aleppo or Damascus or Hama or Homs.

This age-old mind-set is something that raises among those Syrians sensitive to their country's need to build internal cohesion a certain level of anguish. I heard it voiced late one Friday afternoon as I sat on the bank of the slow-moving Orontes River in Homs with a teacher at a nearby girls' school. Looking at the river flow by, she said with a tone of painful resignation, "We all consider ourselves from somewhere in Syria, never from Syria itself. This is the biggest problem of our country and we do not seem to be making very rapid progress in solving it."

As Syria divided by city, it also divided by religion. The geography generally fostered separate, inbred religious communities. But in the western third of Syria, the rugged terrain attracted a variety of religious dissenters and then sealed them within their own exclusive domains. Despite the emotional appeal of Greater Syria, identity stayed frozen in religious affiliation. Little has changed. For religious identity reflects more than theology. It encompasses ties of family, tribe, and clan. It defines geographic area and parochial interests. It describes cultural patterns and ways of life.

The terms "Christian" and "Muslim" are embryonic labels within an intricate religious mosaic. In the history of Christianity, some of the most profound events in the faith took place in Syria. Centuries later, relics of them can still be found. On an obscure, twisting side street in Damascus, a narrow door opens onto a steep set of stairs that leads down through centuries of debris to the house of Ananias. The street called Straight and the wall from which the

280 / PASSION AND POLITICS

Apostle Paul was lowered in a basket to escape his religious opponents are nearby. Outside Damascus, in the isolated hillside village of Maloula, the Christian population still speaks Aramaic, the tongue of Christ. Regardless of these ties to the earliest history of the universal church, great chasms resulting from theology, geography, economics, and family separate Christians into Roman Catholic Maronites, two branches of the Eastern Orthodox Church, and a small contingent of Protestants. These are not simply denominations. They are distinct communal groups willing to subvert the common faith for their own particular interests. Yet the divisions among Christians pale in intensity in comparison to those among the Muslims.

While 85 percent of the people of Syria are Muslim, every fifth Muslim belongs to a schismatic sect. The Sunnis dominate the cities and rural areas of central Syria. The non-Sunni Muslims, principally the Druze and the Alawis, cluster in the southern and northern mountains. Both are loosely attached to Shiism and come out of an eighth-century dispute within that sect over the rightful successor to the Prophet Muhammed. Claiming the succession for Ismail, son of the sixth imam, Jafar al-Sadik, they became known as the Ismailis or "Seveners."*

In the eleventh century, a splinter group of Ismailis seeking refuge from persecution migrated from Egypt to the mountains of southeast Syria. Within the folds of Jebel Druze, they developed their own elaborate set of rituals and distinctive pattern of life. Known as Druze, they came to possess a degree of social solidarity that is legendary.†

The steep hills of Jebel Druze are dotted with the insular villages of the Druze. Physically, the clusters of pale stucco houses that hug the roads look much like other villages of Syria's southern region. But each emits characteristics that make it distinctly Druze. Scattered among the shopkeepers and laborers who gather in quiet sidewalk cafés is the occasional man wearing a red fez bound on the bottom with a length of snowy white cloth. These are the elect of the community, the few to whom the secrets of the religion have been revealed. Yet it is the people, not the chosen of the religion,

---

* The other branch of Shiism became known as the Twelvers. The Islamic government of Iran belongs to this sect.
† The Druze of Lebanon and Israel are a part of this group.

that give Druze villages their distinctive personality. I have never gone into a Druze village where polite and reservedly hospitable people did not express a sharp wariness of strangers. Nor did I ever come away without a clear sense of the closed Druze society, separate and aloof from others sharing the same nationality but not the same heritage.

East of the port of Latakia, Jebel al-Ansariye, rising out of the coastal plain, harbors another of Syria's religious sects—the Alawis. The Alawi faith adds to Islam heavy doses of mysticism and a measure of Christianity. Its secret theology includes the tenet that men were once stars in the world of light. Fallen from the firmament through disobedience, man can return to his place in the heavens only through seven reincarnations and transformations, once in each of the seven cycles of history. Denounced by the Sunnis as heretics and infidels, the Alawis retreated with their faith into the mountains of northwest Syria sometime around the year 1240.

For the Alawis, economic deprivation went hand in hand with religious persecution. Burrowing into the rock-strewn hills, the Alawis existed on goats and patches of grain. Under the Ottomans, many were so poor that they had to walk miles to the sea for a little salt to season their bread. Periodically hunger drove some into the lowlands to work as virtual serfs for wealthy Sunni landowners. Through the centuries, the Alawis remained a despised and oppressed sect until Hafiz Assad turned them into a privileged minority.

Currently Syria's population is composed of roughly 69 percent Sunnis, 12 percent Alawis, 5 percent Druze, and 10 percent Christians. The other 4 percent are Kurds, Armenians, Turkomans, and Circassians, clinging to their own languages and cultures; a half million Bedouin, inhabiting the Syrian desert; and a quarter of a million Palestinians, largely clustered around Damascus. Forcefully identifying not only with religion but with sect, class, region, and ethnicity, every Syrian is in some sense a minority. And every minority possesses a collective psychology that converts every action of an opposing community into a challenge to its own interests or existence. As a result, Syria is less a nation than an archipelago of political islands, each jealously guarding its own interests. In the late 1800s, the wife of a British consul pronounced sentence on Syrian communalism: "They hate one another. The Sunnis excommunicate the Shia and both hate the Druze; all detest the Alawis; the Maronites do not love anybody but themselves and are duly abhorred by all; the Greek Orthodox abominate the Greek Catholics and the Latins; all despise the Jews."* This was the Syria that came to independence in 1946—a virtually ungovernable political entity calling itself a nation.

In 1946, when the French surrendered its mandate, Syria was an agricultural country in which the labor of two million peasants largely supported a million and a half city dwellers. Those who tilled the soil lived in mud-and-stone villages without running water, electricity, or paved roads. They were stalked by disease—typhoid, malaria, and tuberculosis debilitating the adults, diarrhea, measles, and pneumonia killing the children. They were helpless victims of a system in which jobs and land tenure, the currency of survival, lay in the hands of the notables. Nothing changed with independence, because it was still the notables who ran the new state. By 1950, revolt against the whole social, economic, and political system that had come down from the Ottomans to the French to independent Syria gestated. It was led by the Baath.

Syria birthed Baathism, the ideology that the Arab people by nature and history form one nation. During the 1930s, Baathism dwelled in the salons of the intellectuals. Responding to the dismemberment of historic Syria after World War I, Baathist intellectuals debated Syrian national identity and Syria's relationship to other Arabic-speaking communities. Yet the Baath's appeal grew as much out of the realities of the lesser Syria as by the grand vision of a pan-Arab world. Through the Baath's secular ideology, Christians, Druze, Alawis, and the range of Syria's disaffected challenged the domination of Syrian politics by a small number of great urban families and their Sunni clients. And with its fuzzy socialism, Baathism attacked the concentration of wealth and power in the hands of notables. The Baath's call for secularized politics and an equalized economic system drew members of Syria's minorities, including the young Alawi Hafiz Assad.

Hafiz Assad was born to the wife of a fig and tobacco farmer on October 6, 1930, in a two-room rough stone house in Qurdaha in the hills northeast of the port city of Latakia. An Alawi village in the heartland of Alawi territory, Qurdaha was nothing but a knot

* Quoted in Martha Neff Kessler, *Syria: Fragile Mosaic of Power* (Washington, D.C.: National Defense University Press, 1987), p. 23.

of mean, flat-roofed cottages at the end of a dirt path. When Hafiz Assad began his education, it was in an open-air school provided by the French colonial administration. In 1939, the bright son of the local *zaim*, or political boss, came down off the mountain to enter school in Latakia. It was there he confronted head on the reality of what it meant to be an Alawi in Syria.

At the age of sixteen, the class-conscious Assad gravitated to the Baath, which promised the minorities an end to Syria's crushing social and political system. The intellectually gifted Assad rapidly advanced from painting Baathist slogans on stone walls to writing Baathist tracts.*

By the early 1950s, Hafiz Assad had joined the Syrian armed forces that had been developed by the French colonial administration. Offering poor boys a job, the military often provided the only escape from servitude on the land. Furthermore, with the land-owning and mercantile classes rejecting the lowly profession of soldier, the officer corps as well as the ranks filled with minorities and others cut out of the economic system. Seeking social mobility, the same segment of society drawn to the military was also drawn to Baath ideology. Consequently the armed forces and the Baath Party locked together. One controlled Syria's military power and the other its bureaucracy. In 1958, they climbed together to the top of Syria's warped political order.

Since independence, Syria had become synonymous with political chaos. So many coups and countercoups followed one on the other that the international news agencies hardly bothered to report each time tanks rolled into Damascus to oust some government or other from power. The Egyptian newspaper *al-Ahram* went so far as to describe Syria as an insane asylum rather than a state. When it took power, the Baath government found that it could do no better than the others in controlling communal rivalries.

The Baath, confined to the military and the bureaucracy, commanded no mass support either to fulfill its economic agenda or to stay in power. Ideologically committed to the concept of pan-Arabism, the Baath jumped on the idea of union with Nasser's Egypt

---

* In 1948, Assad's pen drew the hostile attention of the rival Muslim Brotherhood, which considered secular Baathism an anathema. One night a group of Muslim Brothers caught the fast-rising Assad alone on the dark streets of Latakia and plunged a knife into his back. It took him several weeks to recover.

as its best hope to outflank the traditional political order dominated by Sunnis. But the federation with Egypt turned out to be a disaster.

The reluctant Nasser's price for union was absolute authority in both the Egyptian and Syrian units of the United Arab Republic. The Syrian Baathists agreed, naively believing that Nasser would have to rule Syria through them. After all, it was they who had sparked the original flame of Arab nationalism. Thus it was they who would teach Arabism to Egypt. Instead Nasser gutted Syrian politics and caged the armed forces, the crucible of Baathist support. Officers suspected of less than total loyalty to Nasser found themselves snatched out of Syria and posted to Egypt. Hafiz Assad who was among them lived much of the history of the UAR lounging in Groppi's Café in Cairo suffering the slights of the imperious Egyptians.* In October 1959, Nasser appointed Field Marshal Abdul Hakin Amer, his closest associate, as virtual governor of Syria. Damascus through its own connivance became a provincial capital in an Egyptian empire. In the caustic words of a Turkish journalist, the UAR was "the first case in history of a black nation colonizing a white nation."†

All the contentious factions within the Syrian body politic began to coalesce against the UAR—merchants, landowners, and businessmen, who detested Nasser's socialism; civil servants, who resented the Egyptian bureaucrats placed over them; the military, who seethed under Egyptian control; and the Baathists, who watched their precious party being dismembered by the ambitious Nasser.

Following panic in the business community ignited by Nasser's nationalization decrees of July 1961, Syria was jerked out of the United Arab Republic on September 28, 1961, by a right-wing putsch led by Lieutenant Colonel Abdul Karim Nahlawi. For the next nineteen months, Syria whirled on another wild merry-go-round of coups and countercoups. Near the center was the Military Committee, a secret organization of young, obscure Baath military officers who possessed their own version of the Baath. Among them was Hafiz Assad.

---

* This was not Assad's first time in Egypt. In 1955 he had taken pilot training there. While landing a plane with bad brakes, Assad realized it was going off the runway. He opened the cockpit, gripped the sides of the fuselage, and waited for the impact. The wheels hit a water conduit, vaulting the plane with Assad inside over a wall and across a main road, narrowly missing a camp of Palestinian refugees.
† Mansfield, *Arabs*, p. 271.

On the night of March 7, 1963, tanks and infantry commanded by the Military Committee began to move on Damascus.* With the swiftness of lightning, the capital fell, and across Syria, an indifferent population accepted the almost bloodless coup. Success came so easily because the existing government, in the words of Hafiz Assad, was "a government without a people and without an army, the rule of a class which had had its day."† A week before the coup the thirty-year-old Hafiz Assad and his five co-conspirators had been living the shadowy and precarious life of obscure plotters. Now they were the strongest force in Syrian politics. As such, the Military Committee began consolidating its position by purging elements in Syria deemed "disloyal." With the goal of building an alternative to the traditional rule of the notables, the military junta dismissed hundreds from government positions and replaced them with party members. It sent Baathists into every unit of the armed forces to further indoctrinate Syria's military with Baathist ideology. Finally, the military and civilian wings of the Baath were fused into a single revolutionary instrument to slay the old order. But for all its energies, the Military Committee was only a fraction of the Baath minority, a military splinter group of an anemic party void of a popular base. Over the next seven years, political turmoil would pit the traditional political order against the Baath, the Baath against the Nasserites and the Muslim Brotherhood, and the Baath against itself.

In May 1963, the Baath drawing on its strength in the military crushed the attempt of Gamal Abdul Nasser and the Syrian Nasserites to overthrow their government in the name of Egyptian-led pan-Arabism. Ignoring Nasser's cries of "fascists and murderers," the Baathist soldiers killed and wounded hundreds of Nasserites in the street in the name of Syrian Baathism.

But one threat was simply replaced by another. In the spring of 1964, the Baath faced a Sunni-centered rebellion against a political regime dominated by minorities. In the cities, prayer leaders associated with the Muslim Brotherhood spat out inflammatory sermons against the secular Baath. Undergirding their religious message was the social message calling the city notables to join the battle against heretics in control of the government. In Hama, the stronghold of landed conservatism and the Muslim Brotherhood, stashes

---

* The Military Committee decided to act after the successful Baathist coup in Iraq on February 8. See Chapter 11.
† Quoted in Seale, *Asad*, p. 72.

of weapons came out of hiding, roadblocks went up, and heavy beatings felled Baath Party members. The Baath sent in its army. After two days of fighting and seventy deaths, the uprising ended.

Having established its dominance over the cities and the Sunnis, the Baath next turned on itself. Following the 1963 coup, the Military Committee, with little experience in how to run a country, had brought Michel Aflaq, Salah Bitar, and others among the original Baathists into the government. Almost immediately, the Baath split between two forces—the old guard and the new, the party of Michel Aflaq and the Military Committee of Hafiz Assad. To Aflaq, the Baath was the font of Arab thought, the guardian of the government's ideological purity. To Hafiz Assad and the Military Committee, the Baath was the engine of social change, the central institution of the state. This was the philosophical dispute. At its gut level, the conflict within the Baath pitted the poor boys from the country against the intellectuals from the city.

On February 23, 1966, the country boys in control of the military purged the party. In an event that amounted to the Communist Party's renouncing Marx and Lenin, the military wing of the Baath sent Salah Bitar to jail and Michel Aflaq fleeing to Lebanon.* In the new regime, the minorities—the Alawis and Druze—held the reins of power. Soon the Druze were ousted, leaving only the Alawis. One further purge left only the Alawis loyal to Hafiz Assad.

On November 12, 1970, Hafiz Assad took the final step that put him in absolute control of the Syrian Baath and the Syrian government. For three days, the country hung suspended, uncertain of what had happened. On the fourth day as Hafiz Assad was putting the finishing touches on a communiqué announcing his ascension to power, Libya's rumor-mongering Muammar Qaddafi arrived unannounced at Damascus airport. Assad, now the only person of suitable rank to receive the chief of Libya, hurried to the airport. Greeting the diminutive Qaddafi, he quipped, "It's a good thing you didn't arrive half an hour earlier."† That evening Syrian radio reported the "Corrective Movement." Hafiz Assad was now forty years old.

---

* Aflaq never saw his native land again. His exile capped the often incomprehensible quarrel between the Syrian and Iraqi branches of the Baath Party. See Chapter 11.
† Seale, *Asad*, p. 165.

Assad had risen to the top of Syrian politics on the name of Baathism. Yet he had never been chained to the pan-Arab ideology of the earlier Baathists. Rather his motivations came from the reality of Syrian society. Just how ungovernable it was perhaps even Hafiz Assad did not understand. In 1970, Assad said to a friend, "Why do you think ruling this country is so difficult? It's really very simple. Let's look at our people. He who has no car wants a car. He who has no house wants a house. A man with a salary wants it doubled or tripled. I can assure you we can satisfy all these demands. If we do, who will remain in opposition in Syria? One or two hundred individuals who take politics seriously. They will be against us whatever we do. Mezza prison has been built for them."* Hafiz Assad would find that ruling Syria would not be that easy.

In its first twenty-five years of independence, Syria had suffered a coup or an attempted coup at the rate of one per year. Now, in open defiance of the centuries-old tradition that power belonged in Sunni hands, an Alawi was in control. The bedrock institution of the state was Hafiz Assad's version of the Baath Party. With its tentacles spreading into every corner of the country, it became the government. Despite some well-intended attempts to bring all elements of Syria's fractured society into the political process, Assad's rule took root among those he could trust—the Alawis. It was because of their tie to Hafiz Assad that the Alawis, rejected, deprived, and persecuted for centuries, would become during the 1970s Syria's economically privileged political elite.

In 1973, the enormous wealth generated by the Arab oil embargo washed across the borders of Syria. In Damascus, the New Umayyad Hotel, furnished with beige Naugahyde sofas straight out of the 1950s, opened. Souk al-Armwam and Souk Hamidiye, Damascus's major markets, underwent modernization that succeeded in robbing them of their enticing atmosphere and timeless color. Only Merjeh Square, more often known as Hanging Square, seemed to escape the monotony created from Syria's secondhand largess from the oil boom. The revenues spun off from the exploding economies of the Persian Gulf continued to erase from Syrian society the ignorant, oppressed Alawi sharecropper of Assad's youth. With government jobs and government contracts delivered by the Assad

---

* Stanley Reed, "Syria's Assad: His Power and His Plan," *New York Times Magazine*, February 19, 1984.

government, the Alawis pushed aside the Sunnis and the Christians to become a new, conspicuously affluent middle class. Some among them became rich. Abandoning all semblance of discretion, Alawis holding senior positions within the Baath cruised around Damascus in gleaming silver Mercedes and drank $100-a-bottle liquor at a string of bistros sporting such improbable names as the Crazy Horse. Yet no one flaunted his wealth as much as Hafiz Assad's brother, Rifaat, a big player in the hashish trade of neighboring Lebanon. Rifaat's fortune was estimated at $100 million, making him the most glaring symbol of corrupt and arbitrary Alawi rule.

The rise of the Alawis offended many Syrians but none more than the Sunnis. Notables stripped of political influence, merchants outclassed by new money, and religious leaders downgraded by the secularism of Assad's regime all seethed with resentment. Their anger spread beyond their class through the long-established networks that linked Sunni families and clans. Leading the opposition against a regime identified with the despised Alawi community was the Muslim Brotherhood.

In 1963, when the Baathists first claimed the state, small bands of Islamic militants went underground to organize an armed resistance against the secular Baath. Over the next sixteen years, clandestine cells stockpiled weapons, assigned *noms de guerre*, and reached into the mosques to recruit fighters to their ranks. By 1979, the Muslim Brotherhood, claiming ten thousand guerrillas, was ready to return Syria to its Sunni majority.

In May, the Muslim Brothers sent their first message to Hafiz Assad when they fired on a car carrying him through the streets of Damascus. The next month, on June 16, 1979, a staff member of the Aleppo Artillery School sympathetic to the Brotherhood assembled the largely Alawi cadets in the dining hall and locked all the doors except one. Through it came Muslim Brothers indiscriminately firing automatic weapons. The trapped students were slaughtered like fish in a barrel. In that one bloody and spectacular act, the Muslim Brotherhood declared open war on the Alawis and Hafiz Assad's Baath political structure.

Insurrection spread east to the Euphrates and west to Latakia, the doorstep of Alawi territory. An array of Syrians outside the fundamentalist fold flocked to its cause, swelling the ranks of the Brotherhood. Baathists displaced by Assad's Corrective Movement joined. The Communist Party added its small weight. In the middle, anchoring the anti-Assad coalition, was the Syrian middle class, led by the merchants of the souks, the backbone of traditional Syrian society.

From mid-1979 to mid-1980 the insurgents held the initiative. Out of their safe havens deep in the ancient warrens of cities like Aleppo and Hama, the guerrillas came forth. During the day, they whipped up antigovernment demonstrations, closed shops, and set fire to buildings. At night, they sent hit teams against members of Assad's Baath, often murdering them in their beds.

Until 1980, Hafiz Assad had seemed reluctant to face the reality that the Syria he had personally crafted was collapsing into virtual civil war. But when Aleppo shut down in a general strike, Assad came to life. Handing out heavy weapons to his supporters for protection and backup, he sent his security forces to storm the city. Despite the two hundred people in Aleppo who died, the protestors would not quit and Assad would not surrender.

On March 9, 1980, helicopter-borne troops launched a ferocious search-and-destroy operation against Aleppo's neighboring town, Jisr al-Shughur. Then the armed forces turned back on Aleppo. A division of ten thousand men and 250 armored vehicles sealed off whole quarters of the city and General Shafiq Fayadh announced that he was prepared to kill a thousand men a day to rid the city of the vermin of the Muslim Brothers. Unbowed, Assad's opponents defiantly rose up in Hama, Idlib, Dayr al-Zur, and Homs.

Heavy press censorship failed to dam the stream of rumors cascading out of Syria about the showdown between the Alawi-dominated government and its largely Sunni opponents. In Riyadh, where I was living at the time, Syrians cut off from their families in the rebellious cities could do nothing but anxiously await some news of their fate. One day an X-ray technician at the King Faisal Specialist Hospital whose wife and children lived in Homs got in his Toyota Land Cruiser and drove north across the desert, passing into Syria between border checkpoints. Leaving his car three miles from Homs, he penetrated the blockade on foot. Darting from street to street, he reached his house to find his family in no immediate danger. He then retraced his steps, reappearing in Riyadh three days later.

On June 26, 1980, the level of violence ratcheted up again. Hafiz Assad was standing at the gate of the Guest Palace in Damascus waiting to welcome the visiting chief of the state of Mali. Suddenly

290 / P A S S I O N   A N D   P O L I T I C S

a speeding car laid down a barrage of machine-gun fire and unleashed two grenades that landed at Assad's feet. The quick-footed
president kicked one out of the way while a self-sacrificing guard
smothered the other with his body. As the news spread of the president's narrow escape, a wave of fury and thirst for revenge swept
the Alawi community.

The next morning, twenty-two helicopter loads of commandos
descended on Tadmur Prison near the ancient ruins at Palmyra.
Storming into cells holding members of the Muslim Brotherhood
arrested over the last year, the commandos killed at least six hundred
prisoners. The following week, Hafiz Assad declared membership
in the Muslim Brotherhood a capital offense.* But the rebellion
rolled on.

Fear imprisoned Baath Party members in their homes, which
were secured like forts. Hafiz Assad himself cowered in the safety
of his office, one of the best-guarded men in the world. Three years
of effort had failed to eliminate an underground that was killing the
flower of the Alawi professional class and tarring with the charge
of illegitimacy the presidency of Hafiz Assad. The opposition had
proved too weak to topple the Baath and too strong to be stamped
out. On the night of February 2, 1982, the last act of the bloody
saga began to unfold on the stage of Hama.

At 2:00 A.M., a rooftop sniper killed a score of Assad's soldiers
as they swept through the old quarter of the city on nighttime patrol.
Suddenly the lights in the city's mosques switched on and the chilling
cry of *jihad* against the Baath rang out from the minarets. "Allah is
great! All of Syria is rising up against the atheist regime. Come to
the mosques, where arms will be distributed to hunt down the infidels."† Hundreds of Muslim Brothers and their allies came out of
their hiding places. In a frenzy of killing and looting, they ransacked
armories and butchered seventy Baath officials. By morning, the
guerrillas triumphantly proclaimed the city liberated from the hated
Alawi and his Baathist government.

Baath radio in Damascus screamed that the rebels, "driven like
mad dogs by their black hatred, pounced on our comrades while

---

* Revenge was visited not only on the Muslim Brothers. Salah al-Din Bitar, the
cofounder of the Baath, was killed on July 21, 1980, in Paris, probably by the
Assad regime.
† Reed, "Syria's Assad," p. 57.

sleeping in their homes and killed whomever they could of women and children, mutilating bodies of the martyrs in the street."* Out of the public eye, the calculating Hafiz Assad decided that Hama would become the battleground on which the fate of the country would be decided. He understood all too well that if the enemies of the Alawis were allowed to seize control of even one neighborhood in Hama, Alawi blood would flow like water throughout Syria. For behind the insurrection lurked the Syrians' complex, multilayered hostility between town and country, between Sunni and Alawi, between Islam and the Baath.

The battle for Hama raged for three grim weeks. For the first four days, the Muslim Brotherhood held the town, killing hundreds of suspected Assad supporters. On the fifth day, the Brotherhood gave way to the army, which indulged in wholesale killing, pillage, and rape. Round after round of artillery shells blazed into the city's heart, sealing people off within the maze of streets in the old quarter without food, water, or fuel. Others were driven into cold winter weather as tanks destroyed acres of mud-and-wattle houses suspected of concealing the insurgents. Hama, Syria's loveliest city, was pulverized, burying the bodies of between five thousand and twenty thousand victims of Hafiz Assad's wrath. In the destruction and death, the insurrection burned out. But in its aftermath, the name of Hama became a synonym for massacre.

In his first public statement after the carnage, Hafiz Assad simply said, "What has happened in Hama has happened, and it is all over."† Giving substance to his words, Assad made another attempt at building a distinct Syrian nationalism. Swarms of workmen began cleaning the massive honey-colored walls of the Damascus citadel built by the Umayyads, and official government pronouncements addressed the citizens of Syria as the "sons of the Umayyads." But the real symbol of Syrian nationalism was Hafiz Assad. A cult of personality built as huge portraits of the president went up in every public building, school, and army post and at every major intersection and traffic circle. In towns and villages up and down the country, towering statues of the president swung into place. In the absence of any true sense of nationalism, Hafiz Assad set out to establish himself as the guardian of Syria's institutions and arbiter

* *Time*, March 8, 1982.
† Ibid.

between its competing interests. He summed it up himself: "I am the head of the country, not of the government."*

Yet during the same period, Hafiz Assad personally retreated more and more from public view. Part of the reason was physical, part was the personality of the man. Assad has long suffered from diabetes. For years his unremitting work schedule had punished his body. In 1982, it was subjected to the emotional stress of the Islamic rebellion. On November 12, 1983, Assad collapsed. For months he remained out of sight while rumors swirled that he had dropped from exhaustion, gone blind, could not walk. Eventually the Lion of Damascus recovered from what was probably a heart attack. But he still kept his solitude. Never enjoying contact with the crowd, obsessed with security, seldom seen outside his heavily guarded environment, the shy Assad assumed the characteristics of a recluse. Unlike Nasser, Sadat, King Hussein, and the House of Saud, he appears to his subjects only as an image on a television screen. His own cabinet ministers may see him only twice in their term of duty—on being sworn in and on leaving office. And the prime minister, the top generals, and the party bosses know the president best through his telephone calls. Seeming to need no advice, Hafiz Assad governs alone, never forgetting nor forgiving disloyalty or disobedience.

After Hama, Syria became a brutal police state. The man who was respected in 1970 was feared by 1982. The intelligence agencies, unknown before the 1950s, became a constant of Syrian life.

A clone of the man who was watching my hotel room that night I arrived in Damascus followed me as I made my rounds. Since I was in Syria on a tourist visa to escape Syrian restrictions on journalists, I was somewhat anxious but not particularly alarmed. After a few days, my shadow doubled. When he tripled, I did become nervous. That was the morning the desk clerk at the hotel asked me if I was a writer. Always prepared with a cover story, I played to the Syrian love of melodrama by saying I was a novelist and I was in Syria to do research for a romance about a Syrian soldier and a Lebanese girl trapped in the tragedy of the Lebanon war. I never knew if he believed me or not, because I went upstairs, packed my bag, and took the Service, the overland taxi, to Amman. A few weeks

---

* Seale, *Asad*, p. 343.

later when I was back in the United States, I received an excited call from my main contact in Syria, a man connected to the higher echelon of government. He wanted to know what on earth I was doing in Damascus that would prompt the security services to assign eighteen men to track me.

As long as he stays in power, Syria is Hafiz Assad. Complex, Byzantine, possessing what Richard Nixon described as a touch of genius, Assad is a man of his Alawi community and at the same time a man of greater Syria. With the same resolve with which he protects his community, he pursues the interests of Syria. Exercising the survival instincts of a Middle East minority, Assad understands the realities of power in the Middle East and beyond. Unlike his Baathist predecessors who frenetically pushed the forces of pan-Arabism, Assad assigns little value to what ephemeral Arab unity can deliver to Syria. Accepting that his country commands little power beyond what geography has bestowed, he operates from the reality that Syria's position within the Levant and the larger Arab world comes from the skill with which its leader manages his country's limited assets. Through the skillful manipulation of the balance of power, Hafiz Assad has done remarkably well in establishing fragile Syria near the center of Arab politics.

Operating out of the experience of an Arab minority, Assad wields secrecy like a weapon, using it to fog the steps of his decision-making and employing it both to gain and to hold the psychological initiative. Maximizing his own strengths, Assad feeds on the weaknesses of others in the political game—their failure to understand the multiple facets of an issue; their lack of patience and direction; their tendencies to damage long-term strategies by acting impulsively. In everything that he does, Hafiz Assad is cautious. While his moves are labyrinthine, his ultimate goals never change. The pattern of Assad's skilled maneuvering—the refusal to compromise until the eleventh hour and the sudden signs of flexibility that catch his enemies by surprise—have maximized Syria's limited assets and masked its vulnerabilities. No one senses Syria's limited resources nor feels more acutely that his country is under siege than Hafiz Assad. Shocked into political maturity by the 1967 war, Assad has spent the last quarter century seeking territorial redemption for Syria.

In important respects, the Six-Day War was a product of Syria's political schizophrenia of the 1960s. The Baath government returned to power by the coup of 1963 howled for war with Israel at any cost. While Egypt, Jordan, and even Baathist Iraq hung back, zealous Syrian Baathists urged Palestinian guerrillas to attack inside Israel. Like hecklers shouting from the stands at a sporting match, they mocked Nasser as the "paper tiger of Arab nationalism" for refusing to lead the Arabs into another war with Israel. In 1966, Syrian ridicule finally goaded the ambitious, egotistical Nasser into a military alliance. With the stroke of a pen, Nasser obligated Egypt to defend a reckless revolutionary regime that had no sense of the realities of the Levant. While Palestinian commandos out of Syrian training camps struck into Israel, Damascus radio called on all Arabs "to undertake the liberation battle that will tear the hearts from the bodies of the hateful Jews and trample them in the dust."*

When the war it coveted came, Syria proved powerless. The only training or battle experience that the fifty-thousand-man army possessed came from tit-for-tat raids along the Israeli border. In this milieu, Syria's arsenal of cast-off weapons from the Soviet military was adequate. Functioning in the same atmosphere, no one thought much about the officer corps crippled by Hafiz Assad's political purges of 1966. When the fast-moving Israeli war machine came, Syria's military collapsed.

The tiny Syrian air force was destroyed in the first hours of the war. Its loss was symbolic of Syria's inability to mount a defense. By the fifth day, Israeli forces had climbed onto the Golan Heights, sacked Quneitra, a city of seventeen thousand, and cleared the surrounding villages. Ninety thousand Syrians, stripped of everything they owned, were driven off the Golan into tented encampments. Thus the Golan became the badge of Syria's shameful defeat, the burning emblem of Syrian hatred of Israel. For Hafiz Assad, the Golan stands as the definitive statement of Syria's vulnerability, the call to territorial recovery.

A quarter of a century after the Six-Day War, a narrow stretch of the Golan seems ghostly. Cool breezes bend broadleaf grasses that feed no animals, the sun warms land worked by no hand. From the highest point on the Golan plateau, a lone minaret can be seen standing in stately silence within the bounds of Quneitra. Beyond it to the west, an Israeli military post watches over the open route to Damascus. Farther down the escarpment, a rusting, abandoned

---

* *Time*, June 2, 1967.

Israeli tank that clambered toward the heights in the 1967 war testifies to Israel's claim to the territory of the Golan. Housing for Jewish settlers that creeps apartment block by apartment block along the territory's western boundary confirms possession. Israel's presence on the Golan is a fact that neither Syria's leader nor his people accept. Every year, hundreds of Syrians come down the gentle slopes of Mount Hermon to Ain Tine, the last Syrian village on the border of the occupied Golan. Armed with megaphones, they stand on rooftops to call to friends and relatives gathered on their own rooftops in Majdal Shams, the first village inside Israeli territory. In this ritual of separation, the words are both simple and profound: "We greet you. We are with you. Someday we will be together."

It had been Hafiz Assad's job as defense minister to direct the war effort. He failed. The man who had defiantly sent Palestinian guerrillas against Israel, who had participated in the histrionics that forced Nasser to throw down the gauntlet, froze psychologically in the first hours of the war. In six short days, all of Assad's previous concepts of defense dissolved in Israel's highly mobile blitzkrieg. And the core of his political reasoning cracked as the great powers allowed Israel to redraw the map of the Middle East. When the fighting ceased, Assad went home to brood in solitude for three days. He emerged from isolation carrying a new set of convictions: that Israel was by its nature an expansionist power, and that only through immense effort on the part of the Arabs could this expansionism be contained. Carrying these two principles like a pair of swords, Hafiz Assad stepped into the Arab political arena.

Following the Correction Movement in 1970, Hafiz Assad gathered every aspect of Syrian defense and foreign policy under his direct control. His youthful years as a pan-Arabist had implanted in him a basic axiom of Arabism. And it was from this axiom that he worked. Syria and Egypt formed the pivots of Arab history. When Damascus and Cairo were one, the Arabs triumphed. When they were apart, the Arabs faltered. Consequently, Syria, Egypt, and the larger Arab constellation either stand together or fall together. It was this simplistic view of history that led Hafiz Assad into Anwar Sadat's grand scheme for the 1973 war.

The corollaries of Arab unity masked the brutal fact that the tactics of Anwar Sadat and those of Hafiz Assad were not the same. Assad sought war because he believed Israel would never negotiate the territorial results of the 1967 war until the Arabs took back some of their land by force. Sadat, on the other hand, saw war as a primal instrument to unblock the diplomatic process. Assad reached for the Golan and Sinai, Sadat for the conference table. Anwar Sadat well understood his differences with Hafiz Assad, yet he convinced the Syrian president that they pursued a common strategy.

Hafiz Assad spent his forty-third birthday entombed in the war room at Damascus general headquarters. At zero hour on October 6, 1973, the Syrian army crossed the central section of the 1967 cease-fire line on the Golan. Heavy artillery opened the way for tanks that chewed their way through Israeli forces dug in behind artillery batteries and mine fields toward the steep escarpment that drops into Israel's Hula Valley. The advance was short-lived.

For the next three days, Syrian troops on the Golan endured the full fury of the Israeli air force. Each day at first light, wave after wave of aircraft swooped down to bomb and strafe Syrian troop and tank concentrations. Running a thousand sorties a day, Israeli air power succeeded in stopping the Syrian advance. It then turned on Syria proper, hitting power plants, storage depots, the oil refinery at Homs, and the port of Latakia. On October 10, Israeli fire fell on the air force headquarters in Damascus. From his threatened bunker, Hafiz Assad begged Sadat to mount a new attack in Sinai and to send air support to Syria. Sadat refused. Egypt would neither advance nor provide air cover for its Syrian ally.

Neither did Anwar Sadat give Hafiz Assad advance warning of his cease-fire proposal delivered to Egypt's legislative body on October 16. The furious Assad retaliated by firing an angry letter to his ally that preserved more decorum than Assad thought the situation deserved. "I would have preferred to have seen the proposals outlined by you to the People's Assembly before they were made public. . . . It gives me no pleasure to write these words, but I wish to hide none of my thoughts and opinion from you since we are engaged together in a battle of life and death."* But the two-front strategy with which Hafiz Assad had gone to war had already collapsed. The Damascus-Cairo axis constructed in the name of the Arabs disintegrated with Egypt's decision to accept the cease-fire. Assad, so completely committed to the reconquest of territory that he had no fallback position, was hung out to dry. Learning from

---

* Seale, *Asad*, pp. 219–20.

yet another war between the Arabs and Israel, Hafiz Assad, the consummate political strategist, decided to position Syria as the central Arab power of the Levant. He would henceforth intone the cause of Arab unity if appropriate and tear that unity asunder when Syria's own security needs required it.

Henry Kissinger's shuttle diplomacy in 1974 thrust Hafiz Assad, the poor Alawi boy from the mountains of Syria, into the world spotlight. In twenty-six arrivals and departures from Damascus airport, the celebrated American secretary of state and the relatively obscure Syrian president appeared together on television screens across the world. In private, the powerful Kissinger and the all but powerless Assad jousted in 130 hours of face-to-face talks. In his meetings with Kissinger, Assad put together his now notorious negotiating technique. Instinctive at first, it later became deliberate. Assad, known in diplomatic circles as "the Sphinx," opens with a long discourse on history, which can last for hours.* When that phase ends, he moves on to raise a host of irrelevant subjects for the sole purpose of winning the psychological advantage as the prelude to ultimate control of the process. Finally, with a certain degree of quiet humor, he drags these meetings to the point that his negotiating partner is irresistibly tempted to accept whatever Assad says simply to escape. In his well-publicized contest with Kissinger, Assad made his reputation as a dogged champion of Syrian and Arab interests. But he gained more in personal notoriety than Syria gained in territory.

In the Golan disengagement agreement that ended the 1973 war, Syria won nothing but Quneitra and the narrow ribbon of territory that looped around it. Located inside the United Nations buffer zone, almost destroyed by the Israelis before their withdrawal, shorn of the surrounding farmlands from which it derived its life, Quneitra's return to Syria did nothing to assuage the wounds of 1967. Consequently, the city has never been rebuilt. The stark, angular collage created by collapsed roofs, wrecked mosques, and a ruined hospital is maintained like a museum piece. In Assad's mode of thinking, to rebuild Quneitra might imply acceptance of Israel's annexation of the Golan. It is in this context that Quneitra transforms from an abandoned town to the one great representation of

---

* In his first meeting with George Shultz, Ronald Reagan's secretary of state, Assad gave the impatient Shultz a five-hour history lesson on the Levant.

Syrian unity. The recovery of the Golan and the protection of Syrian territory from further encroachment is the one issue that overrides communal strife and political alienation to bind Hafiz Assad and the people of Syria together. And it is in the name of the Golan that Hafiz Assad has been willing to sacrifice the tenuous unity of the Arabs.

In 1975, Hafiz Assad denounced the second Sinai Accord between Egypt and Israel, which in essence ended the state of war on Israel's western front. In Assad's assessment, Syria's acquiescence to Sinai II would have had the effect of making the proud descendant of the Umayyads just another weak state on Israel's borders. Like Jordan, Syria faced the danger of living on handouts and devoting most of its military energies to protecting Israel from Palestinian guerrilla raids. Assad vowed instead to fight back, to challenge an Arab environment that seemed willing to accept Israeli supremacy. But no one answered his call. Anwar Sadat had already betrayed him. His Baath rivals in Iraq automatically opposed anything he did. King Hussein plotted his own accommodation with Israel. And Saudi Arabia, as always, trembled with uncertainty. Thus Syria stood exposed in the shadow of Israel, flanked only by feeble Lebanon and the mass of volatile and desperate Palestinians. In the spring of 1975, Syria's last defense, its fragile western flank, began to disintegrate as Lebanon plunged into civil war.

Religion, tribe, and family divide Lebanon as they divide Syria. Through the 1950s and the 1960s, Lebanon lived the hope that Maronite and Greek Orthodox Christians, Sunni and Shiite Muslims, the Druze, and the Palestinians composed a harmonious whole within the country romantics called the "Switzerland of the Middle East." But on April 13, 1975, a bloody incident between Palestinians and Maronite Christians finally shattered the illusion and put Lebanon on the long road of civil war. It was a conflict from which Syria could not stay separated.

Lebanon is Syria's front yard. In culture, language, family networks, and even what they eat and drink, Syrians and Lebanese are cut from the same cloth. Emotionally, most Syrians and some Lebanese never accepted the severance of Lebanon from Syria proper. Yet one overriding difference defined the two countries—power in Lebanon resided with the Maronite Christians, who regarded themselves more as legendary "Phoenicians" than as Arabs. In early 1976, the war in Lebanon in its most simple form pitted the Maronites against the Arab Lebanese for control of the Lebanese state. The Maronites were losing until June 1, 1976, when Hafiz Assad jolted the Arab world by entering the war on the side of the Christians.

In response to Maronite calls for help, Syrian tanks and personnel carriers rumbled through the Bekaa Valley toward Beirut. The natural allies of the Syrian Baathists—the Lebanese who claim an Arab identity and the Palestinians—became the targets of Syrian military power.* Understanding the perils of intervening in fragmented Lebanon, Assad nonetheless plunged into the whirlpool of communal violence to save Syria's western defenses from the unpredictable consequences of a victory won by an unruly coalition of Lebanese Muslims and Palestinians. In the decision to invade Lebanon, Hafiz Assad put Syrian interests in its own territorial integrity before the requirements of Arab unity. Justifying his action to the Arabs, Hafiz Assad claimed that left alone, the Maronites would seek an alliance with Israel, thereby creating a "Christian Zion" in the Arab heartland. He further argued that in throwing the Maronites a life raft he was encouraging them to stay within the Arab habitat. Most of the Arab states, no more amenable to the carnage in Lebanon than Assad, accepted the rationale. For a while, Assad even won an Arab endorsement. Recognizing Assad as the Arab who cared enough to arrest Lebanon's drift toward anarchy, the Arab states meeting in Riyadh legitimized Syria's presence in Lebanon. But by 1977, Arab tolerance of Assad's "anti-Arab" behavior in behalf of the Maronites gave way to deep resentment against the Syrian presence in Lebanon. With an army operating on the ground, Assad could exert leverage over the Palestinians as well as the contentious Lebanese. He could intimidate Jordan. This in turn roused fears in Egypt, Iraq, and Saudi Arabia about Damascus becoming too powerful. Through Arab capitals, the inevitable whispers buzzed—Hafiz Assad was resurrecting Greater Syria.

The Syrian presence did succeed for a time in restoring some order to Lebanon. In the early fall of 1977, I hired a red-haired Syrian taxi driver in Damascus to take me through the lines to Beirut. Just over the border, the Damascus-Beirut highway crawled with

---

* Assad's support for Lebanon's Christians contributed to Syria's internal disorders that peaked between 1979 and 1982. In the early days of Assad's intervention in Lebanon, demonstrators in Damascus massed to chant, "Assad, we can stomach you as an Alawite but not as a Maronite."

military traffic and bristled with barricaded checkpoints. At each stop, the lean driver took our passports, walked into the wooden huts where Syrian soldiers inspected papers, and returned with the required passes sealed with a mass of brightly colored stamps bearing the emblem of Syria.

We arrived at Martyrs Square, the central point in Beirut, to discover that it had been turned into Syrian-occupied territory. Machine guns positioned behind walls of sandbags stood on every corner. At the square's upper end, one of the graceful old buildings had been turned into a military headquarters complete with a giant portrait of Hafiz Assad. It was a different Beirut from any I had ever seen before.

For days, my driver and I traveled the roads to Sidon and Tyre, Aley and Zahle, encountering usually grim, sometimes hostile, and often nervous Syrian soldiers attempting to hold back the murderous rage of Lebanese against Lebanese and Lebanese against Palestinian.

At last, we headed back to Syria. Inching along behind a string of canvas-top trucks, we reached the first checkpoint. The driver, as he did on the trip over, took my passport. But this time instead of going into the guard hut, he walked around the car and opened the trunk. With care, he extracted four boxes of Kleenex, several loaves of flat Arabic bread, and a water-filled plastic bag containing three goldfish. At the next checkpoint and all the way back to Damascus, he performed the same routine. I understood the Kleenex and bread as functional, low-cost bribes but I never found a satisfactory answer for the goldfish.

Hailed by a few, grudgingly accepted by some, bitterly condemned by others, the Syrian presence in Lebanon confirmed Syria's centrality in the Arab world and Hafiz Assad's growing prominence in the Arab constellation. Whatever Assad's growing internal problems were with his Sunni opponents, his intervention in Lebanon had succeeded in changing Syria from an object manipulated by more powerful neighbors to a major player in its own right. How much of a player emerged as Anwar Sadat prepared to go to Jerusalem.

Hafiz Assad fought his last great duel with Anwar Sadat in Damascus on the night of November 16, 1977. In spite of the bitter experience of 1973, Hafiz Assad still subscribed to Nasser's doctrine that the Arabs could defend themselves only when they united. Thus Sadat could not go to Jerusalem without pulling the struts out of

Arab defenses against Israel. For seven stormy hours, Sadat tried to sway Assad toward his peace overture to Israel. But Assad, calling the move an "outrageous disloyalty by a selfish man," refused to budge.* By the morning, they were too angry with each other to hold a joint press conference and Sadat faced the press alone.† The long bitter night marked the climax of four years of growing estrangement between the pivots of the Arab world that began with the October War. And it was the last time Assad and Sadat ever met.

The day Anwar Sadat flew to Jerusalem, government and business in Syria shut down in observance of a day of national mourning. But the symbolic act did nothing to deter Anwar Sadat, who continued on the path that took him to Camp David and finally to a separate peace with Israel. Hafiz Assad fought him every step of the way.

For Assad, Egypt's final exit from the Arab alignment imperiled Syria. Without the critical mass provided by the Egyptians, Syria, Jordan, and the Palestinians were set adrift to face the unfilled territorial ambitions that Hafiz Assad believed propelled the Israeli state. Another defection from the Arab ranks could sound the death knell over the Arab Levant. Imbued with the image of Bismarck, Hafiz Assad set out to make the map of the Middle East conform to Syria's security needs. On December 5, 1977, two weeks after Anwar Sadat spoke before the Knesset, Hafiz Assad pulled Syria, Libya, Algeria, the People's Democratic Republic of Yemen, and the PLO together into the "Front of Steadfastness and Resistance." With the weakest members of the Arab political configuration as allies, Assad took on the frontline Arab states in a high-stakes struggle to prevent Lebanon, Jordan, or the Palestinians from entering into any negotiations with Israel that might lead to an agreement that excluded Syria. In Assad's frame of reference, peace—real peace—required a revision of the entire power relationship between Israel and the Arabs. Assad sought parity, parity defined as the inability of either Israel or Syria to encroach on the pre-1967 territory of the other.

Clear in his objectives and shored up by an infusion of Soviet weapons, Hafiz Assad went to work to bring the Lebanese, Jorda-

---

* *Time*, August 7, 1978.
† Assad's exasperation was so great that he considered locking Sadat up to prevent him from leaving Damascus.

nians, and Palestinians to heel. In his grand design, which resurrected images of the Umayyads of twelve hundred years before, Assad would create a power bloc in the Arab Levant with Damascus at its center. But as he was unable to control the actions of Cairo, neither could Hafiz Assad control the other point of the Arab triangle—Baghdad.

Dismay over the Camp David Accords initially drew Syria and Iraq into an alliance that defied regional rivalry, party schism, and the bitter personal animosity between Hafiz Assad and Saddam Hussein.* The irony was not lost on Assad. Before signing the Iraqi-Syria "national action charter" on October 26, 1978, Assad turned to Saddam Hussein and quipped, "Brother Saddam, is this not like being born again?"† But the alliance turned out to be just short of stillborn. When Iraq invaded Iran in September 1980, Assad denounced Saddam's war against Iran as the wrong war against the wrong enemy at the wrong time. Yet his real concern was that the detested Saddam Hussein might actually defeat Iran, bestowing on Iraq enormous power relative to Syria. Frantic that a quick Iraqi victory over Iran would trap Syria between stalking Israel and resurgent Iraq, Assad broke with the Arabs to shore up the Persians, the centuries-old ethnic and religious rivals of the Arabs.

Heavy loads of arms flew over Syria to Iran, and Hafiz Assad allowed Syria to become the bridge between the fount of militant Shiism in Iran and the aroused Shia community in southern Lebanon.‡ Arab anger descended on Hafiz Assad. Ideologically, the other Arab states challenged his commitment to Arab nationalism. Economically, Syria's much-needed financial aid from the Gulf states contracted under Arab displeasure. Determined to eclipse Iraqi power, Assad absorbed the blows.

With Iraq contained by his alliance with Iran, Hafiz Assad turned on Jordan's King Hussein. The basic conflict between Hafiz Assad and King Hussein involved the greatest lust of nations—power. Assad drove to project Syria's influence over the whole of the Arab Levant, and Hussein was equally determined to remain an independent player.

---

* See Chapter 11.
† *Economist*, November 4, 1978.
‡ Part of the reason for Assad's Iranian alliance was to discourage Tehran from exporting its revolution to Syria. In mid-1985 Syrian defense minister Mustafa Tlas bluntly stated, "We have no interest in creating enemies of forty million Persians." Quoted in Kessler, *Syria*, p. 88.

Assad boycotted the Amman Summit called by Hussein in November 1980 to gain Arab support for his proposed negotiations with Israel aimed at extending Jordanian administration over the West Bank. To drive home the point that Syria would not allow such an agreement to occur, Assad put troops on Jordan's border. The crisis defused only when Assad, deciding he had gone too far, agreed to withdraw "gallantly in view of the existing situation in the Arab world."* In 1981, Assad torpedoed the plan of Saudi Arabia's King Fahd, which put out tentative feelers to Israel on the issue of Arab recognition. With each move on the diplomatic front, Hafiz Assad demonstrated that he possessed enough power to veto any Middle East peace initiative to which he was opposed. But Assad trod a lonely and dangerous path surrounded by Arab enemies.

Assad had exasperated Egypt with his vitriolic attacks on the Egyptian-Israeli peace treaty. He had sided with Iran against Iraq, prompting Saddam Hussein to send Assad's enemies inside Syria truckloads of arms via the eastern desert. His military move against Jordan's border had put him on intolerable terms with Hussein. And his disfavor among so many Arabs had allowed the Palestinian military/political structure in Lebanon to ignore Assad's attempts to control them. In April 1982, Assad faced his most formidable opponent of all when non-Arab Israel invaded the Syrian preserve of Lebanon.

As the massive assault rolled through south Lebanon, Assad understood two things—Israel's fight was with the PLO, not Syria; and Syria could not resist the Israeli invasion and win. Thus while Israeli troops and tanks pushed north toward Beirut, Syria took its Soviet arsenal and its battered air force and moved east into the Bekaa out of the line of battle. With no organized military force standing in the way, the Israeli pincers closed around Beirut, sealing in Yasser Arafat and his guerrillas. For seventy days, Israeli air power pulverized the defenseless city. Hafiz Assad did little beyond sending a message to the besieged PLO: "Beloved ones, I am living with you day and night. . . . Beirut's Arabism is a trust in your hands. . . . I ask you to remain steadfast: martyrdom or victory!"†

The rest of the Arab world, as powerless as Syria to stop the Israeli assault, nonetheless heaped their abuse on Assad. Yasser Arafat hurled the wounding charge that Assad had saved the Mar-

* *Arab News*, December 16, 1980.
† Quoted in Seale, *Asad*, p. 390.

onites but not the Palestinians. Egypt's Mubarak accused Assad of striking a secret deal with Menachem Begin to divide Lebanon between Syria and Israel. Saddam Hussein charged that Assad was in an undefined but treacherous collusion with Israel. King Hussein indicted him for "liquidating the Palestinian cause." Only his new Iranian allies remained silent.

It was in late summer of 1982 that Hafiz Assad's fortunes reached their low point. At home, he faced the aftermath of his brutality in Hama. Regionally, he confronted the Israeli presence in Lebanon. Realizing that the fear of casualties was the only chink in Israel's armor, Assad set about to exploit it. At the end of September, snipers, booby-trapped cars, and hand grenades lobbed from passing vehicles opened up a terrorist war against the Israeli presence in Lebanon. On November 11, 1982, it reached its emblematic height when a bomb ripped through staff headquarters in Tyre killing sixty-seven Israelis.

Hafiz Assad had found a way to fight back against not just Israel but his Arab enemies. Terror would be the tool with which Assad would create his coveted sphere of influence in the Levant. Within it, Lebanon would be his protectorate, the Palestinians his satrapy, Jordan his satellite. Together they would constitute the political-military encirclement of Israel that Hafiz Assad deemed necessary for Syria's defense.

Assad identified as his first target the Israeli-Lebanese Accord of May 17, 1983. Brokered by the United States, the agreement amounted to a treaty between Israel and the government of Lebanon that presented a crisis to Hafiz Assad. He threw every ounce of cunning and energy, every resource, clean or dirty, into the battle to stop a Lebanese accommodation with Israel. Bomb squads fanned out, and Shiite organizations allied with Iran went into the service of Syria. Zealous and fanatical, they chose their own targets and marched to their own orders. They were embraced by Assad because their goals could service his goals.

The September 14, 1982, assassination of Lebanese President-elect Bashir Gemayel, suspected of being executed by Syria, put the Lebanese treaty with Israel on hold. But American troops were still in Lebanon, acting, in Assad's view, as a surrogate for Israel. It was enough to thrust the United States into Assad's ring of enemies. Within a period of six months, terrorist bombs in Beirut destroyed the American embassy and killed 241 U.S. Marines in a collapsing barracks near the Beirut airport. Syria may not have been involved, but it supported the Islamic fundamentalists who were, and Hafiz Assad benefited from what they did. Perceiving his back to be pinned to the wall, Hafiz Assad was resisting with any means at his disposal. He told the Druze leader Walid Jumblatt, "If they really want us to be terrorists, we can be."*

The United States pulled its troops out of Lebanon in February 1984. On March 5, the Lebanese government abrogated its accord with Israel. Against all odds, Hafiz Assad had frustrated Israel's bid for hegemony over Lebanon. Now he would hold the line across the Levant. But efforts to defend the Arab Levant against Israel also meant overriding the particular interests of the Palestinians and the Jordanians, who were striving to fulfill their own destinies free from the dictates of Damascus.

In Assad's scheme of things, the Palestinians had to be under Syrian control, for the Palestinian problem represented more than disputed land or the fate of the Palestinian people. To Assad, the manner in which the Palestinian issue was eventually settled would determine under whose rule the Levant would live—Israel's or Syria's. Thus he had to stop any deal the Palestinians, Jordan, and Israel might strike that did not include Syria on terms acceptable to him.

Alarm bells sounded in Damascus in late 1982 when Yasser Arafat appeared close to giving King Hussein permission to negotiate under the Reagan Plan on behalf of the Palestinians. Assad charged forth to unseat Arafat and his wing of the PLO. Reaching into the PLO's endemic rivalries, Assad armed and financed a rebellion within the PLO against Arafat's leadership.† In December 1983, the rebels ousted Arafat for a second time from Lebanon, menacing as never before his leadership of the PLO. On April 10, 1984, Arafat, facing his political demise, pulled back from the deal with Hussein.

In 1983, when it looked like Hussein might succeed in forming a joint Jordanian-Palestinian delegation to negotiate with Israel, Assad launched an all-out attack against King Hussein. Under the label "Jordanian national movement," Assad promoted Hussein's enemies within Jordan. But the real force of Assad's war against Hussein was a worldwide campaign of terror. In October 1983, automatic-

* Ibid., p. 420.
† See Chapter 12.

weapons fire wounded the Jordanian ambassadors to both India and Italy. In November, gunfire hit two Jordanian officials in Athens, while in Amman experts defused three bombs. In December, a Jordanian consular official in Madrid fell to an assassin's bullets. Still Hussein marched on, charging Hafiz Assad with heinous crimes intended to divide the Arab world.

In mid-1984, the unity of the Arab world stood at the precipice. King Fahd's Ramadan message reflected the anguish: "Perhaps more than at any other time in the past, the Muslim world stands in need of the true spirit of fasting."* Fahd's appeal bounced off the resolute Assad. The following November, the Jordanian chargé d'affaires in Athens narrowly escaped death when his attacker's gun jammed. In December, the Jordanian consul in Bucharest died from a bullet that hit its mark. In April 1985, following another attempt by Hussein to start a joint Jordan-Palestinian negotiating effort with Israel, gunfire ripped into the Jordanian embassy in Rome and a Jordanian aircraft in Athens airport. In July, gunmen sprayed the Madrid office of Alia, the Jordanian national airline, and killed the first secretary of the Jordanian embassy in Ankara.†

In his campaign to frighten Hussein into compliance with his wishes, Assad pressed into service proxies, including the notorious and feared Abu Nidal. By the fall of 1985, King Hussein had had enough. When the Labor Party, Hussein's prospective negotiating partner, lost the Israeli elections, Hussein dropped his deadly quarrel with Assad. Consequently, on November 10, Jordan officially rejected any partial or separate deals with Israel. In February 1986, when Hussein finally broke off his negotiations with the PLO, he conceded defeat to Syria's president.

In pursuit of his vision of the Levant, Hafiz Assad between 1982 and 1987 repeatedly crossed the fine line between terrorism and the defense of national interests. He was not alone. The mid-1980s saw the Arab world sink to new depths of acrimony that grew out of the accumulated and interrelated effects of the Lebanese civil

---

* *Arab News*, June 1, 1984.
† Syria did not escape retaliation. Syrian installations and personnel were attacked in Athens, Rome, Geneva, Rabat, London, and finally Damascus, where a car bomb exploded in July 1985 outside the offices of the Syrian Arab News Agency and the Ministry of Interior, causing dozens of casualties. No one has yet to determine who was responsible for each specific attack—Assad's Arab enemies, his Syrian opposition, or Israel.

war, the Iranian revolution, the Iraq-Iran War, and the Israeli invasion of Lebanon. Chaos consumed the world of the Arabs as rival intelligence agencies, competing militias, and ad hoc terrorist groups battled each other for supremacy. Hafiz Assad stood as a central figure in the disorder. In the end, his entanglement with terror lost him as much as he gained. After the fact, the Lion of Damascus discovered that those accused of state-sponsored terrorism swam as pariahs in the waters of the international community. Hafiz Assad had been labeled a terrorist, and the label stuck. Having achieved his negative goals of preventing any accommodation between Israel and its Arab neighbors, Hafiz Assad began to engage Syria in a process that would stabilize the Levant and return Syria to international respectability. One of his first steps was to expel Abu Nidal from Syria.

By 1988, Assad felt more comfortable than he had since 1978, when the rebellion led by the Muslim Brotherhood began. After Hama, Syria's internal conflicts had stayed under control. Lebanon seemed reasonably secured. And Saddam Hussein continued to stagger in the quicksand of his war with Iran. In August 1988, that war ended. Iran turned inward and Iraq turned west, toward Syria. Freed from the battlefield, Saddam Hussein set out to settle accounts with those who had opposed him. As a result, Iraqi arms began to flow to the last viable foe of Syrian domination of Lebanon—the Maronite Christians led by Lebanese President Michel Aoun. At the same time, Iraqi trade and money built an alliance with Jordan's King Hussein. These were Assad's problems in the Arab arena. Beyond it, Hafiz Assad was losing his arms supplier as the Soviet empire and Soviet expansionist ambitions disintegrated. Syria once more felt imperiled.

Syrian security could no longer be found in Assad's "Front of Steadfastness and Resistance." Nor could Hafiz Assad continue to live in the Arab wilderness. Making an end run around those he had enraged, Assad began to patch up relations with Egypt and send out feelers to the United States. On August 2, 1990, Saddam Hussein handed Hafiz Assad his ticket back into the Arab fold when Iraq invaded Kuwait. Flying into Cairo to attend the emergency meeting of the Arab League, Hafiz Assad thrust Syria into the coalition against his old nemesis Saddam Hussein. "The Syria of Hafiz Assad, self-styled 'citadel of Arabism,' patron of Palestinian 'radicals,' scourge of Egypt and Camp David . . . bulwark of American domination of the region" had aligned itself with the most conservative Arab regimes and connived with the United States to go to war against a brother Arab country.* Suddenly the inimical Assad was in bed with Egypt, Saudi Arabia, and the United States.

Assad's political crossover took some explaining to his own people. In a speech on September 12, 1990, he acknowledged the existence of "those who wonder how Arab forces can be present on Saudi Arabian territory while the foreign [U.S.] troops are there."† He pulled his explanation straight out of the lexicon of Arab unity. Syria intended "not to fight the other threatening brother, but to prevent him from aggression—thus help him."‡

Syria reaped the harvest of its unlikely alliance. For the four thousand soldiers plus an armored division of ten thousand it dispatched to Saudi Arabia, Syria gained $2 billion in aid from the Gulf states and elevation to American ally. Hafiz Assad also won the freedom to consolidate his grip on Lebanon. In October 1990, Syria with the silent consent of the United States and his new Arab allies quelled the forces of General Michel Aoun, the defiant Maronite president of Lebanon. When the Gulf War ended, Hafiz Assad crushed the Arafat faction of the PLO in Lebanon, thus completing the campaign to control Lebanon begun in 1976.

As the reigning Arab power in the Levant, Hafiz Assad in July 1991 once more astounded his Arab brothers. Having torn Arab unity asunder in order to keep his neighbors from negotiating with Israel, Assad announced his intention to sit down with Israel at an American-Soviet-sponsored peace conference on the Middle East.

On the surface it appeared Hafiz Assad had suddenly changed his whole vision of Syrian interests. But Assad's goals remain the same as they were when he seized power in 1970—restraining Israeli expansionism, regaining the lost Golan, and securing Syria a dominant voice in the affairs of the Middle East. Not even his traditional tactics had radically altered. Assad's game plan has always revolved around unwavering objectives pursued with calculated determination. When the world began to totally transform in 1988, Assad simply made his adjustments to the new realities.

---

* David Hirst, "Arab World Turned Upside Down," *Guardian Weekly*, August 19, 1990.
† *New York Times*, October 11, 1990.
‡ Ibid.

In the wake of the announcement that Syria would negotiate with Israel at least on the issue of the Golan, pictures of Hafiz Assad splashed across the pages of the world's newspapers. Taken at different times, in different settings, they were all remarkably alike, because Hafiz Assad presents only one public pose. Dressed in a conservative business suit, thinning hair brushed to the side of his broad brow, an enigmatic smile on his face, he sits with one foreign dignitary or another. Yet he always seems alone, as if the cameras have captured him psychologically more than physically. Always a loner in the Arab world, Assad remains a loner, acting according to his own definition of Syrian interests. In his quest to make Syria the center of the Arab Levant, Assad harbors no illusions about the sanctity of Arab unity. Nor does he hesitate in isolating Syria from the other Arab states for long periods of time if that furthers his ultimate objectives. Often meddling in their affairs, occasionally thrusting with single-minded determination his own agenda on his Arab neighbors, Assad has made Syria a force within the Arab nation that he so frequently ignores. The Arab banner he sometimes thrusts aloft serves the same function for Assad as it did for Nasser—the advancement of his own country's interests.

Those interests tie into Syria's sense of itself. Suffering from the legacies of history, sensing its vulnerability, Syria is a defensive, suspicious country obsessed with reconstituting itself territorially. The return of the Golan remains the one issue on which Hafiz Assad and all Syrians agree and unite, the one issue that gives Assad a claim of legitimacy within his tightly controlled country. And it is the issue of Syrian security and the future of the Golan that will shape Assad's attitudes and decisions concerning both Israel and the place Syria occupies within the Arab world. Yet the lure of territorial redemption cannot provide escape from the realities of the Syrian body politic. Tormented by a diverse and fractious population that lacks any real internal cohesion, Syria remains a fragile country.

Early in the morning, the massive palace of Hafiz Assad that rises out of one of Damascus's Qassioun Hills absorbs the delicate colors of the rising sun. Below its brooding, fortresslike mass stand two distinctive symbols of Hafiz Assad's Syria—the Sheraton Hotel and Mezza prison. The Sheraton with its Arabesque decor and costumed coffee boy serving international businessmen from a brass pot heated on a brazier attempts to project an image of Damascus as the capital of an authentic nation. Mezza prison, with its high, thick walls strung with rusting, twisted barbed wire confining hollow-eyed inmates languishing as prisoners of an authoritarian state, portrays the reality of Syria.

In Assad's state, there are no real institutions attempting to span the great fissures dividing Sunni and Alawi, town and city, religious and secular. Even the Baath Party in terms of its ideological function is virtually at an end. Over the years, Assad's political base has progressively shrunk from the Syrian Baath Party as a whole, to the military wing of the party, to the officers within the wing who belong to his own minority Alawite sect, and now to members of his own clan within the Alawite group. Hafiz Assad and the Baath have never succeeded in substituting ideology for Syria's traditional social, sectarian, regional, and even tribal ties. In a sense, Hafiz Assad and his party are as much victims of these forces as are the people of Syria. Having abandoned its natal notion of pan-Arabism, the Syrian Baath has become a mechanism through which Hafiz Assad exercises his will over Syria.

Externally, Hafiz Assad has secured for Syria a central place in the affairs of the Arabs. Internally, he has failed to forge a nation. When he dies, all those forces within the country that he has so forcefully subdued could rise again to try to claim Syria for themselves.

C H A P T E R 11

SADDAM HUSSEIN: THE BUTCHER OF BAGHDAD

THE TWO GREAT RIVERS, THE TIGRIS and the Euphrates, trace their separate courses across the flatlands of central Iraq, draw near at Baghdad, separate again, and finally come together in the Shatt al-Arab to flow into the Persian Gulf. Along them lie the markers of Iraq's ancient past—the tel that was once Nineveh, the arch of the Sasanid Palace of Ctesiphon, fabled Babylon, and finally the crumbled ziggurat at Ur of the Chaldees. Each fell to influences and invaders as often from the east as from the west.

To wander from Iraq's mountains in the north to the marshes of the south is to see, to hear, and to feel the magnetic pull of lands and cultures beyond the Arab world. Here the domes of the mosques are a little taller and a little slimmer, representing the classical architecture of Iran more than Egypt. Hallowed Arabic is a little different, resonating with words from Turkish and Farsi. Even Islam is more variegated, reflecting a population that is Shiite as well as Sunni. It is as if Iraq is somehow laboring to stay within the sphere of the Sunni Arab world. At Basra, near the point where the Tigris and Euphrates merge, this perception materializes in the most interpretive monument of modern Iraq. Jutting out from the corniche fronting the Shatt al-Arab, the statues of eighty Iraqi military officers killed in the Iraq-Iran War defiantly point their bronze fingers toward the east. The effect is profound. For to stand above the wide Shatt al-Arab, the "river of the Arabs," is to stand on the eastern front of the Arab world.

Iraq's empty western deserts touch the Arab lands of Syria, Jordan, and Saudi Arabia. But its heavily populated eastern region, the region fed by the Tigris and Euphrates, fronts two giant non-Arab countries—Iran and Turkey. Within Iraq's population, only 20 percent are Sunni Arab, the ballast of the Arab world. Almost all of the remainder belong either to the dissenting Shiite sect of Islam or the Indo-European Kurds. Constantly challenged by a 60 percent non-Sunni majority and a non-Arab minority that equals in number the Sunnis, Iraq has developed an identity that is at the same time Arab and not Arab. Although included in the Arab world, Iraq does not quite fit into the Arab matrix largely shaped by the orthodox Sunni branch of Islam. Patched together by imperial fiat at the end of World War I, Iraq is constantly strained by powerful centrifugal forces within a population sharing neither a common identity nor mutual ideals. Only the steel will and spiked heel of a man like Saddam Hussein have been able to keep the country's component parts from ripping apart.

Iraq evokes a sense of time that stirs a deep consciousness of human history. Before there was an Iraq, there was the mystery and majesty of ancient Mesopotamia. Six thousand years before the Christian era, man sank his hoe into the rich soil fed by the Tigris and Euphrates. The mighty rivers presented their gift of fertility, but they also delivered their terrible vengeance. Every year from March to May, they brought down roaring floods that inundated the plains, destroying everything in their path. Man learned that if he was to live on this fruitful land he had to control the raging water in flood stage and irrigate the parched landscape in the dry season. Both demanded collective management. Thus Sumerian civilization was born. By 3000 B.C., the Sumerians had established the world's first urban society. They had invented the wheel, made bronze, created art of amazing power and delicacy, and developed an early form of writing called cuneiform. Sumerian culture centered first at Ur on the Euphrates, two hundred miles south of the present city of Baghdad. By 1800 B.C., the Sumerians' rivals, the Akkadians, were dominant, establishing themselves to the north in legendary Babylon.*

The great king Hammurabi (1792–1750 B.C.), leading society beyond the confines of kinship, cut his code of law into black stone stelae and erected them throughout his domain. Twelve centuries later, Nebuchadnezzar (605–562 B.C.) presided over Babylon at its peak of empire and grandeur.

Babylon was the marvel of ancient Mesopotamia. Herodotus described the double row of defensive walls, each wide enough to accommodate a four-horse chariot moving at racing pace. Inside the walls, a broad avenue ran through the center of the city, from which temples, shops, and housing radiated. Dominating all was the great southern palace of Nebuchadnezzar. Tier upon tier of flowers and vines draped down the towering walls, creating the fabled Hanging Gardens of Babylon.

In 539 B.C., glorious Babylon fell to Cyrus the Great. Mesopotamia, for two thousand years the stronghold of Semitic-speaking people, now belonged to Persia. Eleven centuries later, culture was again dominant under the Sasanids when the Persian Arab armies charged in from the west and claimed Mesopotamia for Islam in A.D. 637.

For the men of Mecca and Medina, Mesopotamia was the outpost of the early Islamic empire. Even by the measure of the Middle East, the climate is punishing. The winters bite with cold. In the summer, temperatures reach the mid-nineties, creating "a yellowish, corpse-like color over the hills and plains . . . [causing] a certain madness."† Yet the cities of Mesopotamia grew in size as the Arabs from the Arabian peninsula installed themselves as landowners and non-Arab immigrants moved in to till the soil. By the ninth century A.D., Baghdad, approaching Constantinople in size, was the capital of Islam. Looking east to Persia, as well as west to Mecca, the Abbasid caliphs of Baghdad presided over the zenith of Islamic culture. By the tenth century, the Abbasids and their capital began to decline. In the thirteenth, they were destroyed.

In 1258, the Mongols under the barbarous Hulagu rode their

---

* Babylon lasted 1,300 years, first under the Akkadians and later under the Semites.
† Egon Friedell, quoted in Joseph Kraft, "Letter From Baghdad," *The New Yorker*, October 20, 1980, p. 165.

barrel-chested ponies out of the steppes of Asia and into Baghdad. The men of the northern plains kicked the last breath out of the Abbasid caliphate before hacking to death Islam's revered scholars, poets, and religious leaders, stacking their skulls in a grotesque pyramid. For over a week, ordinary people fell to the Mongol sword. One hundred thousand corpses filled the streets, and the Tigris flowed with blood. Like a swarm of locusts, the Mongols devoured the treasures of stately Baghdad, destroying the vestiges of Abbasid culture and learning. With no appreciation or knowledge of the delicate task of managing the irrigation system, the Mongols ruined the land along with everything else.

Although Hulagu's armies marched all the way to the Mediterranean, only Mesopotamia, bludgeoned and bleeding, was incorporated into the Mongol Empire. For three hundred years, it stayed cut off from the world of the Arabs, and for the three hundred years following that, it languished as an impoverished and decaying province of the Ottoman Empire. Serving as a buffer zone, it absorbed the contending claims of the Turks to the west and the Persians to the east. It was only in the decade prior to World War I that Mesopotamia drew the covetous eyes of the imperial West.

The scent of oil lying in the northeastern region of Mosul and the appreciation of Mesopotamia as a communication line to India roused the British lion. Through the Sykes-Picot Agreement and the Treaty of San Remo, Britain stalked its prey. Ignoring the dictates of geography, history, and ethnicity, its powerful paws reached into the wilderness of Mesopotamia to ensnare fragments of three separate provinces of the deceased Ottoman Empire—Baghdad, Mosul, and Basra. Each was dominated by an ethnic or religious group that shared either blood or faith but not both with the other two. Tied together, branded with endemic instability, it was named Iraq.

Sunni Arabs, less than a fourth of the total population, occupied the "Golden Triangle," an area beginning at the western boundary of Iran, roughly fifty miles north of Baghdad, and fanning out to the borders of Syria, Jordan, and Saudi Arabia. If Mesopotamia had a political core, it was here. What little government the Turks had exercised over Mesopotamia had favored the Sunni Arabs. They held most of the military positions, they constituted the sparse bureaucracy, and they benefited from what schools there were. Geographically isolated from the nucleus of the Arab world, their identity nonetheless lay with the Sunni Arabs to the west.

The attitudes of the Sunni towns along the Tigris speak to the western desert and the Arab heartland. On any morning, the waterfront crawls with people and commerce. Men sitting on benches beneath wide striped awnings talk more of Damascus and Cairo than of Tehran or Istanbul or even Basra. Their interest is Arab politics conducted between the Sunni Arab nations. To them, Iraq's place is with the Arabs.

Sunni Iraq gives way to Shiite Iraq south of Baghdad. The thickly settled towns and small villages populated by Shiites spread between the two great rivers and on to the head of the Persian Gulf. Together with the Shiite villages west of the Euphrates, they give Iraq the only Shiite majority in the Arab world other than the small island sheikhdom of Bahrain.* The Shiite presence in Iraq exceeds simple numbers. The original split in the body of Islam took place on the soil of what is now Iraq. In that soil rest the remains of Shiism's two great martyrs—Ali and Hussein. The tomb of Hussein at Karbala and the tomb of Ali at Najaf are the Mecca and Medina of Shiism, drawing Shiite pilgrims from Iran, India, Pakistan, and elsewhere. Karbala, during the pilgrimage season, is a sea of brightly colored flags and tiny flashing lights. In every shop and vendor's stall, the flag of Hussein hangs—the green of Islam, the black of mourning. Some are simple strips of cloth tied around a stick and planted in a pile of pomegranates. Others are elaborate black fringed tapestries that portray the momentous events in the life of the martyr. Led by the somber tones of verse after verse of the Koran carried over loudspeakers mounted on the mosques, people by the hundreds converge on the city. Families too poor to afford the price of a hotel spread their sleeping mats, vinyl suitcases, camp stoves, and teapots on the sidewalks. Above them on the balconies of high-priced hotels are the well-to-do. Yet all focus on the same point—the towering minarets of Hussein's mosque.

For a Shiite, the mosque of the martyred Hussein at Karbala, like the mosque of Ali at Najaf, symbolizes the emotionalism of the sect. Both lie south and west of Baghdad, far inside Iraq's eastern border. For centuries, Persia used the common faith to exercise its influence over the area and to challenge the claims of Ottoman Turkey in southern Iraq. Fearing absorption into the Arab realm overwhelmingly dominated by Sunnis, the Shiites of southern Iraq

---

* Most Shiites in Iraq are Arab, but an unknown percentage are ethnic Persians who speak Farsi.

316 / PASSION AND POLITICS

held themselves apart from the ideal of the Arab nation. Their world was the Persian Gulf, anchored by roughly thirty million Shiites.

As in Syria, a collection of small minorities add their knot to the tangle of religion, ethnicity, and language in Iraq. There are the Assyrians, Nestorian Christians who are linked more closely ethnically to the Iranians than the Arabs. There are Armenians and Turkomans. There is a Palestinian presence that arrived after 1948. And finally there are the Kurds, one-fifth of the population of Iraq.

The Kurds live beneath the snowcapped peaks of northern Iraq. They are an ancient mountain people who speak a group of dialects related to Persian. Indo-European by language, Sunni by religion, they inhabit a great arc of territory from western Iran to eastern Syria that passes through southern Turkey and northern Iraq. Possessing a fierce sense of identity, the Kurds were promised an independent state of Kurdistan in the waning days of World War I. But what the great powers could create they would destroy. The Treaty of Lausanne in 1923 canceled Kurdistan. From that moment on, the Kurds have been a permanent source of dissension in Iran and Turkey. In Iraq, they became a major force of separation. Since 1958, the Iraqi government has been continually either at war with the Kurds or at best living in an uneasy state of armed truce.

Northern Iraq, "Kurdistan," is beautiful and brutal. The gentleness of nature celebrated by the Kurdish poet as the roar and hiss of foam, the shrill song of the brook, is counterbalanced by a people who know war too well. I see this in one of my friends, who is a highly educated, beautifully mannered Kurd from a well-to-do family. Once in musing about his childhood he told me, "I always wanted to play the piano. I begged my mother to buy one and arrange lessons for me. The answer was always no. Like the child that I was I kept asking, 'Why, why?' One day she became very impatient. 'The reason is, Kurds fight. Kurds don't play the piano.' I knew the last word had been spoken on the subject."

Iraq's religious/ethnic mix overlies rivalries between regions, tribes, and extended families within each of the larger divisions. Like a hot glass container plunged into cold water, Iraq is cracked, fractured, and fissured. With a population that lacks any unifying sense of nationalism, it struggles to survive intact. If Iraq identified itself as a unique country at the crossroads of competing cultures, the strains might not be as great. But the Sunni minority that traditionally controls the government more often than not labors to keep Iraq a part of the Arab world. The Kurds, as non-Arabs, want no part of pan-Arabism. The Shiites, largely Arabs, nonetheless want to protect themselves from being swallowed up by the Sunni majorities west of Iraq. Perhaps nothing illustrates the ambiguity of Iraq's curious position in the Arab world more than language. Arabic, the great unifying force of the Arabs, is less universal in Iraq than in any other Arab country. Although 75 percent of the population speak Arabic, the remaining quarter speak Kurdish, Turkish, or Farsi. And those who claim Arabic as their first language speak a unique dialect containing a plethora of words from Kurdish, Turkish, and Farsi, the languages of Iraq's minorities. Thus since its creation, Iraq has vacillated between the call to a specific Iraqi nationalism and the pull of Arab unity. It began with the first king, Faisal, and reached its peak under Saddam Hussein.

In 1920, Britain set about concocting a government for the artificial country it had created. Faisal, oldest son of the sharif of Mecca, the spearhead of the Arab Revolt, had been installed on the embryonic throne of Syria by the British Colonial Office. But out of the deep waters of diplomatic intrigue of 1919–20, France surfaced with Syria. The French government, ridding itself of Britain's legacy, "invited" Faisal to leave Syria in July 1920. A sad and pathetic figure, he arrived in London and deposited himself on the doorstep of an embarrassed British government. Faisal, promised an Arab nation during World War I, had no throne. Britain had no government for Iraq. Suddenly the needs of the Hashemites and the interests of Britain merged. In Baghdad, Britain's previous candidate for king was invited to tea with the governor's wife, only to be whisked off in an armored car for a long stay in Ceylon. On April 23, 1923, Faisal, following a whirlwind tour of the major sheikhs, became king of Iraq.

Faisal's Iraq bore the scars of neglect. The canals that once directed the floodwaters of the Tigris and Euphrates into reservoirs were clogged with silt, causing useless marshes to form in what were once fertile fields. Mosul, across the Tigris from the ruins of ancient Nineveh, was nothing more than a market town of decaying mud-brick buildings where Arabs and Kurds came to trade their meager produce. In once-glorious Baghdad, foot traffic crossed the Euphrates on swaying pontoon bridges that also provided moorings for the round reed boats that Herodotus had described two thousand years before. Within the city, the richly colored tiles decorating the mosques barely clung to structures seemingly untouched since the days of the Islamic empire. When Faisal arrived in his capital, the only signs of the new Iraq were in the people. Sunni Arabs in flowing robes lounged on long wooden benches outside a coffee shop along the river, where Kurds wearing felt caps and turbans worked as cargo handlers and Shiite pilgrims passed on their way to Karbala.

Although handpicked by the British, Faisal turned out to be a remarkably good king for this disparate country. Charming, tactful, broadly tolerant of Iraq's minorities, Faisal kept the opposition in check. Yet Faisal was a Sunni who grew to adulthood surrounded by the rising passion of Arab nationalism. With British concurrence, he linked Iraq more closely to the broader Sunni-dominated Arab world. Controlling the army by limiting advancement into the officers' corps to Sunni Arabs and benefiting from the natural dynamics of tribal politics that kept the Shia divided and subdued, Faisal kept Iraq tenuously tethered in the Arab arena.

In 1932, Iraq became the first of the former Ottoman territories granted independence by a European colonial power. In spite of new oil discoveries that promised to make Iraq the Middle East's second-largest producer, Britain could no longer hold its mandate. The distance between ruler and ruled was too great, making the expense of keeping an army on the ground daunting. Trusting Faisal and retaining the military and economic prerogatives of a mother country, Britain relinquished its mandate. Nationalists across the Arab realm rejoiced, elevating Faisal to a position akin to the founding father of the future Arab state. As a result, Iraq took its place in the forefront of the pan-Arab movement. Faisal injected Syrian and Palestinian teachers with pan-Arab credentials into the educational system and Arab ideologues into the fledgling Iraqi civil service. But Faisal, despite a youth spent in the Arab Revolt, had ceased to be an avid pan-Arabist. Recognizing Iraq's profound diversity, he sought to blend a new nationalism encompassing all Iraqis. But dedication and enlightenment could not overcome the reality that the population was divided between Arabs—themselves separated into a politically dominant Sunni minority and a disenfranchised Shia majority—and a remaining population most of which was not Arab at all. Only resentment of British prerogatives in Iraq could at various times, in varying degrees, overcome divisions of tribe, ethnicity, religion, and region. Acknowledging the problems of his embryonic country, Faisal could only lament, "I say in my heart full of sadness that there is not yet in Iraq an Iraqi people."*

Tired and disillusioned, Faisal died unexpectedly in 1933 at the age of fifty-six. With his death, Iraq lost perhaps the one person with sufficient prestige to begin the difficult process of building the idea of an Iraqi nation and reconciling it with the reality of British power.

Faisal's handsome but shallow son Ghazi became king. Pursuing a playboy existence, he never commanded his father's authority or prestige. On April 4, 1939, he wrapped his sports car around a light pole, leaving the throne to his three-year-old son, Faisal II.

From 1939 to 1958, two men managed the monarchy—Faisal's regent, Abd al-Illah, and Nuri al-Said, the most enduring political figure in Iraq before the rise of Saddam Hussein. Like players in a tragedy, both men became trapped between the monarchy's need of British support and rising Iraqi nationalism built on little but resentment of the lingering presence of imperial Britain. As the situation demanded, al-Illah but more particularly al-Said played to Arab nationalism or steered Iraq away from the political winds west of the Euphrates.† Playing to Arab nationalism immediately after World War II, Nuri al-Said helped create the Arab League. He drafted a proposal for the United Nations that would unite Syria, Lebanon, and Transjordan into Greater Syria, which could then form an Arab union with Iraq and any other Arab state wishing to join. And he sent twenty thousand soldiers into the 1948 Palestine war in the name of the Arab nation. The Arab strategy of Nuri al-Said came to an end the year Faisal II reached his majority and Gamal Abdul Nasser began solidifying his hold on Egypt.

---

* Christine Moss Helms, *Iraq: Eastern Flank of the Arab World* (Washington, D.C.: Brookings Institution, 1984), p. 9.
† The men behind the throne could not always control events. In 1941 the ultranationalist Rashid Ali became prime minister in a military coup that sent both Nuri al-Said and the regent into exile. The grand mufti of Jerusalem, the flaming symbol of Arab nationalism who was himself an exile from Palestine, arrived to set up an "Arab committee." With Rashid Ali's participation, it was to probe avenues of Arab-Nazi collaboration. The British quickly retaliated by landing forces at Basra and advancing on Baghdad. Within two months, British force restored the monarchy and Iraq had declared war on Germany, providing a transit point for goods for the Russian front. Nothing contributed more to nationalist sentiment in Iraq than the British invasion of 1941.

On May 2, 1953, the same day that his cousin became king of Jordan, eighteen-year-old Faisal II took his place before an assemblage of Sunni urban notables, a few Shiite sheikhs, and a token presence of grizzled Kurdish mountain men. As muezzins chanted from the minarets and a 101-gun salute sounded on the banks of the Tigris River, he swore "by God to safeguard the Constitution and independence of the country." The young king in his white tunic with gold braid rode through the streets of Baghdad in a red coach, preceded ironically by a horse-drawn war chariot much like those used by the Persians to invade Mesopotamia.

In 1953, Faisal's Iraq seemed a land of promise. It contained 175,000 square miles, claimed oil reserves of five billion barrels, and, like no other country of the Middle East, possessed fertile soil and ample water for irrigation. Increased oil exports and reasonably responsible government spending were gradually raising the living standard of the masses. But the monarchy, afraid to let loose of its security blanket, stayed firmly attached to Britain. As a result, British troops remained on Iraqi soil, and British and Western oil interests continued to hold Iraq's oil in their grip. It was with this tie to imperialist Britain that Iraq's monarchy faced the forces of pan-Arabism unleashed by Gamal Abdul Nasser.

Nasser's anti-imperialist appeal, delivered over his powerful Cairo radio station, cut across Iraq's religious and ethnic divides. Whatever pan-Arab sentiments lingered within the palace in Baghdad died in the face of Nasser's assault on the lackeys of Western imperialism. On February 24, 1955, Iraq agreed to participate in the British-sponsored Baghdad Pact, the treaty that was such anathema to Nasser. Explaining his leap away from pan-Arabism, Nuri al-Said argued that the security provided by the alliance would allow Iraq to develop economically, creating a society that was Iraqi—not Sunni or Shiite or Kurd. In his enthusiasm, he resurrected the medieval splendor of Baghdad in the days of Harun al-Rashid. What Nuri al-Said did not verbalize was that the price Iraq had to pay for these benefits was to become the vanguard of Western interests in the Arab world.

In July 1958, al-Said sent Iraqi troops into Jordan to stand ready to intervene in Lebanon in support of the besieged pro-Western government of Camille Chamoun. But General Abd al-Karim Qasim, refusing to lead his troops against other Arabs, turned on Baghdad. With this one act of defiance, all the factors of discontent in Iraq came together—poverty, government control by the large landowning class, a deplorable educational system, health conditions that resulted in an infant mortality rate of 341 in every 1,000 pregnancies. But the anger did not stop there. Particular grievances inflamed particular communities. For the Kurds, it was lack of autonomy. For the Shiites, it was the inequity of political and economic power. For the middle- and lower-class Sunnis, it was the call of Arab nationalism. Together they rose up to rid Iraq of monarchy and the legacy of imperialism.

In the early-morning hours of July 28, 1958, Baghdad slept. Silently soldiers loyal to General Qasim moved into the main intersections, the railroad station, the telegraph offices, and the radio station. At the palace, twenty-three-year-old King Faisal II, clad only in his underwear, stood before his shaving mirror. Without warning, gunfire announced the army's encirclement of the palace. With no hope of resistance, the king surrendered in return for a promise of safe conduct for himself and his family out of the country. Halfway across the palace's front courtyard, the officer in command turned and opened fire with a machine gun, killing the king and Abd al-Illah.

The king's body was hurriedly wrapped in a carpet and whisked away for secret burial. Lacking any real political instincts, interested in skiing, modern art, and jazz, the king had never really ruled. The Iraqis knew it. Therefore they vented their anger on the former regent and Nuri al-Said. Abd al-Illah's body was tossed from a palace window into the angry crowd below. Men screaming their pent-up rage dragged it through the street before stringing up what remained for all of Iraq to see. The alarm had already sounded for seventy-year-old Nuri al-Said. The next day, he was found on a street in a Baghdad suburb garbed and veiled as a woman. Stripped of his disguise and impaled alive, he was left to rot in the sun.

Proclaiming that the "corrupt clique subservient to the imperialists" was gone, the new regime declared Iraq a republic. But it was a republic bearing the same internal divisions that tormented the monarchy. Carrying the simplistic notion that overthrowing the monarchy would create a benevolent and forward-looking regime, the new leader, General Abd al-Karim Qasim, little understood just how difficult it was to govern Iraq. The Sunnis, Shiites, and Kurds would continue to pursue their contradictory visions of Iraq while families and tribes within each fought their own private battles. On the periphery, nascent political parties backing opposing ideologies would compete in the street. With the image of imperialism gone, nothing united the political forces in Iraq.

For the Sunni Arabs, General Qasim's revolution promised the fulfillment of Arab unity. In 1958, pan-Arabism led by Gamal Abdul Nasser was at its peak. These were the days when the image of an Arab superstate arching the Nile to the Euphrates seemed within reach. With the three great centers of Arab power—Cairo, Damascus, and Baghdad—under pan-Arab revolutionary governments, Jordan, Lebanon, and other lesser Arab countries could not escape being pulled into the vortex. But it was not to be. Qasim turned out to be more of an Iraqi than an Arab nationalist.

Qasim was a perfect Iraqi, the son of a Sunni Arab father and Kurdish mother and the grandson of a Shiite. Qasim represented that element within Iraq whose agenda was Iraq and the Persian Gulf, not pan-Arabism or the goals of Nasser.* But Qasim could not hold the multiple forces in Iraq in check to build a specific Iraqi nationalism. Within two months of the demise of the monarchy, the bloodletting between Nasserites and Iraqi nationalists, Baathists and communists, and the Kurds and the government began. In September 1958, the communists went on a rampage, killing hundreds of suspected Arab nationalists opposed to the communists' "international" orientation; three months later, communist Kurds massacred Turkomans in Kirkuk; and in October 1959, a Baath hit squad including twenty-two-year-old Saddam Hussein attempted to assassinate Qasim on the streets of Baghdad. In the spring of 1962, the Kurds, demanding independence or at least autonomy in a federalized or decentralized Iraq, exploded into a full-scale revolt. Out of the maelstrom, a pattern emerged which pitted the various forms of pan-Arabism against a fragmented, multi-ethnic society ill suited to the ideology of pan-Arabism. It left General Qasim to preside over a three-way struggle for control of Iraq's destiny among communists on one side, pan-Arab Nasserites and Baathists on another, and Iraqi nationalists on the third, while the Kurds fought their own battle for Kurdistan. In the end, the pan-Arabists won.

On February 8, 1963, a contingent including members of the Iraq Baath Party marched Qasim and his closest aides into the Arabic

---

* In a less enlightened exercise in national pride, Qasim staked a claim to Kuwait on June 25, 1961. He quickly retreated in the face of British and Arab pressure.

music room of the government television station and shot them. Then they turned on the cameras. One body sprawled backward on a spindly chair. Qasim lay on the floor. As if to prove the man who had tried to rule Iraq for five years was truly dead, a member of the execution squad grabbed the dead general's head by the hair and thrust it into the camera lens. Iraqis saw for themselves the glassy eyes and gold-capped teeth of their deposed leader.

The perpetrators of the coup were Arab nationalists, including the Baath Party, the small, tightly organized Iraqi wing of the larger Baath. Formally founded in 1952 as a branch of the Syrian Baath Party, it had no political base and claimed a membership of only three hundred by 1955 and only slightly more by 1958. For the Baathists, meager size was to be expected of a revolutionary movement. According to the Baath's ideological father, Michel Aflaq, "A chasm separates the organization of the party from the society around it. From deep within its own resources, taken in calculated isolation from the rest of society, the party must become 'the nation of the revolution before it achieves the revolution of the nation.' "*
By Baathist doctrine, leadership must remain in the hands of an enlightened minority that "represents the people before the people expressly delegate them to undertake this representation."† One of the enlightened was Saddam Hussein al-Tikriti.

Saddam Hussein comes out of the Sunni lower classes. He was born April 28, 1937, to a miserably poor peasant family in the village of al-Auja near the Tigris River town of Tikrit in the Golden Triangle. His first home was a hut constructed of mud and reeds, heated in the winter by dried cow dung. Hussein's father died either before his son was born or shortly after. His mother remarried, and her son fell under the heel of an illiterate stepfather who Hussein claims dragged him from bed every morning yelling, "Get up, you son of a whore, and look after the sheep."‡ At the age of ten, he escaped to Baghdad to the home of his mother's brother, Khayrallah Tulfah. Baghdad opened a new world for the young Hussein. He entered school for the first time, finishing intermediate school at the age of sixteen. Ambitious, he looked to a military career. But poor grades

* Quoted in al-Khalil, *Republic of Fear*, p. 220.
† Ibid., p. 221.
‡ Judith Miller and Laurie Mylroie, *Saddam Hussein and the Crisis in the Gulf* (New York: Times Books, 1991), p. 27.

324 / P A S S I O N   A N D   P O L I T I C S

kept him from advancing to the Baghdad Military Academy, thus denying him the military credentials that are the near-universal mark of contemporary Arab leaders.* Deprived of a military career, he turned to politics.

Saddam, an Arabic name meaning "the one who confronts," spent his adolescence engulfed in the rhetoric and passion of Arab nationalism that flowed through the Tulfah house. In 1957, at the age of twenty, he joined the Baath Party. In October 1959, he was part of the Baathist hit team that machine-gunned General Qasim's car on a Baghdad street in broad daylight. According to his official biography, which now runs over and over on Iraqi television, the wounded Saddam bravely saved his comrades by commandeering a car at gunpoint. Leading them from house to house, he successfully evaded the police. Continuing on alone, Saddam began a long trek across the desert to Syria, digging a bullet out of his leg with a knife on the way.

He ended his flight in Cairo, where he took advantage of Nasser's generous support of young Arab nationalists to enter law school at Cairo University. Like other political exiles of the era, Saddam Hussein spent much of his time at one of Cairo's cafés. Thirty years later the proprietor of the Andiana said, "He was what we call a troublemaker. He would fight for any reason. . . . We wanted to bar him from coming here. But the police . . . said he was protected by Nasser."† In 1963, Saddam Hussein dropped out of school to return to Iraq to claim a place in the Baathist government that overthrew Abd al-Karim Qasim.

The Baathists faced the same bloody disturbances and reacted with the same violent repression as the Qasim regime. Unpopular and internally divided between those who hewed to Nasser and those who saw in Nasser's ambitions the destruction of the party, the Baath was ousted by an army coup less than a year after it took power. For the next four years, Iraq lived with Nasserism, another Kurdish uprising, and corruption.

On July 30, 1968, the Baath seized power for the second time. Baath membership was still only five thousand. But its numbers

---

* Hussein's lack of military training apparently constitutes a self-imposed blight on his honor. In 1976, he had himself appointed lieutenant general. When he became president of Iraq in 1979 he promoted himself to field marshal.
† *New York Times*, October 23, 1990.

belied its strength. The Baath was an organization of fiercely dedicated ideologues commanding its own security apparatus—headed by Saddam Hussein. Operating from their strength within the military, the Baath established the Revolutionary Command Council (RCC), headed by the party's secretary-general, Ahmad Hasan al-Bakr. Al-Bakr also took the titles of president and commander in chief of the army. Saddam Hussein, assistant secretary-general of the party, was designated deputy chairman of the RCC in charge of internal security.

It was Hussein, wielding the force and terror of the Baath security network, who consolidated the Baath's 1968 revolution. On January 5, 1969, the regime hanged seventeen men as spies, thirteen of them Iraqi Jews, in Baghdad's Liberation Square. In February 1969, the whole politburo of the Iraqi Communist Party, the old nemesis of the Baath, went to jail. The following October, Hussein's security services tortured and imprisoned former prime minister Abd al-Rahman al-Bazzazz. A year later, another forty-four people in another shadowy conspiracy suffered the fate of execution. Then al-Bakr and Hussein turned on their own.

Assassinations and executions rolled like drumbeats. October 1970, Hardan al-Tikriti, former deputy premier and former minister of defense, gunned down in Kuwait; August 1971, Abd al-Karim Nasrat, an early Baathist, one of the militia who overthrew the Qasim regime, stabbed to death in his bed; November 1971, Fuad al-Kikkahi, leader of the Baath until 1959, murdered in prison; July 1973, Nadhim Kzar, chief of internal security, and thirty-five others executed in the wake of an attempted coup. Ruthless against its enemies, the regime eliminated communists, pro-Syrian Baathists, Shiite Iraqis who rejected not only Sunni domination but the secularization of government, and, above all, the irreconciled Kurds.

By 1970, the Kurdish question was economic as well as political. Somewhere between 40 and 50 percent of Iraq's oil production was coming from the gently sloping hills on the southwestern edge of the Kurdish region, and Kirkuk, a Kurdish town, was the oil capital of Iraq. At the time, it was impossible to sit in a sidewalk café in bustling Kirkuk without contemplating the irony of nature's distribution of oil in Iraq. Except for some fields in the south, Iraq's copious oil resources lay in the Kurdish north. With production climbing, Kirkuk throbbed with the rhythms of a boom town. Traffic, hurried businessmen, sidewalks crowded with shoppers—the hallmarks of prosperity—were all there. But it was a prosperity held in the hands of others. The foreign-owned Iraq Petroleum Company regulated revenues, which it passed to the Sunni-dominated government in Baghdad.

The Baath government had inherited the ongoing conflict with the Kurds that neither the Qasim regime nor the military governments had been able to subdue totally. Oil simply fed the long-held hatreds between the government and its most restive minority. In Baghdad's view, the ultimate aim of the Kurdish drive for autonomy was the creation of an independent Kurdistan, which would not only take Iraq's northern tier but deprive the country of the lion's share of its oil revenues. At the same time, the Kurds, denying that they intended to secede from Iraq, seethed as the Iraqi government, from their viewpoint, withheld the Kurds' rightful portion of the country's petroleum income. When the Iraqi government nationalized the Iraq Petroleum Company in 1972, angry Kurdish nationalists charged Baghdad was simply tightening its grip on their oil.

The Baath, wed to its own survival, meant to succeed with the Kurdish problem where others had failed. On March 11, 1970, the Baath government unfurled the Manifesto on Kurdish Autonomy, meant to buy time until the Baath was strong enough to crush the Kurds. In March 1974, when the Kurds declared the promises of autonomy hollow and once again revolted, they faced the full fury of the Baathist state. Artillery slammed its fire into the mountain towns of Zakho and Qala at Diza, reducing them to rubble. Below on the plains, tanks, bombers, helicopters, and artillery supporting eighty thousand troops swung into place. But the Kurds held in the hills. Moving on foot or on surefooted donkeys, from ambush point to ambush point, wiry, mustached guerrillas picked at the Iraqi army with small arms and World War II cannons. Unable to penetrate the mountains with ground forces, the Iraqi military sent in its bombers. Two hundred and fifty thousand terrified Kurds, driving cows, goats, and sheep, straggled over the high hills toward safety in Iran. Those who stayed behind huddled in the deep recesses of mountain caves. The rebellion survived because the shah of Iran, intent on winning Iraqi territorial concessions on the Shatt al-Arab, pumped in money for food and ammunition and kept open Iran's borders to refugees and guerrilla bands. The Kurds could not win, but with Iranian help they forced on the Iraqi government a costly war within its own borders.

On March 6, 1975, Iran deserted the Kurds. Recognizing how

closely they were skirting a war that not only imperiled the oil industries of both but threatened to draw Iraq's Soviet patron and Iran's American patron into the Persian Gulf, Iran and Iraq met in Algiers. Masking the bitter enmity between the two, the stately, patrician Muhammed Reza Shah warmly embraced the stocky, revolutionary Saddam Hussein. With most of the Arab states in attendance, they announced the accord. Iraq acceded to Iranian demands on the Shatt al-Arab, and Iran cut off supplies to the Kurds and sealed its borders.

The wrath of Baghdad descended on the Kurds. Slaughter was followed by mass deportations. Under the cover of darkness, convoys rolled into Kurdish villages. Uniformed soldiers, dragging families from their beds, loaded them on trucks and drove them south into Arab areas. With little provided beyond a tent, between 50,000 and 300,000 Kurds were dumped into designated areas and warned to stay there. In the grand scheme to Arabize Kurdistan, the government moved Arabs north into some of the deserted Kurdish areas. In blood and transfer, the rebellion died.

Since 1962, the Kurdish problem and endemic political instability had kept Iraq focused within its own borders and out of Arab affairs. Iraq escaped the 1967 War. It failed to inject twelve thousand troops stationed in northeastern Jordan into the 1970 civil war on the side of the Palestinians. It watched the October War of 1973. To a degree, whatever regime was in power in Baghdad stayed isolated while it labored to establish control at home. The Baath government, the crucible of pan-Arabism, was no different. From 1968 to 1977 it too concentrated on internal stability. To the Baath, the future of the "Iraqi region of the Arab homeland" lay within its own borders.

The Baath committed itself to building a nation in its own image. Saddam Hussein's security services provided the stick, oil revenues the carrot. Between 1973 and 1978, oil revenues ignited by the Arab embargo expanded from $1.8 to $23.6 billion. With this infusion of money, the Baath began to transform Iraq from a dusty agricultural backwater into a developing country. In the race toward modernization, government allocations for industry increased twelve times, transportation eleven times, housing nine times. Irrigation systems, networks of highways, and electricity spread through the flat landscape into every town and village. Free health care flowed to a population accustomed to neglect. Posters proclaiming "The Campaign for Literacy is a holy *jihad*" went up everywhere from Baghdad to the most humble village on the western desert. Refusing to stop with basics, the government used its oil income to subsidize basic consumption items, putting refrigerators and television sets into almost every house, apartment, and mud hut. In its affluent revolution, the Baath at last defined Arab socialism. "Whoever does more, eats more, but there will never be a hungry person."*

This frenetic drive for modernization was aimed at developing a national consciousness, of wiping out the ancient divisions of tribe and religion, of erasing the regional inequities that would remove the Kurdish grievances. But the Baath tried to build this national consciousness by instilling in every Iraqi an Arab identity. The report of the Eleventh National Congress of the Baath in 1977 asserted that the several-thousand-year-old history of the Arab nation embraced numerous ethnic groups whose contributions to that which is Arab were extensive and profound. From this premise, the party disavowed ethnicity and language to pull into the Arab nation the Kurds. Thus Baath thinking and philosophy put Iraq where the Baathists always believed it belonged—in the larger Arab nation. There it was to fulfill its destiny by providing the Arab world its strategic depth and serving as its eastern flank.

By 1977, Baathist Iraq was ready to thrust itself into the Arab arena, where it was regarded as a pariah. Bellicose, condemning the slightest overture to Israel, considered a political madhouse, Baathist Iraq stood on the outside of the Arab club. That was until Anwar Sadat went to Jerusalem and the specter of Egypt's reaching toward a separate agreement with Israel unhinged the traditional balance of power among Cairo, Damascus, and Baghdad. With Cairo's defection removing its western flank, Iraq was needed to anchor the Arab world in the east.

In the new order, Iraq and Syria, the old enemies, discussed union under the Baathist banner.† The failure of union did little

---

* Helms, *Iraq*, p. 123.
† Although Iraq would have benefited from union by the dilution of minority strength in Iraq, there were also disadvantages. Iraq's oil wealth would have compelled it to assume additional economic burdens for Syria and to become a confrontation state geographically rather than rhetorically with Israel. Saddam Hussein initially flirted with the idea but later opposed it if for no other reason than an abhorrence of a power-sharing arrangement with Syrian President Hafiz Assad.

to slow Iraq's ascension in the realm of Arab politics. On November 2, 1978, Iraq convened the Arab states in Baghdad to deal with Egypt's "treachery to the Arab cause." It was the first major Arab conference ever initiated by the Iraqis. And it was carried off with unexpected success as every member of the Arab League except the scorned Egypt presented itself in Baghdad.

By the time of Camp David, the Syrians, the Saudis, the Libyans, the PLO, and practically everybody else in the Arab world acknowledged Iraq as a leader in the rejection of Egypt's deal with Israel. The Iraqi Baath, spurred on by Saddam Hussein, envisioned Iraq as unifying the Arab world and establishing Baghdad at its core.

Iraq's growing influence was palpable. Almost month by month, I watched it grow. Traveling from capital to capital, I saw Iraq's lengthening shadow extend over a region in which it had exerted no measurable influence since the end of World War II. In Amman, Jordanians happily speculated on what the injection of new Iraqi aid and contracts would do for the economy. In Damascus, tight-lipped Syrians shrugged their shoulders when asked about the rising star of the east. In Riyadh, it felt as if some giant force was rising on Saudi Arabia's northern border. It was a specter the Saudis did not like. In 1978 I noted that Saudi Arabia's Foreign Ministry sent its flowery greeting to Iraq on its national holiday on the same day the passport office denied my request for an exit visa to travel to Baghdad.

At the Arab summit in Tunis in March 1979, Saddam Hussein, by now the real power of the Iraqi regime, celebrated what he regarded as Iraq's succession to Egypt as the preeminent organizing force in the Arab world. As Babylon once reigned over Mesopotamia, as Baghdad under the Abbasid caliph once ruled the Islamic world, Iraq would assume its place as leader of the Arabs. Hussein boasted that Iraq was on "the road toward the building of Socialism, the defeat of imperialism and the creation of this country as a safe base for the Arab struggle in general and a model experiment in illuminating the entire region of the Middle East."*

By 1979, Iraq's oil reserves had reached an estimated 100 billion barrels, second only to those of Saudi Arabia. Able to make or

---

* Kraft, "Letter From Baghdad," p. 140.

330 / PASSION AND POLITICS

break oil export quotas, it ranked as a power broker in the Organization of Petroleum Exporting Countries. Casting off the last traces of the dusty backwater that it was before 1973, Baghdad projected the same image of frenzied construction activity and tone of supreme confidence as Riyadh and Kuwait City. Luxury hotels planted by international chains lined the Tigris. And the towering palms that graced Palace Road evoked a grandness this capital had not known since the tenth century. Even the presidential palace complex, created from the confiscated embassies of several countries plus the United States ambassador's residence with its rambling English garden, challenged the palaces of the Gulf kings. But Baghdad would never radiate the glitz of prewar Beirut or the down-at-the-heels stateliness of Cairo. Baghdad had a tenseness that touched even the most casual visitor. Tanks could suddenly appear, take up a position on a street corner for an hour or two, and then disappear.

The Baath Party and Ahmad Hasan al-Bakr governed Iraq in name, but the real power was Saddam Hussein. Famous for his white suits and black ties, Hussein with his ubiquitous security services drove policy and held the disruptive forces within Iraq's borders in check.

The Baath Party still retained its secret, compartmentalized structure and the clandestine methods with which it had secured and retained power. Direction of the party came from the Regional Command, which represented sixteen provincial units. Its members were elected by a network of sections and cells, chillingly reminiscent of the old Soviet Communist Party system under Stalin. These cells functioned everywhere—in places of work, in neighborhoods, and in all ranks of the military forces. They preached Arab unity, nationalism, socialism, and Arab spiritual revival. Party membership in 1979 was about a half million. But only those at the top, not the party, not the people of Iraq, chose the country's leaders. In mid-1979, the Baath changed leadership.

On July 28, Vice President Saddam Hussein ominously announced the discovery of a plot hatched by some of his closest colleagues in collusion with Syria.* Chills ran through the Baath. Eleven days later, on the evening of August 8, 1979, Saddam Hussein watched as twenty-one members of his Revolutionary Com-

---

* There has never been any clear evidence of just who was involved in the plot or if there was a plot at all.

mand Council were executed. They included the deputy prime minister, the minister of Kurdish affairs, the ministers of education, industry, planning, and health, and the chief of Hussein's own office. As the bloodstains dried, Saddam Hussein al-Tikriti stepped onto the balcony of the presidential palace in Baghdad and raised his arms in salute. Below, fifty thousand demonstrators roared their approval and chanted, "Death to the traitors!"

President Ahmad Hasan al-Bakr, Saddam Hussein's cousin, mentor, and partner in power for the last decade, stepped down for "health reasons." Hussein, the poor boy from Tikrit, assumed the presidency plus the positions of premier, chairman of the Revolutionary Command Council, and leader of the Baath Party. His relatives and longtime associates composed the new cabinet as well as assuming the key posts in the military and security services. The new order was in place. Iraq, which in the previous twenty years had suffered at least ten coups and attempted coups, two armed rebellions, and a full-scale civil war, fell into the iron grip of Saddam Hussein. In forcing his will on his fractious country, Hussein would make himself the state.

In Saddam Hussein's Iraq, the Ministry of Information acted as a media center for the president. One only had to step through the door before eager civil servants manning the reception desk presented "the materials." The prodigious propaganda organs of every Middle East political entity from the House of Saud to the PLO paled by comparison. In room after room, books, pamphlets, brochures, and newspapers sat on shelves, spilled out of boxes, piled on the floor. They spoke in Arabic, French, English, Japanese, Chinese, and a spate of African dialects. By style and content, they ranged from smudged mimeographs of Hussein's speeches to a polished coffee-table book entitled *Mesopotamia Today* to a mass-produced paperback of Hussein's dubious biography, *The Long Days*. Yet paper composed only one aspect of the campaign to wed Saddam Hussein and Iraq.

Iraqi newspapers reported in minute detail Hussein's daily activities. In pursuit of personal prestige and legitimacy, Hussein visited schools, pinned badges on graduating firemen, and inaugurated water mains in obscure villages. Like the star he was, he dressed the part, once turning up at a farm dressed in a peasant's sheepskin vest and carrying a shepherd's staff. These public outings transcended the immediate event to instill both national identity and central authority in the person of Saddam Hussein. But fear was his real tool of unity.

Iraq listed twenty-four offenses punishable by death. In a regime where typewriters were suspect and controlled, the security police lurked everywhere as an unseen presence. The businessman, the teacher, the maid, the vendor selling paper cones full of pistachio nuts—anyone could be a member of the dreaded Mukhabarat. In this atmosphere one Baghdad merchant whispered, "This is radio, but if Saddam says this is refrigerator, it is refrigerator."

The truth was that "Saddam came from a brittle land, a frontier country between Persia and Arabia, with little claim to culture and books and grand ideas. The new contender was a despot, a ruthless and skilled warden who had tamed his domain and turned it into a large prison."*

Hussein controlled Iraq, but he could not control forces beyond its border. In 1979, religious revolution convulsed Shiite Iran and pounded against the door of secular Iraq.

With its concentration of Shiites and possession of the two most important Shia shrines, Iraq could not escape the emotional pull of the Islamic revolution in Shiite Iran.† The flaming words of the Ayatollah Ruhollah Khomeini aroused a powerful sense of Shia identity, stirring the Shiite masses of southern Iraq against the secular government of Baghdad dominated by Sunnis. In the summer of 1979, the Iraqi Shiite leader of Najaf, the Ayatollah Muhammed Baqir al-Sadr, mobilized his followers in mass demonstrations in the name of the Ayatollah Khomeini. And Khomeini himself stabbed at the heart of the Baath's Arab philosophy, which had tried to knit Iraq's Sunnis and Shiites together and attach them to the Arab nation. Like the voice of God, the wrathful ayatollah denounced Arab nationalism as "fundamentally opposed to Islam: because it hinders the ability of Islam to act as a unitary force, religiously and politically."‡

Saddam Hussein retaliated. In October 1979, he became the first major Arab head of state to break with Iran's Islamic regime.

---

* Fouad Ajami, "The Summer of Arab Discontent," *Foreign Affairs,* Winter 1990–91, p. 1.
† In October 1978, Saddam Hussein had expelled the Ayatollah Ruhollah Khomeini from Najaf, where he had lived in exile for twelve years. Four months later, Khomeini returned to Tehran to lead the Islamic revolution.
‡ Helms, *Iraq,* p. 160.

Deriding the revolution as "non-Islamic," slapping at the authority of the ayatollahs, he declared, "The Koran was written in Arabic and God destined the Arabs [not the Iranians] to play a vanguard role in Islam."*

On April 1, 1980, suspected Shia terrorists nearly killed Deputy Premier Tariq Aziz. The act gave Hussein the pretext to begin to stomp the life out of the Iraqi Shiite political movement. Through a campaign of arrests, torture, executions, and forced deportations, the heart was cut out of al-Dawa al-Islamiyah ("Islamic Call").

Muhammed Baqir al-Sadr and his sister Bint al-Huda, the symbols of Shiite opposition, disappeared into the bowels of the Mukhabarat. The next victim was the Shiite community. Sinister trucks belonging to the Iraqi army arrived in Shiite towns and villages to load those whose loyalty to Iraq was suspect. Eventually as many as 300,000 Shiites may have been forced across the border into Iran.

In a speech at Nineveh on April 15, 1980, Saddam drew the sword of Arab nationalism against the offending Iranian clerics. "When a clash is a patriotic and national duty, we shall wage it in all its forms. . . . Iraq is once again to assume its leading Arab role. Iraq is once again to serve the Arab nation and defend its honor, dignity and sovereignty. Iraq is destined once again to face the concerted machinations of the forces of darkness."†

Khomeini roared back, calling on Iraqis to "topple this corrupt regime" and labeling Hussein a "treacherous parasite." Having deposed the shah, he vowed he would next topple Saddam Hussein. Khomeini's deputy, Hussein Ali Muntazari, took up his leader's message, charging that the regime of "butcher Saddam Hussein" was opposed to Islam. "I am confident that the noble blood of the martyrs of Islam will boil in the Islamic Iraqi people. . . . This blood will continue to boil until Saddam Hussein's regime is completely overthrown. . . ."‡

On September 17, 1980, the raging conflict between Arab nationalism and Islamic revival, the centuries-long enmity between Arabs and Persians, and territorial disputes stretching from Ottoman

---

* Claudia Wright, "Iraq—New Power in the Middle East," *Foreign Affairs*, Winter 1979, p. 260.
† Quoted in Shahram Chubin and Charles Tripp, *Iran and Iraq at War* (Boulder, Colo.: Westview Press, 1988), foreword.
‡ Helms, *Iraq*, p. 162.

334 / PASSION AND POLITICS

Mesopotamia to Baathist Iraq joined Saddam Hussein's fear of Shiite unrest in south Iraq. Before the cameras of Iraqi television, Saddam Hussein tore up the 1975 Algiers Agreement in which Iraq surrendered sovereignty over the Shatt al-Arab to Iran. A week later, Iraq invaded Iran. In defending himself against the passions of the Islamic revolution, Hussein called the Arabs to a new war against the Persians. Picking up the shield of Arabism, he declared, "We are Iraqis and are part of the Arab homeland and the Arab nation."* Harboring their own fears that the Islamic revolution might upset their own political regimes, the Arab states fell in behind an unchosen and distrusted leader. Tending his economic and strategic interests, Jordan's King Hussein openly allied himself with Iraq, declaring, ". . . Iraq is the front line, not only for us in Jordan but for the entire area, for the Gulf, Saudi Arabia, and Oman as well."† The Arab Gulf monarchies were more cautious. Long uncomfortable with Iraq's revolutionary and socialistic regime, they at first refused to accept Saddam Hussein as an Arab Bismarck. But in time as they became increasingly afraid the Islamic revolution might spread to their own populations, Saudi Arabia, Kuwait, and the sheikhdoms of the United Arab Emirates wanted Iran contained. Thus the rich and the weak quietly transferred money to Hussein's war effort.

Only Hafiz Assad, the Lion of Damascus, broke Arab ranks. The reasons lay in history, politics, and personality. Damascus and Baghdad were natural rivals. They were two legs of the Arab triad. They shared a common border, divided the waters of the Euphrates, quarreled over economic matters involving the transshipment of Iraqi oil over Syrian pipelines. But they also carried with them the legacy of the Baath's bitter infighting. In 1966, the party split between its Syrian and Iraqi wings. From that time on, the two countries harbored their distrust of each other and played host to each other's exiles.‡ Yet nothing characterized the hostility between Syria and Iraq as much as the personal animosity that existed between Hafiz Assad and Saddam Hussein. It had ultimately prevented union in 1978. In 1980, it would put Arab Syria on the side of Persian Iran.

---

* Ibid., p. 8.
† Ibid., p. 183.
‡ When Hafiz Assad expelled Michel Aflaq, founder of the Baath Party, from Syria, he went to Iraq, from where he attacked the Syrian Baath until his death.

Within days of the invasion, Iraq advanced deep into Iran, taking the port of Khorramshahr and encircling the vital oil complex of Abadan. But the Iranian army was not as chaotic and demoralized by the revolution as Hussein had assumed. For a year, the war bogged down in stalemate. The following year, Iran advanced into Iraq. Iraq held, in large part, because it held its minorities. The Shiites, the people whose questioned loyalty had played such a part in Hussein's decision to invade Iran, stayed with Iraq, providing the bulk of Hussein's infantry. The reasons were multiple. The dangers of war turned the Shiites away from a remote religious hierarchy centered in Tehran and toward the traditional organizations that provided security—tribe and clan. Economically, the fat years of Baathist rule had created if not a true Iraqi nationalism at least a sense of shared economic interests between the Shiites and the Iraqi government. And finally, perhaps the magnetism of Tehran had never been as strong as Saddam Hussein thought. By standing with Iraq, the Shiites in a sense affirmed the Baath's call to Arab nationalism. For the vast majority of Shiites were Arabs, speaking Arabic, not Farsi. In the rage of war, they seemed to have found their identity more with the Arabs than with the Persians.

Even the Kurds, beset by their own internal divisions, stayed quiescent early in the war. Despite their fierce nationalism, the Kurds were no more a monolith than any other group in Iraq. They divide into two major linguistic groups, fragment by village, clan, and tribe, respond to differing economic interests depending on whether they live in the lowlands or the highlands, and follow rival families and ideologies. Between 1980 and 1982, the Kurds boiled in their own disputes, giving Baghdad a respite from its perpetual Kurdish problem.

The first two years of the war proved relatively painless for Iraq. The state media succeeded in drawing clear parallels between Iraq's war with Iran and centuries of Arab warfare against the Persians. Saddam Hussein, in his high-pitched voice, railed at the Iranians as "racist Persians" and defamed the Ayatollah Khomeini as an ignorant, narrow-minded, sectarian Persian fanatic, the "turbaned shah."

Along Baghdad's Karadh Street, stores overflowed with crates and barrels of vegetables, and sheep carcasses crowded the butcher shops. Saddam Hussein's government ensured that goods, except for cigarettes and butane gas, were more plentiful than before the war. That same government addressed personal tragedy by bestowing on the families of lost soldiers enough money to buy a piece of land, a new house, and a car.

Portraits of Saddam Hussein were everywhere, always in some kind of costume ranging from a field marshal's uniform to an Arab sheikh's traditional robes to an ordinary vacationer's open sport shirt and Panama hat. Newspapers spilled out pictures of the president visiting the wounded, consoling the families of the dead, and mingling with the troops. But there was another side of the war just as visible. Day after day, processions of taxis along the roads from the battlefield bore flag-draped coffins on their roofs for delivery to the families of the fallen. Unspoken blame fell on Saddam Hussein. On July 11, 1982, Hussein entered a building in a mixed Sunni-Shiite town forty miles north of Baghdad. Without warning, a group of armed Shiites belonging to al-Dawa attacked. Hussein was pinned down for two hours until heavy reinforcements from the army arrived to rescue him. It was the second assassination attempt in four months. Amid reports of unrest and attempted coups, Saddam Hussein retreated into his palace, relying only on a few trusted relatives and supporters.

The presidential palace reflected a leader under siege. Tanks blocked all entrances and red-bereted paratroopers in camouflage battle dress stood guard. In time, everyone around Hussein came to serve as hostage to his fears. The son of his cook became his food taster. When he traveled, his bodyguards transported his personal chair lest someone insert a poison pin in an alien cushion. Even foreign envoys either never saw Iraq's president or were spirited from airplane to helicopter to car en route to meet him in some undisclosed place. Still Hussein did not feel safe. The German contractor Boswau and Knauer A.G. began constructing an underground bunker capable of withstanding atomic blasts. Buried deep under Baghdad, it is accessible only through two reinforced elevators and a four-ton steel door. Inside, a progression of sparkling chandeliers leads to a swimming pool, a mosque, and the president's bathroom, complete with fixtures adorned with silver fish. Its builders estimate that Hussein could live there for a year without ever coming aboveground.

The war went on. Contained on the land, Hussein reduced his conditions for peace to a cease-fire and a return to the *status quo ante bellum*. Khomeini refused. The brooding ayatollah would end the war only when Saddam Hussein stepped down as president of Iraq and his country agreed to pay stiff reparations to Iran. Hussein, forced to choose between peace and power, chose power. Rooted in his own error, the Iraq-Iran War became Saddam Hussein's war, his personal quest for survival.

But Hussein could not prosecute the war alone. He had to have Arab support. Iraq's ability to supply its army and feed its people depended on the Jordanian port of Aqaba. His weapons of war hinged on the millions of dollars the Gulf monarchies funneled into the Iraqi war effort. Capitulating to this need for Arab support, Hussein issued a definitive declaration regarding Arab unity on September 8, 1982. Casting aside Baath ideology, he formally surrendered the Baathist commitment to a pan-Arab state and recognized both the specific nationalism of individual Arab states and the legitimacy of the traditional rulers in the Gulf monarchies. "The Iraqis are now of the opinion that Arab unity can only take place after the clear demarcation of borders between all countries. We further believe that Arab unity must not take place through the elimination of the local and national characteristics of any Arab country. . . . The question of linking unity to the removal of boundaries is no longer acceptable to present Arab mentality. It could have been acceptable ten or twenty years ago. We have to take into consideration the change which the Arab mind and psyche have undergone. We must see the world as it is. Any Arab would have wished to see the Arab nation as one state. . . . But these are sheer dreams. The Arab reality is that the Arabs are now twenty-two states, and we have to behave accordingly. Therefore, unity must not be imposed, but must be achieved through common fraternal opinion. Unity must give strength to its partners, not cancel their national identity."* Iraq had entered the Iraq-Iran War bearing the standard of Arab unity as defined by classic Baathist doctrine. However, in the stark realities of a stalemated war the only criterion became survival.

By 1984, the war was eating at Iraq's economy like a cancer. Before the war, Iraq exported 3.3 million barrels of oil a day. But

---

* Helms, *Iraq*, pp. 114–15. The statement reflected ideology more than reality. Once he assumed power in 1979, Saddam Hussein never seriously supported a unified Arab state that might infringe on his personal control of Iraq. In another about-face, Iraq promoted Egypt's rehabilitation at the 1987 Arab summit in Amman. Egypt's pariah status had ceased to be relevant to Iraq's needs.

with the Gulf closed by mines dropped by the Iranian navy and the pipeline through Syria shut off, it labored to put 700,000 to 800,000 barrels a day on the market. Most of the $35 billion in foreign reserves on hand when the war started were gone. So were the gold reserves. In four years, Iraq had been transformed from a capital-surplus nation to a debtor nation living on transfusions of money from two major donors—Kuwait and Saudi Arabia. To cope, the generous payments to the families of those killed in battle fell to 5,000 dinars, or about $1,500. It was only the beginning. Iraq banned the import of luxury goods, including cars, watches, television sets, and some clothing. No longer could an Iraqi boast, "Iraq has become a consumer society. We have been spoiled with the good life, a lot of money and no poverty."* Saddam Hussein, whose only legitimacy came from building the modern Iraq, was forced to cancel contracts and scale down all his development plans. In their place, Hussein spun larger and larger the cult of personality.

In a culture that puts little emphasis on birthdays, Hussein's became a national holiday. Poster-sized pictures of the president, now almost exclusively in military dress, adorned cafés, bus windows, utility poles, and the courtyards of mosques. His face decorated wristwatch dials, gold-trimmed cake plates, school notebooks, and calendars. In the realm of visual art, a series of portraits painted in the artist's own blood celebrated the "Great Saddam." In poetry he was "the perfume of Iraq, its dates, its estuary of the two rivers, its coast and waters, its sword, its shield, the eagle whose grandeur dazzles the heavens. Since there was an Iraq, you were its awaited and promised one."†

The cult of personality reached its zenith in the restoration of ancient Babylon, where Saddam Hussein tied himself to the greatness of Nebuchadnezzar. On the road outside the city of Hilla, an enormous portrait of Hussein, wearing a kaffiyeh with a white dove of peace fluttering above his head, pointed west toward the new Babylon. At the entrance, it became immediately obvious that more than 2,500 years separated the old and new Babylon. On top of the reconstructed Ishtar Gate, a giant plywood figure of Saddam Hussein one and a half times the height of the gate itself bids greetings.

---

* U.S. News & World Report, November 17, 1980.
† Elaine Sciolino, "The Big Brother: Iraq Under Saddam Hussein," New York Times Magazine, February 3, 1985, p. 24.

Inside, Babylon was less an archaeological site than the propagation of the idea that Iraq had found in Saddam Hussein the true successor to Nebuchadnezzar. The streets and walls brought out of ancient ruins by the fevered efforts of Egyptian and Sudanese laborers pointed toward a replica of King Nebuchadnezzar's Southern Palace that climbed out of its original site. Where the Hanging Gardens once marveled the ancient world, vast brick walls constructed of millions of baked bricks rose to eighty feet, carrying the inscription: "The Babylon of Nebuchadnezzar was reconstructed in the era of Saddam Hussein."

Away from Babylon, the war went on. Two armies, one Arab and one Persian, bled each other in the marshes of the Shatt al-Arab while artillery rained on the oil-production facilities of both and missiles hurled onto urban populations, terrifying but not defeating. It seemed that neither side could win nor lose. In July 1986 the focus of the war dramatically shifted from land to sea. Iraq sent its planes and missiles against Iranian shipping in the Gulf in a desperate effort to shut off Iran's oil exports from its main oil terminal at Kharg Island. Since Iraqi shipping in the Gulf had already been shut off in 1984, the Islamic Republic responded by hitting the shipping of Iraq's allies. Suddenly Hussein's war touched the Arab Gulf states. Saudi Arabia hunkered down, but Kuwait screamed for help. The United States, sensitive to both the flow of oil out of the Gulf and an Iranian government bent on driving the West from the Islamic world, put a flotilla in the Gulf to keep navigation open. On May 17, 1987, the frigate USS *Stark* was prowling the waters of the Gulf when an Iraqi Exocet missile slammed into its rear starboard side. Tensions and insurance rates skyrocketed. But the "tanker war" failed to break Iran, and the Ayatollah Khomeini vowed to go on until Saddam Hussein stepped down.

By 1987, Babylon had become Saddam Hussein's Disneyland. The southern palace of Nebuchadnezzar was now a concert hall whose roof opened to the sky. On September 22, 1987, five hundred foreign archaeologists, artists, musicologists, art historians, and diplomats gathered for an international music festival entitled "From Nebuchadnezzar to Saddam Hussein." As the last notes of the evening faded, lasers shot into the night sky beaming overlapped images of Nebuchadnezzar and Saddam Hussein. Anyone in Iraq at the time had to ask why the government had spent so much money on a festival during a war that was bankrupting the country. The government archaeologist answered, ". . . this is not just a military war. It is also a cultural war. The enemy has his own idea of what culture is, and he is trying to destroy our culture—Arab culture. . . . This struggle is more a cultural war than a war over a piece of land."*

From the beginning of the Iraq-Iran War, Saddam Hussein had always painted the war as an Arab war against Persian power intent on subjugating the Sunni Arab world. The Arabs only half bought the argument. Their support of the war was against Iran, not in support of Iraq. The Iraqi president and those around him deeply resented what they considered anemic Arab support for a war that was bleeding Iraq white. Over and over to those who would listen, Iraqi officials vented their anger against the Gulf states for their ingratitude for Iraq's sacrifices. As one Iraqi government official grumbled, "We paid in blood while the Saudis paid in cash. . . ."†

At last the terrible war began to close in April 1988. Eight years of air and missile attacks, economic drain, and the dread of Iraq's threatened poison gas attacks had exhausted Iran's will to fight, forcing the Ayatollah Khomeini to drop his demands for a new government in Baghdad. On August 20, 1988, both sides accepted a UN-mediated cease-fire. In Baghdad, a city in which spontaneous gaiety had died, the streets filled with throngs of dancing, chanting people. The celebration went on into the night and the next day and on for another fifteen days.

Saddam Hussein, the man who launched the war and the man who refused to quit, pulled an image of victory from what was a stalemate ended by a cease-fire. He had inflicted humiliation on Tehran and those whose religious revolution so many Arabs had found so threatening. Suddenly the destiny of Saddam Hussein, the Arab who smote the Persians, was in ascent. Switching from his field marshal's uniform, Hussein put on Arab dress, casting himself as the arbiter of Arab purity. Reviving the memories of Gamal Abdul Nasser, Saddam Hussein, the architect of socialist Iraq, held himself out to the Arab masses as their champion against wealthy and aristocratic elites. With a massive battle-hardened army seemingly ca-

---

* Quoted in Milton Viorst, "A View from the Mustansiriyah—II," *The New Yorker*, October 19, 1987, pp. 82–83.
† Peter Fuhrman, "Lose a Son, Drive a Car," *Forbes Magazine*, December 11, 1989.

pable of challenging Israel, he presented himself for leadership of the Arab world.

But the war had inflicted a terrible toll on Hussein's base of power—Iraq. The bloodiest since the Mongol invasion in the thirteenth century, the conflict had left scarcely a family unscathed and the economy in shambles. Iraq carried a debt of $70 to $80 billion. In 1989, the first year of peace, Iraq's oil revenues were estimated at $15 billion. From this Iraq would have to service its debt, finance imports of food, maintain the socialist state, and keep up Saddam Hussein's huge military machine. The country teetered on the edge of bankruptcy while Hussein searched for massive foreign credits to rebuild the socialist state that constituted the only noncoercive element in his political existence. But there were no sources of financing. The Japanese government, looking at $3 billion in unpaid debt, cut off all credit. The Soviet Union pressed for payment on a $9 billion weapons bill. Even Lufthansa and Swissair, due over $150 million, refused to pay the government tax on airline tickets booked in Iraq. Yet what Iraq owed others paled in comparison to the approximately $35 billion it owed Kuwait and Saudi Arabia.

Saudi Arabia accepted that the debts would not be paid and began to quietly remove them from the books. But Kuwait repeatedly raised the debt issue, especially when Hussein made noises about Iraq's need to enlarge its boundaries at the expense of Kuwaiti territory.* The issues of money, land, and power put Saddam Hussein on a collision course with his neighbor and at odds with the norms of inter-Arab behavior.

Iraq's downhill course began in February 1990 when Hussein announced that he needed not only debt forgiveness but $30 billion in new money to jump-start his economy. At the end of June, he demanded $10 billion in aid from each Arab member of OPEC, money he considered he was due. Seeing himself as having acted as the gendarme for the Arab states, he came to collect for services rendered. Refused, he charged that Kuwait was stealing Iraqi oil from the Rumaila field that dipped into Kuwait and demanded compensation of $2.4 billion. In private, Egypt's Mubarak called him a "psychopath" and the Saudis mumbled "psychotic."

---

* In 1990, Hussein proposed to build a naval facility at Umm Qasr, a fishing village on Iraq's narrow coastline. According to Iraq, the new harbor required the Kuwaiti islands of Bubiyan and Warba for protection.

On July 21, amid an avalanche of rumors about triggers for nuclear devices and a mysterious "super gun" capable of delivering giant shells of poison gas, thirty thousand Iraqi troops moved near the border of Kuwait. Hussein lashed out again at the Arab oil producers, this time over prices and production quotas. Hussein charged that every dollar Kuwait and the UAE shaved off the price of a barrel of oil by exceeding production quotas set by OPEC cost Iraq $1 billion a year in lost revenues. On July 26, Kuwait gave in and agreed to lower production in order to raise prices. Hussein responded by moving another thirty thousand troops toward Kuwait.

With a total of 100,000 men and three hundred tanks in position, the Arabs still refused to believe Hussein was doing anything more than bluffing.* On July 31, Kuwait and Iraq met in Jeddah under the auspices of the nervous Saudis. After two hours, they adjourned with no agreement. The Kuwaitis expected another meeting, believing Saddam would never act against the country that had kept so much of his war effort afloat. But Hussein continued to insist that the debt was the Arabs', payment for carrying the Arab struggle against the Iranian revolution.

By August 1, the American CIA had become convinced Iraq might do the unthinkable—invade Kuwait. Hosni Mubarak in Cairo, King Hussein in Jordan, and King Fahd in Saudi Arabia still clung to the creed of Arab unity and the cardinal tenet of that creed that no Arab country would blatantly invade another. William Webster, director of the CIA, would comment ten months later, "The Kuwaitis wouldn't believe it. None of the Arabs would."† Yet it happened.

At 2:00 A.M. on August 2, 1990, 100,000 Iraqi troops rolled across the border into Kuwait. They came in tanks, personnel carriers, and ordinary buses. They came from the elite Republican Guards, the People's Army of undisciplined peasants, and the dreaded Mukhabarat, the secret police. Within five hours, they had conquered Kuwait. By what he called the "revolution of August 2," Saddam Hussein meant to right the old imperialist wrongs against Iraq, erase boundaries that denied Iraq access to the sea, and redress Iraqi grievances against the Gulf Arabs who had lived in luxury

---

* The Arabs were not alone. Both the American and Soviet ambassadors left Baghdad on vacation at the end of July.
† National Public Radio, May 8, 1991.

throughout the Iraq-Iran War while Iraqis bled and died to protect them. For these reasons, Saddam Hussein shattered the crucible of Arab unity.

The Arab world convulsed. Hallowed dogmas, time-honored postures, and traditional alliances dissolved the moment Iraq stepped into Kuwait. Overnight the ideal of Arab unity, cultivated and defended since the last days of the Ottoman Empire, crumbled. Left without their bearings, the Arabs tried to act collectively to contain the blasphemer of Arab accord. The Arab League went into emergency session. But it could not extract a consensus. From the core of the Arab world, Egypt, Syria, Saudi Arabia, Kuwait, the United Arab Emirates, Bahrain, Qatar, and war-battered Lebanon took their position against Iraq. Jordan, Yemen, and the Palestine Liberation Organization stood with Hussein.

Ground and air forces from Egypt and Syria joined Saudi Arabia and the Western guarantors of its security, led by the United States. As the massive military machine opposed to Saddam Hussein's invasion of Kuwait gathered on the sands of Saudi Arabia, Hussein, operating in the mode of tyrant, took thousands of Westerners hostage as shields for his weapons facilities. To neutralize Iran and his worrisome eastern front, he relinquished the Shatt al-Arab. The minimal gains of eight years of bloody war with Iran disappeared.

For six months, the elements of war coalesced. Egypt, Syria, Saudi Arabia, and a constellation of Arab states stayed with the American-led coalition while Hussein played to the Arabs' centuries-old hostility to the West. Gathering the existing resentments of the Arabs, Saddam Hussein told again the Arabs' tale of betrayal at the hands of the West and wove once more the dream of a leader who would restore the Arabs to their rightful place in the world. These were the images Gamal Abdul Nasser of Egypt had raised three decades before. Now Saddam Hussein revived them.

But Nasser was the beneficiary of the cold war. Hussein, on the other hand, had triggered the first crisis of the new world order in which the superpowers played on the same side. One resolution after another went through the United Nations—demanding withdrawal, imposing economic sanctions, setting a deadline for Iraqi withdrawal from Kuwait. Hussein held firm. But for most Arabs and the world, the tyrant from Tikrit had gone too far. At 2:30 A.M. on January 17, 1991, the armed might of the coalition built by

344 / PASSION AND POLITICS

George Bush hit Iraq. Hour after hour, day after day, high-tech weapons delivered a whole new generation of bombs on Iraq's military installations and infrastructure. From his bunker, Hussein spoke to his people: "O glorious Iraqis, O holy warrior Iraqis, O Arabs, O believers wherever you are, we and our steadfastness are holding."* And Iraqi radio beamed, "Saddam Hussein, you are the smile on the lips of the young and old. You are the moon over Mesopotamia."†

Once more, taxis carrying coffins from the front headed toward Baghdad and the Shiite burial sites at Karbala and Najaf. Again Iraqis were forced to pay the price for Hussein's mistakes.

"The Mother of All Battles," Hussein's long-awaited ground war, finally came on February 23. It lasted a hundred hours. As a tidal wave of assault weapons poured over the southern border of Kuwait, Iraqi soldiers, cold, hungry, and terrified by weeks of heavy bombing, poured out of Saddam's defensive trenches. The Republican Guard, trying to escape encirclement, raced north. The way to Baghdad was open. But the allied advance halted. The Americans, British, French, Saudis, Syrians, and Egyptians wanted Iraq's Sunni officer corps to depose Saddam Hussein in order to keep Iraq intact. Right or wrong, an uneasy consensus existed among the allies that removing Hussein with no political force to take his place was tantamount to opening a Pandora's box. With its endemic rivalries, Iraq would likely fragment, becoming a large, unstable frontier region in which the surrounding states could exercise their territorial, ethnic, and religious claims.‡ But Iraq, impaired by the artificial boundaries that had cursed its political integrity from the day of its birth and subjugated by over a decade of totalitarian rule, proved incapable of orderly change. In the holy cities of Karbala and Najaf, in towns like Safwan and villages on the flat desolate desert west of the Euphrates whose names only their residents could recognize, the Shiites rose against Baghdad. Poorly armed, chaotic in organization, they vented their anger against a Sunni-dominated government that denied them their share of political and economic power. In the north, the Kurds, sensing the weakness of Saddam Hussein, once

---

* *New York Times*, January 21, 1991.
† *New York Times*, January 28, 1991.
‡ The fear that Iran would extend its influence or control over southern Iraq played a large part in the allied decision to stop short of Baghdad.

more reached for Kurdistan. In the middle lay Baghdad and the Sunni triangle. Sunni control of Iraq teetered on the edge. The Sunni-controlled army, the only force capable of changing the government, stayed with Saddam Hussein. Though many might hate him, they hated even more their ethnic and religious rivals.

The tanks of the Republican Guards, preceded by helicopter gunships, took aim on the Shiites. Thousands of terrified families fled into the American zone of occupation near the Kuwaiti border, while the core of the rebellion took up positions in the mosques of Ali and Hussein. In Karbala, Iraqi firepower zeroed in, scarring every building within a half-mile radius of the tomb of the martyr Hussein. By the end of March, the rebels surrendered the mosque to the army. In silence imposed by vanquishment, the famous carved golden doors hung on twisted hinges and the delicate turquoise mosaics lay shattered by the barrage of tank fire. Six nooses dangled in the courtyard where once a thousand pilgrims a day gathered in prayer. Pockmarked walls in a side room pointed to where firing squads carried out their executions under scrawled graffiti reading, *Asha qaed Saddam*—"Long live Saddam."

The forces of Hussein turned north to crush the Kurds. Remembering 1986 and 1988 when Saddam Hussein expediently put down another rebellion with poison gas, thousands upon thousands of Kurds fled in terror through rain and cold. They struggled over the mountains, often on bare feet, into Turkey and poured across the border into Iran. Perhaps as many as two million chose hunger and homelessness over the vengeance of Baghdad. By April, the flag of Iraq once more flew over all of Kurdistan.

Saddam Hussein survived, at least for the time. With sixty thousand armed guards and the Tikrit clan pulled in close around him, he celebrated his fifty-fourth birthday. In Tikrit, his supporters drove an immense papier-mâché model of the president's head around the city on the back of a flatbed truck. But Saddam himself was not there. In some undisclosed location, television cameras beamed to the nation the national symbol dressed in a white suit.

"Saddam Hussein is Iraq and Iraq is Saddam Hussein" is a slogan that Hussein himself tried to turn into reality. The irony is that Saddam Hussein succeeded more in making himself an emblem of Arab frustrations than Iraqi nationalism. Regardless of his obvious and profound character flaws, Hussein did, in the early days of the Persian Gulf crisis, stir some of the deepest emotions of the Arabs.

His brashness and stubbornness in confronting the rich and privileged Gulf monarchies and their patrons of the industrialized West gave the Arabs a new hero after almost two decades in which no heroic figure had come forward to voice Arab frustrations and disappointments. The glory of 1973 had long since faded, leaving more Arabs poor than rich and the Arab nation still searching for a way to address the arrogance and power of Israel. Suddenly out of Mesopotamia came a man who was ready again to take up the cause of Arab honor lost to the Mubaraks and al-Sauds and al-Sabahs and others willing to bend to the will of the West in return for aid and markets. Even in defeat, Saddam Hussein preserved his image as the Arabs' new champion by comparing the crushing defeat Iraq suffered in the Persian Gulf War to a woman who chose to be killed rather than raped. Unable to achieve reconciliation with Arab governments, Hussein passed them by to speak to Arabs whose own governments ignore their longing for redemption of the Arab nation. Even in letting his people endure the hardships imposed by the United Nations embargo, Hussein forcefully argued his case to the broad spectrum of Arabs that he would not allow what he characterized as a Western-inspired conspiracy to trample Arab pride and dignity.

Unsure of the level and intensity of support Saddam Hussein commanded on the street and uncomfortable about their own role on the side of the West in the Persian Gulf War, Hussein's opponents did not seek to expel Iraq from the Arab League. The quarrel within the Arab house was left as just that—a quarrel among people who must live together. It helped Saddam Hussein survive what most of the world judged a humiliating defeat. Thus "Saddam Hussein is Iraq and Iraq is Saddam Hussein" achieved validity in the Arab world. But did it have legitimacy in Iraq? Could Saddam Hussein continue to pursue his Arab ambitions and the mistakes engendered by those ambitions and survive politically in Iraq? Iraq is the Arab country that Hussein decreed it to be, but it is also a country of Kurds and Arab Shiites who do not share Hussein's commitment to the Arab world. They are the majority of a country that reaches for the Arab nation and at the same time draws away from it. Iraq, as always, stands at the eastern edge of the Arab world.

CHAPTER 12

YASSER ARAFAT: THE CHAIRMAN

AT 11:00 P.M. THE TELEPHONE IN my Tunis hotel room sounded its urgent, jarring ring. I picked up the receiver and an abrupt voice on the other end simply said, "The chairman will see you tonight. Go to the entrance of the hotel. A car will pick you up." That was all.

I threw on my clothes, grabbed a tape recorder and note pad, and streaked through the lobby of the Tunis Hilton. Just as I reached the revolving door to the outside, a nondescript brown sedan pulled up and the back door flew open. I jumped in. As I grabbed for the gaping door, the driver slammed the accelerator, tore down the long, curving driveway, turned left, rounded a traffic circle, and headed into the maze of tree-lined streets encircling the hills overlooking the Gulf of Tunis. No one said a word.

Five minutes later, the car suddenly slowed to a crawl before a blockade created by two cars parked at right angles to the street. Recognizing the driver, men cradling automatic weapons motioned us through. Half a block farther, the car stopped in front of an ordinary two-story stucco villa that looked like any other in the neighborhood. I was motioned out. The air was heavy with its own silence. Perhaps twenty armed men, delineated by perfect circles of red-orange glowing from the end of cigarettes, scattered out under the trees. Their hushed silence was broken only by sparse, muffled conversation and the sound of heavy metal guns shifting into position as I approached the house.

I stepped through the door and into bedlam. Yasser Arafat's female secretary shuffled fat files in and out of a large suitcase. Around her, aides carrying fistfuls of fax messages crisscrossed as they rushed from office to office between prowling guards in tailored suits with custom-made automatic weapons slung over their shoulders. Within the seeming chaos, dozens of men and women sat around with no apparent purpose. I was led into a midsize reception room, deposited on a metal folding chair, and told to wait. It was now midnight.

At 2:00 A.M. I was still there. By now a stilling calm had settled in. Most of the crowd that milled around me had gone, taking with them their aura of rootlessness, their undercurrent of passion. Without warning, a handsome man with thick silver hair appeared at the door and announced, "The chairman will see you now."

I was ushered into a large, stark office. Yasser Arafat, his bald head shorn of the familiar *khaffiyeh*, rose from behind a large mahogany desk. I was startled at how small he is, not more than five feet four. And when I took his outstretched hand, it was almost delicate. Yet when he spoke of his cause, a raging anger changed him from a bearded man in a perfectly pressed military uniform into the embodiment of the Palestinian people. "You can't imagine what it means to be homeless, stateless. . . . This tragedy of the Palestinian people is a problem from a man's birthday to his death. . . . As we have no homeland, we haven't even a place to [be] buried in. . . . Can you imagine the meaning of living deprived of your home and your national identity, of the most basic rights and rudiments of normal human life? I am such a man."*

For a quarter of a century, Yasser Arafat has reigned as the most visible symbol of Palestinian nationalism. Exercising the negotiating skills of a bazaar merchant and the political stealth of a Richelieu, he has pulled the violently divergent components of the Palestinian people together in an arduous, unbroken quest for "Pal-

---

* Interview with author, March 3, 1988, Tunis, Tunisia.

estine." In that quest, the Palestinians are both the beneficiaries of mythical Arab unity and the victims of the singular interests of the Arab states. While wringing from the emotionalism that the Palestinian issue elicits among Arabs enough diplomatic and economic support to keep the Palestinian movement alive, Arafat fends off a succession of Arab leaders, past and present, who reach out to extinguish the Palestinians' authority over their own destiny. Consequently, Arafat and the Arab states stay locked in a battle for dominance in the Palestinian issue. As a result, the Palestinians are both the touchstone of Arab unity and the verification of the existence among Arab states and people of specific identities separate from the Arab whole.

By the criteria most often used to define ethnic groups—the sharing of common race, religion, language, region, and culture—the pre-1948 Palestinians were an enigma. Ethnically they were the mixed product of all those who had battled over the Levant through the centuries. Religiously, they split between Islam and Christianity. Although they spoke the same language and adhered to the same culture, they possessed little sense of themselves as a whole. Instead each was a member of a family, a village, a clan pitted against other families, villages, and clans. Town and country, merchant and peasant shared no common interests beyond a tenuous and limited economic relationship. When they went into exile, it was more as Arabs than as Palestinians, and it was in the fold of the larger Arab nation that the scattered and confused Palestinians looked for the redemption of their lost land.

Shut out of Palestine, those Palestinians with some resources drifted across the Arab world. Those in search of an education that might secure their future headed toward Alexandria, Luxor, and especially Cairo. Yasser Arafat was among them.

Yasser Arafat was born Muhammed Abdul Raouf Arafat al-Qudwa on August 24, 1929. He has at varying times claimed both Cairo and Jerusalem as his birthplace. Because he has turned himself from man to political symbol, Arafat refuses to discuss his personal history except in the most vague terms. Yet no man can totally hide his past.

The name Yasser, meaning "easygoing," came to him in a childhood that was anything but easy. In 1933, Arafat's mother died in Cairo of a kidney ailment, leaving six children to divide between relatives. The four-year-old Yasser was sent to Jerusalem to live with an uncle. By adolescence, he was back in Cairo. In 1947 as the crisis over Palestine peaked, he returned to Jerusalem.

A member of the Husseini family through his mother, the young Yasser gravitated to Abd al-Qadir al-Husseini, the famous al-Qadir of the 1936 rebellion.* When the 1948 war for Palestine came, the eighteen-year-old Arafat carried a rifle and smuggled desperately needed weapons from Egypt into Palestine. After al-Qadir died in April 1948 and the Palestinian resistance collapsed, Arafat fled to Gaza and then to Cairo, where he became a student of engineering at Cairo University.

The Palestinian students Arafat joined adhered to all the reigning political philosophies of the time, from communism to the Muslim Brotherhood's Islamic fundamentalism. In each, a Palestinian saw himself whether as a Marxist, a Muslim Brother, or a pan-Arabist as a largely unspecified part of the Arab nation. In 1952, Yasser Arafat, running for the executive committee of the Palestine Student Union, presented a starkly simple idea to a membership that thrived on complex political philosophy. Palestinians possessed their own identity, separate and distinct from their identity as Arabs. It was the beginning of a revolution in Palestinian thought that would, by stages, build a distinct Palestinian nationalism often at odds with the political environment around it. The first confrontation was with Gamal Abdul Nasser.

Until his death in 1970, the relationship between Nasser and the Palestinians led by Arafat stayed entangled in a web of compatible and conflicting interests. Each acutely needed the other and yet each intensely feared the other. The Palestinian cause handed Nasser the magnet with which to draw the emotions of the Arab masses to himself. For the Palestinians, Nasser presented the vehicle through which they could pursue the lost Palestine. At the same time, Nasser wanted the Palestinians themselves neither flocking into Egypt nor operating at odds with his agenda. And the Palestinians, while coveting Nasser's backing, defied his control. So the two darted and dodged, embraced and broke as they moved through an era in which Nasserism lured the people of the Middle East.

On the teeming campus of the University of Cairo, there are still glimpses of Palestinian university life in Egypt of the 1950s. In 1989, Fawzi, a heavyset balding man whose eyeglass frames always

---

* Haj Amin al-Husseini, the mufti of Jerusalem, belonged to the same family.

seemed bent out of shape, walked me through one of the decaying buildings that was there in Arafat's time. "It was a hard period for Palestinians. Nasser kept most of the camp population sealed up east of the canal and in Gaza. The rest of us lived under Nasser's eyes. Sometimes he stared, sometimes he looked the other way. But mostly he stared. Anything the Palestinians, especially the students, got from Nasser had to help him more than us."

In 1955, the demands of Nasser's own image as the Palestinians' champion led him to approve the training of a cadre of Palestinian commandos to operate against Israel out of Gaza and East Sinai. Then came the Suez War of 1956. The Palestinians carried Nasser's flag of pan-Arabism against Israel and the forces of Western imperialism. And when Britain, France, and Israel withdrew, Nasser and the Palestinians celebrated their victory together. For the Palestinians, Nasser as the high priest of Arab nationalism would return them once more to Palestine. But the Palestinians' future was not to be found with Nasser but in Kuwait with a nascent organization called Fatah.

Until the end of World War II, Kuwait had been an obscure sheikhdom languishing in the backwaters of the Persian Gulf. For generations, Kuwait lived from the water. Single-sail dhows moved cargoes between India, Iran, Africa, and the Arabian peninsula and sleek, sun-hardened divers working the briny waters brought up oysters holding low-grade pearls. The warped yellowish-white spheres constituted a major portion of the national income. But by 1950, pearls were yesterday. Oil was tomorrow.

With a population short in numbers and education, the government of Sheikh Abdullah al-Salim al-Sabah splashed full-page ads in newspapers across the Middle East seductively dangling fat salaries before the eyes of educated, job-hungry Arabs. Many Palestinians, exiles with nowhere to go, flocked to the Gulf.

Yasser Arafat arrived in Kuwait in 1957 as a civil servant charged with reviewing construction plans for the Kuwaiti government. Smelling big profits, he quickly moved into private contracting. "Truly I was very successful as a contractor. Every hour I was working and getting money. I was a little bit of a millionaire. I was! I enjoyed the good life. I used to go during the summer as a tourist to Europe, to Asia as a tourist with my travelers' checks in my pocket."*

---

* Interview with author.

Kuwait, eight hundred miles from the borders of Israel, lay beyond the twisted and tortured juncture of Israeli, Egyptian, Syrian, and Jordanian interests in the Levant. Essentially apolitical in its view of the Palestinians, Kuwait's government imposed none of the constraints Palestinian political organizations faced in the Arab states confronting Israel. Thus during the long steamy nights in Kuwait City, Yasser Arafat and the circle of Palestinians around him gathered in the coffeehouses atop the flat-roofed shops strung along the waterfront. While the Kuwaitis window-shopped the neon-lighted storefronts and inched their bright new Cadillacs along the narrow streets, the Palestinians around Arafat talked politics. Sometime between 1959 and 1961 the interminable conversations birthed Fatah.*

In its infancy, Fatah appeared to be just another organization of exiles within the Palestinian diaspora. With rhetoric as their only weapon, most of these groups talked of the return to Palestine, a return produced by the united effort of the Arab nation. But Fatah spoke in a different voice. Hurling aside the sacred belief that the Arab nation held the key to the liberation of Palestine, Fatah raised a new concept—the Palestinians must assume responsibility for their own destiny. In simple words sung to a simple tune, Fatah handed the Palestinians their future. "I am an Arab, my address is Palestine."

The goal presented was clear and fundamental—return to lost Palestine. The social, economic, and even territorial makeup of the Palestinian state Fatah vowed to win was deliberately left undefined. Nor did Fatah describe the social context of the Palestinian society it sought to create. Papering over the chasms of families and clans, the religious divisions between Muslim and Christian, and the age-old hostilities between town and countryside, Fatah's only program was the development of pure Palestinian nationalism. Almost thirty years later, Farouk Qaddumi, the foreign minister of the PLO and one of the founding members of Fatah, sat in an office heavily shuttered against the heat of a Tunis afternoon and remembered. "We had to build a sense of Palestinian nationalism. All the Arab states tried to control the Palestinians. And most Palestinians saw themselves as Arabs attached to Arab parties. Fatah's challenge was

---

* Fatah is an acronym created by reversing the first letters of Haradat al-Tahrir al-Falastin, the Movement for the Liberation of Palestine. Fatah is also the Arabic word for "conquest."

to instill a sense of pure Palestinian nationalism. This was the only goal of Fatah at the time."*

In 1959, the embryonic Fatah published the first issue of *Filastinuna*, a thirty-page pulp newspaper/magazine. Propaganda not literature, its columns seethed with bitter indignation about the Palestinian tragedy and stormed at Arab regimes whose intense surveillance paralyzed the Palestinians' political voice. It was through these few pages of print that Fatah gained its fame. *Filastinuna*, rough, patched together, amateurish in style, passed from hand to hand in the exile communities. In every issue, the number of a post office box in Kuwait stood out in bold type. It was a lighthouse for the scattered Palestinians. Across the diaspora, they sent their letters, their poems, and their simple cries of distress to *Filastinuna*. Through an ordinary post office box, Fatah had given Palestinian nationalism an address.

Seeking new recruits to the cause, Fatah's founders plowed the forgotten populations of the Palestinian refugee camps located in Lebanon, Jordan, Egypt, and Syria. Constantly moving from location to location, sharing crowded slum dwellings or living out of their cars, Yasser Arafat and the vanguard of Fatah labored to expand the concept of Palestinian nationalism out of the realm of the intellectuals into the caldron of the masses.

The times demanded great secrecy. The growing influence of Fatah sounded the sensitive alarms of Fatah's major Arab rivals— Gamal Abdul Nasser and Jordan's King Hussein, the two political figures most threatened by an independent Palestinian movement. Hounding Fatah's operatives, the security forces of both Egypt and Jordan picked them up and thrust them into jail. Thus no one came to Fatah without passing through the extended lines of personal relationship and affirmation. No one used telephones, disclosed routes, or prolonged stays. Security resided in motion, the constant movement from place to place, camp to camp.

By 1964, Fatah had developed its organizational skeleton and set its leadership structure in place.† Fatah had been born in the

---

* Interview with author, June 10, 1988, Tunis.
† Fatah is governed by a central committee of which Yasser Arafat is the chairman. It operates under a system of collective leadership, both the strength and bane of the organization. Arafat can never make a decision alone, only through consensus with his colleagues.

354 / PASSION AND POLITICS

heat and humidity of the Persian Gulf. But Kuwait was too far from historic Palestine and its dispossessed. Despite Fatah's frenetic efforts in the camps, recruitment to its ranks was slow. The camps of the early 1960s were cages for the emotionally dead. Whether in Egypt, Jordan, Lebanon, or Syria, vacant eyes betrayed people suspended between the despair of the present and the hopelessness of the future. Over squawking radios in cubes built of cement blocks that served as their houses, the refugees heard Gamal Abdul Nasser's pledge to "never waive the rights of the Palestinian people. . . . their honor is part of the honor of the Arab nation."* But Nasser's rhetoric had yet to return them to Palestine. And Fatah, although exciting in its message, also had yet to prove that it could take the Palestinians home. Words were no longer enough. Those in the camps, the great wellspring of recruits for Fatah, longed for their own Salah-al-Din to drive the usurpers out of Palestine. Thus Fatah's future came to hang on action—in an armed struggle against Israel.

During 1964, Yasser Arafat left Kuwait for the battlefield along the borders of Israel. "It was not easy to leave. I liked engineering. I owned a profitable company and four cars—two Chevrolets, a Volkswagen, and a Thunderbird. The cars I gave to my partners, except the Thunderbird. I drove that to Beirut and left it there. . . . You see it would have been impossible for me to have gone to the revolution in a Thunderbird."†

Gamal Abdul Nasser sullenly watched the growing power of Fatah. Although guerrilla attacks against Israel had preceded Fatah by more than a decade, the groups that ran them were ad hoc, with little organized backing, or were beholden to Nasser for training and arms. Fatah, unaided and uncontrolled by Egypt, loomed as a growing menace to Nasser's domination over the Palestinians and threatened to spark another round of violence with Israel. In January 1964, Nasser acted to neutralize Fatah. At his invitation, thirteen Arab kings, emirs, and presidents gathered in Cairo for the First Arab Summit. At Nasser's direction, they sewed together Fatah and more than forty other Palestinian guerrilla groups into the Palestinian Liberation Organization. Nasser had created his own puppet.

Between 1964 and 1967, the PLO chased the Palestinian cause

---

* Quoted in Vatikiotis, *Nasser*, p. 251.
† Interview with author.

at the end of Nasser's leash. Fatah stood powerless as its recruits withdrew to the Palestine Liberation Army and the little financial and military support it had succeeded in garnering in the past from the Arab states drained toward the PLO. Fatah's choice was to begin its guerrilla war or lose the rest of its guerrilla army.

On the night of December 31, 1964, a Fatah commando unit operating under the fictitious name Asifa struck inside Israel. Hardly noted by the Israelis as a military operation, it was enough for Fatah to issue its communiqué number one: "From our people, steadfast to the limit, and from the conscience of our battling homeland, our revolutionary vanguards burst out, believing in the armed revolution as the way to Return and to Liberty, in order to stress to the colonialists and their henchmen, and to world Zionism and its financiers, that the Palestinian people remains in the field; that it has not died and will not die."* But those fighting the Palestinians' battle did die, both at the hands of the Israelis and at the hands of the Arab states around Israel's borders.

Fatah survived by playing the popular support that its *fedayeen* commanded among the Arab masses against its dependence on Arab regimes for money, weapons, and territory from which to strike into Israel. Although an intricate web of issues, ideologies, and personalities went into the matrix of inter-Arab politics, all touched, at the gut level, on the issue of Israel and its provocative affront to the Arab nation. With Fatah hitting inside Israel almost every day in 1966, the cult of the *fedayeen* built among the Arabs, overshadowing the PLO and everything except Gamal Abdul Nasser.

As the critical year of 1967 dawned, Fatah and the other guerrilla groups knew that the liberation of Palestine lay not with them but with the conventional Arab armies backed by the political legitimacy of the Arab capitals, especially Cairo. All, in some way and at some point, believed the Arabs must have another war with Israel, a war they fervently believed the Arabs would win. Yet when the war came, the Palestinians lost the rest of Palestine and suffered another 100,000 refugees.

The costly conventional war machine in which the Palestinians had placed so much confidence dissipated in the tide of Israel's victory. Their hopes for the restoration of Palestine, nurtured for

* Helena Cobban, *The Palestinian Liberation Organization: People, Power, and Politics* (Cambridge, England: Cambridge University Press, 1984), p. 33.

356 / PASSION AND POLITICS

two long decades, splintered. Within the sudden defeat rested the shattered prestige and moral leadership of the range of Arab regimes from Cairo to Amman to Damascus. Into the void created by despair, anguish, and shame came Fatah.

No longer able to argue that the key to the liberation of Arab land rested on traditional military action by the combined Arab states, Nasser watched as the emotions that his impassioned oratory once roused flowed to the *fedayeen*. The commando, the martyr against Zionism, stood among the ashes of 1967 as the symbol of Arab manhood. From across the Arab world, millions joined the *fedayeen* in spirit and thousands flocked to enlist in body. The cream of Palestinian youth abandoned their universities to enter the armed struggle, while teenagers vowing to liberate Palestine with rifles and grenades walked from Lebanon to commando bases outside Amman. Even two princes from Kuwait's royal family flew into Amman, first class, to take positions in Fatah. With the groundswell of recruits, Fatah prepared what it termed the "second launching" of the armed struggle to recover Palestine. Never seriously believing that the Palestinians alone could retake their territory, Arafat saw the guerrilla movement as the means to fix Palestinian identity so firmly that neither the Arab regimes nor the international community could wash their hands of the Palestinian problem.

Commando exploits executed by Fatah delivered to all Palestinians—those in the camps as well as those outside—a new sense of dignity that stood in sharp contrast to the wailing and breast-beating that followed the 1948 war. Fatah's success in restoring Palestinian honor quickly produced a galaxy of look-alike guerrilla organizations. In ideology some were leftist, some rightist, some religious, some secular. They were pan-Arabist and uniquely Palestinian. And a few consisted of nothing more than gangs extorting money in the name of Palestine. Within the jumble, Fatah controlled 60 to 70 percent of the guerrillas.

Fatah's commandos operated largely out of a string of staging camps in the moonscape of Wadi Araba, the divide between Jordan and Israel's Negev desert. The ground is hard, colorless, and thirsty. Rocks ranging in size from pebbles to boulders overlie the land, tearing at even the sturdiest boots. From the main course of the wadi, narrow fingers formed by violent desert storms extend out, concealing whatever settles between the walls. It is perfect guerrilla country.

One of Fatah's camps of the late 1960s was hidden near the

tenth-century ruins of Petra. Silent guards posted on the approaches to the camp passed visitors through to what was little more than a few olive-colored canvas tents hovering beneath the crumbling shale of the wadi's walls. The commandos, clinging to the little shade provided by the outcroppings of rock, wore the surplus of half a dozen armies and draped the black-and-white *khaffiyeh* of the Palestinian peasant around their necks. They claimed as their standard weapons of war Kalashnikov rifles and field bags of hand grenades. This camp on this day boasted a midsize mortar and an early-generation missile that moved from place to place on the back of a camel. Most of the time the men ate and slept and ate again. But when a raid into Israel was called, the commander drew six to ten men for the three-night walk to the border and three-night walk back. Except for a messenger who accompanied them for the first two nights and waited on a hilltop for the glow in the sky announcing the success of their mission, they were alone. Those who made it back arrived suffering from some injury—sometimes a bullet wound or a broken limb but most often swollen and blistered feet. Often none returned. Yet others took their place, dying like moths attracted to a fire. They came because the Palestinians, not the Arab states, were pressing their own cause.

Brandishing its badge of crossed rifles and a grenade, Fatah fed its propaganda network. Making no distinction between success and failure, Saut al-Fatah, the Voice of Fatah, beamed *fedayeen* exploits into the camps. In these broadcasts, code words and mysterious phrases dramatically punctuated Fatah's message of power while the signature song of the station played over and over again—"The Revolution of Fatah exists, it exists here, there, and everywhere, it is a storm, a storm in every house and village."

In igniting a purely Palestinian nationalism, Fatah challenged those Arab political leaders who sought to incorporate the Palestinians into their own power base. As a result of protecting its autonomy, Fatah confronted the delicate task of standing outside the matrix of pan-Arab politics while at the same time cultivating the Arab states for the support the resistance demanded in order to survive. In essence, Fatah could not live with the Arab states on the terms those states demanded and it could not live without the aid —territorial and financial—that those states could provide. In an uneven contest, Fatah's major weapon was its image as the Arabs' sword against Israel.

In early 1968, Fatah took its popular image to another level.

At dawn on March 21, fifteen thousand battle-clad Israeli infantry-men, advancing under the hovering cover of gun-laden helicopters, crossed the border of Jordan and marched on the West Bank town of Karameh. Their objective was to wipe out the command structure of Fatah. But fifteen hours later Israel retreated, having lost seventy-eight tanks and half-tracks and twenty-three dead to Palestinian ambushes and the firepower of the Jordanian army dug into the hills above Salt. Hussein's Arab Legion had won the military victory, but the symbolic victory belonged to Fatah. Across the Arab world, Karameh hailed the resurrection of the Palestinian people. Within days of the battle, heavy trucks, pickups, and ordinary sedans began to pour into Fatah's main camp at Salt carrying blankets, clothes, and food donated by exiled Palestinian communities. Recruits in-creased fourfold. And money from well-wishers flowed into Fatah's coffers in such volume that a covey of accountants joined the ranks of the commandos. Direct and indirect aid from Arab governments followed. Even Nasser realized that he could no longer ignore Fatah. Reaching out to those he had feared as rivals, Gamal Abdul Nasser, the failed savior of the Palestinians, extended Fatah training facil-ities, arms, and political legitimacy.

With the *fedayeen* fighter and Fatah as one in the popular mind, the imperative of secrecy washed away. Taking advantage of King Hussein's decision to allow it to operate openly, Fatah shifted its headquarters from Damascus to Amman. The new command center of Fatah was nothing more than an ordinary two-story stone house on Jebel Luwebdeh that was usually guarded by a teenage com-mando armed with a rifle and a transistor radio blaring Arabic music. But its very existence opened the way for Fatah's leadership to hold press conferences, appear on television, and strut the streets flanked by contingents of their own bodyguards. Politics and theater became one. Yasser Arafat as Fatah's chairman and principal spokesman seemed to be everywhere, always wearing the heavy dark glasses he had adopted as his trademark.

Armed with Nasser's blessing, Fatah took over the shattered remnants of the Palestine Liberation Organization. Incorporating rival groups under its umbrella, the PLO began the process that would in 1974 establish it as the only legitimate representative of the Palestinian people.

Yet Fatah could not totally control the Palestinian movement. For two groups under the PLO rubric regarded the return to Palestine as only a part of a sweeping revolution that would overturn the social, economic, and political structures of the Arab world. The Popular Front for the Liberation of Palestine (PFLP) and the Democratic Front for the Liberation of Palestine (DFLP) both came out of a 1950s political party, the Arab National Movement (ANM), that was grounded in pan-Arabism and advocated a Marxist-Leninist solution to the impotence and lassitude of the Arab world.* By 1968, the PFLP and DFLP took the philosophy of the ANM and added to it its own guerrilla forces.

The ideological split between Fatah and the PFLP/DFLP pitted Palestinian nationalism against pan-Arabism; nonspecific economic doctrine against Marxist-style socialism; and noninterference with Arab regimes against a dictate to purge the Arab world of all reactionary regimes. Tactically, the two camps clashed over Fatah's designation of Israel as the only target of guerrilla raids and the leftists', particularly the PFLP's, declaration that Zionism as a worldwide phenomenon opened any target deemed supportive of Israel.

On July 23, 1968, the PFLP added another dimension to the armed struggle. Shortly after an El Al Boeing 707 en route from Rome to Tel Aviv took off, three PFLP commandos waving guns and hand grenades ordered the pilot to turn out over the Mediterranean toward Algiers. The PFLP struck again on December 26, 1968. Another commando unit armed with automatic weapons and grenades attacked an El Al plane on the ground at Athens airport.† For a year, from September 1969 to September 1970, PFLP squads delivered the front's blows far beyond Israel. Young boys eight to twelve years old, belonging to the PFLP's special unit the Ashbals, threw grenades into El Al offices in Brussels and Israeli embassies in Bonn and The Hague. PFLP commandos opened fire on the crowded El Al reception hall in Athens airport. They attacked an El Al bus carrying passengers at the Munich airport, put a bomb aboard an Austrian airliner carrying mail for Israel, and blew up a Swissair flight from Zurich to Tel Aviv, killing all forty-seven passengers aboard. They hit an El Al office in Istanbul; the Israeli

---

* The DFLP was originally called the Popular Democratic Front for the Liberation of Palestine.
† Two days later, Israel mounted its retaliation. Claiming the guerrillas came from bases in Lebanon, Israeli commandos assaulted Beirut's international airport. In forty-five minutes, they destroyed thirteen airliners estimated to be worth $96 million.

embassy in Asunción; and a Greek airliner between Beirut and Athens, all in a bloody bid for control over the Palestinian movement.*

In June 1970 when United States Secretary of State William Rogers proposed the "Rogers Plan" to Nasser, alarm bells rang in the PFLP. Believing the Palestinians were about to be bound, gagged, and sold down the river in a peace agreement in which they were not represented, the PFLP's George Habash summoned his "Revolutionary Council." Moving between Amman, Baghdad, and the Wahdat refugee camp in Jordan, Habash and the PFLP's now-seasoned commandos worked out in scrupulous detail plans for the infamous Dawson Field hijackings of September 1970.

Three jetliners sitting in a shimmering mirage riveted the world's attention on a strip of Jordanian desert. It was exactly what the whole exercise had intended to achieve. In the midst of the giant grounded birds stood a huge tent flying the Palestinian banner of red, green, white, and black. A few feet away a camouflage-painted water truck bore the sign "The Popular Front at your service."

PLO chairman Yasser Arafat, losing the propaganda war in the *fedayeen* movement and at the same time taking the heat of the Arab governments for the dangerous brashness of the PFLP, rushed from point to point trying to strike a deal that would free the hostages. The PLO, the shepherd of Palestinian interests, found itself heaped with abuse from almost every Arab government, including the zealous Baathists of Iraq. Ever dependent on Arab goodwill, the PLO could not sustain the stinging criticism. Finally a deal was set.

On day six of the hijacking, the PFLP took the last 141 passengers off the planes, ran explosive charges through the fuselages, and blew the aircraft into the sky. As the dust settled, the commandos climbed in their jeeps and left.

The stunning spectacle of air piracy was as symptomatic of the boiling discord between Fatah and the more radical elements within the Palestinian movement as it was indicative of the Palestinians' discord with King Hussein. But when King Hussein declared war on the commandos five days after the Dawson Field drama, the PLO's quarreling elements became one. As "Black September" descended, Fatah took its place with the leftists against the Jordanian onslaught.

---

* In 1972, Fatah, attempting to check the PFLP's growing popularity, mounted the most infamous terrorist incident of the period—the attack against Israeli athletes at the 1972 Olympic Games.

With Hussein's forces pushing relentlessly against the commandos, the Iraqis refused to offer aid, the Syrians sealed their border in order to make Hussein's job of destroying the Palestinians easier, and the conservative Arab states remained aloof. The Palestinians were alone. All the Arab states had either directly sanctioned the Jordanian effort or simply looked the other way. Their actions depicted the state system's sensitivity to outsiders who play by different rules. From the standpoint of the Arab states, "the audacious radicals had to be taught a lesson; the Arab world had to be purged of Marxists; free-lance guerrillas had to be disciplined if the states were to negotiate with Israel or to respond to the diplomatic initiatives offered by outsiders. States are jealous entities: they protect their monopoly on violence and on order, and the Arab state system was no exception."* Only Nasser, in the last political act of his life, salvaged the Palestinian movement.†

With Nasser dead and King Hussein hostage to his own military, the Jordanian army drove the *fedayeen* from their bases in Jerash and Ajlun and into the hills of northern Jordan. One by one, guerrilla positions were isolated, attacked, and absorbed into the army's sphere of control. Finally the commandos were pushed out of Jordan.

The defeat in Jordan washed away the confidence the Palestinians had gained from the commando movement. Representing a profound loss for the resistance movement in the military sense, Jordan also ranked as a crucial loss in the all-important realm of symbols. Vanquished themselves, the *fedayeen* no longer held high the promise of the return. Yasser Arafat himself pronounced the final word: "Yes, we suffered a serious defeat in Jordan, but the operation was not purely Jordanian. It was an Arab plot."‡

The withered PLO, carrying all of its internal divisions, withdrew into Lebanon, the only remaining field of operations open to it. Coming out of the caves of northern Jordan, Yasser Arafat established his headquarters in a crowded one-square-mile area of Beirut's Fakhani quarter, adjacent to the sprawling Sabra and Shatila refugee camps. From there, Arafat and the PLO began to coax into

---

* Ajami, *Arab Predicament*, p. 9.
† Yasser Arafat mourned Nasser in Cairo. Sitting with Anwar Sadat and Soviet Premier Aleksei Kosygin, he wore his military fatigues, combat boots, a *khaffiyeh*, and his ever-present sunglasses.
‡ *Le Monde*, July 29, 1971.

life a government. From 1971 to 1975, the PLO lived the "Ayyam Beirut"—the Beirut era, the time in which the Palestinians came as close as they have ever come to establishing not only a political capital but the epicenter of their intellectual and spiritual life.

Like any government, the PLO needed revenue. Contributions came out of the diaspora. Kuwait taxed Palestinians working within its borders 5 percent and sent the proceeds to the PLO. Countries with revolutionary governments such as Algeria and Libya provided funds. Saudi Arabia, often the most generous contributor, paid chunks of what amounted to protection money to keep Palestinian-led disorders outside the borders of the kingdom. Personally keeping his hand on the purse, Arafat dispensed monthly stipends to the widows and children of the movement's "martyrs." The Palestinian Red Crescent opened or upgraded health clinics in the camps throughout Lebanon. Money went into scholarships, ensuring a large core of Palestinians an education. And SAMED, a pet Arafat project, built a Palestinian economy. By 1982, small factories within the camps were grossing $40 million a year turning out furniture, clothing, shoes, plastics, blankets, and uniforms. Within all the activity a level of internal calm descended on the PLO as the PFLP shifted its emphasis from its war against reactionary forces in the Arab countries to the struggle against Zionism.

Beirut was like nowhere else in the Arab world. Winking at sin, sitting astride the financial, communication, and transportation routes between the West and the Arab world, Beirut in the early 1970s strutted like a peacock. Yasser Arafat did the same. With the international press corps as his stage, Arafat played to the world. Tossing aside his sunglasses, he became "the Chairman," the celebrity head of the Palestine Liberation Organization.

Although the 1973 war proved just how peripheral the Palestinian commandos were to the institutional strength of Arab armies, the war also bore out the adage "A rising tide lifts all boats." The legendary Arab nation crested with oil prices and the PLO reaped its share of the benefits. The Palestinian question emerged from the intrigue of inter-Arab politics to reign once more as the great emotional emblem of Arabism. At Rabat in October 1974, the Arab states anointed the PLO as the "legitimate and sole representative of the Palestinian people" and Yasser Arafat as their political pope.

A month later, Yasser Arafat, wearing the khaki uniform of a guerrilla fighter, mounted the rostrum of the United Nations General Assembly in New York. Defiant, jabbing the air with his finger, Arafat drummed out the grievances of the Palestinian people. Finally he uttered the challenge, "Today I have come bearing an olive branch and a freedom fighter's gun. Do not let the olive branch fall from my hand." The United Nations, the body that partitioned Palestine, passed Resolution 3236, recognizing the Palestinian people as a "principal party in the establishment of a just and durable peace in the Middle East." The Palestinians were no longer "refugees" living at the sufferance of their Arab hosts. Under the umbrella of the PLO, they had become an internationally recognized political entity entitled to represent their own interests. Yet the pursuit of those interests by their very nature kept the Palestinians in conflict with the rival interests of the Arab states. In 1975, the Palestinian agenda added its own particular weight to the collapse of Lebanon.

Despite its *joie de vivre*, Lebanon had always quivered with instability. Its population fragmented into Maronite, Melkite, and Greek Orthodox Christians, Sunni Muslims, Shiite Muslims, and Druze. The refugees from the war for Palestine added another element, which by 1975 was 14 percent of the population. The guerrilla movement and the rise of Palestinian nationalism in the late 1960s widened the existing chasm between the Palestinians and the rest of Lebanon. Demanding what Lebanon could not give, freedom of action to conduct guerrilla operations from its territory, the Palestinians put fragile Lebanon on the front line against Israel.

As infiltration across the Jordan River became increasingly difficult in 1969, the *fedayeen* began to use southern Lebanon as the staging base for raids into Israel. The Lebanese government was so weak and divided it could do nothing to control the Palestinian swashbucklers beyond border patrols and hand-wringing. So the men of Beirut tried compromise. The Cairo Agreement in 1969 gave the PLO freedom of action in southern Lebanon and total control over the refugee camps. After 1970, when the PLO moved to Beirut, its commandos took over the streets.

Lovely Lebanon felt the heel of the *fedayeen*. Beirut, Sidon, and Tyre seemed to belong as much to the PLO as to Lebanon. Khaki-clad guerrillas toting Kalashnikov rifles swaggered down the sidewalks demanding the right of way from pedestrians. Sidewalk vendors selling fruit had no choice but to stand silent as their produce disappeared into the flak-jacket pockets of men who seemed more interested in proving their power than in eating what they took. Ranking at the top of public irritation were jeeps and Land Rovers driven by armed men that screamed through stoplights and careened down one-way streets in the wrong direction, scattering anyone in the way. It was as if an automatic weapon and the label of *fedayeen* granted carte blanche to run roughshod over the Lebanese. Always resented by the Christians, the *fedayeen* were no longer heroes to most Lebanese. Adding to the hostility rising from behavior on the street, commando raids into Israel brought punishment on Lebanon. In a policy of retaliation that amounted to hitting a mosquito with an anvil, Israel sent the fury of its air power down on Lebanon. Thus, when the Palestinians hit Israel with anything from a border raid to the Munich massacre, Lebanon paid. By 1975, most Lebanese had come to hate the Palestinians. Only a portion of the Sunni Muslims, using the Palestinians as allies in their struggle against the Christian-dominated government, accepted their presence.

In April 1975, civil war exploded in Lebanon. A complex conflict involving the redistribution of economic and political power between the dominant Maronite Christians and the larger body of Sunnis, Shiites, and Druze, the war did not directly involve the Palestinians. But everyone was a part of the problem and no one escaped the conflagration. When Christian forces attacked Kantari, a slum area of Beirut inhabited by a large number of Palestinians, the PLO threw its heaviest and most sophisticated Soviet-made weapons into the war on the side of the Lebanese Muslims. And in a war that would become infamous for its brutality against civilian populations, the Palestinians struck at the Maronite Christian town of Damur, on the coastal road between Beirut and Sidon. As many as five hundred were killed before the Palestinians painted a new sign at the entrance of the town—Mudamara, "the destroyed." In the summer of 1976, the Maronites wreaked their revenge by laying siege to the Palestinian camp of Tel al-Zaatar in Beirut. For fifty-two days, artillery barrages slaughtered people lined up at water spigots or darting through its boundaries for food. Finally, on August 12, 1976, the camp's defensive perimeter collapsed. The Maronites stormed through to massacre the people of Tel al-Zaatar. At that moment, Palestinian survival in Lebanon went on the line.

The events in Lebanon aroused the anxieties of Syria's Hafiz Assad. His agitation extended beyond Assad's basic interests in Lebanon to the Palestinian movement itself, particularly Fatah and its leader, Yasser Arafat. The root of Assad's concern with Fatah was the same as that of the other Arab states contiguous to Israel—control. In the opening stages of the armed struggle, Fatah's relationship with Syria benefited from the ongoing hostilities between the Syrian Baath and Egypt born in the failure of the United Arab Republic. To taunt Nasser, Syria allowed Fatah to squirrel away its headquarters on an obscure side street in Damascus and willingly fulfilled the role of sanctuary when Jordan or Lebanon turned up the heat on the commandos. But soon Fatah was kicking at the restraints Syria imposed on its commando operations. In May 1966, Hafiz Assad, Syria's defense minister and the rising star within the Syrian power constellation, decided to quash Fatah and gain dominance over its cadres. Rounding up Yasser Arafat and most of the rest of the military leadership of Fatah, he tossed them into a dank cell in Mezza prison. After fifty-one days and ten straight hours of negotiations between the PLO's Kuwait-based Farouk Qaddumi and Hafiz Assad, Arafat and the others walked out. From that moment on, the relationship between Arafat and Assad has been marked by mutual antipathy that rises to the level of hatred.*

By 1970, when Hafiz Assad took total control, Syria's policy toward the PLO was fixed. Assad saw the *fedayeen* as squabbling irregulars unable to alter the military balance with Israel but capable of provoking Israeli wrath. For Assad, Fatah's "people's war" was a dangerous delusion and its insistence on Palestinian autonomy an intolerable threat to the Arab states on the borders of Israel. Therefore, Palestinian nationalism could be fulfilled only through a united Arab effort in which the interests of Syria as much as the interests of the Palestinians would be realized. In Assad's own words, "There is no logic to independent Palestinian thinking when it comes to the Arab-Israeli conflict."†

From the beginning of the commando movement, Syria has instituted its own controls over it. The Syrian Baath Party implanted its arm, Saiqa ("Thunderbolt"), into the PLO and still exercises control over its leadership, training, and manpower. No commando actions operate out of Syria. The Palestinians in Syria live as suspect

---

* Assad contemptuously calls Arafat "the juggler," referring to Arafat's way of shifting his position depending on who he is talking to.
† Reed, "Syria's Assad."

subjects of the Assad regime. Finally, Syria's intervention in Lebanon in 1976 included as one of its essential goals the containment of Palestinian autonomy.

Syrian military power imposed an imperfect calm on Lebanon and the Palestinians. In the fall of 1977, the coastal road south out of Beirut stayed open, allowing traffic to pass through the ruins of Damur and on to Sidon. At Sidon, the old Crusader castle on the harbor had been converted into an interception point of Palestinian gunrunners. One perfect fall day, I managed to convince a hostile Syrian army officer to take me through a structure that had served two wars—eight hundred years apart. I crawled over sandbags that protected heavy machine guns threaded with belts of ammunition. To reach the top level, I had to pass through a cordon of Syrian soldiers and navigate around giant floodlights that lit up the narrow harbor at night. When I reached the top of the parapet, I could look out to the blue-green sea and back toward Sidon and the massive Palestinian refugee camp of Ain al-Hilweh, the largest in Lebanon. Nowhere in this unhappy country was the extent of the Syrian presence in Lebanon as a containment of the Palestinians more obvious.

Between 1977 and 1979, the Palestinian movement not only felt the fist of Syria but suffered the desertion of Egypt. In the fall of 1977, Anwar Sadat was preparing to announce to the Egyptian parliament his decision to go to Jerusalem. Without telling Arafat why, he sent the presidential plane to fetch the PLO chairman from an official visit to Tripoli. Because of Sadat's devious courtesy, Arafat was sitting in the hall when Sadat told the world he was going to Israel to meet with those the Palestinians blamed for all of their suffering. Enraged that his presence might be interpreted as approval, Arafat jumped from his seat and stormed out of the hall. Accusing Sadat of "putting a turban on my head," an Arabic expression for being made a fool, he left Egypt. Over the next sixteen months, the Palestinians watched themselves cut out of the Camp David Accords and their cause left out of the bilateral treaty between Egypt and Israel. They joined Hafiz Assad's Rejection Front and continued to mount their attacks on Israel from southern Lebanon.

Out of the hills of southern Lebanon, Palestinian rocket launchers hurled their missiles at Israeli settlements in the Galilee. After four years of civil war, there was no Lebanese government capable of controlling the commandos, nor could the twenty-thousand-man army Hafiz Assad had sent into Lebanon contain them. In June 1982, Israel took its turn.*

At midday on the fifteenth anniversary of the Six-Day War, the armed might of Israel once more rolled across the border of an Arab country. But rather than Lebanon, its target was the entire institutional framework of the PLO. For five days, columns of tanks, half-tracks carrying antiaircraft guns, armored personnel carriers, communications vans, and supply trucks ground northward under the protective umbrella of Israeli air power. Palestinian commandos hardened by three decades of exile and seven years of battle experience in the Lebanon war poured out of the camps of Tyre and Sidon to slow the Israelis' steady march. Losing one position, they pulled back, reestablished another position, and pulled back farther north. Finally there was nowhere else to go but into Beirut itself. Ignoring its original declaration that Israel's only objective was to clear its border of PLO guerrilla units, the Israeli Defense Force plowed into the mountains above Beirut. By June 13, a week after the invasion, it paused. Beirut was encircled. Trapped inside was the military and political structure of the PLO.

From bunkers buried within the heart of Beirut, Yasser Arafat sent out the call to the Arab nation for reinforcements. But none came to take their place at what Arafat described as the "Stalingrad of the Arabs." Hafiz Assad, refusing to risk war with Israel to save the despised Arafat and his PLO, had withdrawn his forces into the Bekaa Valley the day of the invasion. Saddam Hussein was bogged down in his war with Iran. Egypt, the great central weight of any Arab war effort, had forsworn war with Israel. And the conservative Arab monarchies, as suspicious of radical Palestinian nationalism as ever, remained silent. Only Muammar Qaddafi answered, suggesting that Arafat commit suicide in defense of Arab honor. Despite vows of eternal fidelity to the Palestinian people, the Arabs had walked away from the Palestinian cause. Yasser Arafat was left to tell his six-thousand-man guerrilla army, "The Palestinians are alone in the field facing the Israeli Goliath."†

Beirut became hell itself. Refusing to send its army into an

---

* Israel made a previous invasion in 1978 that ended under United States pressure exerted through the United Nations. See the concluding chapter.
† Rashid Khalidi, *Under Siege: PLO Decision-making During the 1982 War* (New York: Columbia University Press, 1986).

urban battlefield, Israeli air power pummeled Beirut in a campaign of devastation that revived memories of wasted Dresden in World War II. For seventy days, Israel tried to annihilate the hated PLO. And for seventy days, the Arab states watched. While the guerrillas hung on in the ravaged streets, the poets penned the Palestinian message on placards around the smoking city: "Tell your children what Israel has done. Tell your children what the Arabs have done."*

With Beirut consumed by fury, Arafat and his PLO had no choice but to leave in order to spare the Lebanese civilians trapped in the city and themselves. The United States offered Arafat and his commandos a way out. With an intensity born of crisis, Philip Habib, the U.S. negotiator, shuttled between the PLO, Israel, and the shell that was the government of Lebanon. At last, all parties agreed. In return for evacuating Beirut and scattering its vaunted guerrilla army, the command structure of the PLO won safe conduct out of Lebanon and the preservation of its institutional structures. The Palestinians left behind in Beirut would go under the protection of a multinational force composed of troops of the United States, Britain, France, and Italy. Thus on August 30, 1982, Yasser Arafat took leave of the city from which he had managed the Palestinian revolution for twelve years.

On that morning an expectant hush fell on shell-shocked Beirut as it awaited the unfolding drama. Yasser Arafat, the central figure, emerged from an apartment block in the bomb-damaged quarter of Fakhani. In a green military uniform, the familiar black-and-white *khaffiyeh* on his head, and a necklace of beads in the colors of the flag of Palestine around his neck, he embraced some of those who had shared his final hours in Beirut. A round of official goodbyes followed. And then just after 11:00 A.M., Arafat's black Mercedes limousine flanked by jeeploads of armed guards pulled up at the port of Beirut. As he stepped from the car, he all but disappeared in a sea of reporters, television crews, weeping women, and commandos defiantly firing their weapons in the air. The chairman of the Palestine Liberation Organization, carrying himself with the dignity of a victor, walked between lines of Lebanese army soldiers and U.S. Marines. At the end, he boarded the Greek cruise liner *Atlantis* bound for Athens. The last glimpse Beirut had of Yasser

---

* Friedman, *From Beirut to Jerusalem*, p. 149.

Arafat, he was standing on deck making a V-for-victory sign. It was Yasser Arafat's finest hour. In simply surviving the blitz that Israel threw against it, the PLO had snatched triumph from defeat. And Arafat, more than ever, reigned as the living embodiment of the Palestinians' refusal to disappear. But beneath Arafat's symbolic victory was the reality that he was now as far from the borders of historic Palestine as he was when he sat in the coffeehouses of Kuwait City plotting the Palestinian renaissance. And when massacre befell Beirut's Palestinians in Sabra and Shatila, the man who metaphorically claims all Palestinians as his children was not there.

The siege of Beirut added another measure to Palestinian bitterness. Its focus "was not Arab passivity but something worse: tacit complicity and even collaboration with the foes of the PLO."* An angry Yasser Arafat denounced those who mouthed the Palestinian cause and then walked away from it at the moment of its greatest crisis. "We did better than all the Arabs in this war. They therefore couldn't let us win. In the past, against the French, the Italians, the British, there was Arab solidarity. But this wasn't the case with the Israelis in this war, after they had all been beaten by them. So we were alone. . . . all of them intentionally left us on our own."†

Those who had followed Arafat from Jordan to Beirut now followed him into exile in Tunis, the internationally agreed-upon site of the new PLO capital. The Lebanon era was gone, the race with time began. To ensure that the PLO survived, Arafat had to rebuild its structure, resume its social programs, and above all prove that the Palestinian movement had emerged from the ashes of Beirut intact. Swallowing the Palestinians' wrath of 1970, Arafat opened discussions with King Hussein on a joint Jordanian-Palestinian response to the 1982 Reagan Plan. And just weeks after the retreat from Beirut, Arafat went to the Arab Summit at Fez. Received with full honors, Arafat nonetheless refused to let his Arab brothers escape their shame. Throwing salt on wounded Arab honor, Arafat claimed that the PLO in Beirut had fought for the "defense not only of Palestine and the Lebanon but of the entire Arab nation."‡

Although the cause of Palestine demanded diplomacy, it demanded even more the military capacity to harass Israel. Arafat had

---

* Rashid Khalidi, *Under Siege*, p. 148.
† Quoted in ibid.
‡ Abdallah Frangi, *The PLO and Palestine* (London: Zed Books, 1982), p. 124.

to pry his way back into Lebanon to reestablish a base on the borders of Israel. But that base was now controlled by Syria's Hafiz Assad, the most durable and dangerous of Arafat's enemies.

The war in Lebanon had forced to the surface as never before that essential conflict between the demands of Palestinian nationalism and the interests of the Arab states. One existed only at the expense of the other. In Lebanon, the Palestinians answered either to Yasser Arafat or to Hafiz Assad, but not to both.

Ironically, it was a revolt in Fatah against Arafat's leadership that gave Hafiz Assad an opportunity to rid himself of the detested Arafat and seize control of the Palestinians in Lebanon. Funneling arms to the rebels, Assad pulled in two other factions of the PLO —the Syrian-controlled Saiqa and the ultraradical Popular Front for the Liberation of Palestine—General Command. Reaching for a gut issue with which to meet the challenge, Arafat glossed over the PLO's internal dissension to focus on Hafiz Assad's treacherous plot against Palestinian autonomy. Suddenly Assad, not Arafat, became the issue, prompting the Islamic leader of East Jerusalem to grant divine dispensation to anyone who murdered the Syrian president.

Arafat kept up the heat against the crouching Lion of Damascus. In July, he gathered the international press corps on a blanket in an olive grove outside his new base in the northern Lebanon city of Tripoli to spew forth his venom. "The Syrians are looking to push the dissenters into creating an alternative PLO. Unbelievable! This PLO was created by the will and the sacrifices of the people. All its prestige, all its strength, cannot be undone by the decisions of any Arab government."*

Hafiz Assad refused to be intimidated. By September, he had made alliance with the Shiite Lebanese organization Amal, which carried its own satchel of vendettas against Yasser Arafat and the PLO.† Between them, Syria and Amal trapped Arafat inside Tripoli. Drawing on the camp population that has always been the core of his support, Arafat mobilized Palestinian nationalism against Hafiz Assad. Beginning in September 1982, Tripoli became Arafat's second Stalingrad in a little over a year.

---

* *Time*, July 25, 1983.
† The Shiites of southern Lebanon, as the main sufferers of Israeli retaliation for Palestinian transgressions, wanted to eliminate a Palestinian armed presence from Lebanon.

Intassir al-Wazir is the widow of Arafat's closest associate, Abu Jihad, who was assassinated by Israeli commandos in July 1988. Better known as Umm Jihad, she is often called the Mother of the Revolution. Attractive, even pretty, she is a remarkably young-looking grandmother. Abu Jihad had been dead a little over a year when I interviewed her in the house in which he was killed in Sidi Abu Said outside Tunis. She had been in Tripoli with Arafat when he made his last stand in Lebanon. "The fighting was terrible, sometimes as bad as Beirut. Many of our people were wounded, many killed. One of the big problems for us was keeping our fighters fed. Since we were alone as we were alone in Beirut, there was no one to turn to but ourselves. I organized the Palestinian women. We prepared three meals a day, seven hundred meals at a time." She described the kitchens, the menus, the logistics involved in acquiring and delivering the food. A basically reticent woman, she closed the subject: "Yes, it was difficult, I would say very difficult, but there was no choice."

In December, Assad, propelled by his implacable hatred of Arafat, ordered the final offensive to drive the leader of the PLO into the sea. This time the Arab states answered Arafat's call from his bunker and negotiated his escape on December 22. Yasser Arafat for the second time sailed out of Lebanon on a Greek ship. But this time he went straight to Cairo. His face wrapped in smiles as if Egypt had never abandoned the Palestinians for peace with Israel, Arafat embraced Hosni Mubarak, the successor to the erstwhile traitor Anwar Sadat. If Assad could drive Arafat from Lebanon, Arafat could pull the pin on Assad's Rejection Front.

In the high-stakes tit-for-tat, Hafiz Assad still held the Palestinian population of Lebanon and the willing hand of the Shiite Amal. In May 1985, Amal with its Syrian-supplied tanks and artillery encircled Palestinian camps. Nowhere suffered more in the ensuing savagery of the so-called Camp Wars than Beirut's Bourj al-Barajneh. For 163 days, Amal kept twenty thousand people cut off from fresh supplies of food and medicine. While men and boys armed with weapons and experience from the now ten-year-old Lebanese war held the perimeters, the women, children, old men, and a handful of foreign medical personnel labored to sustain life. Teams battled rats drawn by the large piles of garbage that could not be cleared. Others gathered what food remained to put into community cooking pots. With no replacements, bandages binding wounds inflicted by constant fighting were washed, dried, and reused. When artillery shells ripped through walls, people went into shelters created by the rubble of previous attacks, with no ventilation or sanitary facilities.

Shatila, already ravaged by the massacre of September 1982, underwent the ordeal of a five-month siege in late 1986 and early 1987. Reduced to eating rats and dogs, its inhabitants, like those of Bourj al-Barajneh, held on in the name of Yasser Arafat. Forced to stay with Arafat or surrender to Hafiz Assad, they gathered behind Arafat. For Arafat was more than the embattled leader of the PLO whose demise was daily predicted in the West. Although he might be a flawed leader to many within his movement, to the people of the camps Arafat was the flag of Palestine, the emblem of the Palestinian resistance that some still believed would one day return them to Palestine. And he was the man willing to defy the Palestinians' tormentors by holding his people up to the world as the wronged victims of Arab state policies and Arab political leaders.

It was the power of the symbol rather than the man that allowed Yasser Arafat to survive a bitter four-year battle against his leadership within the PLO. On April 26, 1987, the PLO held its great unity session in Algiers. In return for the chairmanship, Arafat gave in to radical demands that he withdraw from any joint negotiations with King Hussein and retreat from the developing relationship with Egypt.

The irony was that at the point it pulled itself together, the PLO saw the struggle against Israel pass from its hands into the hands of the Palestinians of the occupied territories. In December 1987, the Palestinians of Gaza and the West Bank picked up simple stones from the soil of Palestine and hurled them against the Israeli occupation. The Intifadah, the "shaking off" of Israeli oppression, affirmed Palestinian society and culture and strained against the captivity of pan-Arab politics. By their actions, the Palestinians in the towns of Nablus, Ramallah, Hebron, and Gaza City and in the camps of Kalandia, Balata, and Khan Yunis declared their intention to secure a Palestinian state. Overnight the "children of the stones" became the new *fedayeen* standing before the power of Israel. Hafiz Assad, understanding that a new force had awakened in the Arab world, lifted the siege of the Palestinian camps of Lebanon.

In the early months of the Intifadah, I experienced both the power and the impotence of stones. Escaping the army press brief-ings in Jerusalem, I drove to Gaza to gauge for myself how many men Israel was calling up to contain the uprising. Overlaid with an air of tension in the best of times, Gaza felt as though a charge of electricity was running through it. Leaden skies dumping buckets of rain added another element to the highly strained atmosphere. On the way to the main road back to Jerusalem, I drove into Gaza City. Ahead, a stretch of the main street was covered by a foot of water, forcing traffic around the block. I followed, not remembering that my rental car bore a yellow license tag indicating that it was from Israel proper. Just as I started to make the second turn in the detour, I confronted a bus and a tangle of cars blocking the way. I went straight, turned left on a dirt through street, made another left, and headed in the direction of the main road. Suddenly a huge mud puddle materialized in front of me. It was too late to stop and there was nowhere to go but straight ahead. The mud reached the axle at the same moment a baseball-size rock shattered the front left-hand glass. Another followed, and then another, spraying jagged shards all around me. Small boys armed with small rocks stood on the front line of a semicircle, but the missiles that broke the car windows came from the teenagers perched in the trees behind. Adults were there too, standing passively in the background as observers. I could either stay in the car as a sitting target or get out and try to talk my way out. A new barrage of rocks rained down on me as I waded into the mass of children. Kneeling down to eye level, I began to tell them my name, where I was from, ask if they went to school, how old they were. The rocks were still flying, but by this time I decided their purpose was intimidation, not injury. After what seemed like an eternity, a Bedouin in a pickup with a winch came by. Tormentors turned into helpers as Palestinian hands helped string the cable through the bumper and push me free.

The next day I was at Kalandia camp on the West Bank. I was climbing the steps of the women's center when the door flew open and a hand grabbed my arm and jerked me through. Picking myself off the floor, I came face to face with a pleasant middle-aged Palestinian woman who simply pointed out the closed and sealed window. Patrols of Israeli soldiers armed with Uzis and wearing gas masks were converging on the center of the camp, firing canisters of tear gas as they walked. By the time the Intifadah entered its fourth year, Uzis and tear gas were outweighing the power of rocks.

The Intifadah is more about the emotion of Palestinian nationalism than about its power. Although the Palestinians can force costs on Israel, they cannot win unless the Israelis decide to compromise. Yet by confirming Palestinian honor, the Intifadah gave Yasser Arafat enough leverage with the radicals in the PLO to drop the ephemeral "return" and to accept the state of Israel as the first step in a two-state solution which would create the longed-for Palestinian state in the West Bank and Gaza.

Within the Arab world, the Intifadah opened the treasuries of the richer Arab states. For the Intifidah not only demanded Palestinian rights, it also spoke to Arab pride. And for the moment, mythology overcame realism, uniting all Arabs against the evils of Zionism and the encroachment of the West. Yet the Arab world was less united than ever. In a milieu in which national identities and national interests grew with each year that separated nation-states from their colonial past, the Palestinian issue annoyed as well as inspired. The pear-shaped man in his *khaffiyeh* and mock military uniform who constantly demanded Arab wealth for what most Arab leaders considered a reckless organization that refused to submit to the control of established Arab states vexed those tired of hearing of their sacred duty to the Palestinian cause. For a quarter of a century, Yasser Arafat had made his rounds of the Arab capitals nimbly dancing to the strains of Arab unity while playing one Arab state against another in defense of a Palestinian movement free of Arab control. In August 1990, he fell off the tight wire.

When Saddam Hussein invaded Kuwait, he pitted Arab against Arab over an issue that concerned something other than trafficking with Israel. Since 1968, the cardinal goal of the PLO had been to prevent any Arab state from making a deal with Israel in which the Palestinians were not a part or which did not promote their interests. King Hussein's flirtations with Israel, the Sinai Accords, and, most infamous of all, the Camp David Accords—all brought the Palestinians down hard against specific Arab regimes. This was expected and accepted in a world consumed by the dishonor of 1948. It was, therefore, politically safe. But that luxury disappeared when Saddam Hussein swallowed up Kuwait. Yasser Arafat and the PLO had to choose between the aggression of Saddam Hussein and most of the rest of the Arab world. They chose Saddam.

The reasons were simple and they were complex. On the simple level, Arafat followed his people. As one Arab diplomat explained midway in the crisis, "In Arabic, we say the world is divided between cocks and chickens. Saddam Hussein feels and many Arabs agree that it is better to be a cock for a day than a chicken for a year. He's the first Arab cock in a long time."* The strutting Saddam Hussein was indeed the best cock the Arabs had seen since Gamal Abdul Nasser. And like Nasser, he sounded his trumpeting crow against Israel. On the West Bank, in Gaza, and in Jordan, Palestinians heard the call. As one explained, "We Palestinians are like someone who is drowning—we look for anything that will save us. That may be why people see Saddam as a great savior."†

On the complex level, Arafat's decision to stand by Iraq came out of his political needs. Saddam Hussein was a counterweight to Hafiz Assad—historically, politically, and geographically. Iraq's president, playing out his own vendetta against Assad, supported Arafat's 1980s fight to retain leadership of the PLO and provided Baghdad as a site for Arafat's military headquarters when he was forced out of Tripoli in 1983.

Within hours of the invasion, Arafat went to Baghdad to embrace the conqueror of Kuwait. Ironically, Kuwait was the place where Palestinian nationalism took form and where Palestinians had prospered most. And Kuwait was the place where the Palestinians would first pay the price for their decision to back the "Butcher of Baghdad."

The 300,000 Palestinian residents of Kuwait took on the aura of collaborators. Palestinians who had lived their whole lives in Kuwait, who had provided much of the brains and muscle of Kuwait's development, would see their jobs and their residency permits evaporate with the restoration of the government. But it was not just the Palestinians of Kuwait who would suffer Arab retribution. As Saudi Arabia and the sheikhdoms of the Gulf canceled employment contracts of their Palestinian workers, $120 million in annual remittances drained out of the economy of the West Bank. Contributions to the Intifadah stopped, affecting hospitals, universities, and charitable and social institutions serving the Palestinians engaged in the uprising. Jordan, for its collaboration with the hated Saddam, felt similar shocks. Finally the Palestine Liberation Organization itself was threatened by those no longer willing to press its cause. Saudi Arabia, the PLO's most generous benefactor, cut off the $6 million

---

* *New York Times*, November 28, 1990.
† *New York Times*, January 21, 1991.

a month that constituted the lifeblood of the organization. From within the PLO itself came a haunting critique of its actions. Arafat and the PLO had committed the most crucial error of the movement's turbulent history by casting the Palestinians' lot to the losing side of a deep Arab blood feud. If the Intifadah released the PLO from the captivity of pan-Arab politics, its support of Iraq threw it right back into the caldron. No longer could Yasser Arafat claim that the struggle for Palestine is "Palestinian in face, but Arab in heart."*

Not a word came out of the Arab states when Hafiz Assad sent the Lebanese army in to destroy the PLO's last stronghold in southern Lebanon. Nor did many dispute the view that most Arab leaders thought it was time for Yasser Arafat to step down from the leadership of the PLO.

The position of Arafat and the PLO was so weak that when the long-sought Middle East Peace Conference convened in Madrid on October 30, 1991, the Palestinians were there as part of a joint Palestinian-Jordanian delegation. The great 1974 declaration of Rabat that established the PLO as the Palestinians' only legitimate representative was suspended.

Arafat and the PLO could survive for a time the rejection of the Arab states. What it could not endure was division within its own ranks. But in 1991 the Palestinian movement, the great unifying force of the Palestinians, began to crack. Although invoking the name of the PLO, the Palestinian delegation at Madrid represented the Palestinians of the West Bank and Gaza, not the Palestinians of the diaspora. A political settlement for the occupied territories threatened to leave the problem of the refugees. And it is the refugee population that has sustained the PLO's twenty-five-year-old political and military agenda, and it was the refugees who were caught up in the Jordanian civil war, who endured the siege of Beirut, and who suffered Tel al-Zaatar, Sabra and Shatila, and Bourj al-Barajneh. But the division in the Palestinian movement is no longer only between those inside and outside historic Palestine. Within the territories, particularly Gaza, the PLO faces the Islamic movement Hamas. Rejecting both Arab nationalism and Palestinian nationalism, its members are looking for identity and security in Islam.

---

* Shaul Mishal, *The PLO Under Arafat: Between Gun and Olive Branch* (New Haven: Yale University Press, 1986), p. 39.

Yasser Arafat, now in his sixties, is approaching his twilight years. In a region governed by personalities, he stands as the most flawed and the most grand of Arab leaders. A gigantic ego who covets his position, Arafat keeps control too much with himself. In the name of Palestine, he feeds an unwieldy and corrupt bureaucracy. Unable to prioritize his time, he spins off enormous amounts of energy for very little return. And in an effort to make the PLO all things to all factions, Arafat often ends up settling for the lowest common denominator, thereby enabling hard-liners to set the political parameters of crucial decisions. Most of all, Arafat has failed to provide for a successor. When the chairman disappeared in a plane over the Libyan desert in February 1992, the PLO went into a state of paralysis. In an organization where one man controls the finances and holds the quarreling factions together, there was no one authorized to assume command. Arafat and the PLO were rescued by the next morning, only to be faced with the succession question again three months later, when the chairman underwent surgery to remove blood clots from his brain. An aging leader whose political and physical health is as fragile as it has ever been, Yasser Arafat seems unwilling to designate a successor, and the PLO appears unable to choose a leader for the next generation. Beyond his shortcomings within the Palestinian movement, Arafat's greatest flaw is his inability to effectively lay the Palestinian case before the West, particularly the United States. Whether from ignorance of American culture or more probably from his consuming anger against the U.S. for its support of Israel, Yasser Arafat turns aside those television networks, newsmagazines, and book publishers best able to put his message before the public. In February 1989, Arafat kept Mike Wallace of CBS's *60 Minutes* cooling his heels for three days in the lobby of the Tunis Hilton. By the time the interview was filmed, Wallace's hostility bristled through the television tube, turning Arafat into a totally unsympathetic character. The unfortunate thing for the Palestinian cause is that Arafat and those closest to him do not seem to understand what they do to themselves. I arrived in Tunis just after Wallace left. The first day I was there, Dr. Sami Musallah, the gnomelike chief of Arafat's office, showed me with great pride "a very important interview" with Arafat that had recently been published in *Penthouse*. And so it has gone through the years of Arafat's chairmanship of the PLO.

Yet Yasser Arafat more than any other person is responsible for creating and nurturing a distinctive Palestinian nationalism. He pulled together a scattered and defeated people, gave them an identity, and infused in them a stubborn pride. Through years of endless maneuvering, Arafat fended off Gamal Abdul Nasser of Egypt, King Hussein of Jordan, Hafiz Assad of Syria, and any other Arab leader who attempted to take from the Palestinians their own destiny. And he has refused to allow Israel, the United States, and the larger Western bloc to regard the Palestinians as simply Arabs. Thus the Palestinian issue has been and remains the central issue of the Arab world. It reigns as the cardinal example of the passion of unity and the reality of specific interests that so torments the realm of the Arabs.

CONCLUSION:
THE ARAB REALITY,
THE AMERICAN
RESPONSE

O N A WARM AFTERNOON IN MARCH 1988, I dropped my luggage on the pallid, nondescript carpet of room 326 of the Tunis Hilton. I had been trapped in airports and encased in airplanes for fourteen hours, and my dulled brain hungered for fresh air. I pulled back the bold coral-and-gray drapes hanging across the glass that formed the room's outer wall and stepped onto the balcony. The heat of the sun and the brisk ocean breeze that comes up every afternoon about three o'clock began to work their healing powers on my tired body. Relishing the feeling, I did not immediately realize that something had changed about the familiar view. The super-structure of a large building now stood between me and the aqua blue of the bay of Tunis. Moving to the far side of the balcony and leaning out over the railing, I was able to read a blue-and-white sign painted with black script. It told me that I was looking at the head-quarters of the Arab League, relocated from Cairo to Tunis in March 1978 in the wake of Egypt's agreement with Israel at Camp David. The move, which at the time seemed temporary, now appeared permanent as the League's new home rose on a hill above Tunis.

In December 1989, I was back at the Hilton. The construction process on the Arab League building had created a distinctive dome flanked by two slender minarets whose tops were touched with gold. The exterior was nearing completion, and the graceful curves of what would be gardens displayed the architecture like a jewel. But before those gardens were established, the Arab world plunged into another crisis that ripped the fabric of its unity. Saddam Hussein invaded Kuwait, fracturing the Arab world yet again as Anwar Sadat had fractured it when he made peace with Israel. In the new order that emerged in 1990, Egypt became once more the core of the Arab world, exerting its customary influence. As a result, the Arab League voted to move back to Cairo, always regarded as its natural home. The building in Tunis became an expensive monument to the forces of unity and division that constantly pull at the Arabs.

In the last decade of the twentieth century, the Arabs are experiencing both their unity and their division in new forms. Despite the exile of Egypt during the 1980s, the formal links between Arab countries have strengthened. The Arab League, the oldest and most noteworthy of Arab organizations, survives as the broad umbrella under which the Arab states gather. Beyond it, a range of other inter-Arab organizations have gained life. Some are cultural, some political, and some attempt to bridge the economic gap between the oil states and non-oil states by employing grants and loans to transfer money from the richer Arab states to the poorer. But the real forces of unity are in everyday life. As a result of the revolution in transportation, roads now connect village and town and every Arab country to every other Arab country. And sleek silver jet airliners effortlessly fly above the punishing desert, moving people and commerce, binding the Arabs physically and economically as they have always been bound emotionally. Massive migrations of labor from the poor countries to the rich countries link Egyptian and Syrian and Saudi as they have never been linked before. Yet it is the strengthening of the common culture that most authentically affirms Arab unity. The expansion of education that began in the 1950s and accelerated in the 1970s created in all the countries of the *mashriq* an educated class that sees the world through the spectrum of Arab culture. To those beyond the elite, newspapers, movies, radio, and television link Cairo and Riyadh, Damascus and Baghdad, delivering popular culture in the Arabic language. The poetry readings and television melodramas of one become that of all, certifying the Arabs' historical bonds of unity.

But as unity grows, so does disunion. The countries of the Arab world, once only lines drawn on a map by others, have developed, in varying degrees, the interests of nation-states. The great divide is economic, separating those with oil and those without. Other conflicts are those that involve all nations—competition for water, for markets, for outlets to the sea, for territorial adjustments, for regional leadership. Yet on no issue do the Arabs divide more than over the nature of their relationship with the West, particularly with the United States.

The seeds of Arab turmoil are within the Arab world itself. But those seeds have been fertilized and nourished by policies of the United States that extend back to World War II. Neither clearly conceived nor executed, American foreign policy in the Middle East has contributed to the turbulence of the world of the Arabs. At the same time, it has endangered the American presence in this crucial land area linking Europe, Africa, and Asia that possesses the most vital element of Western industrialization—oil.

At its root, American damage to the Arab world and the United States' ever-growing problem in protecting its position in the Middle East stem from the basic fact that the United States has never approached the Arab world in terms of Arab realities and Arab problems. From 1945 to 1990, American foreign policy in the Middle East, conducted under nine presidents, was a function of only two factors—the cold war and American domestic politics that demanded support for Israel. It was not until the cold war ended and Saddam Hussein, acting without the Soviet Union, threatened to cut off the industrialized world's lifeblood that the United States was forced to look at the Arab world with new eyes. In that awakening, the Bush administration and certain members of Congress realized that access to oil demanded stability in the region that held that oil. And stability required that the United States alter the practices and assumptions of almost fifty years.

In the nineteenth century and early twentieth, the United States possessed almost no commercial or political interests in the Middle East. The Arab world was largely the sphere of the missionaries, and it was the missionaries in their schools and hospitals who defined the United States to the Arabs. Woodrow Wilson in a sense expressed his own Presbyterian upbringing when he formulated the Fourteen Points. As Wilson's blueprint for international relations related to self-determination for the Arabs, it ran head-on into the colonial claims of Britain and France. As a result, neither would participate in a commission suggested by another Presbyterian,

Daniel Bliss, president of the American University of Beirut, that would gather information on the implementation of self-rule for the Arabs. Wilson went on alone. In the spring of 1919, he sent the King-Crane Commission to Palestine, Syria, and Turkey. In its report, the commission bluntly challenged the ambitions of Britain and France and questioned the claims of the Zionists. Better than anyone else in the West, the King-Crane Commission pointed to the potential problems brewing in Palestine. But its efforts came to nothing. Stricken by a stroke, Wilson probably never saw the report. It was eventually published at the end of 1922, but by then no one really cared. The United States had gone into isolation. With the Harding/Coolidge administration content to allow the Middle East to remain Britain's bailiwick, the missionaries in the Levant, later joined by a handful of oilmen combing the sands of Saudi Arabia, were the principal American presence in the Arab world.

It was not until World War II that the basic tenets of American policy in the Middle East began to take shape. Only in small part did they respond to the hopes and fears of the people of the Arab world. In a country in which Islam was still called "Mohammedanism," few knew or cared what the Arabs thought or needed. For Americans, the Middle East was only the "holy land," the cherished cradle of the Judeo-Christian religion. For Jewish Americans, it was Palestine. Harry Truman, like Franklin Roosevelt before him, felt the pressure of prominent American Zionists. Since Palestine posed no direct challenge to American interests and Palestinians could not vote in American elections, Truman chose to escape the organized anger of American Jews by supporting the Zionist agenda. Yet above interest-group politics, it was the enormous burden of guilt—the specter of Hitler's death camps and the heartrending plight of so many made homeless by the crimes of Nazism—that concentrated American attention on Jewish claims to Palestine. The United States voted in favor of the United Nations Partition Plan of 1947. And on May 14, 1948, Harry Truman, against the advice of his State Department, extended U.S. recognition to Israel within eleven minutes of its declaration of statehood.

American money in the form of government aid and private donations flowed into the new state of Israel. From roughly mid-1950 to mid-1951, the U.S. government granted Israel $65 million in direct aid while the Export-Import Bank extended another $35 million in credits and the United Jewish Appeal pumped in an additional $89 million. In the same period, the U.S. government provided $16 million to the United Nations Relief and Works Administration to help care for Palestinian refugees and a few small loans to the Arab states on Israel's borders. The unequal contest between the Arabs and Israel for American aid and support had begun.

The United States might well have left the Middle East to war-exhausted Britain and to American Jewish organizations if it had not been for the expansionist ambitions of the Soviet Union. Already established in eastern Europe when World War II ended, the Soviet army in 1946 tried to hold on to northern Iran. Failing, the Russian bear looked south, toward Turkey and the Dardanelles and on to Greece. In 1947, overburdened Britain shocked Washington by announcing that it could no longer prop up Greece's anticommunist government. According to the scenario drawn up by American intelligence, once Britain withdrew its support from Athens, Russian-sponsored communist guerrillas would seize control. Greece would thus gravitate into the Soviet orbit, threatening to pull the eastern Mediterranean with it. On March 12, 1947, Harry Truman went before Congress to announce that "totalitarian regimes imposed on free people by direct or indirect aggression undermine the foundations of international peace and hence the security of the United States."* The Truman Doctrine, intended to contain the Soviet Union from further expansion, was the opening gun of the cold war. Across the globe, Soviet moves for influence and territory would be countered economically, politically, and militarily by the United States. The world of the Arabs was no exception.

Dwight Eisenhower became president in 1953. Coming out of the Korean War, which was fought to contain communism in Asia, the president worried that Arab resentments against Israel, coupled with American support for the Jewish state, were providing fertile ground for Soviet exploitation of the Arab Middle East. In an attempt to strike a "balance" between Israel and the Arabs, the United States protested in the early summer of 1953 when the Israeli government began to move its offices from Tel Aviv to Jerusalem on the grounds that this violated the 1947 partition resolution, which recognized Jerusalem as an international city. When Israel began work in the demilitarized zone on its Jordan River project, which diverted precious water from Syria and Jordan into Israel, the

---

* Quoted in Thomas Bailey, *A Diplomatic History of the American People* (New York: Appleton-Century-Crofts, 1964), p. 797.

United States urged that it be stopped. Israel refused. Yet American aid continued, constituting 35 percent of all imports into Israel in 1953. The president ran foreign policy, but Congress appropriated money. And it was in Congress that the friends of Israel most effectively wielded their power. Consequently, the Eisenhower administration was caught between the domestic political need to bend to the intense emotional affinity powerful groups of Americans felt toward Israel and the larger strategic goal of containing Soviet influence. It was in this bind that the United States met Gamal Abdul Nasser.

Historically unsympathetic to both monarchy and colonialism, the United States expressed no opposition to the 1952 revolution in Egypt. In fact, for a year or two after the Egyptian revolution, some policy planners even saw Nasser as "America's man in Cairo." But attitudes toward the man who led that revolution hardened in 1955 when Nasser went to the Bangdung conference and emerged as the virulent anti-Western champion of nonalignment. Anti-Western nationalists were a despised element in the mid-1950s deep freeze of the cold war. And like other nationalists of the time, Nasser fell into the black hole of superpower rivalries.

Ignoring Nasser's own fear of communism as a threat to his power in Egypt, Eisenhower, his secretary of state John Foster Dulles, the U.S. Congress, and the American media clothed Nasser as a Russian bear. Seizing the moment, Israel stepped forward to establish itself as democracy's only shield in the hostile world of the Arabs racing down the road toward communism. Launching an intense public relations drive in the United States in which Nasser lurked as the "Hitler of the Nile," Israel neatly tied the West's strategic interests to the Jewish state. And as the seemingly indispensable ally, Israel reaped the largess of American military, financial, and moral support in its contest with the Arabs. Lost in the imagery was Nasser the nationalist, who led the Arab chorus against the legacies of colonialism.*

The real issues in the Middle East, those between the Arabs

---

* Nasser for his part never seemed able to differentiate between the symbols and the implements of international affairs. Unleashing his oratory to his Arab audiences, he cried, "When Washington speaks I shall tell them, 'Perish in your fury.' Death is preferable to humiliation." Never able to move beyond his anticolonial mind-set or to curtail his propaganda attacks against the United States, Nasser torpedoed any American tolerance for him as a genuine nationalist.

and the lingering presence of Western imperialism and those between Israel and the Arabs, gave way to the single question of alignment in the cold war. For the United States, Nasser's neutrality totally overshadowed in importance a cardinal issue for the Arabs in 1955—the Israeli invasion and occupation of Gaza. More than three decades later, an unnamed Arab would remember, "The U.S. saw everything in black and white. The U.S. was saying you're either with us or against us at a time when we were just coming out of colonial rule. The U.S. was twisting our arms."*

Using his neutrality as poker stakes, Nasser played one superpower against the other. Denied American weapons, he struck a deal with Czechoslovakia, which brought the Soviet Union into the Middle East for the first time. Yet when Nasser nationalized the Suez Canal, prompting Britain, France, and Israel to invade, Eisenhower refused to allow the invasion to stand. Bringing Israel and the United States' closest allies to heel, Eisenhower revived among Arabs across the Middle East the image of Americans as benevolent missionaries. But in his decision to force a withdrawal from Egyptian territory, Eisenhower was acting against the Russians, not for the Arabs. Eisenhower saved Nasser during the 1956 Suez War for one reason—to keep him from drawing the Soviet Union further into the Middle East. Motivated by cold-war strategies, Eisenhower and Dulles rapidly mended fences with America's allies and began to shore up the pro-Western monarchies in Jordan and Iraq to contain Nasser's Arab nationalism.

On January 5, 1957, the administration brought forth the Eisenhower Doctrine. Almost an addendum to the Truman Doctrine, it provided economic aid and armed support to any nation in the Middle East threatened by a communist takeover. The Eisenhower Doctrine was essentially a round plug in a square hole, because it ignored the underlying grievances that encouraged Arab ties to Moscow. Nonetheless, when Iraq's King Faisal, the linchpin of the Baghdad Pact against the Soviet Union, was assassinated in July 1958 by elements sympathetic to Nasser, the Eisenhower Doctrine kicked into operation to save the Western-oriented government of Lebanon.

U.S. Marines splashed on shore at Beirut on July 15, 1958. For

* *Christian Science Monitor*, August 13, 1990.

three and a half months, fourteen thousand American troops patrolled the beaches amid sunbathers and ice cream vendors and shopped the boutiques along Hamra Street. When the continuation of a pro-Western government in Lebanon was assured, they went home. It had all been so deceptively simple. Armed force costing only two lives had restored order and preserved American interests in the Middle East. But it was action detached from the political environment in which it was executed. While demonstrating American will against Nasser and by extension the Soviet Union, the invasion of Lebanon simply secured the status quo, leaving in place all the underlying resentments that had fed the turmoil in Lebanon in the first place. More ominous, it set a precedent for future, more costly interventions by the United States into the world of the Arabs.

Perhaps Dwight Eisenhower saw the writing on the wall. In the last two years of his term, the administration pulled back from its aggressive policy toward Nasserism and began to grope tentatively toward a better understanding with the Arab countries in Nasser's camp. But the president could not weaken the hold Israel and its supporters had on Congress and the American public.

Israel was a jealous ward, angered when its patron trafficked with the Arabs. As a result, Eisenhower's probing into Nasser's orbit ran into the frontal assaults of Israel's friends. It was not just the Jewish lobby. It was also many Christian groups who held on to the errant view that Muslims are outside the Judeo-Christian tradition and are therefore people with no claim to the land of David and of Jesus. They were joined by a broad spectrum of the American public. 1960 was the year Leon Uris's novel *Exodus* became a movie. The dashing Paul Newman and the beautiful Eva Marie Saint brought to life Uris's version of the desperate efforts of the victims of the Holocaust to get into British-controlled Palestine and their heroic struggle to claim the land from the fierce and uncultured Arabs. At the same time, newspapers, magazines, and television unfolded story after story about the miracle taking place in Israel.

Israel was making the desert bloom. With public and private money from the West and with an educated population capable of organizing itself for the task of development, Israel had become a state most in the United States considered as Western as Europe. And it was by the measure of Westernization that the Arabs were judged. Because the Arabs were generally poor and at times politically chaotic, they were labeled as culturally inferior, undeserving of the level of American aid and sympathy that went to Israel. Few who exercised judgment on the Arabs appreciated that the Arabs could not live up to the standards Americans demanded because they did not enjoy the same access to capital as Israel and because their history under the Ottoman Empire had left them grossly unprepared to meet the twentieth century. The Arabs' unequal contest with Israel might have been left at that if the energy demands of the West had not begun to alter perceptively the Arab side of the equation.

When John F. Kennedy came into office in 1961, Arab oil was becoming an increasingly important component in American energy sources at the same time that the Soviet Union was extending its influence into Nasser's Egypt. Although the Kennedy administration had no clearly conceived policy for addressing American problems in the Middle East, it did have an appreciation of the fact that the Arab countries were undergoing fundamental and painful social transformations that were as evident in conservative regimes such as Jordan as they were in radical ones like Syria. From this premise, the administration began to push for a program of American economic aid that would serve as a vehicle for a gradual rapprochement with the more radical Arab countries. The assumption was that as the radical Arab countries developed economically and stabilized politically, hostilities toward the West born of a sense of frustration, despair, and humiliation would gradually dissipate, thereby undercutting the appeal of Nasser.

But Kennedy during his short term in office could not surmount domestic politics to put the theory into operation. Israel's supporters raised their hue and cry against any U.S. overture toward the Arabs. Under the onslaught, Congress revolted against the president. The Foreign Assistance Act of 1963 was amended to withhold American aid to any country "engaging in or preparing for aggressive military efforts" against other countries to which the United States also was giving economic assistance. In other words, those Arab countries the administration most wanted to reach were barred from the very aid intended to encourage their moderation toward both the United States and Israel. In justifying a decision made on the basis of politics, Congress argued that the restriction defended the security interests of the United States. It was a persuasive argument for an American public not really interested in balancing American foreign policy in the Middle East.

While domestic politics stymied a more effective approach to the hostile Arab world, the cold war added its weight to the turmoil of the region. Like foxes and hounds, the United States and the Soviet Union chased each other throughout the Middle East. The Soviet Union plugged massive amounts of military equipment and economic assistance into a range of Arab countries, anxious to find a counterweight to what each saw as the Israeli/American dyad. In response, the United States increased its arms shipments to pro-Western Arab regimes such as Jordan and Saudi Arabia. This in turn guaranteed that Israel received its share of American military aid that was always greater in amount and quality than what went to the Arabs.

In this endless cycle, the United States evaluated the success of its Middle East policies by watching the Soviet Union, not the Arabs. By this gauge, the United States faced serious problems. American intelligence judged by 1967 that the Soviet Union had created the equivalent of a Sixth Fleet in the Mediterranean and enough military facilities in Egypt to service it. Thus when Israel went to war against Nasser and won so astoundingly, most in Washington silently cheered. Beyond Washington, the speed and daring with which the Israelis executed the war made heroes of an entire nation. Increasingly bogged down in the morass of Vietnam, Americans rallied to a country that could not only define the enemy but defeat him in six short days. As a result, Israel became larger than life. On the day the war ended, Lafayette Park across from the White House overflowed with Americans waving the blue-and-white flag of Israel. They were saluting little Israel, which had crippled the hated Nasser and stood up for democracy in the Middle East. And the message they delivered was that no country was more deserving of American money and adulation than the Jewish state. Lost were the complexities that led to the war and those that would follow. Almost unacknowledged in the euphoria was the whole new set of territorial disputes that the war engendered—which are as yet unresolved—and the new flood of angry refugees who vented their hatred on the United States. "America helped Israel. They bombed us. They killed our women and children. . . . Someday we will kill you all."* It was a vow uttered by many across the Arab world, one

* *Newsweek*, June 26, 1967.

that has yet to die. But few heard. For 1967 was the year that the American public, the media, and the Congress began their passionate romance with Israel.

The Johnson administration, infatuated with but not totally blinded by Israel, attempted to strike peace on the basis of United Nations Resolution 242, which called for Israel to swap land conquered in 1967 for recognition of Israel's right to exist within secure borders. The land-for-peace formula failed in a scenario in which both sides were at fault. Israel refused to surrender land until the Arab states extended it recognition, and the Arab states refused to grant recognition before Israel returned the occupied territories. The Johnson administration, consumed by the hell of Vietnam, declined to push. With one set of vociferous critics decrying the war in Asia, the administration was not about to inflame the domestic front further by taking on the friends of Israel over the issue of territorial compromise on the spoils of 1967. Having little leverage with the Arabs, the United States could force compromise from that side only with the participation of the Soviet Union. No desire for an untangling of the Arab-Israeli imbroglio was strong enough to tempt the United States to invite the Soviet Union into the Middle East. Instead, Washington in a naive sense convinced itself that Israel was holding the Middle East against the dreaded Soviets while the United States fought the communist enemy in Asia. Seizing the moment, Israel jumped on the opportunity to strengthen its image as the self-declared outpost of democracy in the unruly world of the Arabs. It was at this point that the United States began to elevate Israel to the status of America's strategic ally in the Middle East. The whole process speeded up with the rise of the Palestinian commando and the advent of international terrorism conducted in the name of the Palestinians.

The armed struggle that Palestinian commando groups launched after the 1967 War became, in the American mind, a David and Goliath story in reverse. Israel, the strongest military power in the Middle East, the country which had just vanquished the armed forces of its three neighbors, was David. The disjointed commando groups who walked to the battlefield armed with little except automatic rifles and bags of hand grenades were Goliath. Missing was the point that guerrilla war is the tactic of the weak. But guerrilla war kills innocent people. When groups within the PLO tried to deliver their rage against displacement and impotence by hijacking airplanes and massacring the guiltless, they accomplished nothing in the West except the acquisition of the label of barbarian.

Israel benefited enormously from the Palestinians' campaign of terror that raged between 1968 and 1972. Golda Meir's statement in 1971 that the Palestinians were not a people and therefore had no claim to a homeland was never seriously challenged in the United States. The following year, the massacre of Israeli athletes at the Munich Olympics so offended civilized society that it gave weight to Israeli arguments that the Arabs are the products of a backward, brutal culture. With a galaxy of political figures like the tough but somehow motherly Golda Meir, the erudite Abba Eban, and the dashing Moshe Dayan who knew and understood the West, Israel carried on its media blitz in the United States. Israel, the bastion of democracy, the United States' indispensable ally against the encroachment of the Soviet Union into the Middle East, was imperiled. Thus it was morally and politically incumbent on the United States to feed and arm it. Americans listened, unaware of just how much the Arabs feared Israel and its American-supplied military might.

It was not long after the debut of high-profile international terrorism in 1968 that Lyndon Johnson completed his term as president. Hounded by Vietnam, he left office without ever addressing the turmoil in the Middle East that was constantly stirred by the United States' unrestrained support for Israel and its chess game with the Soviet Union.

He was succeeded by Richard Nixon, the cold warrior with a passion for foreign policy, who came into office looking at the Arab world and seeing Russians instead of Arabs. The Soviet Union was still ensconced in Nasser's Egypt, running the Egyptian military as its own. To Nixon's credit, he reasoned that the United States could best get rid of the Soviet presence in the Arab world by addressing the grievances that had opened the door to the Soviet Union in the first place. Thus in November 1969, the Nixon administration reaffirmed the Johnson administration's policy of opposition to Israel's alteration of the status of Jerusalem and declared that "there can be no lasting peace without a just settlement of the problem of those Palestinians whom the wars of 1948 and 1967 made homeless."* These statements were widely interpreted to mean that the Repub-

---

* Secretary of State William Rogers, quoted in William R. Polk, *The Arab World Today* (Cambridge: Harvard University Press, 1991), p. 411.

lican administration wanted better relations with the Arabs. This was confirmed by a slowdown in new arms sales to Israel, which was followed by the June 1970 Rogers Plan, aimed at ending the war of attrition between Egypt and Israel along the Suez Canal.

The Rogers Plan was Nixon's first foray into Middle East politics. Conception and execution came largely from William Rogers, who as secretary worked out of the State Department. In the Nixon administration, this was the light side of Nixon's foreign policy apparatus. Origination, direction, and to a great extent implementation of foreign policy came from the duo in the White House—the president and his national security adviser, Henry Kissinger.

The first crisis they faced in the Middle East was the 1970 civil war in Jordan. Trapped in the mode of global politics, Nixon and Kissinger peered at the Jordanian crisis through the binoculars of superpower rivalry. Their view gave little consideration to the stresses and strains tearing at the Arab world in the wake of Israel's 1967 victory or the challenge that the Palestinians' angry impatience with their status posed to Hussein's regime. From Pennsylvania Avenue, the multilayered conflict had only one dimension—the pro-Western King Hussein versus the Marxist-tainted PLO. Indicative of how little the administration was willing to concede Arab emotions, Kissinger envisioned at one point using Israel to block Iraq or Syria if either moved to reinforce the *fedayeen*. In American perceptions, Israel was part of the solution to the United States' anxieties in the Middle East rather than a major part of the problem. According to Middle East specialist William Quandt, it was during this period that Israel came to be regarded "as the helpful junior partner in the successful management of a grave global test of superpower wills." Consequently, the strategic relationship between the United States and Israel moved forward another step. In the decades that followed, other administrations would entrust Israel not only with keeping the peace in the Middle East on behalf of the United States but with carrying out clandestine American policy from Africa to Central America. In these theaters far removed from the Middle East, Israel lent a discreet hand in the promotion of American interests in return for American support for its own regional ambitions.*

---

* During the Reagan administration, this aspect of the relationship between the United States and Israel came to light in the Iran-Contra scandal.

392 / PASSION AND POLITICS

The Middle East, overshadowed by the ongoing agony of Vietnam, moved up on Nixon's foreign policy agenda when Anwar Sadat expelled the Russians from Egypt. And then came the October War. Although Sadat had made numerous attempts to engage the administration in a Middle East peace effort, Nixon and Kissinger failed to consider Sadat's war as an act of diplomacy. Interpreting Israel's forced retreat in the Sinai as a threat to the United States' strategic position in the critical Middle East, Nixon ordered American planes to fly to the battlefield to resupply Israel's losses. The immediate result was the Arab oil embargo and an end to the industrialized world's cheap energy.

Mistakes in war were followed by mistakes in peace. Nixon and Kissinger ignored the possibilities of a comprehensive peace created when the Arab armies for a time held Israel to a standstill on the battlefield. In this brief illusion of victory, the Arabs had regained their honor and lifted some of the psychological burdens of the past. If the United States were ever to address the Arab world as a whole and force concessions on both sides, this was the moment. Instead, Henry Kissinger, the czar of foreign policy in both the Nixon and Ford administrations, married the United States' global concerns to the interests of Israel.

Rather than bringing all parties to the peace conference, which would have required Soviet participation, Kissinger adopted a step-by-step approach in which a series of bilateral negotiations would bring Israel and Egypt and Israel and Syria to the bargaining table as the first level of a process aimed at uncoupling the Arab states from each other and into agreement with Israel. Kissinger won disengagement agreements between Egypt and Israel and Syria and Israel. Then the process stalled.* Ignoring or perhaps never fully appreciating the power that the issue of Israel exercises over Arab unity or the symbolic function the Palestinians serve in that unity, Kissinger's strategy in essence ruled out the search for a comprehensive settlement of the Arab-Israeli dispute. One of the central motivations of that strategy was to shut the Palestine Liberation Organization out of any role in deciding the issues of the region of which the Palestinians are such an integral part.

The man who became secretary of state in Nixon's second term

* Anwar Sadat went on to the Sinai II agreement, which met the specific interests of Egypt.

held a formalistic view of the international system. Diplomacy took place among states. Whatever else they might be, the Palestinians were not a state. In Kissinger's view, to even raise the issue of Palestinian participation in peacemaking would derail the entire process. Believing in addressing only those issues which promise success, Kissinger argued that no one had found the answer to the Palestinian problem and no one would. Consequently, he embraced Israel's position that the PLO be neither recognized nor permitted any role in negotiations that might take place between Israel and its Arab adversaries.

In mid-1973, messages sent from Yasser Arafat to Henry Kissinger asking for a dialogue between the PLO and the United States went essentially unheeded. Vernon Walters, the deputy director of the CIA, did meet with a representative of the PLO in November 1973. It was followed by another meeting in March 1974. Nothing came of either. According to Kissinger, "At this stage, involving the PLO was incompatible with the interests of any of the parties to the Middle East conflict."* To Kissinger, the PLO was an overtly anti-American terrorist group dedicated to the destruction of two important friends of the United States—Israel and Jordan. As such, Kissinger meant to ensure that the Palestinian question remained beyond the horizon.

In the whirlwind of his diplomatic initiative following the 1973 war, Kissinger literally closed the door on American contact with the font of Palestinian nationalism when he promised Israel in writing that the United States would not negotiate with the PLO until it recognized Israel's right to exist and renounced terrorism. Added to the elaborate package of agreements, understandings, and commitments negotiated in connection with Sinai I and II, Kissinger essentially handed Israel control over a crucial aspect of U.S. policy in the Middle East. Although hailed in the United States as a geopolitical wizard, Henry Kissinger and his dazzling diplomacy left the Arabs with great bitterness and a sense of betrayal.

When Jimmy Carter became president in 1977, the United

---

* Henry Kissinger, *Years of Upheaval* (Boston: Little, Brown, 1982), p. 629. In 1975, Arafat sent another message via a former New York City policeman. Handed to Nelson Rockefeller, the message, according to the bearer, outlined what was in essence Arafat's agreement to recognize Israel in return for a Palestinian state in the occupied territories. Rockefeller passed it on to Kissinger, and it died.

States' Middle East policy had reached a dead end. But the instability in the region, which threatened to spill over into war with all of its ramifications for the American stake in the Middle East, had not. From the standpoint of American strategy against the Soviet Union, the Nixon/Kissinger policy of excluding the Soviets from the Middle East had proved self-defeating. Soviet arms continued to flow into Arab countries, and the Russian bear continued to growl its threats, precisely because the United States had blocked to it all responsible avenues of participation in the affairs of the region. Carter initiated a change. A joint statement on the need for a comprehensive settlement of the Arab-Israeli conflict issued by U.S. Secretary of State Cyrus Vance and Soviet Minister of Foreign Affairs Andrei Gromyko indicated that the United States was cracking the door of the Middle East to the Soviet Union.

Carter then turned to the issue of the Palestinians. The Palestinians were not only at the center of the Arab-Israeli dispute, they were also an important component of the war in Lebanon that had begun in 1975. Anwar Sadat told the new president that the Palestinian problem remained the "core and crux" of Middle East instability and that the Arab-Israeli conflict could not be resolved apart from it. For the Palestinian issue, as always, involved more than the Palestinians per se. It reflected the psychological wounds of all Arabs generated by their unequal contest with the West and with Israel. To get the Arabs to the negotiating table, the Palestinians had to be included in any peacemaking process. This was one reality. The other reality was that because of the promises that Kissinger had made to Israel, no one in the administration could speak directly to the PLO, the closest thing the Palestinians have ever had to a government.

Jimmy Carter became the first American president willing to sustain an attack on the domestic front over the issue of the Palestinians. In 1977, the year he took office, Carter dropped a pregnant code word into the United States' diplomatic vocabulary. It was "homeland." The president, commenting on the stalemate in the Middle East, stated that a condition for peace was "a homeland for the Palestinian refugees." With that one word, Carter seemed to set the United States on a new path. But the Palestinians themselves refused to give him the help he needed. In the summer of 1977, the United States, supported by Egypt and Saudi Arabia, made an effort to persuade the PLO to accept, even if only partially, UN

Security Council Resolution 242. In return, the United States pledged its willingness both to support the idea of an "independent Palestinian entity" on the West Bank under UN supervision and to reassess its military aid policy toward Israel. The American and Saudi assessment that Arafat could deliver the PLO was wrong. The offer was rejected.

Events then took on their own momentum. Sadat went to Jerusalem in November 1977. In March 1978, Israel invaded southern Lebanon. Called the Litani operation, it was designed to clear Palestinian commandos off Israel's northern border. But it also promised disaster for Carter's efforts to move the parties to the Middle East conflict toward negotiations. Refusing to condone Israel's crossing into an Arab country, Carter took the issue to the United Nations. Israel pulled back on the ground but kept the skies. Israeli planes streaking northward from bases in Israel continued to drop their bombs on whole villages singled out for retaliation for attacks on Israel. The guiltless paid more often than the guilty. In this regard, air attacks on Palestinian camps and villages populated largely by Shiite Lebanese were no less random or inhuman than the bombs terrorists planted among innocent people. Yet while the American government and public opinion firmly denounced the mortar attacks that fell on Israel from Lebanese soil, little was said about the punishment Israel inflicted on the population of southern Lebanon. When the U.S. intervention in Lebanon came in 1982, the Arabs, particularly the Shiites, would remember.

Keeping one eye on the domestic front and the other on the Soviets, Carter doggedly pursued the only promising scenario in the Middle East—negotiations between Egypt and Israel. In August 1978, Secretary of State Vance delivered letters to Anwar Sadat and Menachem Begin inviting them to meet Carter at Camp David. But the Camp David Accords that emerged were not an American formula but rather the acceptance of the Begin plan of the previous December. In their intense desire to win an agreement, Carter and Sadat failed to pay heed to the old British diplomatic maxim "Never negotiate on the other fellow's draft." The result was the great flaw of Camp David—the failure to address the problem of the Palestinians. In his meetings with the Israelis, Carter had pushed hard for Palestinian autonomy in the occupied territories as a transitional step that would lead to a Palestinian entity tied in some type of confederation to Jordan. As the negotiations ended, Carter thought he had Begin's assent on the principle of autonomy and a freeze on Jewish settlements in the occupied territories for five years while the autonomy talks were under way. But according to Carter, the day after the terms of the accord were announced, Menachem Begin reneged on his pledge to suspend building settlements. In a letter delivered to the president, Begin claimed the freeze applied only to the three-month period between the Camp David agreement and the signing of the peace treaty between Egypt and Israel. Unhappily, the Camp David Accords, which were to lay the foundation of a comprehensive peace settlement between Israel and the Arabs, failed to impede Israel's drive to absorb the West Bank and Jerusalem. By extension, the crucial element in the conflict in the Middle East was left unaddressed—the Palestinians, the icon of Arab unity.

Despite the great rejoicing that greeted Carter, Sadat, and Begin when they came off the mountain, thoughtful Israelis recognized the basic flaw in the agreement. Former foreign minister Abba Eban, writing in *Foreign Affairs*, said, "The harsh truth is that on the most crucial and complex issue—that of the Palestinians and the West Bank—the Camp David signatories did little more than postpone their confrontation by the kind of semantic dexterity that is quick to wear out." Nonetheless Carter moved the parties on to the Egyptian-Israeli peace treaty in March 1979.

By the following August, domestic politics began to exert their force on Carter's empathetic approach to the Arab world. Andrew Young, the ambassador to the United Nations, went quietly one evening to the New York apartment of Zuhdi Terzi, the PLO's UN observer. He was seen. The friends of Israel howled in protest that the promises made by Kissinger had been broken. Carter caved in. Young resigned. In the aftermath, the president who had spoken so warmly of the Palestinian "homeland" upon entering the White House was moved to say, "I am against any creation of a separate Palestinian state. I don't think it would be good for the Palestinians. I don't think it would be good for Israel. I don't think it would be good for the Arab neighbors of such a state."*

Nonetheless, Carter continued to press on toward Middle East stability with what he had—an Egyptian-Israeli peace treaty. It had broken the Arab front, theoretically enabling other Arab states to

---

* Quoted in Polk, *Arab World Today*, p. 442.

follow suit. It was from this viewpoint that Carter and his advisers believed that peace could be achieved without a region-wide peace conference requiring Soviet participation.* But the result was precisely the reverse. Rather than a triumph, the Egyptian-Israeli treaty had left the Arab world bitterly divided and the United States savagely condemned. The Saudis argued with some justification that the United States had so polarized the Arabs that the Soviet Union had been handed its best opportunity in years to reestablish itself in the Middle East. Thus, far from correcting Kissinger's flawed strategy, Carter ended up completing it. And just as Sinai II had cost the American taxpayer billions of dollars, so the Egyptian-Israeli treaty with its huge grants of aid to both sides would cost the same taxpayers billions of dollars more. George Ball, a former deputy secretary of state and ambassador to the United Nations who is an outspoken critic of American foreign policy in the Middle East, said at the time, "We bought the sands of Sinai for an exorbitant price from Israel, then paid Egypt a large price to take them back."†

No matter how well intended, the mistake of the Egyptian-Israeli peace treaty was that it tried to sever one Arab state from another. In solving one problem, the state of war between the neighbors on the Sinai, it increased the immediacy and danger of a host of other problems. Arms expenditures, for example, of both Israel and Egypt actually increased after the peace treaty. Sadat, having isolated himself from his Arab environment, needed to cater to the desires of his armed forces for billions of dollars' worth of the latest and most sophisticated American equipment. Israel responded by gathering in its share of American military hardware. Yet as serious as the arms race was, even more important for the United States' position in the Arab world was the image that emerged of a powerful Western country dividing one Arab from another in the interests of Israel. It all happened precisely at the time that the Iranian revolution struck at the very foundations of American policy throughout the Middle East.

In the presidency of Ronald Reagan, the flawed precepts on which the United States had based its foreign policy in the Arab

---

* U.S. tolerance for a Soviet role in the Middle East which the Carter administration exhibited at the beginning of its term ended after the Russian invasion of Afghanistan in December 1979.
† Quoted in Seale, *Asad*, p. 314.

world found their most ardent supporters. From the aspect of domestic politics, the pro-Israeli lobby was reinforced by the politically energized religious right. The Christian fundamentalists, with clout derived from a covey of religious broadcasters and intense grass roots political organization, had helped put Ronald Reagan in the White House. Now they would flex their muscle in foreign policy. In the world as viewed by the fundamentalists, a militarily powerful United States must stand guard against godless communism, and Israel must be allowed to realize its manifest destiny. Ironically, right-wing American Christians defended Zionist nationalism more zealously than many Israelis, who saw in the expansionist policies of the Likud government in the occupied territories an undermining of the state of Israel both politically and morally. The Christian right of the United States shared no such concerns. To them, Israel is not a state exhibiting the ambitions and foibles of a nation-state but Biblical fulfillment. Hence any challenge to Israeli government policies, no matter how detrimental they are to the stability of the Middle East, is a challenge to God.

From the aspect of cold-war politics, the Reagan administration's dread of Soviet penetration of the Middle East was so great that it all but eclipsed other factors in the region. Promoting national defense as an article of faith, the administration shifted the practice of supplying arms to U.S. allies from a tool of foreign policy to policy in its own right. But Reagan's cold warriors found that arming the United States' Arab allies was not as easy as arming its other allies. Sales or transfers of weapons to Arab countries came under the scrutiny of Congress, always alert to potential threats to Israel. Saudi Arabia, haughty, able to pay cash for its weapons, an American ally of the first order, was consistently forced to cut down its shopping lists in order to satisfy Congress and the ever watchful American-Israeli Political Action Committee (AIPAC), the most powerful lobby in Washington. In 1981, the sale of the AWACs, considered by American defense experts critical to the security of Saudi Arabia and its oil fields in light of the Iranian revolution and the Soviet invasion of Afghanistan, underwent ferocious debate. Israel's supporters in Congress argued that the sale should be denied lest the spy planes be used to overfly Israel. When congressional permission finally did come it carried with it the stipulation that the crews carry a quota of American technicians. The sale of F-18 fighter planes likewise was granted only after a stipulation that the size of their fuel tanks be cut down to limit the plane's range, making it less of a threat to Israel's security. The final phase of the complex arms deal gave Israel enough extra military equipment to ensure that it would maintain its military superiority over its Arab neighbors.

The Reagan administration executed on a grand scale what its predecessors had done. Instead of pursuing arms control, which is equally unpopular with both suppliers and recipients, each administration for thirty years sought to balance at each higher stage of escalation the armaments of its friends. If the United States armed Jordan against Nasser, then it armed Israel not only against Egypt but also against Jordan. By the advent of the Reagan administration, the whole Middle East bristled with tanks, fighter planes, and surface-to-surface missiles. Lurking beneath the more conventional armaments of modern armies were chemical and biological weapons. Buried even deeper was Israel's stock of nuclear weapons, stored in the Negev desert. It was all done in the name of strategic necessity—keeping the Soviet Union out of the Middle East. The United States was far from alone in feeding the arms race in the Middle East, but it had played a major part in arming both Jews and Arabs to the teeth.*

The paradox of the Reagan administration's arms policy was that the Soviet Union sought no confrontation with the United States in the Arab East. Soviet armaments going largely to Syria, Iraq, and the PLO were more in the nature of political devices that continued to work at prying open the door of the Arab world, allowing the Soviet Union a voice in the politics of a region that held some sway over the Islamic provinces on its own southern borders. But the Reagan administration kept the door closed. The White House was not interested in stability—only containment. As a result of this single-minded absorption with Soviet containment, the Reagan administration in 1982 found itself committing American troops to Lebanon to deliver Israel from its ill-advised, ill-fated invasion of an Arab neighbor. In terms of lives, it would lead to the United States' costliest involvement in the Middle East.

The Reagan administration more than any administration that preceded it dealt with Israel as a full partner in the United States'

---

* In addition to the Soviet Union, the other major arms suppliers in the Middle East were Britain, France, Germany, and China.

strategic defense of the Middle East.* Seeing the hand of the Soviet
Union at work in the disorder in Lebanon, Secretary of State Alexander Haig either explicitly or implicitly gave Israel the green light
to cross the border of Lebanon in June 1982. The rationale was that
Israel would satisfy the administration's desire to reduce Syrian influence in Lebanon. Blinded by their strong anti-Soviet bias, which
cast Syria as a Soviet surrogate, Haig and the president never understood that Hafiz Assad possessed interests in Lebanon that were
apart from Soviet interests. What they understood even less was that
the purpose of the Israeli invasion had nothing to do with global
politics. Its aim was to wipe out the entire institutional framework
of the PLO and to put a pro-Israeli government in place in Beirut.

As the invasion progressed, the complexities of Lebanon unfolded. To the surprise of Reagan and Haig, this was not a superpower confrontation that separated with clearly drawn lines the
supporters of one power from the supporters of another power.
Israel's goals were its own. They meshed only with those of the
Lebanese Maronite Christians who were in a death struggle with
Lebanon's Sunnis, Druze, factions of Shiites, and the PLO. Syria,
against whom the United States had assumed the invasion to be
directed, was in Lebanon to try to keep the peace in order to secure
its western border, not to promote the interests of the Soviet Union.
As if to prove the point, Hafiz Assad, refusing to become entangled
in a fight with Israel he could not win, pulled his troops back toward
Syria, leaving Beirut to the PLO.

With Syria out of the way and the intensity and range of the
Israeli operation becoming clear, the United States demanded a
withdrawal. But when the issue came up in the United Nations
Security Council, the United States vetoed a resolution condemning
Israel on the basis of Israeli assurances that Israel would not go on
to Beirut. It did. By August, Israel was petitioning the United States
to extract it from an operation it had begun but could not end. The
American envoy, Philip Habib, negotiated the PLO out of Beirut.
The U.S. Marines sent in to maintain order during the evacuation
had barely withdrawn when the Lebanese Christian Maronite militia,
the Phalange, massacred the Palestinians of Sabra and Shatila while
the Israelis watched. The Marines came back. To protect their po-

---

* On May 14, 1988, the fortieth anniversary of its statehood, Israel signed a
long-sought strategic treaty with the United States.

sition at the Beirut airport, Reagan ordered the battleship USS *New Jersey* to fire its massive shells into the small mountain village of Souk al-Garb, creating another emotional symbol of Western arrogance against the Arabs and another grievance on which the Arabs could nurse their hatred of the United States. The problem of the whole American operation in Lebanon was that Reagan and his current secretary of state, George Shultz, had no concept of the passions and complexities at work in Lebanon.

Shultz pushed ahead with an Israeli-Lebanon treaty that would install the pro-Israeli government in Lebanon that Israel wanted, believing it would stabilize Lebanon. Incredibly, he refused to see that the bulk of the Lebanese, who had just suffered a devastating invasion by Israel, would not accept a pro-Israeli government. But Shultz continued to focus on only one goal—to cut Syria, the perceived handmaiden of the Soviet Union, out of any negotiations aimed at rebuilding the political and military structures of Lebanon, destroyed by seven years of civil war and the invasion of Israel. The United States' refusal to acknowledge the will and ability of Syria to play a useful role in Lebanon's problems doomed the process. Denied a voice in the proceedings, Hafiz Assad would not sit by and see six years of effort in Lebanon come to nothing. To stem the breach, he made alliance with the Shiite Lebanese, the major victims of Israeli military actions in south Lebanon, and seized terrorism as an alternative means of political warfare against the United States.

In April 1983, the United States embassy in Beirut exploded under a terrorist bomb. In October, 241 Marines died in their barracks near the Beirut airport, one of the points the shelling by the *New Jersey* was supposed to protect. The pro-Israeli government for Lebanon was no longer a possibility when the last Marines went home in February 1984 shortly before the first American hostages disappeared into the warrens of Lebanon. In their wake Ronald Reagan assumed a new mission—terrorism.

Angered by terrorism in its first term, the Reagan administration was obsessed by it in the second. Uncoupled from any political or social context, terrorism took on a life of its own, and its suppression became the premier goal of American foreign policy in the Arab world. Left behind was all consideration of the grievances that bred the terrorism and the political milieu from which it came. Reagan never seemed to ask why the *Achille Lauro* was hijacked or why the Shiites of Lebanon pursued their terrible vendetta against the United States. For the Reagan administration never came to terms with the reality that in Arab eyes the United States and Israel are tied together. The sins of one are the sins of the other. From this perspective, the United States shares responsibility for the plight of the Palestinians, the occupation of Arab land, the invasion of Lebanon, and the continued humiliation of the Arabs. Failing to comprehend this central fact of life in the Middle East, the Reagan administration also failed to comprehend either the nature of the Iranian revolution or the threat of Iraq's Saddam Hussein.

When Ronald Reagan took office, the Iraq-Iran War was already four months old. With the images of hostages from the American embassy in Tehran still fresh and the Ayatollah Khomeini pledging, "We shall export revolution to the whole world," the United States found itself facing a threat that did not fit the cold-war model. The Iranian Revolution, venting its own anger against the West, brandished the theology of Islam, not the ideology of Marx. And its force lay not in powerful weapons but in the power of old resentments. The Ayatollah Khomeini was calling the Islamic world to rise up in revolt against the West and its "Great Satan," the United States. Suddenly the socialism of Iraq's Baath Party and its ties to the Soviet Union faded as Iran came to dominate American thinking.

Initially the United States employed the traditional and relatively painless tactic of supplying Israel and the Arab Gulf states with still more weapons to combat the potential threats from the ongoing war between Iraq and Iran. But in October 1983, the National Security Council concluded that American interests would be seriously harmed if Iraq were to collapse at the feet of Iran. With this decision, the United States began to tilt visibly toward Iraq. In 1984, seventeen years after they broke over the 1967 War, the United States and Iraq reopened diplomatic relations. And bit by bit, U.S. loans to Iraq, primarily for the purchase of agricultural products, increased, and then sales of sensitive technology grew. By 1990, loans to Iraq were running at $1.045 billion, purchases of Iraqi oil $5.5 billion, and U.S. exports to Iraq $3.6 billion. Also by 1990, $730 million worth of technology had been shipped to the republic of Saddam Hussein. Inadequately assessing Hussein's long-term aims and his ambitions to become the leader of the Arab world, the administration and Congress chose to overlook the more unsavory aspects of the Iraqi regime in order to use the weight of Iraq against

Iran. According to one Reagan administration official, "It wasn't that we wanted Iraq to win the war, we did not want Iraq to lose. We really weren't naive. We knew [Saddam Hussein] was an SOB, but he was our SOB."*

The United States took an intense interest in the Iraq-Iran War not only because of the ayatollah's vows of vengeance but because it was being waged in the Persian Gulf, a region vital to American interests. Since the end of World War II, U.S. foreign policy in the Middle East had confronted the Soviet Union and responded to the demands of Israel's American constituency. In 1973, after the oil embargo so graphically demonstrated Western dependence on Arab oil, access to petroleum became the third element in United States policy in the Middle East. Overshadowed except in times of high oil prices, oil in the mid-1980s took its place near the front of American concerns. But petroleum, like the other two factors driving the United States' relationship with the Arab world, was removed from the problems and grievances, hopes and aspirations of most of the Arabs. Defense of the West's precious oil imperiled by the war between Iraq and Iran became a military operation separated from the political and cultural issues that fueled the war between Saddam Hussein's Iraq and the Ayatollah Khomeini's Iran. As in Lebanon, American military force preceded U.S. policy.

American ships were showing the flag in the Persian Gulf when an Iraqi missile hit the USS *Stark* on May 17, 1987. With no clearly defined goals other than keeping oil moving through the Gulf, the president ordered the U.S. Navy to begin convoying tankers under the missiles and through the mines deployed by both sides. By the end of July 1987, Kuwaiti tankers were flying American flags as they carefully navigated the waters of the Gulf. The United States was militarily involved in the world of the Arabs for the third time in thirty years, the second in five.

The war ended in the last year of the Reagan presidency because both sides were exhausted. That left the Palestinian issue as the closing act of the administration's foreign policy in the Middle East. Through a series of events apart from any American action, the Palestinians had asserted their anger and their pride in the Intifadah, and a group of private U.S. citizens aided by the foreign

---

* Miller and Mylroie, *Saddam Hussein and the Crisis in the Gulf*, p. 143.

minister of Sweden had coaxed the magic words from Yasser Arafat. On December 14, 1988, the PLO recognized Israel's right to exist and renounced terrorism. Within hours, a grim-faced George Shultz, the unbending warrior against terrorism, grudgingly announced that the United States would open the long-rejected dialogue with the PLO. The chains fastened by Henry Kissinger were at last broken. But the dialogue lasted only until June 1990, when it was ended by George Bush after a renegade faction of the PLO attacked a beach at Tel Aviv. Domestic politics and Arafat's reluctance to denounce the raid combined to end the United States' short liaison with the organization representing the core problem of the Middle East.

When George Bush took office, the central objectives of American policy in the Middle East remained the hallowed triad—to hold the Soviet Union at bay; to satisfy pro-Israeli sentiment in the United States; and to ensure access to oil at acceptable prices. On August 2, 1990, protection of Western access to Arab oil became the consuming force of American foreign policy. The other aspects of U.S. policy in the Middle East either faded or dovetailed with George Bush's determination to defend Saudi Arabia and its petroleum reserves. The Soviet threat in the Middle East had dissipated with the unraveling of the Soviet empire. And the president was freed from the grip of the pro-Israeli lobby in Congress because Israel shared with Saudi Arabia the imperative of crushing Saddam Hussein's war machine. Finally, the always overrated specter of the Arabs united against the West had dissolved in the Arabs' own internal conflicts. Yet despite their own internal disorder, the Arabs' deep resentments against the West were still there and had to be addressed.

George Bush seemed to understand the need to give both an international and an Arab cover to an American-led intervention in the Persian Gulf. Thus after four decades of frustrating the United Nations' efforts in the Middle East, George Bush raised its flag over the allied operation, brought the Soviet Union in as a partner, pointedly excluded Israel, and enlisted as many Arab states as possible to give some legitimacy to what was essentially a Western intrusion into the Arab world. In one of the most bizarre alliances of the twentieth century, the *mashriq* states of Egypt, Saudi Arabia, and the outcast Syria joined the West in a war against Arab Iraq. Saddam Hussein was defeated militarily, if not politically, and Western access to the Persian Gulf was secured—for the moment.

The Gulf War stripped Saddam Hussein of most of his war machine. But at the same time, it fed the resentments of the Arab masses and gave credence to their suspicions that the West always stands on the horizon ready to invade their world. A West Bank Palestinian said with passion bred by centuries, "The Gulf War was a colonial war. It was fought against all Arabs, not Iraq."*

From the day the United States committed troops to Saudi Arabia, it was obvious that if the costly effort in the Gulf to guarantee Western access to oil was to be successful in the long run, it had to begin a process that would give the Middle East some stability. And that stability required that the United States address the Arab world in terms other than cold-war politics or the interests of Israel. Otherwise the defeat of Iraq would simply usher in a new era of disorder. The warning that the newspaper *al-Akhbar* issued as the war ended rang with the lessons of the latter half of the twentieth century: "If it [the Palestinian issue] remains unsolved, then twenty Saddams, not one Saddam, will appear, and the region will be marked by instability and coups."†

In the aftermath of the war, Secretary of State James Baker went on the road to put together the Middle East peace talks that opened in Madrid on October 30, 1991. Meeting the demands of both the Israelis and the Arabs that went back to 1967, the complex set of meetings opened with an international conference—an Arab demand—and then reconvened in Washington for face-to-face talks between Israel and individual Arab countries—an Israeli demand. In the first round, Israel met with the confrontation states of Syria, Lebanon, and Jordan. With the PLO dealt out by Israel's insistence and its own mistake in backing Saddam Hussein, the Palestinians were included as part of the joint Jordanian-Palestinian delegation envisioned by Jimmy Carter in 1977 and pursued by King Hussein during the mid-1980s. These talks were subsequently followed by a third round in Moscow that set a schedule for further talks on regional problems that would include most of the other Arab states as well as nations from Europe and Asia. In February, the principle parties were back in Washington. So the process continued.

These sets of talks, regardless of their ultimate outcome, established a new American mode for dealing with the Middle East. In structure, they followed the pattern set in the Gulf War in which

---

* Conversation with author, July 6, 1991.
† Quoted in *New York Times*, March 1, 1991.

the United States addressed both Arab unity and Arab division. And they confronted the specific issues of the Middle East. Out of these new attitudes and new policies, the Arabs as well as Israel were acknowledged as part of the region. They as well as Israel were recognized as having a claim on its resources, and they as well as Israel were conceded the right to secure borders. Furthermore, by bringing Israel into the same room with representatives from the West Bank and Gaza and indicating that the Palestinians outside the occupied territories had a legitimate role in regional discussions on the refugee problem, the United States put the Palestinian issue on the agenda at a time it had reached a crisis.

The Palestinian issue, always extremely difficult, had by the early 1990s become even more so. The political changes that began cascading over the Soviet Union in 1988 freed Russian Jews to immigrate to Israel. They came by the thousands, bringing to Israel the additional population it had so long sought to counter the demographics of the Arabs.* For the Likud government, the Soviet exodus delivered to Israel the population needed to establish a large Jewish presence in the occupied territories which they saw as eventually securing for Greater Israel the Biblical lands of Samaria and Judea. Yet if Israel annexed the occupied territories, as many of the Likud's supporters demanded, then the whole formula for peace established in 1967 by United Nations Resolution 242 and reaffirmed in 1973 by Resolution 338 would be gutted.

The issue of Arab rights to Arab lands, birthed in the loss of Palestine and concentrated in the lost lands of 1967, has fueled Arab passions since 1948. Territory is important for its land value and for satisfying the emotional needs of a people whose identity is attached to specific locations. But equally important for the Arabs is the symbol that the occupied territories provide concerning both Western intentions toward the Arab world and Israel's privileged relationship with the United States. The occupied territories are in essence the litmus test of American tolerance of Israeli expansionism.

In the fall of 1991, the Bush administration, capitalizing on the deep splits in public opinion in Israel and American Judaism and growing hostility to foreign aid on the part of U.S. taxpayers,

---

* Three hundred and eighty thousand Russian Jews arrived in Israel between 1989 and 1991. Another 600,000 are expected in the period 1992 to 1995.

challenged Israel's policy of increasing Jewish population on the West Bank and in Gaza. The president announced that his support of $10 billion in loan guarantees to build housing for Israel's Russian immigrants would hinge on the cessation of settlement activity in the occupied territories. The president, as the chief of foreign policy, backed by some influential members of Congress, directly confronted Israel over an issue judged contrary to the interests of the United States and the region.

The United States learned in the Gulf War that American policy, always removed from the political, economic, and societal problems of the Arab world, no longer served either the Arabs or Israel. There are approximately eighty million Arabs of the *mashriq*. Vital American interests are there, both economic and geographic. And there is always the danger of war, a war that could engulf the whole region in death and destruction delivered by chemical, biological, and nuclear weapons.

Balancing American foreign policy in the Middle East to address the problems and concerns of the Arabs does not mean deserting Israel. The intertwining of those countries over the last four and a half decades morally commits the United States to the survival of pre-1967 Israel. But at the same time, it is not the obligation of the United States to continue to promote Israel's interests and ambitions to the detriment of its own interests in the Arab world. Whether the United States will continue to nurture a closer relationship with the Arabs remains to be seen. If the various facets of Israel's American constituency again coalesce, the pressure on domestic politics could become irresistible. There is also the very real possibility that the United States will revert to the counterproductive behavior of the past in response to challenges from the Arabs themselves. That threat looms on the horizon in the form of Islamic fundamentalism.

The United States stands on the threshold of another of those great misunderstandings that have so crippled its position in the Arab world. Islamic fundamentalism is on the rise in both the *maghrib* and the *mashriq*. Algeria was on the way to electing an Islamic government in January 1992 when the process was blocked by a coup by the armed forces. In Egypt, the Muslim Brotherhood commands a growing following. Islamic fundamentalists hold 40 percent of the seats in the Jordanian parliament. The House of Saud, the great defender of Islamic purity, is under attack from its own Wahhabi extremists. And in the Palestinian Intifadah, the Islamic fundamentalists are challenging both the moderate leadership of the territories and the PLO. As fundamentalist rhetoric screams against the West, it raises in the United States the bitter memories of the Iranian Revolution and the painful experiences of Lebanon. The temptation is to go on the offensive, to support and arm those regimes under attack from the traditionalists. But the United States must stand back. Islamic fundamentalism is an issue of the Arab world, one that profoundly touches the Arabs' divisions and their unity.

The furious and malignant anti-Westernism of the Islamic fundamentalists is in part an expression of the Arab world's rage at itself. It is in certain respects an outpouring of Arab agony over what is regarded as cultural surrender to the West. From this standpoint, Islamic fundamentalism is a weapon with which a people who feel they have been overpowered by the West for almost three centuries try to strike back. In defense of their greatly damaged sense of self-esteem, the Arabs are attempting to prove that their institutions, their way of life, and in essence their whole culture is not inferior to that of the West.

While Islamic fundamentalism flails at the West, it also assaults contemporary Arab life, striking at the divisions of Arab society. The Arab world as much as any other major geographic and cultural region in the world has been bombarded by the swiftly changing twentieth century. Population has relentlessly increased, causing cities to explode, which in turn has upset the comfortable networks of families that traditionally ran them. Concurrently, the availability of education released many of the middle and lower middle classes from the curse of political impotence, giving them a voice with which to express new convictions, grievances, and hopes. They became the Gamal Abdul Nassers and the Hafiz Assads of the modernizing Arab world. As a result, an enormous gap has developed between the traditional leaders and this new elite on the one hand and between the new elite and the masses on the other. Their conflict is one of identity more than politics. It is identity expressed in terms of the proper relationship between the heritage of the past and the needs of the present. In the tension that surrounds them, all the tormenting questions explored by earlier generations as to whether Islam should define Arab politics or whether the future lies in secularism have once more surfaced. And once more, Arab society seems unable to find an answer.

In striking ways, the Arab world is suffering some of the same social tensions that Mecca suffered at the time of Mûhammed. As in seventh-century Arabia, the rapid growth of commerce and a money economy especially since the 1970s has widened the chasm between the rich and the poor and between the influential and their dependents. New wealth has led to new life-styles that break with the past. The kinship of money supplants that of blood in a milieu in which money and power measure the man. It is all in contradiction to the values Mûhammed laid down for Islamic society.

Mûhammed taught that the pure man was a grateful man who prayed to God for the forgiveness of sin, helped his fellowman, avoided all forms of cheating, led a chaste life, and cleansed himself of the love of wealth. This was Islam—the surrender to God. Those originally drawn to it were men who resented their inferior positions compared to those at the top of the social order.

In the 1980s, Islam became the language of political discourse. Its powerful words denounce Western power and influence, those subservient to Western influence, those governments regarded as corrupt, and society generally, which seems to have lost its moral principles and its direction. To those lost in the present, Islam promises an answer, no matter how imperfect, to the complicated problems of a stagnated society. It calls to men shut out of the political process by the new elites, and it connects the confused and uncertain to the traditions of the past and to the glories of the Arabs.

"To regard Islamic fundamentalism as purely reactionary would be false. For there is at work in it also a praiseworthy constructive endeavor to build a modern society on the basis of justice and humanity, as an extrapolation from the best values that have been enshrined in the tradition from the past. It represents in part a determination to sweep aside the degeneration into which Arab society has fallen, the essentially unprincipled social opportunism interlaced with individual corruption; to get back to a basis for society of accepted moral standards and integrated vision, and to go forward to a programme of active implementation of popular goals by effectively organized corps of disciplined and devoted idealists."* This is Islamic fundamentalism at its best. At its worst, it is a repressive throwback to the past that refuses to come to terms with the present

---

* Mohammed Jalal Kishk, quoted in Ajami, *Arab Predicament*, pp. 60–61.

and expends its energy manning the barricades against the West.

There is a perpetual struggle among Arabs between those who look to Islam and the Arab world for their political culture and those who look to secular government with institutions modeled on those of the West. The secularists, who have been dominant in the twentieth century, have not succeeded in achieving either stability or prosperity. Thus Islamic fundamentalism is on the ascent in part because, having failed to eradicate their problems through modernization, many Arabs believe those problems can be relieved by returning to tradition. Which direction the religious revival in each of the various Arab states goes is anyone's guess. What is certain, though, is that if the United States attempts to confront Islamic fundamentalism militarily or denounces it as simply fanaticism and backwardness, it will only open further the already bleeding wound the Arabs feel the West has inflicted on them. Islamic fundamentalism is divisive, pitting those who are secularists and believe that the Arabs must break the chains of religion in order to modernize against those who see the salvation of Arab society in Islam. But in Islam there is also unity. And in the Arab world there is still a sense of oneness that on occasion transcends the reality of politics.

SELECTED BIBLIOGRAPHY

Abdullah of Jordan, King. *My Memoirs Completed: "al Takmilah."* London: Longman, 1978.

Abu-Lughod, Ibrahim, ed. *The Transformations of Palestine: Essays on the Origin and Development of the Arab-Israeli Conflict.* Evanston, Ill.: Northwestern University Press, 1987.

Ajami, Fouad. *The Arab Predicament: Arab Political Thought and Practice Since 1967.* Cambridge, England: Cambridge University Press, 1981.

———. "Stress in the Arab Triangle." *Foreign Policy*, Winter 1977–78, pp. 90–108.

———. "The Struggle for Egypt's Soul." *Foreign Policy*, Summer 1979, pp. 3–30.

———. "The Summer of Arab Discontent." *Foreign Affairs*, Winter 1990–91, pp. 1–20.

Algosaibi, Ghazi A. *Arabian Essays.* London: Kegan Paul International, 1982.

Antonius, George. *The Arab Awakening*. Beirut: Khayat, 1955.

Baker, Randall. *King Husain and the Kingdom of Hejaz*. New York: Oleander Press, 1979.

Beling, Willard A. *The Middle East: Quest for an American Policy*. Albany: State University of New York Press, 1972.

Bill, James A., and Carl Leiden. *Politics in the Middle East*. Boston: Little, Brown, 1984.

Brand, Laurie A. *Palestinians in the Arab World: Institution Building and the Search for a State*. New York: Columbia University Press, 1988.

Carter, Jimmy. *The Blood of Abraham*. Boston: Houghton Mifflin, 1985.

Chubin, Shahram, and Charles Tripp. *Iran and Iraq at War*. Boulder, Colo.: Westview Press, 1988.

Cobban, Helena. *The Palestinian Liberation Organization: People, Power, and Politics*. Cambridge, England: Cambridge University Press, 1984.

Cooley, John K. *Green March, Black September: The Story of the Palestinian Arabs*. London: Frank Cass, 1973.

Duri, A. A. *The Historical Formation of the Arab Nation: A Study in Identity and Consciousness*. London: Croom Helm, 1987.

Esposito, John L. *Islam and Politics*. Syracuse: Syracuse University Press, 1984.

Eveland, William Crane. *Ropes of Sand: America's Failure in the Middle East*. New York: Norton, 1980.

Fagan, Brian M. *Return to Babylon: Travelers, Archaeologists, and Monuments in Mesopotamia*. Boston: Little, Brown, 1979.

Fernea, Elizabeth Warnock. *Guests of the Sheik: An Ethnography of an Iraqi Village*. Garden City, N.Y.: Anchor Books, 1969.

Friedman, Thomas L. *From Beirut to Jerusalem*. New York: Farrar, Straus & Giroux, 1989.

Fuhrman, Peter. "Lose a Son, Drive a Car." *Forbes Magazine* (December 11, 1989): 256–64.

Gershoni, Israel, and James P. Jankowski. *Egypt, Islam and the Arabs: The Search for Egyptian Nationhood, 1900–1930*. New York: Oxford University Press, 1986.

Hameed, Mazher A. *Arabia Imperiled: The Security Imperatives of the Arab Gulf States*. Washington, D.C.: Middle East Assessment Group, 1986.

Heikel, Mohamed. *Autumn of Fury: The Assassination of Sadat*. New York: Random House, 1983.

Helms, Christine Moss. *Iraq: Eastern Flank of the Arab World*. Washington, D.C.: Brookings Institution, 1984.

Hirst, David, and Irene Beeson. *Sadat*. London: Faber & Faber, 1981.

Hitti, Philip K. *Capital Cities of Arab Islam*. Minneapolis: University of Minnesota Press, 1973.

———. *Islam: A Way of Life*. Minneapolis: University of Minnesota Press, 1970.

Hodgson, Marshall G. S. *The Venture of Islam: Conscience and History in a World Civilization*, Vol. 1. Chicago: University of Chicago Press, 1974.

Holden, David. "At Cross Purposes in the Sands of Yemen." *Reporter* (February 14, 1963): 37–41.

Hourani, Albert. *Arabic Thought in the Liberal Age*. London: Oxford University Press, 1970.

———. *Europe and the Middle East*. Berkeley: University of California Press, 1980.

———. *A History of the Arab Peoples*. Cambridge: Belknap Press of Harvard University Press, 1991.

Hussein ibn Talal, King. "Reflections on an Epilogue: Al-Takmilah to the Memoirs of King Abdullah ibn Al-Hussein." *Middle East Journal*, Winter 1978, pp. 79–86.

Kedar, Benjamin Z. *Crusade and Mission: European Approaches to the Muslims*. Princeton, N.J.: Princeton University Press, 1984.

Kent, Marian, ed. *The Great Powers and the End of the Ottoman Empire.* London: Allen & Unwin, 1984.

Kerr, Malcolm. *The Arab Cold War.* London: Oxford University Press, 1971.

Kessler, Martha Neff. *Syria: Fragile Mosaic of Power.* Washington, D.C.: National Defense University Press, 1987.

Khalidi, Rashid. *Under Siege: PLO Decision-making During the 1982 War.* New York: Columbia University Press, 1986.

Khalidi, Walid. *Before Their Diaspora.* Washington, D.C.: Institute for Palestine Studies, 1984.

al-Khalil, Samir. *The Monument: Art, Vulgarity and Responsibility in Iraq.* Berkeley: University of California Press, 1991.

———. *Republic of Fear: The Inside Story of Saddam's Iraq.* New York: Pantheon, 1989.

Kissinger, Henry. *Years of Upheaval.* Boston: Little, Brown, 1982.

Kraft, Joseph. "Letter From Saudi Arabia." *The New Yorker* (July 4, 1983): 41–59.

Lawrence, T. E. *Seven Pillars of Wisdom.* Garden City, N.Y.: Garden City Publishing, 1938.

Lewis, Bernard, ed. *Islam and the Arab World: Faith, People, Culture.* New York: Alfred A. Knopf, 1976.

———. *The Political Language of Islam.* Chicago: University of Chicago Press, 1988.

———. "The Roots of Muslim Rage." *Atlantic Monthly*, September 1990.

Lippman, Thomas W. *Egypt After Nasser: Sadat, Peace and the Mirage of Prosperity.* New York: Paragon House, 1989.

Mackey, Sandra. *The Saudis: Inside the Desert Kingdom.* Boston: Houghton Mifflin, 1987.

Mansfield, Peter. *The Arabs.* Middlesex, England: Pelican, 1985.

Marr, Phoebe. *The Modern History of Iraq.* Boulder, Colo.: Westview Press, 1985.

————. "Iraq's Uncertain Future." *Current History*, January 1991, pp. 1–4, 39–42.

Miller, Judith, and Laurie Mylroie. *Saddam Hussein and the Crisis in the Gulf*. New York: Times Books, 1991.

Morris, Benny. *The Birth of the Palestine Refugee Problem 1947–1949*. Cambridge, England: Cambridge University Press, 1987.

Newhouse, John. "Monarch." *The New Yorker* (September 19, 1983): 49–120.

Nutting, Anthony. *Nasser*. New York: Dutton, 1972.

Patai, Raphael. *The Arab Mind*. Rev. ed. New York: Charles Scribner's Sons, 1983.

Polk, William R. *The Arab World Today*. Cambridge: Harvard University Press, 1991.

Quandt, William. *Camp David: Peacemaking and Politics*. Washington, D.C.: Brookings Institute, 1986.

Quandt, William B., Fuad Jabber, and Ann Mosely Lesch. *Decade of Decisions: American Policy Toward the Arab-Israeli Conflict, 1967–1976*. Berkeley: University of California Press, 1977.

————. *The Politics of Palestinian Nationalism*. Berkeley: University of California Press, 1973.

Rabinovich, Itamar. *The War for Lebanon, 1970–1985*. Ithaca, N.Y.: Cornell University Press, 1985.

Reed, Stanley. "Syria's Assad: His Power and His Plan." *The New York Times Magazine* (February 19, 1984): 42–64.

el-Sadat, Anwar. *In Search of Identity: An Autobiography*. New York: Harper & Row, 1978.

Safran, Nadav. *Egypt in Search of Political Community*. Cambridge: Harvard University Press, 1961.

————. *From War to War: The Arab-Israeli Confrontation 1948–67*. New York: Pegasus, 1969.

Sayigh, Rosemary. *Palestinians: From Peasants to Revolutionaries*. London: Zed Books, 1979.

Sciolino, Elaine. "The Big Brother: Iraq Under Saddam Hussein." *The New York Times Magazine* (February 3, 1985): 16–34.

Seale, Patrick. *Asad: The Struggle for the Middle East.* Berkeley: University of California Press, 1988.

Sheehan, Edward R. F. "In the Flaming Streets of Amman." *The New York Times Magazine* (September 27, 1970): 22–26.

Shlaim, Avi. *Collusion Across the Jordan: King Abdullah, the Zionist Movement, and the Partition of Palestine.* New York: Columbia University Press, 1988.

Sinai, Anne, and Allen Pollack, eds. *The Hashemite Kingdom of Jordan and the West Bank.* New York: American Academic Association for Peace, 1977.

Snow, Peter. *Hussein: A Biography.* Washington, D.C.: Robert B. Luce, 1972.

Stein, Kenneth. *The Land Question in Palestine 1917–1936.* Chapel Hill, N.C.: University of North Carolina Press, 1984.

Stephens, Robert. *Nasser: A Political Biography.* London: Allen Lane/ Penguin, 1971.

Tibawi, A. L. "Visions of the Return." *Middle East Journal* 17 (Late Autumn 1963): 507–26.

Vatikiotis, P. J. *The History of Egypt.* Baltimore: Johns Hopkins University Press, 1980.

———. *Nasser and His Generation.* New York: St. Martin's Press, 1978.

Viorst, Milton. "The House of Hashem." *The New Yorker* (January 7, 1991): 32–52.

Walker, Tony, and Andrew Gowers. *Behind the Myth: Yasser Arafat and the Palestinian Revolution.* London: W. H. Allen, 1991.

Wilson, Mary C. *King Abdullah, Britain and the Making of Jordan.* Cambridge, England: Cambridge University Press, 1987.

Wright, Claudia. "Iraq—New Power in the Middle East." *Foreign Affairs* (Winter 1979): pp. 257–77.

———. "Iraq." *Atlantic* (April 1979): pp. 12–26.

Wright, Robin. *In the Name of God: The Khomeini Decade*. New York: Simon & Schuster, 1989.

———. *Sacred Rage: The Wrath of Militant Islam*. New York: Simon & Schuster, 1986.

THE
BRITISH MANDATE
OF PALESTINE
1922-48

N

Mediterranean Sea

JERUSALEM

PALESTINE

Dead Sea

EGYPT

SUEZ

SINAI PENINSULA

Jordan River

LEBANON

DAMASCUS

SYRIA

TRANS-JORDAN

Gulf of Suez

Gulf of Aqaba

SAUDI ARABIA

Red Sea

Mideast at close
of 1967 war

Occupied
by Israel

LEBANON

SYRIA

ISRAEL

GOLAN
HEIGHTS

Mediterranean
Sea

Jerusalem

Dead
Sea

GAZA STRIP

WEST
BANK

Suez
Canal

EGYPT

JORDAN

SINAI
PENINSULA

SAUDI
ARABIA

Miles

0   50

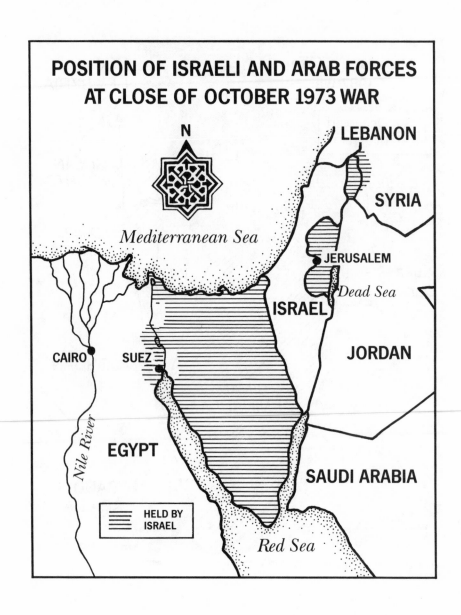

POSITION OF ISRAELI AND ARAB FORCES AT CLOSE OF OCTOBER 1973 WAR

N

Mediterranean Sea

LEBANON

SYRIA

JERUSALEM

Dead Sea

ISRAEL

JORDAN

CAIRO

SUEZ

EGYPT

Nile River

SAUDI ARABIA

HELD BY ISRAEL

Red Sea

TURKEY
ZAKHU
SINJAR
DAHUK
MOSUL
ARBIL
IRAN
SYRIA
KIRKUK
SULAMINIYAH
Euphrates River
Tigris River
MANDALI
BAGHDAD
KARBALA
AMARAH
JORDAN
AL-NAJAF
NAZIRIAH
BASRA
SAUDI ARABIA
KUWAIT
NEUTRAL ZONE

N

MAJOR GROUPS

☰ SUNNI ARAB
⧄ SUNNI KURD
Ⅲ SHI I ARAB
⠿ SUNNI ARAB & SUNNI KURD
▨ SUNNI ARAB & SHI I ARAB

MINOR GROUPS

† CHRISTIAN ▲ YAZIDI ✡ JEWISH
△ TURCOMAN ● SABIAN ○ IRANIAN

DISTRIBUTION OF ETHNIC AND
RELIGIOUS GROUPS IN IRAQ

INDEX

Modernists, 148
Modernization, 81, 93, 327–28, 408
Mohieddin, Khalid, 270
Mongols, 41, 60, 61, 73–74, 74n, 277, 313–14
Moors, 41, 60
Morality, 79
Morgan, John Pierpont, 163
Morocco, 60
Moses, 100
Moshavahs, 112
Mosques, 59–60
Mosul, 92, 314, 317
Mountain, The (Lebanon), 92–93, 278
Mount Nebo, 186
Mount of Olives, 59, 178
Mount Scopus, 59, 137, 178
Moyne, Lord Walter, 129
Muawiyah, Caliph, 52, 54
Mubarak, Hosni, 273–74, 304, 341, 342, 346, 371
Muhammed (Abu al-Qasim Muhammed ibn Abdullah ibn Abd al-Muttalib ibn Hashim, Prophet), 35–39, 41–42, 43, 48–49, 59, 85, 187, 221, 409
party of, 50, 51
Muhammed Ali, Viceroy of Egypt, 157, 161, 165, 277
Muir, Sir William, 3
Mukhabarat, 182, 332, 333, 342
Muna, Princess, 194n, 203
Muntazari, Hussein Ali, 333
Muqtadir, Caliph al-, 56
Musa (nurse), 235
Musallah, Dr. Sami, 377
Muslim Brotherhood (Ikhwan al-Muslimin), 94–95, 134, 166, 167, 215, 272, 283n, 285–86, 288–91, 290n, 307, 350, 407
Muslims, 6, 36, 37, 99n
army, 42–43, 45, 46
in Palestine, 101–2, 105
in Syria, 280
See also Islam

Muslim World League, 67
Mussolini, 5, 162
Mustafa Nahas Pasha, 162–63
Mutanabbi, al- (poet), 81

N

Nabataeans, 20, 186
Nablus, 106, 120, 190, 201, 213, 372
Naguib, Gen. Muhammed, 165
Nahas, Mustafa, 247
Nahlawi, Lt. Col. Abdul Karim, 284
Naif, Prince of Jordan, 193–94
Najaf, 51n, 54, 315, 332, 344
Najran, 229
Napoleon Bonaparte, 76–77, 80, 154, 249
Nashashibis, 110
Nasrat, Abd al-Karim, 325
Nasser, Gamal Abdul, 7–8, 13, 29, 70, 95, 153, 157, 158, 160–83, 184, 185, 195–98, 200–1, 202, 207–8, 225–32, 238–39, 246–53, 254, 269, 283, 284, 285, 295, 300, 319–20, 322, 324, 343, 350, 353, 354, 355, 356, 358, 360, 361, 365, 375, 377, 384–86, 387, 399
Nasserism and Nasserites, 94, 171, 173, 182–83, 227, 250, 253, 272, 285, 322, 324
Nation-state
and divisions vs. unity, 147–49
vs. tribe and family, 13–14, 31, 99
Naziriah, 226
Nazism and Nazis, 7, 121, 130, 136
-Arab collaboration, 319n
death camps, 125, 126, 382
Nebuchadnezzar, 313, 338–39
Negev, 139, 356
Nehru, 8, 167, 169
Nehru, Jawaharlal, 167
Nejd, 221, 222, 223
Neolithic Age, 19

To Mattie With Love and
God's Blessings —

From the ByKota Sunday
School Class —

Christmas 1959

THIS WAY, PLEASE

ROY O. McCLAIN

This Way, Please

FACING LIFE'S CROSSROADS

"I AM THE WAY. . . ." Jesus Christ

FLEMING H. REVELL COMPANY

LIBRARY OF CONGRESS CATALOG CARD NUMBER: 57-13150

Westwood, New Jersey
London E.C.4—29 Ludgate Hill
Glasgow C.2—229 Bothwell Street

To

TWO BOYS AND ONE GIRL
WITHOUT WHOM MY JOURNEY
ON THE WAY WOULD
BE INCOMPLETE

FOREWORD

In this day when one believes that happiness can be prescribed by physicians and dispensed by druggists—a day trying to fight its way to peace, buy its way to eternity, drink its way to pleasure, and filibuster its case before God, the truth needs to be told in forthright clarity. To expect serenity of soul amidst man's designed chaos, to believe that Christian faith can be had in ten easy lessons is to ignore the cross-centered truth which has been the genius of Christianity for twenty centuries. The Way is not by cushions but via crosses.

Christ's clear-cut commands leave no doubt about the fact that mankind does not need salve but surgery; his is not a mild infection but a fatal malignancy. Instead of rebirth, millions are content with reform; rather than being washed white, whitewashing is available in discounted doses. Still remains that unchangeable premise: either He must be God of all or He will not be God at all! This severe "either-or" strikes today's personality as cruelly arbitrary. Man prefers a middle ground on which there is just enough religion to provide a sense of security.

While old systems are crumbling beneath the march of masses, while "wild tongues that have not Thee in awe" are making their bid for place and power, it is imperative that

Christianity look to its ramparts separating substance from shadow. More than duty and expediency are at stake: actually, survival is the issue!

Alternate routes to superlative living are too clearly delineated; Jesus dogmatically contended that there was but one Way. In effect He said, turn right and go straight! If that Way is marked out a bit more clearly by these words, if it is interpreted as an infectious adventure, filled with wonderful danger, rife with soul-rocking surprises, contagious enthusiasm, and replete with song and sacrifice, then this purpose will have been accomplished.

CONTENTS

INTRODUCTION

"Of making many books there is no end." So says Ecclesiastes, the Preacher. "Why don't you write a book?" asked someone of a friend. "I'd rather you would ask me that, than why I *did* write a book," the friend replied.

Not everyone can write a book. Not everyone should. But Roy McClain definitely belongs among those who should write not only a book, but many books. His background eminently qualifies him to discuss the questions he raises in this volume. Raised on a farm, a lover of nature, educated in Baptist colleges and seminaries, a teaching fellow in seminary for a time, a chaplain in the armed forces in World War II, pastor of churches in the South, he is now preaching in the great First Baptist Church of Atlanta, Georgia. He came to this Church when it was predicted that it had seen its best days and was on the way out; people were leaving it to join churches in their own neighborhoods. Dr. McClain's challenging message, his man-to-man approach to the meaning of the Gospel of Christ has turned the tide. The reports show that for more than four years, during his pastorate, there has been an average of one hundred additions to the membership *per month*.

In this book, he deals with many phases of Christian life and church life. The second part of the book brings to the front the one great need of this and any other age in the effort to propagate the Gospel: Dr. McClain insists, and rightly so, that the real trouble with the church today is its *lack of genuine commitment to Christ.* The greatest difficulty the pastor faces in modern America is the complacency and indifference of his church members.

Dr. McClain is free from tradition and dictation from any group or organization. He has a call from God and a message from God which he delivers lovingly but fearlessly. He has a world vision and a world spirit. He sees Christ as the Saviour of the world, including all men and all races. Young pastors and older ones, too, will eagerly read the challenging chapters of this book, and from it receive courage and inspiration to face anew the problems which beset us in an hour when we cannot sing with any real truthfulness, "We are not divided, all one body we." But Dr. McClain makes an appeal to those who love Christ and who love lost men and women to unite in carrying the saving Gospel to all men.

Third Baptist Church,   C. Oscar Johnson
St. Louis, Mo.

PART ONE

The Way Defined

1

THE STRANGER OF GALILEE

THEY CALLED HIM a stranger and rightly so—this Man of Galilee. He undertook the strangest tasks in the strangest way, but in the process He changed the world. One day I met Him in a personal encounter, which changed me; ever since, life has been one inspiring adventure. The path this Stranger follows and the pace He sets is one of rigorous discipline: a demanding pace, exacting, compensating, awe-inspiring. Still I love Him and consider it an esteemed privilege to introduce my Friend through the medium of these words. But I warn the reader: once you encounter Him, you will never be the same. He has a captivating way about Him, getting into your heart if you don't stand guard; not by intrusive invasion but through the portal of unmotivated love. His is an infectious vitality; His magnetic spirit and zest for living will totally disarm you.

Why did they call Him a stranger, this Man whose name is known to millions, by whom time is dated and in whose memory shrines of time are erected? A name of household familiarity—a stranger? Indeed! Twenty centuries have not bridged the chasm 'twixt His uniqueness and our apathetic torpor. The prevailing disenchantment about Him then, as well as now, obscured His real nature. Let me tell you of His strangeness.

Strange forces were fused in this Man of Galilee—forces almost contradictory in nature. Tributaries of fresh virtue flowed into a torrent of personal force. After a few minutes with Him one felt the quality of His compassion. His was more than solicitous pity; He entered into their grief. All of what He said and most of what He did proved His overflowing heart. Such rapport of spirit with the outcasts of life fell like April's dew on the roots of violets, an embarrassing contrast to the insensitive religionists of His day whose cutting edge had been dulled by accommodation and easy conformation. His words, "Come unto me . . ." fell with equal charity on the ears of goat sellers and dissipated womankind—women who, too early in life, had bartered with unholy hands; fell, too, on hardened soldiers and cynical religionists, yet His empathic spirit found no bounds in race or economic preferment. Jesus walked in every man's shoes, the pinch of strictures thus enhancing His universal Saviourhood. Little wonder people wanted to be around Him! Wherever a face reflects the dimension of care, that face will attract others. I think people liked Him, and liked Him immensely! Wearing the recommendation of mercy, His face reflected what was inside of Him. Surely this ring of the real in Him magnetized those who were accustomed to the tinkling symbols of religion; yet, let it be known that this ring of the real, like a sharp sword, cut through the fat into the heart of the truth making inevitable the crucifixion.

Herein is the divine right of Jesus: His loving compassion could not be channeled through human systems, nor stymied by the barriers of creed, class, or culture. In the veiled breast of a Syrophoenician woman lurked a cord of hope just as

valid as the hope of the apostles. The Centurion, with all his
shining brass, received no more preferential treatment at the
hands of Jesus than did a nameless woman who touched the
hem of His garment. This is the peerless forte of Christianity:
every race, every kind came within the province of His love
and care. What a sad fact that this truth is often obscured
by politically inclined opportunists and pseudo-religionists
who, while promoting a "one-world" gospel, practice individual isolationism, fear and demagoguery! Perversion of
His universalism strikes at the taproot of His soul. If anyone
is excluded from the great supper, then everyone is excluded.
Jesus never sits as host to a select fraternity of "do-gooders."
The sooner our world admits this indispensable dictum—the
better.

Nor did His compassion blind Him to man's waywardness.
But He was able to see potential saint in debased sinner! This
facet not only disclosed the quality of His compassion but
also its motive power. Here was no soft sympathy for intentional poverty, no weak-willed itinerant with heart rent by
the throes of ill fortune. His was a positive, genuine concern
not so much for man's losses as for man's lacks. He looked
with shame on hearts of stone that could not melt at the sight
of human anguish. Scorning any pleasure that would give
others pain, He lived out His days in selfless absorption. "A
thousand million lives are his who carries the world in his
sympathies," wrote James Russell Lowell,[1] after having caught
something of the contagion of His spirit. Was there ever a
magnanimous heart that wasn't at the same time tender and
compassionate? But how He has been misread! His genuine,
compassionate mercy has been interpreted as morose despondency—as inevitability in martyrdom, speaking of some
fatal, deterministic rendezvous with death. Not so! Compas-

[1] Charles L. Wallis, *A Treasury of Sermon Illustrations* (Nashville,
Abingdon Press, 1950), p. 270.

sion welled from the spring of a vibrant forthrightness coupled to God's loving heart. That is why He could constrain irresistibly where other leaders could not persuade. He could kindle with ambition anyone who aspired to what the day before seemed inaccessible heights, while another would strive in vain to stir a somnolent mood to cope with the smallest obstacle. In the tenor of this mood one hears Abraham Lincoln say, "I am sorry for the man who can't feel the whip when it is laid on the other man's back."

Once the steamer has received its cargo, the ship's compass must be corrected, so as to neutralize the influence of iron cargo in the hold. Just so the role of compassion in human life: it draws the needle of mercy to the vortex of need, and readjusts the aberrations of mind and soul.

William James told of a Russian noblewoman who wept over the imaginary hardships of certain characters in a theatrical production. There, in the precincts of easy imagination, she entered the travails of hero and heroine, while all the time, as she sat in cushioned splendor, her coachman, whom she might have helped, sat slowly freezing to death outside. Little wonder they called Jesus the Stranger of Galilee. He did the strangest things by becoming a part of other men's miseries. In the words of Oliver Wendell Holmes, He lived His life, for the

> . . . hearts that break and give no sign
> Save whitening lip and fading tresses.

But His was a compassion with teeth in it, sympathy with muscle. No preoccupied priest sauntering the road to Jericho in sophisticated detachment was He. Any effort to catch the mood of Jesus which does not reckon with this truth miserably fails to see the latitude of His great heart. While a little child felt secure in His lap, adults of double-standard lives fled before Him. Like the area of calm in the midst of a hurricane, the core of His compassion centered in typhonic resentments to evil. In the face of social injustice He erupted like a volcano so that few, if any, mistook His empathy for soft indulgence. His disdain for imitations, His indignance to sloth, His vehemence toward play-acting at godliness, His urgency of priorities, and His acute knowledge of human nature—all these made necessary His bastion of vigorous forthrightness. Never did He give the impression that He could prepare a diplomatic statement capable of satisfying both extremes of life. Nor did He practice the art of the tongue of diplomacy in the cheek of discretion.

Such a point of contrast between His life and ours is pointedly specific. There was no nod to approve earthly expediencies, no gesture of assent to the transactions of scheming men, no hand of endorsement to the forces that debase and defile. Our plight of winking at things questionable, walking with unholy men, and sitting in the seats of the scornful marks us as disciples unlike our Master. He, like Amos, denounced the sins of Israel in assiduous words. He spoke of Judgment Day, a day of distinction and separation. He spoke of His mission to bring swords and not peace—of a winnowing fan, an orchard-man's axe, pruning hooks, and a judge's sentence.

No facet more clearly reveals His true self than at the points where compromise was unthinkable. Just here the Damascus steel of His soul is revealed. The temptations in the wilderness found a stubborn, resistive spirit incapable of yielding. Not that He was so exclusively divine that these temptations were mock ritual; they were real to Him. His was no shadowboxing with an imaginative, elusive devil. Here was honest struggle fought out to its triumphant end.

Jesus knew that the wily art of conformity had shorn religion of its vitality, leaving its close-cropped head in the lap of ecclesiastical Delilahs. Religious birthrights were obtainable for a mess of expedient pottage. Life in His day was rife with political preferment, social palavering, religious idolatry, and bone-wearing burdens. Ephraim was wedded to idols, the wine was mixed with water, the cake half-baked and ". . . gray hairs were here and there upon him, yet he knew it not." Life had lost its lustre, and the spirit's cutting edge was dulled by faded vision. An acute consciousness of God was nonexistent. Now, compromise under these conditions was unthinkable to Jesus. Charged by these forces, He steadfastly undertook His mission, a mission demanding not reform but rebirth, not whitewashing but being washed white, not change of pace but a complete about-face. Yielding anywhere would have weakened the cords that bound His stout heart to the task of reconciling man to God.

Today the curse of compromise is shearing us of spiritual power. What with modified convictions, yielded to social pressures, and corroded of courage; visions pruned to the bare nub of cautious realism; conscience seared by repetitious monotony; prayers trimmed by ritualistic esthetics; wrong rationalized to the point of indulgent absurdity; self given the benefit of the doubt at every junction, a palimpsest of lacquered intention over the unregenerate heart—all this but vaguely resembles the original copy of this Stranger of Galilee. To ask one today, "Is it Christian?" hardly activates conversation. To ask, "Is it Christlike?" may introduce a mood of remorse.

When Jesus entered His public ministry, the sores of Roman occupation were well festered. In fact, scars had accumulated from many a conquering army through this bridgeway of Palestine. The stench of a defiling Antiochus Epiphanes lingered in the nostrils of devout Jews while dreams of Jewish patriots to deliver their people from oppressive heels ran back to another Hebrew, Judas Maccabeus. Now this Jesus—was He not a likely candidate for this liberative challenge? A new Judas Maccabeus? So thought the rank and file. It becomes fanciful pastime to imagine what an army Jesus could have raised. Coupling His miraculous power with the forthrightness of command and disciplined rigor (and these in the mood of anguished prayers for deliverance) would have made recruiting easy. John the Baptist characterized by militant fervency did not stand alone in his expectation of a Coming One. The time was ripe, the door open.

Yet Jesus steadfastly and decisively refused this role. Satan's temptation to rule over the kingdoms of the earth is aptly understood when seen in the light of this challenge. Why did Jesus not accept it? Had not another young man, the son of Philip of Macedon, marched over most of the earth? Was entrenched Rome not a justifiable threat to monotheistic religion? In a word, could this cause not be considered "holy"? Hardly! Quite well Jesus conceded that His mission was not displacement of rulers but a call to battle on the fields of mind and soul. His armaments were not of steel and stone but sinews of faith and lancets of love. One more bloody battle—so what? Man's old game has produced no new results, just multiples of pain. Deliverance of one nation by techniques that defeat the common good of both is but re-enacting the time-worn idiom, "The end justifies the means." Thank God that the lure of conquerors with "holy" causes had no lure for the Stranger of Galilee! Among the reasons why many deserted Him was the fact that He fondled no swagger stick, walked in no ostentatious parades, and wore no uniforms with medals, hashmarks, and epaulets.

Do not misunderstand Him: He was no anemic effete who recoiled like a coward from an honest fight. Some have pulled Him out of the camps of real manhood into the orbits of a Lord Fauntleroy, wearing silks and satins in ascetic detachment, and have used Him as a refuge from weathering their own storms—these have dealt violently with a Man who stood His ground in the face of the foe with no thought of harrowing consequences. His admonition to turn the other cheek instead of striking revealed more flexibility of force than all the arguments of militarists. He knew that injury proceeded from hurt to hurt and that more quality of character was involved in sustaining the initial blow than in returning it. No, the fact that He wasn't a master sergeant does not bespeak His manliness or mission. Had He recruited a conglomerate army and waged a local skirmish, the last part of this point never could have been written: i.e., multimillions have followed Him.

Most of these disciples have marched since He became invisible. Think of it: a veritable host of soldiers following a general whom they have never seen! Who was the dreamer after all: Herod? Pilate? Annas? Certainly not this Man of Galilee! He turned out to be the practical realist after all, a fact still confounding infantile conceptions of reality. A ragged, few hundred from the hills of northern Palestine or multimillions from all over the world? How many are following Him today? Ah, this involves many estimates, but it is safe to say that several hundred millions serve this invisible Leader in the camps of His Kingdom in the middle of this twentieth century. And these—compared to all soldiers, sailors, marines, generals, and admirals combined of all time— make the latter look puny by comparison. Who recruits an army for Alexander the Great today? Are not Ptolemy's generals all dead? No torch is carried for Hannibal in this modern age nor is any menial task rendered in the name of Caesar. But with this Man Jesus it is a different picture. From all walks of life they come. Down dusty mountain trails of the Andes, across the broad boulevards of great metropolises, through the jungles of Sumatra to the plains of the West, marches this maze of militant, imperfect, generous, awe-inspiring humanity, a turbulent band called Christians. His privates (who come from the down-and-outs—the hordes of

"the great unwashed,") these are the untouchables so akin to
dust as destiny that a nexus with things holy seems absurd.
Yet they are there, a whole brigade of Nathanaels and
Marthas, of Philips and Andrews. These are the anonymous
masses who shoulder the housekeeping chores of an ever-increasing army wrought with pains of mass growth and commensurate mass contradictions; these whose names are known
mostly to God; these who aforetime were freighted with futility—these are the genius of the faith.

Though fewer in number, and far harder to reach, there
are the "up-and-outs," the prosperous, who have no consciousness of a need for God and the things of God. Some of these
are finding their places in the line behind this unseen General. To this preacher's way of thinking, the great mission
field of America consists right at this point. While the light
of community consciousness through slum clearance, community drives, local mission projects, is ever turned on the
down-and-outs, little is being said or done about the be-
hemoth-like growth of the near-rich, the pseudo-sophisticates,
who have not God in their conscience. These are the suburban
sinners—equidistant from the heart of town and the heart of
God! Their cushions and Cadillacs have given them a specious
security from ill fortune, doom, or death. When a devout
Christian disciple responds to a call to serve in such a modern
Sodom, the snare drums among the orthodox seldom, if ever,
beat; yet for one to go to Equatorial Africa elicits the highest
priority of virtue. Equatorial Africa may seem as a Brigadoon
of ease compared to some of the world-encrusted paganism
of a typical American suburban community. But when did the
intensity of difficulty become a detriment to those of the Way?
The challenge is but intensified.

There is another type of upper stratum which is supplying
personnel for this multitude of disciples: those who represent
the cream of the mental crop, Phi Beta Kappa Christians—

those who are ever learning and *are* coming to a knowledge of the truth. Five-talent soldiers, those who have a reason for the hope within them and know its nature; multilingual recruits who, in fine fettle and mental acumen, offer Christ and religious faith its intellectually respectable dimension. And all of these are not professional religionists. They are astrophysicists, medical researchers, aero-dynamicists, and teachers of philosophy. Like the young man at the Georgia Institute of Technology who, having made the highest scholastic average in the history of that educational institution, walked the aisles of Atlanta's First Baptist Church one morning to say, "My major is mathematics, but my mission in life is to be a full-time Christian." Such is the quality of these whom I prefer to call, "God's automatics."

Moreover, this invisible Leader has inspired more volunteers for hazardous duty than any other singular figure. This in no respect belittles the superhuman fortitude exemplified by many a serviceman on fields of battle. The ground at Thermopylae, Suribachi, the Argonne, and Okinawa was covered by men who spoke of valor, and gallantry in the face of death-duty. But I doubt if Suribachi with all of its banzai charges—and I was there—held any more courage per man than the five missionaries who were slain by the Aucua Indians of South America, or William Wallace, a medical missionary, who resisted the impertinences of wicked inquisitors in Communist China, and who suffered death at equally infamous hands. As a matter of fact, the way of the cross has always been a way of pain, and the steep ascent to heaven still is through "peril, toil, and pain."

He has no recruiting office for volunteers, yet as I write these lines our seminaries and colleges have thousands who, having heard the still small voice, are marching to His cadence. Last summer at Ridgecrest, that summer assembly area for religious youth, scores of high-browed, clean-faced lads responded to a call to follow Jesus wherever He led, and what is more, they are sticking to it with intelligent direction. There was no high-powered evangelism, no noxious emotional miasma; just a forthright, clearly-defined invitation to yield their whole lives to this Stranger of Galilee. There is no counterpart to this response in a single military institution the world over!

And the equally strange thing about it is that they have no battle cry, no Geronimo, no Banzai; instead, they are singing, "A Mighty Fortress Is Our God," "The Son of Man Goes Forth to War," "Am I a Soldier of the Cross?" They declare with Richard Gilder:

> If Jesus Christ is a man,—
>   And only a man,—I say
> That of all mankind I cleave to him,
>   And to him will I cleave alway.
>
> If Jesus Christ is a god,—
>   And the only God,—I swear
> I will follow Him through heaven and hell,
>   The earth, the sea, and the air! [2]

During the Second World War, Don Blanding, the poet laureate of Hawaii, in his little book, *Pilot Bails Out*, wrote these militant lines:

What did you see, Soldier? What did you see at war?
I saw such glory and horror as I've never seen before.
I saw men's hearts burned naked in red crucibles of pain.
I saw such godlike courage as I'll never see again.

What did you hear, Soldier? What did you hear at war?
I heard the prayers on lips of men who had never prayed before.

[2] Richard W. Gilder, "The Song of a Heathen," in Caroline M. Hill, ed., *The World's Great Religious Poetry* (New York, Macmillan Company, 1924), p. 323.

I heard men tell their very souls, confessing each dark stain.
I heard men speak the sacred things they will not speak again.

What did you eat, Soldier? What did you eat at war?
I ate the sour bread of fear, the acrid salt of gore.
My lips were burned with wine of hate, the scalding drink of Cain.
My tongue has known a bitter taste I would not taste again.

What did you think, Soldier? What did you think at war?
I thought, how strange we have not learned from wars that raged
before,
Except new ways of killing, new multiples of pain.
Is all the blood that men have shed, but blood shed all in vain?

What did you learn, Soldier? What did you learn at war?
I learned that we must learn sometime what was not learned
before,
That victories won on battlefields are victories won in vain
Unless in peace we kill the germs that breed new wars again.

What did you pray, Soldier? What did you pray at war?
I prayed that we might do the thing we have not done before;
That we might mobilize for peace . . . nor mobilize in vain.
Lest Christ and man be forced to climb stark Calvary again.[3]

One never gets the impression that anything Jesus thought or did was half-hearted. From one's initial introduction, He began to talk in totals, saying: "If any man come to me, and hate not his father, and mother, and wife, and children, and brethren, and sisters, yea, and his own life also, he cannot be my disciple." To a rationalizing, would-be follower He answered, "Let the dead bury their dead." And even went so far as to say, "He that is not with me is against me." What means this demanding totalitarian? What means this One who gives no alternative to complete self-renunciation? Not a single note

[3] Reprinted by permission of Dodd, Mead & Company from *Pilot Bails Out* by Don Blanding. Copyright © 1943 by Don Blanding.

of apology accompanied His saying that there was no other road to God than by Him.

Why such monopolistic designs on man? He readily admitted that God must be God of all, or He will not be God at all. Partial allegiance and seasonal devotions could never change the pagan world. People not only needed to be counted but also to count. Too, divided allegiance would but continue dual masters; one of the two must be slighted in the end. Nor could He ever convey the life of the Spirit to schizophrenic disciples, who were torn between duties of lesser loyalties and priorities of God. Poly-altars, submission in convenient varieties, doxologies of dollars: all spoke of the impossibility of serving two masters. In its natural state, human nature is so constituted as to follow some leader; if not God, then someone less than God. This fact was illustrated recently by the inmates of a Texas prison who elected a leader to speak and plan for them, even while confined by steel bars. I think God resents His creation's following a blind leader who is unfit for the role. At no place is God's zealous care more apparent than when Jesus made a complete bid for men's hearts. Yes, He sounded like a totalitarian! Still we readily admit that unless all life is under the sovereignty of His purpose, there will be no unity of effort, no serenity of soul.

It is right at the point of partial surrender that most of our modern tensions arise. What with dual standards, ulcer-induced fears; one eye on the barometer of God and the other on our own calculations; one foot in the camps of the redeemed and the other in pagan tents; little wonder we are distracted to the point of self-annihilation. Many eat His bread, but not many drink His cup. Cushions are far more expedient than crosses—and much less painful!

When my soul clears the fogbank away, I readily can see

that His demand that I give up all to follow Him was a great compliment. The fact that He had faith in my being able to do it compliments this weak ego to the point of actual effort. There's something about a hard task that arouses deep reserves of energy and determination. Never would He have suggested our doing something that was outside the province of possibility.

Responding to His demands in total allegiance is no acquiescence to doom. No scandal of Christianity is more defeating than the belief that the will of God is a type of enforced slavery, ascetic chains that bind man's initiative from free expression. The prayer, "Thy will be done," should be accompanied by delight in eager expectation. Some of the stuffy creeds of Christendom and its cloistered walls that confirm this erroneous impression are a far cry from the simple life of the Nazarene who shunned in His own day such artificiality. He refused to wear a cloak of ostentatious "holiness." One needs to look no further to find a good part of the reason as to why many young people have little interest in following this Stranger of Galilee. Many think Him to be too clerical, too antithetic to their natural loves and hates, too removed from the flow of common life. Here the clergy and the church at large must concede their guilt: that the words of Jesus should be disbelieved is to be expected; that many would have no natural appetite for things spiritual, that the church should fail to reach certain ones is a foregone conclusion; but that the life of Jesus should be considered trite is without any justification. He was no kill-joy then who thrived on mortification; nor is there any comfort in Him today for those who use Him to hide their own insecure, negative sublimations. Were He here today, such negative reasoning would receive less refuge than rebuke!

The strait and narrow way, though of rigid dimensions, still knows nothing of the psychological and religious strictures perpetrated on modern Christendom by some self-appointed watchdogs of orthodoxy. Even though such self-conjuring gets by in the name of religion, it never is justified to sail under the name of New Testament Christianity. Oh, there must be a difference between Christ's followers and unredeemed man-kind—a life of separateness without doubt, one that knows nothing of pharisaical detachment from the world of sin in which we are to be shining lights. If the spokesmen of God started talking more about what is "taken up" rather than about what is "given up," what a new day there would be for the Kingdom when this surrender is effected. The contagious words, ". . . be of good cheer; I have overcome the world," hardly sound like the monotoned chant of priestly liturgies.

Then something wonderful happens: as one yields to the persuasive Presence, a reciprocal response is immediate: God gives Himself completely. But never believe that God's giving is contingent upon man's yielding. His is no market-place bar-ter, nor an exchange in kind. If divine love were motivated, it would be but another edition of human love. His self-giving is part of His self-loving. That is why it is divine love. Oh, what comfort for us mortals: that any sacrifice made on man's part is always in the context of a nobler, completer sacrifice on God's part. Though He asks of me my all, He already has given Himself in completeness.

He is with me not only in the big moments of life where major decisions, decade-involving, are to be made, but also in the little moments where day-by-day routine events are in-volved—that level on which most of life is lived out. To exclude Him here would deal violently with His omnipres-ence. No finite set of priorities activate His attendant mercies. God is not erratically related to human events. In every con-dition involving human response He is there to guide and sustain.

Early one morning I was aroused by the plaintive nicker

of a palomino Shetland stallion in a field some distance from the house. During the hours of the night he had cut the main tendon in one back leg. When I found him, he was slowly bleeding to death. With expert help of a good veterinarian, we stitched, transfused, and finally placed his leg in a cast. Months of patient care saw the young stallion restored to full vigor without the slightest trace of a limp. To imply that I felt a nearness of God in an event so commonplace and mundane as a pony stable may seen to many as more naïveté than wisdom, but this much to me is clear: His nearness is not restricted to the pulpit, nor to the sacred precincts of crypt, cathedral, or chapel. If He is anywhere, He is everywhere, and if in anything and in any place, then in all things and in all places.

Just here I admit of a pronounced danger in things both great and small: awareness of His presence never permits the sin of presumption—that excessive familiarity with the divine. Constant handling of the sacred vessels must hold in balanced perspective one undeniable truth: man and God are not one; man's thoughts are not God's thoughts; and man must forever keep a respectable distance. No laxity of moral muscles is permitted on the supposition that His proximity is a thing of special license nor does His proximity permit one a special dispensation of indulgence. Actually, the exact opposite is the case!

This Stranger of Galilee said the worst things about sin, things which left no doubt as to which side He was on. He knew that sin was more than priestcraft stricturing human conduct, or more than a preacher's semantics enforcing unwilling adherence to staid theology by clothing his preachments in the presumed authority of "thus saith the Lord." Nor was it figments of the imagination like the negative feedback of psychological frustrations, fears, and guilt complexes. On this subject there was no shooting marbles of

ecclesiastical minutiae. Hear His definitions: Sin, in the teachings of Jesus, means *missing the mark*. There stands the
archer with bow drawn, then the arrow is released toward the
eye of the target. Instead of hitting the center, the arrow
shoots off in a leftward direction. So in life, the arrow of
self-determination is released and fails to hit God's target center—whatever contributes to that, that failure is sin. This
"eye" is nothing short of the prescribed purpose of God for
the individual's life, and failing this purpose, all other ex-
cellencies of one's nature notwithstanding, he fails all.

Moreover, sin to Jesus was *perversion of purpose*—life
thrown out of gear by majoring on minors, by the tail wagging
the dog of confused values. Jesus met many such people in
His daily walks: a young ruler given to mammon, a young
woman given to lust. Intentional leaving home in exchange for
the sordid pleasures of sin's specious freedom attests to per-
versions of divine purpose. Said a senior devil in bitter com-
plaint, "We work under a cruel handicap; nothing is naturally
on our side. Everything has to be twisted before it is of any
use to us."

To complete the trilogy of definitions, sin was the *rupture
of relationship*. Sin severs a filial bond between father and
son; fellowship is broken at the lifeline 'twixt man and God.
Of course, Jesus could stand and preach with sound authority
because He saw man severed from the source of life.

Now for centuries man has waged a campaign to soften the
tenor of these condemnations. He has sought soothing syn-
onyms to extract from "sin" its crudeness of sound. To call
black "black" today, produces a response of resentment. Many
prefer to call it "gray" or "off-white." The worst kind of sin
is consciousness of no sin; the worst effects: not poverty,
pain, and purposelessness, but dethroned reason, self-love,
low aims, and impoverished spirits. Let someone rise up to tell
this generation of libertines that there is more satisfaction in

resisting temptation than in committing the sin! "No man is compelled to evil; only his consent makes it his," reminds the preacher.

While His words about sin cut like a razor, they were suffused with kindness for sinners. Every "Thy sins be forgiven thee" was accompanied by a look of redeeming grace. Forever keeping sin and sinner in clear contradistinction, He was able to denounce one and direct the other. Whereas one stirred in Him a volatile indignation, the other elicited a Saviour's pity.

The primacy of His mission sent Him into the darkened alleys of the city, down rocky hillsides of sheep keepers, to cultivate His friendships among sinners for whom He was to die. Like a talisman impressed into the archives of history was this epithet He earned from contact with the least, the last, the lost: "Friend of sinners." Not a single honor graduate in the seminary at Jerusalem, with all of his medals of general excellence, rated such cosmic compliment as "friend of sinners." In eternity's hierarchy of values, this epithet takes precedence over every other summa cum laude. And what variety of sinners: a Judean visionary who wormed his way into the inner circle; a cold logician who became earth-bound by conventional proofs; two brothers who were propelled by a mother's vain ambition; a respectable sinner who "had it made" financially, yet whose generosity found expression only in a post-mortem expression; a haggard daughter of Israel who was caressed by multiple hands—these He lived to love, and died to save.

Little wonder they called Him the Stranger of Galilee.

2

IF I HAD BUT ONE DAY
TO LIVE

IF YOU KNEW this were your last day on earth, what would you do, say, and think? Such a question isn't quite as fanciful as it may sound. Indeed, today will be the last for many! Would the hours be filled with erratic fears, last-minute agreements, feverish debt adjustment, and stupefying regrets? Or, routine pleasures, a sense of purposeful resignation, and packing of one's grips for a friendly journey to a known destiny? If this were my last day I think I should like to do four things.

I would begin the day in communion with God. The role of right beginnings is difficult to exaggerate. Whether it be a horse, tightly reigned, waiting the thud of a paddock's release; the water skier, with angular tilt anticipating the initial moment to balance himself on top of the water; or a plane crowding its horsepower to leave the ground—beginnings are all important. This last day, as every day, should commence in the mood of prayerful communion—communion that places parentheses around the day for safekeeping. In a sense these first few moments are like the preface to the book

33

where an author sets forth his intention and offers a word of explanation as to how one should explore its contents. Begin the day with Christ, you need no other. Sir William Osler, as he spoke to the Yale student body, contended that what one does the first twenty minutes of the day sets the moral tone for the rest of his day. This art, like a tuning fork, sets the tenor of life in proper perspective so that one may go into his day suffused with heavenly presence like the fragrance of a *fleur d'amour*. This is the regimen by which great men have blocked their days off in "daytight compartments," and have not borrowed from tomorrow the interest that must be paid in advance. No hour is more consequential than the first hour; it must be shared with God to assure the right consequences for the remaining hours. In the province of a day lies all "the varieties and realities of your existence; the bliss of growth, the glory of action, the splendor of beauty; for yesterday is but a dream, and tomorrow is only a vision; but today well lived makes every yesterday a dream of happiness, and every tomorrow a vision of hope. Look well, therefore, to this day! Such is the salutation of the dawn." [1]

I am not thinking so much about formal worship but rather the quiet place of one's own choosing, whether in the corner of a garden, edge of a bedroom, or nook in an office, in which the heart begins its journey Godward. As the soul begins its informal projection toward God, the wires of life are lifted off the ground. Mind is dredged of all foul deposits left from yesterday and the tired preoccupations so uncomplimentary to the spirit of man. Dr. Johnson commented on man's harrowing circumstances, "Not by an ascendant planet, a predominating humor, but by the first book which they read, some early conversation which they have heard, or some accident which excited ardour and enthusiasm." [2] This initial activity in the

---

[1] A poem from Sanskrit in *A Way of Life*, by Sir William Osler.
[2] *Ibid.*, p. 18.

morning is best conceived as spontaneous outflow of life. To me this is real praying since there is no fumbling for words; no stage fright that accentuates a consciousness to be heard of men; and no ulterior desire to impress God with one's ecclesiastical—and often borrowed—rhetoric. Gilding a key doesn't make it unlock the door any better. Best that we leave off such erudite semantics so as to convey the core of our souls. As a matter of fact, it is often better not to speak at all; vertical thoughts are prayers and "there are moments when, whatever be the attitude of the body, the soul is on its knees."

The belief that our human conception of needs must be outlined in minutest detail and expressed in elaboration is also a misconception, since the thoughts moving us to prayer are easily transmitted to God's consciousness during this communion while the lips may vehicle only a meager minimum of gratitude and praise. Babbling voices profit little—other than implying one's superiority to God's knowledge. The deeper secrets of the heart seldom rise to the surface in formal prayers; for instance, the Lord's Prayer is easily memorized, but oh, so slowly learned by heart. But let the early riser neutralize his own feverish activism, and prayer becomes a transcendental, sublime experience. There is no higher point of view from which life's values can be contemplated. Prayer is not eloquence but earnestness, desire turned with a Godward angle.

Beginning the day in any other fashion admits a shoddy substitute which results in a day of things piling up, like a singer who never quite gets on the right key; much like the issues that are fed into the machine of life in ever-choking fashion, where the wheels get clogged in hypertensive distraction. Without a talk with God early in the day, things run together, and everything is reduced to the same common denominator. Who has not lived too many days like these already? Far too many are hard pulls even with the tonesetter of prayer, but to immerse oneself in the relentless sea of "much ado about nothing" without this middle "C" is to write a prescription for misery. Waste of energy, mental distress, ulcerated worries can dog man's pace from minute to hour. He is a fool to walk them alone!

It should go without saying that one must fight for the privilege of these right beginnings. What with the world's ever-accumulating demands, pressures from without and tensions within, the soul is often pulled from its altars even under the guise of religious priorities. Nothing short of Spartan discipline will provide for these meditative moments. The soul that rationalizes by saying he is too busy to pray is too busy indeed. A honey bee does not dart in and out of a flower; instead, it tarries with the flower for a while and thus draws out the fragrance that results in honey. Our day would greatly profit by this advice given David Livingstone by a Scotsman, "Religion is not a matter of fits, of starts and stops, but an everyday affair."

The psychological advantage of beginning each day aright is measured through many dividends during the day. That old feeling that one is ahead of the game serves as wings to the feet. After such an experience becomes habitual, you then anticipate the early rising because you know that you have a rendezvous to keep with the Master. Were there nothing else to be gained than the conquering of a down-in-the-mouth dread of early rising, this would be dividend enough. Some people are congenitally unhappy for the first few hours of each day as though the brilliant sunlight were a source of offense. He who constantly awakens in such a dark-blue pall either needs a thorough orientation of attitude or needs to improve the quality of activity of the previous night. It comes as no chagrin to anyone that all life spent in dissipating conduct will never greet the early hours with any modicum of eagerness. Actually, most of the "last week's" taste in the mouth is but the unpleasant residue of an infamous trilogy: Nicotine, Bacchus, and Aphrodite. Or, if one desires to make it four: then add the fact that the physical body has simply been driven beyond any reasonable pace. A clean, healthy body can be introduced to a new day with zestful willingness. One should fight to keep from bringing a dyspeptic attitude into the new day just as he would fight off infectious diseases! This day sees as desperate a pursuit of peace of mind as is made by researchers after uranium. The nearly positive antidote to our fears and worries consists in this simple premise: a few minutes with God early in the morning before the machines of life are humming in full speed will insulate us from the heat of pursuit and passion. Just how frequently one should approach his sacred shrine of communion depends upon the disarranged schedule and hectic pace. If one doesn't come apart from the world to be with God, then he will come apart within. The rarest soul, short-circuiting this essential, will lose its bloom. Oh, many are its rich benefits—benefits which transcend all the contemporary fuzziness that accompanies the average man's conception of God. God becomes a daily encounter, not a sophomoric subject for debate.

It matters little what is the nature of the weather or what coalition of circumstances challenges both might and main. God never breaks an appointment; He is ever accessible. Like the Ediles among Romans who had their doors standing open so that those who had petitions might have free access to them, God's willingness to meet one three-fourths of the way ought to be enough to convince the vilest skeptic.

This daily coming to God is not an act of presumption that makes of God a grandiose commissary for human need, or an apothecary for man's ills. Instead, it is love in action, a reaffirmation of relationship and sincere wanting to be together.

An incalculable tragedy of our day is that the art of meditation is hard for us to come by! Our nervous dispositions would rather place higher premium on doing something, as though turning one's hands was a lever by which the soul grows! A God-discerning discipline will elevate time into eternity, will divert wandering thought back into the main stream of significance, and will probe the depths for soul shallowness. This is the vocabulary of the spirit: knowing that God is never deaf unless man is dumb.

Let it be known that the whole experience loses its value if the communion degenerates into egomania. To make prayer an occasion for airing personal grievances, selfish desires, etc., also defeats such communion; God gets tired of all our whinings! One should ask Him not to remove the load but to strengthen the back, not to transplant mountains but to give strength to climb them. Occasionally one lives long enough to thank God for the prayers which He ignored—and that for our own good. An old Russian proverb warns, "What men usually ask for when they pray to God is that two and two may not make four." I cannot earnestly implore that my ignorance should take precedence over His wisdom, all my innocence notwithstanding. A Christian knows that he can never astonish the world by his own power; he knows something better; that he can win the world through God's astonishing power!

> I met God in the morning,
>   When my day was at its best,
> And His presence came like sunrise,
>   Like a glory in my breast.
>
> All day long the presence lingered;
>   All day long He stayed with me;
> And we sailed in perfect calmness
>   O'er a very troubled sea.

Other ships were blown and battered,
Other ships were sore distressed,
But the winds that seemed to drive them
Brought to us a peace and rest.

* *

So I think I know the secret
Learned from many a troubled way:
You must seek Him in the morning
If you want Him through the day.[3]

If this were my last day on earth, I would balance the
books: I would forgive and be forgiven. What danger por-
tends of more fright than that of facing an endless eternity
with the books of this life out of balance? In silent reflection
I would take stock of my mental and moral inventory; I would
walk again the labyrinthine paths of decision, choice, omis-
sion and commission—back to the times when advantage was
taken of my fellow man, or self was given the benefit of the
doubt; to times when the ego demanded right of way in
advancement at the expense of another; to times when preferential treatments gave me the edge in this worldly deception called "success." And all this because judgment is up
ahead: that day of God-human reckoning when man shall
give account of the deeds done in the flesh; that day of divine
fixing; that one inevitable appointment for all mankind. Then
the true record will be read; the sheet shall be exposed,
whether clean or cluttered, like film in a camera: once the
shutters have opened, an impression is made.

Entering eternity with the books out of balance is the essence of human folly. Surely Satan's cleverest weapon is to
exploit man's vagueness about the future, and to influence him
in believing that judgment is really nonexistent. Man is a
gambler indeed, but in this game there is no possible way for

[3] Ralph Spaulding Cushman, "His Presence Came Like Sunrise," in
Janus Gilchrist Lawson, comp., *The Best Loved Religious Poems* (Westwood, N. J., Fleming H. Revell Company, 1933), p. 147.

him to win unless he admits God's prerogative in the judgment. Let none of these be shown in that final record: short weights, debit entries without commensurate credits; unpaid debts, secret partners, spiritual Yaltas; shady deals, unkept promises and a soul that never grew beyond its infantile babyhood. At least one should be able to stand before God with a clear conscience. Ragged reputations, or illegitimate children left to face a cruel world; a home without a spiritual legacy, an influence which left its foul deposit to the already overladen human burden—these must not appear in that reckoning day! (I refer not so much to the bundle of minor aggravations as to the rupture of relationships, those anchored souls that never broke loose from ego's moorings.)

Under the cathode ray of divine scrutiny, a spirit of unforgiveness will show up in the first test. Just at this point the human race has perfected itself but a bit; it has come but a stone's throw from the time when Cain killed Abel. Hear the words of Jesus on the matter: "If thou bring thy gift to the altar, and there rememberest that thy brother hath ought against thee; Leave there thy gift before the altar, and go thy way; first be reconciled to thy brother, and then come and offer thy gift." For years I read this passage without noticing the pronoun—"If *thy* brother hath ought against *thee.*" Instead, I consoled myself in the belief that the initiative in forgiveness was certainly with the offender. Not so, according to Jesus. The initiative in reconciliation is with the innocent, not the guilty. Why? Simply because the guilty will never display enough soul dimensions to do it; and were he of such character, chances are that he never would have inflicted the harm in the first place. But a better reason: here is an ideal opportunity of winning the offending brother to Christ. His seeing that one who goes the mile which is not required and shields his hurt from pride's acid is apt to wonder what it is in a person that can subdue the animal and vent his spirit.

Impractical? Precisely! Yet this world of woes and unrepented hurts—man's inhumanity to man, cutting words, festering injustices—these are no arguments that favor a worldly definition of "practical." There is nothing practical about endless litigation with all its parasitic "legal" expenses; nothing too sensible about the fact that our day's biggest business is how to kill efficiently. More moral courage is displayed in one act of this suggested procedure than in all the "I'll get even with him if it kills me" tactics. But here is where the going is tough: to swallow one's wounded pride, to look askance at losing face, and to plow right ahead in order to effect reconciliation—this is the measure of a man. But will one not consider you a weakling, or suspect you of ulterior motives? What does it matter? The suspicion is quickly allayed when the real motive, love, is on display.

Doubtless the prime reason why an unforgiving spirit will arouse in God such indignation is that He has given us the perfect pattern by which we are to cut our brief lives. Our sins were forgiven by God's initiative and inexplicable sacrifice. We had committed wrong—not God. And in that fact He sent His Son to reconcile the world unto Himself. Our being forgiven is predicated on our forgiving our debtors. Anyone who saunters into eternity freighted by a hardened heart will suffer threefold at God's hand for this very reason.

When the soul foregoes revenge, there is nobility at its greatest. But little, narrow-gauged souls seek revenge and remain adamant in the face of every effort to set the record straight and to effect understanding. No sight is uglier in the church of Jesus Christ than the presence of a pious veneer which covers an obstreperous, incalescent, unforgiving spirit! And their number is legion. Jesus left no doubt that retaliation is out of the question for a true Christian. Remembering that mud will brush off better after it has dried, the follower of the Nazarene fails to aggravate, inflame, or irritate the points at which friction occurs. Instead of turning the other cheek, it has become habit to turn the other point of logic, the other machine gun or the other legal suit.

Having lost his temper with the exasperating slowness of his private, a major in the Civil War kicked the private with muddy boots, and left not only physical wound and dirty uniform, but also hurt pride and humiliation among his fellow soldiers. Next morning the major found, beneath his cot, his muddy boots highly polished and neatly laced by the same private orderly. Such an act of forgiving grace was indictment enough to an officer who acted with less discipline than the man whom he kicked. Should God return but a meager portion of our due in this respect, who would survive?

Life is far too short to harbor any grudge, to nurse any wounds, no matter what their source. The heart has no room to hold the memories of yesterday's miseries. Just our kind of life will see to it that this day will have its share without ushering in those behind us. Of one thing we can be dogmatically certain: the heart that loses its pardoning power is not ready to meet God! This will stand in any religion. When injury begins on the part of one, let kindness begin in the others knowing that man never stands so tall as when he kneels and asks God to set his record straight. Let us be in haste about this matter; the uncertainty about tomorrow and the brevity about today argue clearly in favor of balancing the books before the setting sun. Warns the Book, ". . . let not the sun go down upon your wrath." Shakespeare proves to be a better prophet than many, "Who from crimes would pardoned be, in mercy should set others free."

Those wandering, questioning Greek scholars, who followed their itinerant teacher, had a habit of entering into debate at such a heated pace that they all but came to blows over some minor point of logic. But it was said of them that before their day had closed, they fell into an affectionate embrace, lest the day would close on some ill will. Would that this human forum refuse sleep until the wrong of ill will was righted. If this were my last day, I would set the books straight.

Would one's last day produce morbidity of conversation, would the hours pass in the proverbial small talk so characteristic of most conversation? Modern man is vocal on most issues, and the slightest provocation produces a "I will say a few words on the subject." Today the world is being told its destiny through many a soothsayer, prophet, or priest. One would think from the incessant voices on radio, television, and other media that man's salvation consisted in certain brands of beverage, a particular kind of tobacco, specific types of automobiles, or one special make of toothpaste. The ardor and zeal with which these things are promoted leaves one prostrate in the wake of their monotonous sincerity. The eardrum is bombarded night and day with a staccato urgency; little wonder in this babel of vocality, the human race has a confused sense of values. Now, in this maze of words, man needs to be told the good news that the most wonderful thing has happened, something mystifying, unfathomable yet real: Jesus has come to save man's soul. Yet, the very tongues which are glibly vocal on all things else become confusingly thick on this subject. No proof is more positive of one's own religious experience than the fact that he thinks enough of it to recommend it to someone else, and that without the professional propaganda and hoopla of organized activism. We generally speak of the things in which we have a pronounced interest, be it cars, cash, clothes, or courage. Could it be that this sin of silence among us is the modern blight of Christendom?

What is the answer to this dilemma? Perhaps multifold: some never give verbal expression to the good news of salvation but think that such sacred things should not be given over to promotionalism; or think that religion, like dew, should be quietly and personally lived without the fanfare so obnoxiously apparent in our day. While this attitude has a note of commendation, it so flagrantly violates Jesus' commands to "go tell" that it reveals far more the dimension of disobedience than that of admirable emulation. Others remain silent in the face of the good news on the pretext that they do not know how to say it. Lest they blunder in the process, they refrain from the effort. No credence is placed on this obvious skirting of privilege and duty. Nowhere does Jesus require a masterful elocutionist to tell the good news. As a matter of fact, He warned against erudition and public display of semantics, lest the ability to say it finely detract from the thing said. When words become ornamental bric-a-brac to be tasted in the mouth of the pronouncer instead of channels through which living ideas flow, they become man's impeder instead of expediter.

Still others fail to vocalize the glad tidings because of their disdain for the methods and techniques of many who do. The indiscriminate, mass approach of seeing all sin without relatives; the bass drum of semi-jazz, corny "gospel music" edition; the hurrying pace of literature distributors; the negative wail of the condescending soul-winner—professional soul winning's less pleasant side, a noxious, emotional miasma insulting reason; the indiscretion of improper time and place; the lack of rapport between saved and sinner; the coercive zeal of the "decision now or never"; the perennial idolatry of statistics inaccurately compiled and gloatingly reported; the equally ignored "once-I-have-won-him leave-him-alone" lethargy; the hard-to-live-with pharisaism so easily the nature of a third-grade Christian—all these argue in favor of silent lips on the part of throngs. While conceding some plausibility of such an analysis, perhaps God's hierarchy of value would still give precedence to a poor method over no method at all. Rather one would murder the King's English by using it than spill the

King's blood by abusing it. Fanaticism may be tempered by good judgment, but there is no known cure for indifference! A qualifying epitaph for any decadent religion would include the fact that they did not missionize their faith. Sum up the history of Christianity from any vantage point, and each time the answer of its amazing spread consists of the fact that the invitation to the open tomb, "Come see" was followed by the imperative, "Go tell." Had not the Holy Spirit in the first century found free and ready tongues to give utterance to its power, there would have been no significant Pentecost.

What a sobering thought: that one's last conversation on earth would be centered around the One whom he would first meet at the end of the day! The only time some people ever call His name is in the colloquial antics of profanity; or in some emergency, or like the soldiers in midnight combat who had a way of crawling along the wet beaches of the Pacific and saying, "Chaplain, pray that God will let us live through just one more of these Banzai charges, and we promise Him through you that we will live for Him the rest of our days." Of course, the prayers were offered and most of them did come through; yet, a few months later when the war was over, the same well-intended men were lined up outside the geisha house of prostitution for a city block! Emergency religion: the name called only when one can do nothing else.

Now there is a vicious alternative to our not telling the world this news: the world is being told a shoddy edition of Marxism, secularism, and materialism. Like an engulfing tide that goes beyond its boundary, this cancer of thought and deed is rolling over millions. No longer can our take-it-or-leave-it attitude toward Christianity suffice. To rise up and tell the truth right now is incumbent upon us all.

By having lived the day in the methods just described, then it follows as night follows day, the end should hold no last-minute desperation. No time now to violate all the premises practiced through the day: rather, an opportunity to draw the interest accrued by each previous hour's devotion. This I know, that faith has its own anesthesia for the solemn walk (if such were ever needed) and God imparts grace for dying at the time of death—not before. Christian faith poignantly affirms that death is no monster of negation before which all hope falls in defeat; no impenetrable mystery drawing the nerve of life; not a hot Sahara into which the flow of love is lost; no detour through purgatorial fires, nor is it a tenure in tomb, mausoleum or crypt; no mingling of suspended ghosts in ether; no "paying the debt of nature," nor is it a sacred trance or abridgement of life. Death is the process of being born into life that shall not die.

This being true, the right attitude, devoid of any woebegone fatalism, must hold. An attitude of anticipation, while not discounting this earthly life, still prepares for the long journey in restrained eagerness. This is the conditioner of mind and soul that causes one to go about his normal routine unsullied and unhurried, knowing that a child of God is not made for time but for eternity. Such rare disciple knows that One so sovereign in life would not be impotent in death; and though the act of dying may hold a modicum of dismay, the state of death is devoid of danger. Believing this, Christians have marched into the mouths of lions, have faced the withering fire of machine guns, have stood up to death sentences with steel-like fortitude, knowing that bullets may destroy the brains but never the soul of man. Things don't run away with you like this:

> When the anchors that faith has cast
>   Are dragging in the gale,
> I am quietly holding fast
> To the things that cannot fail.[4]

[4] Washington Gladden, "Ultima Veritas."

The approach of this would-be finale points up the conviction that they who know the way to God can find Him in the dark. Faith will stand its final examination and will pass it! Surely anything so inevitable, so vastly personal, so universal as death could not be other than purposive in the plan of a wise Creator. Death holds no advantage to anyone unless it comes as a stranger. Let it come when it will; it can do the Christian no harm, because he knows: if he die he shall be with God, if he live he shall be with Him.

It is not the glitter of this earth that has produced so glum an attitude toward death for so many—rather, subscription to paganistic teachings at the expense of Christ's clear words on the subject. There is more real truth in the statement of Lucan than in most religious outlooks, "The gods conceal from men the happiness of death, that they may endure life."

For the sake of conjecture, suppose this is not my last day— what does this attitude engender? It neither discounts earthly significance nor engenders disconsolation. It induces vigilance, sobriety, a zest for things holy, and an appetite for things eternal.

Said the surgeon to the young parents, "Your little daughter is incurably ill." After days of searching agony, the devout Christian couple answered, "God's will be done." "Should we tell her? After all, she is nine years of age and has accepted Jesus as her Saviour three years ago. She is older than her years, and why should we not prepare her?" There in the quiet room with their only daughter the father said, "Darling, I want to talk to you about something that is very hard for me to say. The doctors say you have a disease that they cannot cure. We have prayed that God would heal you, but it seems to be His will that He take you to heaven to live with Him. Pretty soon He will send a long train to get you and take you to the beautiful city of angels and God's throne." Quick as a flash, the little face lighted as she looked into her daddy's eyes and said, "Will Jesus be at the station to meet me?" "You bet He will!" the father quickly replied, "and what's more, Mother and Daddy will be on the very next train to join you."

I would come to the end of the day with a nondesperation outlook, admitting that weariness of this life is no qualifying virtue for the next; instead, my attitude should be one of wholesome anticipation that I was going home! From the Book of Common Prayer is that memorable prayer of John Henry Newman, "O Lord, support us all the day long of our troublous life, until the shadows lengthen and the evening comes, and the busy world is hushed, and the fever of life is over, and our work is done. Then in thy mercy grant us a safe lodging and a holy rest, and peace at the last."

One day, after I had preached this sermon, a lady condensed it to a few poetical lines and mailed it to me. This is the way she wrote it:

> I'd greet God gladly at rise of sun.
> Grateful to have a good race to run,
> Had I but a single day to live.
> I'd balance my account of shortcomings and sin
> By forgiving, since forgiveness I'd hope to win,
> Had I but a single day to live.

> And I'd tell that wondrous "sweet story of old"
> To a sordid hoarder of silver and gold,
> Sorely bereft of kindly ties;
> Or, to a child with wistful eyes—
> Had I but a single day to live.

> Calmly, I'd set about such chores
> As would vouchsafe wide-open doors
> To a house in order, once I was done.
> And so be ready at setting of sun
> To meet my Maker, face-to-face,
> Shielded by my Redeemer's grace,
> Had I but a single day to live.

3

WELLS WITHOUT WATER

IN AN EFFORT to commemorate their lives, two brothers sought a medium to defy passing time. One erected a granite obelisk with a poetical epitaph carved on four sides. The other dug a well! After their deaths, curious passers-by admired the symmetrical art of the obelisk but were unmoved by its coldness. In the hot, dry climate others stopped to draw water from the well. Each time as their thirst was satiated, the younger brother's memorial became validly useful. What cruel disappointment to drop a bucket and rope into a well on a scorching day and find no water there! The singular purpose for which a well exists is to yield water; when it is dry, the purpose is mocked.

Today men are attempting to pull up water from dusty bottoms—shafts in which no real water exists. Yet, despite repeated testimony that the efforts are futile, nonetheless, millions continue.

Recently a research foundation sent into one of America's larger cities a man armed with a bag of one thousand silver dollars. He was instructed to be out early at office buildings, near depots and busy intersections, and to give a silver dollar to everyone who looked happy. All day the man observed thousands of people who went their busy ways from place to place. When the day was over, the man had given away only seven hundred and sixty-three dollars! What a commentary! Was his conception of happiness too idealistic? Do people not convey their real inner selves on their faces? Happiness without holiness is a waterless well!

To ask some people, "Are you happy?" is an interrogation of offense—not that the question is interpreted as meddling in personal affairs, but it puts them on a spot where a quick flush of pink speaks of an indictment against the shoddy state of affairs being interpreted as "happiness." Few like to be reminded of their shortcomings, especially in an area so vital as happiness. To be happy in one's work, worship, and play as a means to a higher end is the birthright of everyone who has experienced a new birth. Let us be done with the crisis school of theologians, those who maintain that all life is summed up in tensive stress, in paradoxes and complexes, in strife and disenchantment. True, that in the vortex of gripping tensions creative works have been wrought by some, that by the bloody whip and from the maddening dreams have come poetical utterances which confound interpretation. But if the real truth were known, more nightmares and manic depressives have resulted from such frustrative curricula than great oratorios, sonnets, or songs. Destructive crises are bad for the soul, and few will ever do effective work unless they are happy in what they are doing.

Few, if any, people ever were as prosperous as American people who have a prosperity which has made possible freedom from the grinding rigors of earning daily bread, and free time to pursue hobbies and recreational interests; yet, one must be honest to admit that this prosperity has not brought commensurate amounts of enjoyable happiness. Irrefutable indices abound on every hand to prove such conclusion. The fact that twenty thousand people committed suicide in a recent year—and more in the month of May at that—is an alarming index to this ugly truth of unhappiness. Tons of aspirin speak of a national headache while millions must be kept awake by chemical stimulants; others, though lying on innersprings and silken sheets, must be forced to sleep by equally potent chemicals. Every other bed in American hospitals is occupied by a patient whose "illness" is psychosomatic without any perceptible organic origin. To say that unhappiness is the culprit in most cases is perhaps nearer the truth than any other diagnosis. There are functional suicides, chronic in nature, who would never think of something so crude and uncouth as arsenic, or lead, but who through the leeway given to the death impulse are nonetheless taking their lives by small digits, half-steps at a time. Though it may take them ten or twenty years to gnaw out the vitals of superlative living, nonetheless they are responsible for suicide in the long run. What is time to God? All such irrational activities speak of a national wave of prosperity and its inevitable adjunct: misery translated into a disconcerted, unhappy state of affairs.

Any effort to solve this riddle should beg for clear delineation of terms lest specious definitions cloud the issue to the point of futility. Happiness eludes many because they are looking for the wrong thing. Pleasure is not necessarily happiness. To hordes of people, pleasure is merely gratification of the senses: appetites satiated by food, drink, sex and sound. Man's emotions are ridden in roller-coaster fashion—rising on tides of artificial elation, then the dizzy descents into depression and occasional remorses as consequential appendages to unholy stimulation. Now and then pleasure is the lot of all men, but who will say that such is happiness? A good percent-

age of the human race would easily settle on a role of animal
sensuality as a good enough definition for happiness. As a
matter of fact, few get any valuable returns from an activity
that fails to produce sensual gratification or arouse the animal
instinct. To learn the folly of this criterion is to approach the
wisdom of those philosophers who, through the ages, knew
that true happiness never lay at the door of the beast!

Moreover, neutral conditioning is not to be pawned off in
the name of real happiness. Some have so equated, developing
a sort of Stoicism which works in Spartan discipline, building
dams to the tear ducts, forcing smiles from one's face, taking
the high hurdles of elation in the same stride as the low valleys
of despair, while running an average through both to come
out with a neutral, if not a downward, graph. This art of the
Orientals in whose life "too much rain has fallen," while being
a bit commendable in that it doesn't permit the emotions to
escalate, is poor fare for exuberance in honest happiness.
When a person practices neutral conditioning long enough,
a protective mechanism "strait jackets" the soul to the point
where the sharp edge of hara-kiri produces little more than
will power to force a knife through the entrails. This indeed
is a far cry from the Christian admonition, "Weep with them
that weep, and rejoice with them that rejoice." To sit in stolid
detachment when the wine of springtime is subtly inebriating
every living creature—when saffron showers of pungent odors
pervade the air in competition with lyrical notes of a mocking
bird; when summer clouds ride the ether with gliding ease—
speaks of no happiness fit for human life. It merely endorses
the fearful conclusion of the Greek philosopher, "Let no one
be called happy until his death."

There is an unphilosophic approach to life which knows
not the academic dimensions of neutral conditioning but
works much the same way, a type of conformation to circumstances through no design, no election, merely drifting with

the flow of things. A man gets a job, marries a woman, rents a house, eats his three meals a day, piddles along in minor, peripheral things, lives out his three-score-and-ten years, dies and is soon forgotten. But to mistake this as happy living is much beside the point. Quite beside the point! Such is of no recommendable value. If sheer existence is the issue of living, then I contend it isn't worth the effort. If no great obsessions grip life in inextricable hold, if life isn't lost in some undertow other than meat and bread, if no rosy vistas or generous indiscretions sweep life off its feet, then mutual suicide would speak of more wisdom than the effort to continue! Conforming habits that make a treadmill of life without rhyme or reason, giving in to this demand and that, rounding the edges and corners of individuality, acquiescing before the onrush of presumed fate, rationalizing the status quo as the predestined "right thing," and all of these tied into one bundle as a means of getting through another day, another week, another year: these nowhere come close to the point of creative happiness. Though happiness knows dimensions of adaptability and adjustment, never does it bargain its unique qualities for ersatz limitations.

Nor is happiness living on the high realm of the wheel all the time. Herein most adults stand indicted: they refuse body, mind, and soul the needed moments of dull neutrality wherein life, like a motor which idles in overdrive, renews itself for the next high hurdles. They are apt to drive, to stoke, and to force life back to its unaccustomed heights. Perhaps no other thing so accounts for the millions of gallons of alcohol consumed by people every month in an effort to escape the dull drabness which is as essential to real happiness as the moments that are pink and glowing. Were it not for the former, there would not be the latter. Caught in a cross fire of cause and effect tension, happiness begins its justifiable exodus insomuch that its absence is misinterpreted as being present

—hence the dilemma and deception. Every individual should indulge himself to the point of one hour per day in which nothing is planned—not even meditative thinking—an hour wherein all the wires are unplugged from the switchboard of daily preoccupations, just to sit, lie, stand, or walk with no purpose in mind whatsoever. Taut muscles would relax; fidgety hands always turning to some chore would droop in open detachment; irritable tempers triggered by pressured concern would yield to calm reason, while the mania for more and the passionate fevers of life would subside.

While many people are disappointed in their quest by virtue of looking for the wrong thing, more are disquieted in that they may be searching for the right thing in the wrong places. Just as gold ore is not apt to be found in desert sand, happiness isn't to be found in certain arid deserts. To forego the search is conservation of energy as well as prevention of disappointment. Since millions are spending fortunes to be happy, some voice needs to be raised against the deceiving promises lest we all be duped by the economic mirages. A casual listening to radio commercials, or glancing at billboards, or viewing television crudities would give the gullible searcher the impression that happiness is easily within reach of anyone who is willing to make the down payment! Conversely, this most frequently asked question in America, "How much is the down payment?" may be among the reasons for so much unhappiness.

Let it be said with dogmatic certainty that among the wrong sources of happiness is the delusion that it can be prescribed, taught, or bought. This is a waterless well, a vain delusion to believe that happiness is a chemical balance in man's body needing only additional chemical resuscitation when its quantity ebbs. Let proper deference be shown the galloping gains of research chemists et al; let there be a doxology of gratitude sung for all those scientific wonders which have enhanced the quality of living while alleviating needles of pain. Let no thin religion presume that an excursion through the ether of superstition is justifiable fare for one whose aches and pains are as real as life itself—and this to the detriment of those whose sacrifices to discover the cause and cure of diseases are as qualitative in devotion as their religious adherents.

But the fearful extreme of man's enthroning capsule and prescription as the way to happiness is today's danger in extreme. Tranquilizers know nothing about the stimulation of ardent faith; Reserpine, while allaying the jig of anxiety, cannot pronounce the words of Jesus, "Do not be anxious about tomorrow. . . ." In the process of consciousness oozing into the twilight of sleep by chemical stimulants, personality is robbed of the residue which comes by nature's voluntary entrance into that valley of repose which is natural pay for everyone who has done an honest day's work.

"Why is it that one seldom, if ever, hears of deathbed repentance nowadays?" asked a puzzled church member. Part of the answer may lie in the fact that most patients are under the merciful grip of sedation prior to death: a merciful balm indeed for those who are ready to die. For those who should cry out in desperation for God's saving power to heal them— not so merciful.

Happiness cannot be found in the tyranny of things. To a people who are consumed by an obsession that automation will usher in the millennium, it is nigh impossible to convey the truth that things, while reducing the sweat of toil, cannot assure peace of mind and tranquillity of soul. So long as electric appliances, air-conditioners, and auxiliary aids are means to higher ends, just so long do things deserve a rating in a hierarchy of values. When things reduce life to an unrelenting quest on their behalf, then man is mastered by his machines and life knows no multidimension in value.

Who today heeds the warning of Epictetus, "The one way to tranquillity of mind and happiness: to account no external things thine own, but commit all these to God"? Future historians will interpret history's vainest delusion: we were misled to believe that finer houses, bigger automobiles, antique furniture, and an imposing façade of stocks and bonds would produce that tenor of life-zest so desired by all. They will not! Too often things are impedimenta, blocking the way to happiness. What with weariness of possessions and inordinate desire for what one does not possess, there is an overriding lust which knows no satisfaction. Who ever heard of a contented millionaire?

Happiness is not bought in a bottle—the fact that millions believe it notwithstanding! What irony: the very process designed to induce that inner state of life contributes to its disappearance—and that as early as the next morning's hangover. The measurable effects of alcohol are not stimulating, but depressing. Acting in the role of a narcotic, it sends life into a pink Valhalla for a miserly brief tenure, and there the ooze of mild sedation reduces one's problems tremendously. For a few moments the world is painted pastel while personality yields to the calloused hands of inebriation. But such hands are impersonal hosts insomuch that a Japanese proverb begs for recognition: "First the man takes a drink, then the drink takes a drink, then the drink takes the man." And lo, the very state of affairs which seemed so intolerable that escape was sought through alcohol is compounded in misery and intolerance. Hence, the deep-seated habit from which few ever are released.

The new psychology toward drinking among the population of this mid-twentieth century—a psychology of tolerance, associated with the thing to do—is but studied, heavily-financed subterfuge, designed to flush the economic till, not to contribute happiness to a nation. So to admit is to challenge forces that would place a higher value on profit than on personality.

It is not enough to denounce and negate; however, one must analyze, understand, and approach any problem in an effort to see its many components. In this day when "scientism" has been enthroned, one should look at the scientific facts. If seventy million Americans drink to some extent, surely there must be a reason.

The following has been gleaned from personal testimonies, most of which are easy rationalizations: to many this habit provides an avenue of psychological escape. Life's ever-whirling pace, its competitive demands, its ulcerated societies, all drive men to the point of despair. Having no real sense of inner calm, they seek it in external prods. When the workday is over, the ragged nerves, acutely accentuated by bumper-to-bumper traffic, dirty tenements, noisy voices, cry out for some balm. The sight of congested flats prods the mind to some imaginary Brigadoon, or some Tahitian island of escape. Then vaunted desire gives way to realism. One simply cannot afford the island jaunt, and there are no Brigadoons; hence, he seeks the nearest saloon to approximate what the mind demanded. So, over the second and third martini, personality gambols through its make-believe world. Then, one asks, "Isn't this escape from the humdrum existence justified?" Hardly! Any technique which compounds the very misery it is designed to alleviate is vain deception. The embarrassingly specific fact remains that the problem still awaits the sobering process. Instead of removing the difficulty, one more problem is added. Perhaps there is no better admission than the fact that man must face himself and his world of circumstances just as they are, if ever they are to be as they should.

Many drink with the notion of bolstering their personalities. In a day of frequency of contact, where the "glad" look becomes an index of "success," who can afford the sour scowl?

Cursed by a bad disposition, one reasons that he can compensate his clogged vocabulary or corroded mind by enough alcohol to "loosen" him up. But as objective as this appears on the surface, just the opposite is accomplished. Instead of stimulating, it stupefies; it retards the mental process rather than inciting sensitivity of thought and decision. And it does *not* enhance the affability of one's personality. As to making him a man of distinction, his low estate is better characterized by deleting the "di." Incoherence of thought, montonous vocality, and the presumption that one can speak on all subjects with authority—these mark the inebriated as stupid.

Insecurity accounts for its share of those who resort to this medium for little ravellings of "happiness." Dream worlds remaining increasingly elusive, inevitable approach of old age and its uncertainties, the certainty of death, contradictions of adversity, momentum of time and events, and the rupture of domestic relationships leave an engulfing deposit in the lives of many insecure souls, sending them by the millions to grog shops.

There are some misinformed drinkers who believe that alcoholic beverage provides aphrodisiac qualities, compensating their lack of sexual potency. On behalf of this myth many an erotic sexualist has written or testified. The folklore of every nation has its records and quotas of sensualists who, in their efforts to exploit man's animalistic tendencies, have contended that alcohol contained sexually empowering properties. Though no scientific data is available by way of statistical proofs, the generally accepted facts that the sensory tracts are stultified under such sedation holds true in this contention.

Still others drink in the hours of adversity when the world gets them down and the high tides of fortune turn against them. Life's gales blow in from cold seas, and they are chilled, and need a drink to help them "buck up." Instead of a bucking up, they gain no firmness of the knees; they only give in to the onslaught of a worse malady. Whatever else may be said for the habit of drink as an avenue to happiness, let this be known in dogmatic finality: happiness can never be bought in a bottle!

A poem, composed by a twenty-five-year-old convict in prison in Joliet, Illinois, and published in the *Chicago Tribune*, occupied two and a half inches of space. However, the same edition ran 169 inches of advertisement for alcoholic beverages. The poem reads:

> The name of every saloon is bar,
> The fittest name by far;
> A bar to heaven, a door to hell,
> Whoever named it, named it well.
>
> A bar to manliness and a bar to wealth,
> A door to sorrow and broken health;
> A bar to honor, pride, and fame,
> A door to sorrow, grief, and shame.
>
> A bar to hopes, a bar to prayer,
> A door to darkness and despair;
> A bar to useful, manly life,
> A door to a brawling, senseless strife.
>
> A bar to heaven, a door to hell,
> Whoever named it, named it well.

This increasingly illusive state—happiness—is not a matter of geography, though some places challenge the best of minds merely to exist in their niggardly environment where nature ran out of Eden inventory. While a leisure trip through mountain forests, down to the beaches, or other resorts will refresh the tired spirits and recharge the batteries of life-glow, the truth remains that long jaunts from island to island, continent to continent, job to job, result in the same disconcerting misery one attempts to evade. Even on a Tahitian island one finds his old self. Happiness is not in places, but in people, in one-self; it is not position, but disposition; not accumulation, but outlay. If it were a matter of geography, then the inhabitants of the rock-strewn coasts of Maine should be miserable, and those of sunny Miami should be enraptured. Neither is the case. We, like the searcher of the Holy Grail, may travel the world over only to find on our return that the vague, indefinable drive within was satiated nearer home when one discovers his Holiest Grail in the hands of some anonymous mendicant begging for a pittance. But some strange talk this, in a day when millions know not where they are going but still are on their way.

One word of caution should be recorded about the realm of thought as a reservoir of happiness. Standing like a dark sentinel in the night is the irrefutable reminder, "There are no happy philosophers." Deep within the labyrinths of thought and meditation, one should surely mine up the raw materials of this coveted state of mind. Should not the residue of great minds be poured into a hopper, distilling from them an essence to perpetuate soul happiness? To some extents this is possible. But the rub comes in at the point where one searches in vain through their findings, discovering no evidence of their happiness—all logical wits and rationalizations notwithstanding, one is loathe to continue his search. While objective thinking frees the mind from many palimpsests, it fails miserably to produce that inner sterling of equipose and equanimity.

Then: what is genuine happiness, and from whence is it obtained? The best advice on the art of being happy is about as easy to follow as advice on how to be well when one is sick. But at least here is a start: happiness is not a thing in itself, but a by-product of something else. At this juncture the pagan world makes its departure. No one can ever be happy until he forgets himself—self is acquiring, demanding, preoccupying; and these are the forces which rob the virtue of its presence. None of Andrew Carnegie's millions amounted to the wealth contained in these six words which he spoke toward the end of his life: "The secret of happiness is renunciation." There it is! Most of what Jesus had to say about abundant, superlative living is summed up in that sentence. Forsaking father and mother, brother and sister, yea, houses and lands: all were tantamount to His disciples. Then the strange alchemy occurred: the very process of giving up was the means by which the disciples took up a rare dimension unknown to them in their former enslavement to things. Life must be peeled of its wrappings if it is to be lived in rightful tenor. Who can know such enraptured glory without severing the earth-bound cords? That lowly Nazarene, devoid of those encumbering weights that so easily beset us, was determined to make each day rich, for He knew that eternity is now, and that man need not wait for translation to some unknown land and future rendezvous in order to wake up and live here and now! His radiance was what Whitman called "an evanescent tinge," imputing to word, thought and deed pungent significance. Little wonder His was teaching with ringing authority, which defied the crusty molds of dull, listless religion. His was the dictum that no one is happy by trying to be happy; that thinking positively is vain semantics if man insists on living negatively; and that concluding that happiness is possible in an unregenerate life is to contend that darkness is light.

The Caliph Abdelraham left a verbal legacy to all who would imbibe of its chilling wisdom. Said he: "I have now reigned about fifty years in victory and peace, beloved by my subjects, dreaded by my enemies, and respected by my allies. Riches and honors, power and pleasures, waited on my call, nor does any earthly blessing appear to have been wanting to my felicity. In this situation, I have diligently numbered the days of pure and genuine happiness which have fallen to my lot; they amount to *fourteen*. O man, place not thy confidence in the present world!" A greater than Caliph minted the same truth into gospel coin: "Lay not up for yourselves treasures upon earth . . . for whosoever will save his life shall lose it."

When a godly man seeks the holy work of duty, then happiness follows like shadows the sunshine. A Christian disciple confronts each day as a God-given trust of hours, minutes and seconds—each a holy requiem for duty and delight. Baffled by the beauties of nature, a Christian staggers in his efforts to choose the best of seasons. Which is the happiest season of the year: spring, summer, autumn, or winter?

Springtime: when life revolts from its prisons of ice and snow, insinuating itself through crocus buds and robin eggs; when floral filigrees of nature's lace and dogwoods like whitened umbrellas are raised over carpets of violets; when the wobbly frolic of a newborn colt speaks of gangling life. Springtime, with its intimations of immortality, like a perennial resurrection from nature's grave, an unconscious memory of Eden reminding one of the words of van Dyke: "If we should find another Eden, we would not be fit to enjoy it perfectly nor stay in it forever." Surely springtime is the happiest season!

Then summer comes with its *laissez-faire* fever, its resplendent indulgence for man and beast, suffusing sluggishness with energy, luring landlubbers to the nearest waterway, refurbishing life with new, fresh thought, ignoring man's mechanical time clocks for vacation jaunts while nature paints the desert and perfumes the countryside—and then I think summer receives the vote.

Yet, autumn's determined bid to excel Raphael's painted variety, its pungent odor of scuppernongs, its delicate sachet of herbs and spices, a mellow aroma from forest and field—all these demand the prize for autumn.

But alas, the vote is withheld as winter enters with a touch of melancholy, denuding nature of foliage, drawing back the drapes from trees and shrubs, unblushingly, nakedly revealing a high-vaulted stage of wonder: the sky and its transluscent challenge for man to sever the cords which bind him to the earth. Winter, with the subdued tones of a holy requiem as it enters the sanctuary of nature's silence. Then the vote for the happiest season is cast: *no one season can be chosen.* The quartet, all four, must be rated with equal uniqueness as God's accommodation to man's unconquerable appetite for variety; these are ingredients of happiness to the seeing eye, the hearing ear, and the soul sensitive to supernal beauty.

To be happy is not the purpose of existence; instead, it is to be worthy of happiness when it comes. If happiness is made the *summum bonum* of life, Christians are in for major disappointments. Preponderance of pagan majorities, the capricious whims of nature, the ineffable mysteries of mind and soul, brevity of life, problems of evil and suffering, the seeming indifference of God to crushing tyranny—all these will induce a sense of unhappiness which, if used as the true goal of living, will fall short of the mark. No, the end of Christian discipleship is not happiness but perfection—a perfection defined in terms of usableness and growth toward one's highest possible realization. Along the way of this often remorseful, awing, magnificent process, there will be strewn occasional flowers of happiness. These grow nowhere else! Were happiness the end of superlative living, the world would never have progressed to its present junction since the forward thrusts of human achievement have come from some of the unhappiest mortals. No divine discontent is known to the contemporary "happy" man.

Happiness to the child of God is a tenor of life based on creative delight: it is personality played in its intended key with corresponding varieties of sharps, flats, and naturals. It is confronting each day with the lung-expanded conviction that "This is the day the Lord has made, let us rejoice in it." It means seeing some constructive work undertaken, knowing that the main thing is not whether it is finished in one's lifetime but that some fine craft should be undertaken. It means the art of contentment where true wealth is defined as the poverty of desire, a consciousness that one is on the winning team, annexed to the greatest cause, affiliated with the greatest Leader. The ingredients of happiness are simple: a loaf of bread, a consuming thought, a holy awe of things beautiful, a rare and trusted friend, a little held in reserve, the itch to know, a sense of belonging, and a roster of aesthetic values. Happiness is equipment whose anchors hold, no matter how tempestuous the gale, a keel that maintains equilibrium despite what may come: adversity, disappointment, fiasco, or death. These hold no final sway over the happy person in whose life a holy cause has come alive and whose allegiance is mortgaged to the One whose last thought was happiness while doing the will of His God.

Real happiness is grounded in holiness, that exclusive spring of sweet water which flows from one's devotion to God. Byron was right when he contended that "Happiness was born a twin." Holiness and happiness are inseparable. One is the native dialect of the other, and it is vanity to speak of a state of happiness without subduing life's impulses to holy awe. Where a union of life with dedicated purpose is effected, one may logically expect a quality of happiness to ensue. Even death can be happiness if approached via the highways of holiness.

The strictly biblical meaning of holiness is "set aside"— dedicated for prescribed purposes. But what a contrast to colloquial usage where the range of holiness seldom exceeds that of sanctimoniousness. The word has a dissonant ring to most ears because of such shoddy demonstrations in history.

When not associated with untutored fanaticism, it li
mant on the counter of taught virtues rather tha..
caught up in a contagion of purposeful living. To Jesus, holiness was a kind of sacred halo placed around all places, all
people, and all pursuits. He robbed life of a vulgar interpretation by seeing in every class, in every culture, the germinal
quality for real potential. Such is the appropriate climate for
spiritual maturity. All the veneer happiness in the world will
never grow a single stalwart character as will holy dedication
to a supremely important cause.

Just here one needs to be reminded that a holy life must be
a near impression of the original—that of Christ's—lest it
degenerate into sordid mortification, deviation into endless
labyrinths of priestcraft, conjecture and superstition. The
world knows too many "holy" men who disdain earning their
daily bread while being ensconced in a marathon of prayers.
Surely these are not the need of the world. Christ's kind of
holiness was faith with muscle in it, trust with concrete pilings
under it, hope with better eyesight than reason, and dynamic
belief that admitted no impossibility. A far cry from the pious
Essenes of His day!

The dedicated life set aside to God is one of symmetrical
submission to divine grace, placing no premium on asceticism,
claiming no merit for gloom; rather, fidelity regulated by
God's edicts and a granitic stability in its apology. It is the
process by which God's glance is claimed in unwary direct-
ness as He sees His creation shaping up in His likeness. Holiness is clear delineation 'twixt conformation to the world and
transformation of the world. It is faith in coveralls, love with
biceps, ethical principle coined into conduct, an empathic
urge toward every downtrodden creature, a consecration of
all things secular. Holiness is a blushing contrast when laid
alongside vulgar sacrilege. What man, place, or circumstance
is profane when holiness sounds a note of significance? Holi-

ness is the process by which the metal of the soul is embossed to a shining finish. It is an ennobling sentiment, vulgarized only by impiety which disdains distance from God and sets up a rarefied antagonism to every form of paganism.

Just such holy life has won more wars than all regiments combined, made more converts than all sermons, spread the good news of salvation farther and wider than all printing presses, and stands at this moment as Christianity's most persuasive filibuster. One single, solitary life, when totally dedicated to the highest purpose, serving the greatest God, is a stronger argument for Christian faith than every other medium within the province of human knowledge. Such a witness speaks though tongues be silent, proclaims though words be none, wins though effort be unperceptive.

It was said of the brothers in their monastery that when they were feeling morose, when a depressive gloom seemed to etch itself into their day, all they had to do to get a lift was to look on the face of Francis Xavier. Why? Because his very profile enunciated a course of holiness, setting at ease every violent impulse and passion. The same tenor of quality coursed through Fanny Crosby, who, though blind, had twenty-twenty vision to see the spiritual skyline of transforming values. Among her musical legacies are: "Praise Him! Praise Him!"; "Blessed Assurance, Jesus Is Mine"; "All the Way My Saviour Leads Me"; "I Am Thine, O Lord"; "Jesus, Keep Me Near the Cross"; "Pass Me Not, O Gentle Saviour," and many others. Said she, on the occasion of some light, solicitous remark intended to convey a modicum of pity, "Don't weep for me. I'm the happiest person on earth."

In cruder expression is the testimony of a floor-sweeper after conversion. "But how do you know that your life has been changed?" queried her employer. "Now I feel better when I feel bad than I did before when I felt good." There you are— and much to the point!

While Mrs. Wilson was waiting for someone to help her across the street, a well-dressed gentleman approached her and asked, "Seeing that you are blind, may I escort you across the street?" The blind lady gratefully accepted the offer and was safely led across. She thanked him profusely, her gratitude conveying the overriding freight of self-pity. Whereupon the man replied, "Lady, when you have been blind as long as I have, it is a big favor for one to help you across a busy street." Such is the artful beauty of a holy life.

But let no one mistake the fact that such grace comes with ease or speed. Not so. It is a learned art, taught and caught, and is no more suddenly acquired than education is suddenly acquired. Like the sun: a faint insinuation at dawn—then a crescent—next, full round—high noon—sinking—and alas, a crimson rim before it escapes. Just so with the holy life: little manifestations of growth through trial and error, a little less chafing under the weight of necessity, a bit more ease in turning the other cheek, and by painful digits the life is refined into graceful holiness.

Among such waterless wells is the quest for power without commensurate purity. The pages of history are replete with man's struggle for power, but auxiliary to that repleteness is the monitoring finger of judgment—a judgment expressed through timely defeat of all such quests which were not based on purity. Seeking to strengthen his hold on others, man has evolved a long way from the crudity of oxwheels and stone axes. No mean jump from flint sparks to acetylene torches! An Indian pony, used to transport the chieftain's son to Bald Rock Mountain in order to fan smoke signals, seems like naïveté compared to the Pentagon's radarscopes.

Within the province of this muscular quest for more power, human personality becomes indispensable. To achieve its goal, the elevation of human life, personality became secondary to semirespectable ends; hence we see the all-too-familiar

curse of demagogues, despots, totalitarians, bigots, rationalized slavery, subjugation, group deportation, oppressive taxation, and mass annihilation.

When power is seated in purity, the world sees a rare coalition of virtue, an unbeatable combination which is history's
rarest union. Power in its rightful hue, used as a force for
righteousness, is akin to the Creator; when prostituted on
selfish interests, it is man's curse.

Valid power is the force of resilient ideas, a thrust of
creative passion issuing in the expulsive activity of an energizing affection. It is the momentum by which society is im-
pregnated with noble purpose, a certain residual strength
which comes to dwell in one whose conduct knows singular
honesty. It is the force of faith which does a job without
quibbling or counting the cost. Such is the need of our world
—and the only need devoid of "pleasures" which in their
deceptive allure mislead the unwary and inordinately ambitious. In constructive expression, power is pure duty.

When power is not compounded with the virtue of purity
the resulting woe is that vice which corrupts and wreaks
misery. The magnitude of this evil is not measurable on any
slide rule. Confounding the wildest of guesses, it points to one
succession of attempts and failures after another. The strongest test of a man is at that point where he is given a modicum
of authority—then every dormant vice rallies to expression.
Seneca commented for all would-be rulers, "A dwarf is small,
even if he stands on a mountain; a Colossus keeps his height,
even if he stands in a well." Just as wine intoxicates the
strongest heads, so does power the best of hearts, resulting in
inebriation of purpose and plan and corruption of the best
personalities. And what often is forgotten is that power is no
divine right; instead it is the grapes of labor and the price of
valorous virtue.

Power without purity—a waterless well! To limit this evil to dictators and glaring examples in history is to overlook the fact that power-madness is equally vice when it shows itself not only in generals, tyrants, and self-appointed demagogues, but also in county seat precincts, principals of rural schools, third vice-presidents, corresponding secretaries, file clerks, and dish washers. Too easy it is to condemn Hitler, Hannibal, and Mao; and though condemnation is in order, the same sin exists all about us wherever power is used to advance unholy causes, to champion desecrated goals, and to imbrute life by falling far below its God-directed destinies.

Ours is a day which has given vent and encouragement to a generation of politicians whose statesmanship is short-circuited by expediencies of the moment. Once a dribble of power and authority is acquired, then the campaign promises wear thin. These are they who with the alloy of "public interest" actually seek their own interest under the guise of the common good, loud champions of intercession who, while appearing to pioneer for social betterment, actually confirm the entrenched prejudices of the masses while insuring the politician's own entrenchment in office. Many politicians but few statesmen! What is needed is to surrender the plaudits of the crowds for the approval of Christ and decency!

Under this condition of entrenchment, security becomes the criterion of highest value; progress for the common welfare is relegated to some lower concern, if it is considered at all. Then follows such a quagmire of contradictory factors that an analytical genius cannot extricate a people from its magnetic grip. Little wonder Shakespeare remonstrated, "But man, proud man! drest in a little brief authority. . . . plays such fantastic tricks before high heaven as make the angels weep." [1]

Those who love power should never have it, especially when

[1] William Shakespeare, *Measure for Measure*, Act II, scene 2, line 107.

the desire for it stems from a fear of being controlled by despots. The champion of reform so easily becomes a counterpart of the despot who should be ousted.

Doubtless one of the contributing factors to today's rise of communism is the economic power blocks which have a minimum of enlightened conscience. Despotic economic domination wherein the wealth of the world is concentrated in fewer than a thousand hands, where cartels and monopolies can move their strangling chessmen at will and can determine inflation or deflation, fame or fortune, prominence or obscurity —such is the incubator which caused the rebellion of downtrodden millions. Rebellion has been mothered by other equally subjugated throngs insomuch that nearly a billion people are dedicated to the task of enthroning a way of life which would reduce God to mythology and human significance to meaningless production digits.

God has dated for defeat every personality who attempts to drink from this waterless well. Unless power is other than an avaricious means to self-aggrandizement, unless purity protects itself from corruption—defeat is inevitable. No lesson in history is so irrefutable. The nomenclature in history's cemeteries is remorsefully familiar: Pharaoh and his hardened heart mummified in his casket of gold with his ruling sceptre still in hand; Antiochus Epiphanes' dust mingled with the ashes of his destroyed domain; Genghis Khan, Oriental master of brutality, now a mere puff, smaller than an opium smoke ring; Pompey, boasting that "one stamp of his foot would arouse all Italy," as dismembered as the city which bore his name, buried beneath the molten lava of Vesuvius; Alexander, man of moods and mystery, whose blood was mixed in the democracy of death like any private lancer, whose life was lost for some vainglorious fling; Hannibal; Ashurbanipal; Pancho Villa; Lenin and company—these speak of men who, maddened by corrupt power, proved that only dust lay at the bottom of such a well.

Still stands that divine dictum: "Not by might, nor by power, but by my spirit, saith the Lord of hosts." God is not necessarily on the side of the biggest battalions. It is as sensible to build a skyscraper on a sandbar as to try to build a republic on impure power. God's gavel will surely fall!

But oh, the agonies of life while the gavel is falling—tyranny has nine lives. Just here it is easy to lose faith. Dictators have a way of dying so slowly! Stalin stayed in office and in life longer than a dozen devils should! By what soul-wearing pace does the devil die! The mills of God seem to grind so slowly, especially when evil men call the plays for righteous men. The wisdom of Kipling's "Recessional" reminds:

> If, drunk with sight of power, we loose
> Wild tongues that have not Thee in awe—
> Such boasting as the Gentiles use
> Or lesser breeds without the law—
> Lord God of Hosts, be with us yet,
> Lest we forget—lest we forget! [2]

The church of Jesus Christ unfortunately is not exempt from the temptation of corrupting power. One of the major and justifiable roadblocks in the path of organizational unity among major denominations is the fear of centralized power in the hands of men who, though professedly devoted disciples, nonetheless are human; and human nature, too often like the Swiss mercenaries, is willing to fight for the side which seems most profitable. Many a church has known a Diotrephes, lay or ordained, who was a one-man empire to throttle, control, and condemn. There is an old proverb: "Better to have

[2] From *The Five Nations* by Rudyard Kipling. Copyright 1931 by Rudyard Kipling, reprinted by permission of Mrs. George Bambridge and Doubleday & Company, Inc.

a lion at the head of an army of sheep than a sheep at the head of an army of lions." The truth of the matter is that sheep need an intelligent shepherd. A lion is out of order.

Henry Ford once answered a question, "Who ought to be boss?" by saying, "It is like asking, 'Who ought to be the tenor in a quartet?' Obviously, the man who can sing tenor." Just so in society. Only the one capable of using power for the common good should be entrusted with it.

Purity stands without peers as a singular giant among virtues. Generating its own power, this virtue knows more strength than a regiment of powerful dictators. Yet, too often it is conceived of as a pale, effete virtue, bereft of virility and strength. Such misconception accounts for history's revolt against Puritanism. Yet that revolt has bred a type of impuritanism which is worse in its extreme than the counterpart. Actually, prudishness is to be preferred to libertines who with license admit of no boundaries beyond which they fear to tread. Purity is not moral perfectionism; instead, it knows that quiet serenity of a governor at the stern, charting his course without feverish splashing of oars. Rising in easy effort over courage, purity passes the censor board of conscience, judgment, and sense. It is no ostentatious virtue. It is unknown to gusto and bravado. "The most virtuous of all men is he who contents himself with being virtuous without seeking to appear so," reminded Plato. Without power, purity often is little more than insipidity.

Jesus accented the note of purity as of loftiest rank among virtues. To the pure in heart He offered congratulations with the promise that ". . . they shall see God." Appearing twenty-eight times in the New Testament, the word "pure" in ten cases means: clean as white linen; clear as glass; unmixed; without alloy. The metal is devoid of foreign agents that would dilute the true nature. Wax used to fill holes in wooden columns was another example common to craftsmen in the day of Jesus. Often a carpenter would nick the wood grain as he planed the column to a smooth finish. To cover his error he would pour in hot wax. But when the sun would shine, sooner or later, the wax would melt and run out, revealing the imperfection. No wonder Jesus warned against a process that glosses over life's imperfection with the wax of impurity. He left no doubt about the fact that in the final judgment, as well as in the judgment of time, all that is imitative, incomplete, and impure would be brought to light. No afterthought that the person who stands the test of God would eventually see God! God is pure, and no other kind of vision than singular purity can see Him. "When the heart is clean, the eye is clear," says a bit of ancient wisdom. Nothing so irked the patience of Christ as that veneering of life's imperfections which was pawned off as the "real thing." Whited walls! Blind guides! There is no known rabbinical antecedent for these words of Christ.

Herein is an admitted difficulty: life is a fusion of good and bad, fair and foul, pure and impure. Any effort to distinguish them often results in the exercising of a faculty more dangerous in import than impurity itself. But the fact remains that dualism and duplicity reside in all mankind. There are times in the life of a Christian when the condition and the promise of that pointed beatitude elude us all. Singleness of heart— one's total being oriented to the divine plan and purpose— means everlasting antagonism at the points of severest friction. Motives have a way of getting all mixed up even in Christian service. Honesty inspired by fear of jail bars; church affiliation motivated by desire for public acceptance; giving as a lever to trigger publicity; flag-waving as a sop thrown to patriotism while currying favor with the casters of votes; these outwardly admirable things can spring from the rankest sort of motive: self-aggrandizement, the desire to belong, proving ground for psychological complexes, and adherence to accepted standards of expectation. This is like the restraint which comes to one who drives past the rubber line of a speed trap, or while passing a patrolman. For a few moments his conduct is beyond reproach; but ah, the motive is not from voluntary respect for speed laws but from fear of being apprehended and fined. Just so with many in religion. It was no afterthought in the mind of Jesus that singled out one group who was assured of seeing God, the pure in heart.

The third waterless well is expectation of a crown without bearing a cross—this, too, is utter folly. The Christian faith is not understood at all apart from that rough-hewn beam on which the Founder of the faith was nailed. Central to all its claims is that shaft dividing time, spanning eternity, and reconciling estranged man to his Creator. Try as one may to explain the sacrifices of Jesus Christ, there still remains the baffling mystery of a thief's cross as integral to His total life and death. He had borne it all through His ministry; it became wood only the last day of His life. Agony of care, spikes driven by impiety, beams hewn by hands that preferred mammon to God, infamous lips puckered for easy betrayal, fickle crowds turning from soup-line discipleship to any other filler of stomachs—these were the points of conflict where His life came at cross currents with men estranged from their Maker. These then constituted His cross and its inevitable exactitude.

The endless query rises in each generation: "But could not God have worked out a more painless method for redemption? Why did Jesus have to die?" A good question indeed! Why He died is easy to answer: anyone living as He did—teaching the things of authority, setting such an embarrassing precedent— either had to change the world, or the world would not tolerate such an example. Obviously, the latter happened. Running athwart currents of vested interests, upsetting financial applecarts of the status quo, ploughing roughshod over the religious niceties of His day, challenging the authority of those who were self-appointed interpreters and arbiters for God— these hammered out the spikes for His palms. When light intrudes darkness, one or the other must give way. When honesty and truth are held alongside the crooked wall of half-truths and dishonest dealings, the slanting angle becomes a source of irritation for the builders of the wall. Better to remove the plumb line than tear down the wall—at least so reasoned the high priests! To say that He had to die for His convictions is without equivocation.

Then how about us? Is the servant better than the Master? If His bearing a cross was a necessity, then by what stricture of rationalizing can a similar fate be escaped by men living in the same kind of world? His evident necessity was no whimsical God proving allegience by wielding a chastising whip. Not that at all. Instead, it was an honest admission that crowns and crosses were forged in the same crucible, and eternal life cannot have one without the other. Little wonder He spoke in imperative forthrightness: "If any man will come after me, let him . . . take up his cross. . . ." No easy options here; no elective based on whim or fancy—instead, a direct command is given to everyone who would become a follower of His way.

There is an appropriate cross for every type of personality. God's sense of fairness, whatever else may be involved, sees to it that not one splinter too many shall constitute that spiritual load. The fact that He permits the weight is axiomatic of the faith; but what is often obscured is that the divine scales accurately test the back, then the load. Only the insensate conclude that such theology speaks of tyrannical cruelty, sadistically gleeful of man's struggles. God knows that man cannot be polished any other way; ease is the sorriest school for soul growth, and spiritual acumen is commensurate

only with struggle and forbearance. To be "carried on beds of
ease while others fight to win the prize" is to admit a condition which God disavows.

Hobbles on the feet of horses induce surefootedness; governors on motors prevent their incessant whine; stabilizers on
ships control the lurch in the cradle of the waves; alloy
strengthens pewter; tension is the force by which a hinge
closes the door. A cross astride man's spiritual shoulders
produces an Apostle Paul, a Helen Keller—a Saviour of mankind.

So easily man's attitude to a cross-centralized religion degenerates into mythology and into medievalism with all its
negative blights. Lest that fate befall some reader of these
lines, be it known that cross-bearing is not hypochondria or
chronic depression induced by intemperance or weak judgment. Nor is it a Gordian knot tied by selfish interests, ex-
trication from which seems impossible. The nature of the
cross is not self-righteous martyrdom conjured by alternate
elation and morbidity; nor is it even vicarious suffering stemming from overactivated imagination, nor a sophomoric conclusion that life is an unfathomable mystery and that any
efforts to solve the riddle are wasted. Instead, it is that cross
fire which naturally results from one's being in the world yet
not of it, the persecution which comes for His sake—all the
Johns who rebuke Herods, all Stephens proclaiming judgment
on evil men and subsequent stoning, disciples upsetting
silversmith's rackets out of deference for human personality
and its worth, all modern Samaritans whose preoccupation
about business deals in Jericho do not blind them to the man
who has been beaten and robbed in the ditch of life. These
exemplars of virtue who, because of no restraint in market
places, are dragged before heathen judges; runaway slaves
returned to their masters; withered hands and leprous faces

eliciting the kind of pity that sometimes breeds contempt; medical missionaries whose blood coursed down their weary faces and whose only crime was to minister in the name of Jesus rather than be ministered unto, paraded before grimacing Communists: these then are the splinters of a rugged cross akin to that which jutted in the rocky crevasse on the Place of the Skull.

When man staggers beneath the load of his cross—whether that cross be circumstantial or otherwise—God usually has two recourses. Either He can remove the load or He can strengthen the person's back. Usually He does the latter. No artesian well pours forth more refreshing waters of inspiration than the remembrance that God never overloads, all human disposition to complaining notwithstanding. Let every child of God who thinks his lot unbearable take new courage in the conviction that God has appropriate strength for each extra pound of human weight. When asked why God should permit such a staggering weight on him, Billy Sunday answered: "Better limp all the way to heaven (under your cross) than not get there at all."

A crossless discipleship is a tragic misnomer, totally alien to that of the Son of God. Today's edition of light allegiance, easily sidetracked by the slightest turn of circumstance; a chameleon conduct, diluting the ethic of Jesus to nice manners, courteous palaver and ecclesiastical mumblings, are part and parcel of a religious movement that saw no need of or significance in the sacrificial crucifixion. To them the ethical code of Jesus rates a high berth in religious literature; but this business of a horrendous cross—no! But they hold that opinion to their own undoing. Such a loose-knit system has a way of falling apart at the seams when the acid test of realism is put to it. The cross is to religion what a rudder is to a ship.

Says an ancient legend: "Three trees prayed that they might

choose what they would be converted into when they were cut down. One prayed to be made into a palace, one a large ship, and the other to stay in the forest and point men to God. One day an axeman came and cut down the first tree. Instead of a palace it was made into a common stable wherein was born the fairest Babe in all creation. The second tree was made into a ship that was launched on the Sea of Galilee. On the deck of the ship stood a tall Young Man who said: 'I am come that they might have life, and that they might have it more abundantly.' The third tree was made into a cross, and to it men nailed that same Young Man, the loveliest personality of all time. But ever since, that tree—that cross—has been pointing men to God."

When one has borne his cross willingly in time, then he may expect to wear his crown in eternity. The two were hammered out on the same anvil—one is heaven's counterpart of the other. But the idea of reward religion strikes us as having a bit of ulterior motive. A peppermint heaven with "pie in the sky bye and bye"—as well as now; service motivated by anticipation of celestial compensation; God conceived of as a quartermaster general or as an apothecary to whom one may run for relief from all life's strictures: these do not speak of the kind of crown assured those who chafe beneath a cross. The objection to reward religion pleads for service in the name of Christ for Christ's sake; it pleads for work just for the sheer joy of working, for lifting a fallen brother, not for approbation but because the brother is down and needs lifting —as Kipling says in "L'Envoi":

And no one shall work for money, and no one shall work for
    fame;
But each for the joy of working, and each, in his separate star,
Shall draw the Thing as he sees It for the God of Things as They
    Are.[3]

[3] From *The Seven Seas* by Rudyard Kipling. Reprinted by permission of Mrs. George Bambridge and Doubleday & Company, Inc.

As noble as this sentiment of objective service sounds, it smacks of a dualism and inconsistency. The very people who frown on reward religion will strike for incentive pay, reward their children for work rendered, look for high grades in school, rebel at the absence of bonuses, while the thought of approaching old age without security is frightening! What inconsistency! It is true that Christian service should be rendered for the glory of God and in the voluntary joy of doing it, but it should never be forgotten that the logical result of such activity is a crown of glory and not the purpose for which service was done. If one seeks heaven's reward to save his soul, such egomania already has inured him to hell.

The "something for nothing" attitude of today's millions has crept over into theology. Man's ego, inordinately inflated, is brash enough to presume on God for an endowment of eternal life with or without preparation. What folly: to believe that one has anything worth perpetuating in heaven who has not learned something of heavenly living on earth! The diluted theologians who, with more charity than truth in judgment, have led many to believe that at the end of time God will overlook human history and will take us all to heaven, give the lie to most of what Jesus had to say.

He made it succinctly clear that at the end of a devout life of cross-bearing was the certainty of a crown. Said He, "I go to prepare. . . ." Replete with this assurance is the biblical record: ". . . to obtain . . . [not handed down without reasons, but achieved through rigorous service] an incorruptible (crown)" (1 Corinthians 9:25). "Henceforth there is laid up for me [passive voice] a crown of righteousness . . ." (II Timothy 4:8). ". . . and I will give thee [on basis of divine love and human response] a crown of life" (Rev. 2:10). The objectors to such contention are usually those who do so out of disdain for literalism. But too often such objection is camouflage for puny effort which would never earn a crown.

So to expect is similar to the one running counter to the law being the first to object to the law's validity. Two indispensable requisites are imperative for reaching heaven: first, one's sins must be pardoned, and second, his nature must be changed. There is no known method other than by the Cross of Jesus Christ by which both can be achieved.

Unshakable confidence in this future certainly is endorsement enough to encourage man through this earthly pilgrimage. Knowing that his future is secure in God, one should live each day in radiating, compulsive love. The little dividends received each day are but interest; the principal is reserved for eternity. God doesn't settle His accounts on the first of the month but on the first of eternity. That is why heaven must wait. In the meantime, duty brings delight, and heaven attracts to itself those who have affinities with its nature. Any apparent delay is sufficiently interpreted by these lines of John Greenleaf Whittier: "Forever from the hand that takes one blessing from us, others fall; and soon or late, our Father makes his perfect recompense to all." [4]

[4] James Mudge, *Poems with Power to Strengthen the Soul* (Nashville, Abingdon Cokesbury Press, 1907, 1909).

4

LIFE'S OVERFLOW

THERE IS IN life a principle of overflowing abundance. Nature, in addition to supplying the basic necessities for survival, is freighted with cargoes of nonessentials: cascading vapors, color harmonies, gentle symphonies, and radiant sunsets. The soil of life is inundated by fertile bounty, and only the spiritually uninitiated or color-blind fails to see this panorama of plenty. The fact that "the world is too much with us" is commentary enough to explain man's unawareness. Archibald Rutledge has called them "life's extras." They are not indispensable to living. One could live his allotted years without them; yet, they are here: a fact with which we take delight in reasoning.

Take color. One could live out his allotted time if everything he saw was olive-drab or dark gray. All matter could be monotonously neutral without hindering life's propagation. But the fact remains that the universe is suffused with a riot of color speaking of a Master Painter. The two colors which one can look at the longest are blue and green; God put one overhead in the sky and the other under foot. What Raphael or Titian could produce so golden a sunset? There is but one Old Master: the original artist. Faint shades of purple and lavender; overtones of crimson and orange; basic browns in Indian summer; delicate tenderness of wild violets; contrasts of light and shadows as sunrays burst through a canopy of live oak trees: these are the color charts of the Master Painter. And to go one better, the prisms of the eyes are focused so as to admit automatically the quantity of light and color conveyable to the brain.

In the chambers of sound, man discovers one of God's extras. Few sounds are harsh and discordant other than those of man's creation. Shrill, raucous commercials on radio and television; car horns blaring down concrete canyons; screams emitted by nervous children; the discords of unholy cities, thunder of mass response in bleacher ovation—these are the sounds that bombard man's eardrums into pain and frenzy. Not so with Nature! She knows the symphony of gentle breezes, the rhapsody of robins. Oh, the thrill of strolling through live-oaked forests at dusk to hear the sweet oboe of an oriole, the flute of a nightingale, or vox humana of chirping sparrows! Now and then in summer's uneven lull, the sharp crack of lightning (like electric dynamos suddenly loosed from their chains) dances across the sky with a resounding amen of thunderous sforzando. Few sounds break with more pleasant grace than the roaring fire on a cold wintry night untying the knot of bundled nerves and inducing blissful sleep.

Last night I walked under the stars and there, gazing into limitless space, I saw a new dimension: God's high-vaulted canopy above, respecting my minute stature! Then I thought, God could have made this universe with low, cramped ceiling more akin to man's posture and nature in dust, more of man's actual size; yet He didn't. It is high and strewn with sparkling stars as diamonds in black velvet. In these templed dimensions of grandeur there is room enough to absorb earth's carbon monoxides, her fumes and smokes exuding from chimney and pit. There, in this celestial orb rests the rainbow, that golden diadem of divine assurance. A high sky embraces rain clouds which draw up and give back moisture in reciprocal generosity. A high sky, challenging man to lift his eyes, to hold his head high, and look beyond his earth-bound status, knowing that whenever the outlook is dark, the uplook is always bright!

Any poll of human tastes would reveal man's universal love for two things: children and flowers. One is a necessity, the other an extra. I suppose man could hoe his row in life without a single violet. These are not tantamount to existence, yet they are here speaking of a benevolent Creator. There is an endless variety of flowers both native and cultured: the rich formality of camellias, the unsung glory of blackeyed susans, the prolific abundance of all sizes and colors. Tiny violets, debuting from shrouds of leaves, leaving their perfume on the heels of the one who crushes them; rare brown orchids, smiling behind moss-covered leaves in the jungles; the blushing brevity of a night-blooming cereus—all these dazzle the eye in endless varieties of beauty.

Jesus must have been standing in a garden when He said, "Blessed are the eyes which see the things that ye see." What better place for the story of the Creation to be located than in a Garden! Man in his modern dilemma cannot accuse God of lack of provision—at least, man was given a good start. Man's contemporary jungle-like estrangement is a commentary on his distance from the garden. Maybe religion can be understood better as God's reconciling effort to restore the garden and man's place therein. At least we are all in the debt of botanists and horticulturists for their labors in mutation, budding, cross-pollination, and grafting. These have provided accentuated colors and odors, giving man a pastel technique for expressing his heart's sentiment. And as if flowers were not enough, the Lord put a spring of perfume between stamen and pistil as a special dividend.

If the personality of man has a master-key, it must be the warmth of a smile. For a smile dispels more gloom and depression than a whole apothecary shop full of pills! The wider the shutters of a camera are opened, the more light is admitted to the film; so with life: the smile is an index of warmth, radiance, empathy, and inner peace. There are those who equate Christian devotion with somber expression and rigid sternness. They have consigned laughter and gaiety to the province of "worldliness" as though Christianity were an invitation to doom. Not so with Jesus! His was an infectious gaiety. Part of the day's fatigue could be foregone by remembering that three times as many muscles are involved in frowning as in smiling. Why all the extra work? The dimple in a little child's face speaks more nearly of convincing sincerity than the scowl of a towering theologian. "You can smile when you can't say a word, you can smile when you cannot be heard, you can smile when it's cloudy or fair, you can smile anytime, anywhere," says a familiar song.

Music, either that which sets feet in motion or that which stills the heart's tempest, is an undeniable extra. When God got ready to please Himself, He distilled sound and called it music. When He infused His soul into man's soul, He knew that man had a craving which could be satisfied only by the harmonies of symphonic excellence. The human soul needed a vocabulary foreign to the babble of phrases and clauses, so he was given a voice box and pursed lips to whistle the simple melodies, and thereby lighten the load of life. In the folklore of all peoples is a place for music: some of it simple, some of it complex and heavy. Whether it is the hum of a consoling mother to the fevered brow of a child at the end of a day, or an Aeolian organ swelling the last refrain of the

"Hallelujah Chorus," music is a universal idiom. Man's musical mechanics—sharps and flats, tone poems, major and minor chords—are feeble efforts to imitate the Master composer who has written the song of life in natural key.

Nature is suffused with a system of checks and balances, immutable laws that control all things seen and unseen. In the microscopic world, myriads of forces are waging their battles, but they are usually following clearly delineated lines of battle. A veritable catalog of interrelated conditions is necessary for life to exist on earth. Such a list is mathematically impossible if explained on the basis of sheer chance. The relation of earth to other planetary bodies; the fact of four seasons; gravitational pull; the curious relation between oxygen and carbon dioxide; an inexplicable complement of chemicals so essential to biological existence—all these speak of a life force so everywhere apparent that man in casual ease takes it for granted.

A. C. Morrison, in his excellent little book, *Man Does Not Stand Alone,* points up this amazing balance in nature, by citing the case of eels. From the lakes and ponds of America, as well as Europe, go the eels to the water depths off Bermuda. After the parents breed and die, the tiny, young eels begin their long journey back to the same ponds and lakes from which their parents came. This process continues but never has an American eel been found in European waters or a European eel in American waters. This could hardly happen by sheer chance!

When disease attacks the human body, the heart, nerves and muscles, like a regiment of well-armed soldiers, act in concerted unity to ward off the assault. Our bodies are wonderfully made, and they take a terrific pounding from cradle to grave. What with all the stress and strain of modern living, the wonder is not that so many are dying, but that so many are living. If the body becomes chilled, hormones constrict the arteries and raise blood pressure, thereby providing increased warmth. Incident to bacteria invading the body, glands provide hormones to produce inflammation, which wall off infection, while during severe injury they hasten the clotting of blood, lower blood pressure to control hemorrhage, increase blood sugar to provide quick energy and decrease sensitivity to pain. The pituitary and adrenal hormones go into action like assault troops on an entrenched enemy, fighting off stress and any threat to the body's welfare.

Recounting the principle of life's overflow leads to the inevitable "why?" Are all these part of a master design? Does man deserve such superfluity? Life is oversupplied with the extras to inspire man to do his extra best. The divine stencil has been cut, and we are to run off the copies by the divine pattern. God in nature has set a norm for our conduct—a sort of check valve against skimping, exactitude, and meticulous caution. God never intended man to degenerate to miserly egoism; instead, He wants man to mature into magnanimity. The words of Jesus serve as a direct rebuke to the one who insists that there are only twelve inches to a foot: "Give, and it shall be given unto you; good measure, pressed down, and shaken together, and running over, shall men give into your bosom. For with the same measure that ye mete withal it shall be measured to you again." Are we to take this literally? What would it do to our philosophy of mathematics? Ah, there is the rub! It is absurd to defend orthodox conceptions while failing to learn the deeper lesson. Little wonder Jesus was met with rebuttal, rebuke, and crucifixion. It is axiomatic of the faith that life cannot be doled out in niggardly fashion without commensurate response. Beware the conservative, Zacchaeus-like economist in the kingdom; he has no affinity with the spirit of the Nazarene.

Much of what Jesus had to say consisted of direct attacks upon this negative attitude. He found it easier for a camel to go through the eye of a needle than for a rich man to enter the Kingdom. Warning against laying up earthly treasures, He pointed man to the divine depository. To the acquisitive temperament He showed the way of sacrifice, while making it clear that a miser with a dime is no more to be preferred than a miser with a dollar. What a tragedy that no one should ever be accused of the indiscretion of impulsive generosity!

The rebuke from nature is embarrassingly specific: here the sunshine is in profusion; the rain falls indiscriminately on just and unjust; oxygen exists for all. Snowflakes are not doled out for moisture content, nor is the ripening fruit measured to the bushel. Not a single violet demands subtraction from income taxes; no song of the bird mails a statement for services; no exuding perfume expects credit on the books. Hence, Gray's "Elegy": "Full many a flower is born to blush unseen and waste its sweetness on the desert air." Such is the rebuke to man's mediocrity. It is with glib ease that the substantives and modifiers of Jesus are used, but the verbs *love, obey, give,* are hard to come by. These are irregular, demanding. Hence, the trouble.

Life is not measured by accumulation but by outlay. This fact seemed to immunize Jesus against the tyranny of things. He exhorted that man walk the second mile in cross-bearing. After having carried the Roman soldier's dufflebag the required mile, he was to carry it on into camp for him and perhaps in the process the soldier would ask why he was doing it. There was the golden opportunity to tell him about One whose spirit went all the way. This is poignant to the duty-type religion so characteristic in this day. Currently there is a *laissez-faire,* time-clock attitude toward Kingdom things, a level of discipleship which contents itself with doing just what is expected and little more. Walking half a mile is taxing for most latter-day saints, and the suggestion that they go two brings forth a resounding howl of dissent. But life's advances

are always made by those courageous souls who do not sum
up discipleship in terms of costs counted or hours spent. They
pause to ask, "How many miles did Jesus walk?" The answer
is apparent: He went all the way! Beyond the call of duty
there lie the wide vistas, the vast panorama of vision never
seen by the eyes of spiritual sluggards. These are God's
automatics—self-starting Christians who are never pushed off
by homiletical threats or theological coercives.

This resounding advice, given by no other than Albert
Schweitzer, I keep on a small card under the glass of my
study desk, "Only a person who can find a value in every sort
of activity and devote himself to each one with full consciousness of duty, has the inward right to take as his object some
extraordinary activity instead of that which falls naturally
to his lot. Only a person who feels his preference to be a
matter of course, not something out of the ordinary, and who
has no thought of heroism, but just recognizes a duty undertaken with sober enthusiasm, is capable of becoming a
spiritual adventurer such as the world needs." [1]

The abundant presence of every good thing should inspire
us to do our maximum in life.

Man's wandering in the waste places of the earth speaks of
his estrangement from God and His garden. An accommodating
Creator has sown the desert with flowers, sprinkled the pathway with beauty by saying through gentle zephyrs, "Come
home." It is not God's design that man miss his final destina-
tion. He has seen to it that every means necessary has been
made available to conduct safe passage. But some have
difficulty finding God even with the extras! This is intentional
blindness; even a little child can see the way. If man fails to
find God, let him never say that it was because he didn't know
the way. Orchid anthems, antiphonal choirs, air waves re-

[1] Charles R. Joy, *Albert Schweitzer, An Anthology* (Boston, Beacon
Press Inc., 1947), p. 157.

plete with sermonic admonition, kind faces indicating the direction—these all, like signposts, are saying, "This is the way, walk ye in it." And just to think of it: all these and Calvary, too!

If ever our nation needed another symbol for her banners, let her adopt the overflowing cup. No Israel ever knew as much about milk and honey as these United States. No psalmist ever had more right to extol the goodness of God than any man or boy of these streets. The economic cup is running over—and for that matter, the educational, social, and religious cups are all brimming full. If Eden had anything superior to our surroundings, surely it must have been a keener sense of appreciation than ours!

While sitting at his desk an atheist idly scribbled the words, "God is nowhere." After having read these words, his daughter, in an unwatched moment, took the same letters and rewrote them to read, "God is now here." Some men take the tools and circumstances of life, see in them no hidden or apparent meaning, and arrange them to read, "God is no where." Others take the same words with purposeful living and make them to read, "God is now here." With all these extras you would think that no one would be lost!

5

THROW OUT THE TRASH!

My knock on the door was answered by a feeble voice in an adjoining room, "Come on in." My walk from the door to her bedside became a winding path around stacks of yellow papers (some dating back fifty years); old boxes; wrapping twine; tin cans, and bits of a thousand things discarded by other people. I found her sick amidst all that rubbish. After a few consoling words I left the place with a compulsion to tell her, "Throw out the trash!"

Life, like that old house, can become cluttered with remnants, odds and ends, leftovers, irrelevancies, and minutiae which are unworthy furnishings. Every corner of the mind can become a catchall for undeserving thoughts. Speech can harbor all types of derelict vessels, and like barnacles, it can corrode, impede, and destroy. Look at some of the areas where the trash should be thrown out.

If the mind is a catchall, an oversized trashbasket filled with degraded thoughts, risqué attitudes, and indulgent rationalizations, then life will be lived out on a commensurate plane. One's actions in life are based on one's thoughts. There are mental gymnastics which have a way of clogging the channels of life, while making deep deposits in the unconscious self, which, like old discarded rags thrown in the basement, eventually show up in unlikely ways. Instead of a forthright facing of facts, man so easily files them away on the shelves of memory where they are "buried too deep for tears." Out of this subterranean chasm comes the double ego—Dr. Jekyll and Mr. Hyde—that curses existence. "Why did I think such thoughts?" one often asks. Many times the answer involves involuntary choices, those unconscious desires that rise to betray one in the hour of real judgment. Fed on a diet of trash, the mind responds like an automaton in mechanical rhythm. "The mind grows narrow in proportion as the soul grows corrupt," reminds a timeless prophet. A clean mind makes the body impregnable to the fiery darts which otherwise find easy mark.

Today there is an endless variety of mental rubbish which needs to be thrown out. Discouragement, the devil's handle fitting all the tools in his shed, is mental trash. When effort is expended and rebuffed by failure, the mind will flounder in self-pity, that handmaiden of discouragement, that type of mental trash which ignites and destroys. Fear is mental débris. If one borrows on trouble before it happens, an untimely interest is often paid in advance. Life knows no worst paralysis than numbing fear, a shrinking mental timidity that fences life off from its higher and fuller destiny. Fear is a quiver of the mind, causing it to recede when it should be advancing; acquiescing when it should have a firmness of the knees; yielding in compromise when it should stand in dogmatic certainty; questioning the fundamentals when it should be declaiming the goodness of God; imputing to life negation and gloom when it should be exuding the dynamics of triumph. These are the ugly children of fear—mental trash which should be thrown out.

Anxiety, the mental débris so foreign to creative faith, excels only in the capacity of corrosion and rusts out life. Meeting trouble halfway, anxiety is the secret mother of many sins. Let it be known anew that vibrant faith cannot co-exist with pagan anxiety. A singular heart that loves God and trusts Him implicity is raised above the turbulence of anxiety. What absurdity in the thought that finite man, by being anxious, can hold the world together! God has not abdicated His throne. And if He had, this feverish effort would be to no avail.

Perhaps no trash in the mind is more unsightly than *neurotic desire*—a type of mania for more, the craze for cash and all the things it can buy. This compulsion neurosis, which is man's new atheism, the creed of the twentieth century, is a sad requiem to portend a death knell for our kind. By "getting and spending we lay waste to our powers." Human nature is so constituted that it never knows a stopping place in its desires. What once were considered luxuries now are considered essentials; there seems to be no plateau wherein one concludes: "This is enough." Oh, in this day which has enthroned gadgets as gods, where is the man who, like the Apostle Paul, can honestly say, "I have learned, in whatsoever state I am, therewith to be content"?

Negativism is so much worthlessness in the precincts of the mind. Confronting life with broken pinions, it refuses to soar above the sordid. This backhanded desire for defeat, more accurately identified as death impulse, erases smiles out of deference to frowns; questions the worth of all things recreative; exults in pronouncing "no"; disdains the warmth of empathy; chortles and heckles; casts aspersions and ridicules. Peace of mind is but the figment of someone else's imagination. It is never real to the negativist!

Close on the heels of negativism follows its cousin: depression. This mental disease is aggravated by lives that insist on stoking the furnace too often. Running roughshod over the fact that life turns much as a wheel, with its cycles of elation and depression in a comparatively regular rhythm, one insists on all elations and no depressions. Hence, there follows the inevitable collapse into the slough of despondency, despair, and depression. Desperate efforts to combat depression usually result in experiments with another type of tranquilizing drug or with a return to the grog shop. Like so much trash stacked against a wall, this mental accretion saps life of its zest and pungency. A parasite it is, and a despicable one at that!

Given time enough, the aforementioned will eventuate in a form of chronic suicide which, though functional in nature, is nonetheless fatal as poison. The mind knows its own unique snake pit wherein it would obliterate its existence were it not for the loss of face, orphaned children, or personal pride. To work beyond endurance, drink excessively, eat disproportionately to one's needs, veto every movement to enhance the quality of life, these speak of chronic suicidal tendencies.

An obsessive preoccupation about one's own health is the most tedious of diseases, a sort of mental trash. Hypochondria is but a high-falutin' name for the mental rubbish of imaginary illnesses, vicarious pains, ethereal surgery, functional diagnoses, et al. I have no brief to carry against the whole miasma of psychosomatics; as a matter of fact, many a frontier in this direction must be crossed if our day is to know the meaning of health, but there is little store to be placed in the grunts and groans of shallow people whose ills are of their own conjuring. Mental trash! And when it is left in the mind long enough, real sickness is inevitable!

And a host of assorted odds and ends clutter the rooms of the mind. Feelings of being hurt, wounded pride nourished like a fat child who refuses to walk, unwillingness to learn "grief's slow wisdom," exhuming and reinterring deceased loved ones, detailed analyses of the last operation at the slightest evidence of interest—these need to be thrown out.

Few people deliberately choose to collect the wastes of life; many such acquisitions are unintentional. Of what value are old razor blades, wrapping twine, or brown paper? If the mind doesn't have a periodic stocktaking, then hard stock will occupy all the space. Little chains of habits are generally too small to be felt until they are too strong to be broken. With no pattern to follow, no board of censure for thoughts to pass, a mental hodge-podge results.

Jesus spoke with cutting severity about man's mental rubbish. Knowing that deeds are preceded by thoughts, He said that man could be guilty of adultery in his mind without touching a woman; that mental murder, though not taking the life of the hated person, would kill nonetheless. ". . . whosoever looketh on a woman to lust after her hath committed adultery with her already in his heart." Such servile inclinations throttle man's thrust toward his Godlike destiny. Love needed singular enunciation; hence, Jesus drew the clear line of demarcation 'twixt love and lust. Love is the union of souls; lust the union of senses, and "If we live in the kingdom of sense, we shall die in the kingdom of sorrow." It is hard to lust after man without loathing God because lust holds reason captive, and things holy become the first casualty. An old Arabian proverb warns: "An enemy to whom you show kindness becomes your friend, excepting lust, the indulgence of which increases its enmity." To think polygamously and to act monogamously sets up dualism better known as hypocrisy! The maturer virtues extolled in the New Testament will remain unknown to mankind until he differentiates love from lust in the clarity of Butler's words: "One a golden spur, urging the spirit to nobler aims; the other but a foul and miry pit, o'erturning in the midst of its career."

An evil thinker loose in the world is worse than an evil disease. Whereas antibiotics are potent in combating one, nothing short of rebirth can combat the other. Woe unto him whose evil mind is scratched over with obscenity—God will read it all out in the Judgment Day. All these streaks come out in the final washing, as evidenced in the story of Henry II: after visiting his secret mistress as she sat knitting with scarlet thread on the front porch, he was chagrined to find that the scarlet thread remained on the sole of his shoe, a tell-tale evidence of his infidelity, as he walked down the street to his life's partner. One never should be able to think before God what he is unable to do before men. Little wonder there is spiritual indigestion after a diet of salty selfishness and the starch of immoral severity.

Herein one needs a sensitized conscience, a "ruling foible" of the mind. When conscience is conditioned by a God-given capacity for cleanness, the old house is apt to be ridded of its rubbish. When passions, the voice of the body, contradict conscience, the voice of the soul, there is no alternative to positive action. To yield to one's lower self is to crown the animal at the expense of the spirit. Conscience is God's gift to man like a hearth to a house which keeps the hot coals from burning it down.

It is within the domain of mental discipline that muscles sag. This day of libertines sees an ever-mounting number who know little or nothing about a real moral fight. The quality of resistance is shoddy and puerile. Instead of a present-day David's going into the valley to meet his Goliath with sling in hand, he goes to embrace him; and like Samson, luxuriating in the lap of Delilah, he divulges the secret of moral strength rather than resisting the onslaughts of the inquisitor. As a matter of fact, we are not quite convinced of the necessity of resisting.

There are many people confused about the presence of degrading thoughts in their minds: those thoughts involving other people, those circumstances which are contrary to moral standards. Often a sense of cutting guilt plagues such folk and induces despair. It should be made clear that one is no more guilty of such things if the thoughts come out of "thin air" than one is guilty of sinning when he is only tempted. Temptation, though not of God, is no sin in itself. If so, then Jesus sinned, for He was sorely tempted! An evil thought passes your door first as a stranger; second, it enters your room as a visiting guest; third, it installs itself as lord and master. Like a beard, evil thoughts come again and again. The fact is: an evil mind, like other faculties, can be brought into line by forthright discipline. The mind yields to contraction as well as to dilation. Setting it above the appetites, a firm regimen serves to curb, redirect, sublimate, and substitute. Knowing not this mental setting of the house in order, one is enslaved to every passion, every subterranean mental labyrinth. It is a total impossibility for man to think in low and to live in high, because "As he thinketh in his heart, so is he. . . ." But to conclude that "these are just my thoughts" is to rationalize the old injunction "Get thee behind me, Satan."

Immediate dismissal of an evil thought is the way of intelligent Christian action. To trifle with such a thought at its inception is to encourage its residence. To tinker with wrong is not the way to expel it. All a camel wants to do is to get his head in the tent in order to assure entrance of his whole body later. Evil's direction is down, and that is degradation: first it walks with the ungodly, then stands with sinners before sitting in the seats of the scornful. The Devil is never done, and what better place for him to chart his course for the soul than in the precincts of the mind.

Today's parlance, the new-found psychological nomenclature, has served to confirm man's foolish notion that his evil thoughts constitute no area of his own responsibility. He is being led to believe that a passion is an "obsession" or "compulsion" neurosis with the degree of compulsion determined by its repetition. In no sense of the word does he think that he is to be accused of "guilt"; hence we see the evolution of the wayward libertine to whom all thoughts are liberty and license. If one is not accountable for what he thinks, there is no area of accountability. Such is his real soul.

To sharpen the cutting edge of mental discipline, a Christian can always ask, "What would Jesus do?" Can Christ dwell in your kind of mind? Certainly He will not take up residence amidst mental trash. Just as the balance wheel of a watch reacts to the pull of a magnet, so the mind, magnetized by any predilection, acts irregularly.

> My mind to me a kingdom is;
>   Such present joys therein I find,
> That it excels all other bliss
>   That earth affords. . . .

Nothing short of mental excellency makes the body impregnable.

No modern gimmicks work half so well in this effort to discipline the mind as that which Jesus taught twenty centuries ago. Said He that the dismissal of the Devil is but half the process of victory. Throw the Devil out in "wondrous potency"; but then the house is to be swept and garnished, furnished with new furniture, fresh occupants, positive thoughts, creative desires, worthy aspirations—or else a mental vacuum results, and the time will come when the Devil returns in legion with seven worse devils to invade the house and the "last state of that man is worst than the first." Replace degraded thoughts with elevated ones; substitute the lustful for the lovely; fix the mind on things above; stay it on God in trusting belief. Pleasant thoughts can become part and parcel of everyone who soldiers on this field of battle. Like a lever that turns the bright and glowing, worthy thoughts direct the mind in quest of the best. This has been the faith of great thinkers during all ages; knowing the intellectual force of mental disciplines and their derivatives, they reposed in the security of a communion of thinkers who rose above the flats of mental trash. "Give me," said Herder to his son, as he lay in the parched weariness of his last illness, "give me a great thought, that I may quicken myself with it."

In the arena of amusements there has accumulated much débris. Quite naturally the mind that is stoked on evil thoughts will seek, soon or late, expression in the bordel of entertainment.

The right kind of recreation and fun is both good and wholesome; the mind ought to be diverted so it can do its best thinking. The body needs to participate in order to realize its maximum usefulness. No tragedy takes precedence over that which contends for religion a colorless resignment to dullness. Why should religion strip mankind of all his pleasures? One reason the Devil took over so many places of amusements is that religion has been too afraid to have a good time. It is hard to conceive of Jesus as a kill-joy, always finding something wrong with every kind of human good time. No, He surely was one in whom laughter found full latitude, levity was given ordinate berth, and zest found consummate expression. He knew life was meant to be lived, that everything which God made was good. Yet, these were but means to a nobler end. Whatever obstructed that higher purpose and caused personality to forfeit its heavenly destiny was not tolerated.

The wrong kind of amusements, like so much trash, serves to retard instead of advance man's quest of the eternal. Many an activity in our day is to be indicted, not on the basis of its vulgarity or intrinsic wrongness, but in that it is nothing but a pastime for idle souls. Being neither moral nor immoral this neutral activity sounds no depths of profundity, calls for no higher content. Little wonder this age has been accused of the "disease of nothingness." Whatever absorbs thought, taxes patience, and becomes taskmasters of idleness is nothing but trash so far as entertainment is concerned.

Mankind is keeping company with the lesser breeds when he develops the habit of dissipating every serious thought by a succession of sensations, a process that is fatal to spiritual maturity. If a given activity does not excite unusual emotional depth, it is considered too tame for endorsement. What better index of waywardness is needed than this: the cutting edge of spiritual sensitivity is dulled by an inordinate insistence on sensuality as the criterion of worth for most entertainment! One notch more—our day demands a bit more sordid edition, not quite so puritanical is the cry of the rabble. Then appetite is whetted on rawness; conventional things lose their feeble grip.

The midway mark of the twentieth century witnessed a heresy within the Christian church: duty in Kingdom service was replaced by ecclesiastical entertainment. People, who were amused and toasted on every hand at the slightest provocation, cajoled, and entertained, could hardly be expected to take stock in the strange demands of self-sacrifice, servility to objective realism, cross-bearing, or losing the ego in the ground swells of God's eternal purpose! Evangelizing the heathen was "one for the books," or at best it was the nicety of an ancient emphasis with little or no bearing on this technical day. The raw meat of the gospel was replaced by ecclesiastical pablum. No rare stuff to test the molars! No sinewy savour for the palate! Appealing to this semi-pagan nature in man, a jazz band was heard in some churches nearly as often as the organ. The clarion call of the prophet gave way to the chant of the priest with the ugly adjunct of spiritual poverty, juxtaposition of values, and downright paganism. Whatever else can be said of this type of ecclesiastical entertainment, never let it be pawned off as being "Christian."

A great part of the scandal of Christianity is that those who go in the name of Christ are not markedly different from those who do not. The line of delineation should be so clearly drawn that no mistake would be made as to identity—not a line of puritanical exclusiveness, nor setting one up as a model of perfection, but in the natural hallmarks which set themselves on the personality of one who follows in the footsteps of the Lord as His Christ. Still remains the pointed imperative: ". . . come out from among them. . . ." Some never have been convinced of these truths: that it is hard to breathe fresh air in foul places, that it is better to overcome the world than to retreat into it, that "he buys honey too dear who licks it from thorns." An old Spanish proverb contends: "Live with wolves, and you will learn to howl." Like a hot stab in the flesh are the words of Jesus: "Can the blind lead the blind?"

The youth of our land desperately need the guiding light in their choices of recreation, lest a neo-paganism capitalize on the "free thought" cult by exploiting every facet of indulgence and shaming the Parisian *laissez-faire* as infantile. The fact that seven out of eight boys and girls in America drop out of church and Sunday school before their sixteenth birthday is cause for alarm even among the most calloused or optimistic!

Every life needs a board of censure for its amusements. Obviously all that is condemned is not wrong any more than all that is condoned is all right. Some board of measurement, some telling criterion, should serve as a screening process to separate the sensual from the spiritual and the pagan from the pure. It has helped me in such an endeavor to ask the following questions about entertainment: Does it produce moderate excitation or does it result in dissipation? Is it recreation or exhaustion? Frequent or habitual? Does it return me to duty with renewed perspective or does it set up competition with my primary duties? Can I partake of it in front of my most respected friends? Is it conducive to self-respect? Knowing that self-gratification is but one consideration, does it bring harm to others? Is it actuated by right principles that dignify the purpose for which it is intended? Is it accompanied with the knowledge that life has a higher end than to be amused? Does it hold in consciousness the fact that sinful pleasure is paid for before and after: that sensuality is akin to flowers which die when gathered; that when senses are seered, nothing is left and counterfeit pleasures mock the Christian conscience? In a word, throw the trash out of social amusements!

It would take a fleet of trucks to haul off the trash that is current diet in much reading material. Could there be a more telling commentary on the nature of thoughts than what is in current print? Many dark chasms would remain unexplored by thousands were it not for graphic, detailed directions on the part of an "author." Desultory reading explains much waywardness and comes in for its rightful share of the blame for moral degeneracy. Not that what is read *forces* the reader to sin, but it gives him detailed instruction as to *how* to sin! Three-fourths of popular novels enfeeble the intellect, impoverish the imagination, vulgarize the taste, initiate false values, and waste time. In the literature of the world not one popular immoral book continues to exist two centuries after publication: a fact made possible, not by improvement of human taste but by the intrinsic worthlessness of immorality.

The literary diet of the average man is unpalatable indeed. Finding no time for the classics and rushing headlong in his mania for more, man takes time only for "pocket editions"— in the main, light doses of fantasy and foible with just enough ethical content to point up the freighted load of immorality. As a matter of fact, unless it is flavored with sex, glamour, crime or inversion, it is seldom bought. A casual glance at the captions on the "slicks" will reveal the modern play for Aphrodite which disdains clothes, and accentuates biology to the detriment of personality. Pornography found a legal conduit in bikinis, the lives of private stars, and the sex life of native tribes! Of course, the cry on every hand that this situation is the doings of commercial booksellers, and all one needs to do is to ban their products and haul them into courts of censure is but absurdity! Why have sales skyrocketed into such astronomical figures that supply cannot meet demand? It all goes back to the first pile of trash cited: that of vulgar thoughts. The mind needs a source of slag if the furnace is to be stoked. It is embarrassingly specific to point out that in the same year that America boasted of one hundred million church members it also sold more literary trash than it printed in Bibles and religious literature combined for all those hundred million church members. The contradiction consists in the fact that to the same church members went both Bibles and literary trash!

The disclosure by Senate investigators of a $500,000,000-a-year traffic in pornography in this country presents a shameful target for lawmakers and law-enforcement officers. The report stated: "The quantity and quality of the material beggars description. It is wanton, depraved, nauseating, despicable, demoralizing, destructive and capable of poisoning any mind of any age." Serious indictment indeed against those who are so enslaved by the profit motive that they will stoop to this form of degradation for the sake of a dollar.

In painful exorcism, many parents scrutinize the texts used by their children in school but say little or nothing about the extracurricular reading in "comics," "facts of life slicks," etc. Herein is overlooked a fundamental psychological premise: that early preadolescents who consume the pages of adult indulgence are apt to move in the same direction. What emotional system of thirteen years of age is stabilized to read the case of the missing mistress? Or the secret partner? Or sexual imbalance? This is no plea for the equally erroneous prudery so characteristic of a preceding day that threw the mantle of hush-hush over every effort to educate youth. But it is an unapologetic indictment of the literary trash which finds lodging on the shelves, in the bedrooms, and within the attics of millions of homes, dormitories, and children's rooms. Let us throw the trash out of what we read with forthright severity!

Incident to excitation of thought and deed is the desire for expression—to put into words the course of thought, decision and judgment. This vehicle of expression, which at one and the same time can commend and condemn, comes in for its share of trash. Speech can become rife with verbal vice—vocal rubbish which curses personality and mocks its nobler destiny. On top of the pile of this speech-trash is the infamous habit of finding fault. In a day of accelerated paces, quick tempers, and nervous dispositions, it has become habitual to sharpen criticism and to sit in judgment on one another. With frequency of contact and excessive familiarity, this old evil brooks no quarter to kindness. Moral perfectionism is preached as the *summum bonum* of discipleship; hence, the impasse to which many have come. "Be ye therefore perfect" is taken for literal value while failing to know that the word "perfect" means "usable." The church of Jesus Christ is not regarded as a school wherein some are in the second grade, some in the sixth, and others in graduate school. Unfortunately, newly-confessed Christians are expected to work college-level geometry of Christian maturity. We are merciless in our judgment of a weaker brother. The admonition to "bear one another's burdens" is ignored with smug finality. So speech becomes cluttered with cutting remarks, razor-edge sarcasm and assiduous cant.

Against such verbal débris, the best and fairest of souls have spoken. Warned that British bard, "Forbear to judge for we are sinners all." One may know that the aptest censor has less virtue or merit than the one being censured, a fact which should be reckoned with when one is prone to denounce another. Censure of others is often nothing more than indirect description of his own faults, running roughshod over the wisdom of ages which contended that nothing is so much an index of one's own nature as that which he deems ridiculous in others. Close your ears against the person who would open his mouth against other persons! I keep these lines under the glass on my office desk as poignant reminders of a searching truth:

> In men whom men condemn as ill
> I find so much of goodness still,
> In men whom men pronounce divine
> I find so much of sin and blot,
> I do not dare to draw a line
> Between the two, where God has not.[1]

Nothing is withheld in the Epistle of James to cite the magnitude of danger inherent in an unbridled tongue: it is worse than fire, serpent, or poison.

It is an axiom of the faith that one cannot raise his own posture by reducing that of others, though each day finds a multitude who try it. A subtle edition of this sin (far less blatant and obvious than gutter vocality, yet far more consequential because of its truculent subtlety) prevails among professionals—often religious professionals—who, ignoring the biblical dictum, "in honour prefer one another," climb the ladder of ecclesiastical success by low blows to their brethren. The prefatory question, "Have you heard?" may initiate a conversation in which the verbal paring knife whittles away the sacred posture of one's character. Criticism, the worst of

[1] Joaquin Miller, "Byron."

cants, saps life of its sweetness, and reduces all to a monotonous common denomination of human opinion. Certainly no capital is needed to set one up in this business—the cruelest of professions!

Closely allied with fault-finding and criticism is the verbal rubbish of gossip, that activity by which the commonly accepted theory of mathematics is changed into making two plus two equal five. History is rife with records of wounded pride, crippled characters, and paralyzed personalities who are victims of vocal slander. Actually, to the mind of Jesus this was a type of assassination; one could be guilty of murdering the reputation of another by deceitful slander. One word, inaptly spoken in the right place, can be as deadly as a bullet. "Slander is the revenge of a coward." There ought to be an eleventh commandment: "Thou shall not slander thy neighbor." At least, if one cannot say something good, he should be constrained to say nothing at all. The pioneers had a saying, "If you don't chase a lie, it will run itself to death." But it is at the point of being unjustly accused that one of the hardest of Christian virtues is to be practiced, i.e., in one's attitude toward the accuser. Reconciliation is to be effected by the innocent. The initiative will not be taken by the guilty; hence, the big lump of pride must be swallowed. ". . . if thou . . . rememberest that thy brother hath ought against thee; Leave there thy gift before the altar, and go thy way; first be reconciled to thy brother, and then come and offer thy gift," warned Jesus. A safe attitude to take when one slanders you is to ignore it. To seem disturbed by it to the point of striking back at one's defamer is not to prove innocence. "Ill deeds are doubled with an evil word." [2]

Many jokes need the trash thrown out of them. Whenever intimacies of life are hung out on the public clothesline of indiscreet speech—either in mixed or unmixed company—the

[2] William Shakespeare, *Comedy of Errors*, Act III, scene 2, line 20.

trash needs to go. Many a "corny" joke that masquerades under the banners of "cute" "flavored" "risqué" often depicts the inner nature of the joker. Just here this reaction of a Christian is noted—how he responds to trashy jokes. Does he laugh to be popular, giving assent at least by passivity, or is he offended? Has his moral sensitivity become so calloused that nothing activates revulsion within him?

Profanity is verbal trash. That awkward effort to phrase one's feeble thoughts speaks of an insecure soul that flounders in its compensating efforts to measure up. If some people were to throw out this vocal garbage, they would be mistaken for being mute, having little or no vocabulary left! No! Authority is not accentuated by the bellow of a profane sitting bull, nor for that matter, is one considered more masculine, integrated or in command of his wits when he barks in thunderous profanity. The converse is true. There rests more real authority in discreet speech, spoken in the restraint of wisdom, than in all the blabber-mouths who have not learned how to speak without cursing. Bitter and sweet, prayer and profanity, condemnation and commendation, all from the same mouth, belie a life of singular adherence to Him. In the whole rhetoric of life one should strive to cleanse his speech and purge every offending phrase, every vulgar clause, insomuch that what one says as well as the tone of voice conveys the indwelling Spirit of the Holy God.

One of the loveliest communities of the old South is Orangeburg, South Carolina, a community which boasts, in justifiable pride, of its famed Edisto Gardens. There, along the banks of the dark waters of the Edisto, sleep several acres of cultured gardens in geometrical symmetry and floral beauty. Wisteria trailing up the stately pines; dogwoods spread like crowding umbrellas over mounds of variant azaleas; clumps of second-fiddle flowers hiding beneath their more imposing camellia cousins; tea roses in experimental wonder—these bloom most of the year. But what a visitor doesn't see is the fact few years ago the gardens were a dumping ground for de and trash. Swamp lands were considered too low and marsh for cultivation; but determined residents went to work, build-ing levees, draining, terracing, and planting. Today instead of trash there are trellises, instead of rodents there are roses, and in the place of débris there are donkolarii camellias. Just so with life! A trash pile or a garden? And life in Christ deter-mines which.

6

WHEN WE DIE

BELIEF IN IMMORTALITY is as fundamental to life as air is to breathing. Who will purposefully live through this brief moment of time without believing that immortality is real? In the province of these pages it is not possible to reduce eternity to a timetable or to survey the streets of heaven, but man needs more than inspired memory; he needs to penetrate theological abstractions in an honest attempt to answer the question, "Does life actually survive beyond the grave?" George Santayana's "The Soul's Invincible Surmise" needs to give way to Jesus' "I go to prepare a place for you."

To approach the subject in a funereal attitude is to belie the Christian conviction: life does survive beyond time and the grave in a state of conscious continuity. Armed with this invincible conviction, one is buoyed up from psychological snake pits of pessimism and despair. Death is not a chasm but a triumph. Contemplation of its victory should not induce a mood so mournful as a Wagnerian dirge as though death were the consummate victor of life. Though universal, it is not an

engulfing undertow, drowning man's soul indiscriminately; no swan song of life, no sadness of farewell, no sickly sweet tuberoses, no sentimental finale, no entree to mausoleum, crypt or casket, no pagan chant extolling the heathen gods of the River Styx, no mournful catastrophe to characterize our procession "like dumb driven cattle." If death is the logical bridge spanning the time-eternity ratio, then why all the pagan fuss? "May it not be that some day from this dream of time, this chronicle of smoke, this strange and bitter miracle of life, in which we are the moving and phantasmal figures, we shall awake?" [1]

The contemplation of death is not unconscious longing for it. I like this life—this digit of time—with its illusive "realities": the flush of a covey of quail, the nicker of a Shetland pony, the pungent odor of new-mown hay, the somber clarity of an old church bell, the disconcerting hum of the wheels of progress, the wholesome laughter at our own absurdities, the tight grip of a friend's hand when a job is well done—these are time's royalties which are intrinsically valuable here and now. No, there should be no discounting of this life out of deference for the next. Just the opposite! Weariness of this life is no more a qualifying virtue for the next than it is for this one. Spurgeon often reminded his listeners, "When you talk about heaven, do so with a smile on your face." Going home is always a pleasant journey.

The old school of "finalists," the school that taught life's extinction at the grave, continues to diminish in size. To them, man, like any other animal, merely ceased to exist when breath left his lungs. It was the end of the journey; the final period to the sentence beyond which there was no more rhetoric, no more composition, no prose, no poetry. Out of honesty one must admit that most people have at one time or another

[1] Thomas Wolfe, *The Face of a Nation* (New York, Charles Scribner's Sons, 1939).

trifled with this belief. Theirs was the inspiration of the "Rubaiyat" of Omar Khayyam,

> I sent my Soul through the Invisible,
> Some letter of that After-life to spell:
>   And by and by my Soul return'd to me,
>   And answer'd, "I Myself am Heav'n and Hell."

Despite the magnitude of fatalism engendered by such beliefs, it no more answers the question than it satisfies the soul's longing.

On what hinges shall we swing the doors of belief in immortality? Are there proofs intellectually respectable which do not contradict the premises of faith? Where shall we go for the indices of immortality? I have consulted the booths of media, the intriguing labyrinths of parapsychology, the dualistic contentions of phantasms and poltergeists, but alas, these leave me with no solid ground on which to stand. Nor is wishful thinking any more than projection of one's inflamed ego into the immensity of time and space. Are the verbal remnants of sacred literature the only fingers of authority?

The soul of man instinctively speaks of a "more" and "other" than this earthly habitat. After the finest food has been eaten, the rarest music heard, the strangest sights seen, the happiest moments experienced, he knows something is still lacking, some "i" remains undotted, some "t" uncrossed. This "lack" is God's way of teaching that man is not made for time but for eternity. Were all the goals of man fulfilled here, God would have no chance with him. Woe to him who eats and is completely filled! Beware the person who has no hunger left for things beyond! Bound to the dust of earth, he is a slave serving the sentence of time. The soul, like birds with a natural instinct for warmer climates at winter's advent, knows its migratory direction.

On board an ocean freighter a group of Australian sheep became restive. While trying to explain the sheep's nervous movements, the sailors caught a glimpse of the Australian shoreline. The sheep already had smelled the fresh fields of grass. Sheep were made for green fields, not the ocean waves. Nor is man the creature of dust but a citizen of the city four-square.

Were this instinct more pronounced, man would turn from this stage of time in haunting dismay. God pulls back the curtains of immortality just far enough to let us see what can be appropriated by inspiration without distraction from our present tasks—just enough to nettle the curiosity, and to goad us to nobler heights.

Mankind has never been satisfied with any other conclusion than believing in immortality. Despite the baffling mysteries so ever attendant to the subject at hand, somehow the argument keeps coming up. Facing the reasonings of philosopher and cynic, nonetheless he will not accept any other conclusion than that his soul is stenciled for continuity. Since the dim twilight of primitive history, this belief has been the leitmotiv of all cultures. Before there was a clear-cut belief in God, man, confronted with the loss of a child by disease, lifted his low-browed head to gaze into the face of death with a searching query. Given the fact of rigor mortis, he refused to embrace it as the end of life. Whether Indian, Egyptian, Andean, Slav, or Neanderthal, the belief in immortality finds its place among them all. Long before the authority of religion or the logic of philosophy, man was believing this basic truth. His intuitive feelings were there all the time—the structures of formal thought merely confirmed them.

The best thing that ever happens to one in this life is not to be wealthy, praised, informed, or to live long, but to love and to be loved. Oh, the miracle that transforms dull routine into zestful delight, the elixir that tones one's attitudes and finds the common daylight sweet! That cohesive force welding people into a unity of purpose! Then to say that this life-energizing force can be committed to the grave is preposterous! The scissors of death cannot sever the steel cords that tie life together in the bundle of love. There is no force in this universe which can terminate this wondrous obsession.

I speak not of the animalism in turbulent passions which, under the guise of love, so mocks the word in this twentieth century. No juke-box mania can be elevated to such dignified levels. Even the lower stratum of animal life knows the metabolic secretions of glandular excitation. But only man can pronounce *agape*—God's kind of love. Man can reciprocate or fail to retaliate, and in this unmotivated initiative, human society discovers its own soul. Does this not explain why Jesus could die at thirty-three instead of sixty-three? He knew that transcendent love would assure continuity of purpose, that the mocking mask of death would end nothing but habitation in flesh and blood, and that nothing is lost which is begun here in the labors of love. If this be true, one does not lose a loved one by death, he merely yields him to the broader outreaches of love's pursuits. If this fresh conviction were to take roots in our thinking, becoming a part of our hourly thoughts, it would yield dividends beyond compare. The fear of death for self or others would disappear, and the paganism of worry, so attendant to most professing Christians, would vanish overnight. Such could be our lot without "grief's slow wisdom."

The nature of God is the clearest index for believing in immortality. God's divine, providential magnetism draws His own creation to Himself. This is the act of redemption actively at work in the process of history. Creation is compulsive, and continuity is indispensable to its sustained purpose. Earthly life is but the prologue of existence, the preface of a long volume unfolded through eternity. Were God a permanent discarder of His highest creation, atheism would be preferred to worship. God is no whimsical extinguisher of His own children, grinding them into dust. Man could never worship such a God as that! Instead, "God was in Christ, reconciling the world unto himself." The kind of God revealed in Jesus Christ is a heavenly Father, who insists that the dimensions of eternity are superior to earth and that love will never content itself in any activity other than redeeming the human race. Christ resolves the dilemma by revealing the nature of God as solicitous care and sacrificial love. He proves that God is no distant potentate indulging in an exclusive fraternity of celestial bliss.

The provisions God makes for life on this earth stagger the imagination of those who are sensitive to beauty. The multiflora of garden and jungle; the iridescence of sea foam; enchanting aurora borealis; pupils of the eye admitting color and light in mathematical precision; the alternation of spring, summer, fall and winter; the beige-black plumage of Chukkar quail—all these testify to a bountiful Provider. Now, if all this elaborate handiwork, so obviously existing for man's procreation and pleasure, is provided by God for the brief three-score and ten, why should one falter in believing that God has made commensurate provisions for the soul? I feel quite certain that the botanical splendor of the Versailles will look like patches of weeds when compared to the meadows of heaven!

If God were stultified by death, He is not the Master of life. Here we must admit a cosmic truth: immortality is not a natural endowment of mankind but a gift of God through regeneration. This pontoon was placed by God across Jordan to assure safe passage for those twice born, who were made over in His likeness. Death cannot nullify the greatest work on earth: that of Jesus in His atoning love.

The disquieting news reached Naval headquarters that a submarine had failed to surface and lay helpless on the bottom of the ocean off the New England coast. Soon a diver went down and landed on the side of the submarine. From within he could hear a tapping. Listening intently he heard the frantic, yet deliberate, code taps, "Is there hope?" Instantly he replied, "Yes, there is hope!" Imprisoned in the darkness of egomania, man tapped out the agonizing query to God, "Is there hope?" The answer came back in the form of Jesus Christ saying, "I am the way, the truth and the life . . . he that believeth in me, though he were dead, yet shall he live."

The nature of personality argues with convincing vigor in favor of immortality. The nexus of personality and soul is at best a blurred line, but, suffice it to say, man may be changed in form without extermination of form. Transition is one thing; annihilation, another. As a match is struck, electromagnetic radiation results. In a second or two the flame goes out, but the light will strike spectra of other planets and will become a part of eternal light. In the apparent disintegration of an acorn, an embryonic oak is born. From the center of a rotting tulip bulb comes a new shoot of tender life. The soul's season of metamorphosis, which looks like death, actually is the shucking off of a coat that has served its purpose in time. Actually, nothing in life is lost: solids become liquids or gases, while all matter in transition is the rearranging of atoms, molecules, and protons. Nor can life's transition, so erroneously called "death," extirpate its prime quality: life itself.

One of the intriguing studies in recent years has concerned itself with the distinction of brain-waves and mind-states. Once it was concluded that the mind was but electric impulses triggered by a highly sensitive nerve track, and that coordination of glandular secretions with nerve and muscle tissue resulted in thought. Obviously, if this were the case, man is reducible to test tube analysis, and a surgeon's scalpel could lay bare his "soul." Today, in an advance outpost of psychical research, it is accepted knowledge that the mind is an entity in contradistinction to the brain. If the fleshy mass of the brain dies, then in no sense does it follow that the mind has died. Herein we are impoverished by the limitation of terms. Trying to characterize by the poor mechanics of speech something so multifarious as man's soul is an undertaking of presumption. Whether one calls it "nous," spirit, soul, personality, ego, et al, there is a sixth dimension—a third estate—which cannot be committed to the grave.

Man's spiritual history is replete with the gropings for a wider dimension, a new dimension for personality's expression. Confronted with time-obsession, the soul agonizes for an undated rendezvous devoid of alarm clocks, calendars, and almanacs. Here, like a butterfly imprisoned in a cocoon, personality convulses, writhes, and sometimes ruptures in the struggle for release. It feels its potential wings and resents crawling like a caterpillar! And the silken thread, though smooth to the touch, is still a prison of darkness. There is not enough room here—nor time enough—for life to be lived out in its fullest forte. Friction mounts in proportion to longevity. Little wonder that immortality bids so convincingly to these distraught souls! Ours is the need for a wider tract, a deeper berth. Life on earth is a single manual organ providing minimal stops—stops producing a monotonous tone which causes one summarily to dismiss the jig as "one dern thing after another." But to those who have built dimensions in their souls by selfless service, immortal life will be as a five-manual organ equipped with its vox humana, aeolian harps, celestial chimes, flutes, and full crescendo activated by thunderous sforzando.

When consciousness disdains the idea of dissolution, it must not be construed as sentimental subjectivism. Instead, could it not be one's most objective outreach, since a vigorous defense of life's continuity is actually an endorsement of life's quality, a sure sign that such a life has discovered something worth living for? Who ever hears a gloomy pessimist reveling in the anticipation of immortality? He often would much prefer extinction here and hereafter. Finding this "vale of tears" a miserable mockery, he has no point of reference for life's unceasing aspect. What an embarrassing contrast to the vibrant words of Jesus, "I am come that they might have life, and that they might have it more abundantly."

If one concedes that immortality is a reality, will we know each other as individual personalities? Most individuals insist on this type of immortality, a reunion with those who were known personally to us here: Grandma, the younger brother who died of scarlet fever, the sergeant killed on Iwo Jima, the quaint old school teacher with such unique patience. It is all right for mystics and professional philosophers to dream of immortality in group terms like corporate goodness or one life being reabsorbed in the reservoir of life much as one drop of rain eventually returns to the ocean, but the man of the street who sweats, laughs, prays, and cries, wants to believe that he will continue to live beyond the grave as the person he now is. His special set of emotions and relations, and his well of special affection for certain people is part of the "he" which he wants to survive. Who cares about an ethereal wonderland of disembodied ectoplasm? Such strange environment would strike no happy chords of response in my heart—I would be a total stranger to that heavenly citizenry if the "changed bodies" of which Paul speaks were changed beyond recognition. Oh, not that I am arguing for the same pain-racked physiques nor for the time-dated forms that reek of aging imperfection. But why the other extreme? Who would not settle for his present life devoid of the minus elements and the impulse of death which works within, making one ugly, hard to live with, and unhappy?

Granted that we shall retain our present essential make-up, then these faculties will assure our knowing each other as we do now, though on a maturer basis which shall be devoid of rancor or consequent misunderstanding. Not that we shall be omniscient—that is God's special prerogative—but that "we shall know even as also we are known."

Right at this juncture it should be made clear that love's relationship continues in heaven in its own unique way. But what of those with plural marriages? Will heaven be a divisive sphere wherein broken ties of earth are resumed? The Sadducees posed this question to Jesus when they asked about the woman who had seven husbands. But this, like many other hypotheses, was designed not for an intelligent answer but as a snare to Jesus. The Sadducees did not believe in heaven. But, nonetheless, the answer throws light on our query. Said He, "(There) they neither marry, nor are given in marriage. . . ." The primary purpose of earthly marriage is to consummate love through procreation and to provide an environment for rearing the young. Obviously, heaven's citizenry comes from earth or from other spheres of existence as the result of redemptive love. On this sure postulate one can bank his faith: that the narrow gauge of earthly love with its attendant limitations—jealousy, inordinate affection, fretting protectiveness, turbulent passions, time-obsession, and space cramps— will be changed in heaven, though in the changing there will be retained that residue of pure quality that is distinctive to the love relationship here and now. I mean that one will love his wife and children as his wife and children—he will embrace his mother and father as his own. How shall this be? Because it is heaven!

But suppose there are friends or even life partners conspicuously absent—could it be heaven for the one who felt so alone? Surely heaven will not be a search party for the one whom you loved best! True love would rather be in hell with the object of its affection than in heaven without it. It is nothing short of cruelty to conclude, as some have, that such loneliness is the punitive aspect of heaven for those who did not show enough zeal on earth to win the lost to the heavenly portal. No, I think it nearer the truth to conclude that one of the providential mercies of God is that under such conditions He would block from memory anything that would limit or hurt by a superfluity of provision, compensating tenfold. That's what heaven is like. And God.

Jesus made it explicit that there would be degrees in the next life. A surface glance at immortality by the average modern (whose thinking seldom transcends the plateau of "fair play") will dismiss the notion that heaven is a grandiose rank system where there are priorities of living ranging from private to five-star general. Yet, with no passion to labor the analogy, our whole system of justice on earth is based on a concept that compensation is to be commensurate with effort. The sluggard who is a parasite on society is not offered the garlands of accomplishment. The ardent researcher who conquers poliomyelitis is given national praise. So in heaven. Those who enter the portals by the "skin of their teeth" will hardly exercise a latitude of those who enter with all the bugles blowing. The incisive words of Jesus point up this truth, "that servant, which knew his lord's will, and prepared not himself, neither did according to his will, shall be beaten with *many* stripes. But he that knew not, and did commit things worthy of stripes, shall be beaten with *few* stripes. . . ." On such fair reasoning the laws of this land are based. One does not receive life imprisonment as a sentence for stealing a loaf of bread nor sixty days confinement for committing murder. When the due processes of law are not impeded by ulterior forces, the punishment is in proportion to the crime. Equally pertinent are the words, "For unto whomsoever much is given, of him shall be much required. . . ." Every facet of ability must shine in purpose lest that outlet be darkened. Nothing is ours for waste. We merely hold it in escrow for God. And the divine economy shall take into account every thought and deed.

But one asks, "How could it be heaven if all would not share and share alike? Who would be happy with positive, comparative, and superlative degrees?" This question represents the typical rationalizing so common to egotistical man. The degree of reward in heaven is determined by the quality and quantity of service in the name of God while on earth. Our "something for nothing" is not transferable to the other side. Here is a father who loves string music; the simple melodies played on four strings constitute the repertoire of his enjoyment. But the son, with wider range of study, travel and experience, has come to appreciate great symphonies, among which are string instruments, too. But to the father symphonies are strictly "high brow" because he has no capacity for such appreciation. In a sense, heaven will be that way. Those who only walked the first mile in discipleship, who took a "punch-the-clock" attitude toward Kingdom service, who equated discipleship in terms of one hour on Sunday morning in church, whose souls were never charged by a great indiscretion of impulsive generosity: they shall know a reward of four strings—simple music without addenda. But that rare, saintly soul who walked the second mile, gave not until it hurt but because it hurt, turned the other cheek, stooped to lift, stood fast in the face of adversity, yielded no quarter to the death impulses, fought with tenacity knowing that courage is ever in close proximity to a cross, kept his footing despite the slippery time, knew that compromise with one's weaker self is unthinkable, undertook his hard task in life with no sense of nobility knowing that in obedience to the will of God he could do no otherwise, sought not the plaudits of the crowd—this type of soul shall find a heaven awaiting him that is like a majestic symphony. His reward will be a many-splendored thing. Yet, he shall have no consciousness that one is circumvented by a smaller radius, nor will the four-string citizen know that some abler spirit exults in symphonic splendor. You see, that is what makes it heaven.

To this last question we must come with trepidation. Who goes to heaven? Everybody? Is that school of theologians correct which contends that in the end all will be saved? On this question hinge centuries of dispute, exegesis, and the resultant rise of sects and cults. At least the Universalists who would become self-appointed gate openers can be credited with the sentimentalism of charitableness. Those who would wrest the keys of the gates and become the watchdogs of orthodoxy admitting only those who conform to their little sectarian molds can be credited with bigotry and exclusiveness. The question remains, who goes there?

To contend that everyone is worthy of immortality is absurd! It is hardly playing the role of judge to conclude that the common bum who goes through life with no sense of purpose is not worth living forever, or the miserly egoist who climbs the economic ladder on the back of suffering humanity —what ridiculous sense of value would perpetuate that type? There is no mystery in the Bible as to who goes to heaven. The conditions for entrance are understandable to a little child. NO ONE WILL EVER GET INTO HEAVEN UNTIL HEAVEN FIRST GETS INTO HIM! Eternal life becomes a possession in time as a sinner contritely repents and confesses. At that starting point heaven becomes his destiny and from that point his life does an "about face." Salvation is a point and a process—a process of growing, maturing, and serving. It is flagrant mockery to assume that one who lives on the level of the five senses will have any nature or right for immortality. The loveliest music means nothing to an unmusical ear, nor have flowers, sunsets or landscapes any allure to the unseeing eye. A sinner would be in hell in heaven because he has no nature for the place.

The logic of such a position is seen in the dilemma of an employee who missed the boat by half an hour. His party, made up of employees from a large brewery, had chartered a river boat for a weekend excursion. Another group—a Sunday school class—had chartered another boat and had headed for the same city. Since the second group left a few minutes after the first, they offered the brewery employee a place with them, and added that he could join his group after they docked. Thanking them for their courtesy, he rejoined his group who asked how he got there so quickly. He told them of the Sunday school group that offered him a ride. "A Sunday school class! What kind of a time did you have with them?" He answered, "A hell-of-a-time!" "Why?" they asked. "Because their jokes were too tame, their perspective too high, their company too dull." He simply was not in his crowd. The same way in heaven. One must be in his crowd, speaking his language, sharing in his interests to be in heaven. Who goes there? No one will ever get into heaven until heaven first gets into him! As an unknown author says:

> Then let us learn the language of that home,
>   Whilst here on earth we be,
> Lest our poor hearts for want of words be dumb,
>   In that high company.[2]

It was with impatient curiosity that the parents slowly removed the bandage from the eyes of their young son who had never seen. The surgeon had highest hopes of the operation's being successful. The first sight of light was blinding to him. Then, as his eyes focused on the outstretched meadows

[2] Charles L. Wallis, *op. cit.*, p. 162.

and the faint shades of autumnal pastels, the ten-year-old exclaimed, "But why didn't you tell me it was so beautiful?" "We tried to," his father answered. When the bandages of earthly dust are removed from the eyes of the soul, and the first glimpse of heaven's extended vistas comes in view, the first question will be "But why didn't you tell me it was so beautiful?" God will reply, "I tried to."

PART TWO

Sins of the Church

7

THE SIN OF SILENCE

IT WAS SAID of the German General VonMoltke that "he could be silent in seven languages." It does look as though Christians could be vocal in at least one! In the midst of a desperate famine four Syrian lepers decided to fall into the hands of the enemy in order to keep from starving. Expecting arrest at any moment, they sauntered through the enemy camp grabbing bits of food wherever they could find them. But to their dismay no soldiers were near the camp, so the lepers sat down and gorged themselves into satisfaction. While they sat dozing from overeating, they remembered their families who were back home, consumed by hunger. This incident is recorded in the seventh chapter of II Kings where the spokesman finally admits, "We do not well: this day is a day of good tidings, and we hold our peace: if we tarry till the morning light, some mischief will come upon us: now therefore come, that we may go and tell the king's household. So they came and called unto the porter of the city: and they told them. . . ." Equal guilt must be shared by the Christian church in the midpoint of this century because we do not well; this is a day of good tidings, and we hold our peace. For nearly two thousand years we have known the good news of salvation, yet enjoying it for ourselves, we have failed to propagate it. But inability to transmit news is not our problem. When a former President of the United States died, the news of his death was known around the world in less than thirty minutes.

The fact that the church is committing the sin of silence is apparent everywhere. For instance, in one of the major evangelical denominations it takes the efforts of thirty-one church members to win one other person to Christ in a year's time. In some of the "non-evangelical" groups that ratio is increased by forty to one. And yet this is the one thing that all professed Christians are called to do. Seeing is for the purpose of telling. If the experience with Jesus Christ is not of sufficient import to recommend it to someone else, then the whole structure of the Kingdom is in question.

In one of those post-resurrection appearances near Galilee, Jesus left a spiritual legacy to the unwon millions when He commanded His followers to "go teach all nations." Taking Him at His word, they spread over the pagan world like wildfire, waiting for no other impetus than that forthright command. Sellers of figs, dealers in pearls, importers of dates and spices, handlers of purple, camel and oxen traders, tent dispensers, cosmetic peddlers—all were told of the wonder-working way of life: a life suffused by love and loyalties which figured no expense too costly for its devotees. Strange sounding things, this new talk of a Nazarene who had died in order that others might live. Hearing it was like hearing subdued harmonies after a thunderstorm while this concordant note in a world of Caesarean discord served as a tuning fork for the sagging strings of humanity. The old gods, like poorly washed clothes on a line when snow fell, looked dingy and curiously out of date. While they listened to the clarion words, "Hear, O Israel: the Lord our God is one Lord," the polytheism of

Greece and Rome paled into insignificance. Here was set in motion a tidal wave inundating the arid deserts of philosophy and crusty religions. Resulting from that inundation came moisture to the dry roots which had all but parched in the blistering sun of godless noons and heathen nights—moisture that revived the potential verdancy while flowers began to bloom in the desert! Who is amazed at such wonder? And until this day that metamorphosis is taking place where the worm of life, transformed into a butterfly, resents the cramped, silken cell and bursts forth into firmamental glory. Whatever impedes the telling of this story is spiritual crime!

In the past hour, while thinking through this phase of discipleship, the radio in my car has been playing. Within this hour no fewer than thirty-seven commercials blared forth in exciting urgency. Were it not for a type of conditioning, partially immunizing the listener, one would get the impression that his very life and salvation depended upon buying a particular kind of soap, smoking a specific type of tobacco, trading for one firm's used cars, exchanging last year's washing machine, attending the society for the propagation of doodlebugs, giving to the fund for preserving the monument of General Fungus or running for your life because an atomic bomb is imminent. The point: we are vocal on everything else save the important thing! The same tongue that thickens when it comes to the wares of the gospel is astoundingly agile and glib with Caesar's wares. Americans are known the world over as good salesmen, a fact borne out by the presence of American gadgets in practically every port and hinterland of the world.

While tramping through the remote mountains of Mindanao in the southern Philippines, one saw in the thatch-roofed, one-room dwellings the only piece of furniture to be an American-made sewing machine. Some smooth-talking itinerant had sold a shipment of electric toasting machines to a community that doesn't have and probably won't have for the next generation any type of electricity. Nor could their bread fit into the narrow sluices of the toasting machine, even if they had electricity. No, there is no perceptible delinquency in the art of salesmanship; psychology has come to its rescue in its gospel of putting the best foot forward, of understanding the potential purchaser, of not overselling the point or product, etc. But what an ironical commentary that goods and gadgets should receive such preferential treatment over the gospel!

My reaction to the news that the Japanese had surrendered and the war was over lives in my memory as a daily emotion. As I stood in a little ravine in Okinawa, the news came from a private who was sitting at a switchboard in communication with Manila. Reaction to the news was one spontaneous outburst of joy, gratitude, and tears; but this fusion of emotion in no sense of the word hindered or delayed my shouting down the ravine at the top of my voice, "The war is over! The war is over!" Upon hearing such news the next man relayed that momentous news on down the valley until every man from signal post, through motor pool, to command tower, into the mess hall, and to every pup tent had heard, insomuch that a chorus of unrestrained emotion echoed from hill to hill. Why? Because it was a personal issue to every man there: homes were involved, future plans were to be formulated, unseen children to be rocked, and loved ones to be embraced. We are always vocal on the things that matter.

But such a conclusion points up an embarrassing consideration: then do the things of the gospel matter to us? Do they matter sufficiently for one to go beyond the perfunctory, casual, "take-it-or-leave-it" attitude? In many cases—yes! But to conclude that even a sizable minority of professed Christians are busy at the job of telling the good news of salvation is to conclude an absurd error. They simply are not! The empty pews, the unwalked aisles in thousands of churches, dry eyes, pursed lips, unbent knees, and the rage of the heathen in his deceived folly: all speak of the sin of silence —a sin indeed.

Why the muteness? Surely so widespread an observation should be subjected to intense, honest analysis. If these contentions are not exaggerated, what forces have played the field to mute Christian testimony? The forces are multifold, interwoven, and difficult to pinpoint. Among the more obvious one is the fear of extremes. When in the historical process zeal got the better hand of judgment, and a fanatical demonstration buttonholed people on street corners with the frontal interrogation, "Are you a Christian?"; when poorly printed tracts became substitutes for kind, warm, personal telling; when an unholy, amateurish tone crept into the voice to destroy natural individuality and peg the witness as a bit otherworldly; when self-righteousness appended its obnoxious self as an indispensable adjunct to the activity thus alienating the "heathen"; when the fires of hell were described with more telling erudition than the lustre of the gates of heaven; when no doubt was left but that the wrath of God was always present in sadistic glee, whether His love was or not; when the impression was left that divine grace could be manipulated, dispensed, and monopolized by one particular sect or cult—it was at these times that many froze over in their willingness to tell the glad tidings. While understanding such a response, no justification remains for it. Which extreme is worse: the one just described or the opposite which regards the moving drama of life being converted, budgets stabilized, families reunited, minds built up in the admonition of the Lord and faith revived, with the succinct smugness of "no comment"? Gallio still lives today on some boards of deacons, and among some vestrymen, stewards, and elders. Better to admit the honest truth than to skirt the issue as though it didn't exist; or if admitting its existence, to regard it as being of such meager import that one should never get "worked up" over it. Let excessive zeal be chosen any day in preference to its opposite.

Why the sin of silence? A growing suspicion that He no longer is the Way contributes its share to silence. Lodged in the net of doubts, the floundering member never quite gets to the place where any belief assumes the proportions of conviction; hence, he really has nothing to say. Is man a sinner? He isn't quite sure. After all, maybe this belief is nothing more than theological priestcraft, a perpetuated system of ministers and priests, who have duped the human race by their coercive threats and fears and have used such techniques to intimidate, control, and commercialize. Such is the reasoning of throngs who no longer are convinced that He is the Way, the Truth, and the Life. While not daring openly to declare it in business, home or on street corner, silently, in the inner precincts of their hearts, they are secretly disagreeing with God.

Christendom has yet to see a vocal disciple who didn't believe that man without God is lost. Who seeks a child playing in his own backyard? One doesn't run for a streetcar that he has already caught, nor does a follower of Him go in pursuit of one who is not considered lost. Gone with the wind are more things than Spanish moss, magnolias, and old lace; gone also is the staggering conviction that there is a hell, and man is logically its future occupant until he is made over by the shaping hands of a loving God. All the gimmicks, novelties, and pressure campaigns combined will never accomplish the privileged job of testifying to unsaved people as will the simple conviction that man without God is a hopeless equation. So to believe is so to tell. Whatever activates Satan's glee, I know not; but surely nothing in the church would please him more than to observe a uniform shout of silence!

"No comment!" is doubtless the surest index to a vacuous soul wherein a saving encounter with the Son of God never happened.

Events took a happier turn in the case of the Syrian lepers. At a certain point of saturation they decided, "Some greater mischief may befall us if we tarry until morning." The same probability, though with horrendous dimension, may befall us because of our tarrying at the job. Among two and a half billion people, better than half that number are under Communistic domination. In 1904 one man kept preaching an infamous sermon, a sermon that produced seventeen converts. By 1917 these seventeen had become forty thousand. By 1933 their fold had swollen into the millions insomuch that in 1955 there were nine hundred million plus! What phenomenal laws of growth account for this multiplication? Is the content of that godless belief such that it recommends itself to so many millions? Hardly! If ever the human race was sold a bill of goods—a pig in the poke—it is in this first half of the twentieth century. It is true that communism has had the aid of the sword; but more important, it has had the nigh unbeatable ally of vocal lips. Its story has been told in staccato monotony to anyone who would hear and to many groups who were in forced audiences. And while not endorsing a single technique involved, one must admire the zeal by which the tenets were disseminated. Into the sugar cane fields of the East they went with crusading urgency; down the ragged rows of hemp they witnessed; in sampan and rickshaw the *Das Kapital* was recited; on communal farms and collective experiments the *Communist Manifesto* was chanted in rote; to lecture hall and study dormitory went the apostles of Marx; and in this present age the whole world fears this virus with justifiable dread. The tightest noose of censorship can never silence man's undying quest to disseminate his beliefs.

Until the church admits that man refuses to live in a

vacuum, it will have no potent authority in this kind of world. Pessimists are multiplying, believing that it is too late to stem this contaminated tide, that the greater mischief has already befallen us. Yet, others remember: if each Christian won one other to Christ, the whole world could be won in less than twenty years! No index is more telling than the average church's emphasis on missions, that agency which is designed to tell the good news over the world in the most effective, continuing way. If but a modicum of the finances spent for military defense were funneled into this soul-winning agency, the real defense of man would be a permanent *spiritual* possession.

Were there no other consideration than the economic, Christian missions would still be the best business bet under the sun. When China closed her doors to the western world, there were multimillions in assets that were quickly liquidated, frozen, or stolen outright. Quite an unprofitable venture financially! Yet, the most bigoted provincial knows that had business been suffused with real ethics and had Christian teachers, farmers, medics, and preachers outnumbered businessmen, communism would never have gotten a foothold, nor would business have lost its investments. "But we can't afford it," is the plaintive and quick reply to the plea for more missionaries. The positive fact is that we can't afford not to. One would think that all the acumen of Wall Street would have given rise to a bit more vision along this line. Not that missionaries can be used as front men for lucrative business deals, but that when human hearts are changed and minds rightly are positioned toward a world of cooperative harmony, then sound business is an inevitable adjunct. Could it be that the future will witness the realization of this new frontier approach? Or must the biblical interrogation be repeated, "Is it nothing to you, all ye that pass by?"

If the church is willing to admit its sin of silence, then three suggestions are offered. First, encourage a sense of urgency about the task. Sitting until morning may be too late. The night always is of determined duration, and day comes of its own initiative: the day of doom or delight, depending upon man's cooperative efforts with God's good pleasure. Jesus knew some things could not wait, a fact that explains His working "while it is day: the night cometh, when no man can work." Characterizing everything He did was a consciousness of immediacies. The danger is not that the world might end, but that it might continue. Regardless of what one thinks about the program of eschatology, last things, or whether he believes in a millennium and Christ's coming before, during or after, the fact remains: man's going is imminent, whether Christ comes tomorrow or never! That meeting in judgment is the most certain rendezvous of time, and urgency about one's preparation should be a consuming interest of the church.

In the back of a floral shop my friend showed me a long tray of chalky-white orchids—some with yellow throats, others with shades of lavender fragile as silk—but the sixty orchids were all limp and worthless. When asked what happened, he told me that after they were picked in Central America, the shipping clerk failed to stencil "PERISHABLE—RUSH BY AIR." Instead, they came by a slow boat and upon arrival they were wilted. The Bread of Life in the kitchen of the Christian church cannot be delivered by slow boat—it is highly perishable! More urgency about the good news is prerequisite to survival.

Paralleling this requirement should be a nonprofessional approach. Pentecost was that cataclysmic event in early history when down-to-earth laymen took the initiative in telling the story of their Saviour. It was not a group of trained theologians but a group of men who still had the smell of fish on their boots, women whose hands spoke more of goat hair and mutton than of satins from Damascus. But it was these uncouth folk who caused curious bystanders to marvel, when they saw that they had been with Jesus. Not because of their lack of formal schooling was such an observation made, but despite it. And so today. One doesn't have to approach a fellow bookkeeper in the nicety of memorized jargon, quoting verses of Scripture and interspersing emotional froth. A better way is to use one's own words and one's own voice in the propitious time and place. Like a deaf-mute who had a habit of standing in a foyer of the church as the people came in and left, and when asked why, answered in sign language, "To let people know what side I am on." Anybody can witness for Jesus—much like our little elevator operator who tells every group of people she brings down from the upper floors, "Be sure your last trip is up." Or like a crippled lady in our church whose foot is twisted at pathetic angles when it receives the weight of her body. She requires two walking canes for balance, yet in a recent revival I saw her come early to supper, go from the church in pouring rain, and limp along, up and down steps, in the big city to tell some lost soul that Jesus had died for him. If a paralytic can go in drenching rain, it looks as though the rest of us could, too!

When the issue becomes personal it will become purposeful. If it is taken to heart one need not be cajoled, coerced, and browbeaten in order to do the job. Spontaneously the desire and motive power well up in his heart, and he reaches for his hat, making it primary business. Just such sincerity was in evidence when a young lawyer asked an attractive lady on the train, "May I sit beside you?" Having talked in lighter vein for several miles, they discussed in an honest, yet nonobnoxious way, the wonderful business of being a Christian. Soon the train pulled into the station; the young lady walked down the steps and was greeted by her husband. The man with whom she had talked followed a few paces behind and bade her good-bye. "Who was that?" the inquisitive husband asked. "Oh, just someone I met on the train with whom I talked to kill time." "What did you talk about?" he pressed. "Just weather and nothing in particular. But you know, he asked me the strangest thing: he asked, 'Are you a Christian?'" Without the slightest twinge of reverence her husband continued, "Well, why didn't you tell him to mind his own business?" "That's just the point," she answered. "Had you heard him talk, you would have thought it was his business."

The Bible, in more than eleven hundred editions says in every one of them six hundred times: "Come." Let us not go about our business in this world saying: "Look what the world has come to." Instead, let us say: "Look what has come to the world!"

8

THE SIN OF DULLNESS

THAT THE CLAIMS of Christ would be difficult to achieve, that a negative response to its demands from many would be anticipated, that a resounding "no" to its challenging commissions when many disbelieve them would be expected, but that Christianity would be dull is unforgivable! Nothing could more misrepresent this dynamic, status-changing way of life! Sparkling with the fire of soul-brightness, Christianity energizes every facet of life's interest. Understood aright, it impregnates sluggishness with vitality, torpor with momentum, and futility with purpose. Yet, twenty centuries have wreaked havoc with this uncomplicated idea. The church has suffered partial severance of its vital nerve, becoming content in many places with drab inertia—that pall which comes over such an organization to denude it of its power and to make destitute its spiritual generators. The resultant state is well known: while not lacking in disposition to activity, it spends its energies in spur-line values, majoring on minors, while being content with a complexion which is phlegmatic, supine, and torpid. To many this institution challenges little more than nice manners—a type of ecclesiastical conditioning concerning itself with reform instead of regeneration, respectability rather than rebirth.

Her sins have been legion, yet few list the sin of colorlessness where pastels of purity are reduced by ascetics to olive drab and dismal gray! Herein many a cynic sees far more affinities of monasteries with morgues, cathedrals with crypts, and churches with catacombs, than he sees of radiant sunrises, empty tombs, and gravebands laid aside.

One is ever at the point of oversimplifying the condition when the church is accused of anemia, yet who would doubt such diagnosis? With one hundred million Americans claiming membership in church, synagogue, or cathedral, still this Republic is beset by contradictory waste, charity, crime, and waywardness. Who fears the voice of the church as an instrument of mediation? What churchly sanctions would deter organized monopolies in their madness for more at the expense of human life? Unfortunately, only a few! Why not? The church knows too much pale effeteness, as though the red blood of a Man had never flowed down the gray stones of Golgotha. This life quality giving authority to the church, this same dunamis loading her votaries with pulsating power which activates life, evoking that Gibraltar-like prophecy that "the gates of Hades shall not prevail against her"—this is the historical genius of that redeemed fellowship. Hers is to be not only a fervor but also a fever setting up antagonism wherever right is on the scaffold and wrong is on the throne. What justifiable dread when the rosy cheeks of a growing child pale into colorlessness, when food only produces rebellion! Life is ebbing away. So the church, often cursed by the plague of soul-anemia, is too weak to sustain the suffering and too impotent to rebuke the strong.

In frantic desperation for a rare type of blood, a visiting

tourist in Miami sought help from the editor of a local paper. Knowing no one and being far from home, he asked, "Would you help me locate blood for my wife who is desperately ill in a local hospital?" Searching his wits, the editor suddenly remembered that Walter Winchell's broadcast would originate in Miami that very night—just a short while from the time of the man's request. Taking a long chance, he called Winchell's secretary and relayed the request. The newscaster opened his broadcast by making a simple request for the type of blood needed by a visiting stranger. Within a few minutes the switchboard at the hospital was clogged by calls, each offering blood without cost. From distant states several people sent blood while two men, one chartering a plane in Augusta, Georgia, another flying from west of the Mississippi, brought blood to the suffering woman. Finally, radio once again became the means by which an announcer said, "No more blood, please; several hundred pints have been donated and the woman is fast recovering." Such impulsive generosity is characteristic of the American people; yet, the same folks seldom are alarmed at the anemic condition of the church of Jesus Christ, refusing to give the needed transfusion of personal sacrifice, unstinting devotion and common sweat.

Indifference, like a main tributary, feeds the stream of inertia. Few, if any, compliments ring with assuring vigor as do those which were voiced by Jesus to His early disciples— shining lights to illuminate and salt to season and to preserve. He told them that they should be so filled with divine strength that their very nearness to weakness should suggest power, and their sway over men's hearts would be called miracles. But, alas, indifference crept in, first stealthily, then with unapologetic bravado; hence the present sin of apathy and spiritual senility. It is reported that while the merits of a state church were being disputed, a British lord insistently urged, "If we are going to have a state church, by all means make it an indifferent one." Though few would be so verbally forthright, so caustic, in our day of "revivalism" where throngs flock the church, still remains the cynic's query, "Church of Jesus Christ, where is thy strength?"

It was such a deplorable condition that caused one to summarize in more uncharity than accuracy a previous generation whose allegiance to the church was little more than academic, "They slept, dozed, waited for public opinion, shunned hardships, dreaded sacrifices, and died weaklings." What a telling commentary! What a disdainful epitaph!

Midway in this twentieth century there is being acted out a moving drama of staggering dimensions. Masses are on the march; old empires with their traditional wrongs and rationalized "rights" are crumbling like dried-out pottery; ends that once justified any means are being discounted in the hopper of enlightened consciences; geopolitics, embarrassed by its totalitarian advocates, now is being integrated by metaphysical mechanics; techniques are being subjected to the end of human personality; religious servility is being questioned by those on whom priestly heels have stood with grinding severity—all these constitute a three-dimensional drama, inspiring courage, evoking pathos, eliciting sympathy, arousing anger, and changing the profile of status quo. Just to be alive in this day is a thrilling privilege as well as an awesome responsibility. But to be indifferent and apathetic to this mighty march of men, to be a spectator rather than a participator, to remain insensate in the wake of this charged emotion, is to forfeit one's right to lead or to be led. His not even is the right to criticize. The world is being remade— being turned right-side-up—and to have no role in the effort is to be marked as wooden.

Such was the stupidity of a Bavarian merchant when Hitler's Gestapo came juggernauting through the land, raping, pillaging, murdering. The merchant's one consuming concern was to save his collection of Bavarian china, while human life and transcendent values were at stake. Cups and saucers or boys and girls! Just so with life in the church. It can become so immersed in concern for theological bric-a-brac, so ensconced in ecclesiastical mumbo-jumbo, in the rigmarole of "do" and "don't," in the falderal of divisive cultism, that its eyes can be dimmed to the presence of a type of spiritual sedation which wreaks more havoc than a regiment of dictators.

Any minister would prefer fluctuating extremes of interest to no interest. Let there be response! Let hearers either be angered or made glad, moved, worried, made solicitous, awakened, or awed! Any observable reaction is preferred to stolidity. What penetrates soul-chilling neutrality? When detachment stems from freedom from prejudice, or from wrong methods, such detachment is commendable. Herein is a certain emancipation of the soul from the rigors of involvement, a freedom from tightness of the Gordian knots tied by a pagan world; yet when aloofness is volitional—a studied effort to be a nonparticipant with the corresponding rationalized justification—such detachment is a curse to the person and the church in which he attempts to worship. Beneath much of today's church activity is a sort of bravado which, by honest analysis, is affected unconcern. Such was the wellspring of Macaulay's flippant yet truthful remark, "Rome contemplated the spectacle with the detached, intelligent amusement of the . . . theater-goer." Whatever the fate that befalls the church: huge debts saddling its members with year-in and year-out mortgages, gypsying of its members from shambles to sanctuary, perennial bazaars and their noisy commercialism as substitutes for New Testament stewardship, lost vision—whatever the fate, none is more lethal in effect than indifference. This is the coup de grâce—the fatal stroke.

The history of Christendom consistently has divided its

disciples into two categories: the doers and the talkers—those who make history and those who attempt to interpret it. Though the division is arbitrary, obviously less courage and acumen are required for the latter. Hardly can the hindsight of religious "interpreters" lay more claim to wisdom than the valiant foresight of the prophet who is willing to take a leap into the future despite its often dark foreboding. Trial and error have won many more battles than has reluctant neutrality.

Luke, writing of another day when the world was "burning down," gave a severe summary statement of Gallio, the proconsul of Achaia. This petty politician was fortunate enough to be living while Christendom was first budding, insinuating itself like a spring crocus in cold earth. He had a grandstand seat in this beautiful tragedy. The only crime of those early Christians was to claim a love for Jesus. And what effect did this have on Gallio? Said Luke, "And Gallio cared for none of these things." There you are! Remembered in history, not for his magnanimity, nor for his cooperation with the movement that supplanted his little half-acre domain and a thousand others like him; remembered not for what he could have done to avert a modicum of brutality; instead, remembered for that sterility of mind and heart: indifference—he didn't care for any of those things! Yet, verbal chastizing is poor compensation for the same evil in today's Gallios. Conditioned by the same "old stuff" of the gospel, the corners of care rounded out by habitual reference, the cutting edge of incisive value dulled by vulgar usage, a generation has developed wherein cultured care is rare.

Last year one of the South's large department stores staged a mock air raid after having assigned each of its employees an exit to the building and an improvised bomb shelter. At the sound of a siren each was to go immediately to his assigned place. But to the chagrin of the organizing committee, the siren was not heard because a disc jockey was playing Brahm's "Lullaby" over a public address system in the store! It is often so in the church. In thunderous rudeness the voice of prophetic judgment cries for justice and mercy, only to be countered by soothing lullabies that induce specious peace of mind and lethargy of soul.

Whatever credence history or historians may give to indifference, one thing is sure: indifference charted no new worlds, raised no columns of architectural splendor, composed no sublime music, recorded no arts of man on canvas, clay or stone. Failing to rebel at servitude, it did not become indignant to cruelty; it never lifted its finger to pluck the first thorn from His crown nor to remove a single splinter from His cross. Not by one digit did indifference lift the human soul toward its divinely appointed plateau. All these grandeurs were born of enthusiasm—accomplished by the zeal of singular abandonment.

Enthusiasm is an antidote for indifference, a generator from which flows power that refuses to quench Godlike passion. Failing to imbrute the capacities for heavenly things, it will not permit the heart to be interred in the trash pile of the world. It is at the point of zealous, arduous enthusiasm that God enters to endorse human effort. Yet, the word in our day has a certain "go easy" connotation; to many churchly groups it belongs to the lesser breeds, the cults and sects, as though it were tainted by some foreign virtue to Christian ethics. Not so! Lacking enthusiasm, faith usually lies dormant in the morass of human intention; programs become staid and perfunctory, reducing momentum to cautious realism. Fear of fanatical extremes in zeal has given the green light to an earthly walking by sight, disdaining any amount of emotion, while enthroning thought as the *summum bonum* of Christian discipleship. God can be apprehended through all three: thought, will, and emotion. But who fears the opposite extreme: that of a chilling detachment, charting its own course regardless of God's say in the matter? If the choice must be made between enthusiasm that leans a bit too much toward zeal and an unfeeling "take-it-or-leave-it" apathy, let us choose, for the sake of posterity, the former every time!

Such a state of affairs partly explains the attitude that the church primarily is an institution to be kept, protected, defended by blushing apologists—a sort of aesthetic museum piece depending upon the erratic and often desperate loyalties of its members—lest it too, like other nice, old institutions, goes with the wind. Quite naturally would such protectiveness justify the mumbo-jumbo of priestcraft which perverts purpose, subverts personality, and diverts the main stream into the desert of futility.

It was the midnight of enthusiasm which gave rise to a hybrid religion: Islam—that amalgam of plagiarized ethics and asceticism, that compound of superstition and severe chastity, holding in its grip millions of souls who otherwise could have been emancipated by the truth that sets men free. But the missionary fires of Christianity were largely extinguished; the church occupied itself with minutiae of housekeeping niceties, confirming its own gains, indulging in the same evils against which it had been so articulate. Hence, the mills of the gods grind out their fine grist to thwart, subvert, and delay the coming of the Kingdom.

Dr. Huxley contends that the soil in Great Britain contains all types of tropical seeds brought there by birds, wind currents and other agents. Rainfall is sufficient to make the tropical plants flourish and the island blossom into pastel magnificence. Yet one item is lacking: warmth, without which germination is impossible. A favorable temperature, as well as moisture, is essential to make those bleak Islands look like Tahiti. Potential lies dormant in every church, the possibilities of bleak ineffectiveness being supplanted by bright, colorful harmony, of little goals giving way to higher mountains of accomplishment, of waters treaded, loaves multiplied, sick healed, and depressions relieved. But to accomplish these things there must be the warmth of a contagious enthusiasm.

It is as impossible to understand the life of Jesus apart from a radiant glow as it is to contend that there can be day without light. Jesus glowed with radiant life in the manner of His early antecedent Moses, who, after having come down from the mountain, was transformed. What appalling misrepresentation to strip Him of His humanity in one's efforts to deify Him! Of course, He was the Son of God, but this in no sense robbed Him of His humanity. This is no effort to immortalize flesh but to sanctify it. Would that the Christian church dispense with its dichotomy set up 'twixt flesh and spirit; the two should be bound in the same bundle of total devotion with resultant loss of dualistic conduct. Puritan severity's inflexible austerity may have inspired admiration, but it never aroused affection or caused many to want it as a way of life. So to foist upon Jesus and His unaffected naturalness this restrictive product of demented minds is little short of tragedy. No little Lord Fauntleroy, Jesus! No lavender and old lace Lord! Life's votaries are to be pregnant with pulsating life—so was His!—not effete, but virile and virtuous. Little wonder that few take note that "We have been with Jesus" when contact with Him fails to show! There is not enough starlight in our eyes!—the starlight that shone on the hills around Bethlehem, making radiant glow in a darkened world. We are not before a wailing wall but an opened door; ours is not a call to weep but a challenge to speak.

Enthusiasm needs to go back to its early antecedents, to stand for a moment with feet firmly planted on the slippery sod where the first Christians stood. It needs to sit in the seats of arena ruins where despots and demagogues witnessed the helpless slaughter. It needs to walk the Appian Way, to sail across to Crete, to stand in Pilate's chambers, and to grope through darkened catacombs. Here twentieth-century enthusiasm would receive a stern rebuke for its softness, its mumbling complaints of "hard lots"; and if it looked long enough, it could see the remains where torture, tyranny, and trouble rode like wild stallions across the hearts of those followers of the Way. If effort were suffused with imagination, it could distill from ether the words of Peter and John still ringing with frantic certainty, "We cannot but speak the things which we have seen and heard." That little band whose main virtues consisted of consuming enthusiasm and a firsthand experience with the Holy Spirit knew that some tides are inevitable—they must flow; that human efforts, though ensconced in garbs of magistrates, centurions, or gestapo, ultimately are powerless to restrain the streams that God has designed to flow. Trying to quench the impetus of this new-found faith was folly at its worst. Suffused with the vigor of expanding, custom-rending life, theirs was an uncontrollable catalyst which lifted them from the pits of oppressive slavery, from the trammels of torture, from the traumata of defeat, and from the deadly venom of paganism. They knew a fervent devotion inherent in attachment to a worthy cause, a grip of spiritual reality which dumbfounded the lesser breeds without the law. Defying all reason and limitation, a type of holy madness took hold of them making it impossible to separate the message from the messenger. These magnificent "fools," whose contagious fever reached pandemic proportions, insisted on dwelling in an aura of visions, voices and revelations. Such concentration of devotion was like an acetylene torch penetrating the steel of crustaceous religion. Losing their direction, they redoubled their efforts, earning the ugly epithet "fanatic." But what cared they, if their monomania identified them as Christ-followers? What was lost if their inflexible determination undermined the old gods, toppling them from pedestals made crimson by blood of human sacrifices? Just such a singular eye accounted for the blinding partisanship which is womb for vigilance and faith. Say what one wills, it was this holy inebriation which made them valiant in the valley while encountering Goliaths and made them mighty on the mountains while battling Baal. Nothing short of this propulsion could have supplanted the Roman Empire by the fourth century. Said Pope, "Harmonic twange! . . . Such as from lab'ring lungs th'enthusiast blows!" But the blowing was another's bugle, the one that fell from the lips of a young Man at thirty-three whose reveille still rang in their ears, who never sounded the taps of defeat—not even in the seven last "notes" of the cross!

9

THE SIN OF A THREE-
TABERNACLE KINGDOM

AT THE PEAK of a Galilean mountain stood Peter, James, and
John in an aura of transfiguration. Jesus had taken them there
to share a preview of God's radiating presence. Hardly had
they stopped panting from the steep climb before the place
was filled with inexplicable wonder, shining lights, and
celestial voices which evoked fear, awe and sublime mystery.
To commemorate that once-in-a-lifetime experience, Peter
suggested that they build three tabernacles: one for Moses,
one for Elijah, and one for Christ. But the gospel account of
this incident adds, ". . . Peter said (this): . . . not knowing
what he said." Why not? What was wrong in wanting to erect
a pile of stones or a brush arbor over the hallowed spot where
they had heard God endorse His Son? After all, weren't
Moses and Elijah in the lineage that led to Jesus? A tent for
Moses, Elijah, and Jesus and that on a high mountain removed
from the rank and file of people was too small, too exclusive;
such a tent needed to be big enough for all the human race,

not for just three! A three-tent kingdom or heaven is too small to stretch over the whole human race. This is the lesson which our world and church have never known.

No picture in Christendom is more disconcerting than the multitudinous tents of cults and sects, each raising its monuments of authority, claiming exclusive inerrancy, promoting and propagandizing to the detriment of the other—all in the name of One who prayed ". . . that they may be one. . . ." The fact remains that any tent claiming God's presence should be big enough to cover all. Anything else knows no nexus with Christ whose heart was big enough for the whole wide world.

Our world never has known a sense of oneness, and there are few world citizens, those rare individuals who think globally instead of locally. Boundaries that divide are tragically tall, like the Chinese wall, suggesting to the outside that our one-tent heaven is big enough only for ourselves. India isn't alone in her exclusive temples over whose doors is written, "Not allowed: Low Castes and Dogs." Note their company!

Sociologically, man is divided into a multitude of camps: Jews and Gentiles; Occidentals and Orientals; Barbarians and Scythians; blacks and whites; rich and poor—so much divided that God's family concept is strained to the point of breaking. Until the church challenges this divisive concept with forthright authority, the church will remain as a little-feared, muted voice.

If the Christian faith is understood at all, it is understood as a universal blessing. God saw to it that within the province of His provision there was room for all. The Great Supper has been prepared, and His engravers have been working overtime to see that the list includes all mankind: every clime —East, West, North, South; every class—the oppressed, downtrodden, disappointed, weak, sick, young, and old. No provincial limits are reflected in this invitation; no exclusive four hundred; no social snob hill; no special, favored, religious group; no elect people. Around that banquet table a chair has been placed for everybody. Oh, how this world with its tired systems, its age-old contradictions, this world of side-taking, mutual pacts, and secret agreements, desperately needs to be told that the love of God is shed for all. Let it be shouted from the housetops that the table of salvation is set. "Come and buy without money, come and eat without price." "And let him that heareth say, Come . . . And whosoever will, let him take the water of life freely." Here is one good thing that everyone can get in on, costing not a cent! What appalling tragedy that prejudice, bigotry, and heat, instead of light, should remove the invitation from the table which God has set for millions! When one thinks that all the places have been filled, there still is room: a picture of the inexhaustible capacities of God's provisions, confounding our wildest dreams. Still He is preparing for the unborn, for other nations, perhaps other planets; and if the gospel had nothing else to recommend than this, it would stand as the champion of human reform, binding the human equation into one inseparable bundle. No other religion claims so wide a berth for the world as this.

Had God not loved all, He could not have loved any. Nothing gives significance to the nameless masses of humanity as does telling them that they are in the circle of divine love, that their legacy is a place in the eternal Kingdom made possible by redeeming grace. Just in case some benighted bigot forgets, let him read anew that classic: "God so loved the *world*. . . ." Not just America, not only the Occident, nor this generation, but the world! This scarlet thread of identity runs through the warp and woof of the Bible in uninterrupted rapier thrusts. To Jesus Christ we owe an eternal debt for refusing to falter at national boundaries, racial animosities, group cleavages, and religious partitions. His words still ring in deafened ears, "And they shall come from the east, and from the west, and from the north, and from the south, and shall sit down in the kingdom of God." The fact that Jesus talked with a Samaritan woman—to say nothing of the fact that He made a Samaritan the hero in His parable of neighborliness—was enough to initiate the via dolorosa. He loved the unlovely, the unclean, the helpless, the impotent, the forgotten, and the outcast. But let us not fool ourselves: this is dangerous business, this conviction that God's love is universal. Like a two-edged sword it will cut through sham and pretense, exposing men for what they really are. As a matter of fact, it cost the Son of God His life on a cross!

It is so painless to see the vertical relationships of His love, but when it comes to loving my brother, the horizontal—there is the rub! Like an embarrassing sequel comes that second commandment which is liken unto the first, "Thou shalt love thy neighbour as thyself." Boyd McKeown is exactly right in saying, "We may not be our brothers' keepers, but we certainly are our brothers' brothers." It is by snail-paced, painful steps that the human race is having to learn the hard way that God meant this world to be a home in which a redeemed family would share in His provident love and grace. No other concept is worthy of God.

> No one could tell me where my soul might be;
> I sought for God, but God eluded me;
> I sought my brother out and found all three.[1]

Though Macedonia is still calling, Troas is too convenient to most of us. So down with the barriers that impede the flow of this mighty army! Down with iron curtains, bamboo curtains, curtains of sects and cults—the Kingdom of God knows no ugly partitions!

[1] Crosby, Ernest, *The Search.*

It is one of our most singular tragedies that religion, the one great force which should unite us, has contributed to the division! Like a rough-hewn wedge in a log, splitting it into many staves and ribs, religion, through the annals of history, while claiming the cohesive qualities of unity has been the axe to split the log of human devotion. The results are too familiar: duplication of effort, a miasma of activity, fog banks of suspicion, violence in the name of God, propelled by a delusion that service can be rendered in His name by persecuting those who bear His name. And all this without the slightest compunction that the means did not justify such despicable ends. Why aren't we honest enough to admit that there exists very little true unity in the church of Jesus Christ? That brotherhood is something daily proclaimed but hourly denied? One observer was never more right when he concluded that one-half of Christendom is not on speaking terms with the other half.

Let this truth not be prostituted: there is no room in ivory towers for an "ecumaniac" to dwell who is foolish enough to believe that if the church were one grandiose body all the problems would be solved. Indeed not! As a matter of fact, the problems might be intensified. Oh, that a small percentage of the momentum engendered by dreams and conclaves to make the church one in organization were spent in making it one in spiritual unity. Diversity of form and ritual, of organization and affiliation often is not only natural but desirable. Yet, when that diversity becomes the means by which spiritual unity is sacrificed, then the former is man's curse—not his blessing. "The more we get together the happier we'll be" is true only in the sense that when we get together in the family of redeemed men made over in the likeness of our Father, then the differences between theological tweedledum and tweedledee seem trivial by comparison.

In this day the concept of brotherhood is political fare, a

source of much heat but little light, a day in which conformity is disciplined by coercion—a fact which in itself militates against the very nature of the Christian approach. Compulsive brotherhood is contradiction; spontaneity makes for a natural friendliness that isn't trying to be friendly. Is the human race supposed to be a fraternity? In what sense are all men "brothers"? Now it is common conviction that all Christians are brothers in Christ. "In Christ there is no east nor west." But to say that such a brotherhood implies equality outside this redeemed fellowship is to impute to it a pale complexion which it fails to claim for itself. Brothers are equal in a family only in the sense of status; beyond that, one must admit that some are older, wiser, or better endowed. While not speaking of superiority or favoritism, differences exist which give virile significance to the term "brotherhood" instead of the slick usages so common to lecture hall, pulpit, and editorial. Though this word has been mouthed to death, nonetheless there still remains the fact: God's plan envisages its inclusion. Christianity concerns itself not with the many divergencies but with the one point of unity: common Fatherhood. While admitting marked differences in cultures, color, and characteristics, it makes these irrelevant to redemption. The grand delusion that social amalgamation is prerequisite to the coming of His Kingdom or that such should be made a test of fellowship, obscures the imperative by which the Kingdom must come in a redeeming fellowship! "Christian brotherhood sets up no pre-emptive right of intrusion."

Inescapable is the universal fact that everyone is actually or potentially a child of God, a category depending largely upon the efforts of those who are unquestionably the children of God. In creative origin, in the universality of sin, in potential sharing of the atonement, in a common destiny in dust, and in candidacy for the final judgment—all men are as one.

Strolling through a Russian alley went Tolstoy among the hungry masses. One lean-faced beggar approached him with the plaintive cry, "Give me a ruble for bread." Tolstoy reached in his pockets but found no coin in them. Putting his arms on the shoulder of the beggar, Tolstoy replied, "Don't be angry with me, my brother, because I have no ruble to give you." "But you have given to me," he said. "You called me 'brother.'" A poor fare, to fill the stomach with "brother." Yet many a mendicant prefers just such salutation to all the bakeries of bread, because the stomach knows a satisfaction that leaves the heart hungry.

The armies of God's church are divided into too many platoons, each marching under its own command, unable to hear the orders of the General. Who fears the authority of the church today? Business? Commerce? Education? Hardly! One would think that the keys of the Kingdom were in the possession of the chambers of commerce instead of the church founded by Jesus against which the gates of Hades are not to prevail. Shorn of much of her strength, the church tolerates the sin of three-tent heavens without pining over the ground which could be covered were her armies united in spiritual endeavor to wage decisive conflict against entrenched evil.

At midnight, as a full moon shone over the Ryukyuan seas, we heard the shrill cries of Japanese infantrymen flashing samurai swords in their banzai charge. All night the charge continued until daylight revealed a ghastly sight of mutilation. During the heat of battle and intermittent lulls this chaplain could hear a sergeant praying to his Jewish God, another praying to his Methodist God, a corporal entreating his Presbyterian God, and a Roman Catholic imploring his God. The thought riveted itself in my memory: why should such common realization be engendered only by a baptism of death in trenches? Said one in succinct conviction, "The Devil displays little terror when he sees a Presbyterian forefinger, or a

Baptist middle finger, or an Episcopalian thumb, or a Methodist third finger, or some other denominational little finger pointed at him. But when those fingers and that thumb are all doubled up in one compelling fist, then the Devil begins to take notice." Thank the Almighty that the day has come when we pay more attention to our points of unity than to our differences! Yet what barren acres are yet to be traversed. The sin of division is one for which the church should be on its knees in penitence.

> He drew a circle that shut me out—
> Heretic, rebel, a thing to flout.
> But Love and I had the wit to win:
> We drew a circle that took him in.[2]

Religious exclusiveness is a contradiction to the nature of God. There are many things on earth on which there are monopolies: certain real estate, oil cartels, industrial empires; but on one thing there is no monopoly: divine truth. Let every pontifical prophet speak to the contrary, every watchdog of orthodoxy, every self-appointed arbiter cry to the four winds, still God is not divided, and He is no respecter of persons. His word cannot be tinkered with any more than His grace can be manipulated for man's benefit. There is but one true church: the ecclesia—those who are "called out of the world," the transformed, the reborn, the regenerate. But these are in every communion. No one organizational group composes it, no one race nor creed. From the four corners of the universe come the godly to populate the church of Jesus Christ. The keys of the Kingdom are given to those who are indisputably the sons of the Kingdom, a prerogative of divine favor, not an historical vantage.

Religious bigotry mocks the name that it desires to worship.

[2] Markham, Edwin, "Outwitted." Reprinted by permission of Virgil Markham.

A rereading of the account of the Jerusalem conference will point up anew this ugly fact. The crux of the matter at that first-century conference was whether or not the Gentile was worth saving. Was the gospel for the chosen house of Israel, or by some strange stretching of the facts did the non-Jew have significance in the plan of the ages? Think of it: the leaders of the church debating such an issue! But many will recall when the issue of foreign missions was considered fantasy for fanatics, a sort of otherworld foolishness having nothing to do with ecclesiastical housekeeping on this side of the ocean. The common delusion ran, "If God wants the heathen saved, He will save him." Then came Pearl Harbor. Would that one could conclude: then came the death of provincialism!

What a startling disclosure when the Apostle Paul announced his intentions of giving his life to win the very people whom many thought were not worth winning. What ironical confessions that one can rally more forces to the support of orthodoxy than he can to the cause of the Saviour. More money can be raised to defend the home plate any day of the week than to tell the glad tidings out in left field.

"Isn't that too big a load for you?" asked a bystander to a little boy who was carrying another boy almost his size. "Oh, no, sir, he ain't heavy, mister; he's my brudder!" The load never is heavy when one is carrying his brother.

Prejudice has a nauseatingly ugly face, a profile of blind animosity which, while seeing what it pleases, cannot see what is plain. This is an universal disease which eats away at one's sense of values until judgment is destroyed. When judgment is weak, prejudice is always strong. "All looks yellow to the jaundiced eye," quipped Pope in a flash of revealed wisdom. Prejudice should be regarded as personal disgrace on the part of Christians. Like a relic of a benighted past, it should be consigned to that dark cellar of infamous memories. "It is with narrow-souled people as with narrow-necked bottles; the less they have in them the more noise they make in pouring it out." [3] When this alkali of progress is paraded as "convictions," it is defended with the greatest violence. But one is as guilty as the other when his contempt of another's prejudice assumes like proportions. Trying to reason one out of his prejudices is folly, since he wasn't reasoned into them. There is no known exit other than the bold intrusion of truth that would erase, uproot, and eradicate.

Herein Christians must share in the responsibility for such universal prevalence of prejudicial thinking; if not for its inception, then surely for its continuity, by tolerating it in side-stepping silence and encouraging the deception that it will work itself out if given time. This no more is the case than that weeds will uproot themselves by their own initiative. Public utterances are comparatively easy, but encountering a prejudiced individual on the field of verbal combat is a challenge from which most Christians are prone to shrink. There are times when silence is golden; there are also times when silence is yellow! To mock the creation of God, all one must do is to observe that activity by which worship is intended but wherein one merely rearranges his prejudices. The golden rule, while committed to memory, now needs to be committed to life.

What to do about it? Can the leopard change its spots? If Christian love be prostituted exclusively on its own, then it is neither love nor Christian. Any way one looks at it, the ground at the foot of the cross is level ground. Suffused with the contagion of good will, one can meet prejudice head-on while not quivering one iota in the battle, and with steady aim, release the stones of truth to the head of this Goliath. Too long have the armies of our God stood on the mountains estimating the height and strength of this Goliath. Now let

[3] Alexander Pope, *Thoughts on Various Subjects.*

some David descend the valley with the will to win, and he'll do it.

> There are thousands to tell you it cannot be done,
>   There are thousands to prophesy failure;
> There are thousands to point out to you one by one,
>   The dangers that wait to assail you.
> But just buckle in with a bit of a grin,
>   Just take off your coat and go to it;
> Just start in to sing as you tackle the thing
>   That "cannot be done," and you'll do it.[4]

To the ears of those early disciples came the strange words of Jesus, "And other sheep I have, which are not of this fold. . . ." Who can measure the limits of His love, or count the heads crowned thereby? To conclude that man as he is known is the only or final creation is to limit God absurdly. From yesterday, today, and tomorrow; from now and then; from here and there; from the given and the unknown; from the real and the imaginary will come the pilgrimages whose common destiny is at the feet of the Almighty. To believe this explodes the narrow-gauged boundaries which would build only three tents for the favored and transfigured. So long as we Americans have our "election" complex about our destiny and churches, so long as individual denominations are obsessed by their presumed "Divine preferential standings," just so long will the world travail and groan in her error. Each community, each church must prove to the world that the gospel is inherently universal in content and claim—a fact that would neutralize the Marxist myth that there is no God. All that degrades and impugns must go if God would come.

As he paced before a colored map of Europe, Napoleon nervously stroked his forehead. He had rolled over the European landscape like a virus of vultures. Stymied by his inabil-

---

[4] "It Couldn't Be Done" from *The Path to Home* by Edgar A. Guest, copyright 1919, The Reilly & Lee Co., Chicago.

ity to conquer England, he turned to one of his lieutenants and pointed to the British Isles, which were represented in red color on a map, and said, "Were it not for that red spot, I would conquer the world." The red spot known as Calvary, where a young Nazarene poured out His blood for His cause, stands as the sole deterrent to a modern despot who would conquer the world. In this frightening consideration, fear is harnessed as faith proclaims: I know not what the future holds, but I know who holds the future!

10

VESTIBULE VIRTUE

A MINISTER IN Seattle during the Second World War held a
phone in his hand and asked a sergeant on the other end of
the line, "Are you ready?" A nervous, distant voice answered,
"Yes, sir." Then the minister began reading familiar words,
"Dearly beloved, we are gathered together here in the sight of
God, and in the face of this company, to join together this man
and this woman. . . ." A nervous young lady stood beside the
minister as he held the phone in his hand and performed the
rites of matrimony for two people who were five thousand
miles apart. A young man stood beside the bride as proxy for
his soldier brother on a distant Pacific island. They were
getting married by remote control, with none of the warmth
of immediate nearness at hand!

In the church of Jesus Christ there are thousands whose
religion is proxy relationship with no immediate warmth of
personal experience to traverse the distance 'twixt God and
them.

Some time ago three couples from the deep South stood in

a long queue before a marquee in an eastern city in hopes of getting tickets to a popular stage production. As they stepped up to the window, they were told the discouraging news that no tickets were available. Some enterprising young boys, seeing their dilemma, picked up cancelled stubs and used programs, clipped them together, and approached the disappointed couples with the proposition, "Why don't you give us twenty-five cents for these cancelled stubs and used programs and go back home and tell your friends you saw the show? They won't know any difference, and you'll have a lot of fun making them believe you saw the real show." The boys were doing a brisk business in selling their worthless wares, a note of comedy were it not a telling commentary on what is wrong with many people of the church: they are content to buy cancelled stubs to use them as proof that they have seen the show. Out in the vestibule of the church stand throngs of people who design their distance from the altar. Amidst the small talk of pots and pans they feel a specious security much akin to their unregenerate natures. When approached about the real thing, in glib facility they are quick to reply, "See, I'm a Christian . . . here is the proof: I have been to church, sung doxologies, tipped God or perhaps tithed, said my prayers . . . see, here are the cancelled stubs and used programs . . . these are my proof." Used programs indeed, held by these who know but a mild, effete faith, whose sporadic spurts of generosity are triggered only by supercharged appeals from the pulpit. But the question keeps coming up: Have they seen the show? Have they ever gone to the foot of Calvary and watched that infamously tragic drama played out to its crucial, horrendous finale? Though singing, "Were you there when they crucified my Lord?" they honestly know that they were not. "Were you there when they laid Him in the tomb?" must be answered in embarrassing negation. This is vestibule virtue that never goes into the sanctuary of total commitment.

Now and then a mood of penitent contrast comes over such discipleship; and amid the milling mediocrity of the masses, one is arrested by some strange sight or eerie sound coming from the holy of holies where others have gone in and surrendered their all. For a moment a type of spiritual nausea is generated by the foyer observer, only to be forgotten as a crescendo of babbling voices acclaim: "It must be all right since everybody is doing it." To the chagrin of those inside the fact is that the vestibule is under the same roof as the sanctuary, pointing up the fearful truth that one can be lost from God in the house of God. In His parable of the lost coin, Jesus taught that the coin was lost, not on the pathway, but in the house. Could it be that He meant one's soul is apt to be lost in its home harbor? Out of God in the house of God! What presumptive arrogance that Satan should undertake to do business in the precincts of God Himself!

This hearsay type of discipleship is a major stumbling block in that it is a masquerade—the ring of the real isn't there. Content with secondhand editions, many are willing to have their religion piped to them via television in the comfort of a living room or served à la carte by some religious novelist. Like the Ephesian elders, they have not even heard of the Holy Spirit. The biggest mission field in the world is in the vestibule of the Christian church where those who bear the name of Christian do not bear commensurate fruit. Churches —filled with empty people!

Lest someone conclude this contention is an overstatement, let the facts speak for themselves: one hundred million Americans claim membership in church or synagogue; but parallel to this claim is the incontestable fact that the jails are overcrowded, one of three marriages eventuates in divorce, over a million children are born illegitimately every year, eighteen thousand Americans committed suicide in a recent year, there are more barmaids than college girls, seventy-six per cent of the boys and girls from American homes have dropped out of Sunday school and church before their sixteenth birthday, more money is paid for toys than for textbooks, more spent for dog food than for Christian education, more bubble gum is bought than three denominations gave to home and foreign missions in a total year, and blacksmiths receive more remuneration than some college professors. All this is proof enough that all the hundred million people have not gone from the vestibule into the sanctuary to see the moving drama that would change society.

This impressive number has deceived many into believing that the nation is enjoying a great outburst of religious devotion, that true revivalism is sweeping the land. They cite the filled stadiums, the stacks of decision cards, and the Herculean budgets of churches and crusades as proof of their contention. One easily could conclude that the millennium is just around the corner. Would that it were! Yet never has there been a people so religiously interested, but whose religion is so nearly divorced from life. Small talk in the vestibule is tragic babble compared to the penitent wail of those who, prostrate before the altar, entreat God's loving forgiveness. Against such shallow profession Jesus warned that part-time and partial religion had no place in His Kingdom; "forsaking all" was prerequisite to discipleship. No doubt was left in the minds of those who heard Him that He expected each to walk on through the vestibule into the temple of faith. No stymying in the foyer, lest one never enter the sanctuary of meaningfulness. Little courage is required for vestibule virtue simply because no great causes are championed there, no devils are exorcised in those environs, no tears of penitence are shed out there. Little wonder this anteroom speaks of dry eyes, unbent knees, and unopened pocketbooks—a comfortable precinct for the uncommitted. Such was the climate of inspiration for the assiduous words:

I'd rather see a sermon than hear one any day;
I'd rather one should walk with me than merely tell the way.
The eye's a better pupil and more willing than the ear,
Fine counsel is confusing, but example's always clear;
And the best of all the preachers are the men who live their creeds,
For to see good put in action is what everybody needs.

I soon can learn to do it if you'll let me see it done;
I can watch your hands in action, but your tongue too fast may
    run.
And the lecture you deliver may be very wise and true,
But I'd rather get my lessons by observing what you do;
For I might misunderstand you and the high advice you give,
But there's no misunderstanding how you act and how you live.[1]

When one remains in the foyer long enough, resisting the entreaties to come in, his religion will be little more than dull habit—something he can take or leave with equal ease. The pain of struggle, the bliss of resignation, and the exhilaration of walking the second mile are unknown to him. Half a heart is worse than no heart in Christianity in that it deceives the halfhearted into believing he is all right.

Nervously fidgeting the phone dial, a sailor, upon arrival from the Korean War, called his parents on the east coast and nearly shouted with joy, "Mom, I'm coming home!" Then, in more temperate tones he added, "I am bringing a buddy home with me who got the worst end of the deal. He has but one eye, one arm, and one leg. I want him to live with us and make our home his home." The mother on the other end of the line said, "Why, of course, son, we will be glad to have him come and stay a while with us." "But Mom, I didn't say for a while; I want him to make his home with us . . . to live with us from now on." A second time the fashionable lady assured her sailor son, "We'll be happy to have him live with us for

---

[1] "Sermons We See," from *Collected Verse* of Edgar A. Guest, Copyright 1934, The Reilly & Lee Co., Chicago.

several weeks or months if you like. Then perhaps he would like to go to his own home." The mild argument went on for a few seconds until the young sailor hung up the phone in rude finality. Two days later the parents on the east coast received a telegram from the Naval Command saying that their son had jumped out of a hotel window from the tenth floor in San Diego. When they received their *son's* body, it had one eye, one arm, and one leg! You see, you just can't be halfhearted in your sympathies and ever count for much.

An inevitable adjunct to vestibule virtue is a religion that is short on morality. With delicate social relations, friction points ever mounting because of the burgeoning population, masses on the march demanding solid substance for morality which the law can never provide, it is high time that the note of authority be put back into religious truth. A man's faith must be grounded in honest morals, else he joins the ranks of those whose practice is at variance with their professions. This is what Jesus called hypocrisy, play acting, make believe. Every overture in religious history which was delinquent in common morality—whether that experiment was through metaphysical fantasy or through an individual's role of practicing conduct in antagonism to his higher self—has first floundered, then fallen before the scrutiny of the Almighty.

Religion can be the most immoral thing in the world, and is, when it induces comfort without crosses, rewards self without service, indulges iniquity without rebuke, condones profits without principles, endorses compromise at the expense of convictions, substitutes reform for regeneration, resorts to evil that good might result, builds partitions between God's people as though any one group had a monopoly on the grace of God, encourages peace of mind without purity of heart, and dims its vision about the one thing it is called to do: to lift the human race to its rightful standing in reconciliation before God Almighty. Man needs a moral religion as a plumb line dropped

alongside the crooked wall of society, straightening its leaning
convictions, shoring up its tottering institutions, and solidifying
its adolescent gains. But society rebels at stringent morals just
as an unruly child rebels at the hand of correction. Rebels
from morals object to rigid codes in adamant consistency,
while all the time overlooking the fact that even a musical
instrument must be tuned a bit sharp since it is apt to fall
in playing. Here is no plea for pharisaism; instead, a positive
admission of an elementary fact in human nature: declaring
faith in God while refusing to keep His commandments, calling oneself Christian without exemplifying a Christlike spirit,
addressing one as "brother" while not doing a stranger's service—all these constitute an irony of contradiction.

How can one be a partaker of divine grace who doesn't
know common morality? Saved and immoral? No, sir! When
religion becomes a substitute for common morality, then religion is man's curse and not his blessing. Better for him never
to have heard of the church than to stand in the vestibule with
no sense of wrong and no compunction to repent of it if he
did admit it. Christian faith without morality is as likely as
fire without heat. While religion talks, convenes, presides, par-
rots, and splits hairs, morality lifts, looks, listens and loves.

Under closer scrutiny this type of disciple reveals a life, not
of peace and inner harmony—all his casual unconcern notwithstanding—but a life of strife and disconcerting misery.
The very thing he searches for can never be found because of
his distance from the center of the real drama. He is too far
removed from the heat of the Nazarene's heart to feel its
warmth. Beneath a thin façade of good intentions and lesser
loyalties is the original sinner who was whitewashed instead
of being washed white. The slightest test or most minor crisis
will reveal true identity. Such dualism is described by the
Dutch phrase: "Howling with the wolves in the woods and
bleating with the sheep in the fold." This is the deference that

vice pays to virtue. Such is the case of the Hindu student who made an "A" on his examination in the theories of sanitation but returned to filth in his own home. Or like a Bible student who in blasé detachment reads the Sermon on the Mount but operates a loan company whose policy it is to charge exorbitant rates of interest without the slightest genuflection of conscience! But let this much be known anew: any force that will not change one who stands in the vestibule now, will not save him in the hereafter.

One day on a south Pacific island as a chaplain, I noticed a sergeant with whom I had talked for weeks about his relation to God, strip to his waist for a volley ball game. As I stood beside him on the other side of the net, I saw that the Lord's prayer had been tattooed on his chest—every line of it. What a stunning surprise! But it was all on the outside! To him the most poignant memory was nothing more than the pain of the electric needles that imbedded the color in his epidermis. What a shame that it didn't sink on in! The disparity 'twixt saying and doing is the church's heaviest drag. What is the worth of a profession when a life tells one story and the lips another?

A memorable day awaits the church if vestibule disciples were to come in as participators instead of spectators in the tragically beautiful drama of God reconciling man unto Himself.

11

HORSE AND BUGGY
EVANGELISM

A HOLY CURIOSITY has swept through the rank and file of American people in the last decade—curiosity expressing itself in a gypsying from church to church, sporadic giving, theological deviation into cultisms, and card-signing by the thousands. But to mistake this interest as real revivalism is to misread the handwriting for the future. Filled churches can mean empty people. Despite proper credence which must be placed on all this curiosity, the fact remains that along with crowded churches there are also overflowing jails and mammoth budgets. Yet poverty and destitution and the song of the heathen remain unmuted. Still rises the specifically embarrassing question: How many people fear the judgment of God as criterion for determining human conduct? Is it an ever-increasing majority who believes the prayers of the church can heal the sick or change the flow of history? Hardly! The steep ascent to heaven is still perilous, exacting, and unpopular; and dimensions of the strait gate have not been altered nor has a bulldozer widened that narrow pathway which leads upstairs. Despite the stampede of millions who seek, there are comparatively few who go through that gate.

This day needs a resurgence of New Testament evangelism which will transcend the veneer of popularity so characteristic of this decade. What with three out of five people in our world under Communist domination, all our plans need to be reevaluated. Rethinking, reworking, and recommitting ourselves to a type of evangelism which will do the job not only is in order but is urgently imperative. If the whole world were won to Christ in this generation, the job would have to be done all over again in the next generation. Far-reaching plans for a world awakening in evangelism demands revision of goals, methods, and techniques. The horse and buggy techniques of the nineteenth century, though somewhat workable in their day, hardly speak the tongue of people who live behind a modern façade of bebop, trailer camps, escalators, jet propulsion, and religious hors d'oeuvres. Sawdust trails may have a pioneering allure to the reminiscent, but will have little relevancy to this day which would require definition of the terms to be mildly conversant. Most efforts to reproduce Pentecost result in disquieting gloom. Why? Could it be that the basic factors, so apparently present in that first-century experience, are obscured by our chamber of commerce psychology, our "we-can-do-it-ness," our externals that smack of humanism, and the curse of a conditioned behaviorism? Honest analysis reveals some glaring weaknesses.

To say that one is going to hear an evangelistic sermon would hardly alert the interest of the honorary scholastic fraternity. And why not? Is it that evangelistic truth lacks profundity? No! It is an admission that many evangelistic messages lack intellectual content, thereby failing to convey the real import of the greatest thing that has happened to the world. Failing to enlist the interests of the best informed, the announcement of an impending revival meeting nowadays is strangely coincidental with a wholesale exodus of the Phi Beta Kappas. This alarming fact should send one back to re-examine the methods, reappraise the content of each message, and point up the bold truth, rent free from deceiving façades of ecclesiastical mumblings. The good news of the gospel is news that can hold its own in any corridor of *Who's Who*— academic or otherwise. The phrase "gospel preaching" to millions means a dull discourse on cloister wares with about as much appeal as an orange crate. Reasons are obvious: too often such preachments are but coveralls for lack of preparation, mildly good intentions, and ambiguous admonitions to "go out and do good." This is proclamation at its thinnest point, and the wonder is not that so few come to hear it but that so many come!

The word "evangelism" rates a low berth in many churchly circles with its stock held in unpreferred status. Being associated with emotions running wild; fantastic claims of conversions; pressure tactics; erratic discipleship; literalisms; and more fever than fervor, evangelism has come in for more than its share of disdain. Rightly understood, evangelism means the telling of the good news. Further, it is the sob of God expressed in anguish for wandering humanity, the wail of a father at midnight over his prodigal child—the lament of the Apostle Paul, "I could wish that myself were accursed from Christ for my brethren, my kinsman according to the flesh," —and the secret of every great disciple who got his sense of value in rightful proportion.

There is nothing about telling the good news that contradicts reason. It, like the faith that propels it, is suprarational —going beyond the point where reason cannot go. What appalling tragedy that this energizing force, which sent the young church in that first century into the farthest-flung provinces claiming adherents wherever it went, should today be deemed by millions as inconsonant and irrelevant! That the profoundest truth of the universe should be so misconstrued is human folly of first magnitude!

To see a well-informed Christian standing at his post of duty in qualitative service is a talisman of beauty. When all the talents of a well-endowed disciple are on the altar of usefulness, he, like a mighty bulldozer, can do more in an hour than a brigade of shovels can accomplish in a week. But Sunday school classes, in the main, are not being taught by the best-informed adults. Youth groups, training unions, mission societies—with admitted exceptions—are not engineered by those who have had the best advantages of formal education. A part of the explanation for this condition lies in the fact that evangelism has majored on "down and outs" and has developed a method and approach in the process which fails to win the "up and outs." Let this not be misunderstood: skid row, the bowery, the dirty, back alleys are still catchalls for the underprivileged—the "great unwashed." And from this group, sincerest sympathies must be elicited, lest one mocks the name of Him who came to save all kinds, including the least, the last, and the lost. Some Kingdom it would have been for these twenty centuries had not most of its proponents come from the lower strata! Jesus spent most of his time among that kind. Yet such being granted, it is equally important to win the upper strata, the well-heeled, the social register who feel little or no sense of need. No poverty of the spirit prompts their seeking the Master. Many times their only compulsion is triggered by alcohol or chemicals as tranquilizing substitutes for Christian faith. But the fact remains that their need, though often subtly obscured, perhaps is more pronounced than their unbathed cousins on the other side of the tracks. At least Jesus thought so. Any proportionate sense of value points up the potential value to the Kingdom of the upper strata, in that they have talents which would advance the Kingdom in a way that a converted bum could never do. Nuclear giants who are moral infants could come from behind their microscopes and slide rules to project a new law of physics: the relativity of every man's heart to his Creator. Many an honorary alumnus from the best universities counts for little in the Kingdom of God, and that fact in itself is enough to prompt the winning method in their direction.

Horse and buggy methods in evangelism will not win the worldly wise. Not that there are two gospels, one for the dull of mind, and one for the keen; not that our religious overtures are to be display counters for philosophical bric-a-brac or theological erudition; but that the only gospel is intellectually respectable. It needs no crutches to support it in a climate of thinking people, for the simple reason that it doesn't limp!

God can be apprehended through the vestibule of one's mind as well as through the foyer of his emotions and feelings. Herein modern evangelism flunks much of the test: failing to point to the transcending nature of God, proclaiming a love that is predominately sentiment instead of love with muscle in it, refusing to call for all-out revolution within the soul, showing delinquency in promoting His unmotivated love which sets forth supernal beauty in reconciling grace while making restitution for the sinner's transgression. What contrast to the common stock so widened in sectional antipathies and sectarian "do's" and "don't's." To love "the Lord thy God with all thy . . . mind" is still a part of the first commandment.

Certain impedimenta block the road of ready advance when any stratum of people is sought for redemption. Few such road blocks are higher than the hindrance afforded by a miasma of theological rigmarole: archaic expressions, negative departures, horse and buggy pitches that take none of the elemental psychological fundamentals into account. What irony that the processes designed to clarify can so easily cloud the issue. Thought structures intended to convey divine truth clog the conduits with resultant sterility. Phrases and clauses tooled as vehicles of conveyance become ground wires which are unable to transmit the current.

A sharp paring knife is indispensable equipment for every religious worker who would speak in fresh, pungent words—a paring knife to prune away archaic shibboleths, meaningless trappings that have a way of hanging on with as little justification as crusty barnacles do on the side of a ship. "Thee," "thine," and "thou" may speak of traditional deference, but they say little to the ears of this jet age. What sense of pronominal value gives leeway to such type when one is trying to communicate eternal truth to the rank and file of lost people? Legends and myths of the eighteenth century may trigger a bit of tearful reminiscence about frontier fervor; but they hardly hold a modicum of relevancy for a day which trusts its future to economic soothsayers, political bigots, and the delusion that happiness can be prescribed by physicians and dispensed by druggists.

At no place do the modern methods of evangelism fall to such ineffectual lows as when slick nomenclature is voiced in a tone that speaks more of medieval chants and sonorous twang than of joyous, eternal certainties. Who can imagine Jesus talking to a group of farmers and fishermen in the tone that is common stock in church and cathedral? Had He done so, the response would have evoked sniggers, jest, and unconcealed ridicule. Some salesman of patent medicine, some carnival hawker, or some prefectural politician has done the world of religion incalculable harm by setting a cadence of intonation which impedes rather than enhances. A method of speaking, adopted to give effect, often produces the very opposite results. Oh, the message of Jesus was so imperatively simple: "Feed my sheep," "Compel them to come," "Come, follow me,"—but it was a simplicity wrought with meaning. Today the plea to make it simple is often a concession to the plea of ignorance—ignorance which mistakes simplicity for dull, commonplace, meager content. The current quip that "He preaches above their heads" should be rebuffed by, "Then raise their heads."

Over the surface of an exquisite Louis XVI electric sconce, an antique dealer painted cheap, dime-store, gilt paint. The "finished" product had all the ersatz glitter that forty-nine cents could produce! But little did he know that beneath the thin veneer of gaudy gilt was solid brass and bronze, needing only buffing to bring out its brilliance. Just so with the real metal of the Word. All the theological rigmarole designed to gild the lily is unnecessary—the lily doesn't need gilding; it has a radiance and fragrance uniquely its own. Whatever impedes, hinders, or renders impotent the gospel and its presentation should be discarded in forthright honesty and that with immediate dispatch.

One of the major areas of deception appears when salvation is offered as a cure-all for man's problems—a kind of permanent panacea. True, the major problem of sin's alienation is solved when a sinner is accepted by God's forgiving grace into the family of those who have been twice born; then that day he has learned the criteria by which life's other problems are to be solved. Yet, to contend that by being saved one is miraculously changed in nature, thought, and habit is to claim for salvation something it never claimed for itself. It simply is not so. What fakery is more of a travesty on divine truth than the current jargon of peace-of-mind sedatives designed to soften the import of life? While such deception may absorb a bit of its shock, still, like an alcoholic who takes the third drink to escape his second, he must awaken to face a compounded problem. No, the invitation "Come to Jesus" is not an invitation to blissful detachment nor immunity from hurt and harm. As a matter of fact, Jesus taught nothing which suggests that His followers would have a sure panacea for every problem; He did something better: He told them of the court of highest appeal where they could take their problems no matter how great or small.

Being a Christian means knowing an inner harmony when there is outer discord, a soul-pacing peace when the world is at sword's points. And though many of our problems have easy solutions, the indisputable fact remains that there are problems by virtue of one's being a Christian that makes those of the early Galilean fishermen seem pale by comparison. Hear Jesus repeatedly saying, "Are ye able to drink of the cup that I shall drink of?" Among the few things that He promised to those who would wash their fishy hands as they hung up their nets were: they would get in trouble, they would suffer much, but they would be serenely happy in the process.

It is at the point where a redeemed person's life touches the world that conflict arises. Like a plumb line held alongside a crooked wall is the life of an honest man when it parallels dishonesty. The process of carrying a cross assures trouble when its beams are hewn from the stuff that calls for heroic action despite the cost or consequence. Every vestige of effort which pulls new life away from its old moorings, warns against looking back, and encourages firm grip on the handle of life, which comes by disciplined effort and without which there is no deepening of spiritual life. Washing feet, turning the other cheek, plucking out the offending eye with stern severity, cutting off the hand that turns to evil, surrendering both cloak and coat in uncontesting grace, walking the second mile without drudgery or compulsion, resisting not the evil one, choking the viper of prejudice, extricating the virus of fear, replacing cowardice with courage, condemning evil while complimenting good, standing with firmness of the knees in Herod's court while saying, "It is not lawful for you to live with your brother's wife,"—these are the staples of a Christian's gear; these are the components of trouble, trial, and triumph.

Oversimplifying the human equation is an ever-present temptation. Man is a complex aggregate of changing attitudes. While attitudes change with more facility than habits, the new convert is not sufficiently led to believe that salvation is a point and a process—a point in that it can happen in a moment, but a process in that it involves the rest of his normal life, living each day in the realization of a divine presence which encourages, rebukes, exacts, and sustains. It is dishonest to say that being saved is synonymous with conversion. Just as a child receives his education through the long progression of grade to grade, so a Christian develops into the fullness of maturity by the same slow, educative process. Human personality no more becomes saintly by instant action than a block of granite instantly becomes a statue. In both cases, incessant activity of chiseling, polishing, and bevelling is involved.

The old fear of not being able to hold out is founded on a limited conception of salvation. No one holds out in the sense that he isn't inclined to lapse back into his old patterns. The essential difference is that he now knows what to do about it, once he does lapse. Resenting the former climate, he now moves with courageous expedition to return to the new relationship near the Father. God can pull out the nails, but He cannot pull out the holes—a fact which cripples many a person's faith when, after conversion, he suddenly discovers the same old scars of sin. Let it be remembered that to practice exorcism—the expulsion of the soul's undesirables—requires biceps which are constantly flexed by intelligent will power. Every new convert should be alerted to this danger lest the house of life vacated by repentance is soon occupied by seven other devils whose expulsion is seven times harder than the original.

Suppose one is converted; does this mean he has suddenly

been translated to a new world? Not at all. There still remains the problem of evil, and though one may be saintly himself, still he must live on and serve in an evil society of scheming men. This fact guarantees the existence of problems. And human suffering is still here despite one's recent baptism. Though he possesses robust health himself, his sense of empathic concern, which is part and parcel of regenerate life, means that he too must suffer, if in no other way than by mutual burden-bearing. Then the complex art of tolerating despotism, tyranny, and hatred, in a world that should know better, creates a vortex of tensions. Added to these inevitables is the mystery of divine discontent which propels that one who knows this world is not his home. Growing up in the fullness of the faith is rife with pain; its derivatives are: the sweet misery of disenchantment; the soothing security of a now-then dualism; the awful mystery of human-divine partnership, an aura of invisible accompaniment; the sublime paradoxes: gaining while losing, standing while kneeling, succeeding while failing, and living while dying. Like an artist who is always touching up his painted works, never quite satisfied with his last stroke of the brush, so is the way of a conscientious Christ-follower who remembers that his salvation is not a problem-solver but a soul-saver.

That man of Tarsus thought that his security in God's salvation was the perfect condition for removing his thorn in the flesh, only to discover that persistence in prayer meant nothing so long as he appended: ". . . not what I will, but what thou wilt." It may be that God has in mind man's glorious acceptance of what appears to be a weight of necessity of human limitation, and at the very point of one's weakness this becomes the place of God's power. At any rate, this is the interpretation that the man himself put upon his thorn and thereby converted a stumbling block into a stepping stone. Conversion may confirm the existence of a thorn; but instead of pulling it out, it assures that it be more deeply seated in the flesh.

The reward note is much too dominant in twentieth-century evangelism. Offering the prospective convert the world and heaven too is alien to the selflessness of Jesus. Man, in this spoiled day, actually listens for a cataloging of the assets which may accrue to his account in case he responds to the invitation. "Pie in the sky by and by" as well as now is paramount, in many acceptances. Prayer so easily can degenerate into a conduit of one-way blessings—always vertical and in descent. The old hymn, "Just as I am" is good for a starting point: God takes a man just as he is, but to remain "just as I am" mocks the promise to which he has responded. He is to go from just as he is to just as he ought to be. But here is where the rub comes in: seeing little immediate reward, the glories of a nebulous tomorrow are too illusive. From this stems the rupture of relationships and the many discords all too familiar in the church. To expect peace of mind while having a guilty conscience; to live like hell and anticipate heaven in the end; to try saintliness and sin simultaneously, without admitting or fearing the dichotomy is to invalidate the contention that one has been with the Saviour. So, while conversion is no panacea for every problem, it does admit that man's final need is in God; and bringing this truth to bear at every junction of the way is to assure enough leverage to lift the load—no matter how galling the gait or wearisome the way.

Twentieth-century evangelism stands indicted on another score: its minimal social dynamic. Social betterment is not commensurate to the hundreds of decision cards which otherwise indicate great spiritual awakening. It is too bottled up and too concerned with inner experience to the detriment of energies released to convert society. Once again we are witnessing the pendulum of extremes swinging away from the opposite pole. One extreme placed the major emphasis of evangelism on a social gospel and in the process mistook the nature of the Kingdom, equating its worth in terms of seminars, renovated tenements, and drained swamps. The twenties and thirties heard the disconsolate query of a former wilderness voice, "Are you the coming one. or shall we look for another?" Its rosy idealism, though dwelling in Machaerian castles, still was to be commended, its failure to relate the whole story notwithstanding. The unremitting premise still stands inviolate: trying to change society without changing individuals who make up society is as futile as trying to dry up the ocean with a mop! Painting shanties on muddy alleys did little to alleviate the misery of unsanitary conditions so long as the tenants insisted on personal filth as a necessary adjunct to their way of life. The inner man must be washed white before it does any good to whitewash his picket fence. Clean wallpaper and painted lintels are sorry substitutes for the forthright imperative, "You must be born again." Little wonder the social gospel, reduced to such narrow-gauge dimensions, fell short of its admirable objectives.

Today's opposite extreme is equally fragmentary. Instead of concentrated interest in renovating society there is the highly individualistic cult with its strange coalition of personal experiences, existentialism, and egomania—an amalgam which has produced a hybrid of neo-ascetics who see little need for *koinonia* and who feel no compunction to relate their individual oddities to the mass equation. Insisting that theirs is the Kingdom, they manifest but a dribble of effort to populate the Kingdom with redeemed men. While claiming to have the balm of Gilead, still they show no urgency in applying such balm to humanity's sores.

If theirs is the way, there is no clear delineation for others to find it. And poor rationalizing it is to think that community chests and penny arcades can suffice for one's duty to society; a Christian is obligated to his environment by virtue of his profession. Personal experience is validated in the process of sharing and alleviating consumptive fevers of the human race. Salt and light mean little if they are confined to hydroelectric plants and storage vats; only as salt is spread on meat does it act dually in flavoring and preserving. Kilowatts must course through steel veins and arteries to make the machine churn its pistons. There is little recommendable value for one whose faith claims to live on better terms with God than he does with his fellow man.

Christianity can't be bottled up. Any effort to do so results in garments torn from their warp and woof by the tensive nature of the new force. New wine with its fermenting potential is turbulent content for wineskins which are dried out and cracked by use and age. If the true faith is understood at all, it is understood as explosive—an explosive that may lie dormant in seeming sterility but which may be easily detonated by the least cap of vibrant faith. Like fermenting yeast it diffuses through the wet wad of dough, raising, lighting, enriching, while being content to lose its own identity in the process.

Such was the technique of a Chinese farmer who, after having cataracts removed from his eyes, made his way from the Christian compound to the far interior of China. Only a few days lapsed, however, until a missionary doctor looked out of his bamboo window and noticed the man from whose eyes cataracts had been removed, holding an end of a long rope. In single file holding to the rope were several dozen blind Chinese who had been rounded up and led for miles to the doctor who had worked the "miracles" on his eyes. What a recommendation! Restored sight was cause enough to share what had happened to him with those of like condition.

Just so with the Gospel of Christ. What one will not share he cannot keep; Christian faith is no end in itself but the means by which man struggles upward and onward.

Whatever else may be said for the cloister approach to religion, such an approach is not the way of that Nazarene who, while finding Himself in the world, refused to be of the world. Not behind forbidding walls is the genius of the faith—all logical arguments of the meditative life notwithstanding—but in the shambles where variant men with unclean hands and lying lips need the cleansing power of the gospel. Like money or fertilizer, faith has to be spread around to render potent action; it is not a nicety of possession—some bric-a-brac to be admired—but a power to be let loose. More real good is accomplished for God and His purposes by beads of sweat that course down faces of toiling men who still believe that work is a sacred requiem than by all mystics who gaze into crystal balls or who genuflect at every station of the aisle while praying every hour on the hour! Herein is no decrying judgment on those who walk the way of the cloth; instead, an unapologetic reminder that if one is to fashion his life after that Nazarene, one should walk the way He walked—at the busy intersections and down on market streets where men, consumed by tempests in teapots, pour their lives into the hopper of dissipation. Here a disciple of the Redeemer is to be found translating into deeds the words so fitly spoken in synagogue and church.

One day, after having dropped a bit of chocolate on a kitchen counter, I noticed an ant came from nowhere to taste the sweetness. But hardly had it tasted before it left and started a zigzag course into unknown labyrinths. A few minutes later a single file of ants in tandem came to the pile of sweetness. Than followed a feast for all as each small tentacle clutched its microscopic portion. Then the thought: if human life would go to the ants, consider their ways, and be wise,

what a difference! The sweetness of the gospel should be sufficient stimulant to recommend it to someone else. The inclination to feast to satisfaction and then go our way until hunger
reappears speaks of an activity which is alien to historical
Christianity.

Man's religion must change his environment as well as his
inner nature lest the blind continue his futile effort to lead the
blind. In fact, the validity of the inner change is determined
by the outward expression. Sympathies which fail to alleviate
poverty, doxologies that stop short of praise expressed in
sweat, tithes content to ignore how the remaining nine-tenths
is spent, brotherhood daily proclaimed but hourly denied,
teaching the golden rule while worshiping the golden calf,
dreaming of a great, big, bright world without brightening the
corner where one is: this is hardly a faith to help the millions
whose major deterrent is religion itself. An English maid,
when asked for some evidence that she had been saved,
answered, "Now I sweep under the rugs." Deeds, not words,
separate sacred substance from superstitious shadow.

It is so easy to get lost in today's crowds. Mass techniques,
assembly-line serials, the deception that numbers are essential
to achievement, a growing suspicion that it is a crime to be
alone, and the subsequent feeling of guilt when one takes off
a few hours for himself, the proverbial "cheaper by the dozen"
index—all tend to discount the individual. Creative uniqueness
receives nauseatingly meager compensation, indicating the
scourge of creeping inclusiveness engendered by socialism.
"Let the government do it" has become a substitutionary alternative to personal achievement or personal responsibility.

Into this climate of anonymity it is quite natural that mass
evangelism should make its entry. Observing the reactions of
people at circuses and theaters, evangelists have learned many
variant group responses. The infant schools of psychology and
parapsychology have provided new levers on which the hu-

man equation can be turned. For those who dismiss mass evangelism as amateurish theatrics, let this be made clear: when the psychology of man is right and the Spirit of God chooses to move through an assembly of people, incalculable good can be achieved. Those who would decry such as emotional froth would also overlook not only one of the basic laws of human nature but also the testimony of Christendom for twenty centuries. Success in the effort involves publicity, visitation, prayer meetings and deep study. Yet, with a publicity committee that would shame an international cartel; with visitation excelling that of a brush salesman; and with music that would confound the crankiest esthete, the desired results are not always assured because such efforts speak too much of human initiative and ulterior motives of excellence in performance or subscription to the worldly standards of success. It is at this point that one of the glaring weaknesses of evangelism is revealed: when failure in effort seems apparent, one wants to hire a better public relations expert or another evangelist!

On the level of the mass approach, activity so easily degenerates into professionalism. "Let preachers and the paid staff members do it. Why expect laymen who are busy with beans and bonds to be witnesses?" Such an attitude leaves little leeway for the Holy Spirit to work through people as God's agents of communication. Whatever else may be said for the mass technique, one must conclude that Jesus preferred the personal approach. He didn't win people, but persons; and while the masses in Jerusalem evoked from Him tears of solicitation, His call was to Andrew, the man; to Matthew, the tax collector. Mary and Martha were not swallowed up in the anonymity of the ladies aid society in Bethany. Perhaps no other factor better explains why so comparatively few adults are being won today than this admission: we substitute for the personal encounter a mass front which depends largely upon preaching missions and perfunctory concern, usually one week a year. This method will not reach many. The best of orators can never orate a man into the Kingdom; but as he shows individual heart-care toward another man, then the greatest force in heaven or earth is brought to bear in persuasive encounter.

The great moments of life usually are personal. While an individual has nothing to do with his own birth, still the experience is uniquely his own—a very personal one. Rebirth is vastly personal. Whereas a man had nothing to do with his first birth, in rebirth he has everything to do. Both are accompanied by rigorous pain—a fact that individualizes the experience. The moment when a life partner says "I will" is a great moment of personal import, freighted with tender emotions—emotions that obliterate all competitive concerns. Then, the moment of death is specifically personal. All the solicitations of loved ones who create a climate of security in which to die notwithstanding, the fact remains: there are no proxy deaths. Everyone must walk that lonesome valley alone.

Likewise, the great accomplishments of life have been personal triumphs. George Handel, wrestling through the midnight hour in quest of the ground swell in sharps and flats, struggling to blend musical excellence with spiritual triumph, finally fused the best of both in a crescendo of hallelujahs! Eve Curie, shamed by failure in a thousand experiments, making a laboratory a veritable altar, at the point of her seeming failure turned in the late hour of the night to see the rebuking glow of radium! The crusading knight, wandering through forest and field, ignored in his pursuit the rightful source of his Holy Grail, in the face of a mendicant with tin cup in hand! The shout of Eureka came from ten thousand lips when discovery was made of chemical, mathematical, philosophical, or theological treasure! These, with few exceptions, have been personal climaxes.

Gethsemane was a personal victory. Narrowing like the apex of a pyramid were the crowds that followed Him for hunger's gratification or curiosity's satiation. Across the Jordan River He fed five thousand, but on the opposite side the number had narrowed to twelve. As He entered the garden of Gethsemane, He reduced the twelve to three. Then these were left to pray at a distance as He went alone to wrestle with the will of God. Even the endearing qualities of John or Peter were not equal to that struggling drama which involved a single solitary soul. And though He was crucified in the company of two robbers, still there was no room left on that rough-hewn cross with its suggestive dualism: the vertical shaft pointing to God in whose love He was dying; the horizontal shaft with one of its ends pointing to a sinner on the left and the other end pointing to a sinner on the right—graphic indices for a world which needed such loving sacrifice. This was the method of Jesus— living and dying for individual persons, knowing that if the individual were saved, society in the long run would be too. Working from the center to the circumference assures total coverage, but the distance from circumference to center is too far.

Like chain reaction through electrons, neutrons, protons, and atoms, one life stoked into consuming heat can suffuse society with its radiant warmth.

Just such magnetizing influence was felt when Hitler placed a persuasive Nazi agent in a cell next to that of Martin Nie-moller, with the hope of converting the Christian minister to totalitarianism. After some days of observing the equipoise of God's prisoner, his habit of devotions, and his unfettered faith in the ultimate triumph of righteousness, the Nazi officer called for a copy of the Holy Bible, whereupon he was promptly removed from the jail. No prison bars can contain the magnanimous force of Christian personality!

Horse and buggy evangelism gives rise to an inadequate relationship to the church. The mushrooming of cults and sects can syphon off many potentially useful Christians, a mania of divisiveness equating its worth in terms of separateness, lack of cooperation, and vain babblings. Such mushrooming is accounted for by the efforts of many itinerant evangelists who feel little need for the church of Jesus Christ just so long as they pack them in some wayside enclosure. The untimely birth and inordinate growth of many heretical cults is attributable to two causes. One is the fault of the larger denominational groups who fail to feed all the sheep. They ignore those who could not eat the strong meat of the gospel and refuse to serve milk out of fear that such a process is beneath their ecclesiastical dignities. On the other side of the ledger is the frank admission that one-sided conversions give rise to thousands who retain enough of their former paganism to resist the operations of charity which would have graciously included them in the fold of belonging. There is a type of paganism that chooses to sail under the colors of egotism, a sort of pooled ignorance masquerading under the ambiguous guise of "gospel truth" without remotely knowing what such profound words entail. Many of the religious cults that demand a hearing today are little more than an obnoxious amalgam of superstition; commercial trappings; personal, obsessional neuroses; cantankerous natures that refuse to be softened by Christian graces; and the dispositions of a Diotrephes who, loving "to have the preeminence among them [the brethren]" never read for the first time that Scriptural imperative, "Be kindly affectioned . . . with brotherly love; in honour preferring one another!" What interesting pastime to speculate how fewer sects there would have been had their leader or leaders been elected third vice-president in some established denomination! It seems to be the nature of some that they cannot survive without being included in preferential favor—a far cry from the One who "made himself of no reputation, and took upon him the form of a servant. . . ."

That the church is in line for justifiable criticism is beyond dispute; that the organic institution possesses no saving powers, no one will deny; but to expect perfection from anything composed of human beings is to flaunt the accepted facts.

The stock question, "Is it necessary to belong to a church in order to be a Christian?" rises every day. "Does the church hold the master-key to the door of eternity?" On the right answer hangs the weight of divine truth. To say that one must belong to the Church down on the corner of Broadway and Second Street in order to be saved is to admit of error. The thief on his cross didn't have time for catechisms, confirmations, and office holding; but he did have time for confession, confession of the most valid type: "Lord, remember me . . ." Yet, who will doubt that God ignored his plea?

Still, what is the nature of the church, and is that nature antithetic or a hindrance to being a Christian? Is it a choice between Christian discipleship and church affiliation? Once again the authority lies not in creeds and councils but in the One who founded His church. The word *eklesia* which He used to denote His church means "called out of"—those who are called out of the world by the redeeming voice of the Saviour, who constituted the church. Now, to say, "Must I belong to this in order to be a Christian?" is as much beside the point as one asking, "Must I get in uniform in order to fight for my country?" A professing Christian who sees no need for challenge in a local church is just about as useful as a citizen who says, "I am patriotic, I believe in my country's objectives, and I am sympathetic with those who fight, but I will not get in uniform." Some fighting he will do—some patriotism! The fighting is good all along the line at any time and at any place: in the city cathedral, at the wayside chapel, in the county-seat church—anywhere. It isn't the place but the person who matters. And if one waits until he thinks the church is going to be an acre of heaven transplanted to earth, isolated from the flotsam of society wherein meek and perfect people congregate to count their intangible assets, then he will wait from now on. The church was never intended to be a mutual admiration society, but a bulwark never failing; not an assembly of moral perfectionists, but salt and light; not a congregation of good, bad and indifferent people, but those who are twice-born, speaking the language of love, seeing the invisible, and handling things which fingers cannot touch. It is a pilgrimage of magnificent "fools" who refuse to see the impossible, maddened by a dream, magnetized by a vertical Presence, charged by an energizing force which knows no exhaustion, who, despite the straitness of the gate and narrowness of the way, are climbing the steep ascent to heaven "through peril, toil and pain." Must one belong to such a group if he is a Christian? Precisely! One cannot do otherwise without contradicting the very thing he professes to have happened to him. God does not have churches and CHRISTIANS ANONYMOUS. To be unknown to other cooperating, fellowshipping Christians is altogether too much privacy!

What is the upshot of all these efforts? Why try to win the world? Duty? Self-advancement? Fear of human extinction? Blind obedience? Why? Twentieth-century evangelism needs to give its motives a good scrubbing and to hang them out to dry. What strange components make up the complexity of motivation! For instance, a casual glance at the negative motives causes disconcerting dismay. Mental assent propels some people a certain distance but not far. Soon spent, as other competitive interests creep in, this type knows no durable continuity.

Reputation and the advancement thereof will not cohere for a sustained period of time in the art of evangelizing. It is embarrassingly interesting to speculate how many religious workers go after the lost people because they are interested in them as persons or because the winning of them will accrue to the account of a local church's baptismal record. If such speculation produces one case, this is one too many. A sure prognosis for such effort is failure.

Will statistics and what they represent motivate one's efforts to evangelize? The reading of the annual report which discloses the number of additions to the church may be an experience of excruciating self-condemnation by virtue of their diminution to some, whereas to others the size of numbers may be a gusher of elation and pride. It is commonplace to hear throngs discount statistics and deprecate the worth of numbers; as a matter of fact, the only ones usually found running down numbers are those who are not running them up— a self-incriminating commentary. Matthew Arnold insists that the best known book in the Bible to most Christians is the Book of Numbers. Yet all such provender will not activate intelligent diligence in the task.

Then what will? What artesian well pours forth clear, sweet water to satiate the thirst of parched throats? Just this: a zealous delight in doing the job which is undergirded by the power of divine compulsion. This is it! To work for the sheer love of doing it, for no other reason than that it needs to be done! Finding time where there is no time becomes relatively easy when a life is motivated by this obsession. This love of work is the lever which lifts it from the duty level to privileged joy. Transforming it from perfunctory task, zealous delight is the effective motivation, a holy contagion which must be caught—it cannot be taught. Approached by one whose life is thus characterized, a sinner is at a disadvantage in that the Christian (combining sincerity of effort with delight in motive) invades the personality of the one to whom he is witnessing. This is the unbeatable combination. No sense of well-being takes precedence over that state of affairs when a Christian knows that the Lord goes before him and that his rear guard is Israel's God. Such a sense inspires conviction that a regiment of strength is available when one witnesses in the power of the Unseen Presence. The history of successful evangelism is replete with those who did the job because they reveled in the process. All other motives fall as flat as flounders, and the task remains undone.

"Give your heart to Christ" often means little more than surrender of one's emotions at that particular time. To imply that such a surrender involves an about-face, a stock-taking of one's vocabulary, expulsion of vulgarity in "wondrous potency," the choice of new associates, surrender of certain personal bastions of conduct which do not become a regenerate life, bringing under the sway of divine aegis the back half-acre of stubborn will, yielding to God's sovereignty all of one's future plans, sharing in communal miseries without counting the cost, giving not until it hurts but because it hurts—ah, this is something else altogether!

Thousands of modern "converts" know little more than the fact that they walked down the aisle of a church, or met with the session, or attended classes in church instruction. "Did you have an experience with Jesus?" may mean an interrogation of offense to some of these, who then counter with a vacuum query, "What do you mean?" A horse and buggy evangelism that doesn't convert the whole man results in a fragmented personality which is of little worth to the Kingdom of God. A dissected soul is poor fare for service to either master. The old dichotomies of body and spirit, heaven and the world, now and then, here and hereafter, have encouraged a division of man's nature and interests; hence, the fragmentary conversions. Integration of every facet of man's nature presents a whole through which divine energy can operate. "It doesn't take much of a man to be a Christian, but it takes

all there is of him." The fact of the tear ducts working overtime is no justification for the mind to hibernate—God wants
all of a man: mind, body, soul. Busy hands are no substitute
for unbent knees; nor is a swivel chair conducive to easy devotions, in that it is a proxy for shoe leather which should be
worn thin by steps to the despairing, destitute, and dejected.

What a day to cut the cords that bind us to the earth and
earthy loves, freeing man so that he may be bound by the
love of God which involves his emotions, thought, and will!
Herein is superlative living; herein is unsurpassed wisdom.

12

CATERING WITHOUT CONVICTING

STRAIGHT AS BULLETS, the words of Jesus found a ready target in the minds and hearts of men, unimpeded by verbal embroidery or apologetic tone. No one got the idea that He was lacking in authority; His was not the wily art of speaking out of both sides of His mouth at the same time, nor trying to prepare a statement to the satisfaction of opposing parties. Reconciliation? yes; compromise? never! In fact, the words of Jesus are among the most dogmatic in all religious writ, giving no quarter to alternatives, leaving no doubt about the fact "He that is not with me is against me. . . ." He never implied if the human race missed His train that another nearly or equally as good would come along a little later.

To propagate Christianity as one among many religions is to impute to it an insipid charity which it fails to claim for itself. Let its dynamic ethic be thrown into the arena with other religions, and let each see for himself which is victor. If it cannot fight its own battles, how can it fight those of its weak adherents? The indisputable fact is that it never fails to assert its superlative worth wherever it is harnessed to human life.

Yet many in the church have insisted that this position of Christ in its raw, undiluted form is too strong. Man, floundering in the historical process of growth, is embarrassed, then discouraged, by so lofty an ideal and Personage; hence, the presumed necessity of accommodation, modification, and dilution. Pages of history are replete with this infamous effort insomuch that what is too often observed is a pale palimpsest only faintly resembling the original.

Look at the anatomy of the sin of catering: it is best understood as the activity by which crowds are served a diet bereft of spiritual nourishment—a type of subserviency to popular standards and prejudices. While not purveying desires that are morally debasing, catering is content with a sort of moral truckling, that godparent of servility. It may not wink at entrenched evil, but turning its head the other way is more confirming than if both eyes were winked. The church is shorn of its strength when it acquiesces in the wake of social bulldozing, political squeeze plays, and organized ignorance which masquerades as religious convictions. Majority rule in a democratic country has given rise to an adamant belief that majorities make theological issues right on the basis of sheer numbers. Not so! Truth can be, and often is, at the door of a single individual or a small minority. How many were there at Calvary? Hardly a corporal's guard. It was not the noisy Sorbonne student body that discovered radium but the solitary figure of Eve Curie. The dungeon of Mamertine Prison was not crowded as the Apostle Paul shivered in its dampness. Bedford Jail's majorities may have been rodents and seraphim, but the fact remains: John Bunyan, in singular adherence, was the cell's only occupant. Spiritual altitudes usually are cold, isolated, and populated by some courageous Elijah standing in stable contrast to the will of the masses.

The field of His Kingdom is much like a jungle which persists in encroaching; vines, bushes, and weeds grow wider and taller while claiming the cultivable land. What a providential time to take gospel machetes in hand, whacking away at social débris, reclaiming for God the rabble of humanity! In order to do this, the nerve of compromising catering must be cut. Let it be cut with decisive forthrightness while admitting that this generation which is trying to drink its way to happiness, fight its way to peace, buy its way to heaven, and filibuster its case before God, will never know the calamitous dimensions of such folly unless the church in militant action convinces and convicts man of this evil.

Right here one should stop to check the genesis of compromising catering—its headwaters must be located and dried up if the streams are to cease to flow. Taking the cues from the world instead of God is the first dribble of that tainted water. Now, it is true that the church of Jesus Christ can learn much from the world by way of efficient business methods, crowd psychology, and changing tastes; it stands to reason that the affairs of the church should be as free from slipshod methods and archaic system as any topflight business corporation. But successful businessmen may be least qualified to dispense the things of His Kingdom—the two are not synonymous. Presuming that agility with gadgets, dexterity with machines, or acumen with stocks and bonds are qualifying virtues for determining foreign missions quotas or leading adolescents to the Saviour is a bit of arrogance. Spiritual things must be spiritually discerned, a process possible only among the spiritually regenerate. Woe to that church whose spiritual temperature is determined by the city fathers when true humility and Christian love are not there! The result is something of a hybrid, a country club with a pulpit and choir loft in one end, where people come and go in perfunctory habit, seldom if ever sensing the high and holy Presence. No, the plays can't be called by the wrong quarterback lest the team flounder in confusion and loss of yardage.

In such predicament the explosive nature of faith is de-capped into dull neutrality. Power that would remove mountains falters before mole hills. Rather than the prophetic plea, "Let judgment run down as waters, and righteousness as a mighty stream" a mild alternate is offered: "Take it easy, brother, everything is going to be all right." The worst state of affairs that possibly can exist in a church is that state in which everything is under control. What a shame! Who can harness the flood tide of divine power? What human control is sufficient to that divine dunamis?

Common sense—that enemy of Christianity! There is nothing common about dying for another or walking beyond the required distance, nothing usual about loving the unlovely. He had no thought of keeping a firm grip on Himself; letting Himself go in one burst of generosity didn't look much like the tame, self-composure so characteristic of many disciples today. Fanaticism has two facets: one is dogmatic, intensified, and when it loses its way, redoubles its efforts. This must be shunned as being detrimental to progress. But fanaticism has a second desirable facet: that which leaves no alternative to obedience, counts no cost, and deems no mountains too high to climb for God. In this sense of the word, everything the Nazarene did was fanaticism. Let there be more fanaticism of self-forgetting which commits the great indiscretion of generosity, in some hot-hearted lad foolish enough to believe that nothing is impossible with God! This is the stuff of which saints are made and by which the world is turned right side up. Without it, the church in calm self-control will sit and rot!

Still another headspring of compromising catering is failure to declare the full mandates of God's Word out of deference to expediency. It is common practice for some to hop, skip, and jump through the Bible in order to reach those appeasing pages where all is sweetness and light. The many series of sermons on "peace of mind" should be interrupted by a "thus saith the Lord" on judgment, sowing and reaping. Herod still insists on living with his brother's wife; Diotrephes continues his love for pre-eminence among the brethren; Judas holds membership in the inner circle; Sadducees still deny the resurrection. And, so long as those persist, the full force of gospel truth must be heard and heeded.

In the light of sin's unblushing face in the pews, the jewel-laden trappings which are put in to cover lack of convincing preaching are insulting substitutes. The sin of catering often is justifiably placed at the feet of the minister. His is the role of both prophet and priest. But when the prophetic voice is muted to a priestly chant, then no one hears the certain ring of prophetic judgment. There are not two gospels—one for clergymen and one for laymen. The same truth pertains to all; and despite constant handling of sacred vessels and excessive familiarity with the Divine, no sense of immunity from accountability is granted. If the minister takes one step into the world, he can be sure that laymen will take two. It was said of one who preached rather well but lived rather ill that it was a shame he ever went out of the pulpit. And, when he was out, it was a shame that he ever went in. What telling indictment! Catering is the process by which this sorry state of affairs occurs.

To every professing follower of the Stranger of Galilee there comes the moment when he must decide whether or not he will conform or transform—whether he will be a shaper of his world or be shaped by it. Pagan society has its own molds into which it fits mankind; and if Christians have no specific form of their own, the world will rush in to claim its right to impress. If the wisest of saints should rise from his grave, he would shout again in dogmatic certainty, "Be not conformed to this world: but be ye transformed. . . ."

The policy of accommodation as a method of approach in Christian missions stands out as treacherous warning. Upon entering new mission fields where civilization was minimal, missionaries would try new seeds, sanitary methods, and medicines before mentioning the gospel and its cleansing power. Education was tried, and then the gospel was presented. The best of the native culture was interwoven into missionary efforts, and what were the results? Indescribable! Cornish game chickens brought in to improve the strain were killed and eaten; soap was buried as ill omen to the gods; education was used to enhance economic standing while accentuating a mania for more; medicine became a fiery goad which infuriated witch doctors—while missionaries were regarded as foreign devils who came to pronounce a curse. Wherever a policy of accommodation continues, the result is a synthesis of paganism, faint dashes of Christian ethics, brutality, reconfirmed prejudices, and deep-seated, malignant nationalism.

On the other hand, when the policy of accommodation has been ignored and the gospel in its pure form presented as the first appeal, then supplemented by penicillin, hybrid corn, Guernsey heifers, and vacation Bible schools, these results followed: eroded land was terraced to preserve the topsoil, mortality rate of children was cut in half, a sense of communal superstition gave way to a degree of sanitation and beauty, while an indigenous church grew to replace those who were regarded as outsiders. A religion of appropriation, accommodation, blending the new and the old, is little more than common stock which man has possessed from the beginning.

Transformation seldom comes easily. Requiring revolution within the soul of man, it demands that the old house be torn from its foundations and that a completely new structure replace it. Admittedly, this process is wrought with rigor, regimentation, and dangerous cost. The natural inclination of human nature is to follow lines of least resistance.

Current in the thinking of many young people today is the reasoning: try anything once—what harm does it do?—everybody is doing it. The necessary presence of checks and balances to many seems like Victorianism. Why not live your life here and now, forgetting the consequences? The reasoning runs: when in Rome do as the Romans do. Better advice would be: when in Rome do as the Romans do—only when the Romans do right! Caught in a vortex of two citizenships, earth and heaven, Christians must ever be cognizant that they are in the world but cannot be of it, and that their nexus to God through Christ prohibits proximity to some things and some people. Not in self-righteous judgment but for the same reason that lilies do not grow in cesspools. So long as a ship is in water, the law of balance is intact but when water gets in the ship, catastrophe is ahead. Just so with the followers of the Way; their being in the world is a necessary tenure lived out in the context of Divine intention, but when the "world" gets in them, the purposes are foiled and God takes leave of the individual's life.

Off the coast of South America, sweet waters of one of its major rivers meet the churning, salty waves of the ocean with thunderous embrace. It looks as though the tidal force of the ocean Goliath would force the river water back into its channel for miles. Not so. Even at flood tide the saline waters are held back. At low tide the river is seen to flow unabated. To the millions who insist that only brackish water is possible in this kind of world—that separation from contamination is idle fancy—let it be known anew that this is possible only by positive identity with that which is the superlative in height and holiness—God Himself.

What the church needs in order to save it from conforming to worldly standards is more enemies. She stands in too much favor with Caesar. In some cases, the two appear to be interchangeable in loyalties and standards; not enough marked delineation is observable. Enemies! The kind created as a result of independence from governmental support—when a spade is called nothing else; when sin is admitted and condemned. Enemies—because of indignation to social evil, the voice of one crying in a metropolitan wilderness, "Prepare ye the way of the Lord" instead of preparing the way for despots, distilleries, and dealers in junk. Enemies—by virtue of shining lights which set in bold contrast the darkness of treachery, providing counterpoint to sin's monotony. The fine deference shown the church by the world is a source of alarm, in that the only times when the church militant broke out of rusty molds and evangelized the world were when it stood in disfavor with the contemporary way of life. One wonders whatever happened to the two-edged sword of the Spirit, a sword never intended to substitute for a scepter. Where is the truth that was to take precedence over love of father, mother, brother, or sister? Is it that this truth has been interwoven in the fabric of other skeins so that it can be but faintly traced in an ambiguous, ecclesiastical design? Conforming, instead of transforming!

To a farmer's dismay, a wild duck broke ranks from a flock going south and lighted in his barnyard with a dozen tame ducks. Nervously panting in its new surroundings like some winged visitor from another planet, the duck soon relaxed a bit and snatchingly ate from scattered grain. As another flock of wild ducks came over, the stray mallard stretched its wings and joined their flight. Hardly had it gone a short distance but it returned to the barnyard and the tame ducks. With winter over and spring in the air, the mallards winged their way back to Canadian heights. But the stray duck stretched his wings to join them, yet never left the ground. Next winter as they came over, the lone duck merely looked up. Man, like that one stray duck, can putter around in the barnyard muck, whereas all the time he was made for loftier altitudes and cleaner environs. Not by sudden thrust of choice or habit does life become conformed to ugly shapes, but by unintentional descents to the barnyard of life, ignoring admonition to regain altitude and to join the pilgrimage to celestial heights.

13

PRAYING WITHOUT PAYING

"No matter what I do, it seems that everything goes against me. Even when I pray, my prayers don't seem to get beyond the ceiling of my bedroom," complained a tired businessman to his minister. A few minutes of querulous comment caused the minister to ask, "Do you have any trouble with your paying?" "What do you mean?" he asked, somewhat stunned. "Just this: there are multitudes of people who are familiar with prayer books, but who think that there is no relationship to pocketbooks. They are content to pray, but they seldom pay. Not that praying is by the dollar, but when one prays, 'Thy will be done,' he is asking for his own hands to be opened and his pocketbook along with them."

This is one of the major sins of the church: praying without paying—as though Christianity were some fragmented, partial allegiance. If it is understood at all, it is understood as a total way of life, not religion *and* business, but religion *in* business, pervading every facet of one's activities. There is more said in the Bible about stewardship than about anything else other than salvation. Five times as much appears in Holy Writ about this phase of living as about prayer; yet prayers are mouthed in endless rhetoric while the one praying often is penurious. This ought not to be! No conversion is genuine until the pocketbook has been converted. The essence of faith is summed up in the verb "to give." "For God so loved the world, that he gave . . ." not that He lent, or borrowed, or promised, but that He "gave."

Jesus' most forthright words dealt with a man's relationship to his money and the things represented thereby. Recognizing man's inordinate love for things, He warned against that tyranny with forceful vehemence: "Ye cannot serve God and mammon."

A singular stroke of rhetorical beauty are the words in Malachi, ". . . prove me now herewith, saith the Lord. . . ." Think of it: God putting Himself in position where finite, imperfect man should put to test that which is infinite and perfect! Yet that is exactly what God has invited us to do. What is He up to? Just this: to make man His junior partner with all the privileges that accrue from such a wonderful relationship. Taking man in his low estate with no capital to invest, God suffuses him with health, vigor, vision, muscle, opportunity, and material prosperity, saying, "Now you are blessed to be a blessing. Don't get any foolish ideas that you are sole owner; the deed is held in escrow. You are trusted with the management, but in the end there will be an accurate audit." And God's only motive in the partnership is that of interested love for the people involved. Oh, that many a suspicious cynic could see it! God needs nothing from man, but man needs to give—the only process by which the conduits of growth are kept open.

But many want prosperity to precede their liberality, and God refuses such a proposition. Instead, He says, "But seek ye first the kingdom of God, and his righteousness; and all these things shall be added unto you." The sequence is as important as the promise: preceding our prosperity is a demonstration on our part that we mean business. Many a Christian has promised God that in the event prosperity came his way he would share it with the needy masses of people, only to receive the prosperity and to forget his promise.

In every congregation there are those self-pitying souls who live from hand to mouth, envying those who have more than they, while luxuriating in the slough of penury. In one accord they acclaim, "We never had a chance." Now it is true that in some cases there was such an ugly coalition of circumstances that they did not have a chance. Yet, in most cases these questions should be raised, "Did you ever give God a chance? Did He ever have first call on self and substance?" Still stands that ancient reminder: "Behold, I stand at the door, and knock: if any man hear my voice, and open the door, I will come in. . . ." Refusing to bolt the door, He stands outside—while inside the person can continue in wanton poverty by refusing divine partnership. In this sense of the word, poverty is criminal. It must be remembered: it was no more Lazarus' poverty that took him to Abraham's bosom than it was Divese's wealth that took him to Hades: it was attitude in each case. For a Christian to remain in financial want throughout his life—unless he is of that meager fraternity where ill-fortune, like a recurrent toothache, curses his life— is to question that promise of the psalmist: ". . . and whatsoever he (the righteous man) doeth shall prosper." It is not the good pleasure of God that His children always be begging bread.

There is a time in the affairs of men when ignorance is criminal. Just such a time is that described in Malachi, "But ye say, Wherein have we robbed thee?" And like a rifle shot to the mark came the honest answer, "In tithes and offerings." To call some members of the church of Jesus Christ "robbers" is strong talk; yet the truth knows no affinity with anemia—ever!

Last year a thief broke into my office study and with rude hands pried open drawers, rummaged through desk and papers, and scattered things in whirlwind fashion all over the place. Pictures were removed from the wall during the search for anything of value. But one picture over a kneeling altar was left untouched: Sallman's "Head of Christ," beneath which a light burns all the time. That picture was left untouched. Was it that the thief, seeing those honest eyes, was arrested in his burglary? I know not—all I know is that it was left in its place without being touched. The same eyes look down in penetrating grief and wrath upon those who, while plundering through God's world, selfishly snatch for themselves the good things without acknowledging His divine right.

Who can look at this fabulous Republic of America and restrain his exuberance? Its bulging granaries; its teeming cattle; its verdant meadows; its humming industries; its lakes of black gold buried beneath the surface; its tall fir fortunes like silent sentinels pointing to the sky; its world of invisible wealth awaiting the delayed decade in which nuclear energies will be released by the finger of a child; its amalgam of people, claiming for its residue the best and worst of all; its vaunted freedoms proclaimed, though taken for granted and misunderstood; its smoking funnels; its laboratories of labor— all speak of a wonderful nation whose God ought to be the Lord! Some shortsighted prophet would conclude from this aura of material splendor that surely such merit has prevailed in ratio to its stocks and bonds, that doubtless some deserving facet of its nature accounts for this modern Eden. Not so! Through the eons of time God has blessed a variety of people and nations for one prescribed purpose: that they might be a blessing. When such a condition was met, prosperity continued; when turned to its own consumption, it was abruptly terminated.

Now lesser men than Amos are predicting the future of this Republic to be one of unlimited prosperity, unsurpassed wealth! But as a dissident note from unwelcome quarters comes the timeless wisdom of Goethe: "A nation can endure anything except continuous prosperity." Why? Because man has never yet learned the lesson of stewardship as being partnership with God. Things get in man's way; then they get in his heart, and crowd God out. History has yet to display a nation in the throes of financial plenty which has continued over a long period of time without a spiritual antecedent.

Who originated the yarn that Americans are generous? Up to a point they perhaps are the world's most generous, but that point is so far behind even a representative minimum that it shames the face of such prosperous folk. To thousands of people such a contention may seem at variance with the facts. Pointing to the all-time high in church finances, construction, mission gifts, etc., one easily concludes that this generation will be recorded as one of the open palm. Let any pastor of a church in lowly hamlet or city metropolis speak the facts: probably twenty per cent of the members do ninety per cent of the giving. While salaries for most have increased from ten to five hundred per cent over the last ten years, the percentage of giving has not increased in the overall picture. Millions who gave fifty cents a Sunday during the depression are giving about the same in 1957. If the average member gave twice as much as he was giving ten years ago, he would still be giving the same amount in light of the purchasing power of today's dollar. A quick glance at the Sunday evening offering plates is a pretty good index to America's "generosity." Today's minister, like Xerxes who prayed, "Would that I had as many soldiers as I have men," now prays, "Would that I had as many payers as I have prayers."

There is little difficulty or delinquency about rendering to Caesar his share; as a matter of fact, he is getting both his share and God's, nowadays. Whether one likes it or not, this country is ensconced in a web of politico-military expediencies which involve not only our destinies but also those of unborn generations—involvements which represent personal ambition, hindsightedness, partisan blundering, and the delusion that an intelligent, long-range national policy can be formulated and substituted every four years. All this has led to a demand on the part of "Caesar" that the citizens finance every wild-goose-chase from Afghanistan to Morocco. Taxes, which have drained the lifeline of its people through all ages, are mounting now in frightful proportions. In every loaf of bread there are fifty-one hidden taxes. And the end is far from view.

Such is the sorry state of things when Caesar is rendered the things which are God's. Said a desperate businessman, at the point of bankruptcy: "Man, you can't talk to me about tithing. I can't afford it. Don't you see that I am having to borrow money to pay my taxes now?" One will recall that a previous generation said that to have ten per cent of one's income taken would ruin the budget. Now about thirty per cent and perhaps more is taken, whether one likes it or not.

To mention the biblical practice of tithing is to alert all the fears of "legalism." But it is just such so-called fears that have constituted a wall behind which millions have hidden while dodging their responsibility. Jesus made it succinctly clear that unless the righteousness of the new disciples exceeded that of the scribes and Pharisees—which in their case meant tithing as a minimum—they would never see the Kingdom of God. In Christ's "These (things) ought ye to have done, and not to leave the other undone" fits the activity by which one is to give a tenth of his resources to his Lord. It is an interesting thing that the only person who argues against tithing is the one who does not tithe! A self-indicting commentary!

206 SINS OF THE CHURCH

Why tithe? A catalogue of "why's" is easy reference: tithing is necessary primarily to prove where one's heart is. One's heart can't be in the First National Bank and in the Eternal City simultaneously. One's affections can be on his acres with justifiable pride, but his heart must be on heavenly real estate if he ever is to be severed from earth-bound ties. "Lay not up for yourselves treasures on earth . . ." was no verbal prohibition against thrift, saving, and diligence; but against negation, occasioned by the fact that man's chief interests are going to be fixed on his fortune, whether it be in cash or character. This is the process by which the follower of the Supreme Giver matches idealism with realism. Knowing that it costs the Kingdom as many cents per kilowatt hour as it does the state, a Christian, though known for dwelling in ivory castles and dreaming of bright new tomorrows, never permits his ethereal existence to blind him to the realities of meat and bread, prisons visited, backs clothed, and penicillin administered. These require money; and the old advice, "Preach on spiritual things" needs to be rebuffed by a reminder that these are the things of the spirit for ". . . Inasmuch as ye have done it unto one of the least of these my brethren, ye have done it unto me." Praying without paying is poor religion indeed! Money is not the supreme necessity, but it is an imperative necessity. Too long has the church of Jesus Christ had to back into its commitments, contingent upon the whims, moods, and fancies of its adherents.

God's recurrent judgments in time are calling to task the church's contentment with little fish, widows' mites, and hard loaves. It is true that miracles have been wrought by the use of little things: a child's picnic lunch, a cruse of oil, a bit of meal. As a matter of fact, anything in the hand of God is power untold; but why must the business of the Owner be done on little fish, cold loaves, and mites of the many? Vested with divine authority, the church should move in militant might, asserting her divine authority over pagan enunciators and claiming the allegiance of the people for whom Christ lived and died. The present defensive attitude which approaches the subject of a man's accountability to his Creator is little short of apostasy: no crutches by way of verbal apologies are needed to support this eternal truth—no crutches because the truth does not limp. Such truth is forged in the crucible of divinity, and man can bank his life on that! Now is the time when man's "counselor corners" need to give way to "thus saith the Lord." Man must be called back to that early allegiance when all things were deemed "as dung" in the process of winning Christ; this alone will stem the mania for more and the infamous tide that sweeps man down before the altars of greed and gadgets.

In many phases of church activity, stock needs to be taken: in evangelism, organization, her teaching ministry, mission vision—but in none more than in her stewardship. What with a strange juxtaposition of values, motion is often mistaken for progress, and "much ado about nothing" is pawned off as worship. A statistical schizophrenia has invaded the holy precincts insomuch that altar incense is replaced by the odor of baked ham in the kitchen with the hope of attracting five more to break last week's record. Strange discipleship that can attend Sunday school without ever limbering up the muscles to reach for one's wallet; a type of nice conformity which seldom, if ever, lowers the azimuth of pride, or bends the knee, or oscillates the smitten cheek, or unclenches the fist, or walks the second mile, or turns the skull into a sanctuary of obedient meditation. Still, God doesn't judge one so much by mileage covered as by direction taken and motives employed. If the verb "to do" received less emphasis and "to be" became the number one, the grand old church would revive from her pale anemia, shake herself from lethargy, and recognize the presence and power of the Senior Partner. In sarcasm that militant hymn has been paraphrased:

> Like a Freshman forum
> Moves the Church of God;
> Brothers we are talking
> Where the saints have trod.
> We are not decided
> Whether we shall be
> One in deed or doctrine
> Or futility.[1]

On an occasion of showing the Hall of Bishops at the Sorbonne, a guide dryly commented, "This is where theologians have argued for five hundred years." Just a modicum of that energy spent in the direction of honest laboring with God to lift fallen humanity to its rightful standing in reconciliation would have availed far more than the theological rigmarole which, to many, becomes easy substitute for the common act of obedience!

Why tithe? Because it is a stopgap to selfishness. To give less than a tenth is to join the ranks of those who see the price in everything and the value in nothing. Placing more value on creature comfort than on creeds and crosses, one goes his way, living out his three-score-and-ten, without ever fathoming the depths of that which is the superlative in holiness. Who ever heard of an outstanding Christian who wasn't generous? Who ever heard of a penurious person who was at the same time a good Christian? We are supposed to be examples—the blind still can't lead the blind.

Those who frequent the congregation of the righteous have been classed in three categories so far as gifts are concerned: those who are like flint, the incorrigible misers, who despite all types of pleas and despite Herculean powers of persuasion,

[1] Charles L. Wallis, *op. cit.*, p. 70.

remain impervious and unresponsive and refuse to give. Others, like sponges, give only when they are "squeezed," a squeeze which is the result of pressure campaigns, emotional miasma, or coercive threats. God does not love a coerced giver; He does not because He knows that the motive is ulterior, a response to a stimulant other than love. Current in many financial programs are gifts that are contingent upon matching amounts from local sources. While such conditional gifts may encourage local generosity, they do not speak of that magnanimity which Jesus endorsed. Just imagine the widow saying in the temple, "I'll drop in my last farthing if someone else will come and match it!" She gave without others saying a word—other than commenting on her generosity— and she didn't even hear that. If one is able to give much, he should give it in the name of Christ, with little or no thought of tax advantages, matching amounts, or what others give.

Gifts without strings! Such was the attitude of the Metropolitan Opera officers when offered a gift of $100,000, providing the opera company would present an original composition of the donor. After studying the music, the quality was found to be beneath the standards of the company. The gift was refused because of the condition. May their tribe increase! Many a prosperous donor to the church needs to have his gift for a rose window or memorial organ denied because the money was accumulated from exorbitant interest rates, foreclosures, and dealings in unholy things.

The third type of giver is like a honeycomb all covered by a thin protective coat, yet beneath which is a well of sweetness. The slightest scratch penetrates this type of personality. Every appeal is heard and weighed in the light of his ability to give. Then without counting costs, hedging or rationalizing, such a one gives with joy and generosity. This is the only type of giver God has promised to bless. While the gracious invitation of God's plenteous mercy is free, acceptance entails obligations and responsibilities including the total life of man. The invitation, "Ho, every one that thirsteth . . . come, buy . . . without price," needs to be read in the same context as, ". . . for we receive the due reward of our deeds. . . ."

Investment in human life for the glory of God is the only investment that never fluctuates on Wall Street and never fails to pay dividends. When such bread is cast upon the waters, it always returns—buttered.

Like children on the fourth of July were those American servicemen who were ordered to take wheelbarrows and to roll out the millions of dollars stored in the vaults on Corregidor. Japanese infantrymen were but a few miles to the north where the island bastion would surely fall into their hands. Lest the money be captured and used to finance the Japanese machine of destruction, an order was given to burn all the money. Privates, whose monthly salary was about forty dollars, used one-hundred-dollar bills to light their cigarettes; and for several hours remarks were made which should have been recorded for posterity. But one remark, though commonly prosaic, spoke a kernel of abiding truth. Said a sergeant to his buddy, "You know, I didn't know the stuff was so worthless after all." Would that more than one sergeant could learn that difficult lesson: there is no pocket in a shroud.

Stingy people need to be reminded of a negative note in stewardship; namely, if they do not respond in willing generosity, then God is the surest of collectors. He doesn't settle all of His accounts in October. Man isn't punished in time, but God metes out judgment at the end of time. So, the prosperity of the wicked is no occasion for a Christian's faith to sag nor any grounds for a pagan to boast—the settlement is ahead!

Praying without paying! This is sin indeed; for within the province of the church's stewardship potential is enough to finance the cause of Christ around the globe in thorough, immediate, life-changing discipleship.

14

WORSHIPING WITHOUT SACRIFICING

WORSHIP IS A learned art wherein man encounters the Spirit of God, an encounter which produces a harmony of beating hearts and singing voices inspirited by a unity of purpose and destiny. Worship, as seen in the limitless aspirations of youth borne on dreamer's wings to the court of highest appeal; as seen in the aged, whose last digits of time are placed in selfless abandonment on the holy altar for God's own pleasure; as seen in tiny tots with faces untainted by dread of futility, bowed by instructed reverence, unconscious of alternatives; worship, the mighty organ let down by God on lease from heaven as an instrument for earth's accommodation, now thundering in heavy sforzando, now like a gentle, consoling zephyr through vox humana communicating the wisdom of the ages! Worship is the rapport where heart meets heart in mystic unity generating a sense of belonging to a victorious pilgrimage which is freighted with undying conviction and a do-or-die finality. Yet this mystical, ethereal, awe-inspiring activity does not replace the recurrent necessity of contrition, confession, and implored forgiveness. This is worship in its purest form.

Such reverent activity is impossible without sacrifice, that mood of mind and condition of spirit essential to its existence. The one singular event of history was an act of sacrifice: God's Son given into the hands of murderous men. If on that anvil the sublimest truth were wrought, then on the same basis true worship must be hammered out. Any other type is sacrilege. Herein the church tolerates a sin worse than impiety: an activity called worship which often is a hodge-podge of songs, sermons, sentences, and salve; a type of ecclesiastical entertainment designed for the plaudits of men and general standards of excellence. There is a profanity of attitude which renders true worshiping impossible. It was a bit of profound wisdom in a child who asked if a certain church were God's house. "Yes, this is God's house," she was hastily assured. "Then if it is God's house, why doesn't He move in?" she unabashedly asked. God doesn't move into some worshiping situations for the sole reason that no attitude or deed of sacrifice exist. When hearts do not go with the spoken words; when gifts do not represent the capacities of heart or mind; when brevity becomes the primary index of value; when washing priestly pots and pans takes precedence over handling the sacred vessels of Word and prayer; when falderal is mistaken for faith and joy is assigned too low a berth; when man's wisdom outshines the truth of God; when music is an end instead of a means to the end of God-directed adoration; when few if any are made dissatisfied with themselves—such is not sacrificial worship. Such a holy hush should fall over an assembly that one could hear the angels sing. The very word sacrifice comes from *sacer,* "sacred" plus *ficare,* "to make"—to make sacred.

The Turks have a habit of collecting every scrap of paper

because they believe the name of God may be written on it. What would it do to the quality of worship if something of that same concern pervaded our efforts from prelude to postlude?

But sacrifice is neither pleasant nor easy, and present-day man insists that his birthright guarantees him both pleasure and ease. Even a sophomoric concept of history would recount how the milestones of progress were passed by sacrificial efforts. Paul's "Present your bodies a living sacrifice" was advice made possible only after he had sacrificed his own will and way. So Shakespeare says, "Brave conqueror; for so you are, that war against your own affections and the huge army of the world's desires." [1] Brave conquerors indeed, that regiment of men and women who braved the yawning jaws of death to serve their unseen God.

Integral to the practice of Judaism was the slaying of lambs, goats, and doves. Such ritual did not grow out of cruelty to dumb animals nor from bloodthirsty sadism of tribal mores. The central meaning was not in the dying of the victim but in the giving of its life. Blood was the visible sign of life. Today, though no smoking altars receive the blood of sheep and goats, nonetheless, it is possible to achieve the same spiritual results when a life says "I will" to the claims of God and substantiates his "I will" by "I love, I pray, I go, I tell, I lift, and I trust." In each verb the life of the person is involved in purest sacrifice.

When asked to speak on the nature of Christian sacrifice, Albert Schweitzer, who has shown a cynical world that scholarship can be an ally rather than an obstacle to service, who regarded wealth and prestige with the deference the average man would pay to a lump of clay—Schweitzer, who knew that life's riddle could be solved only in terms of detachment and deposits in human life, a man to whom age is a vista ever-

[1] William Shakespeare, *Love's Labour's Lost*, Act I, scene 1, line 10.

214   SINS OF THE CHURCH

becoming to renewed effort and selfless devotion, answered: "I cannot speak on sacrifice because I know nothing about it."

The absence of this emptying out of self accounts for so much dullness in worship. When no sacrifice is rendered in advance, the worshiper comes with the "What can I get out of it?" attitude instead of "What can I put into it?" No verb so impedes the art of effectual worship as does the verb "to get." It is true that in some situations there is little or nothing to get; but there is also the fact that some professing Christians have nothing to take it away in had there been anything there to get!

Once on the island of Ie Shima, that small dot in the Ryukyuan Chain south of Japan, I stood early one Sunday morning in pouring rain, rain that gave the impression that God had a spite at the world and was whipping it with water. Time came for religious services, and the men were close to the front lines. In halting apology I halfheartedly asked the men if they wanted to have a service. To the last man they replied "Yes." With no books to sing from, we hummed familiar tunes; with no Bible to read, we recited the twenty-third Psalm. Then I thought, surely we must go since the water on my steel helmet chased itself down my face so fast that my eyes were filled. "Shall I preach?" I asked them. "Preach!" they said in one accord, and there for fifteen or twenty minutes a hundred men stood in mud and water ankle deep. Since returning to a civilian pulpit where cushions line the pews and air-conditioned splendor surrounds the worshipers, where it is as painful as pulling a front tooth for some to walk two blocks to church, I have thought of the zeal of my GI parishioners standing in the rain and mud saying, "Preach!" One lad from Arizona assured me, "That was the best sermon I have heard you preach." As I recall it, the outline was a hodge-podge; and its structure would have been poor stock in any department of homiletics. In all likelihood, the sergeant's remarks were prompted by the fact that he had paid a price to hear the message—a sacrifice of personal comfort—hence, the breakthrough to things worthwhile.

When one's unregenerate nature is brought under full sovereignty of God, creature comforts take a back seat. Weather, position, geography, age, circumstance, or condition mean little as determiners of loyalties. The choice often is between two goods; and the wisdom to know the difference is incumbent upon every disciple who knows that sacrifice is man's hope for sitting in the presence of the Sacrificer.

In all recorded art there are few works that tell the story of human shrinking from dreaded sacrifices as well as an artist's canvas that was painted to depict the contrast between Christ's sufferings and ours. In the background of the oils stand three shadowed crosses nearly eclipsed by dark paint. In the foreground stands a man who has picked up the crown of thorns which has fallen from the head of Jesus. There, in puny sympathies that took the form of curiosity, he pricks a tiny place on his index finger by one of the thorns just to see how it would feel. One puny prick to draw a microscopic speck of blood from one man—three spikes and a Roman sword to draw all the blood from Another!

Any cataloging of the sins of the church should include this fact: the church calls for so little heroic service; consequently, this institution claims the allegiance of too few able men. Pale societies hold little challenge to brawny men; mutual admiration clubs dealing in petit point will hardly develop the loyalties which endure through fire or flood. It is no argument against the stars that some are blind; nor against medicine that some are sick; nor against law that some are renegade. The fact that so little heroic service is called for, while indicting the caller, does not indict the case. Many have discarded their satin cushions and have shouldered a cross whether such process was called for or not.

To hang up one's nets and follow Him is always a challenge to the difficult—like the man from New England who sold his rocky farm and went to the black acres of the river bottoms, only to return the next year to repurchase the rocky farm. When asked why, he answered, "When I sink my shovel into the soil, I like to feel the rocks. They challenge my best efforts, and these hills give me something to hang my affections on." Indeed God has put the valuable things of life out of immediate reach: a soft peach can be plucked during a casual stroll through an orchard, but the iron ore is in the entrails of the earth; diamonds are locked in their rocky vaults beneath the strata of stone, and pearls are imbedded in oysters on the bottom of the sea; an education is achieved after long and arduous effort. And for good reason: that which man achieves too cheaply is esteemed too lightly. There is something in the struggle that enhances the accomplishment. Sweat is as indispensable to a sense of value as sweetness is to a cup of tea. Oh, the glory of "annexing your strength to a cause greater than yourself." [2]

George Eliot represents Stradivarius as saying about his violins:

> . . . when any master holds
> 'Twixt chin and hand a violin of mine,
> He will be glad that Stradivari lived,
> Made violins, and made them of the best.
> The masters only know whose work is good;
> They will choose mine, and while God gives them skill,
> I give them instruments to play upon
> God choosing me to help Him . . .
> . . . He could not make
> Antonio Stradivari's violins
> Without Antonio.[3]

[2] Fosdick, H. E., *The Secret of Victorious Living* (New York, Harper & Brothers).

[3] George Eliot, "Stradivarius," from *Complete Poems* (New York, Doubleday, Page & Co., 1901).

Today's minister would run the risk of shock if he approached some of his members with a proposition to do something really heroic such as championing an unpopular cause, defending an unlucrative issue, or closing a business that contradicts good ethics. Poor economy—all this strength for climbing, and no hills to climb! Many are now convinced that the time is ripe for the strong meat of the gospel to be served medium-rare. Too long has the church of Jesus Christ insisted on grinding it three times and sometimes precooking it as though man's belly were a tissue-lined fragility! Ecclesiastical hamburger produces no bulging biceps of faith—only sagging stomachs, effete smiles, and soft sympathies. The breastplate of righteousness is replaced by pastel vests of "the best dressed man of reason." Feet, instead of being shod with the preparation of the gospel of peace, are shod by the sandals of specious securities. The shield of faith is exchanged for a jacket of doubt while the helmet of salvation is readily pawned for the enlightenment of behaviorism. The sword of the spirit is returned to its scabbard by tranquilizing drugs insomuch that the full armor, which would resist the fiery darts of the wicked, would leave today's man vulnerable on every flank.

Percy Buck tells of a mining town in Bolivia where a small church was constructed from the odds and ends of crating boxes shipped in by several large firms. The pulpit desk was made of one packing crate and remained unpainted. As the minister stepped up to preach the first sermon, he noted the words, stenciled on the boards of the stand, "Explosivos Peligrosos"—Dangerous Explosives. So it is! There is enough explosive potential in the Word of God which, if preached in clarion certainty, would blast away all that divides, hurts, and grieves. But so to do demands three-dimensional, heroic service in the face of incalculable odds.